ADVANCED COMPUTER ORGANIZATION AND ARCHITECTURE

CONCEPTS AND DESIGNS

AF527390

ADVANCED COMPUTER ORGANIZATION AND ARCHITECTURE

CONCEPTS AND DESIGNS

SECOND EDITION

Dr. Ikvinderpal Singh

KHANNA BOOK PUBLISHING CO. (P) LTD.

Publisher of Engineering and Computer Books

4C/4344, Ansari Road, Darya Ganj, New Delhi-110002

Phone : 011-23244447-48 **Mobile:** +91-9910909320

E-mail : contact@khannabooks.com

Website : www.khannabooks.com

Dear Readers,

To prevent the piracy, this book is secured with HIGH SECURITY HOLOGRAM on the front title cover. In case you don't find the hologram on the front cover title, please write us to at contact@khannabooks.com or whatsapp us at +91-99109 09320 and avail special gift voucher for yourself.

Specimen of Hologram on front Cover title:

Moreover, there is a SPECIAL DISCOUNT COUPON for you with EVERY HOLOGRAM.

How to avail this SPECIAL DISCOUNT:

Step 1: Scratch the hologram
Step 2: Under the scratch area, your "coupon code" is available
Step 3: Logon to www.khannabooks.com
Step 4: Use your "coupon code" in the shopping cart and get your copy at a special discount
Step 5: Enjoy your reading!

Thanks,
Khanna Publishing House

Price: ₹ 549.00

Advance Computer Organisation and Architecture
by **Dr. Ikvinderpal Singh**

ISBN: 978-93-5538-701-1

First Edition: 2013
Second Edition: 2024

To view complete list of books, please scan the QR Code:

Published by:
Khanna Book Publishing Co. (P) Ltd.
CIN: U22110DL1998PTC095547

Visit us at: www.khannabooks.com
Write us at: contact@khannabooks.com

Printed in Bharat.

Copyright © Publisher

No part of this publication may be reproduced, stored in a retrieval system or transmitted, in any form or by any means, electronic, me-chanical, photocopying, recording or other-wise without prior permission of the publisher.

This book is sold subject to the condition that it shall not, by way of trade, be lent, re-sold, hired out or otherwise disposed of without the publisher's consent, in any form of binding or cover other than that in which it is published.

Disclaimer: The website links provided by the author in this book are placed for informational, educational & reference purpose only. The Publisher do not endorse these website links or the views of the speaker/ content of the said weblinks. In case of any dispute, all legal matters to be settled under Delhi Jurisdiction only.

Dedicated to

MY GRANDMOTHER

ADVANCED COMPUTER ORGANIZATION AND ARCHITECTURE

- **Paradigms of Computing:** Synchronous – Vector/Array, SIMD, Systolic.
- **Asynchronous – MIMD, reduction Paradigm, Hardware taxonomy:** Flynn's classification, Software taxonomy: Kung's taxonomy, SPMD.
- **Parallel Computing Models:** Parallelism in Uniprocessor Systems: Trends in parallel processing, Basic Uniprocessor Architecture, Parallel Processing Mechanism.
- **Parallel Computer Structures:** Pipeline Computers, Array Computers, Multiprocessor
- **Systems Architectural Classification Schemes:** Multiplicity of Instruction-Data Streams, Serial versus Parallel Processing, Parallelism versus Pipelining
- **Pipelining:** An overlapped Parallelism, Principles of Linear Pipelining, Classification of Pipeline Processors, General Pipelines and Reservation Tables.

ADVANCED COMPUTER ORGANIZATION AND ARCHITECTURE

» **Paradigms of Computing:** Synchronous – Vector/Array, SIMD, Systolic

» **Asynchronous – MIMD, Reduction Paradigm, Hardware taxonomy:** Flynn's classification,

» **Software taxonomy:** Kung's taxonomy, SPMD.

» **Abstract Parallel Computational Models:** Combinational circuits, Sorting Network, PRAM Models, Interconnection RAMs.

» **Parallelism in Uniprocessor Systems:** Trends in parallel processing, Basic Uniprocessor Architecture, Parallel Processing Mechanism.

» **Parallel Computer Structures:** Pipeline Computers, Array Computers, Multiprocessor

» **Systems Architectural Classification Schemes:** Multiplicity of Instruction-Data Streams, Serial versus Parallel Processing, Parallelism versus Pipelining

» **Pipelining:** An overlapped Parallelism, Principles of Linear Pipelining, Classification of Pipeline Processors, General Pipelines and Reservation Tables

» **Principles of Designing Pipelined Processors:** Instruction Prefetch and Branch Handling, Data Buffering and Busing Structures, Internal Forwarding and Register Tagging, Hazard Detection and Resolution

» **Superscalar and Superpipeline Design:** Superscalar Pipeline Design, Superpipelined Design

» **Structures and Algorithms for Array Processors:** SIMD Array Processors, SIMD Computer Organizations, Masking and Data Routing Mechanisms, Inter-PE Communications

PREFACE

Single processor supercomputers have achieved great speeds and have been pushing hardware technology to the physical limit of chip manufacturing. But soon this trend will come to an end, because there are physical and architectural bounds, which limit the computational power that can be achieved with a single processor system. In this book, we study advanced computer architectures that utilize parallelism via multiple processing units. While parallel computing, in the form of internally linked processors, was the main form of parallelism, advances in computer networks has created a new type of parallelism in the form of networked autonomous computers. Instead of putting everything in a single box and tightly couple processors to memory, the Internet achieved a kind of parallelism by loosely connecting everything outside of the box. To get the most out of a computer system with internal or external parallelism, designers and software developers must understand the interaction between hardware and software parts of the system. This is the reason we wrote this book. We want the reader to understand the power and limitations of multiprocessor systems. Our goal is to apprise the reader of both the beneficial and challenging aspects of advanced architecture and parallelism. The material in this book is organized in 10 chapters, as follows.

Chapter 1 is a survey of the field of computer architecture at an introductory level. We first study the decades of computing and the changes that have led to obtaining high performance computing via parallelism. An introduction to classes of parallel computers and various trends in hardware, software, computer design, applications and networking.

Chapter 2 covers the paradigms of computing: synchronous – vector/array, SIMD, systolic arrays.

Chapter 3 describes the paradigms of computing: asynchronous – MIMD, reduction paradigm, hardware taxonomy: Flynn's classification, software taxonomy: Kung's taxonomy, SPMD.

Chapter 4 discusses the abstract parallel computational models: combinational circuits, sorting network, pram models, interconnection RAMs.

Chapter 5 covers the parallelism in uniprocessor systems: trends in parallel processing, basic uniprocessor architecture, and parallel processing mechanism.

Chapter 6 navigates through a number of parallel computer structures: pipeline computers, array computers, multiprocessor systems, architectural classification schemes: multiplicity of instruction-data streams, serial versus parallel processing, parallelism versus pipelining.

Chapter 7 is about pipelining: an overlapped parallelism, principles of linear pipelining, classification of pipeline processors, general pipelines and reservation tables.

Chapter 8 illustrates the principles of designing pipelined processors: instruction prefetch and branch handling, data buffering and busing structures, internal forwarding and register tagging, hazard detection and resolution.

Chapter 9 gives description of superscalar and superpipeline design: superscalar pipeline design, superpipelined and VLIW.

Chapter 10 explains the design structures and algorithms for array processors: SIMD array processors, SIMD computer organizations, masking and data routing mechanisms, inter-PE communications.

This book is intended for students in computer engineering, computer science, and electrical engineering. The material covered in the book is suitable for a one semester course on "Advanced Computer Organization and Architecture" and a one semester course on "Advanced Computer Architecture." Most of the material used in the book has been used in our undergraduate and postgraduate classes. In what follows, we provide a chapter-by-chapter review of the material covered in the book. In doing so, we aim at providing course instructors, students, and practicing engineers/scientists with enough information that can help them select the appropriate chapter or sequences of chapters to cover/review.

We welcome comments from all readers to improve this book as a useful guide for the community of engineers and technologists who will become knowledgeable about the potential of Advanced Computer Organization and Architecture for their use in solving the problems that challenge us each day.

DR. IKVINDERPAL SINGH

CONTENTS

CHAPTER - 1

INTRODUCTION TO ADVANCED COMPUTER ARCHITECTURE AND PARALLEL PROCESSING

CHAPTER - 2

PARADIGMS OF COMPUTING: SYNCHRONOUS

CHAPTER - 3

PARADIGMS OF COMPUTING: ASYNCHRONOUS

CHAPTER - 4

ABSTRACT PARALLEL COMPUTATIONAL MODELS

CHAPTER - 5

PARALLELISM IN UNIPROCESSOR SYSTEMS

CHAPTER - 6

PARALLEL COMPUTER STRUCTURES

CHAPTER - 7

PIPELINING

CHAPTER - 8

PRINCIPLES OF DESIGNING PIPELINED PROCESSORS

CHAPTER - 9

SUPERSCALAR AND SUPERPIPELINE DESIGN

CHAPTER - 10

DESIGN STRUCTURES AND ALGORITHMS FOR ARRAY PROCESSORS

"Computing is not about computers anymore. It is about living. . . . We have seen computers move out of giant air-conditioned rooms into closets, then onto desktops, and now into our laps and pockets. But this is not the end. . . . Like a force of nature, the digital age cannot be denied or stopped. . . . The information superhighway may be mostly hype today, but it is an understatement about tomorrow. It will exist beyond people's wildest predictions. . . . We are not waiting on any invention. It is here. It is now. It is almost genetic in its nature, in that each generation will become more digital than the preceding one."

CHAPTER 1

INTRODUCTION TO ADVANCED COMPUTER ARCHITECTURE AND PARALLEL PROCESSING

1.1 INTRODUCTION

This book presents details on various aspects of computer system design and programming. We discuss organization and architecture of advanced computer architecture, how they are designed, and how they are programmed. In order to clarify the scope of this book, we need to explain these terms: computer architecture, computer organization, computer design, and computer programming.

Computer architecture refers to the aspects with which a programmer is concerned. The most obvious one is the design of an instruction set for the computer. For example, should the processor understand instructions to process multimedia data? The answer depends on the intended use of the system. Clearly, if the target applications involve multimedia, adding multimedia instructions will help improve the performance. Computer architecture, in a sense, describes the computer system at a logical level, from the programmer's viewpoint. It deals with the selection of the basic functional units such as the processor and memory, and how they should be interconnected into a computer system.

Computer organization is concerned with how the various hardware components operate and how they are interconnected to implement the architectural specifications. Computer organization addresses issues such as control signals (how the computer is controlled), signaling methods, and memory types. It encompasses all physical aspects of computer systems. The study of ***computer architecture***, on the other hand, focuses on the structure and behavior of the computer system and refers to the logical aspects of system implementation as seen by the programmer. Computer architecture includes many elements such as instruction sets and formats, operation codes, data types, the number and types of registers, addressing modes, main memory access methods, and various I/O mechanisms. The architecture of a system directly affects the logical execution of programs. For example, if the architecture specifies a divide instruction, we will have a choice to implement this instruction either in hardware or in software. In a high-performance model, we may implement the division operation in hardware to provide improved performance at a higher price. In cheaper models, we may implement it in software. But cost need not be the only deciding criterion. For example, the Pentium processor implements the divide operation in hardware whereas the next generation Itanium processor implements division in software. If the next version of Itanium uses a hardware implementation of division, that does not change the architecture, only its organization.

Computer design is an activity that translates architectural specifications of a system into an implementation using a particular organization. As a result, computer design is sometimes referred to as *computer implementation*. A computer designer is concerned with the hardware design of the computer.

Computer programming involves expressing the problem at hand in a language that the computer can understand. As we show later, the native language that a computer can understand is called the machine language. But this is not a language with which we humans are comfortable. So we use a language that we can easily read and understand. These languages are called high-level languages, and include languages such as Java and C. We do not devote any space for these high-level languages as they are beyond the scope of this book. Instead, we discuss in detail languages that are close to the architecture of a machine. This allows us to study the internal details of computer systems.

The distinction between computer organization and computer architecture is not clear-cut. People in the fields of computer science and computer engineering hold differing opinions as to exactly which concepts pertain to computer organization and which pertain to computer architecture. In fact, neither computer organization nor computer architecture can stand alone. They are interrelated and interdependent. We can truly understand each of them only after we comprehend both of them. Our comprehension of computer organization and architecture ultimately leads to a deeper understanding of computers and computation—the heart and soul of computer science.

Computer architects have always strived to increase the performance of their computer architectures. High performance may come from fast dense circuitry, packaging technology, and parallelism. Single-processor supercomputers have achieved unheard of speeds and have been pushing hardware technology to the physical limit of chip manufacturing. However, this trend will soon come to an end, because there are physical and architectural bounds that limit the computational power that can be achieved with a single-processor system. In this book we will study advanced computer architectures that utilize parallelism via multiple processing units.

Parallel processors are computer systems consisting of multiple processing units connected via some interconnection network plus the software needed to make the processing units work together. There are two major factors used to categorize such systems: the processing units themselves, and the interconnection network that ties them together. The processing units can communicate and interact with each other using either shared memory or message passing methods. The interconnection network for shared memory systems can be classified as bus-based versus switch-based. In message passing systems, the interconnection network is divided into static and dynamic. Static connections have a fixed topology that does not change while programs are running. Dynamic connections create links on the fly as the program executes.

The main argument for using multiprocessors is to create powerful computers by simply connecting multiple processors. A multiprocessor is expected to reach faster speed than the fastest single-processor system. In addition, a multiprocessor consisting of a number of single processors is expected to be more cost-effective than building a high-performance single processor. Another advantage of a multiprocessor is fault tolerance. If a processor fails, the remaining processors should be able to provide continued service, albeit with degraded performance.

1.1.1 BASIC TERMS AND NOTATION

The alphabet of computers, more precisely digital computers, consists of 0 and 1. Each is called a *bit*, which stands for the binary digit. The term *byte* is used to represent a group of 8 bits. The term *word* is used to refer to a group of bytes that is processed simultaneously. The exact number of bytes that constitute a word depends on the system. For example, in the Pentium, a word refers to four bytes or 32 bits. On the other hand, eight bytes are grouped into a word in the Itanium processor. The reasons for this difference are explained later. We use the abbreviation "b" for bits, "B" for bytes, and "W" for words.

Sometimes we also use *doubleword* and *quadword*. A doubleword has twice the number of bits as the word and the quadword has four times the number of bits in a word. Bits in a word are usually ordered from right to left, as you would write digits in a decimal number. The rightmost bit is called the *least significant bit* (LSB), and the leftmost bit is called the *most significant bit* (MSB). However, some manufacturers use the opposite notation. For example, the PowerPC manuals use this notation. In this book, we consistently write bits of a word from right to left, with the LSB as the rightmost bit. We use standard terms such as *kilo* (K), *mega* (M), *giga* (G), and so on to represent large integers.

TABLE 1.1: Terms to Represent Large Integer Values

Term	Decimal (base 10)	Binary (base 2)
K (kilo)	10^3	2^{10}
M (mega)	10^6	2^{20}
G (giga)	10^9	2^{30}
T (tera)	10^{12}	2^{40}
P (peta)	10^{15}	2^{50}

Unfortunately, we use two different versions of each, depending on the number system, decimal or binary. Table 1.1 summarizes the differences between the two systems. Typically, computer-related attributes use the binary version. For example, when we say 128 megabyte (MB) memory, we mean 128×2^{20} bytes. Usually, communication-related quantities and time units are expressed using the decimal system. For example, when we say that the data transfer rate is 100 megabits/second (Mb/s), we mean 100×10^6 Mb/s. Throughout the text, we use various number systems: binary, octal, and hexadecimal. If the number system used is not clear from the context, we use a trailing letter to specify the number system. We use "D" for decimal numbers, "B" for binary numbers, "Q" for octal numbers, and "H" for hexadecimal (or hex for short) numbers. For example, 10110101B is an 8-bit binary number whereas 10ABH is a hex number.

1.2 FOUR DECADES OF COMPUTING

Most computer scientists agree that there have been four distinct paradigms or eras of computing. These are: batch, time-sharing, desktop, and network. Figure 1.1 is modified from a table proposed by Lawrence Tesler. In this table, major characteristics of the different computing paradigms are associated with each decade of computing, starting from 1960.

1.2.1 BATCH ERA

By 1965 the IBM System/360 mainframe dominated the corporate computer centers. It was the typical batch processing machine with punched card readers, tapes and disk drives, but no connection beyond the computer room. This single mainframe established large centralized computers as the standard form of computing for decades. The IBM System/360 had an operating system, multiple programming languages, and 10 megabytes of disk storage. The System/360 filled a room with metal boxes and people to run them. Its transistor circuits were reasonably fast.

Power users could order magnetic core memories with up to one megabyte of 32-bit words. This machine was large enough to support many programs in memory at the same time, even though the central processing unit had to switch from one program to another.

1.2.2 TIME-SHARING ERA

The mainframes of the batch era were firmly established by the late 1960s when advances in semiconductor technology made the solid-state memory and integrated circuit feasible. These advances in hardware technology spawned the minicomputer era. They were small, fast, and inexpensive enough to be spread throughout the company at the divisional level. However, they were still too expensive and difficult to use to hand over to end-users. Minicomputers made by DEC, Prime, and Data General led the way in defining a new kind of computing: time-sharing. By the 1970s it was clear that there existed two kinds of commercial or business computing:

(1) centralized data processing mainframes, and (2) time-sharing minicomputers. In parallel with small-scale machines, supercomputers were coming into play. The first such supercomputer, the CDC 6600, was introduced in 1961 by Control Data Corporation. Cray Research Corporation introduced the best cost/performance supercomputer, the Cray-1, in 1976.

Feature	Batch	Time-Sharing	Desktop	Network
Decade	1960s	1970s	1980s	1990s
Location	Computer room	Terminal room	Desktop	Mobile
Users	Experts	Specialists	Individuals	Groups
Data	Alphanumeric	Text, numbers	Fonts, graphs	Multimedia
Objective	Calculate	Access	Present	Communicate
Interface	Punched card	Keyboard and CRT	See and point	Ask and tell
Operation	Process	Edit	Layout	Orchestrate
Connectivity	None	Peripheral cable	LAN	Internet
Owners	Corporate computer centers	Divisional IS shops	Departmental end-users	Everyone

FIGURE 1.1: Four Decades of Computing

1.2.3 DESKTOP ERA

Personal computers (PCs), which were introduced in 1977 by Altair, Processor Technology, North Star, Tandy, Commodore, Apple, and many others, enhanced the productivity of end-users in numerous departments. Personal computers from Compaq, Apple, IBM, Dell, and many others soon became pervasive, and changed the face of computing.

Local area networks (LAN) of powerful personal computers and workstations began to replace mainframes and minis by 1990. The power of the most capable big machine could be had in a desktop model for one-tenth of the cost. However, these individual desktop computers were soon to be connected into larger complexes of computing by wide area networks (WAN).

1.2.4 NETWORK ERA

The fourth era, or network paradigm of computing, is in full swing because of rapid advances in network technology. Network technology outstripped processor technology throughout most of the 1990s. This explains the rise of the network paradigm listed in figure 1.1. The surge of network capacity tipped the balance from a processor-centric view of computing to a network-centric view. The 1980s and 1990s witnessed the introduction of many commercial parallel computers with multiple processors. They can generally be classified into two main categories: (1) shared memory, and (2) distributed memory systems. The number of processors in a single machine ranged from several in a shared memory computer to hundreds of thousands in a massively parallel system. Examples of parallel computers during this era include Sequent Symmetry, Intel iPSC, nCUBE, Intel Paragon, Thinking Machines (CM-2, CM-5), MsPar (MP), Fujitsu (VPP500), and others.

1.2.5 CURRENT TRENDS

One of the clear trends in computing is the substitution of expensive and specialized parallel machines by the more cost-effective clusters of workstations. A cluster is a collection of stand-alone computers connected using some interconnection network. Additionally, the pervasiveness of the Internet created interest in network computing and more recently in grid computing. Grids are geographically distributed platforms of computation. They should provide dependable, consistent, pervasive, and inexpensive access to high-end computational facilities.

1.3 PARALLEL COMPUTING

Parallel computing is a form of computation in which many calculations are carried out simultaneously, operating on the principle that large problems can often be divided into smaller ones, which are then solved concurrently ("in parallel"). There are several different forms of parallel computing: bit-level, instruction level, data, and task parallelism. Parallelism has been employed for many years, mainly in high-performance computing, but interest in it has grown lately due to the physical constraints preventing frequency scaling. As power consumption (and consequently heat generation) by computers has become a concern in recent years, parallel computing has become the dominant paradigm in computer architecture, mainly in the form of multicore processors.

Parallel computers can be roughly classified according to the level at which the hardware supports parallelism, with multi-core and multi-processor computers having multiple processing elements within a single machine, while clusters, MPPs, and grids use multiple computers to work on the same task. Specialized parallel computer architectures are sometimes used alongside traditional processors, for accelerating specific tasks.

Parallel computer programs are more difficult to write than sequential ones, because concurrency introduces several new classes of potential software bugs, of which race conditions are the most common. Communication and synchronization between the different subtasks are typically some of the greatest obstacles to getting good parallel program performance.

Traditionally, software has been written for serial computation:

- To be run on a single computer having a single Central Processing Unit (CPU);
- A problem is broken into a discrete series of instructions.
- Instructions are executed one after another.
- Only one instruction may execute at any moment in time.

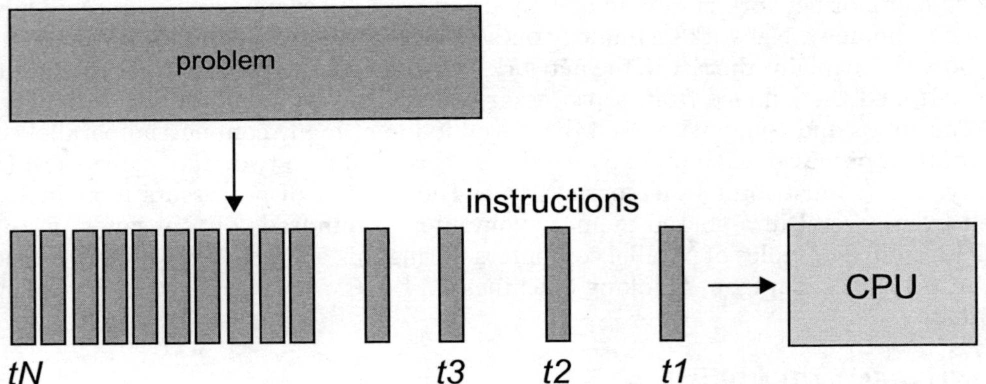

For example:

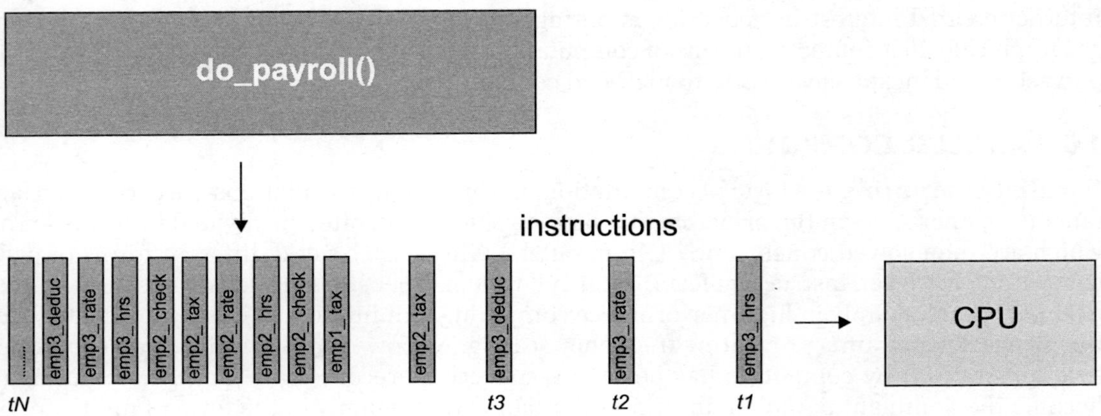

In the simplest sense, parallel computing is the simultaneous use of multiple compute resources to solve a computational problem:

- To be run using multiple CPUs
- A problem is broken into discrete parts that can be solved concurrently
- Each part is further broken down to a series of instructions
- Instructions from each part execute simultaneously on different CPUs

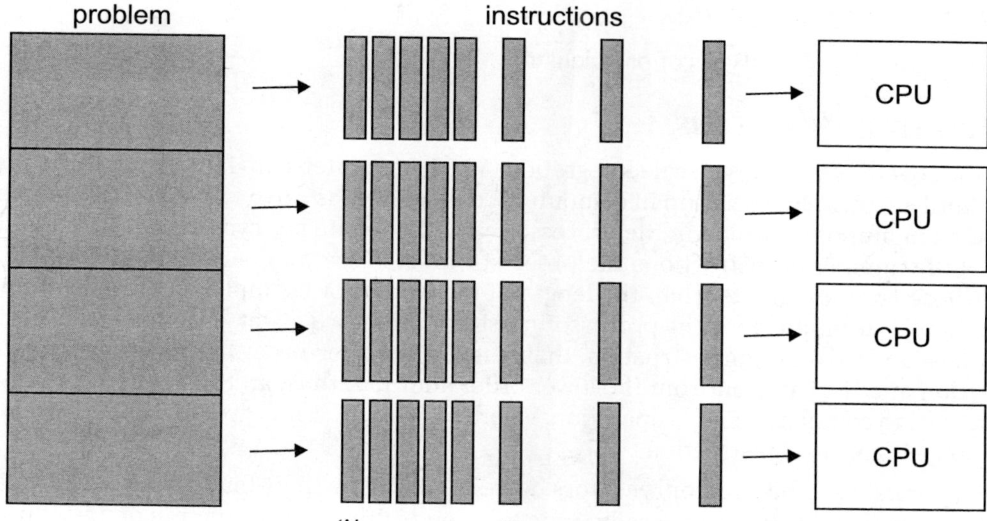

For example:

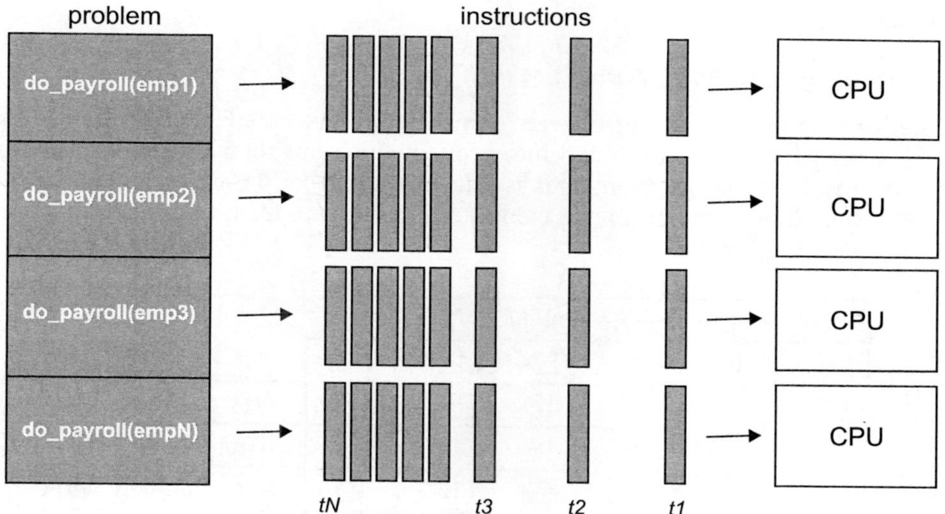

The compute resources might be:

- A single computer with multiple processors;
- An arbitrary number of computers connected by a network;
- A combination of both.

The computational problem should be able to:

- Be broken apart into discrete pieces of work that can be solved simultaneously;
- Execute multiple program instructions at any moment in time;
- Be solved in less time with multiple compute resources than with a single compute resource.

1.4 TYPES OF PARALLELISM

Following are the various types of parallelism:

1.4.1 BIT-LEVEL PARALLELISM

From the advent of very-large-scale integration (VLSI) computer-chip fabrication technology in the 1970s until about 1986, speed-up in computer architecture was driven by doubling computer word size—the amount of information the processor can manipulate per cycle. Increasing the word size reduces the number of instructions the processor must execute to perform an operation on variables whose sizes are greater than the length of the word. For example, where an 8-bit processor must add two 16-bit integers, the processor must first add the 8 lower-order bits from each integer using the standard addition instruction, then add the 8 higher-order bits using an add-with-carry instruction and the carry bit from the lower order addition; thus, an 8-bit processor requires two instructions to complete a single operation, where a 16-bit processor would be able to complete the operation with a single instruction.

Historically, 4-bit microprocessors were replaced with 8-bit, then 16-bit, then 32-bit microprocessors. This trend generally came to an end with the introduction of 32-bit processors, which has been a standard in general-purpose computing for two decades. Not until recently (c. 2003–2004), with the advent of x86-64 architectures, have 64-bit processors become commonplace.

1.4.2 INSTRUCTION-LEVEL PARALLELISM

A computer program is, in essence, a stream of instructions executed by a processor. These instructions can be re-ordered and combined into groups which are then executed in parallel without changing the result of the program. This is known as instruction-level parallelism. Advances in instruction-level parallelism dominated computer architecture from the mid-1980s until the mid-1990s.

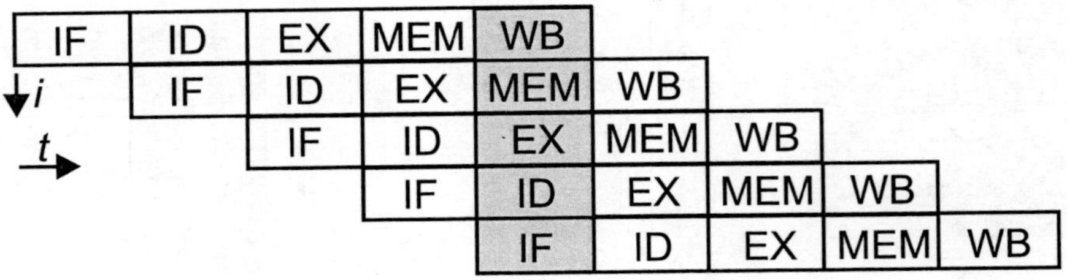

IF	ID	EX	MEM	WB				
	IF	ID	EX	MEM	WB			
		IF	ID	EX	MEM	WB		
			IF	ID	EX	MEM	WB	
				IF	ID	EX	MEM	WB

↓ *i*   *t* →

FIGURE 1.2: A canonical five-stage pipeline in a RISC machine (IF = Instruction Fetch, ID = Instruction Decode, EX = Execute, MEM = Memory access, WB = Register write back)

Modern processors have multi-stage instruction pipelines. Each stage in the pipeline corresponds to a different action the processor performs on that instruction in that stage; a processor with an N-stage pipeline can have up to N different instructions at different stages of completion. The canonical example of a pipelined processor is a RISC processor, with five stages: instruction fetch, decode, execute, memory access, and write back. The Pentium 4 processor had a 35-stage pipeline.

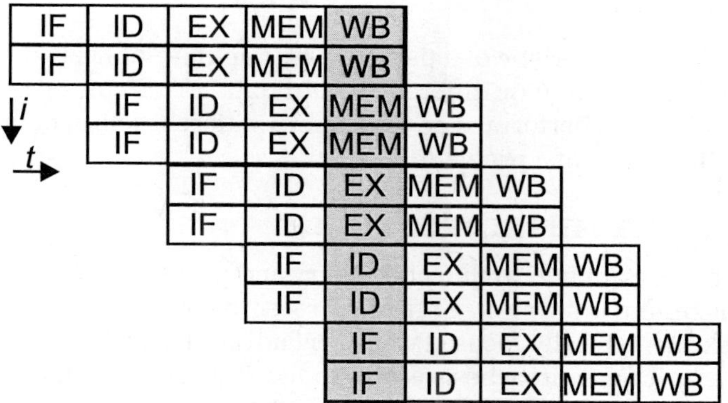

FIGURE 1.3: A five-stage pipelined superscalar processor, capable of issuing two instructions per cycle. It can have two instructions in each stage of the pipeline, for a total of up to 10 instructions (shown in green) being simultaneously executed.

In addition to instruction-level parallelism from pipelining, some processors can issue more than one instruction at a time. These are known as superscalar processors. Instructions can be grouped together only if there is no data dependency between them. Scoreboarding and the Tomasulo algorithm (which is similar to scoreboarding but makes use of register renaming) are two of the most common techniques for implementing out-of-order execution and instruction-level parallelism.

1.4.3 DATA PARALLELISM

Data parallelism is parallelism inherent in program loops, which focuses on distributing the data across different computing nodes to be processed in parallel. "Parallelizing loops often leads to similar (not necessarily identical) operation sequences or functions being performed on elements of a large data structure." Many scientific and engineering applications exhibit data parallelism.

A loop-carried dependency is the dependence of loop iteration on the output of one or more previous iterations. Loop-carried dependencies prevent the parallelization of loops. For example, consider the following pseudocode that computes the first few Fibonacci numbers:

```
PREV1:= 0
PREV2:= 1
do:
CUR: = PREV1 + PREV2
PREV1:= PREV2
PREV2:= CUR
while (CUR < 10)
```

This loop cannot be parallelized because CUR depends on itself (PREV2) and PREV1, which are computed in each loop iteration. Since each iteration depends on the result of the previous one, they cannot be performed in parallel. As the size of a problem gets bigger, the amount of data-parallelism available usually does as well.

1.4.4 TASK PARALLELISM

Task parallelism is the characteristic of a parallel program that "entirely different calculations can be performed on either the same or different sets of data". This contrasts with data parallelism, where the same calculation is performed on the same or different sets of data. Task parallelism does not usually scale with the size of a problem.

1.5 EXISTING ARCHITECTURAL TECHNIQUES

One of the main goals of computer architects is to try and produce architectures in which the functional units have maximum utilization. Until fairly recently, processor speeds have been increasing so fast that this task was typically focused on taking advantage of instruction level parallelism on a uniprocessor system. Two approaches were introduced that, between them, are found in almost every processor produced today--superscalar and VLIW architectures. However, with decreasing gains on higher clocking, refining these architectures has become less important, and approaches such as multithreading, multiprocessing, and multicomputing have shifted to be the forefront of research interests.

1.5.1 THE SUPERSCALAR APPROACH

Superscalar refers to the process of issuing multiple instructions at the same time. The goal is to allow instructions to be executed out of order and in parallel if functional units are available and no true data dependencies are violated (i.e. exploit instruction-level parallelism). Superscalar relies on sophisticated hardware to dynamically schedule and manage the issuing, execution, and completion of multiple instructions simultaneously. In doing so, it has increased on chip complexity, power dissipation, and heat production. However, unlike VLIW processors, it does not require any extra software (compiler) support, which is likely a key reason that it has been a tremendous success. Most desktop and workstation architectures are superscalar.

1.5.2 VERY LONG INSTRUCTION WORDS

Another approach to the parallelism problem is to exploit instruction level parallelism by having the compiler create bundles of instructions that take advantage of the chip's known functional units. For instance, if the processor is capable of executing two ALU operations, one load/store operation, and one multiply operation simultaneously, the compiler can do its best to arrange the instructions in such a way that groups consisting of all these elements will be formed. Together, the group will be issued as a very long instruction.

This technique is not as popular as superscalar because of the high dependency on compiler support, and the initial lack thereof. VLIW avoids the chip complexity issues that are present in superscalar, but it is hindered by the fact that if there is no compiler capable of efficiently created very long instructions, the architecture is basically useless. The VLIW technique is probably most useful in certain implementations of high-performance computers where the types of programs that will be executed are known in advance and that extensive compiler support is not needed.

1.6 MULTI-THREADING

Multithreading is the process of executing multiple threads concurrently on a processor. It takes the idea of processes sharing the CPU to a lower level, and allows threads to be switched off and on the processor without any latency. There are a number of ways that multithreading can be implemented, including: fine-grained multithreading, coarse-grained multithreading and simultaneous multithreading.

1.6.1 FINE-GRAINED MULTITHREADING

Fine-grained multithreading involves instructions from threads issuing in a round-robin fashion--one instruction from process A, one instruction from process B, another from A, and so on (note that there can be more than two threads). This type of multithreading applies to situations where multiple threads share a single pipeline or are executing on a single-issue CPU.

1.6.2 COARSE-GRAINED MULTITHREADING

The next type of multithreading is coarse-grained multithreading. Coarse-grained multithreading allows one thread to run until it executes an instruction that causes a latency (cache miss), and then the CPU swaps another thread in while the memory access completes. If a thread doesn't require a memory access, it will continue to run until its time limit is up. As with fine-grained multithreading, this applies multiple threads sharing a single pipeline or executing on a single-issue CPU.

1.6.3 SIMULTANEOUS MULTITHREADING (SMT)

Simultaneous multithreading is a refinement on coarse-grained multithreading. The scheduling algorithm allows the active thread to issue as many instructions as it can (up to the issue-width) to keep the functional units busy. If a thread does not have sufficient ILP to do this, other threads may issue instructions to fill the empty slots. SMT only applies to superscalar architectures which are characterized by multiple-issue CPUs.

1.7 PARALLELISM AND COMPUTING

A *parallel computer* is a set of processors that are able to work cooperatively to solve a computational problem. This definition is broad enough to include parallel supercomputers that have hundreds or thousands of processors, networks of workstations, multiple-processor workstations, and embedded systems. Parallel computers are interesting because they offer the potential to concentrate computational resources—whether processors, memory, or I/O bandwidth—on important computational problems.

Parallel Processing *refers to the concept of speeding-up the execution of a program by dividing the program into multiple fragments that can execute simultaneously, each on its own processor. A program being executed across n processors might execute n times faster than it would using a single processor.*

Parallelism has sometimes been viewed as a rare and exotic subarea of computing, interesting but of little relevance to the average programmer. A study of trends in hardware, software, applications, computer architecture, and networking shows that this view is no longer tenable. Parallelism is becoming ubiquitous, and parallel programming is becoming central to the programming enterprise.

1.7.1 TRENDS IN HARDWARE

Following are the various trends in hardware:

1.7.1.1 MEMORY AND COMMUNICATION

Main memory in a parallel computer is either shared memory (shared between all processing elements in a single address space), or distributed memory (in which each processing element has its own local address space). Distributed memory refers to the fact that the memory is logically distributed, but often implies that it is physically distributed as well. Distributed shared memory and memory virtualization combine the two approaches, where the processing element has its own local memory and access to the memory on non-local processors. Accesses to local memory are typically faster than accesses to non-local memory.

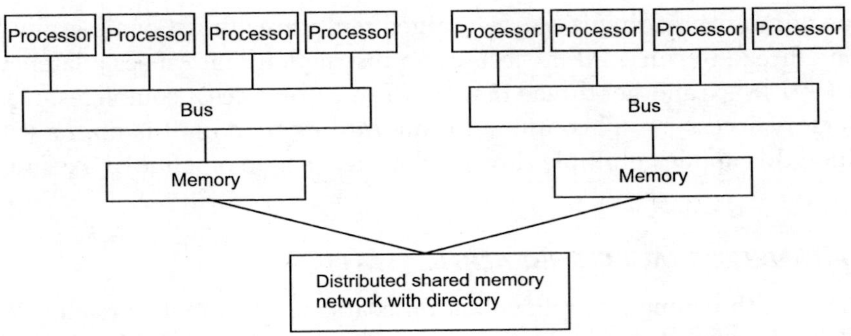

FIGURE 1.4: A logical view of a Non-Uniform Memory Access (NUMA) architecture. Processors in one directory can access that directory's memory with less latency than they can access memory in the other directory's memory.

Computer architectures in which each element of main memory can be accessed with equal latency and bandwidth are known as Uniform Memory Access (UMA) systems. Typically, that can be achieved only by a shared memory system, in which the memory is not physically distributed. A system that does not have this property is known as Non-Uniform Memory Access (NUMA) architecture. Distributed memory systems have non-uniform memory access.

Computer systems make use of caches—small, fast memories located close to the processor which store temporary copies of memory values (nearby in both the physical and logical sense). Parallel computer systems have difficulties with caches that may store the same value in more than one location, with the possibility of incorrect program execution. These computers require a cache coherency system, which keeps track of cached values and strategically purges them, thus ensuring correct program execution. Bus snooping is one of the most common methods for keeping track of which values are being accessed (and thus should be purged). Designing large, high-performance cache coherence systems is a very difficult problem in computer architecture. As a result, shared-memory computer architectures do not scale as well as distributed memory systems do.

Processor–processor and processor–memory communication can be implemented in hardware in several ways, including via shared (either multiported or multiplexed) memory, a crossbar switch, a shared bus or an interconnect network of a myriad of topologies including star, ring, tree, hypercube, fat hypercube (a hypercube with more than one processor at a node), or n-dimensional mesh.

Parallel computers based on interconnect networks need to have some kind of routing to enable the passing of messages between nodes that are not directly connected. The medium used for communication between the processors is likely to be hierarchical in large multiprocessor machines.

1.7.2 CLASSES OF PARALLEL COMPUTERS

Parallel computers can be roughly classified according to the level at which the hardware supports parallelism. This classification is broadly analogous to the distance between basic computing nodes. These are not mutually exclusive; for example, clusters of symmetric multiprocessors are relatively common.

1.7.2.1 MULTICORE COMPUTING

A multicore processor is a processor that includes multiple execution units ("cores") on the same chip. These processors differ from superscalar processors, which can issue multiple instructions per cycle from one instruction stream (thread); in contrast, a multicore processor can issue multiple instructions per cycle from multiple instruction streams. Each core in a multicore processor can potentially be superscalar as well—that is, on every cycle, each core can issue multiple instructions from one instruction stream.

Simultaneous multithreading (of which Intel's HyperThreading is the best known) was an early form of pseudo-multicoreism. A processor capable of simultaneous multithreading has only one execution unit ("core"), but when that execution unit is idling (such as during a cache miss), it uses that execution unit to process a second thread. IBM's Cell microprocessor, designed for use in the Sony PlayStation 3, is another prominent multicore processor.

1.7.2.2 SYMMETRIC MULTIPROCESSING

A symmetric multiprocessor (SMP) is a computer system with multiple identical processors that share memory and connect via a bus. Bus contention prevents bus architectures from scaling. As a result, SMPs generally do not comprise more than 32 processors. "Because of the small size of the processors and the significant reduction in the requirements for bus bandwidth achieved by large caches, such symmetric multiprocessors are extremely cost-effective, provided that a sufficient amount of memory bandwidth exists."

1.7.2.3 DISTRIBUTED COMPUTING

A distributed computer (also known as a distributed memory multiprocessor) is a distributed memory computer system in which the processing elements are connected by a network. Distributed computers are highly scalable.

1.7.2.4 CLUSTER COMPUTING

A cluster is a group of loosely coupled computers that work together closely, so that in some respects they can be regarded as a single computer. Clusters are composed of multiple standalone machines connected by a network. While machines in a cluster do not have to be symmetric, load balancing is more difficult if they are not. The most common type of cluster is the Beowulf cluster, which is a cluster implemented on multiple identical commercial off-the-shelf computers connected with a TCP/IP Ethernet local area network.

FIGURE 1.5: A Beowulf cluster

Beowulf technology was originally developed by Thomas Sterling and Donald Becker. The vast majority of the TOP500 supercomputers are clusters.

FIGURE 1.6: Blue Gene/L MPP

1.7.2.5 MASSIVE PARALLEL PROCESSING

A massively parallel processor (MPP) is a single computer with many networked processors. MPPs have many of the same characteristics as clusters, but MPPs have specialized interconnect networks (whereas clusters use commodity hardware for networking). MPPs also tend to be larger than clusters, typically having "far more" than 100 processors. In an MPP, "each CPU contains its own memory and copy of the operating system and application. Each subsystem communicates with the others via a high-speed interconnect."

A cabinet from Blue Gene/L, ranked as the fourth fastest supercomputer in the world according to the 11/2008 TOP500 rankings. Blue Gene/L is a massively parallel processor.

Blue Gene/L, the fifth fastest supercomputer in the world according to the June 2009 TOP500 ranking, is an MPP.

1.7.2.6 GRID COMPUTING

Grid computing is the most distributed form of parallel computing. It makes use of computers communicating over the Internet to work on a given problem. Because of the low bandwidth and extremely high latency available on the Internet, grid computing typically deals only with embarrassingly parallel problems. Many grid computing applications have been created, of which SETI@home and Folding@Home are the best-known examples.

Most grid computing applications use middleware, software that sits between the operating system and the application to manage network resources and standardize the software interface. The most common grid computing middleware is the Berkeley Open Infrastructure for Network Computing (BOINC). Often, grid computing software makes use of "spare cycles", performing computations at times when a computer is idling.

1.7.2.7 SPECIALIZED PARALLEL COMPUTERS

Within parallel computing, there are specialized parallel devices that remain niche areas of interest. While not domain-specific, they tend to be applicable to only a few classes of parallel problems.

1.7.2.8 RECONFIGURABLE COMPUTING WITH FIELD-PROGRAMMABLE GATE ARRAYS

Reconfigurable computing is the use of a field-programmable gate array (FPGA) as a co-processor to a general-purpose computer. An FPGA is, in essence, a computer chip that can rewire itself for a given task. FPGAs can be programmed with hardware description languages such as VHDL or Verilog. However, programming in these languages can be tedious. Several vendors have created C to HDL languages that attempt to emulate the syntax and/or semantics of the C programming language, with which most programmers are familiar. The best known C to HDL languages are Mitrion-C, Impulse C, DIME-C, and Handel-C. Specific subsets of SystemC based on C++ can also be used for this purpose.

AMD's decision to open its HyperTransport technology to third-party vendors has become the enabling technology for high-performance reconfigurable computing. According to Michael R.

D'Amour, Chief Operating Officer of DRC Computer Corporation, "when we first walked into AMD, they called us 'the socket stealers.' Now they call us their partners."

1.7.2.9 GENERAL-PURPOSE COMPUTING ON GRAPHICS PROCESSING UNITS (GPGPU)

General-purpose computing on graphics processing units (GPGPU) is a fairly recent trend in computer engineering research. GPUs are co-processors that have been heavily optimized for computer graphics processing. Computer graphics processing is a field dominated by data parallel operations—particularly linear algebra matrix operations.

FIGURE 1.7: Nvidia's Tesla GPGPU card

In the early days, GPGPU programs used the normal graphics APIs for executing programs. However, several new programming languages and platforms have been built to do general purpose computation on GPUs with both Nvidia and AMD releasing programming environments with CUDA and Stream SDK respectively. Other GPU programming languages are BrookGPU, PeakStream, and RapidMind. Nvidia has also released specific products for computation in their Tesla series. The technology consortium Khronos Group has released the OpenCL specification, which is a framework for writing programs that execute across platforms consisting of CPUs and GPUs. Apple, Intel, Nvidia and others are supporting OpenCL.

1.7.2.10 APPLICATION-SPECIFIC INTEGRATED CIRCUITS

Several application-specific integrated circuit (ASIC) approaches have been devised for dealing with parallel applications. Because an ASIC is (by definition) specific to a given application, it can be fully optimized for that application. As a result, for a given application, an ASIC tends to outperform a general-purpose computer. However, ASICs are created by X-ray lithography. This process requires a mask, which can be extremely expensive. A single mask can cost over a million US dollars. (The smaller the transistors required for the chip, the more expensive the mask will be.) Meanwhile, performance increases in general-purpose computing over time (as described by Moore's Law) tend to wipe out these gains in only one or two chip generations. High initial cost, and the tendency to be overtaken by Moore's-law-driven general-purpose computing, has rendered ASICs unfeasible for most parallel computing applications. However, some have been built. One example is the peta-flop RIKEN MDGRAPE-3 machine which uses custom ASICs for molecular dynamics simulation.

1.7.2.11 VECTOR PROCESSORS

A vector processor is a CPU or computer system that can execute the same instruction on large sets of data. "Vector processors have high-level operations that work on linear arrays of numbers or vectors. An example vector operation is $A = B \times C$, where A, B, and C are each 64-element vectors of 64-bit floating-point numbers." They are closely related to Flynn's SIMD classification. Cray computers became famous for their vector-processing computers in the 1970s and 1980s.

FIGURE 1.8: The Cray-1 is the most famous vector processor.

However, vector processors—both as CPUs and as full computer systems—have generally disappeared. Modern processor instruction sets do include some vector processing instructions, such as with AltiVec and Streaming SIMD Extensions (SSE).

1.7.3 TRENDS IN SOFTWARE

Following are the various trends in software:

1.7.3.1 PARALLEL PROGRAMMING LANGUAGES

Concurrent programming languages, libraries, APIs, and parallel programming models (such as Algorithmic Skeletons) have been created for programming parallel computers. These can generally be divided into classes based on the assumptions they make about the underlying memory architecture—shared memory, distributed memory, or shared distributed memory. Shared memory programming languages communicate by manipulating shared memory variables. Distributed memory uses message passing. POSIX Threads and OpenMP are two of most widely used shared memory APIs, whereas Message Passing Interface (MPI) is the most widely used message-passing system API. One concept used in programming parallel programs is the future concept, where one part of a program promises to deliver a required datum to another part of a program at some future time.

CAPS entreprise and Pathscale are also coordinating their effort to make HMPP (Hybrid Multicore Parallel Programming) directives an Open Standard denoted OpenHMPP. The OpenHMPP directive-based programming model offers syntax to efficiently offload computations on hardware accelerators and to optimize data movement to/from the hardware memory. OpenHMPP directives describe remote procedure call (RPC) on an accelerator device (e.g. GPU) or more generally a set of cores. The directives annotate C or FORTRAN codes to describe two sets of functionalities: the offloading of procedures (denoted codelets) onto a remote device and the optimization of data transfers between the CPU main memory and the accelerator me

1.7.3.2 AUTOMATIC PARALLELIZATION

Automatic parallelization of a sequential program by a compiler is the holy grail of parallel computing. Despite decades of work by compiler researchers, automatic parallelization has had only limited success.

Mainstream parallel programming languages remain either explicitly parallel or (at best) partially implicit, in which a programmer gives the compiler directives for parallelization. A few fully implicit parallel programming languages exist—SISAL, Parallel Haskell, and (for FPGAs) Mitrion-C.

1.7.3.3 APPLICATION CHECKPOINTING

The larger and more complex a computer is, the more that can go wrong and the shorter the mean time between failures. Application checkpointing is a technique whereby the computer system takes a "snapshot" of the application—a record of all current resource allocations and variable states, akin to a core dump; this information can be used to restore the program if the computer should fail. Application checkpointing means that the program has to restart from only its last checkpoint rather than the beginning. For an application that may run for months, that is critical. Application checkpointing may be used to facilitate process migration.

1.7.4 TRENDS IN APPLICATIONS

As computers become ever faster, it can be tempting to suppose that they will eventually become "fast enough" and that appetite for increased computing power will be sated. However, history suggests that as a particular technology satisfies known applications, new applications will arise that are enabled by that technology and that will demand the development of new technology. As an amusing illustration of this phenomenon, a report prepared for the British government in the late 1940s concluded that Great Britain's computational requirements could be met by two or perhaps three computers. In those days, computers were used primarily for computing ballistics tables. The authors of the report did not consider other applications in science and engineering, let alone the commercial applications that would soon come to dominate computing. Similarly, the initial prospectus for Cray Research predicted a market for ten supercomputers; many hundreds have since been sold.

Traditionally, developments at the high end of computing have been motivated by numerical simulations of complex systems such as weather, climate, mechanical devices, electronic circuits, manufacturing processes, and chemical reactions. However, the most significant forces driving the development of faster computers today are emerging commercial applications that require a computer to be able to process large amounts of data in sophisticated ways. These applications include video conferencing, collaborative work environments, and computer-aided diagnosis in medicine, parallel databases used for decision support, and advanced graphics and virtual reality, particularly in the entertainment industry. For example, the integration of parallel computation, high-performance networking, and multimedia technologies is leading to the development of *video servers,* computers designed to serve hundreds or thousands of simultaneous requests for real-time video. Each video stream can involve both data transfer rates of many megabytes per second and large amounts of processing for encoding and decoding. In graphics, three-dimensional data sets are now approaching 10^9 volume elements (1024 on a side). At 200 operations per element, a display updated 30 times per second requires a computer capable of 6.4×10^{12} operations per second.

Although commercial applications may define the architecture of most future parallel computers, traditional scientific applications will remain important users of parallel computing technology. Indeed, as nonlinear effects place limits on the insights offered by purely theoretical investigations and as experimentation become more costly or impractical, computational studies of complex systems are becoming ever more important. Computational costs typically increase as the fourth power or more of the ``resolution" that determines accuracy, so these studies have a seemingly insatiable demand for more computer power. They are also often characterized by large memory and input/output requirements. For example, a ten-year simulation of the earth's climate using a state-of-the-art model may involve 10^{16} floating-point operations---ten days at an execution speed of 10^{10}floating-point operations per second (10 gigaflops). This same simulation can easily generate a hundred gigabytes (10^{11} bytes) or more of data. Yet as Table 1.2 shows, scientists can easily imagine refinements to these models that would increase these computational requirements 10,000 times.

TABLE 1.2: Various refinements proposed to climate models, and the increased computational requirements associated with these refinements. Altogether, these refinements could increase computational requirements by a factor of between 10^4 and 10^7.

Current State	Needed Capability	Cost
100-km resolution	10-km resolution	10^2-10^3
Simple process representations	Improved process representations	2-10
Simple ocean	Fully coupled ocean	2-5
Simple atmospheric chemistry	Improved atmospheric chemistry	2-5
Limited biosphere	Comprehensive biosphere	about 2
Tens of years	Hundreds of years	10-10^2

In summary, the need for faster computers is driven by the demands of both data-intensive applications in commerce and computation-intensive applications in science and engineering. Increasingly, the requirements of these fields are merging, as scientific and engineering applications become more data intensive and commercial applications perform more sophisticated computations.

1.7.5 TRENDS IN COMPUTER DESIGN

The performance of the fastest computers has grown exponentially from 1945 to the present, averaging a factor of 10 every five years. While the first computers performed a few tens of floating-point operations per second, the parallel computers of the mid-1990s achieve tens of billions of operations per second (Figure 1.9). Similar trends can be observed in the low-end computers of different eras: the calculators, personal computers, and workstations. There is little to suggest that this growth will not continue. However, the computer architectures used to sustain this growth are changing radically---from sequential to parallel.

The performance of a computer depends directly on the time required to perform a basic operation and the number of these basic operations that can be performed concurrently. The time to perform a basic operation is ultimately limited by the "clock cycle" of the processor, that is, the time required to perform the most primitive operation. However, clock cycle times are decreasing slowly and appear to be approaching physical limits such as the speed of light (Figure 1.10). We cannot depend on faster processors to provide increased computational performance.

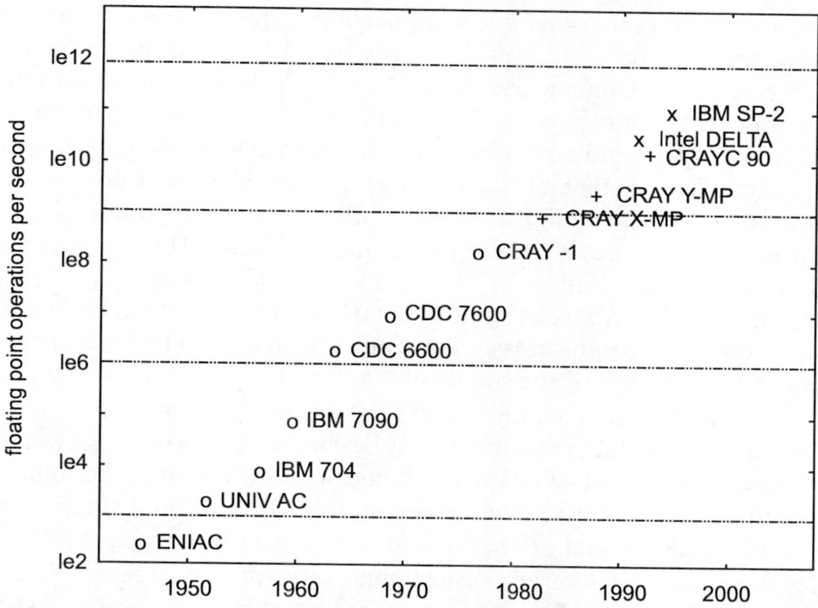

FIGURE 1.9: Peak performance of some of the fastest supercomputers, 1945–1995. The exponential growth flattened off somewhat in the 1980s but is accelerating again as massively parallel supercomputers become available. Here, "o" are uniprocessors, "+" denotes modestly parallel vector computers with 4–16 processors, and "x" denotes massively parallel computers with hundreds or thousands of processors. Typically, massively parallel computers achieve a lower proportion of their peak performance on realistic applications than do vector computers.

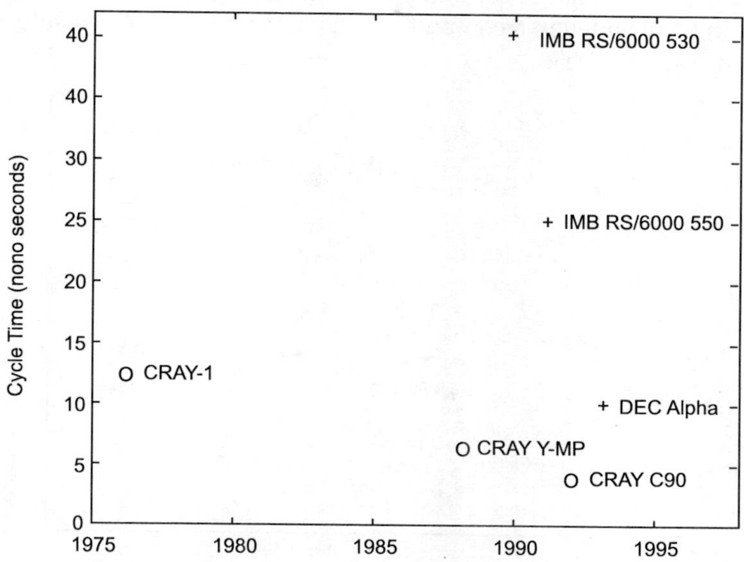

Figure 1.10: Trends in computer clock cycle times. Conventional vector supercomputer cycle times (denoted "o") have decreased only by a factor of 3 in sixteen years, from the CRAY-1 (12.5 nanoseconds) to the C90 (4.0). RISC microprocessors (denoted "+") are fast approaching the same performance. Both architectures appear to be approaching physical limits.

To circumvent these limitations, the designer may attempt to utilize internal concurrency in a chip, for example, by operating simultaneously on all 64 bits of two numbers that are to be multiplied. However, a fundamental result in Very Large Scale Integration (VLSI) complexity theory says that this strategy is expensive. This result states that for certain transitive computations (in which any output may depend on any input), the chip area *A* and the time *T* required to perform this computation are related so that AT^2 must exceed some problem-dependent function of problem size. This result can be explained informally by assuming that a computation must move a certain amount of information from one side of a square chip to the other. The amount of information that can be moved in a time unit is limited by the cross section of the chip, $\sqrt{A}$. This gives a transfer rate of $\sqrt{AT}$ from which the AT^2 relation is obtained. To decrease the time required to move the information by a certain factor, the cross section must be increased by the same factor, and hence the total area must be increased by the square of that factor.

This AT^2 result means that not only is it difficult to build individual components that operate faster, it may not even be desirable to do so. It may be cheaper to use more, slower components. For example, if we have an area n^2 of silicon to use in a computer, we can either build n^2 components, each of size *A* and able to perform an operation in time *T*, or build a single component able to perform the same operation in time *T/n*. The multicomponent system is potentially *n* times faster.

Computer designers use a variety of techniques to overcome these limitations on single computer performance, including pipelining (different stages of several instructions execute concurrently) and multiple function units (several multipliers, adders, etc., are controlled by a single instruction stream). Increasingly, designers are incorporating multiple ``computers," each with its own processor, memory, and associated interconnection logic. This approach is facilitated by advances in VLSI technology that continue to decrease the number of components required to implement a computer. As the cost of a computer is (very approximately) proportional to the number of components that it contains, increased integration also increases the number of processors that can be included in a computer for a particular cost. The result is continued growth in processor counts (Figure 1.11).

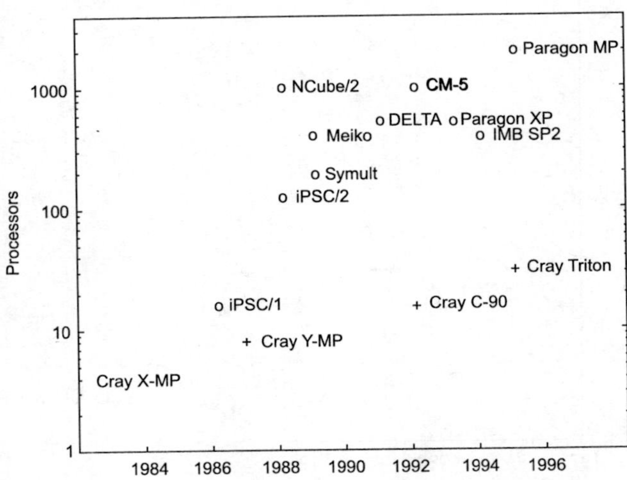

FIGURE 1.11: Number of processors in massively parallel computers ("o") and vector multiprocessors ("+"). In both cases, a steady increase in processor count is apparent. A similar trend is starting to occur in workstations, and personal computers can be expected to follow the same trend.

1.7.6 TRENDS IN NETWORKING

Another important trend changing the face of computing is an enormous increase in the capabilities of the networks that connect computers. Not long ago, high-speed networks ran at 1.5 Mbits per second; by the end of the 1990s, bandwidths in excess of 1000 Mbits per second will be commonplace. Significant improvements in reliability are also expected. These trends make it feasible to develop applications that use physically distributed resources as if they were part of the same computer. A typical application of this sort may utilize processors on multiple remote computers, access a selection of remote databases, perform rendering on one or more graphics computers, and provide real-time output and control on a workstation.

We emphasize that computing on networked computers ("distributed computing") is not just a subfield of parallel computing. Distributed computing is deeply concerned with problems such as reliability, security, and heterogeneity that are generally regarded as tangential in parallel computing. (As Leslie Lamport has observed, "A distributed system is one in which the failure of a computer you didn't even know existed can render your own computer unusable.") Yet the basic task of developing programs that can run on many computers at once is a parallel computing problem. In this respect, the previously distinct worlds of parallel and distributed computing are converging.

1.8 A PARALLEL MACHINE MODEL

The rapid penetration of computers into commerce, science, and education owed much to the early standardization on a single machine model, the von Neumann computer. A von Neumann computer comprises a central processing unit (CPU) connected to a storage unit (memory) (Figure 1.12). The CPU executes a stored program that specifies a sequence of read and write operations on the memory. This simple model has proved remarkably robust. Its persistence over more than forty years has allowed the study of such important topics as algorithms and programming languages to proceed to a large extent independently of developments in computer architecture. Consequently, programmers can be trained in the abstract art of "programming" rather than the craft of "programming machine X" and can design algorithms for an abstract von Neumann machine, confident that these algorithms will execute on most target computers with reasonable efficiency.

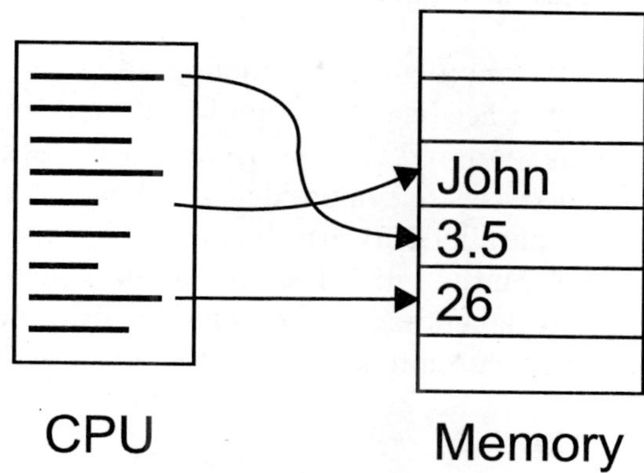

FIGURE 1.12: The von Neumann computer. A central processing unit (CPU) executes a program that performs a sequence of read and writes operations on an attached memory.

Our study of parallel programming will be most rewarding if we can identify a parallel machine model that is as general and useful as the von Neumann sequential machine model. This machine model must be both simple and realistic: *simple* to facilitate understanding and programming, and *realistic* to ensure that programs developed for the model execute with reasonable efficiency on real computers.

1.8.1 THE MULTICOMPUTER

A parallel machine model called the *multicomputer* fits these requirements. As illustrated in Figure 1.13, a multicomputer comprises a number of von Neumann computers, or *nodes*, linked by an *interconnection network*. Each computer executes its own program. This program may access local memory and may send and receive messages over the network. Messages are used to communicate with other computers or, equivalently, to read and write remote memories. In the idealized network, the cost of sending a message between two nodes is independent of both node location and other network traffic, but does depend on message length.

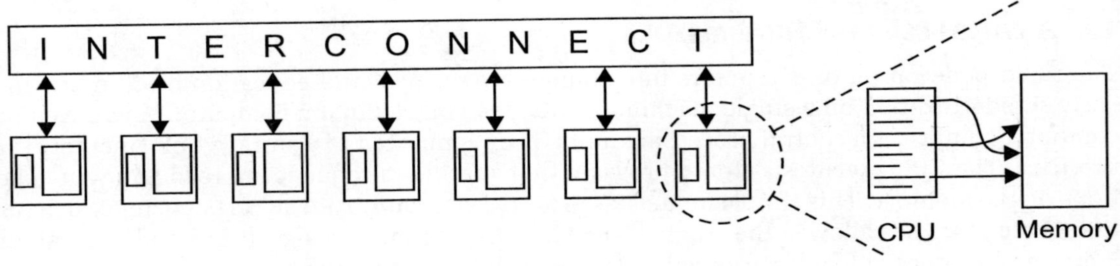

FIGURE 1.13: The multicomputer, an idealized parallel computer model. Each node consists of a von Neumann machine: a CPU and memory. A node can communicate with other nodes by sending and receiving messages over an interconnection network.

A defining attribute of the multicomputer model is that accesses to local (same-node) memory are less expensive than accesses to remote (different-node) memory. That is, read and write are less costly than send and receive. Hence, it is desirable that accesses to local data be more frequent than accesses to remote data. This property, called *locality*, is a third fundamental requirement for parallel software, in addition to concurrency and scalability. The importance of locality depends on the ratio of remote to local access costs. This ratio can vary from 10:1 to 1000:1 or greater, depending on the relative performance of the local computer, the network, and the mechanisms used to move data to and from the network.

1.8.2 OTHER MACHINE MODELS

We review important parallel computer architectures (several are illustrated in Figure 1.14) and discuss briefly how these differ from the idealized multicomputer model.

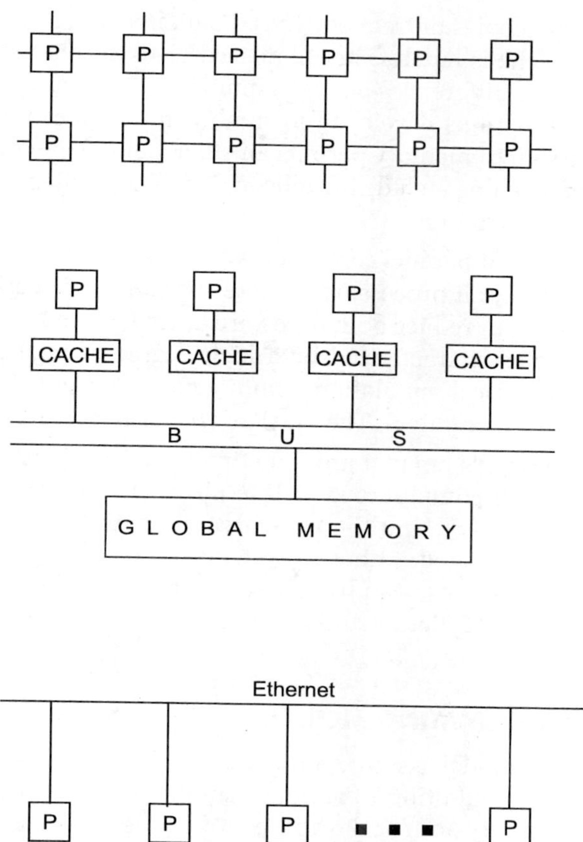

FIGURE 1.14: Classes of parallel computer architecture. From top to bottom: a distributed-memory MIMD computer with a mesh interconnect, a shared-memory multiprocessor, and a local area network (in this case, an Ethernet). In each case, P denotes an independent processor.

The multicomputer is most similar to what is often called the *distributed-memory MIMD* (multiple instruction multiple data) computer. MIMD means that each processor can execute a separate stream of instructions on its own local data; distributed memory means that memory is distributed among the processors, rather than placed in a central location. The principal difference between a multicomputer and the distributed-memory MIMD computer is that in the latter, the cost of sending a message between two nodes may not be independent of node location and other network traffic. Examples of this class of machine include the IBM SP, Intel Paragon, Thinking Machines CM5, Cray T3D, Meiko CS-2, and nCUBE.

Another important class of parallel computer is the *multiprocessor* or shared-memory MIMD computer. In multiprocessors, all processors share access to a common memory, typically via a bus or a hierarchy of buses. In the idealized Parallel Random Access Machine (PRAM) model, often used in theoretical studies of parallel algorithms, any processor can access any memory element in the same amount of time. In practice, scaling this architecture usually introduces some form of memory hierarchy; in particular, the frequency with which the shared memory is accessed may be reduced by storing copies of frequently used data items in a *cache* associated with each processor. Access to this cache is much faster than access to the shared memory; hence, locality is usually important, and the differences between multicomputers and multiprocessors are really just questions of degree. Programs developed for multicomputers can also execute efficiently on multiprocessors, because shared memory permits an efficient implementation of message passing. Examples of this class of machine include the Silicon Graphics Challenge, Sequent Symmetry, and the many multiprocessor workstations.

A more specialized class of parallel computer is the *SIMD* (single instruction multiple data) computer. In SIMD machines, all processors execute the same instruction stream on a different piece of data. This approach can reduce both hardware and software complexity but is appropriate only for specialized problems characterized by a high degree of regularity, for example, image processing and certain numerical simulations. Multicomputer algorithms *cannot* in general be executed efficiently on SIMD computers. The MasPar MP is an example of this class of machine.

Two classes of computer system that are sometimes used as parallel computers are the local area network (LAN), in which computers in close physical proximity (e.g., the same building) are connected by a fast network, and the wide area network (WAN), in which geographically distributed computers are connected. Although systems of this sort introduce additional concerns such as reliability and security, they can be viewed for many purposes as multicomputers, albeit with high remote-access costs. Ethernet and asynchronous transfer mode (ATM) are commonly used network technologies.

1.9 A PARALLEL PROGRAMMING MODEL

The von Neumann machine model assumes a processor able to execute sequences of instructions. An instruction can specify, in addition to various arithmetic operations, the address of a datum to be read or written in memory and/or the address of the next instruction to be executed. While it is possible to program a computer in terms of this basic model by writing machine language, this method is for most purposes prohibitively complex, because we must keep track of millions of memory locations and organize the execution of thousands of machine instructions. Hence, modular design techniques are applied, whereby complex programs are constructed from simple components, and components are structured in terms of higher-level abstractions such as data structures, iterative loops, and procedures. Abstractions such as procedures make the exploitation of modularity easier by allowing objects to be manipulated without concern for their internal structure. So do high-level languages such as Fortran, Pascal, C, and Ada, which allow designs expressed in terms of these abstractions to be translated automatically into executable code.

Parallel programming introduces additional sources of complexity: if we were to program at the lowest level, not only would the number of instructions executed increase, but we would also need to manage explicitly the execution of thousands of processors and coordinate millions of interprocessor interactions. Hence, abstraction and modularity are at least as important as in sequential programming. In fact, we shall emphasize *modularity* as a fourth fundamental requirement for parallel software, in addit

1.9.1 TASKS AND CHANNELS

We consider next the question of which abstractions are appropriate and useful in a parallel programming model. Clearly, mechanisms are needed that allow explicit discussion about concurrency and locality and that facilitate development of scalable and modular programs. Also needed are abstractions that are simple to work with and that match the architectural model, the multicomputer.

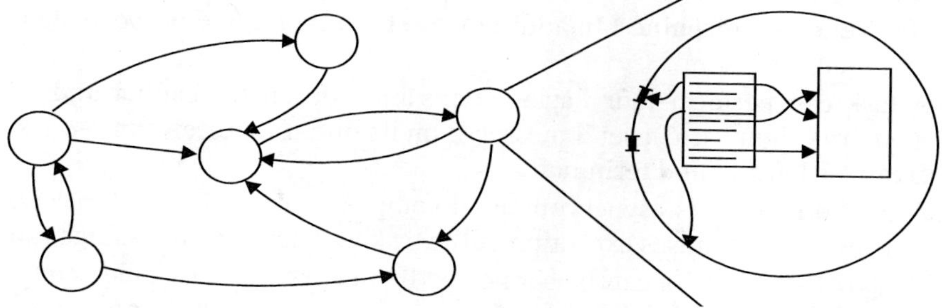

FIGURE 1.15: A simple parallel programming model. The figure shows both the instantaneous state of a computation and a detailed picture of a single task. A computation consists of a set of tasks (represented by circles) connected by channels (arrows). A task encapsulates a program and local memory and defines a set of ports that define its interface to its environment. A channel is a message queue into which a sender can place messages and from which a receiver can remove messages, "blocking" if messages are not available.

While numerous possible abstractions could be considered for this purpose, two fit these requirements particularly well: the *task* and *channel*. These are illustrated in Figure 1.15 and can be summarized as follows:

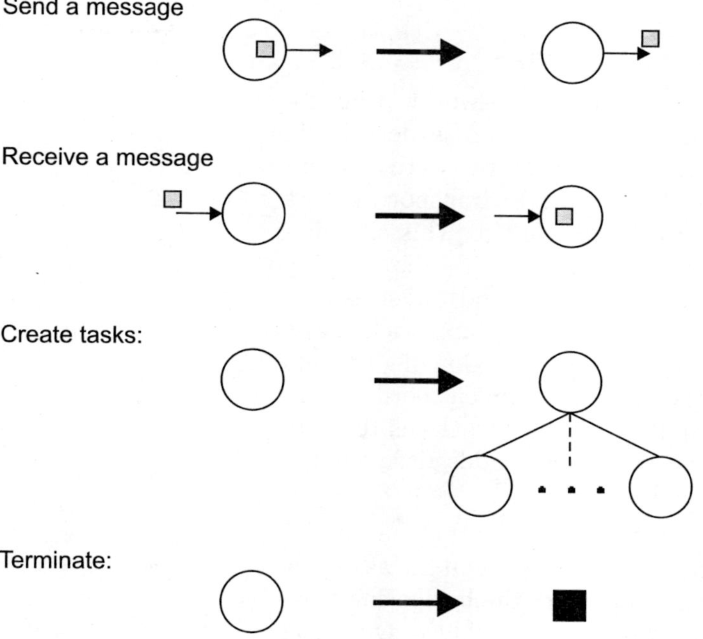

FIGURE 1.16: The four basic task actions. In addition to reading and writing local memory, a task can send a message, receive a message, create new tasks (suspending until they terminate), and terminate.

1. A parallel computation consists of one or more tasks. Tasks execute concurrently. The number of tasks can vary during program execution.
2. A task encapsulates a sequential program and local memory. (In effect, it is a virtual von Neumann machine.) In addition, a set of *inports* and *outports* define its interface to its environment.
3. A task can perform four basic actions in addition to reading and writing its local memory (Figure 1.16): send messages on its outports, receive messages on its inports, create new tasks, and terminate.
4. A send operation is asynchronous: it completes immediately. A receives operation is synchronous: it causes execution of the task to block until a message is available.
5. Outport/inport pairs can be connected by message queues called *channels*. Channels can be created and deleted, and references to channels (ports) can be included in messages, so connectivity can vary dynamically.
6. Tasks can be mapped to physical processors in various ways; the mapping employed does not affect the semantics of a program. In particular, multiple tasks can be mapped to a single processor. (We can also imagine a single task being mapped to multiple processors, but that possibility is not considered here.)

The task abstraction provides a mechanism for talking about locality: data contained in a task's local memory are "close"; other data are "remote." The channel abstraction provides a mechanism for indicating that computation in one task requires data in another task in order to proceed. (This is termed a *data dependency*). The following simple example illustrates some of these features.

Example: Bridge Construction

Consider the following real-world problem. A bridge is to be assembled from girders being constructed at a foundry. These two activities are organized by providing trucks to transport girders from the foundry to the bridge site. This situation is illustrated in Figure 1.17(a), with the foundry and bridge represented as tasks and the stream of trucks as a channel. Notice that this approach allows assembly of the bridge and construction of girders to proceed in parallel without any explicit coordination: the foundry crew puts girders on trucks as they are produced, and the assembly crew adds girders to the bridge as and when they arrive.

A disadvantage of this scheme is that the foundry may produce girders much faster than the assembly crew can use them. To prevent the bridge site from overflowing with girders, the assembly crew instead can explicitly request more girders when stocks run low. This refined approach is illustrated in Figure 1.17(b), with the stream of requests represented as a

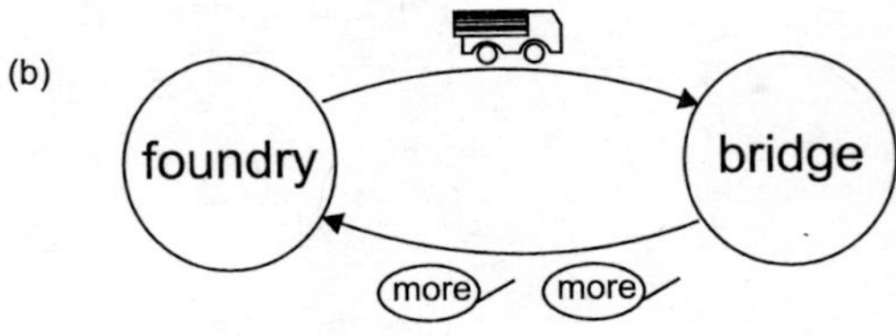

FIGURE 1.17: Two solutions to the bridge construction problem. Both represent the foundry and the bridge assembly site as separate tasks, foundry & bridge. The first uses a single channel on which girders generated by foundry are transported as fast as they are generated. If foundry generates girders faster than they are consumed by bridge, then girders accumulate at the construction site. The second solution uses a second channel to pass flow control messages from bridge to foundry so as to avoid overflow.

second channel. The second channel can also be used to shut down the flow of girders when the bridge is complete.

We now examine some other properties of this task/channel programming model: performance, mapping independence, modularity, and determinism.

Performance: Sequential programming abstractions such as procedures and data structures are effective because they can be mapped simply and efficiently to the von Neumann computer. The task and channel have a similarly direct mapping to the multicomputer. A task represents a piece of code that can be executed sequentially, on a single processor. If two tasks that share a channel are mapped to different processors, the channel connection is implemented as interprocessor communication; if they are mapped to the same processor, some more efficient mechanism can be used.

Mapping Independence: Because tasks interact using the same mechanism (channels) regardless of task location, the result computed by a program does not depend on where tasks execute.

Hence, algorithms can be designed and implemented without concern for the number of processors on which they will execute; in fact, algorithms are frequently designed that create many more tasks than processors. This is a straightforward way of achieving **scalability:** as the number of processors increases, the number of tasks per processor is reduced but the algorithm itself need not be modified. The creation of more tasks than processors can also serve to mask communication delays, by providing other computation that can be performed while communication is performed to access remote data.

Modularity: In modular program design, various components of a program are developed separately, as independent modules, and then combined to obtain a complete program. Interactions between modules are restricted to well-defined interfaces. Hence, module implementations can be changed without modifying other components, and the properties of a program can be determined from the specifications for its modules and the code that plugs these modules together. When successfully applied, modular design reduces program complexity and facilitates code reuse.

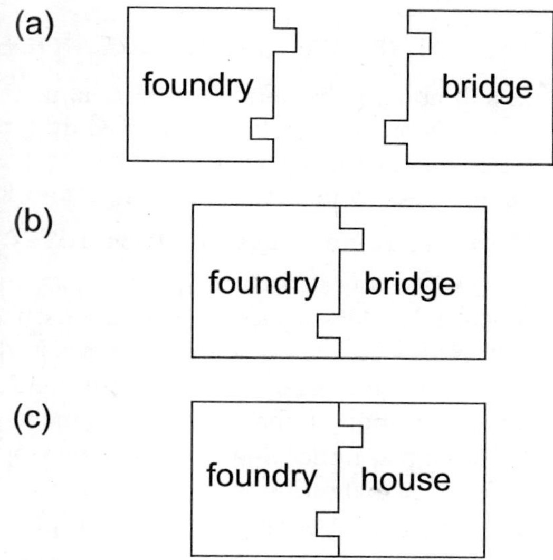

FIGURE 1.18: The task as building block. (a) The foundry and bridge tasks are building blocks with complementary interfaces. (b) Hence, the two tasks can be plugged together to form a complete program. (c) Tasks are interchangeable: another task with a compatible interface can be substituted to obtain a different program.

The task is a natural building block for modular design. As illustrated in Figure 1.18, a task encapsulates both data and the code that operates on those data; the ports on which it sends and receives messages constitute its interface. Hence, the advantages of modular design summarized in the previous paragraph are directly accessible in the task/channel model.

Strong similarities exist between the task/channel model and the popular object-oriented programming paradigm. Tasks, like objects, encapsulate data and the code that operates on those data. Distinguishing features of the task/channel model are its concurrency, its use of channels rather than method calls to specify interactions, and its lack of support for inheritance.

Determinism: An algorithm or program is deterministic if execution with a particular input always yields the same output. It is nondeterministic if multiple executions with the same input can give different outputs. Although nondeterminism is sometimes useful and must be supported, a parallel programming model that makes it easy to write deterministic programs is highly desirable. Deterministic programs tend to be easier to understand. Also, when checking for correctness, only one execution sequence of a parallel program needs to be considered, rather than all possible executions.

The "arms-length" interaction supported by the task/channel model makes determinism relatively easy to guarantee. As we shall see in Part II when we consider programming tools, it suffices to verify that each channel has a single sender and a single receiver and that a task receiving on a channel blocks until a receive operation is complete. These conditions can be relaxed when nondeterministic interactions are required.

In the bridge construction example, determinism means that the same bridge will be constructed regardless of the rates at which the foundry builds girders and the assembly crew puts girders together. If the assembly crew runs ahead of the foundry, it will block, waiting for girders to arrive. Hence, it simply suspends its operations until more girders are available, rather than attempting to continue construction with half-completed girders. Similarly, if the foundry produces girders faster than the assembly crew can use them, these girders simply accumulate until they are needed. Determinism would be guaranteed even if several bridges were constructed simultaneously: As long as girders destined for different bridges travel on distinct channels, they cannot be confused.

1.9.2 OTHER PROGRAMMING MODELS

In subsequent chapters, the task/channel model will often be used to describe algorithms. However, this model is certainly not the only approach that can be taken to representing parallel computation. Many other models have been proposed, differing in their flexibility, task interaction mechanisms, task granularities, and support for locality, scalability, and modularity.

Here, we review several alternatives:

1. Message passing: Message passing is probably the most widely used parallel programming model today. Message-passing programs, like task/channel programs, create multiple tasks, with each task encapsulating local data. Each task is identified by a unique name, and tasks interact by sending and receiving messages to and from named tasks. In this respect, message passing is really just a minor variation on the task/channel model, differing only in the mechanism used for data transfer. For example, rather than sending a message on "channel ch," we may send a message to "task 17." We explain that the definition of channels is a useful discipline even when designing message-passing programs, because it forces us to conceptualize the communication structure of a parallel program.

The message-passing model does not preclude the dynamic creation of tasks, the execution of multiple tasks per processor, or the execution of different programs by different tasks. However, in practice most message-passing systems create a fixed number of identical tasks at program startup and do not allow tasks to be created or destroyed during program execution. These systems are said to implement a *single program multiple data* (SPMD) programming model because each task executes the same program but operates on different data. As explained in subsequent chapters, the SPMD model is sufficient for a wide range of parallel programming problems but does hinder some parallel algorithm developments.

2. Data Parallelism: Another commonly used parallel programming model, data parallelism, calls for exploitation of the concurrency that derives from the application of the same operation to multiple elements of a data structure, for example, "add 2 to all elements of this array," or "increase the salary of all employees with 5 years service." A data-parallel program consists of a sequence of such operations. As each operation on each data element can be thought of as an independent task, the natural granularity of a data-parallel computation is small, and the concept of "locality" does not arise naturally. Hence, data-parallel compilers often require the programmer to provide information about how data are to be distributed over processors, in other words, how data are to be partitioned into tasks. The compiler can then translate the data-parallel program into an SPMD formulation, thereby generating communication code automatically. We show that the algorithm design and analysis techniques developed for the task/channel model apply directly to data-parallel programs; in particular, they provide the concepts required to understand the locality and scalability of data-parallel programs.

3. Shared Memory: In the shared-memory programming model, tasks share a common address space, which they read and write asynchronously. Various mechanisms such as locks and semaphores may be used to control access to the shared memory. An advantage of this model from the programmer's point of view is that the notion of data "ownership" is lacking, and hence there is no need to specify explicitly the communication of data from producers to consumers. This model can simplify program development. However, understanding and managing locality becomes more difficult, an important consideration (as noted earlier) on most shared-memory architectures. It can also be more difficult to write deterministic programs.

1.10 PARALLEL ALGORITHM EXAMPLES

We conclude this chapter by presenting four examples of parallel algorithms. We do not concern ourselves here with the process by which these algorithms are derived or with their efficiency. The goal is simply to introduce parallel algorithms and their description in terms of tasks and channels.

The first two algorithms described have an SPMD structure, the third creates tasks dynamically during program execution, and the fourth uses a fixed number of tasks but has different tasks perform different functions.

1.10.1 FINITE DIFFERENCES

We first consider a one-dimensional finite difference problem, in which we have a vector $X^{(0)}$ of size N and must compute $X^{(T)}$, where

$$0 < i < N-1, 0 \le t < T: X_i^{(t+1)} = \frac{X_{i-1}^{(t)} + 2X_i^{(t)} + X_{i+1}^{(t)}}{4}$$

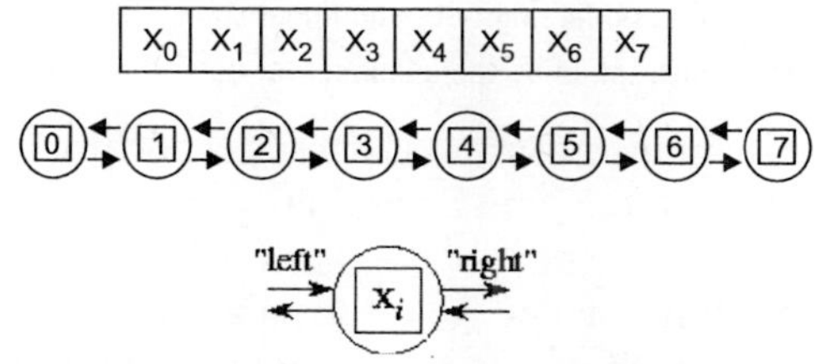

FIGURE 1.19: A parallel algorithm for the one-dimensional finite difference problem. From top to bottom: the one-dimensional vector X , where N = 8 ; the task structure, showing the 8 tasks, each encapsulating a single data value and connected to left and right neighbors via channels; and the structure of a single task, showing its two inports and outports.

That is, we must repeatedly update each element of X, with no element being updated in step $t+1$ until its neighbors have been updated in step t.

A parallel algorithm for this problem creates N tasks, one for each point in X. The i th task is given the value $X_i^{(0)}$ and is responsible for computing, in T steps, the values $X_i^{(1)}, X_i^{(2)}, \ldots, X_i^{(T)}$. Hence, at step t, it must obtain the values $X_{i-1}^{(t)}$ and $X_{i+1}^{(t)}$ from tasks $i-1$ and $i+1$. We specify this data transfer by defining channels that link each task with "left" and "right" neighbors, as shown in Figure 1.19, and requiring that at step t, each task i other than task 0 and task $N-1$

1. sends its data $X_i^{(t)}$ on its left and right outports,
2. receives $X_{i-1}^{(t)}$ and $X_{i+1}^{(t)}$ from its left and right inports, and
3. uses these values to compute $X_i^{(t+1)}$.

Notice that the N tasks can execute independently, with the only constraint on execution order being the synchronization enforced by the receive operations. This synchronization ensures that no data value is updated at step $t+1$ until the data values in neighboring tasks have been updated at step t. Hence, execution is deterministic.

1.10.2 PAIRWISE INTERACTIONS

Our second example uses a similar channel structure but requires a more complex communication algorithm. Many problems require the computation of all $N(N-1)$ pairwise interactions $I(X_i, X_j)$ $i \neq j$, between N data, $X_0, \ldots, X_{N-1}$. Interactions may be symmetric, in which case $I(X_i, X_j) = \pm I(X_j, X_i)$ and only $N(N-1)/2$ interactions need be computed. For example, in molecular dynamics we may require the total force vector f_i acting on each atom X_i, defined as follows:

$$fi = \sum_{j=0}^{N-1} F(Xi, Xj)$$

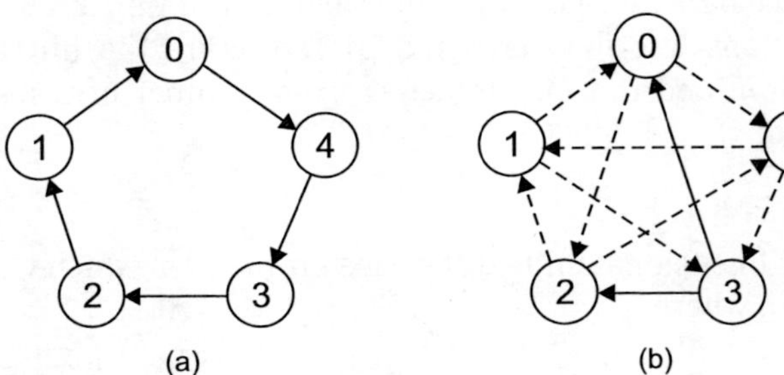

FIGURE 1.20: Task structures for computing pairwise interactions for N = 5. (a) The unidirectional ring used in the simple, nonsymmetric algorithm. (b) The unidirectional ring with additional channels used to return accumulated values in the symmetric algorithm; the path taken by the accumulator used for task 0 is shown as a solid line.

Each atom is represented by its mass and Cartesian coordinates. $F(X_i, X_j)$ denotes the mutual attraction or repulsion between atoms X_i and X_j; in this example, $F(X_i, X_j) = -F(X_j, X_i)$, so interactions are symmetric.

A simple parallel algorithm for the general pairwise interactions problem might create N tasks. Task i is given the datum Xi and is responsible for computing the interactions $\{I(Xi, Xj) \mid i \neq j\}$. One might think that as each task needs a datum from every other task, $N(N-1)$ channels would be needed to perform the necessary communications. However, a more economical structure is possible that uses only *N* channels. These channels are used to connect the *N* tasks in a unidirectional ring (Figure 1.20(a)). Hence, each task has one inport and one outport. Each task first initializes both a buffer (with the value of its local datum) and an accumulator that will maintain the result of the computation. It then repeatedly

1. sends the value contained in its buffer on its outport,
2. receives a datum on its inport into its buffer,
3. computes the interaction between this datum and its local datum, and
4. uses the computed interaction to update its local accumulator.

This send-receive-compute cycle is repeated *N-1* times, causing the *N* data to flow around the ring. Every task sees every datum and is able to compute all *N-1* interactions involving its datum. The algorithm involves *N-1* communications per task.

It turns out that if interactions are symmetric, we can halve both the number of interactions computed and the number of communications by refining the communication structure. Assume for simplicity that *N* is odd. An additional *N* communication channels are created, linking each task to the task offset [N/2] around the ring (Figure 1.20(b)). Each time an interaction $I(X_i, X_j)$ is computed between a local datum X_i and an incoming datum X_j, this value is accumulated not only in the accumulator for X_i but also in another accumulator that is circulated with X_j. After [N/2] steps, the accumulators associated with the circulated values are returned to their home task using the new channels and combined with the local accumulators. Hence, each symmetric interaction is computed only once: either as $I(X_i, X_j)$ on the node that holds X_i or as $I(X_j, X_i)$ on the node that holds X_j.

1.10.3 SEARCH

The next example illustrates the dynamic creation of tasks and channels during program execution. Algorithm 1.1 explores a search tree looking for nodes that correspond to "solutions." A parallel algorithm for this problem can be structured as follows. Initially, a single task is created for the root of the tree. A task evaluates its node and then, if that node is not a solution, creates a new task for each search call (subtree). A channel created for each new task is used to return to the new task's parent any solutions located in its subtree. Hence, new tasks and channels are created in a wavefront as the search progress **Algorithm 1.1:** A recursive formulation of a simple search algorithm. When called to expand a search tree node, this procedure checks to see whether the node in question represents a solution. If not, the algorithm makes recursive calls to the same procedure to expand each of the offspring nodes.

```
procedure search (A)
begin
if (solution (A)) then
score = eval (A)
report solution and score
else
for each child A(i) of A
search (A(i))
endfor
endif
end
```

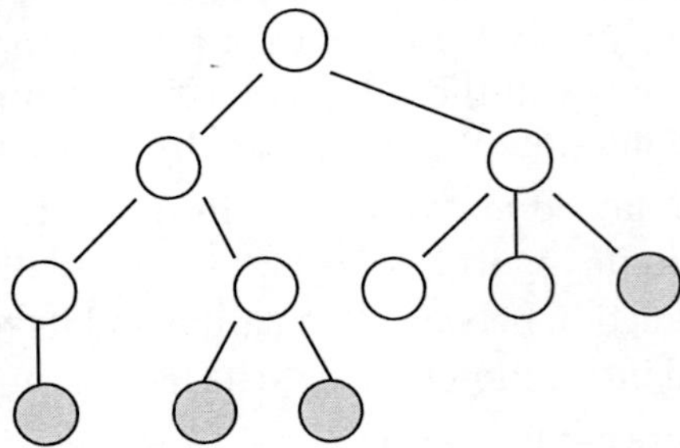

FIGURE 1.21: Task structure for the search example. Each circle represents a node in the search tree and hence a call to the search procedure. A task is created for each node in the tree as it is explored. At any one time, some tasks are actively engaged in expanding the tree further (these are shaded in the figure); others have reached solution nodes and are terminating, or are waiting for their offspring to report back with solutions. The lines represent the channels used to return solutions.

1.10.4 PARAMETER STUDY

In so-called embarrassingly parallel problems, a computation consists of a number of tasks that can execute more or less independently, without communication. These problems are usually easy to adapt for parallel execution. An example is a parameter study, in which the same computation must be performed using a range of different input parameters. The parameter values are read from an input file, and the results of the different computations are written to an output file.

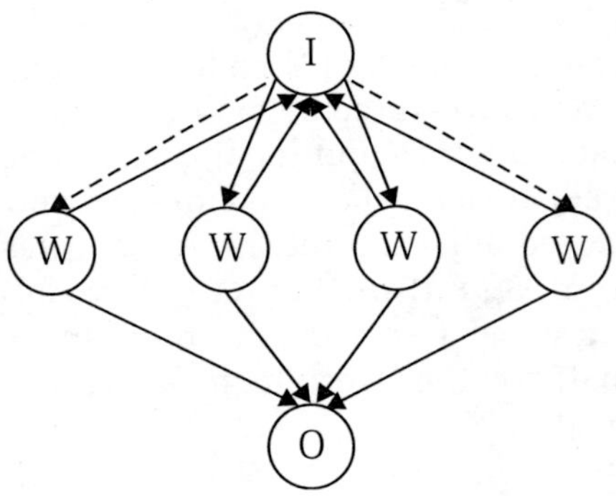

FIGURE 1.22: Task structure for parameter study problem. Workers (W) request parameters from the input task (I) and send results to the output task (O). Note the many-to-one connections: this program is nondeterministic in that the input and output tasks receive data from workers in whatever order the data are generated. Reply channels, represented as dashed lines, are used to communicate parameters from the input task to workers.

If the execution time per problem is constant and each processor has the same computational power, then it suffices to partition available problems into equal-sized sets and allocate one such set to each processor. In other situations, we may choose to use the task structure illustrated in Figure 1.22. The input and output tasks are responsible for reading and writing the input and output files, respectively. Each worker task (typically one per processor) repeatedly requests parameter values from the input task, computes using these values, and sends results to the output task. Because execution times vary, the input and output tasks cannot expect to receive messages from the various workers in any particular order. Instead, a many-to-one communication structure is used that allows them to receive messages from the various workers in arrival order.

The input task responds to a worker request by sending a parameter to that worker. Hence, a worker that has sent a request to the input task simply waits for the parameter to arrive on its reply channel. In some cases, efficiency can be improved by *prefetching*, that is, requesting the next parameter before it is needed. The worker can then perform computation while its request is being processed by the input task. Because this program uses many-to-one communication structures, the order in which computations are performed is not necessarily determined. However, this nondeterminism affects only the allocation of problems to workers and the ordering of results in the output file, not the actual results computed.

QUESTIONS

1. What do you understand by computer architecture and parallel processing?
2. Explain the four decades of computing?
3. What do you mean by parallel computing?
4. Explain the various types of parallelism?
5. Explain the various existing architectural techniques?
6. What do you mean by multi-threading?
7. Explain the relationship between parallelism and computing?
8. Explain the various classes of parallel computers?
9. Explain the parallel trends in hardware?
10. Explain the various trends in software?
11. Explain the various trends in applications, computer design and networking?
12. Explain the parallel machine model?
13. Explain the concept of multicomputer?
14. Explain the parallel programming model in detail?
15. Explain the task/channel model in detail?
16. Explain the various parallel algorithm examples in detail?

CHAPTER 2

PARADIGMS OF COMPUTING : SYNCHRONOUS

2.1 SYNCHRONOUS ARCHITECTURES

This chapter includes all the parallel architectures that coordinate concurrent execution in lockstep fashion and do so via mechanisms such as global clocks, central control units or vector unit controllers. Further subdivision of this chapter is made primarily on the basis of the synchronization mechanism.

Synchronous complex systems are a direct generalization of SIMD parallel computers. Technically, synchronous systems consist of more or less identical members which evolve synchronously with identical time evolution algorithms. We can also introduce *associative systems* as a special case of the *synchronous class*. This class includes content-addressable memories and associative processors, but we will not discuss this topic further in this book.

2.2 VECTOR PROCESSORS

Vector machines are special-purpose systems targeted for high-performance scientific computations in which matrix and vector arithmetic operations are quite common. Vector is a linear array of numbers: integers or floating-point numbers. From a programming language perspective, a vector is a one-dimensional array. That does not mean that vector processors work only one-dimensional arrays. As we show later in this section, we can treat a column of a two-dimensional matrix as a vector.

A vector processor consists of a scalar processor and a vector unit, which could be thought of as an independent functional unit capable of efficient vector operations. Various pipelined vector processing methods are Horizontal Processing, in which vector computations are performed horizontally from left to right in row fashion. Vertical processing, in which vector computations are carried out vertically from top to bottom in column fashion. Vector looping, in which segmented vector loop computations are performed from left to right and top to bottom in a combined horizontal and vertical method.

2.2.1 VECTOR PROCESSING REQUIREMENTS

A vector operand contains an ordered set of n elements, where n is called the length of the vector. Each element in a vector is a scalar quantity, which may be a floating point number, an integer, a logical value or a character. A vector processor consists of a scalar processor and a vector unit, which could be thought of as an independent functional unit capable of efficient vector operations.

2.2.2 VECTOR HARDWARE

Vector computers have hardware to perform the vector operations efficiently. Operands can not be used directly from memory but rather are loaded into registers and are put back in registers after the operation. Vector hardware has the special ability to overlap or pipeline operand processing.

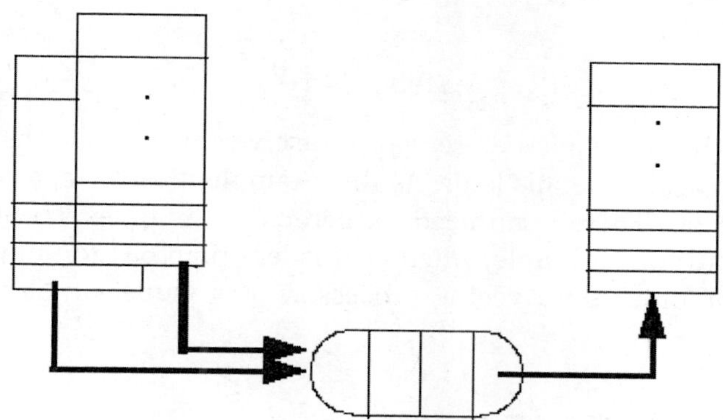

FIGURE 2.1: Vector Hardware

Vector functional units pipelined, fully segmented each stage of the pipeline performs a step of the function on different operand(s) once pipeline is full; a new result is produced each clock period (cp).

2.2.3 VECTOR PROCESSING

Vector machines are designed to operate at the vector level. To vector operations, let's assume that we have two vectors A and B, each with 64 elements. The number of elements in a vector is called the vector size. In our example, the vector size is 64. We write our vectors A and B as

$$A = a_0, a_2, \ldots\ldots\ldots\ldots, a_{n-1},$$

$$B = b_0, b_2, \ldots\ldots\ldots\ldots, b_{n-1}.$$

Suppose that we want to add these two vectors and place the result in vector C. Note that adding two vectors involves adding the corresponding elements as shown below:

$$C=A+B=a_0+b_0, a_1+b_1, \ldots\ldots\ldots\ldots, a_{n-1}+b_{n-1}.$$

In high-level programming languages, we perform the vector addition by using a loop that iterates n times, where n is the vector size. In the C language, we can write this code as

```
for(i=0; i<n; i++)
```

C[i] = A[i] + B[i];

This for loop iterates n times. The addition operation in this code is called the scalar operation. Vector processor instructions specify vector operations. For example, we just need one vector instruction to add vectors A and B. A typical vector instruction specifies four fields three registers and an operation:

VOP Vd Vs1 Vs2

Which performs Vd = Vs1 VOP Vs2. As you can see from this format, it uses the three address format. Here is what a vector addition instruction V3=V2+V1 looks like in the Cray X-MP assembly language:

V3 V2 + V1

We need some more details before we can use vector instructions for A + B. We discuss the necessary Cray machine details later. As this example illustrates, a single vector instruction replaces the entire loop. There is no need to increment the index variable i and test it for the boundary condition (in our example, whether it is less than 64) to jump back. Due to this and their exploitation of pipelining, vector processors give superior performance for scientific computations.

2.2.4 *ARCHITECTURE OF VECTOR MACHINE*

A vector machine consists of a scalar unit and a vector unit. The scalar unit works on scalars and has architecture similar to that in the traditional processors. The vector unit is responsible for performing vector operations. The first vector machines used the memory–memory architecture. In this architecture, all vector operations receive the input operands from memory and store the result in memory. The first vector machine CDC Star 100 used this architecture. Most of the current vector machines including the machines from Cray, NEC, Fujitsu, Hi-tachi, and Convex use the vector–register. All vector operations are done on vectors located in vector registers. As with the RISC processors, special load and store instructions move vectors between vector registers and memory. It consists of five components: vector registers, scalar registers, vector functional units, vector load/store unit, and main memory.

2.2.4.1 VECTOR REGISTERS

The most vector processors have eight vector registers. Each register can hold 64 elements of 64 bits each. Some processors such as the Fijitsu VP 200 allow the total available register space of 8 K elements into a programmable set of vector registers ranging from 8 to 256. When using eight vector registers, each register can hold 1024 64-bit elements; at the other end, with 256 registers, each can hold only 32 elements. As shown in Figure 2.2, each register has two read ports and one write port to allow a high degree of overlap among vector operations on different vector registers.

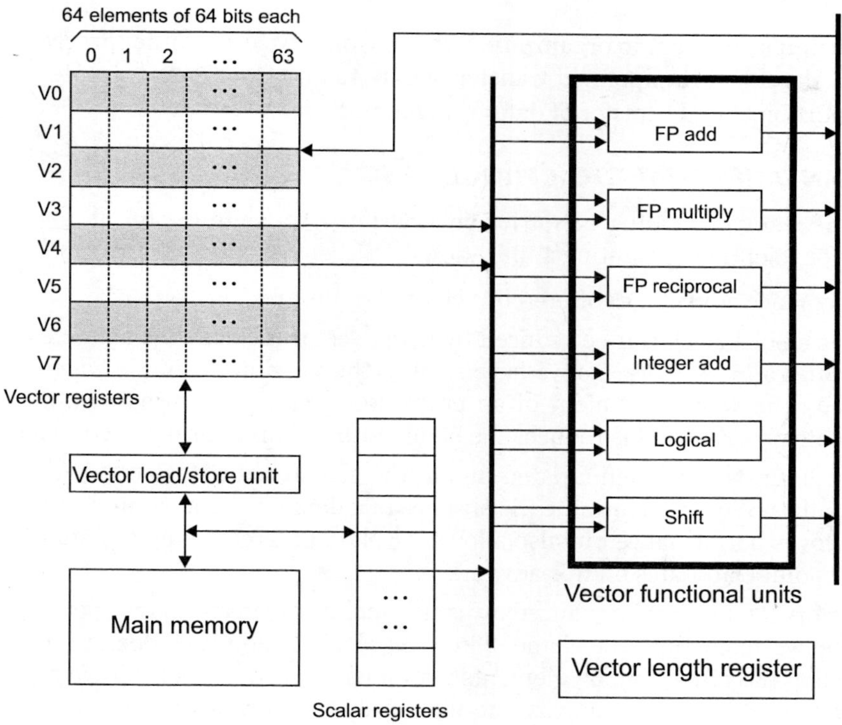

FIGURE 2.2: Vector Processor Architecture

2.2.4.2 SCALAR REGISTERS

The scalar registers provide scalar input to vector operations. For instance, when multiplying all elements of a matrix by a constant, a scalar register supplies the constant. For example, to compute

$$B = 5*X + Y$$

The constant 5 is stored in a scalar register, and vectors X and Y are stored in two vector registers. The scalar registers are also used to compute addresses for the vector load/store unit.

2.2.4.3 VECTOR LOAD/STORE UNIT

This unit is responsible for movement of data between vector registers and memory. This unit is pipelined to facilitate overlapped read and write operations from memory. As well, it will mask the high latency associated with main memory access. This unit supports two basic operations: a load vector operation to move a vector from memory to a vector register and a store vector to move a vector to the memory. However, several vector processors have more than one such unit. For example, the NEC SX/2 has eight vector load/store units.

2.2.4.4 VECTOR FUNCTIONAL UNITS

Vector processors contain several vector functional units for floating- point, integer, and logical operations. For example, the Cray 1 has 6 functional units as shown in Figure 2.2. The NEC SX/2 has 16 functional units: 4 integer add/logical, 4 FP multiply/divide, 4 FP add, and 4 shift units.

2.2.4.5 MEMORY

The memory unit is different in organization than the ones we use in other processors. The memory organization should allow pipelined transfer of data to and from memory. Interleaved memory is used to support pipelined transfer of data from memory.

2.2.5 ADVANTAGES OF VECTOR PROCESSING

Even though vector processing is not for general-purpose computation, it does offer significant advantages for scientific computing applications.

To the performance advantages offered by vector systems are:

1. Flynn's bottleneck can be reduced by using vector instructions as each vector instruction specifies a lot of work. As we have seen in the previous example, vector instructions can specify the work equivalent of an entire loop. Thus, fewer instructions are required to execute programs. This reduces the bandwidth required for instruction fetch.
2. Data hazards can be eliminated due to the structured nature of the data used by vector machines. We can determine the absence of a data hazard at compile-time, which not only improves performance but also allows for planned prefetching of data from memory. The next point elaborates on this advantage.
3. Memory latency can be reduced by using pipelined load and store operations. For example, when we fetch the first element in a 64-element addition operation, we can schedule fetching the remaining 63 elements from memory. By using interleaved memory designs, vector machines can amortize the high latency associated with memory access over the entire vector.
4. Control hazards are reduced as a result of specifying a large number of iterations in a single vector instruction. The number of iterations depends on the size of the vector registers. For example, if the machine has 64-element vector registers, each vector instruction can specify work equivalent to 64 loop iterations.
5. Pipelining can be exploited to the maximum extent. This is facilitated by the absence of data and control hazards. Vector machines not only use pipelining for integer and floating-point operations but also to feed data from one functional unit to another. This process, known as chaining. In addition, as mentioned before, load and store operations also use pipelining.

2.2.6 VECTOR STRIDE

The vector stride elements are stored in memory. Since vectors are one-dimensional arrays, storing a vector in memory is straightforward: vector elements are stored as sequential words in memory. If we want to fetch 40 elements, we read 40 contiguous words from memory. These elements are said to have a stride of 1. That is, to get to the next element, we add 1 to the current element. We will need non unit vector strides for multidimensional arrays. We want to store a two-dimensional matrix in memory. There is one of two ways: row-major or column-major order. Most languages, except FORTRAN, use the row-major order. In this ordering, elements are stored in row order: row 0, row 1, row 2, and so on. In the column-major order, which is used by FORTRAN, elements are stored column by column: column 0, column 1, and so on. As an example, consider the following 4 X 4 matrix:

$$A = \begin{bmatrix} 11 & 12 & 13 & 14 \\ 21 & 22 & 23 & 24 \\ 31 & 32 & 33 & 34 \\ 41 & 42 & 43 & 44 \end{bmatrix}$$

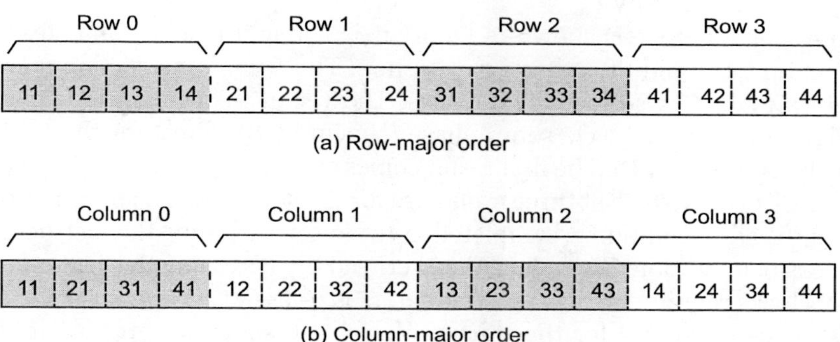

FIGURE 2.3: Memory layout of vector A

Figure 2.3 row-major orders for storing; access all elements of column 0? Clearly, these elements are not stored contiguously. We have to access 0, 4, 8, and 12 elements in the memory array. Since successive elements are separated by 4 elements, we say that the stride is 4. Vector machines provide load and store instructions that take the stride into account. For example, the instruction Vi, A0, Ak loads vector register Vi with stride Ak. Since unit stride is very common, a special instruction Vi, A0, 1 is provided. Similar instructions are available for storing vectors in memory.

2.2.7 VECTOR OPERATIONS

All vector units produce a result on each clock once the pipeline is full. Pipelined operations on the Cray X-MP proceed in three phases: setup, execution, and shutdown. During the setup phase, the functional unit is programmed to perform the appropriate operation and the connections to the source and destination vector registers are established. The setup time for all vector units is three clock cycles. The pipeline performs the computation during the execution phase. The number of cycles required to complete the computation depends on the vector length and the number of stages in the functional unit. The final shutdown phase represents the time difference between when the final result comes out of the pipeline and when the destination register can be used for another operation. For the X-MP, the shutdown phase also takes three clock cycles.

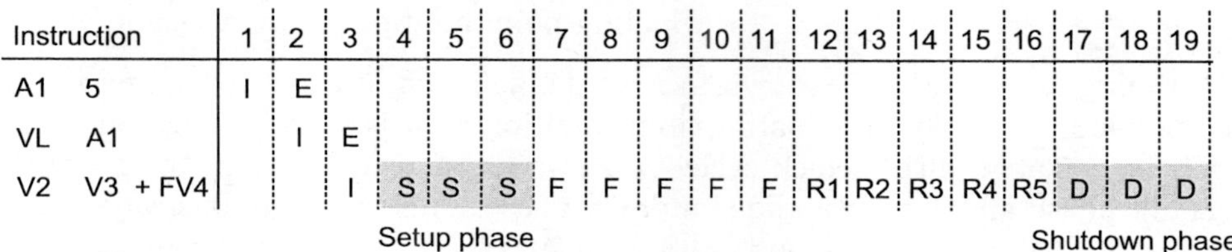

FIGURE 2.4: Timing analysis of a simple vector addition operation

Example: Simple Vector Add Operation.

As a first example, consider the following code that adds the first five elements of vectors V2 and V3 and places the result in V1:

A1	5	
VL	A1	(VL = 5)
V1	V2+FV3	

The timing for this code is shown in Figure 2.4. The first instruction takes two clock cycles: one for instruction fetch and the other for execution. The second instruction fetch is done during the second clock cycle. It also takes two clocks. The vector instruction is fetched in clock cycle 3. This is followed by a three-cycle setup phase (shown by S). Thus, for the next five clocks, the pipeline gets filled (shown by F). The first result comes out during clock 12. We get one result out for the next four clock cycles. The last three cycles are for the shutdown (D) phase. From this example, we can see that the add operation is completed in 16 clocks, excluding the instruction fetch. That is, 16/5 = 3.2 clocks per addition. We reduce the overhead by increasing the vector length. In general, the number of clocks required to add VL size vectors is 3+6+(VL - 1)+3.

The first three cycles are for the startup phase. The six cycles are the number of stages in the add pipeline. Thus, by nine clocks, the result is out. The remaining (VL- 1) results will require (VL - 1) clocks as we get one result per clock. The last three cycles are for the shutdown phase. For example, if we use 64 element vectors, the number of clocks for each addition reduces to 75/64 ≈ 1.2 clocks.

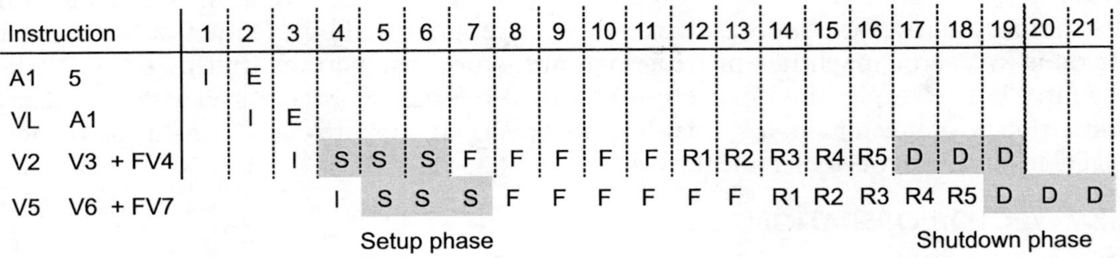

FIGURE 2.5: Overlapped execution of floating-point addition and multiplication operations.

Example: Overlapped execution of vector operations.

In this example, we consider two vector operations that are independent. These instructions can be executed in any order.

A1	5	
VL	A1	(VL = 5)
V1	V2+FV3	(Floating-point addition of V2 and V3)
V4	V5*FV6	(Floating-point multiplication of V5 and V6)

The timing for this code is shown in Figure 2.5. The first three rows are exactly the same as in the previous example. The floating-point multiply unit is a seven-stage pipeline. Thus, the first result is available during clock cycle 14. As in the add instruction, there are three clocks for the setup phase and three for the shutdown phase. This example illustrates the overlapped execution of the floating-point add and multiply units. We get significant performance gains by this overlapped execution. Without overlapping these two operations, we would have required 16 clocks for the addition and 17 clocks for the multiplication. Using overlapped execution, we complete both operations in 18 clocks.

2.2.8 CHAINING

There is no conflict on the vector registers used by the addition and multiplication operations, we could overlap the execution of the two operations. What happens if there is a conflict as in the following example?

A1	5	
VL	A1	(VL = 5)
V1	V2+FV3	(Floating-point addition of V2 and V3)
V4	V5*FV1	(Floating-point multiplication of V5 and V1)

The multiplication operation takes values from V1, which are produced by the addition operation. Due to this dependency, we cannot independently schedule these two instructions. As we have seen, sequential execution of these two instructions takes 16 + 17 = 33 clocks. This is where chaining is useful.

Instruction	1	2	3	4	5	6	7	8	9	10	11	12	13	14	15	16	17	18	19	20	21	22	23	24	25	26	27	28
A1 5	I	E																										
VL A1		I	E																									
V2 V3 + FV4			I	S	S	S	F	F	F	F	F	R1	R2	R3	R4	R5	D	D	D									
V5 V6 + FV7				I	S	S	S	H	H	H	H	H	H	H	F	F	F	F	F	F	R1	R2	R3	R4	R5	D	D	D

Multiply unit on hold

FIGURE 2.6: vector chaining example.

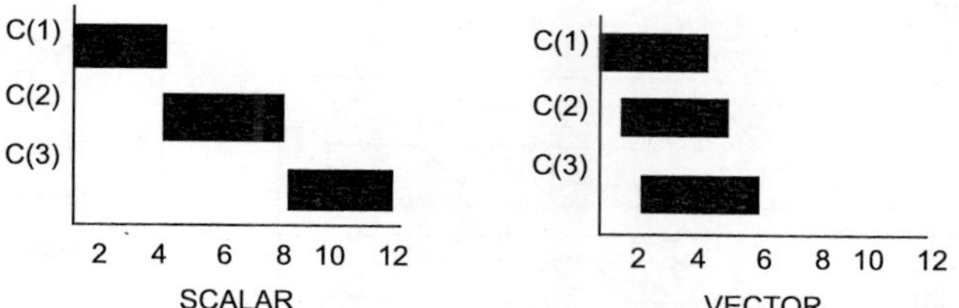

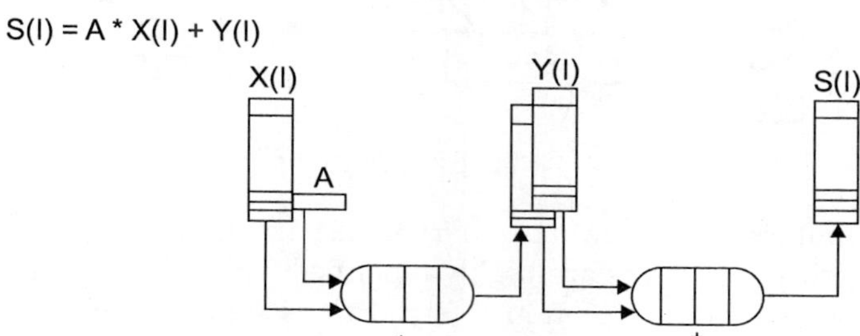

FIGURE 2.7: Pipeline Chaining

Chaining allows feeding of data from one operation to the next without waiting for the first operation to complete. For example, once the first result of addition is placed in V1, we could make that value available for the multiplication instruction. Example execution timing is shown in Figure 2.6. The vector multiplication instruction uses chaining to get values from the V1 vector register. The addition operation produces the first result R1 during clock cycle 12. This result is available for use by the multiplication two clocks later. Until that time, the multiplication pipeline is in the hold (H) state. From that point onward, execution proceeds in the normal fashion. Thus, by using chaining, we complete both operations in 25 cycles. This is significantly faster than executing without chaining: 33 cycles versus 25 cycles, about 24% improvement.

2.2.9 *VECTOR COMPUTERS*

Many scientific and engineering computations require the same operation to be performed on every element of a list or matrix. To satisfy the demand for this specialised type of computation, the class of 'vector computers' was built which includes the Cray computers, the Cyber 205, the ETA10, SX1 and SX2 from NEC, Hitachi's HITAC S-810, and Fujitsu's FACOM VP series. The high performance of most supercomputers comes from their ability to perform vector operations.

Rather than working on single data words (scalars), these processors have instructions which work on lists of such words (vectors). A vector instruction might, for example, add the contents of one vector to the contents of another vector and place the results in a third vector. Several arithmetic units are usually available for the execution of these instructions, see figure 2.8.

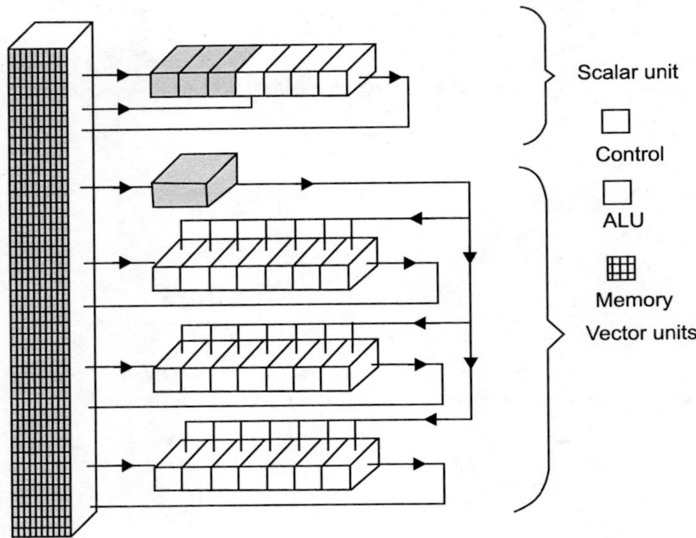

FIGURE 2.8: Vector Processor

Vector computers are split into two parts, one part works on scalars and the other part work on vectors. The arithmetic units are highly pipelined which further increases performance. For this reason these computers are often referred to as pipelined vector computers. The control system schedules operations so that all of the arithmetic units are kept fully active during vector operations.

Every data item that passes through a scalar processor requires the pipeline to be reconfigured to execute a new instruction. Once a vector pipeline has been configured it does not need to be reconfigured until the whole vector has passed through. The time saved by not having to reconfigure the pipeline for every data item to pass through it allows the overall clock speed to be increased. High clock speeds along with multiple pipelines account for most of the high performance of vector computers.

Simple memory systems are unable to deliver data at a high enough rate to keep a vector computer fully loaded. Once a memory system has been accessed, there is a short period during which that memory bank is unable to respond to another access. This period is called the 'latency time'. Vector computers overcome the latency time by splitting the memory system into several independent banks. Vectors are stored so that consecutive elements are in different memory banks. Immediately after accessing a vector element in one memory bank, the next vector element can be accessed from the next memory bank whilst the first memory bank is still serving out its latency time. A high speed memory system is vital to the performance of vector computers.

The Cray-1 derives its operands from seven register files, each of which can store 64 words of 64-bits. The Cyber 205 takes its vector operands directly from main memory. These vectors can have up to 64K elements. Vector instructions include:

```
VectorC  = VectorA + VectorB            -- diadic operations
VectorC  = VectorA + ScalarB
VectorC  = VectorA * (Scalar + VectorB) -- triadic operations
VectorC  = VectorA + (Scalar * VectorB)
```

Vector elements are taken sequentially and pushed through the arithmetic pipeline. A new element is required every clock cycle. Hidden registers automatically keep track of how many more elements are left to be processed. The destination address for the results are calculated automatically and made available as soon as every result leaves the pipeline.

Scalar pipelines suffer serious performance degradation from jump instructions. Vector operations do not include jump operations, and so vector pipelines are much more effective.The efficiency of vector computers begins to suffer when the application problem is bigger than the vector size of the computer. This can be detected by the compiler, which breaks the problem up as best it can into manageable chunks.

Vector computers are large machines built from very high speed components and are the most expensive class of computers available. High clock speeds allow scalar and vector computations to be executed quickly. Applications with a high scalar content, however, are not usually run on a vector processor because they under-utilise the processor so much that it is not economically viable.

2.3 ARRAY PROCESSOR

An array processor is a processor that performs computations on large arrays of data. It may be composed of a group of special processors designed to calculate math procedures at very high speeds, often under the control for another central processor. Some computers use array processors to speed up video operations or for fast floating-point math operations. The term is used to refer to two different types of processors, an *attached array processor* and a *SIMD array Processor*. A processor capable of executing instructions in which the operands may be arrays rather than data elements. An array processor is a processor that performs computations on large arrays of data. There are two different types of processors; a) an attached array processor b) SIMD array processor.

Array processor, also called a vector processor, is a microprocessor or computer that is capable of performing simultaneous computations on elements of an array of data in some number of dimensions. Common uses of such processor include analysis of fluid dynamics and rotation of 3D objects as well as data retrieval, in which elements in a database are scanned simultaneously that executes one instruction at a time but on an array or table of data at the same time rather than on single data elements.

The term 'array processor' is not well defined and has been used as a label for many different computer architectures. Generally, the term can refer to any computer architecture that has been enhanced in some way for the processing of arrays. This includes architectures with arrays of arithmetic units under the direction of one control unit, arrays of processors each with their own control unit, and vector computers.

2.3.1 VECTOR/ARRAY PROCESSORS

The vector processors, described in section 2.2, fit the term array processor in its general sense. They are, however, such an important sub-category that they retain their own identity and are referred to as vector computers rather than being lumped in with array processors.

2.3.1.1 VECTOR-LIKE PROCESSORS

There is a class of computers which are called either array processors or 'attached processors'. Their architecture is similar to vector processors, but they do not directly implement vector instructions. The AP-120B made by Floating Point Systems is an example of such a computer. It was designed to perform well on numerically intensive problems which have their data organised into vectors or arrays. It is a specialised unit that has to be attached to a general purpose computer - called the host.

Like vector computers these processors have multiple pipelined functional units. The FPS AP-120B has ten such functional units. Instructions are stored as 'long words'. The long words are divided into ten blocks, each of which act as a micro-instruction for a single functional unit. In this way every functional unit is given a task to perform every clock cycle. All the functional units can pass data between themselves but only some can move data to or from main memory. The high performance of vector-like processors comes from every functional unit being able to work on a different piece of data at the same time.

Vector operations are synthesised by carefully micro-programmed subroutines supplied by the manufacturer in a library. The library contributes significantly to the high performance of the computer. The processor cycle time is high compared to a vector computer, consequently the performance is lower. The throughput is much higher than that of the host computer, and, due to their relatively low cost they are sometimes called the 'poor man's vector computer'. Another, more modern, name for a processor exhibiting this type of parallelism is Very Long Instruction Word machine, or VLIW.

2.3.2 ARRAY PROCESSOR MACHINES

The term array processor is also used for the class of computers that have a single control unit with many identical processing elements under its control, see figure 2.9. Examples of this group include the DAP, PEPE, Illiac VI, MPP and CM-1. These machines are also attached processors and need a host computer to provide a backing store and feed them with instructions and data.

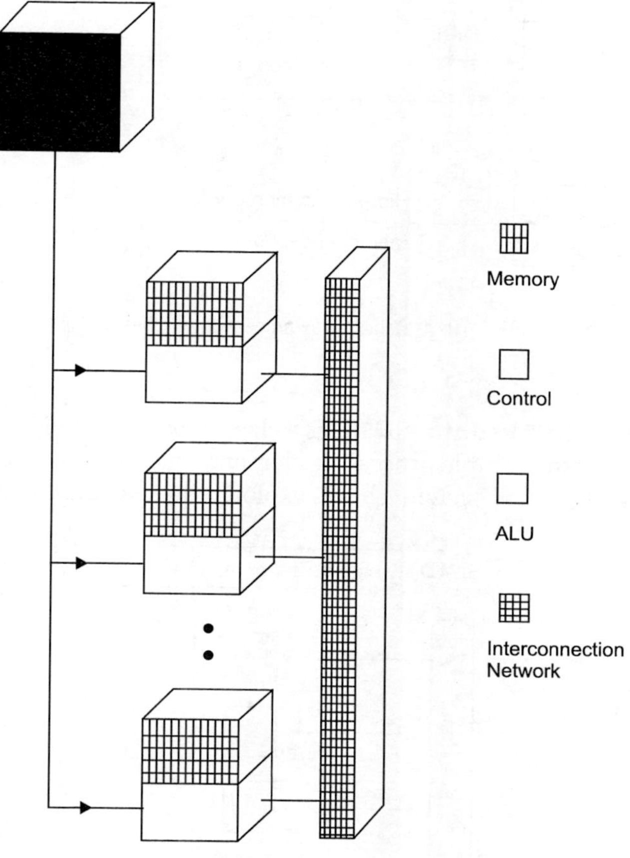

FIGURE 2.9: Array Processor

Each processing element has a small amount of memory and an arithmetic and logic unit. The central control unit transmits the same instruction simultaneously to all the processing elements. They, in turn, execute the instruction working on data from their local memories. Instruction processing is, therefore, synchronous. The processing elements tend to be simple and slow. However, since there are so many of them, there is high overall throughput.

2.3.3 ATTACHED ARRAY PROCESSOR

An *attached array processor* is an auxiliary processor attached to a general-purpose computer, designed as a peripheral for a conventional host computer. The array processor can be programmed by the user to accommodate a variety of complex arithmetic problems. The host computer is a general-purpose commercial computer and the attached processor is a back-end machine driven by the host computer. The array processor is connected through an input output controller to the computer and the computer treats it like an external interface. The data for the attached processor are transferred from main memory to a local memory through a high-speed bus. The general-purpose computer without the attached processor serves the users that need conventional data processing.

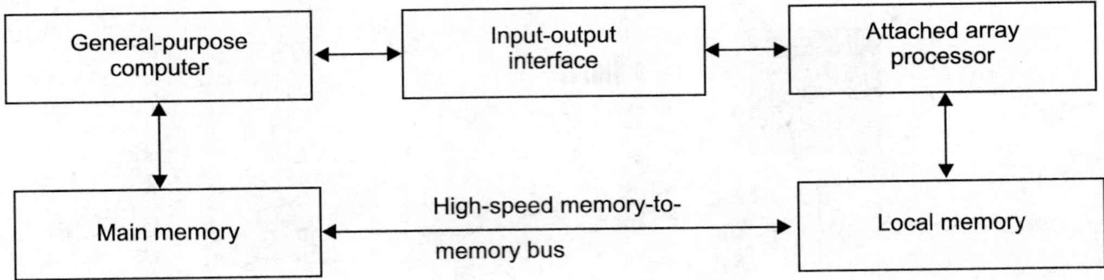

FIGURE 2.10: Attached array processor with host computer

2.4 SIMD

Single instruction, multiple data (SIMD) is a class of parallel computers in Flynn's taxonomy. It describes computers with multiple processing elements that perform the same operation on multiple data simultaneously. Thus, such machines exploit data level parallelism.

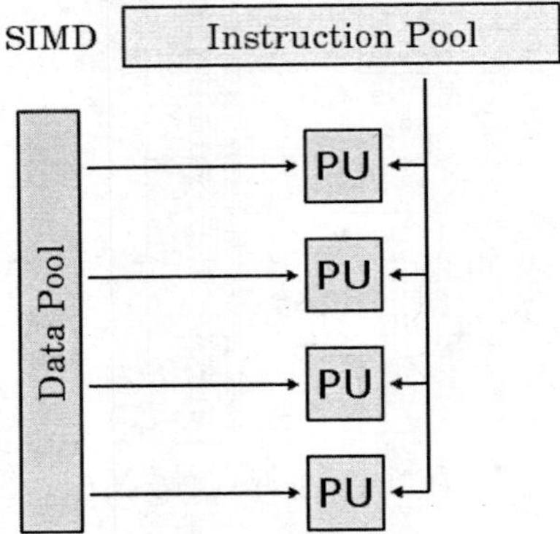

FIGURE 2.11: SIMD structure

2.4.1 SIMD ARRAY PROCESSOR

A synchronous array of parallel processors is called an array processor, which consists of multiple processing elements under the supervision of one control unit. An array processor can handle single instruction and multiple data stream streams. In this since, array processors are also known as SIMD computers. SIMD machines are especially designed to perform vector computations over matrices or arrays of data. In this book, the terms array processors, parallel processors, and SIMD computers are used interchangeably.

This scheme uses the *SIMD* (Single Instruction Stream, Multiple Data Stream) category from Flynn's Taxonomy as a root class for *Processor Array* and *Associative Memory* subclasses. SIMD architectures are characterized by having a control unit broadcast a common instruction to all processing elements, which execute that instruction in lockstep on diverse operands from local data. Common features include the ability for individual processors to disable an instruction and the ability to propagate instruction results to immediate neighbors over an interconnection network.

An SIMD *array processor* is a processor that has a single-instruction multiple-data organization. It manipulates vector instructions by means of multiple functional units responding to a common instruction. It contains a set of identical processing elements (PEs), each having a local memory M. Each processor element includes an ALU, a floating-point arithmetic unit, and working registers. The master control unit controls the operations in the processor elements. The main memory is used for storage of the program. The function of the master control unit is to decode the instructions and determine how the instruction is to be executed. Scalar and program control instructions are directly executed within the master control unit. Vector instructions are broadcast to all PEs simultaneously. Each PE uses operands stored in its local memory. Vector operands are distributed to the local memories prior to the parallel execution of the instruction.

Consider, for example, the vector addition $C = A + B$. The master control unit first stores the ith components a_i and b_i of A and B in local memory M_i for $i = 1, 2, 3, . n$. It then broadcasts the floating-point add instruction $c_i = a_i + b_i$ to all PEs, causing the addition to take place simultaneously. The components of c_i are stored in fixed locations in each local memory. This produces the desired vector sum in one add cycle. To control the status of each PE during the execution of vector instructions, Each PE has a flag that is set when the PE is active and reset when the PE is inactive.

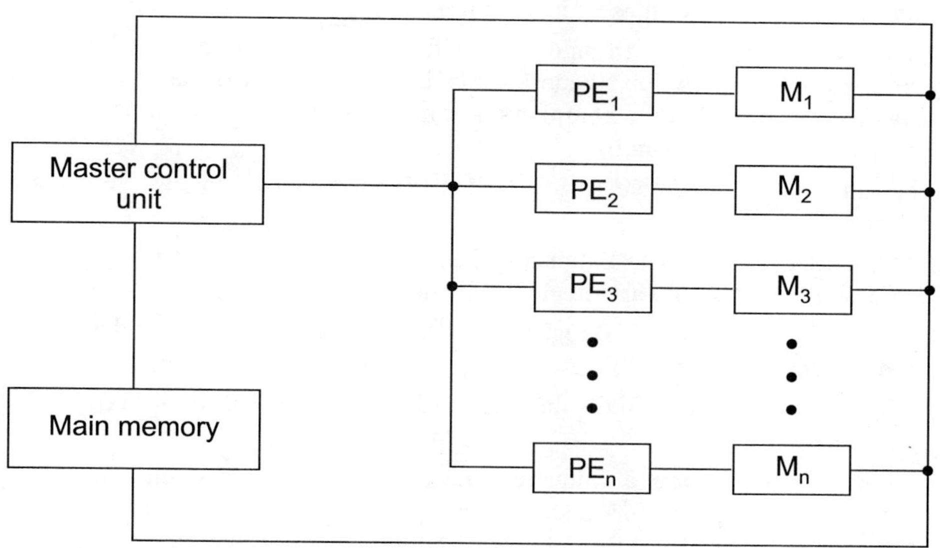

FIGURE 2.12: SIMD Array Processor Organizations

2.4.2 ADVANTAGES

An application that may take advantage of SIMD is one where the same value is being added to (or subtracted from) a large number of data points, a common operation in many multimedia applications. One example would be changing the brightness of an image. Each pixel of an image consists of three values for the brightness of the red (R), green (G) and blue (B) portions of the color. To change the brightness, the R, G and B values are read from memory, a value is added to (or subtracted from) them, and the resulting values are written back out to memory.

With a SIMD processor there are two improvements to this process. For one the data is understood to be in blocks, and a number of values can be loaded all at once. Instead of a series of instructions saying "get this pixel, now get the next pixel", a SIMD processor will have a single instruction that effectively says "get lots of pixels" ("lots" is a number that varies from design to design). For a variety of reasons, this can take much less time than "getting" each pixel individually, as with traditional CPU design.

Another advantage is that SIMD systems typically include only those instructions that can be applied to all of the data in one operation. In other words, if the SIMD system works by loading up eight data points at once, the add operation being applied to the data will happen to all eight values at the same time. Although the same is true for any super-scalar processor design, the level of parallelism in a SIMD system is typically much higher.

2.4.3 *DISADVANTAGES*

Following are the disadvantages of SIMD processor:

- Not all algorithms can be vectorized. For example, a flow-control-heavy task like code parsing wouldn't benefit from SIMD.
- It also has large register files which increases power consumption and chip area.
- Currently, implementing an algorithm with SIMD instructions usually requires human labor; most compilers don't generate SIMD instructions from a typical C program, for instance. Vectorization in compilers is an active area of computer science research. (Compare vector processing.)
- Programming with particular SIMD instruction sets can involve numerous low-level challenges.
    - SSE (Streaming SIMD Extension) has restrictions on data alignment; programmers familiar with the x86 architecture may not expect this.
    - Gathering data into SIMD registers and scattering it to the correct destination locations is tricky and can be inefficient.
    - Specific instructions like rotations or three-operand addition aren't in some SIMD instruction sets.
    - Instruction sets are architecture-specific: old processors and non-x86 processors lack SSE entirely, for instance, so programmers must provide non-vectorized implementations (or different vectorized implementations) for them.
    - The early MMX instruction set shared a register file with the floating-point stack, which caused inefficiencies when mixing floating-point and MMX code. However, SSE2 corrects this.

Note: Detailed description of SIMD Array Processor is given in Chapter 3 and 10.

2.5 ASSOCIATIVE PROCESSORS AND MEMORY

Associative processors were built for high speed information retrieval from databases. Items to be retrieved from a database are usually read into a processor and compared with a 'key' to see if they are required. The procedure is repeated with the same key until the relevant part of the database has been exhausted. It was noticed that the critical part of most keys is only several bits wide.

Associative processors comprise a simple control unit, several registers and a small amount (eg 8 KBytes) of 'associative memory' which replaces normal random access memory. Under the direction of the control unit processing is performed by the associative memory itself.

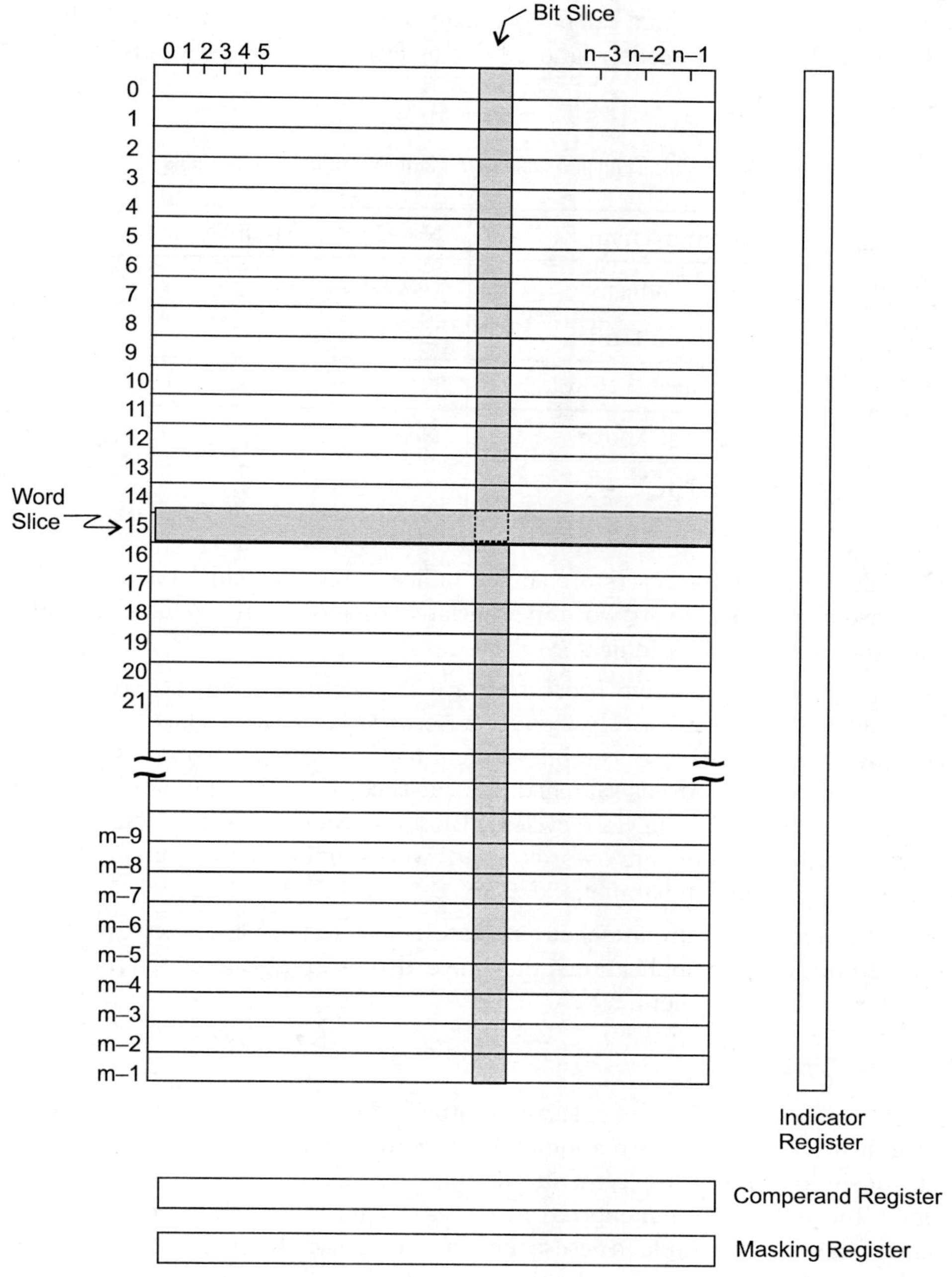

FIGURE 2.13: Associative Memory

Associative memory is also called 'content addressable memory', 'parallel search memory', or 'multi-access memory'. Its function is to allow memory items to be selected by reference to their contents rather than by an address. Every word in the associative memory is searched in parallel against a key held in the comperand register which is the same width as memory, see figure 2.13. There is also a masking register that can be used to overlay the comperand register. It allows certain parts of the key to be either forced or ignored during a search. Associative processor instructions include;

TABLE 2.1: Typical Associative Memory Primitive Operations

Greater Than,	Not Greater Than
Less Than,	Not Less Than
Between Limits,	Exact Match
Smallest	Largest
Nearest Above	Nearest Below
Median	

The result of every operation is stored in the 'indicator register' which has a single bit associated with every word in memory. Every word in associative memory that produced a valid comparison sets its corresponding bit in the indicator register.

Two examples of associative processors are the 'Parallel Element Processing Ensemble' (PEPE) by 'Bell Labs' and STARLAN by Goodyear Aerospace. STARLAN has 32 modules containing 256 processing elements. Each processing element has 256 256-bit memory words, and operates in bit-serial mode. The memory is searched one 'bit-slice' at a time; therefore a 256 x 32-bit slice of memory can be searched in 32 clock cycles. PEPE has 288 processing elements, each with 1024 words of 32-bit associative memory words. PEPE works in 'bit-parallel' mode. Every bit-slice in every word can be searched in parallel.

Associative processors are attached processors, and require a host computer to administer them. Apart from database applications, they have also been used in image processing and real-time signal processing equipment.

2.6 SYSTOLIC ARRAYS

Systolic arrays are another form of specialised attached processor. And as such, they need a host computer to provide control information and access to peripherals. Systolic arrays comprise several chains of similar processing elements with either a memory bank or an I/O link at the chain ends. None of the processing elements have any local memory. Only the processors at the beginning and the end of the chains are able to access the main-memory. The arrangement can be regarded as a macro-pipeline. All the processing elements perform essentially the same computation, which is repeated for every item of data to pass through the array.

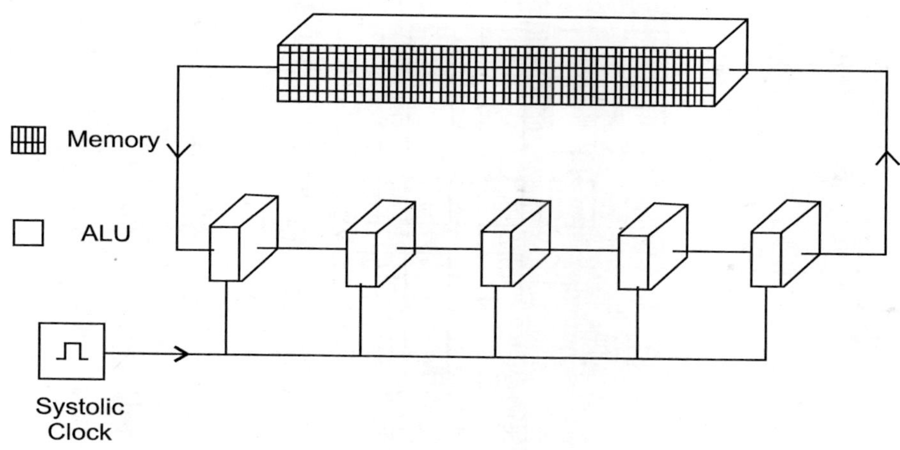

FIGURE 2.14: Chain of Processors in a Systolic Array

The reasoning behind this architecture centres on the bottleneck between a CPU and its main-memory. Having issued a memory request, a processor has to wait a short time for the memory system to deliver the data item. Once they have a piece of data uniprocessors perform one calculation with it and then either return the result to main-memory or request another data item. Systolic arrays, however, use that data item to perform a calculation at every processor in the chain before returning a it back to main-memory, see figure 2.14. The memory access penalty is not paid for every instruction, and so, systolic arrays are much faster than uniprocessors.

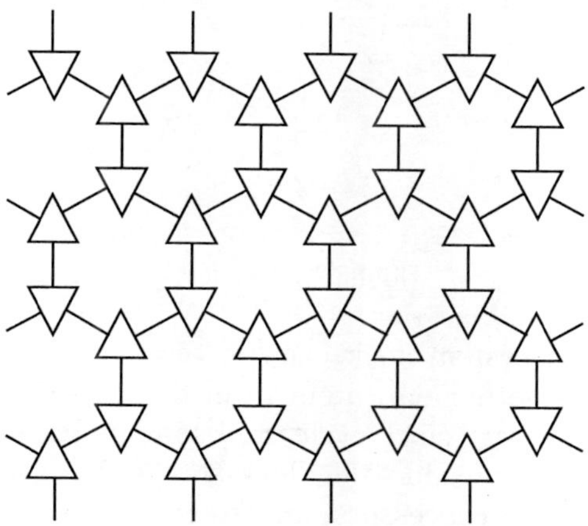

FIGURE 2.15: Systolic Array

Each processing element comprises a simple arithmetic and logic unit and a communications unit. The arrays are made up of single type of processing element, ie they are homogeneous. Systolic arrays are usually wired into two dimensional grids with only the adjacent elements being able to communicate directly, see figures 2.15, 2.16 and 2.17. Systolic arrays can be programmed to allow data to flow in several dimensions and several directions around the grid.

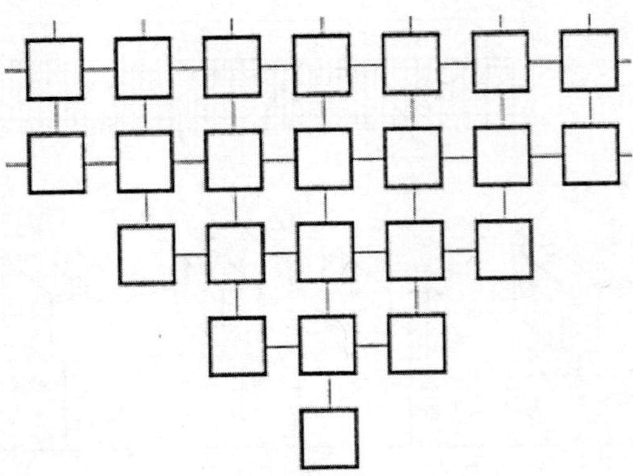

FIGURE 2.16: Systolic Array

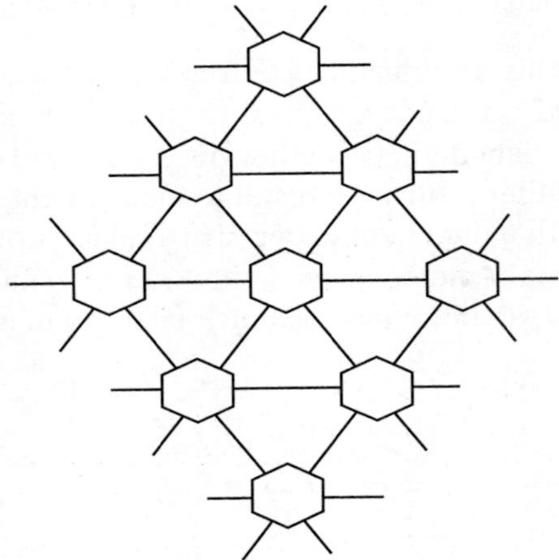

FIGURE 2.17: Systolic Array

On every beat of a global system clock, each processor passes its results to the next processor in the chain, and receives another data item from the previous processor in the chain. Each processor produces a result every clock cycle, and so complex multi-cycle instructions are not implemented. Systolic arrays are said to be 'lock-stepped' or synchronous. There is no master controller, as found with array processors, and so control is effectively distributed across the network.

The periodic pumping of data around the systolic array is the feature by which systolic arrays get their name. A systole is the name given to a contraction of the heart. When the heart contracts blood moves along the vanes and arteries coming to rest at the end of the contraction. During the brief pause between beats the blood does its work - distributing oxygen and nutrients. When the work is being done the network of vanes and arteries is still. This is followed by another contraction and the whole cycle starts again. Note that when the network is active no 'work' is being done and vice-versa.

Computations that require more operations to be performed than there are data items (ie data items or intermediate results are reused) are said to be 'compute bound'. Furthermore, if a function's operands are near neighbours in a given data structure there is said to be 'data locality'. Systolic arrays are used in compute bound applications with data locality.

Systolic arrays come in a variety of different topologies, as shown in the figures. These topologies reflect either the flow of data in an algorithm, or the structure of the incoming data. Systolic arrays tend to be built for a specific application, often where real-time digital signal processing (DSP) is needed. However, some topologies have been found which are either optimal or efficient for many different algorithms.

The modular and regular design of systolic arrays means that more processing elements can be added to the arrays without any effect on the memory bandwidth.

Examples of general purpose systolic arrays are the Matrix-1 by Saxpy Computer Corporation, and the Warp by Carnegie Mellon University.

2.6.1 WAVEFRONT ARRAYS

Everything that has been said about systolic arrays can also be said about wavefront arrays. The only difference is that wavefront arrays do not have a global pulse used to synchronise all the processing elements. Instead wavefront arrays pass on intermediate results or data items whenever they are ready. The receiving processing element confirms it has been sent a data item by returning an acknowledging signal, called the handshaking signal. Wavefront arrays are said to be self-synchronising or asynchronous.

Wavefront arrays allow a multiple or variable number of instructions to be performed at each stage, hence they can be more generally applied than systolic arrays. The price for this extra flexibility, however, is reduced performance due to the need to send handshaking messages.

2.6.2 SYSTOLIC ARCHITECTURES

Kung (1982) proposed systolic architectures as a means of solving problems of special purpose systems that must often balance intensive computations with demanding I/O bandwidths. Systolic arrays (architectures) are pipelined multiprocessors in which data is pulsed in a rhythmic fashion from memory through a network of processors and the results returned to the memory (see Figure 2.19). A global clock and explicit timing delay synchronize this pipeline dataflow, which consists of operands obtained from memory and partial results to be used by each processor. The processors are interconnected by regular, local interconnections. During each time interval, the processors execute a short, time invariant sequence of instructions. Systolic architectures address the performance requirements of special purpose systems by achieving significant parallel computation and by avoiding I/O and memory bandwidth bottlenecks. A high degree of parallelism is achieved by pipelining data through multiple processors, typically arranged in a two-dimensional fashion. Systolic architectures maximize the computations performed on a datum once it has been fetched from the memory or an external device. Once a datum enters the systolic array, it is passed to any processor that needs it without an intervening store to memory.

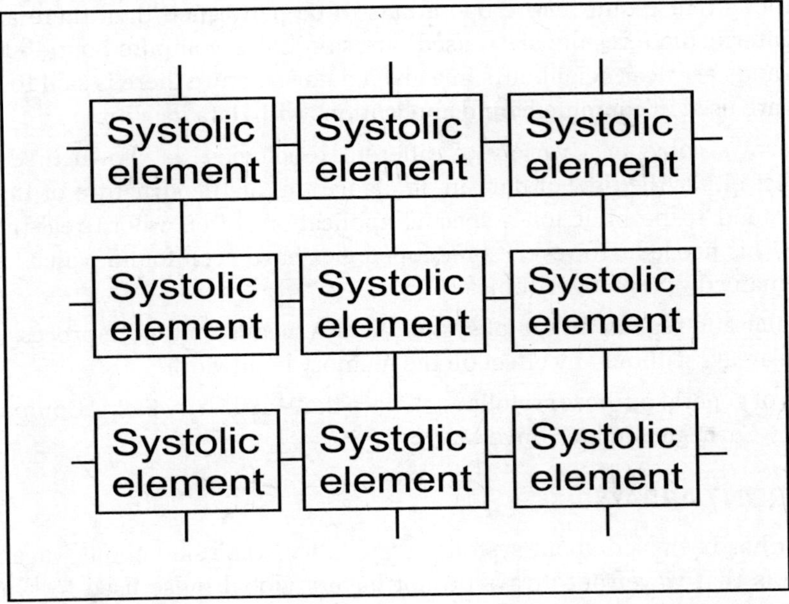

FIGURE 2.18: General systolic organization

$$A = \begin{bmatrix} a & b \\ c & d \end{bmatrix} \quad \text{and} \quad B = \begin{bmatrix} e & f \\ g & h \end{bmatrix}$$

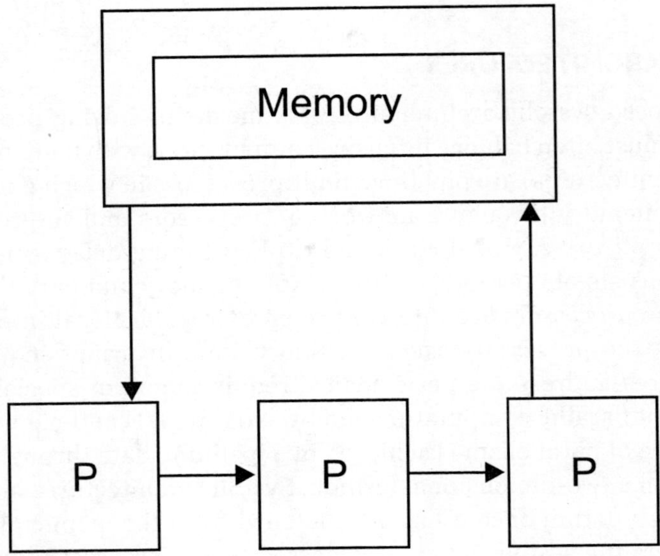

FIGURE 2.19: A systolic architecture.

Example: Figure 2.20 shows how a simple systolic array would calculate the product of two matrices,

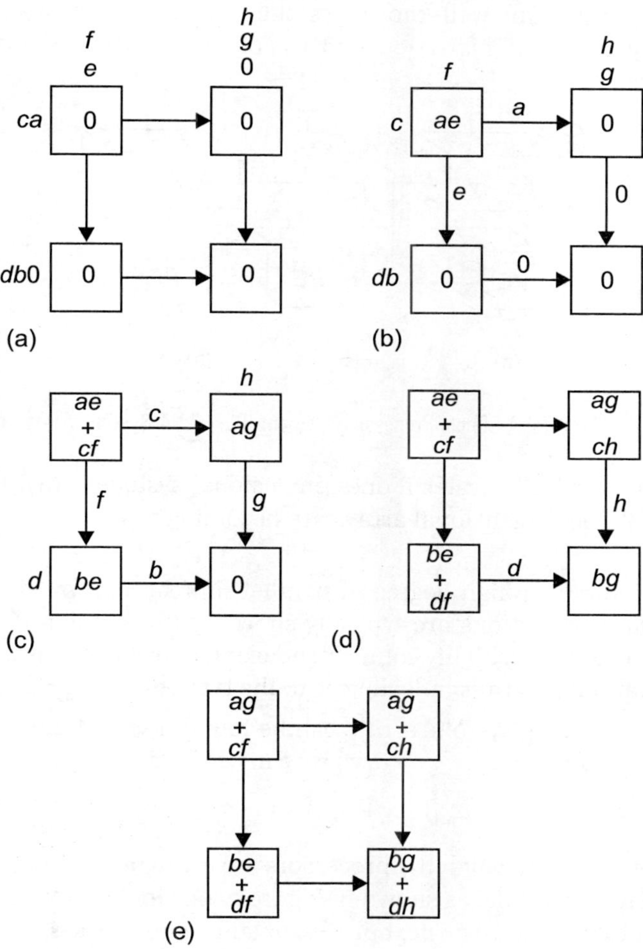

FIGURE 2.20: Systolic matrix multiplications.

The zero inputs shown moving through the array are used for synchronization. Each processor begins with an accumulator set to zero and, during each cycle adds the product of its two inputs to the accumulator. After five cycles the matrix product is complete.

A variety of special purpose systems have used systolic arrays for algorithm specific architectures, particularly for signal processing applications. Programmable (reconfigurable) systolic architectures (Intel iWarp, Saxpy Matrix) have been constructed.

2.6.3 SYSTOLIC ARRAY PROCESSOR

Systolic array computers derive their name from drawing an analogy to how blood rhythmically flows through a biological heart. They are a network of processing elements that rhythmically compute data by circulating it through the system. Systolic arrays are a variation of SIMD computers that incorporates large arrays of simple processors that use vector pipelines for data flow, as shown in Figure 2.21b. Since their introduction in the 1970s, they have had a significant impact on special-purpose computing. One well-known systolic array is CMU's iWarp processor, which was manufactured by Intel in 1990. This system consists of a linear array of processors connected by a bidirectional data bus.

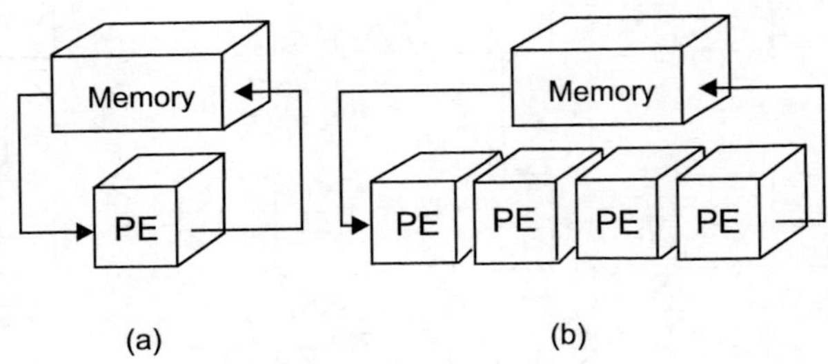

FIGURE 2.21: (a) A Simple Processing Element (PE) (b) A Systolic Array Processor

Although Figure 2.21b illustrates a one-dimensional systolic array, two-dimensional arrays are not uncommon. Three-dimensional arrays are becoming more prevalent with the advances in VLSI technology.

Systolic arrays employ a high degree of parallelism (through pipelining) and can sustain a very high throughput. Connections are typically short, and the design is simple and thus highly scalable. They tend to be robust, highly compact, efficient, and cheap to produce. On the down side, they are highly specialized and thus inflexible as to the types and sizes of problems they can solve.

A good example of using systolic arrays can be found in polynomial evaluation. To evaluate the polynomial $y = a_0 + a_1x + a_2x^2 + \ldots + a_kx^k$, we can use Horner's Rule:

$$y = ((((a_nx + a_{n-1}) \times x + a_{n-2}) \times x + a_{n-3}) \times x \ldots . a_1) \times x + a_0$$

A linear systolic array, in which the processors are arranged in pairs, can be used to evaluate a polynomial using Horner's Rule, as shown in Figure 2.22. One processor multiplies its input by x and passes the result to the right. The next processor adds a_j and passes the result to the right. After an initial latency of $2n$ cycles to get started, a polynomial is computed in every cycle.

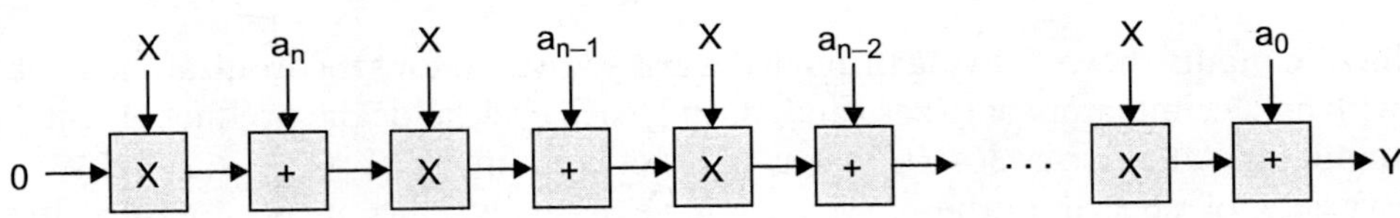

FIGURE 2.22: Using a Systolic Array to Evaluate a Polynomial

Systolic arrays are typically used for repetitive tasks, including Fourier transformations, image processing, data compression, shortest path problems, sorting, signal processing, and various matrix computations (such as inversion and multiplication). In short, systolic array computers are suitable for computational problems that lend themselves to a parallel solution using a large number of simple processing elements.

2.6.4 FEATURES OF SYSTOLIC ARRAYS

A Systolic array is a computing network possessing the following features:

- **Synchrony** means that the data is rhythmically computed (Timed by a global clock) and passed through the network.
- **Modularity** means that the array (Finite/Infinite) consists of modular processing units.
- **Regularity** means that the modular processing units are interconnected with homogeneously.
- **Spatial Locality** means that the cells have a local communication interconnection.
- **Temporal Locality** means that the cell transmits the signals from one cell to other which require at least one unit time delay.
- **Pipelinability** means that the array can achieve a high speed.

2.6.5 ADVANTAGES OF SYSTOLIC ARRAYS

Following are the advantages of systolic arrays:

1. Regularity and modular design (Perfect for VLSI implementation).
2. Local interconnections (Implements algorithms locality).
3. High degree of pipelining.
4. Highly synchronized multiprocessing.
5. Simple I/O subsystem.
6. Very efficient implementation for great variety of algorithms.
7. High speed and Low cost.
8. Elimination of global broadcasting and modular expansibility.

2.6.6 DISADVANTAGES OF SYSTOLIC ARRAYS

Following are the disadvantages of systolic arrays:

1. Global synchronization limits due to signal delays.
2. High bandwidth requirements both for periphery (RAM) and between PEs.
3. Poor run-time fault tolerance due to lack of interconnection protocol.

2.6.7 APPLICATIONS OF SYSTOLIC ARRAYS

Following are the applications of systolic arrays:

1. Matrix Inversion and Decomposition.
2. Polynomial Evaluation.
3. Convolution.
4. Systolic arrays for matrix multiplication.
5. Image Processing.
6. Systolic lattice filters used for speech and seismic signal processing.
7. Artificial neural network.

2.6.8 SUPER SYSTOLIC ARRAY

The super systolic array is a generalization of the systolic array. Because the classical synthesis methods (algebraic, i.e. projection-based synthesis), yielding only uniform DPU arrays permitting only linear pipes, systolic arrays could be used only to implement applications with regular data dependencies. By using simulated annealing instead, Rainer Kress has introduced the generalized systolic array: the super systolic array. Its application is not restricted to applications with regular data dependencies.

2.6.9 KRESSARRAY

The KressArray is the reconfigurable version of the super systolic array. More information about the background may be obtained from the articles about Systolic array, Reconfigurable Computing, Configware Compiler, super systolic array and Configware/Software Co-Compiler. Because of the wide applicability of the super systolic array its reconfigurability makes sense: the Kress Array, having been pioneered by Rainer Kress for reconfigurable computing.

Note: Detailed description of Systolic array is given in Chapter 3.

QUESTIONS

1. What do you mean by synchronous architectures?
2. What is vector processor? Explain the various requirements of vector processing?
3. Explain the architecture of vector machine?
4. What are the advantages of vector processing?
5. Explain the various vector operations?
6. Explain the example of vector computers?
7. What do you mean by array processor?
8. Explain the array processor machine in detail?
9. Explain the concept of attached array processor?
10. Explain the concept of SIMD array processor in detail?
11. What are the advantages and disadvantages of SIMD array processor?
12. Explain the concept of associative processor and memory?
13. Explain the concept of systolic arrays?
14. Explain the concept of wavefront arrays?
15. Explain the concept of systolic architectures?
16. Explain the concept of systolic array processor?
17. Explain the various features and applications of systolic arrays?
18. What are the advantages and disadvantages of systolic arrays?
19. Explain the concept of super systolic array
20. What do you mean by kressAraay?

CHAPTER 3 PARADIGMS OF COMPUTING: ASYNCHRONOUS

3.1 ASYNCHRONOUS ARCHITECTURES

Asynchronous complex systems contain, for the most part, disparate members which evolve dynamically in time with changing interconnect and usually different evolution algorithms for each member. This corresponds to a general distributed-memory MIMD machine with each node typically executing distinct programs and with varying and unsynchronized internodes message traffic.

When we consider computer hardware and software systems, we will need to consider other temporal classes which can be thought of as further subdivisions of the asynchronous class.

- *Static asynchronous* (or *static* MIMD) systems consist of fixed members whose interconnect-or in the application to parallel computers, message traffic-is varying. This translates into a MIMD software model of static processes interacting with a general dynamic message-passing system. We have a fixed number of processes which are spawned and then execute a particular program which remains unchanged. This leads to the important SPMD (Single Program Multiple Data) model of computation. SPMD is the natural implementation of synchronous or loosely synchronous problems on MIMD distributed-memory parallel computers. In SPMD, each process runs the same program but operates on different data sets. In synchronous implementations, the different processes execute the same instructions at each computer cycle. In loosely synchronous problems, the processes are at different points of the same program at each time.
- *Dynamic asynchronous* systems generalize the above example with processes and messages able to spawn new processes dynamically. For instance, *reactive* systems are dynamic asynchronous systems that spawn services as needed in a distributed operating system. Generally, we define such systems to have both an irregular time-dependent interconnect and members which can be created and destroyed at any time.
- *Shared-memory* MIMD complex systems are defined to represent this model of parallel computer. One could include shared-memory systems as examples of *static MIMD* or *dynamic asynchronous* systems with a particular form for information to be transferred between processes or processors. In distributed-memory machines, information is transferred via the construction of messages; in shared memory by memory access instructions. Indeed, the so-called NUMA (non-uniform memory access)

shared-memory machines are implemented in machines like the Kendall Square as distributed-memory hardware with (from the point of view of the user) memory access as the communication mechanism. Uniform memory access (UMA) shared memory machines, such as the Sequent; do present a rather different computational model. However, most believe that NUMA machines are the only shared-memory architectures that scale to large systems, and so in practice scalable shared-memory architectures are only distinguished from distributed-memory machines in their mechanism for information transfer.

- *Dataflow* can be considered as a special dynamic asynchronous complex system describing the dataflow hardware and/or software model. Here, members of the complex system are dormant until all data needed for their definition is received when they "fire" and evolve according to a predetermined algorithm.

3.2 MIMD

This is the most general and most powerful of our classification. We have N processors, N streams of instructions and N streams of data. Each processor operates under the control of an instruction stream issued by its own control unit. (i.e. each processor is capable of executing its own program on a different data. This means that the processors operate **asynchronously** (typically) i.e. can be doing different things on different data at the same time. As with SIMD computers communication of data or results between processors can be via a shared memory or interconnection network.

MIMD computers with shared memory are known as **multiprocessors** or **tightly coupled machines**. Examples are ENCORE, MULTIMAX, SEQUENT & BALANCE.

MIMD computers with an interconnection network are known as **multicomputers** or **loosely coupled machines**. Examples are INTEL iPSC, NCUBE/7 and transputer networks.

3.2.1 *MIMD SCHEMES*

MIMD machines use a collection of processors, each having its own memory, which can be used to collaborate on executing a given task. In general, MIMD systems can be categorized based on their memory organization into shared-memory and message-passing architectures. The choice between the two categories depends on the cost of communication (relative to that of the computation) and the degree of load imbalance in the application.

Multiple-instruction multiple-data streams (MIMD) parallel architectures are made of multiple processors and multiple memory modules connected together via some interconnection network. They fall into two broad categories: shared memory or message passing. Figure 3.1 illustrates the general architecture of these two categories.

Processors exchange information through their central shared memory in shared memory systems, and exchange information through their interconnection network in message passing systems.

A shared memory system typically accomplishes interprocessor coordination through a global memory shared by all processors. These are typically server systems that communicate through a bus and cache memory controller. The bus/ cache architecture alleviates the need for expensive multiported memories and interface circuitry as well as the need to adopt a message-passing paradigm when developing application software. Because access to shared memory is balanced, these systems are also called SMP (symmetric multiprocessor) systems. Each processor has equal opportunity to read/write to memory, including equal access speed.

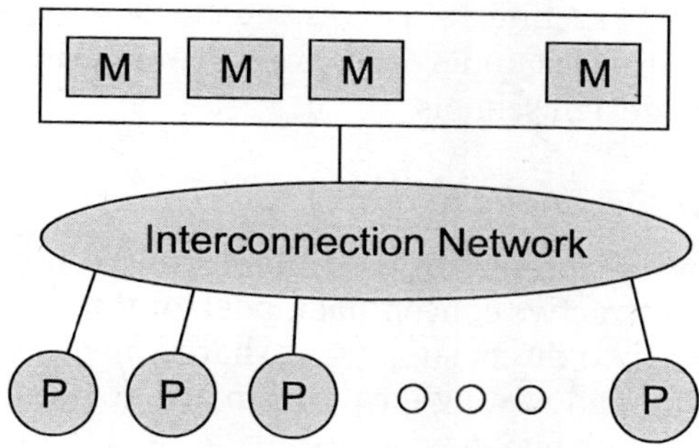

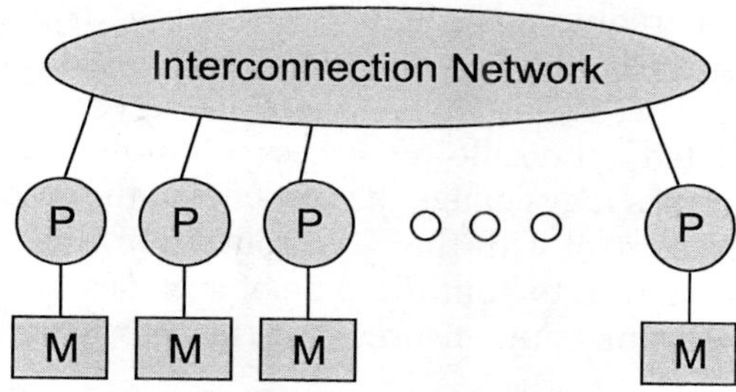

FIGURE 3.1: Shared Memory Versus Message Passing Architecture.

Commercial examples of SMPs are Sequent Computer's Balance and Symmetry, Sun Microsystems multiprocessor servers, and Silicon Graphics Inc. multiprocessor servers.

A message passing system (also referred to as distributed memory) typically combines the local memory and processor at each node of the interconnection network. There is no global memory, so it is necessary to move data from one local memory to another by means of message passing. This is typically done by a Send/Receive pair of commands, which must be written into the application software by a programmer. Thus, programmers must learn the message-passing paradigm, which involves data copying and dealing with consistency issues. Commercial examples of message passing architectures c. 1990 were the nCUBE, iPSC/2, and various Transputer-based systems. These systems eventually gave way to Internet connected systems whereby the processor/ memory nodes were either Internet servers or clients on individuals' desktop.

It was also apparent that distributed memory is the only way efficiently to increase the number of processors managed by a parallel and distributed system. If scalability to larger and larger systems (as measured by the number of processors) was to continue, systems had to use distributed memory techniques. These two forces created a conflict: programming in the shared memory model was easier, and designing systems in the message passing model provided scalability. The distributed-shared memory (DSM) architecture began to appear in systems like the SGI Origin2000, and others. In such systems, memory is physically distributed; for example, the hardware architecture follows the message passing school of design, but the programming model follows the shared memory school of thought. In effect, software covers up the hardware. As far as a programmer is concerned, the architecture looks and behaves like a shared memory machine, but a message passing architecture lives underneath the software. Thus, the DSM machine is a hybrid that takes advantage of both design schools.

3.2.2 SHARED MEMORY ORGANIZATION

There has been recent growing interest in distributed shared memory systems. This is because shared memory provides an attractive conceptual model for interprocess interaction even when the underlying hardware provides no direct support. A shared memory model is one in which processors communicate by reading and writing locations in a shared memory that is equally accessible by all processors. Each processor may have registers, buffers, caches, and local memory banks as additional memory resources. A number of basic issues in the design of shared memory systems have to be taken into consideration. These include access control, synchronization, protection, and security. Access control determines which process accesses are possible to which resources. Access control models make the required check for every access request issued by the processors to the shared memory, against the contents of the access control table. The latter contains flags that determine the legality of each access attempt. If there are access attempts to resources, then until the desired access is completed, all disallowed access attempts and illegal processes are blocked. Requests from sharing processes may change the contents of the access control table during execution. The flags of the access control with the synchronization rules determine the system's functionality. Synchronization constraints limit the time of accesses from sharing processes to shared resources. Appropriate synchronization ensures that the information flows properly and ensures system functionality.

Protection is a system feature that prevents processes from making arbitrary access to resources belonging to other processes. Sharing and protection are incompatible; sharing allows access, whereas protection restricts it. Running two copies of the same program on two processors will decrease the performance relative to that of a single processor, due to contention for shared memory. The performance degrades further as three, four, or more copies of the program execute at the same time.

A shared memory computer system consists of (1) a set of independent processors, (2) a set of memory modules, and (3) an interconnection network. The simplest shared memory system consists of one memory module (M) that can be accessed from two processors Pa and Pb (Figure 3.2). Requests arrive at the memory module through its two ports. An arbitration unit within the memory module passes requests through to a memory controller. If the memory module is not busy and a single request arrives, then the arbitration unit passes that request to the memory controller and the request is satisfied. The module is placed in the busy state while a request is being serviced.

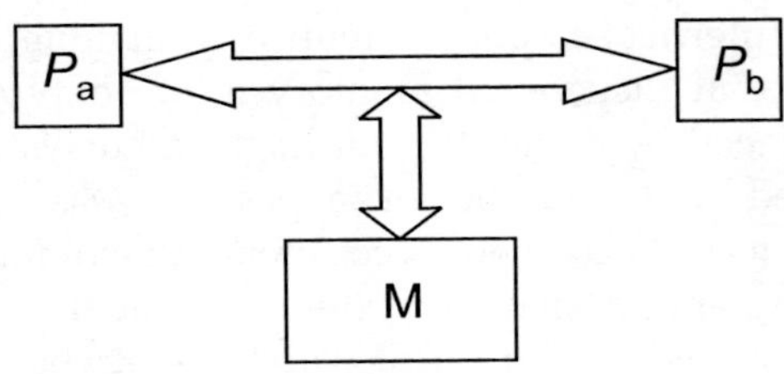

FIGURE 3.2: A Simple Shared Memory Scheme

If a new request arrives while the memory is busy servicing a previous request, the memory module sends a wait signal through the memory controller to the processor making the new request. In response, the requesting processor may hold its request on the line until the memory becomes free or it may repeat its request some time later. If the arbitration unit receives two requests, it selects one of them and passes it to the memory controller. Again, the denied request can be either held to be served next or it may be repeated some time later.

The arbitration unit may not be adequate to organize the use of the memory module by the two processors. The main problem will be in the sequencing of interactions between memory accesses from the two processors. Consider the following two scenarios for accessing the same memory location M(1000) by the two processors Pa and Pb (Figure 3.3). Let us also assume that the initial value stored in memory location M(1000) is 150. Note that in both cases, the sequence of instructions performed by each processor is the same. The only difference between the two scenarios is the relative time at which the two processors update the value in M(1000). A careful examination of the two scenarios will show that the value stored in location M(1000) after the first scenario will be 151 while the stored value following the second scenario will be 152. The above illustrative example presents the case of a nonfunctional behavior of this simple shared memory system. Such an example should demonstrate the basic requirements for the success of such systems.

These requirements are:

1. A mechanism for conflict resolution among rival processors
2. A technique for specifying the sequencing constraints
3. A mechanism for enforcing the sequencing specifications

The use of different interconnection networks in a shared memory multiprocessor system leads to systems with one of the following characteristics:

1. Shared memory architecture with a uniform memory access (UMA)
2. Cache-only memory architecture (COMA)
3. Distributed shared memory architecture with nonuniform memory access (NUMA)

Cycle	Processor P_a	Processor P_b
1	$a \leftarrow M(1000);$	
2		$b \leftarrow M(1000);$
3	$a \leftarrow a + 1;$	
4		$b \leftarrow b + 1;$
5	$M(1000) \leftarrow a;$	
6		$M(1000) \leftarrow b;$

Scenario 1

Cycle	Processor P_a	Processor P_b
1	$a \leftarrow M(1000);$	
2	$a \leftarrow a + 1;$	
3	$M(1000) \leftarrow a;$	
4		$b \leftarrow M(1000);$
5		$b \leftarrow b + 1;$
6		$M(1000) \leftarrow b;$

Scenario 2

FIGURE 3.3: Potential Shared Memory Problem

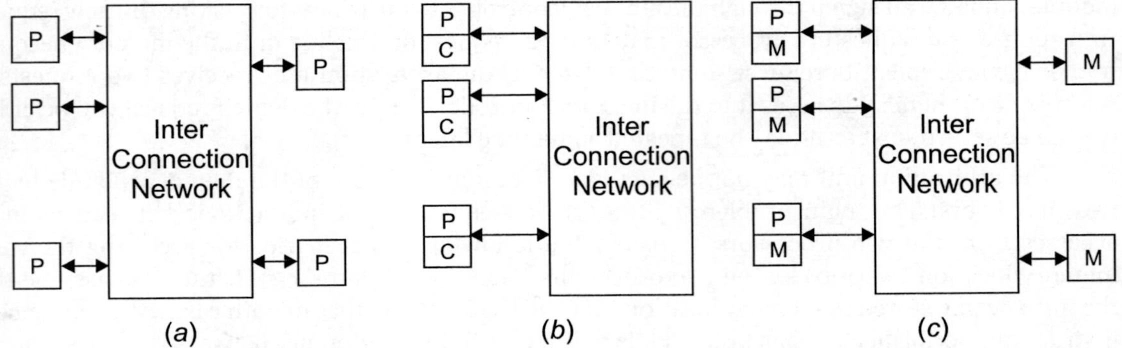

FIGURE 3.4: Three examples of Shared-Memory Architectures. (a) UMA, (b) COMA, (c) NUMA

Figure 3.4 shows typical organization for the abovementioned three shared memory architectures. In the UMA system, a shared memory is accessible by all processors through an interconnection network in the same way a single processor accesses its memory. Therefore, all processors have equal access time to any memory location. The interconnection network used in the UMA can be a single bus, multiple bus, a crossbar, or a multiport memory.

In the NUMA system, each processor has part of the shared memory attached. The memory has a single address space. Therefore, any processor could access any memory location directly using its real address. However, the access time to modules depends on the distance to the processor. This results in a nonuniform memory access time. A number of architectures are used to interconnect processors to memory modules in a NUMA. Among these are the tree and the hierarchical bus networks.

Similar to the NUMA, each processor has part of the shared memory in the COMA. However, in this case the shared memory consists of cache memory. A COMA system requires that data be migrated to the processor requesting it.

3.2.3 MESSAGE-PASSING ORGANIZATION

Message passing represents an alternative method for communication and movement of data among multiprocessors. Local, rather than global, memories are used to communicate messages among processors. A message is defined as a block of related information that travels among processors over direct links. There exist a number of models for message passing.

Examples of message-passing systems include the cosmic cube, workstation cluster, and the transputer. The introduction of the transputer system T212 in 1983 announced the birth of the first message-passing multiprocessor. Subsequently the T414 was announced in 1985, while Inmos introduced the VISI transputer processor in 1986. Two subsequent transputer products, the T800 (1988) and T9000 (1990), have been introduced. The cosmic cube message-passing multiprocessor was designed at Caltech during the period 1981–1985. It represented the first hypercube multiprocessor system that was made to work. Wormhole routing in message passing was introduced in 1987 as an alternative to the traditional store-and forward routing in order to reduce the size of the required buffers and to decrease the message latency. In wormhole routing, a packet is divided into smaller units that are called flits (flow control bits) such that flits move in a pipeline fashion with the header flit of the packet leading the way to the destination node. When the header flit is blocked due to network congestion, the remaining flits are blocked as well. The elimination of the need for a large global memory, which is usually a reason for a slowdown of the overall system, together with its asynchronous nature, give message-passing schemes an edge over shared-memory schemes. Similar to shared-memory multiprocessors, application programs are divided into smaller parts; each can be executed by an individual processor in a concurrent manner.

A simple example of a message-passing multiprocessor architecture is shown in Figure 3.5. As can be seen from the figure, processors use local bus (internal channels) to communicate with their local memories while communicating with other processors via an interconnection networks (external channels). Processes running on a given processor use internal channels to exchange messages among themselves. Processes running on different processors use external channels to exchange messages.

Such a scheme offers a great deal of flexibility in accommodating a large number of processors and being readily scalable. It should be noted that the process and the processor, which executes it, are considered as two separate entities. The size of a process is determined by the programmer and can be described by its granularity, given by:

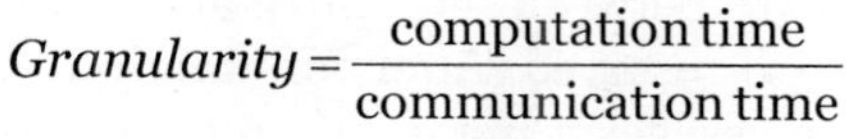

$$Granularity = \frac{\text{computation time}}{\text{communication time}}$$

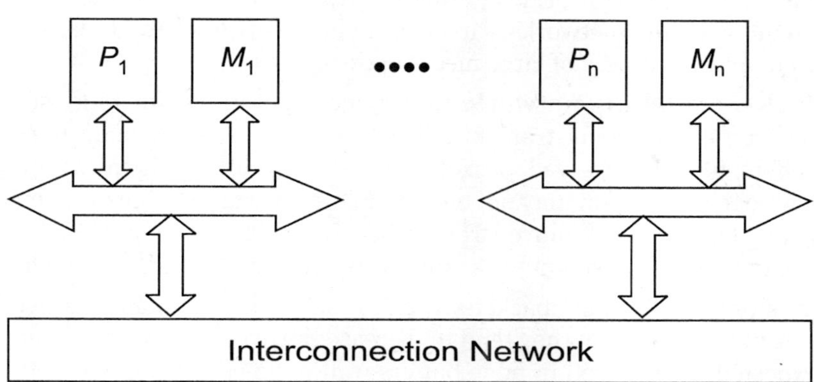

FIGURE 3.5: Example of a Message-Passing Multiprocessor Architecture

Three types of granularity can be distinguished. These are:

1. **Coarse granularity:** Each process holds a large number of sequential instructions and takes a substantial time to execute.
2. **Medium granularity:** Since the process communication overhead increases as the granularity decreases, medium granularity describes a middle ground whereby communication overhead is reduced in order to enable each nodal communication to take less amount of time.
3. **Fine granularity:** Each process contains a few numbers of sequential instructions (as few as just one instruction).

Message-passing multiprocessors use mostly medium or coarse granularity. Message-passing multiprocessors employ static networks in local communication. In particular, hypercube networks have been receiving special attention for use in a message-passing multiprocessor. The nearest neighbor two-dimensional and three-dimensional mesh networks have the potential for being used in a message-passing system as well. Two important factors have led to the suitability of hypercube and mesh networks for use as message-passing networks. These factors are (1) the ease of VLSI implementation and (2) the suitability for two and three-dimensional applications.

Two important design factors must be considered in designing such networks. These are (1) the link bandwidth and (2) the network latency. The link bandwidth is defined as the number of bits that can be transmitted per unit time (bits/ second). The network latency is defined as the time to complete a message transfer. For example, links could be unidirectional or bidirectional and they can transfer one bit or several bits at a time. To estimate the network latency, we must first determine the path setup time, which depends on the number of nodes on the path. The actual transition time, which depends on the message size, must also be considered.

The information transfer from a given source through the network can be done in two ways:

1. **Circuit-switching networks:** In this type of network, there is no buffer required in each node. The path between the source and destination is first determined. All links along that path are reserved. After information transfer, reserved links are released for use by other messages. Circuit-switching networks are characterized by producing the smallest amount of delay. Inefficient link utilization is the main disadvantage of circuit-switching networks. Circuit-switching networks are, therefore, advantageously used only in the case of large message transfer.
2. **Packet-switching networks:** Here, messages are divided into smaller parts, called packets, before being transmitted between nodes. Each node must contain enough buffers to hold received packets before transmitting them. A complete path from source to destination may not be available at the start of transmission. As links become available, packets are moved from a node to a node until they reach the destination node. The technique is also known as the store-and-forward packet-switching technique.

Although store-and-forward packet-switching networks eliminate the need for a complete path at the start of transmission, they tend to increase the overall network latency. This is because packets are expected to be stored in node buffers waiting for the availability of outgoing links. In order to reduce the size of the required buffers and decrease the incurred network latency, wormhole routing (see above) has been introduced. Having touched on some of the machine categories based on the Flynn's classifications, we now provide an introduction into the interconnection networks used in these machin

3.2.4 *MIMD MACHINES*

MIMD is a parallel computer structure composed of multiple independent processors. MIMD machines are the most common type of parallel machines in use today. In this architecture, each processor has its own copy of a program and it can work on different data streams. The programming model for MIMD resembles the way processes interact in UNIX, but the obvious difference is that they are actually executing concurrently.

One factor that can have great impact on the performance of parallel systems is the interconnection of the processors. Because processors need to interact, some way to share information must be implemented. The study of the topological properties of the communication network and the way processors share common resources, as memory, generates further division in parallel computer architectural classification.

The two extreme cases for the way MIMD machines share information are shown in Figures 3.6 and 3.7. Figure 3.6 shows the general architecture of a *shared memory* MIMD machine. In this model all the processors have equal access to the memory, and the memory is seen as a single address space by every processor.

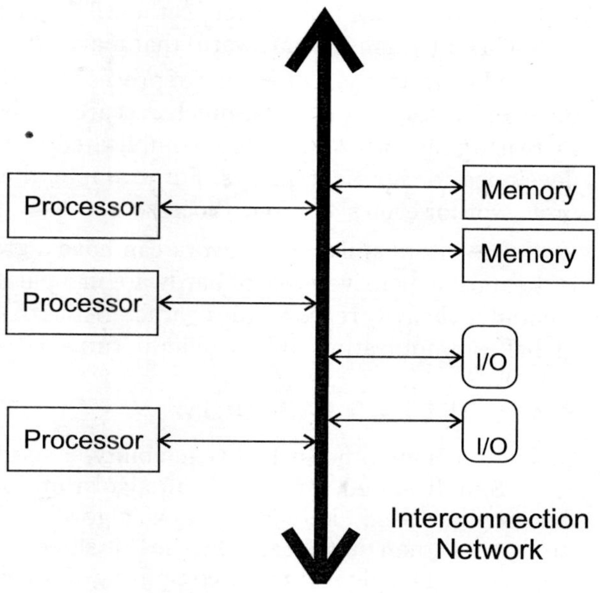

FIGURE 3.6: General Architecture of a Shared Memory MIMD.

In Figure 3.7, we have the general model of a *distributed memory* MIMD. In this model each processor has its own memory. This memory may be accessed by other processors but it is clear that the interconnection network will impose different access constraints to the different processors.

Shared memory machines have the advantage of allowing the same programming model as a UNIX workstation. The main drawback of pure shared memory machines is high contention for the memory bus and the speed of dynamic RAM, which is known to have high latency. This further limits the scalability of shared memory machines.

Actually, pure systems are rare and most large shared memory machines are in fact distributed memory MIMD with special hardware for accessing memory. The reason is that the bus to memory interface becomes a bottleneck when just a few processors need to access the same shared memory limiting the scalability of the system. For this reason the largest MIMD machines have distributed memory.

To build scalable shared memory architectures, several researchers have been trying novel interconnection techniques. Early optimizations employed caches (single and double level caches greatly improved the performance of the systems by reducing the use of bus bandwidth). The drawback of this approach is the complexity associated with cache coherence in multiprocessor architectures. Several shared memory

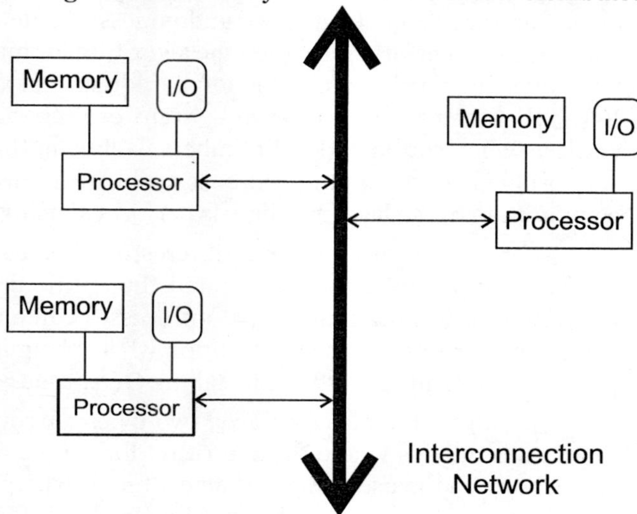

FIGURE 3.7: General Architecture of a distributed Memory MIMD.

architectures in use today, such as the BBN TC2000, are really distributed memory architectures with a layer (usually in hardware) that makes the communication transparent.

When more than a few tens of processors are put together, contention for the communication bus can be very high. Thus, much research is being devoted to minimizing bus contention and increasing bus utilization. Very complicated communication topologies and protocols have been developed for multicomputers. For example, the Intel Paragon uses a dedicated communication processor for each set of four processors.

The interconnection network can have a great impact on performance and in most cases; it is the most expensive piece of hardware in a parallel machine. The study of algorithms for parallel computers heavily relies on the characteristics of such networks. For instance, algorithms that need global communication will, in general, run slower on network with large *diameter*

3.3 REDUCTION PARADIGM

Reduction, sometimes called reducibility, is used in complexity theory for solving decision problems. Simply stated, "If there is an algorithm for deciding X, and then there is an algorithm for deciding Y." Often, there is no known algorithm for X; yielding a result that says that deciding Y is no "harder" than deciding X. We use this same notion for computing solutions to problems. Simply stated, given an algorithm for computing X, we use this algorithm for X in the algorithm for computing Y. We specifically imply that there is already a known algorithm for computing X. Not only does this say that Y is no harder to compute than X, but that in solving Y, we do not need to solve X again. Also, by using the algorithm for X, we may have made the solution to Y much easier. It may also be that if a better algorithm for X is found, there will be a better algorithm for Y.

This notion is used in the theory of parallel computation. Anderson gives an algorithm for the maximal path problem that uses an algorithm for matching. Although **N** the underlying model of computation is the PRAM, it is an example of the reduction paradigm. An interesting point about this algorithm is the fact that the known algorithm for matching uses randomness. This makes the algorithm for maximal path use randomness. If a deterministic algorithm for matching was found with the same performance, then the algorithm for maximal path would be deterministic. There are CTA algorithms using the reduction paradigm. The topological sort algorithm is a good example. Recall that the problem is solved by transforming the graph into vertices with level numbers. The vertices, when sorted by level numbers, will be in topological order. This changed the topological sort problem into a numerical sort problem for which there are known algorithms. Also, the computation of the level numbers is performed using matrix multiplication.

There are several points of interest in this algorithm. First, the time and resources of the matrix multiply algorithm dominated the entire algorithm. For the fastest solution, the matrix multiply algorithm required $\mathbf{O(n^3)}$ processes while the remaining part of the algorithm required only $\mathbf{O(n^2)}$ processes. For the solution where the matrix multiply algorithm was limited to $\mathbf{O(n^2)}$ processes, it dominated the time, taking $\mathbf{O(n)}$ time.

This algorithm also displayed two types of reduction. The first type, shown in the use of the matrix multiply, is where the algorithm for Y uses that algorithm for X many times. The second type, shown in the use of the sort algorithm, is where the algorithm for Y transforms the input into an instance of the problem for X. The algorithm for X needs to be used only once and after the algorithm for Y has completed its work. Schwartz gives two algorithms for the shuffle-exchange Ultracomputer using reduction. He shows how matrix inversion of a lower triangular matrix can be done using matrix multiply. For general matrices, he shows how to change the general matrix into a lower triangular matrix and use the algorithm for inversion of lower triangular matrices. The other algorithm is for connected components and uses matrix multiply for repeated squaring.

Dekel, Nassimi and Sahni also use reduction in several algorithms. These include all-pairs shortest-paths, several spanning tree problems, and topological sort, the algorithms used to solve these problems include matrix multiply, sorting and several of the graph algorithms just given.

3.3.1 REDUCTION PROCESSING OR DEMAND DRIVEN PROCESSING

"Demand driven processing" (also called "reduction processing") is a variant of data flow processing in which the indiscriminate execution of instructions is avoided. An operand is executed only when its results are needed by another operation, therefore, only the operations needed to get the results are executed. The details of a demand driven computer are significantly more complicated than those of a data flow machine.

Data flow computers have not yet moved into the commercial market place. However, they are an active area of research, and the data flow model is an important influence on the field of parallel computers. The data flow computers built to date has all been attached processors.

3.3.2 DEMAND-DRIVEN MECHANISMS

Data-driven machines select instructions for execution based on the availability of their operands; this is essentially a bottom-up approach. Demand-driven machines take a top-down approach, attempting to execute the instruction (a demander) that yields the final result. This triggers the execution of instructions that yield its operands, and so forth. The demand-driven approach matches naturally with functional programming languages (e.g. LISP and SCHEME). Pattern driven computers: An instruction is executed when we obtain a particular data patterns as output. There are two types of pattern driven computers String-reduction model: each demander gets a separate copy of the expression string to evaluate each reduction step has an operator and embedded reference to demand the corresponding operands each operator is suspended while arguments are evaluated Graph-reduction model: expression graph reduced by evaluation of branches or subgraphs, possibly in parallel, with demanders given pointers to results of reductions based on sharing of pointers to arguments; traversal and reversal of pointers continues until constant arguments are encountered.

3.3.3 REDUCTION ARCHITECTURES

Reduction or demand architectures implement an execution paradigm in which an instruction is enabled for execution when its results are required as operands for another instruction already enabled for execution. Most reduction architecture research began in the late 1970s to explore new parallel execution paradigms and to provide architectural support for applicative (functional) programming languages.

Reduction architectures execute programs that consist of nested expressions. Expressions are recursively defined as literals of function applications on arguments that may be literals or expressions. Programs may "reference" named expressions, which always return the same value (the referential transparency property). Reduction programs are function applications constructed from primitive functions.

Reduction program execution consists of recognizing reducible expressions, then replacing them with their calculated values. Thus, an entire reduction program is ultimately reduced to its result. Since the general execution paradigm only enables an instruction for execution when its results are needed by a previously enabled instruction, some additional rule is needed to enable the first instruction(s) and begin computation.

Practical challenges for implementing reduction architectures include synchro-nizing demands for an instruction's results (since preserving refer-ential transparency requires cal-culating an expression's results once only) and maintaining copies of expression evaluation results (since an expression result could be referenced more than once but could be consumed by subsequent reductions upon first being delivered).

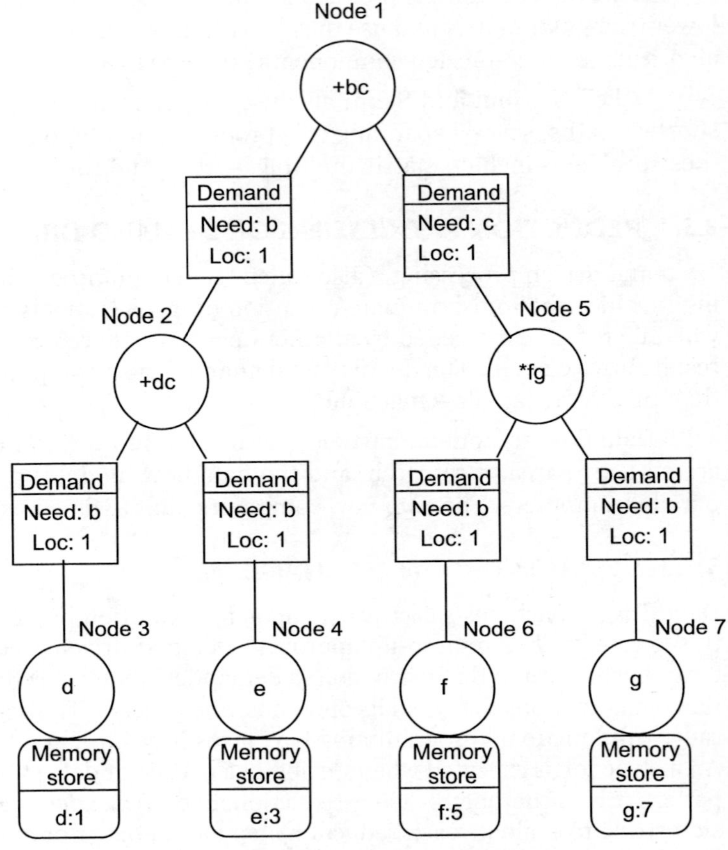

FIGURE 3.8: Reduction Architecture demand token production.

Reduction architectures employ either string reduction or graph reduction to implement demand driven paradigms. String reduction involves manipulating literals and copies of values, which are represented as strings that can be dynamically expanded and contracted.

Graph reduction involves manipulating literals and references (pointers) to values. Thus, a program is represented as a graph, and garbage collection reclaims dynamically allocated memory as the reduction proceeds.

Figures 3.8 and 3.9 shows a simplified version of a graph-reduction architecture that maps the program below onto tree-structured processors and passes tokens that demand or return results.

Figure 3.8 depicts all the demand tokens produced by the program, as demands for the values of references propagate down the tree. In figure 3.9, the last two result tokens produced are shown as they are passed to the root node.

a= +bc;

b= +de;

c= *fg;

d=1; e= 3; f=5; g=7.

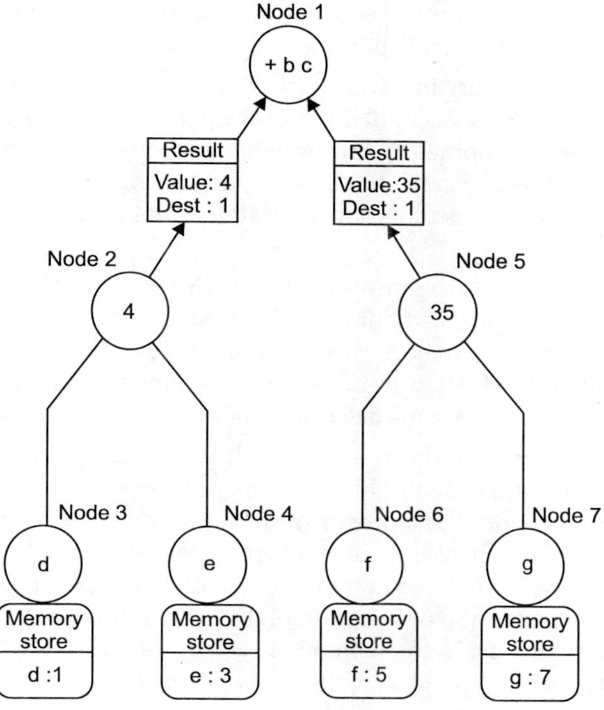

FIGURE 3.9: Reduction Architecture Result token production.

Rather dissimilar architectures (such as the Newcastle reduction machine, north Carolina cellular tree machine, and utah applicative multiprocessing system) have been proposed to support both string and graph reduction approaches.

3.4 OVERVIEW OF FLYNN'S TAXONOMY

Over the years, several attempts have been made to find a satisfactory way to categorize computer architectures. Although none of them are perfect, today's most widely accepted taxonomy is the one proposed by Michael Flynn in 1972. *Flynn's taxonomy* considers two factors: the number of instructions and the number of data streams that flow into the processor. A machine can have either one or multiple streams of data, and can have either one or multiple processors working on this data. This gives us four possible combinations: *SISD* (*single instruction stream, single data stream*), *SIMD* (*single instruction stream, multiple data streams*), *MISD* (*multiple instruction streams, single data stream*), and *MIMD* (*multiple instruction streams, multiple data streams*).

Uniprocessors are SISD machines. SIMD machines, which have a single point of control, execute the same instruction simultaneously on multiple data values. The SIMD category includes array processors, vector processors, and systolic arrays. MISD machines have multiple instruction streams operating on the same data stream. MIMD machines, which employ multiple control points, have independent instruction and data streams. Multiprocessors and most current parallel systems are MIMD machines. SIMD computers are simpler to design than MIMD machines, but they are also considerably less flexible. All of the SIMD multiprocessors must execute the *same* instruction simultaneously. If you think about this, executing something as simple as conditional branching could quickly become very expensive.

Flynn's taxonomy falls short in several areas. For one, there seem to be very few (if any) applications for MISD machines. Secondly, Flynn assumed that parallelism was homogeneous. A collection of processors can be homogeneous or heterogeneous. A machine could conceivably have four separate floating-point adders, two multipliers, and a single integer unit. This machine could therefore execute seven operations in parallel, but it does not readily fit into Flynn's classification system.

Another problem with this taxonomy is with the MIMD category. An architecture with multiple processors falls into this category without consideration for how the processors are connected or how they view memory. There have been several attempts to refine the MIMD category. Suggested changes include subdividing MIMD to differentiate systems that share memory from those that don't, as well as categorizing processors according to whether they are bus-based or switched.

Shared memory systems are those in which all processors have access to a global memory and communicate through shared variables, just as processes do on a uniprocessor. If multiple processors do not share memory, each processor must own a portion of memory. Consequently, all processors must communicate by way of message passing, which can be expensive and inefficient. The issue some people have with using memory as a determining factor for classifying hardware is that shared memory and message passing are actually programming models, not hardware models. Thus, they more properly belong in the domain of system software.

The two major parallel architectural paradigms, SMP (symmetric multiprocessors) and MPP (massively parallel processors), are both MIMD architectures, but differ in how they use memory. SMP machines, such as a dual-processor Intel PC and the 256-processor Origin3000, share memory, whereas MPP processors, such as the nCube, CM5, and Cray T3E, do not. These particular MPP machines typically house thousands of CPUs in a single large cabinet connected to hundreds of gigabytes of memory. The price of these systems can run into millions of dollars.

Originally, the term MPP described tightly coupled SIMD multiprocessors, such as the Connection Machine and Goodyear's MPP. Today, however, the term MPP is used to refer to parallel architectures that have multiple self-contained nodes with private memories, all of which have the ability to communicate via a network. An easy way to differentiate SMP and MPP (by today's definition) is the following:

MPP = many processors + distributed memory + communication via network

and

SMP = few processors + shared memory + communication via memory

Distributed computing is another example of the MIMD architecture. *Distributed computing* is typically defined as a set of networked computers that work collaboratively to solve a problem. This collaboration, however, can occur in many different ways.

A *network of workstations* (*NOW*) is a collection of distributed workstations that works in parallel only while the nodes are not being used as regular workstations. NOWs typically consist of heterogeneous systems, with different processors and software that communicate via the Internet. Individual users must establish the appropriate connection to the network before joining the parallel computation. A *cluster of workstations* (*COW*) is a collection similar to a NOW, but it requires that a single entity be in charge. Nodes typically have common software, and a user that can access one node can usually access all nodes. A *dedicated cluster parallel computer* (*DCPC*) is a collection of workstations specifically collected to work on a given parallel computation. The workstations have common software and file systems, are managed by a single entity, communicate via the Internet, and aren't used as workstations. A *pile of PCs* (*POPC*) is a cluster of dedicated heterogeneous hardware used to build a parallel system. Whereas a DCPC has relatively few, but expensive and fast components, a POPC uses a large number of slow, but relatively cheap nodes.

The BEOWULF project, introduced in 1994 by Thomas Sterling and Donald Becker of Goddard Space Flight Center, is a POPC architecture that has successfully bundled various hardware platforms with specially designed software, resulting in an architecture that has the look and feel of a unified parallel machine. The nodes on a BEOWULF network are always connected via a private network. If you have an old Sun SPARC, a couple of 486 machines, a DEC Alpha (or simply a large collection of dusty Intel machines!), and a means to connect them into a network, you can install the BEOWULF software and create your own personal, but extremely powerful, parallel computer.

Flynn's taxonomy has recently been expanded to include *SPMD* (*single program multiple data*) architectures. An SPMD consists of multiprocessors, each with its own data set and program memory. The same program is executed on each processor, with synchronization at various global control points. Although each processor loads the same program, each may execute different instructions. For example, a program may have code that resembles:

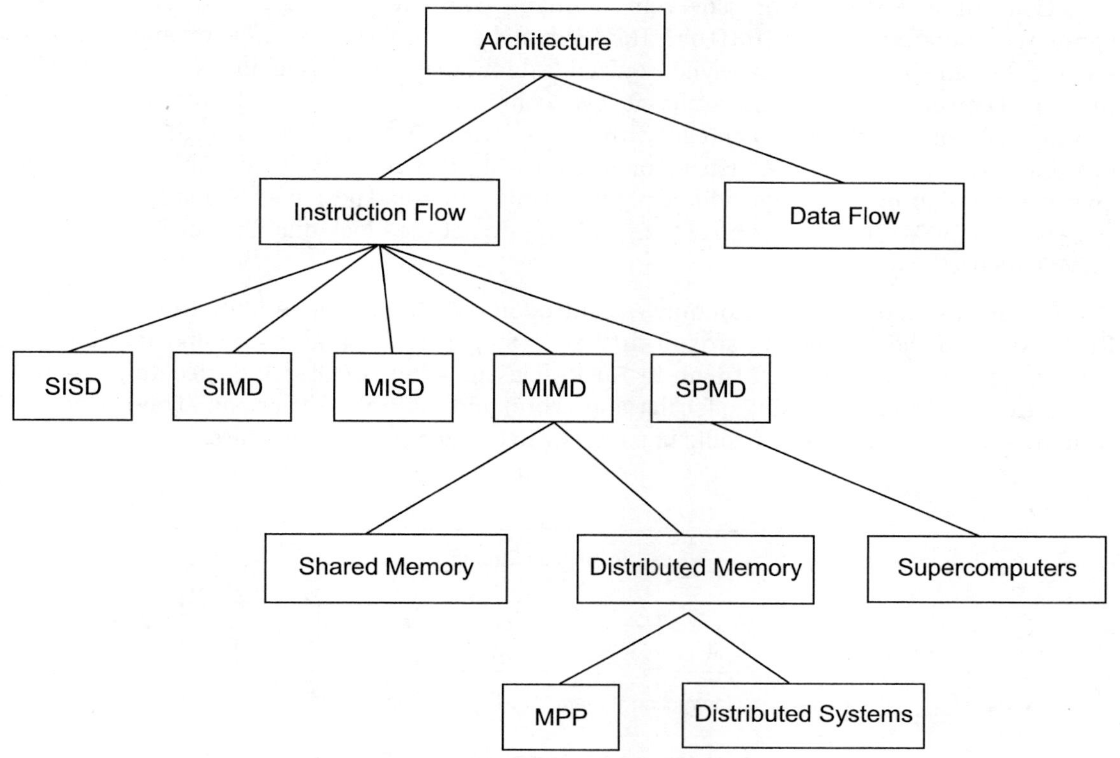

FIGURE 3.10: Taxonomy of Computer Architec

If myNodeNum = 1 do this, else do that

In this way, different nodes execute different instructions within the same program. SPMD is actually a programming paradigm used on MIMD machines and differs from SIMD in that the processors can do different things at the same time. Supercomputers often use an SPMD design.

At a level above where Flynn begins his taxonomy, we need to add one more characteristic, and that is whether the architecture is instruction driven or data driven. The classic von Neumann architecture is instruction driven. All processor activities are determined by a sequence of program code. Program instructions act *on* the data. Data driven, or *dataflow*, architectures do just the opposite. The characteristics of the data determine the sequence of processor events. With the addition of dataflow computers and some refinements to the MIMD classification, we obtain the taxonomy shown in Figure 3.10. You may wish to refer to it as you read the sections that follow. We begin on the left-hand branch of the tree, with topics relevant to SIMD and MIMD architectures.

3.4.1 HARDWARE TAXONOMY: FLYNN'S CLASSIFICATION

The most popular taxonomy of computer architecture was defined by Flynn in 1966. Flynn's classification scheme is based on the notion of a stream of information. Two types of information flow into a processor: instructions and data. The instruction stream is defined as the sequence of instructions performed by the processing unit. The data stream is defined as the data traffic exchanged between the memory and the processing unit.

Conventional single-processor von Neumann computers are classified as SISD systems. Parallel computers are either SIMD or MIMD. When there is only one control unit and all processors execute the same instruction in a synchronized fashion, the parallel machine is classified as SIMD. In a MIMD machine, each processor has its own control unit and can execute different instructions on different data. In the MISD category, the same stream of data flows through a linear array of processors executing different instruction streams. In practice, there is no viable MISD machine; however, some authors have considered pipelined machines (and perhaps systolic-array computers) as examples for MISD. Figures 3.11, 3.12, and 3.13 depict the block diagrams of SISD, SIMD, and MIMD, respectively.

An extension of Flynn's taxonomy was introduced by D. J. Kuck in 1978. In his classification, Kuck extended the instruction stream further to single (scalar and array) and multiple (scalar and array) streams. The data stream in Kuck's classification is called the execution stream and is also extended to include single (scalar and array) and multiple (scalar and array) streams. The combination of these streams results in a total of 16 categories of architectures.

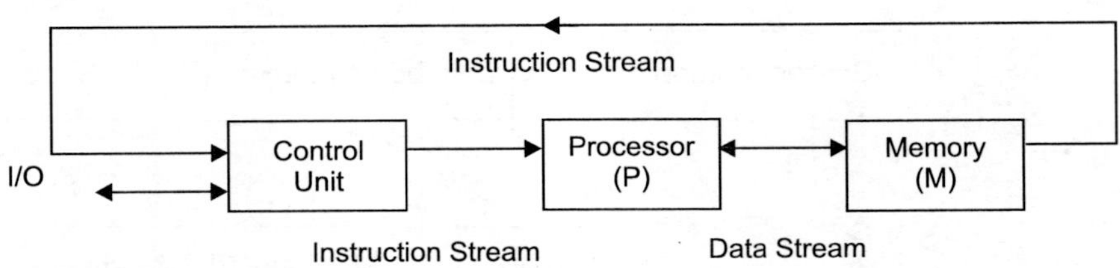

FIGURE 3.11: SISD Architecture.

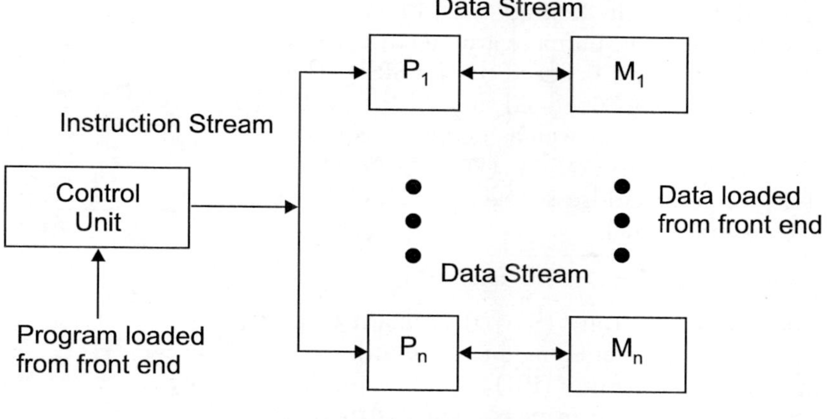

FIGURE 3.12: SIMD Architecture.

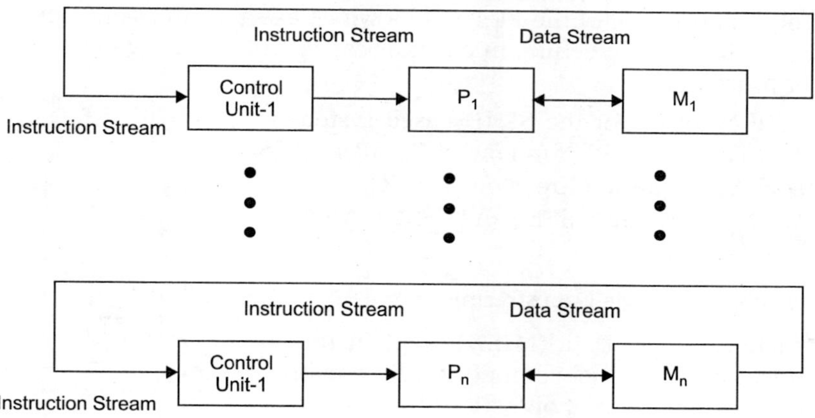

FIGURE 3.13: MIMD Architecture.

According to Flynn's classification, either of the instruction or data streams can be single or multiple. Computer architecture can be classified into the following four distinct categories:

- single-instruction single-data streams (SISD);
- single-instruction multiple-data streams (SIMD);
- multiple-instruction single-data streams (MISD); and
- multiple-instruction multiple-data streams (MIMD).

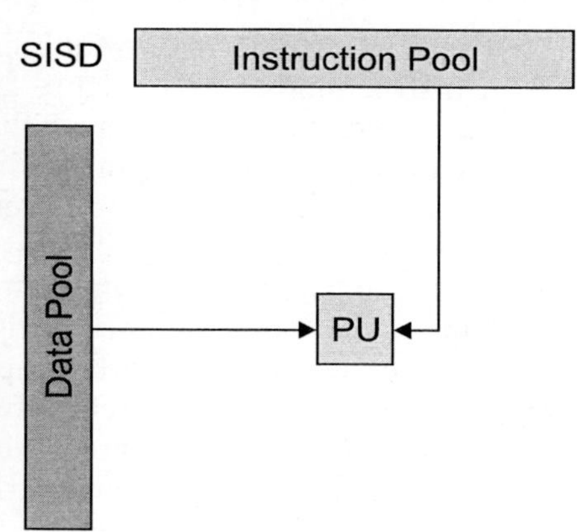

SISD (Single Instruction, Single Data stream)

Single Instruction, Single Data (SISD) refers to an Instruction Set Architecture in which a single processor (one CPU) executes exactly one instruction stream at a time and also fetches or stores one item of data at a time to op-

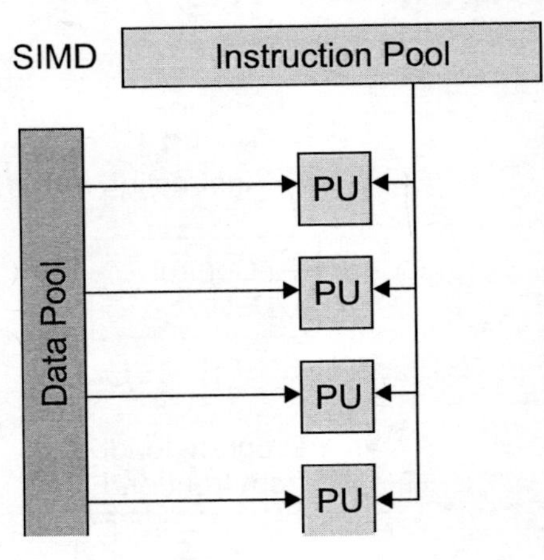

erate on data stored in a single memory unit. Most of the CPU design, based on the von Neumann architecture, from the beginning till recent times is based on the SISD. The SISD model is a typical non-pipelined architecture with the general-purpose registers, as well as dedicated special registers such as the Program Counter (PC), the Instruction Register (IR), Memory Address Registers (MAR) and Memory Data Registers (MDR).

SIMD (Single Instruction, Multiple Data streams)

Single Instruction, Multiple Data (SIMD) is an Instruction Set Architecture that have a single control unit (CU) and more than one processing unit (PU) that operates like a von Neumann machine by executing a single instruction stream over PUs, handled through the CU. The CU generates the control signals for all of the PUs and by which executes the same operation on different data streams. The SIMD architecture, in effect, is capable of achieving data level parallelism just like with vector processor.

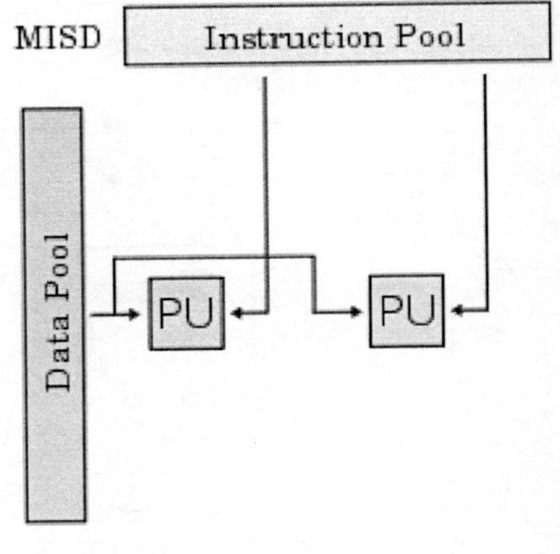

Some of the examples of the SIMD based systems include IBM's AltiVec and SPE for PowerPC, HP's PA-RISC Multimedia Acceleration eXtensions (MAX), Intel's MMX and iwMMXt, SSE, SSE2, SSE3 and SSSE3, AMD's 3DNow! etc.

MISD (Multiple Instruction, Single Data stream)

Multiple Instruction, Single Data (MISD) is an Instruction Set Architecture for parallel computing where many functional units perform different operations by executing different instructions on the same data set. This type of architecture is common mainly in the fault-tolerant computers executing the same instructions redundantly in order to detect and mask errors.

MIMD (Multiple Instruction, Multiple Data streams)

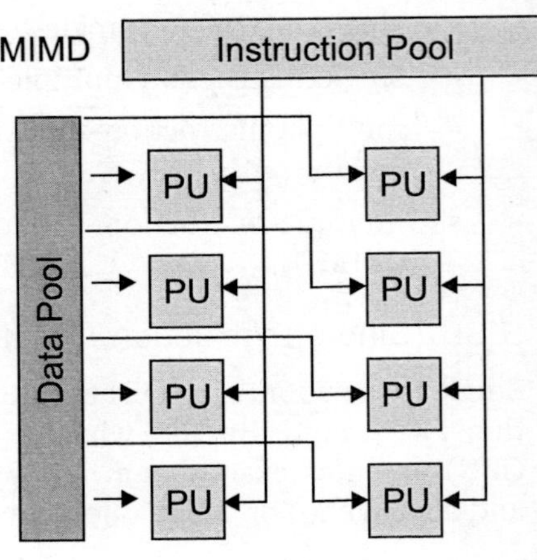

Multiple Instruction stream, Multiple Data stream (MIMD) is an Instruction Set Architecture for parallel computing that is typical of the computers with multiprocessors. Using the MIMD, each processor in a multiprocessor system can execute asynchronously different set of the instructions independently on the different set of data units. The MIMD based computer systems can use the shared memory in a memory pool or work using distributed memory across heterogeneous network computers in a distributed environment. The MIMD architectures is primarily used in a number of application areas such as computer-aided design/computer-aided manufacturing, simulation, modeling, communication switches etc.

Some further divide the MIMD category into the following categories:

Single Program, Multiple Data (SPMD)

Multiple autonomous processors simultaneously executing the same program (but at independent points, rather than in the lockstep that SIMD imposes) on different data. Also referred to as "Single Process, multiple data" - the use of this terminology for SPMD is erroneous and should be avoided, SPMD is a parallel execution model and assumes multiple cooperating processes executing a program. SPMD is the most common style of parallel programming. The SPMD model and the term were proposed by Frederica Darema. Gregory F. Pfister was a manager of the RP3 project, and Darema was part of the RP3 team.

Multiple Program Multiple Data (MPMD)

Multiple autonomous processors simultaneously operating at least two independent programs. Typically such systems pick one node to be the "host" ("the explicit host/node programming model") or "manager" (the "Manager/Worker" strategy), which runs one program that farms out data to all the other nodes which all run a second program. Those other nodes then return their results directly to the manager. An example of this would be the Sony PlayStation3 game console, with its SPU/PPU processor architecture.

3.4.2 PARALLEL ARCHITECTURES

Parallel or concurrent operation has many different forms within a computer system. Using a model based on the different streams used in the computation process, we represent some of the different kinds of parallelism available. A stream is a sequence of objects such as data, or of actions such as instructions. Each stream is independent of all other streams, and each element of a stream can consist of one or more objects or actions.

We thus have four combinations that describe most familiar parallel architectures:

(1) **SISD:** single instruction, single data stream. This is the traditional uniprocessor [Figure 3.14(a)].

(2) **SIMD:** single instruction, multiple data stream. This includes vector processors as well as massively parallel processors [Figure 3.14(b)].

(3) **MISD:** multiple instruction, single data stream. These are typically systolic arrays [Figure 3.14(c)].

(4) **MIMD:** multiple instruction, multiple data stream. This includes traditional multiprocessors as well as the newer networks of workstations [Figure 3.14(d)].

Each of these combinations characterizes a class of architectures and a corresponding type of parallelism.

SISD

The SISD class of processor architecture is the most familiar class and has the least obvious concurrency of any of the models, yet a good deal of concurrency can be present. Pipelining is a straightforward approach that is based on concurrently performing different phases of processing an instruction. This does not achieve concurrency of execution (with multiple actions being taken on objects) but does achieve a concurrency of processing— an improvement in efficiency upon which almost all processors depend today.

Techniques that exploit concurrency of execution, often called instructionlevel parallelism (ILP), are also common. Two architectures that exploit ILP are *superscalar* and VLIW (very long instruction word). These techniques schedule different operations to execute concurrently based on analyzing the dependencies between the operations within the instruction stream—dynamically at run time in a superscalar processor and statically at compile time in a VLIW processor. Both ILP approaches trade off adaptability against complexity— the superscalar processor is adaptable but complex whereas the VLIW processor is not adaptable but simple. Both superscalar and VLIW use the same compiler techniques to achieve high performance.

The current trend for SISD processors is towards superscalar designs in order to exploit available ILP as well as existing object code. In the marketplace there are few VLIW designs, due to code compatibility issues, although advances in compiler technology may cause this to change. However, research in all aspects of ILP is fundamental to the development of improved architectures in all classes because of the frequent use of SISD architectures as the processor elements in most implementations.

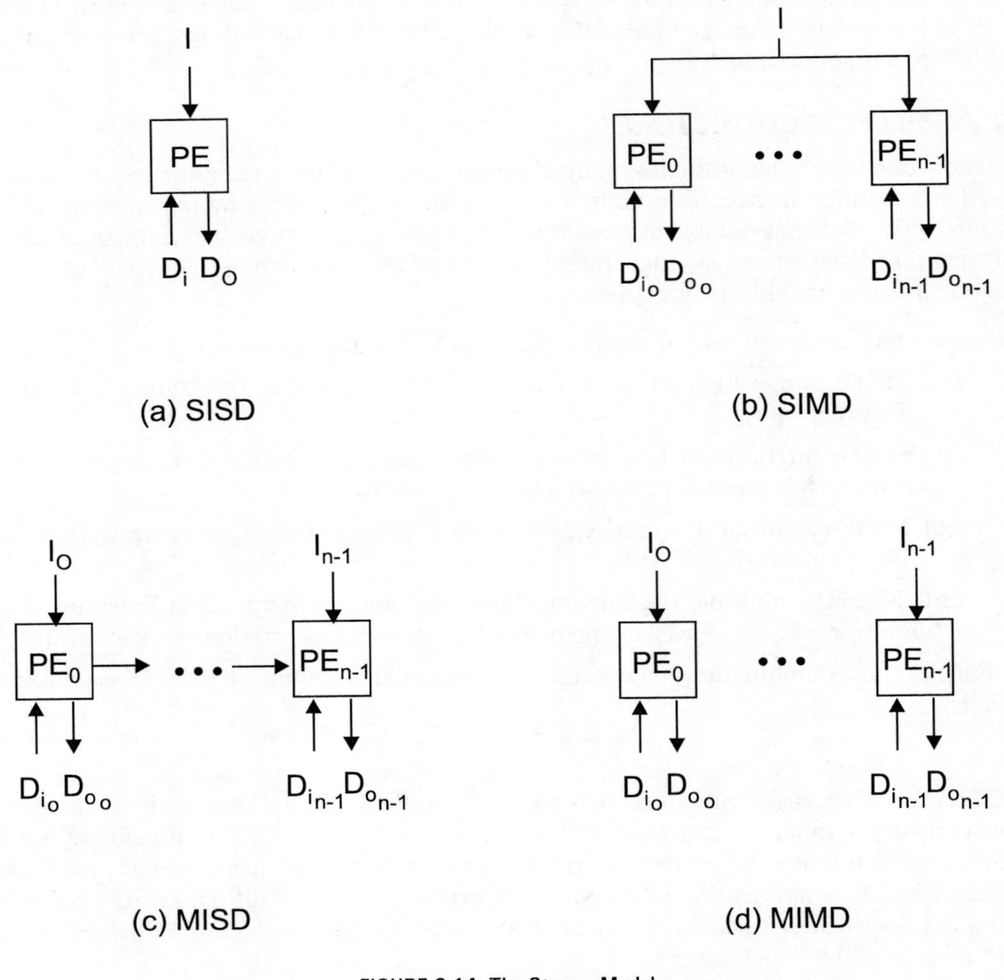

FIGURE 3.14: The Stream Model

SIMD

The SIMD class of processor architecture includes both array and vector processors. This processor is a natural response to the use of certain regular data structures such as vectors and matrices. Two different architectures, array processors and vector processors, have been developed to address these structures. An array processor has many processor elements operating in parallel on many data elements. A vector processor has a single processor element that operates in sequence on many data elements. Both types of processors use a single operation to perform many actions. An array processor depends on the massive size of the data sets to achieve its efficiency (and thus is often referred to as a massively parallel processor), with a typical array processor consisting of hundreds to tens of thousands of relatively simple processors operating together. A vector processor depends on the same regularity of action as an array processor but on smaller data sets and relies on extreme pipelining and high clock rates to reduce the overall latency of the operation.

There have not been a significant number of array architectures developed due to a limited application base and market requirement. There has been a trend towards more and more complex processor elements due to increases in chip density, and recent array architectures blur the distinction between SIMD and MIMD configurations.

On the other hand, many different kinds of vector processors have developed dramatically through the years. Starting with simple memory-based vector processors, modern vector processors have developed into high-performance multiprocessors capable of addressing both SIMD and MIMD parallelism.

MISD

Although it is easy to both envision and design MISD processors, there has been little interest in this type of parallel architecture. The reason, so far anyway, is that no ready programming constructs easily map programs into the MISD organization.

Abstractly, the MISD is a pipeline of multiple independently executing functional units operating on a single stream of data, forwarding results from one functional unit to the next. On the microarchitecture level, this is exactly what the vector processor does. However, in the vector pipeline the operations are simply fragments of an assembly-level operation, as distinct from being a complete operation in them. Surprisingly, some of the earliest attempts at computers in the 1940s could be seen as the MISD concept. They used plug boards for programs, where data in the form of a punched card was introduced into the first stage of a multistage processor. A sequential series of actions was taken in which the intermediate results were forwarded from stage to stage until at the final stage a result was punched into a new card.

MIMD

The MIMD class of parallel architecture is the most familiar and possibly most basic form of parallel processor: it consists of multiple interconnected processor elements. Unlike the SIMD processor, each processor element executes completely independently (although typically the same program). Although there is no requirement that all processor elements be identical, most MIMD configurations are homogeneous with all processor elements identical. When communications between processor elements are performed through a shared memory address space (either global or distributed between processor elements, called distributed shared memory to distinguish it from distributed memory), two significant problems arise. The first is mainlining memory consistency—the programmer-visible ordering effects of memory references both within a processor element and between different processor elements.

The second is maintaining cache coherency— the programmer-invisible mechanism to ensure that all processor elements see the same value for a given memory location. The memory consistency problem is usually solved through a combination of hardware and software techniques. The cache coherency problem is usually solved exclusively through hardware techniques. There have been many configurations of MIMD processors that have ranged from the traditional processor described in this section to loosely coupled processors based on networking commodity workstations through a local area network. These configurations differ primarily in the interconnection network between processor elements that range from on-chip arbitration between multiple processor elements on one chip to wide-area networks between continents, the tradeoffs being between the latency of communications and the size limitations on the system.

3.5 SOFTWARE TAXONOMY: KUNG'S TAXONOMY

The exploitation of parallelism created a new dimension in computer science. In order to move parallel processing into the mainstream of computing, H.T.Kung (1991) has identified the need to make significant progress in three key areas:

- Computational models for parallel computing
- Interprocessor communication in parallel architectures, and
- System integration for incorporating parallel systems into general computing environments

A theoretical treatment of parallelism is thus needed to build a basis for the above challenges. In practice, parallelism appears in various forms in a computing environment. All forms can be attributed to levels of parallelism, computational granularity, time and space complexities, communication latencies, scheduling policies, and load balancing. Very often, tradeoffs exist among time, space, performance, and cost factors.

3.5.1 DATA FLOW COMPUTERS

Data flow computers are the hardware realisation of a general "data flow graph". These graphs reflect how data is used in an algorithm or a computational process. Data flow graph nodes indicate what is done to the data, while the arcs show which nodes the results are to be transferred to, see figure 3.15.

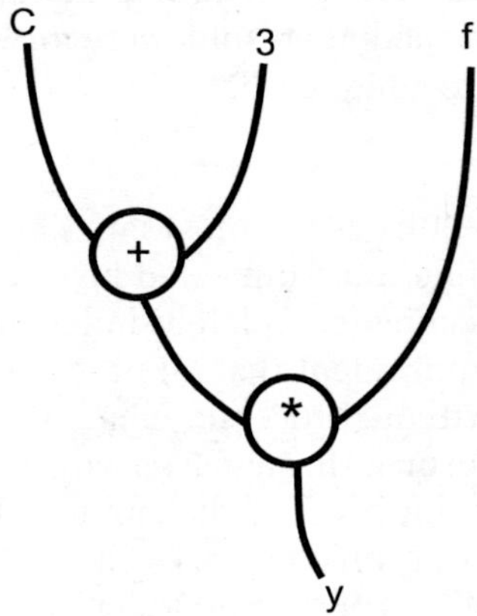

FIGURE 3.15: Data Flow Graph for y=(c+3)*f

Instruction	Operand	Operand	Result Address

FIGURE 3.16: Operation Taken for Data Flow Computer

Data flow computers execute 'tokens' rather than instructions. A token contains an instruction, several operands, and a destination address for the result, see figure 3.16. Once compiled the entire program is represented by a list of tokens. At compile time, however, not all of the operands will be present. The missing operands are the results of other tokens and are filled in as the corresponding source tokens produce their results. A program completes when all the missing operands have been filled in and the resulting tokens executed. Figure 3.17 shows how the memory contents change during the execution of a the data flow graph in figure 3.15.

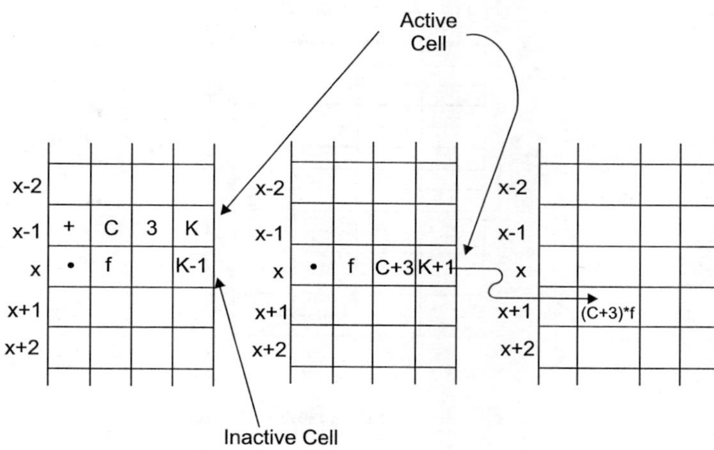

FIGURE 3.17: Three Memory Snapshots during the Execution of y = (c + 3)*f by a Data Flow Computer.

Only complete tokens are offered for execution. There is nothing in the list of complete tokens to indicate which order they will be executed in. Execution proceeds as data becomes available.

Data flow computers are split up into three major sections:

1. A collection of simple processors, each of which has enough memory to execute a few machine code instructions.
2. A memory section which is divided into addressable cells, each of which may use several bytes and store a single token.
3. A communications network that moves tokens from memory cells to available processors and the results back again.

The memory system contains the control section of the computer. It accepts "result tokens" and inserts the data items into the corresponding memory cell. Once a cell has all its operands it becomes active, and the memory controller creates an "operation token" which can be queued ready for execution, see figure 3.18. The communications network sends the operation tokens to any processing elements that are free.

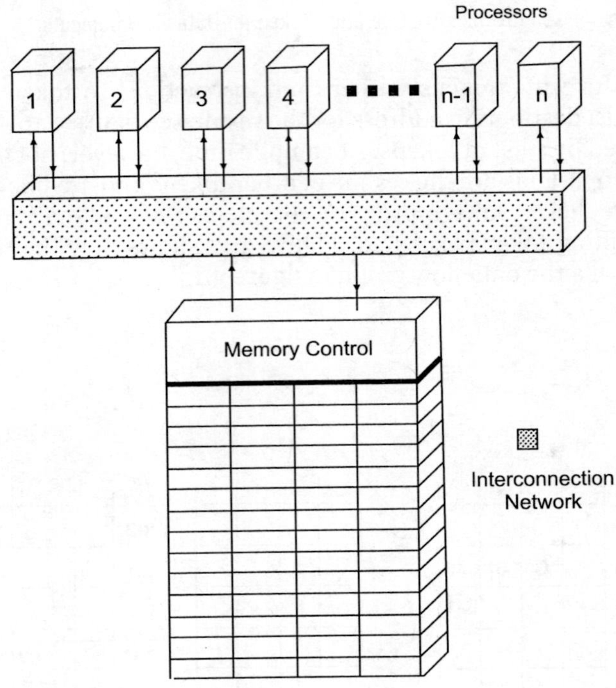

FIGURE 3.18: Data Flow Computer

Once a processing element receives an operation token it is decoded and the instruction executed on its operands. The result(s) are then placed in a result token and are sent back to the memory system which places them in the memory cell(s) indicated by the result pointer. Result tokens contain the operands for other instructions which lead to the generation of new operation tokens and so process repeats until the program is complete.

Once a result token has been sent to the memory system the processing element must wait for another operations token from the memory system. The computer can be enhanced by having a token buffer in front of every processing element. Once the processing element has sent out its result token, it can collect the next operation token from this buffer without delay.

The data flow hardware model of a parallel computer is particularly suitable for being programmed in "functional languages". Functional languages are characterised by expressions feeding their results directly into other expressions, which in turn feed other expressions - variables are avoided.

A particular problem in programming many types of parallel computer is "load balancing" which involves keeping all the processors equally busy. Another problem is that of data dependency and only scheduling instructions when their operands are available. Data flow computers do not face these problems.

All data dependencies are resolved by the data flow graph description of the program. There is no need for explicit parallel declarations in a data flow program, and they have nothing to indicate the order of execution. There is also no need to find parallel algorithms. A suitable order of execution is revealed at run-time by the availability of data. The order of execution is not controlled by the instructions as in a normal computer, but rather by the availability and flow of data.

Load balancing is taken care of by the data flow model and need not be addressed by the programmer. Idle processors simply request more work and this happens at a fine enough level as to balance the work evenly amongst the available processors.

The size of data flow computers is limited by the communications network, which grows faster than the number of processors. At some point it will become the dominating part of the computer and make it uneconomical to add more processors.

One disadvantage of data flow computers is the relatively large program storage requirements. Tokens take up more memory space than simple instructions and data. A given problem will need more main memory on a data flow computer than on a conventional computer.

Another disadvantage of data flow computers is the indiscriminate execution of instructions. On a conventional computer, some of a program's instructions will usually not have been executed by the time it completes. Branch and jump instructions bypass sections of code which often never need to be returned to. The strategy of data flow computers dictates that all instructions are to be executed, and the unnecessary ones are only distinguished when the results come to be used. Data flow computers, therefore, waste some processing power.

3.5.2 SYSTOLIC ARCHITECTURES

Kung (1982) proposed systolic architectures as a means of solving problems of special purpose systems that must often balance intensive computations with demanding I/O bandwidths. Systolic arrays (architectures) are pipelined multiprocessors in which data is pulsed in a rhythmic fashion from memory through a network of processors and the results returned to the memory (see Figure 3.19). A global clock and explicit timing delay synchronize this pipeline dataflow, which consists of operands obtained from memory and partial results to be used by each processor. The processors are interconnected by regular, local interconnections. During each time interval, the processors execute a short, time invariant sequence of instructions. Systolic architectures address the performance requirements of special purpose systems by achieving significant parallel computation and by avoiding I/O and memory bandwidth bottlenecks. A high degree of parallelism is achieved by pipelining data through multiple processors, typically arranged in a two-dimensional fashion. Systolic architectures maximize the computations performed on a datum once it has been fetched from the memory or an external device. Once a datum enters the systolic array, it is passed to any processor that needs it without an intervening store to memory.

$$A = \begin{bmatrix} a & b \\ c & d \end{bmatrix} \quad \text{and} \quad B = \begin{bmatrix} e & f \\ g & h \end{bmatrix}$$

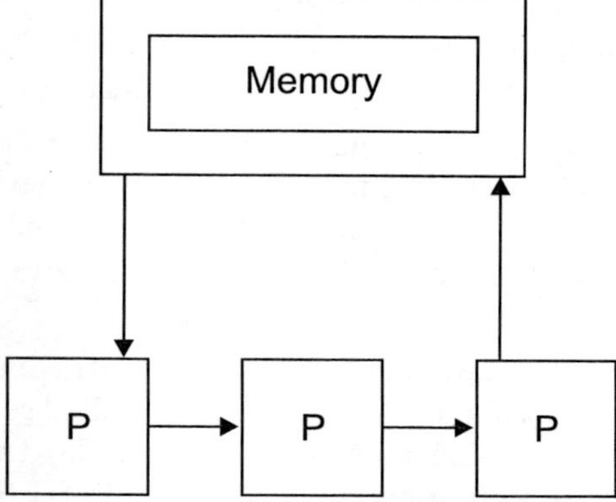

FIGURE 3.19: A Systolic Architecture

Example: Figure 3.20 shows how a simple systolic array would calculate the product of two matrices,

The zero inputs shown moving through the array are used for synchronization. Each processor begins with an accumulator set to zero and, during each cycle adds the product of its two inputs to the accumulator. After five cycles the matrix product is complete.

A variety of special purpose systems have used systolic arrays for algorithm specific architectures, particularly for signal processing applications. Programmable (reconfigurable) systolic architectures (Intel iWarp, Saxpy Matrix) have been constructed.

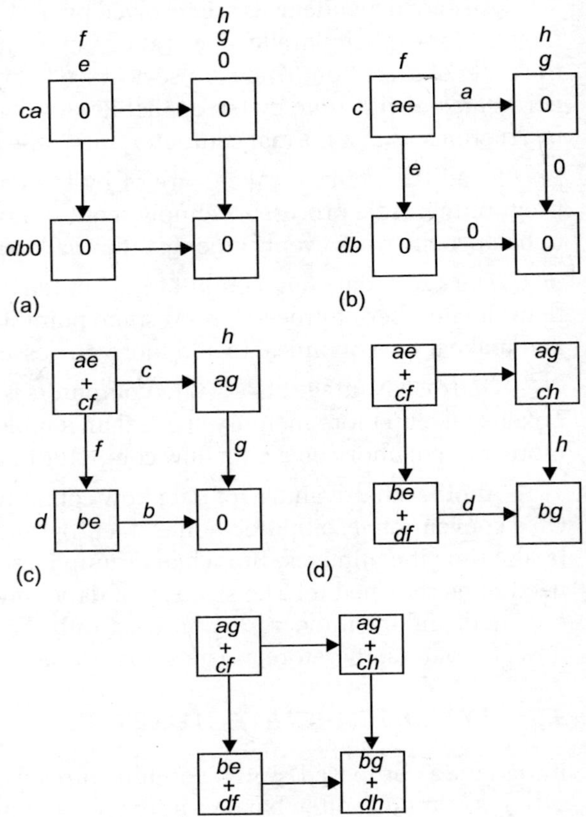

FIGURE 3.20: Systolic Matrix Multiplications.

3.5.2.1 DESCRIPTION OF SYSTOLIC ARRAY

The systolic array paradigm, data-stream-driven by data counters, is the counterpart of the von Neumann paradigm, instruction-stream-driven by a program counter. Because a systolic array usually sends and receives multiple data streams, and multiple data counters are needed to generate these data streams, it supports data parallelism. The name derives from analogy with the regular pumping of blood by the heart.

H. T. Kung and Charles E. Leiserson published the first paper describing systolic arrays in 1978; however, the first machine known to have used a similar technique was the Colossus Mark II in 1944.

In computer architecture, a **systolic array** is a pipe network arrangement of processing units called cells. It is a specialized form of parallel computing, where cells (i.e. processors), compute data and store it independently of each other.

A systolic array is composed of matrix-like rows of data processing units called cells. Data processing units DPUs are similar to central processing units (CPU)s, (except for the usual lack of a program counter, since operation is

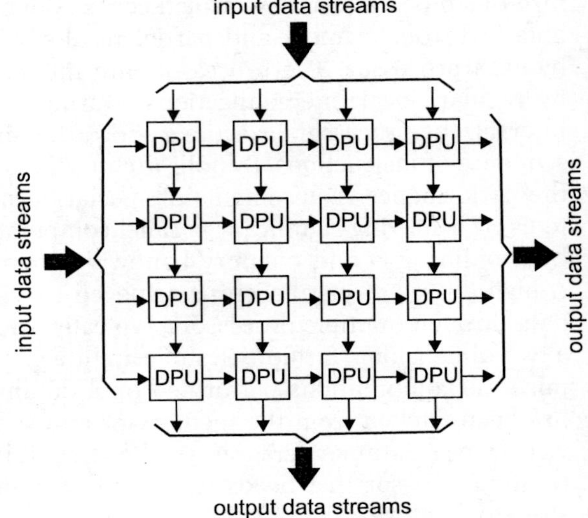

FIGURE 3.21: Description of Systolic Array

transport-triggered, i.e., by the arrival of a data object). Each cell shares the information with its neighbours immediately after processing. The systolic array is often rectangular where data flows across the array between neighbour DPUs, often with different data flowing in different directions. The data streams entering and leaving the ports of the array are generated by auto-sequencing memory units, ASMs. Each ASM includes a data counter. In embedded systems a data stream may also be input from and/or output to an external source.

An example of a systolic algorithm might be designed for matrix multiplication. One matrix is fed in a row at a time from the top of the array and is passed down the array; the other matrix is fed in a column at a time from the left hand side of the array and passes from left to right. Dummy values are then passed in until each processor has seen one whole row and one whole column. At this point, the result of the multiplication is stored in the array and can now be output a row or a column at a time, flowing down or across the array.

Systolic arrays are arrays of DPUs which are connected to a small number of nearest neighbour DPUs in a mesh-like topology. DPUs perform a sequence of operations on data that flows between them. Because the traditional systolic array synthesis methods have been practiced by algebraic algorithms, only uniform arrays with only linear pipes can be obtained, so that the architectures are the same in all DPUs. The consequence is that only applications with regular data dependencies can be implemented on classical systolic arrays. Like SIMD machines, clocked systolic arrays compute in "lock-step" with each processor undertaking alternate compute communicate phases. But systolic arrays with asynchronous handshake between DPUs are called wavefront arrays. One well-known systolic array is Carnegie Mellon University's iWarp processor, which has been manufactured by Intel. An iWarp system has a linear array processor connected by data buses going in both directions.

Applications

An application Example - Polynomial Evaluation

Horner's rule for evaluating a polynomial is:

$$y = (\ldots(((a_n * x + a_{n-1}) * x + a_{n-2}) * x + a_{n-3}) * x + \ldots + a_1) * x + a_0$$

A linear systolic array in which the processors are arranged in pairs: one multiplies its input by X and passes the result to the right, the next adds a_j and passes the result to the right.

3.5.2.2 WAVEFRONT ARRAY ARCHITECTURES

Wavefront array processors combine systolic data pipelining with an asynchronous dataflow execution paradigm. S.Y. Kung developed wavefront array concepts in the early 1980s to address the same kind of problems that stimulated systolic array research –producing efficient, cost-effective architectures for special purpose systems that balance intensive computations with high I/O bandwidth.

Wavefront and systolic architectures are both characterized by modular processors and regular, local interconnection networks. However, wavefront arrays replace the global clock and explicit time delays used for synchronizing systolic data pipelining with asynchronous handshaking as the mechanism for coordinating interprocessor data movement. Thus, when a processor has performed its computations and is ready to pass data to its successor, it informs the successor, sends data when the successor indicates it is ready, and receives an acknowledgement from the successor. The handshaking mechanism makes computational wavefronts pass smoothly through the array without intersecting, as the array's processors act as a wave propagating medium. In this manner, correct sequencing of computations replaces the correct timing of systolic architectures.

Figure 3.22a-c depicts wavefront array concepts, using the matrix multiplication example used earlier to illustrate systolic operation. The example architecture consists of processing elements (PEs) that have a one-operand buffer for each input source. Whenever the buffer for a memory input source is empty and the associated memory contains another operand, that available operand is immediately read. Operands from other PEs are obtained using a handshaking protocol.

Figure 3.22a shows the situation after memory input buffers are initially filled. In figure 3.22b PE(1,1) adds the product ae to its accumulator and transmits operands a and e to neighbors; thus, the first computational wavefront is shown propagating from PE(1,1) to PE(1,2) and PE(2,1). Figure 3.22c shows the first computational wavefront continuing to propagate, while a second wavefront is propagated by PE(1,1).

Kung argued that wavefront arrays enjoy several advantages over systolic arrays, including greater scalability, simpler programming, and greater fault tolerance. Wavefront arrays constructed at johns Hopkins University and at the standard telecommunications company and royal signals and radar establishment (in the United Kingdom) should facilitate further assessment of wavefront arrays proposed advantages.

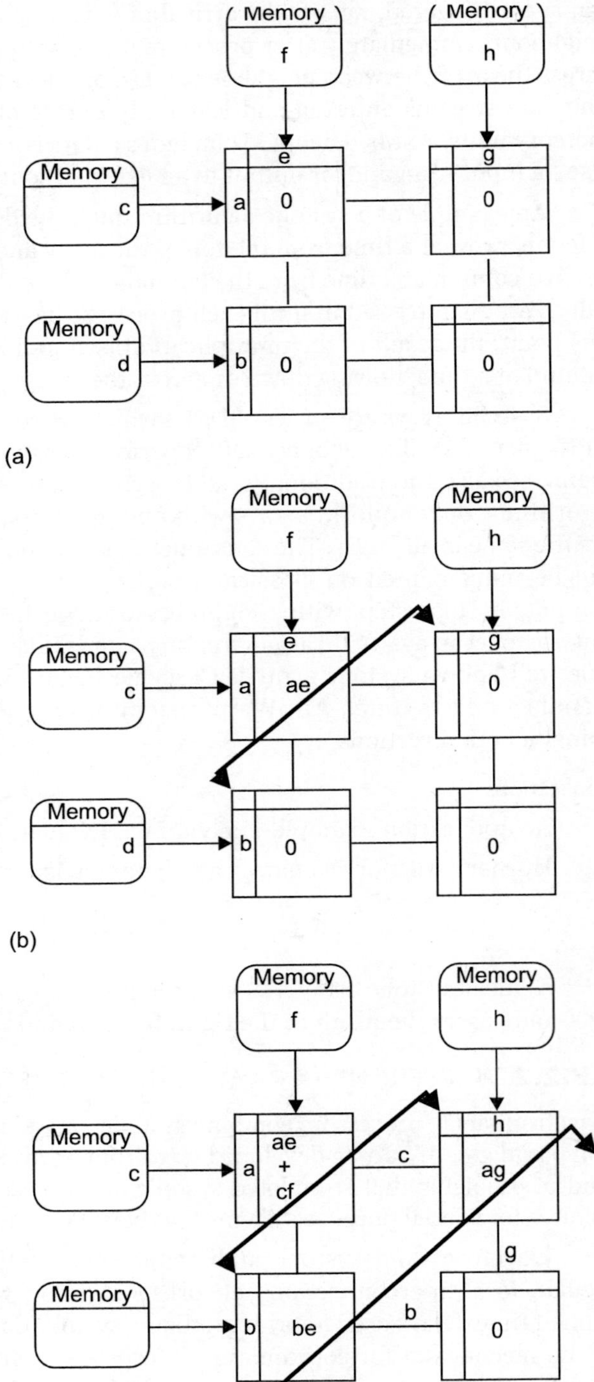

FIGURE 3.22: Wavefront array matrix multiplication

3.5.3 INTERPROCESSOR COMMUNICATION AND SYNCHRONIZATION

The term interprocess communication (IPC) refers to a predefined library or set of interfaces that allow processes to communicate with each other. IPC gives the appearance of programs that run concurrently in the background of an operating system and allow computer users to conduct multiple tasks at one time on a computer. IPCs have evolved to being able to share memory, run synchronized with other processes, message passing, and to conduct remote procedure calls. The specific method of IPC will vary based on Operating System (OS), latency of communication between program threads, and the type of information being exchanged between the processes.

The various processors in a multiprocessor system must be provided with a facility for communicating with each other. A communication path can be established through common input—output channels.

3.5.3.1 SHARED MEMORY MULTIPROCESSOR SYSTEM

In a shared memory multiprocessor system, the most common procedure is to set aside a portion of memory that is accessible to all processors. The primary use of the common memory is to act as a message center similar to a mailbox, where each processor can leave messages for other processors and pick up messages intended for it.

The sending processor structures a request, a message, or a procedure, and places it in the memory mailbox. Status bits residing in common memory are generally used to indicate the condition of the mailbox, whether it has meaningful information, and for which processor it is intended. The receiving processor can check the mailbox periodically to determine if there are valid messages for it. The response time of this procedure can be time consuming since a processor will recognize a request only when polling messages.

3.5.3.2 INTERRUPT SIGNAL

A more efficient procedure is for the sending processor to alert the receiving processor directly by means of an interrupt signal. This can be accomplished through a software-initiated interprocessor interrupt by means of an instruction in the program of one processor which when executed produces an external interrupt condition in a second processor. This alerts the interrupted processor of the fact that a new message was inserted by the interrupting processor.

In addition to shared memory, a multiprocessor system may have other shared resources. For example, a magnetic disk storage unit connected to an IOP may be available to all CPUs. This provides a facility for sharing of system programs stored in the disk. A communication path between two CPUs can be established through a link between two IOPs associated with two different CPUs. This type of link allows each CPU to treat the other as an I/O device so that messages can be transferred through the I/O path.

3.5.3.3 ASSIGNING RESOURCES

To prevent conflicting use of shared resources by several processors there must be a provision for assigning resources to processors. This task is given to the operating system.

There are three organizations that have been used in the design of operating system for multiprocessors:

1. **Master-slave configuration:** In this configuration, one processor, designated the master, always executes the operating system functions. The remaining processors, denoted as slaves, do not perform operating system functions. If a slave processor needs

an operating system service, it must request it by interrupting the master and waiting until the current program can be interrupted.

2. **Separate operating system:** In this configuration, each processor can execute the operating system routines it needs. This organization is more suitable for loosely coupled systems where every processor may have its own copy of the entire operating system.
3. **Distributed operating system:** In this configuration, the operating system routines are distributed among the available processors. However, each particular operating system function is assigned to only one processor at a time. This type of organization is also referred to as a floating operating system since the routines float from one processor to another and the execution of the routines may be assigned to different processors at different times.

In a loosely coupled multiprocessor system the memory is distributed among the processors and there is no shared memory for passing information. The communication between processors is by means of message passing through I/O channels. The communication is initiated by one processor calling a procedure that resides in the memory of the processor with which it wishes to communicate. When the sending processor and receiving processor name each other as a source and destination, a channel of communication is established. A message is then sent with a header and various data objects used to communicate between nodes. There may be a number of possible paths available to send the message between any two nodes. The operating system in each node contains routing information indicating the alternative paths that can be used to send a message to other nodes. The communication efficiency of the interprocessor network depends on the communication routing protocol, processor speed, data link speed, and the topology of the network.

3.5.3.4 METHODS USED IN INTERPROCESS COMMUNICATION

There are several methods used to support interprocess communications on OSs. These include:

1. **Message queuing:** Where messages can be sent between running processes using one or more message queues and are managed by the OS kernel.
2. **Pipes:** Information can only be sent in one direction and will be buffered until received.
3. **Named pipes:** Where a pipe consists of a certain name and can be used amongst processes not sharing a common origin.
4. **Shared memory:** Permits the exchange of information through a predefined area of memory and has to allocate before data can gain access to the memory location.
5. **Semaphores:** Solves problems when synchronization or race conditions arise between processes.
6. **Socket:** Used by processes to communicate over a network via a client/server relationship.

3.5.3.5 INTERPROCESSOR SYNCHRONIZATION

Communication refers to the exchange of data between different processes. For example, parameters passed to a procedure in a different processor constitute interprocessor communication. Synchronization refers to the special case where the data used to communicate between processors is control information. Synchronization is needed to enforce the correct sequence of processes and to ensure mutually exclusive access to shared writable data. Interprocess communication (IPC) includes thread synchorization and data exchange between threads beyond the process boundaries. If threads belong to the same process, they execute in the same address space, i.e. they can access global (static) data or heap directly, without the help of the operating system. However, if threads belong to different processes, they cannot access each others address spaces without the help of the operating system.

There are two fundamentally different approaches in IPC:

- processes are residing on the same computer
- processes are residing on different computers

The first case is easier to implement because processes can share memory either in the user space or in the system space. This is equally true for uniprocessors and multiprocessors.

In the second case the computers do not share physical memory; they are connected via I/O devices (for example serial communication or Ethernet). Therefore the processes residing in different computers can not use memory as a means for communication.

Multiprocessor systems usually include various mechanisms to deal with the synchronization of resources. Low-level primitives are implemented directly by the hardware. These primitives are the basic mechanisms that enforce mutual exclusion for more complex mechanisms implemented in software. A number of hardware mechanisms for mutual exclusion have been developed. One of the most popular methods is through the use of a binary semaphore.

3.5.4 INTERCONNECTION NETWORKS

In parallel MIMD systems, communication is essential for synchronized processing and data sharing. The manner in which messages are passed among system components determines the overall system design. The two choices are to use shared memory or an interconnection network model. Shared memory systems have one large memory that is accessed identically by all processors. In interconnected systems, each processor has its own memory, but processors are allowed to access other processors' memories via the network. Both, of course, have their strengths and weaknesses.

Interconnection networks are often categorized according to topology, routing strategy, and switching technique. The network *topology*, the way in which the components are interconnected, is a major determining factor in the overhead cost of message passing. Message passing efficiency is limited by:

- *Bandwidth:* The information carrying capacity of the network.
- *Message latency:* The time required for the first bit of a message to reach its destination.
- *Transport latency:* The time the message spends in the network.
- *Overhead:* Message processing activities in the sender and receiver.

Accordingly, network designs attempt to minimize both the number of messages required and the distances over which they must travel.

Interconnection networks can be either *static* or *dynamic*. Dynamic networks allow the path between two entities (either two processors or a processor and a memory) to change from one communication to the next, whereas static networks do not. Interconnection networks can also be *blocking* or *nonblocking*. Nonblocking networks allow new connections in the presence of other simultaneous connections, whereas blocking networks do not.

Static interconnection networks are used mainly for message passing and include a variety of types, many of which may be familiar to you. Processors are typically interconnected using static networks, whereas processor-memory pairs usually employ dynamic networks.

Completely connected networks are those in which all components are connected to all other components. These are very expensive to build, and as new entities are added, they become difficult to manage. *Star-connected networks* have a central hub through which all messages must pass. Although a hub can be a central bottleneck, it provides excellent connectivity. *Linear array* or *ring networks* allow any entity to directly communicate with its two neighbors, but any other communication has to go through multiple entities to arrive at its destination. (The ring is just a variation of a linear array in which the two end entities are directly connected.) A *mesh network* links each entity to four or six neighbors (depending on whether it is two-dimensional or three-dimensional). Extensions of this network include those that wrap around, similar to how a linear network can wrap around to form a ring.

Tree networks arrange entities in noncyclic structures, which have the potential for communication bottlenecks forming at the roots. *Hypercube networks* are multidimensional extensions of mesh networks in which each dimension has two processors. (Hypercubes typically connect processors, not processor-memory sets.) Two-dimensional hypercubes consist of pairs of processors that are connected by a direct link if, and only if, the binary representation of their labels differs in exactly one bit position. In an n-dimensional hypercube, each processor is directly connected to n other processors. It is interesting to note that the total number of bit positions at which two labels of a hypercube differ is called their *Hamming distance*, which is also the term used to indicate the number of communication links in the shortest path between two processors. Figure 3.23 illustrates the various types of static networks.

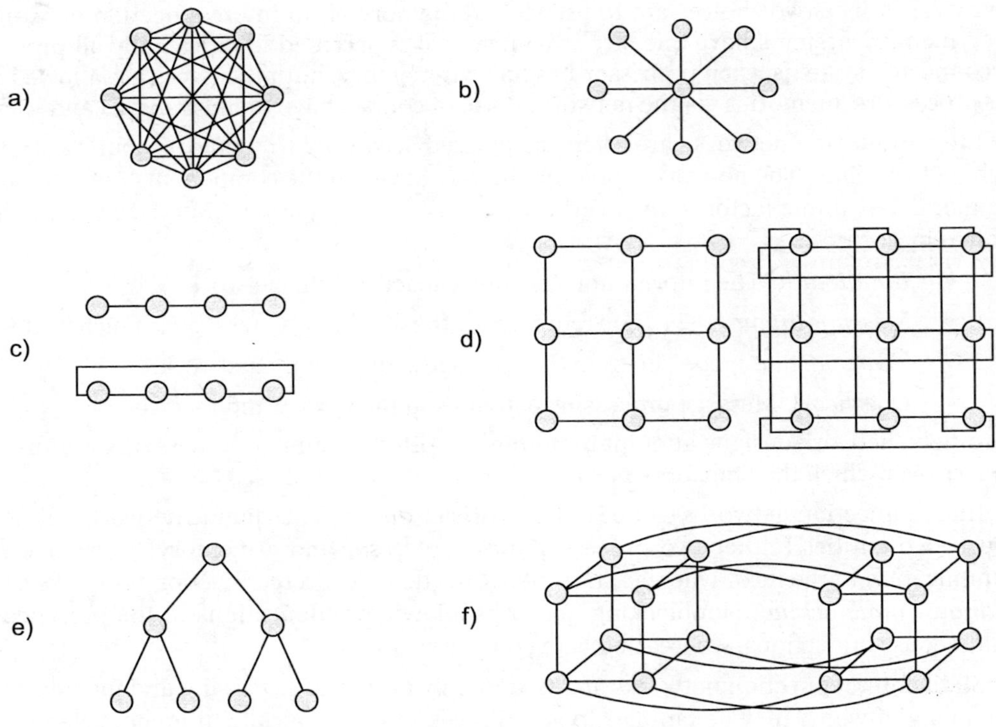

FIGURE 3.23: Static Network Topologies (a) Completely Connected (b) Star (c) Linear and Ring (d) Mesh and Mesh Ring (e) Tree (f) Three-Dimensional Hypercube

Dynamic networks allow for dynamic configuration of the network in one of two ways: either by using a bus or by using a switch that can alter the routes through the network. *Bus-based networks*, illustrated in Figure 3.24, are the simplest and most efficient when cost is a concern and the number of entities is moderate. Clearly, the main disadvantage is the bottleneck that can result from bus contention as the number of entities grows large. Parallel buses can alleviate this problem, but their cost is considerable.

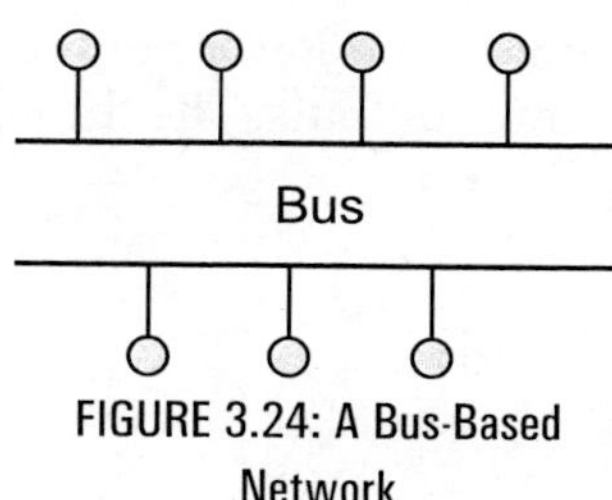

FIGURE 3.24: A Bus-Based Network

Switching networks use switches to dynamically alter routing. There are two types of switches: crossbar switches and 2 × 2 switches. *Crossbar switches* are simply switches that are either open or closed. Any entity can be connected to any other entity by closing the switch (making a connection) between them. Networks consisting of crossbar switches are fully connected because any entity can communicate directly with any other entity and simultaneous communications between different processor/memory pairs are allowed. (A given processor can have at most one connection at a time, however.) No transfer is ever prevented due to a switch being closed. Therefore, the crossbar network is a nonblocking network. However, if there is a single switch at each crosspoint, n entities require n^2 switches. In reality, many multiprocessors require many switches at each crosspoint. Thus, managing numerous switches quickly becomes difficult and costly. Crossbar switches are practical only in high-speed multiprocessor vector computers. A crossbar switch configuration is shown in Figure 3.25. The blue switches indicate closed switches. A processor can be connected to only one memory at a time, so there will be at most one closed switch per column.

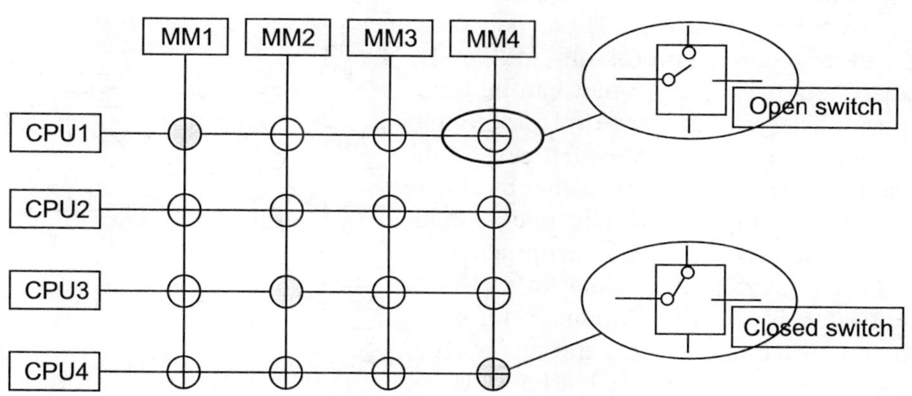

FIGURE 3.25: A Crossbar Network

The second type of switch is the 2×2 *switch*. It is similar to a crossbar switch, except that it is capable of routing its inputs to different destinations, whereas the crossbar simply opens or closes the communications channel. A 2×2 interchange switch has two inputs and two outputs. At any given moment, a 2×2 switch can be in one of four states: *through*, *cross*, *upper broadcast*, and *lower broadcast*, as shown in Figure 3.26. In the through state, the upper input is directed to the upper output and the lower input is directed to the lower output. More simply, the input is directed through the switch. In the cross state, the upper input is directed to the lower output, and the lower input is directed to the upper output. In upper broadcast, the upper input is broadcast to both the upper and lower outputs. In lower broadcast, the lower input is broadcast to both the upper and lower outputs. The through and cross states are the ones relevant to interconnection networks.

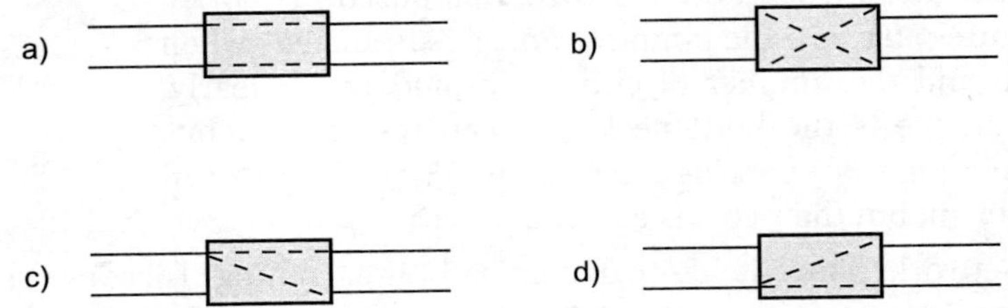

FIGURE 3.26: 2 Interchange 3 States of the 2 Switch (a) Through (b) Cross (c) Upper Broadcast (d) Lower Broadcast

The most advanced class of networks, *multistage interconnection networks*, is built using 2×2 switches. The idea is to incorporate stages of switches, typically with processors on one side and memories on the other, with a series of switching elements as the interior nodes. These switches dynamically configure themselves to allow a path from any given processor to any given memory. The number of switches and the number of stages contribute to the path length of each communication channel. A slight delay may occur as the switch determines the configuration required to pass a message from the specified source to the desired destination. These multistage networks are often called *shuffle networks*, alluding to the pattern of the connections between the switches.

Many topologies have been suggested for multistage switching networks. These networks can be used to connect processors in loosely coupled distributed systems, or they can be used in tightly coupled systems to control processor-to-memory communications. A switch can be in only one state at a time, so it is clear that blocking can occur. For example, consider one simple topology for these networks, the *Omega network* shown in Figure 3.27. It is possible for CPU 00 to communicate with Memory Module 00 if both Switch 1A and Switch 2A are set to through. At the same time, however, it is impossible for CPU 10 to communicate with Memory Module 01. To do this, both Switch 1A and Switch 2A would need to be set to cross. This Omega network is, therefore, a blocking network. Nonblocking multistage networks can be built by adding more switches and more stages. In general, an Omega network of n nodes requires $\log_2 n$ stages with switches per stage.

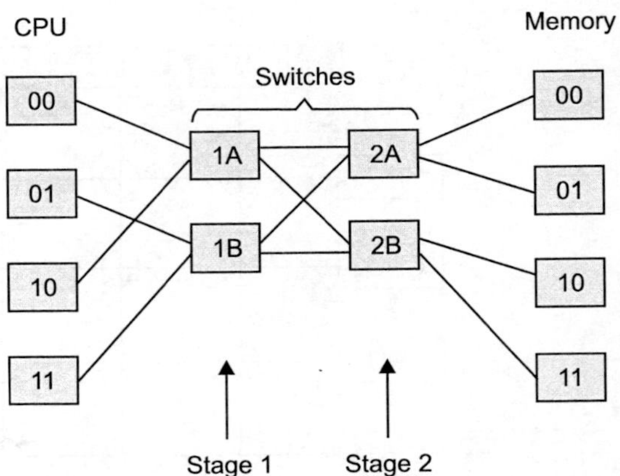

FIGURE 3.27: A Two-Stage Omega Network

It is interesting to note that configuring the switches is not really as difficult as it might seem. The binary representation of the destination module can be used to program the switches as the message travels the network. Using one bit of the destination address for each stage, each switch can be programmed based on the value of that bit. If the bit is a 0, the input is routed to the upper output. If the bit is a 1, the input is routed to the lower output. For example, suppose CPU 00 wishes to communicate with Memory Module 01. We can use the first bit of the destination (0) to set Switch 1A to through (which routes the input to the upper output), and the second bit (1) to set Switch 2A to cross (which routes the input to the lower output). If CPU 11 wishes to communicate with Memory Module 00, we would set Switch 1B to cross, and Switch 2A to cross (since both inputs must be routed to the upper outputs).

Another interesting method for determining the switch setting is to compare the corresponding bits of the source and destination. If the bits are equal, the switch is set to through. If the bits are different, the switch is set to cross. For example, suppose CPU 00 wishes to communicate with Memory Module 01. We compare the first bits of each (0 to 0), setting Switch 1A to through, and compare the second bits of each (0 to 1), setting Switch 2A to cross.

Each method for interconnecting multiprocessors has its advantages and disadvantages. For example, bus-based networks are the simplest and most efficient solution when a moderate number of processors are involved. However, the bus becomes a bottleneck if many processors make memory requests simultaneously. We compare bus-based, crossbar, and multistage interconnection networks.

Table 3.1: Properties of the Various Interconnection Networks

Property	Bus	Crossbar	Multistage
Speed	Low	High	Moderate
Cost	Low	High	Moderate
Reliability	Low	High	High
Configurability	High	Low	Moderate
Complexity	Low	High	Moderate

3.6 SPMD (SINGLE PROGRAM, MULTIPLE DATA)

In computing, SPMD (Single Process, Multiple Data) or (Single Program, Multiple Data) is a technique employed to achieve parallelism; it is a subcategory of MIMD. Tasks are split up and run simultaneously on multiple processors with different input in order to obtain results faster. SPMD is the most common style of parallel programming. It is also a prerequisite for research concepts such as active messages and distributed shared memory. SPMD was proposed in 1984 by Frederica Darema at IBM for highly parallel machines like the RP3 (the IBM Research Parallel Processor Prototype), in an unpublished IBM memo by late 1980s, there were many distributed computers with proprietary message passing libraries. The first SPMD standard was PVM. The current de-facto standard is MPI. The Cray parallel directives were a direct predecessor of OpenMP.

3.6.1 BASIC STRUCTURE OF SINGLE-PROGRAM MULTIPLE-DATA (SPMD)

The SPMD paradigm is the most commonly used paradigm. Each process executes basically the same piece of code but on a different part of the data. This involves the splitting of application data among the available processors. This type of parallelism is also referred to as geometric parallelism, domain decomposition, or data parallelism. Figure 3.28 presents a schematic representation of this paradigm. Many physical problems have an underlying regular geometric structure, with spatially limited interactions. This homogeneity allows the data to be distributed uniformly across the processors, where each one will be responsible for a defined spatial area. Processors communicate with neighbouring processors and the communication load will be proportional to the size of the boundary of the element, while the computation load will be proportional to the volume of the element. It may also be required to perform some global synchronization periodically among all the processes. The communication pattern is usually highly structured and extremely predictable. The data may initially be self-generated by each process or may be read from the disk during the initialization stage. SPMD applications can be very efficient if the data is well distributed by the processes and the system is homogeneous. If the processes present different work loads or capabilities, then the paradigm requires the support of some load-balancing scheme able to adapt the data distribution layout during run-time execution. This paradigm is highly sensitive to the loss of some process. Usually, the loss of a single process is enough to cause a deadlock in the calculation in which none of the processes can advance beyond a global synchronization point.

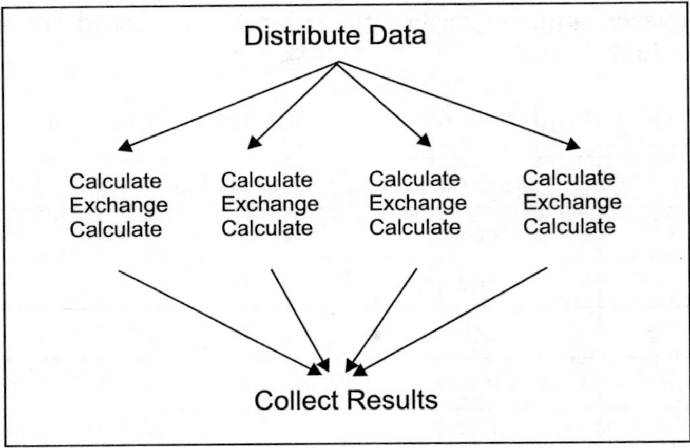

FIGURE 3.28: Basic Structure of a SPMD Program

3.6.2 *SPMD VS SIMD*

In SPMD, multiple autonomous processors simultaneously execute the same program at independent points, rather than in the lockstep that SIMD imposes on different data. With SPMD, tasks can be executed on general purpose CPUs; SIMD requires vector processors to manipulate data streams. Note that the two are not mutually exclusive.

SPMD - Single Program Multiple Data

The SIMD paradigm is an example of synchronous parallelism - each processor operates in lockstep. A related asynchronous version is SPMD. This is where the same program is run on the processors of an MIMD machine.

SPMD is not a hardware paradigm, it is the software equivalent of SIMD.

Because an entire program is executed on separate data, it is possible that different branches are taken, leading to asynchronous parallelism. The processors no longer do the same thing (or nothing) in lockstep; they are busy executing different instructions within the same program.

Consider

```
IF X = 0            Assume X = 0 on P1
THEN S1             X! = 0 on P2
ELSE S2
```

Now P1 executes S1 at the same time P2 executes S2 (which could not happen on an SIMD machine)

3.6.3 DISTRIBUTED MEMORY

SPMD usually refers to message passing programming on distributed memory computer architectures. A distributed memory computer consists of a collection of independent computers, called nodes. Each node starts its own program and communicates with other nodes by sending and receiving messages, calling send/receive routines for that purpose. Barrier synchronization may also be implemented by messages. The messages can be sent by a number of communication mechanisms, such as TCP/IP over Ethernet, or specialized high-speed interconnects such as Myrinet and Supercomputer Interconnect. Serial sections of the program are implemented by identical computation on all nodes rather than computing the result on one node and sending it to the others. Nowadays, the programmer is isolated from the details of the message passing by standard interfaces, such as PVM and MPI.

Distributed memory is the programming style used on parallel supercomputers from homegrown Beowulf clusters to the largest clusters on the Teragrid.

3.6.4 SHARED MEMORY

On a shared memory machine (a computer with several CPUs that access the same memory space), messages can be sent by depositing their contents in a shared memory area. This is often the most efficient way to program shared memory computers with large number of processors, especially on NUMA machines, where memory is local to processors and accessing memory of another processor takes longer. SPMD on a shared memory machine is usually implemented by standard (heavyweight) processes.

Unlike SPMD, shared memory multiprocessing, also called symmetric multiprocessing or SMP, presents the programmer with a common memory space and the possibility to parallelize execution by having the program take different paths on different processors. The program starts executing on one processor and the execution splits in a parallel region, which is started when parallel directives are encountered. In a parallel region, the processors execute a single program on different data. A typical example is the parallel DO loop, where different processors work on separate parts of the arrays involved in the loop. At the end of the loop, execution is synchronized, only one processor continues, and the others wait. The current standard interface for shared memory multiprocessing is OpenMP. It usually implemented by lightweight processes, called threads.

3.6.5 COMBINATION OF LEVELS OF PARALLELISM

Current computers allow exploiting of many parallel modes at the same time for maximum combined effect. A distributed memory program using MPI may run on a collection of nodes. Each node may be a shared memory computer and execute in parallel on multiple CPUs using OpenMP. Within each CPU, SIMD vector instructions (usually generated automatically by the compiler) and superscalar instruction execution (usually handled transparently by the CPU itself), such as pipelining and the use of multiple parallel functional units, are used for maximum single CPU speed.

3.6.6 *SPMD VS MPMD*

Following are the differences between SPMD and MPMD:

Single Program Multiple Data (SPMD):

- SPMD is actually a "high level" programming model that can be built upon any combination of the previously mentioned parallel programming models.
- SINGLE PROGRAM: All tasks execute their copy of the same program simultaneously. This program can be threads, message passing, data parallel or hybrid.
- MULTIPLE DATA: All tasks may use different data
- SPMD programs usually have the necessary logic programmed into them to allow different tasks to branch or conditionally execute only those parts of the program they are designed to execute. That is, tasks do not necessarily have to execute the entire program - perhaps only a portion of it.
- The SPMD model, using message passing or hybrid programming, is probably the most commonly used parallel programming model for multi-node clusters.

Multiple Program Multiple Data (MPMD)

- Like SPMD, MPMD is actually a "high level" programming model that can be built upon any combination of the previously mentioned parallel programming models.
- MULTIPLE PROGRAM: Tasks may execute different programs simultaneously. The programs can be threads, message passing, data parallel or hybrid.
- MULTIPLE DATA: All tasks may use different data
- MPMD applications are not as common as SPMD applications, but may be better suited for certain types of problems, particularly those that lend themselves better to functional decomposition than domain decomposition.

QUESTIONS

1. What do you mean by asynchronous architectures?
2. What do you mean by MIMD?
3. Explain the concept of various MIMD schemes?
4. Explain the concept of MIMD machines in detail?
5. Explain the concept of reduction paradigm?
6. Explain the concept of reduction processing or demand driven processing?
7. Explain the concept of reduction architectures?
8. Explain the concept of Flynn's taxonomy?
9. Explain the various parallel architectures in detail?
10. Explain the Kung's taxonomy in detail?
11. Explain the concept of dataflow computers?
12. Explain the concept of systolic arrays

13. Explain the concept of wavefront arrays?
14. Explain the concept of interprocessor communication and synchronization?
15. Explain the various types of MIMD interconnection networks?
16. What do you mean by SPMD?
17. Explain the basic structure of SPMD?
18. Explain the difference between SPMD and SIMD?
19. Explain the concept of Shared and distributed memory in SPMD?
20. Explain the difference between SPMD and MPMD?

CHAPTER 4 ABSTRACT PARALLEL COMPUTATIONAL MODELS

4.1 INTRODUCTION

Computational models define the usage patterns of a computer. They can be used to derive the architecture of the machine, provide guidelines for programming tools, and suggest how the machine should be used in applications. Identifying computational models is especially important for parallel computers, because their architectures and usages are still not well understood in general. This section describes a number of computational models for parallel computers like combinational circuits, sorting Network, PRAM Models, interconnection RAMs. These models characterize the communication patterns under which processors exchange their intermediate results during computation.

4.2 OVERVIEW OF COMBINATIONAL CIRCUITS

There are various computational models for representing the parallel computers. In this section, we discuss various models. These models would provide a platform for the designing as well as the analysis of the parallel algorithms. It is another model of parallel computers. Combinational circuit refers to a family of models of computation. A combinational circuit can be viewed as a device that has a set of input lines at one end and set of output lines at the other. And each component, having received its inputs, does a simple arithmetic and logical operations in one time and produces the results as output.

4.2.1 COMBINATIONAL CIRCUITS

Combinational Circuit is one of the models for parallel computers. In interconnection networks, various processors communicate with each other directly and do not require a shared memory in between. Basically, combinational circuit (cc) is a connected arrangement of logic gates with a set of m input lines and a set of n output lines as shown in Figure 4.1. The combinational circuits are mainly made up of various interconnected components arranged in the form known as stages as shown in Figure 4.2.

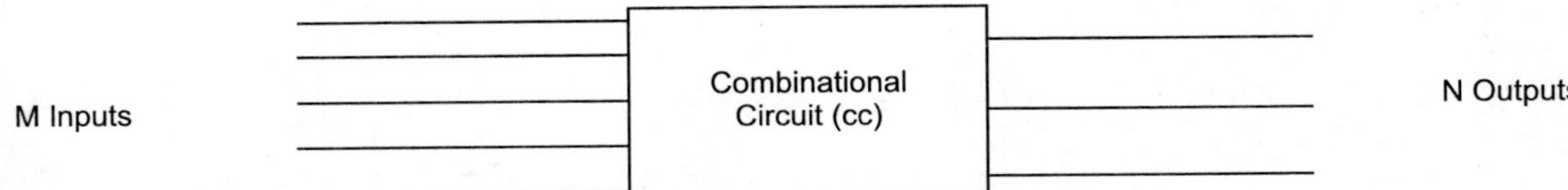

FIGURE 4.1: Combinational circuit

It may be noted here that there is no feedback control employed in combinational circuits. There are few terminologies followed in the context of combinational circuits such as fan in and fan out. Fan in signifies the number of input lines attached to each device and fan out signifies the number of output lines.

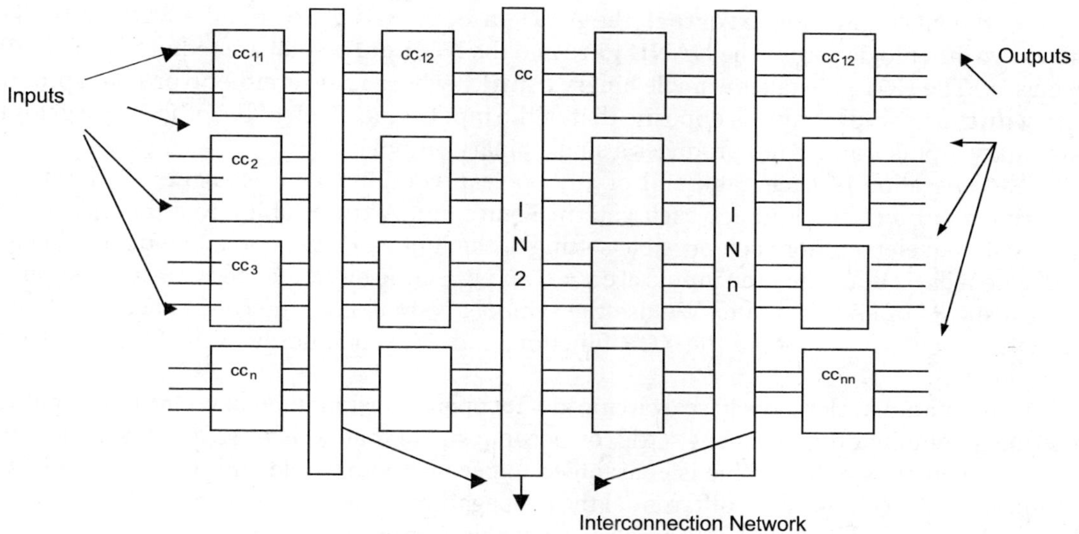

FIGURE 4.2: Detailed Combinational Circuit

In Figure 4.2, the fan in is 3 and fan out is also 3. The following parameters are used for analysing a combinational circuit:

1. **Depth:** It means that the total number of stages used in the combinational circuit starting from the input lines to the output lines. For example, in the depth is 4, as there are four different stages attached to an interconnection network. The other form of interpretation of depth can be that it represents the worst case time complexity of solving a problem as input is given at the initial input lines and data is transferred between various stages through the interconnection network and at the end reaches the output lines.
2. **Width:** It represents the total number of devices attached for a particular stage. For example in Figure 4.2, there are 4 components attached to the interconnection network. It means that the width is 4.
3. **Size:** It represents the total count of devices used in the complete combinational circuit. For example, in Figure 4.2, the size of combinational circuit is 16 i.e. (width * depth).

4.2.2 COMPONENTS OF COMBINATIONAL CIRCUITS

Combinational circuits operate in parallel: many elements can compute values simultaneously as a single step. In this section, we define combinational circuits and investigate how larger combinational circuits can be built up from elementary gates.

4.2.2.1 COMBINATIONAL ELEMENTS

Arithmetic circuits in real computers are built from combinational elements that are interconnected by wires. A **combinational element** is any circuit element that has a constant number of inputs and outputs and that performs a well-defined function. Some of the elements we shall deal with in this chapter are **boolean combinational elements**--their inputs and outputs are all drawn from the set {0, 1}, where 0 represents FALSE and 1 represents TRUE.

A boolean combinational element that computes a simple boolean function is called a **logic gate**. Figure 29.1 shows the four basic logic gates that will serve as combinational elements in this chapter: the **NOT gate** (or **inverter**), the **AND gate**, the **OR gate**, and the **XOR gate**. (It also shows two other logic gates—the **NAND gate** and the **NOR gate**—that are required by some of the exercises.) The NOT gate takes a single binary **input** x, whose value is either 0 or 1, and produces a binary **output** z whose value is opposite that of the input value. Each of the other three gates takes two binary inputs x and y and produces a single binary output z.

The operation of each gate, and of any boolean combinational element, can be described by a **truth table**, shown under each gate in Figure 4.3. A truth table gives the outputs of the combinational element for each possible setting of the inputs. For example, the truth table for the XOR gate tells us that when the inputs are x = 0 and y = 1, the output value is z = 1; it computes the "exclusive OR" of its two inputs. We use the symbols ¬ to denote the NOT function, ^to denote the AND function, v to denote the XOR function, and ⊕ to denote the XOR function. Thus, for example, 0 ⊕ 1 = 1.

Combinational elements in real circuits do not operate instantaneously. Once the input values entering a combinational element settle, or become stable that is, hold steady for a long enough time--the element's output value is guaranteed to become both stable and correct a fixed amount of time later. We call this time differential the propagation delay of the element. We assume in this chapter that all combinational elements have constant propagation delay.

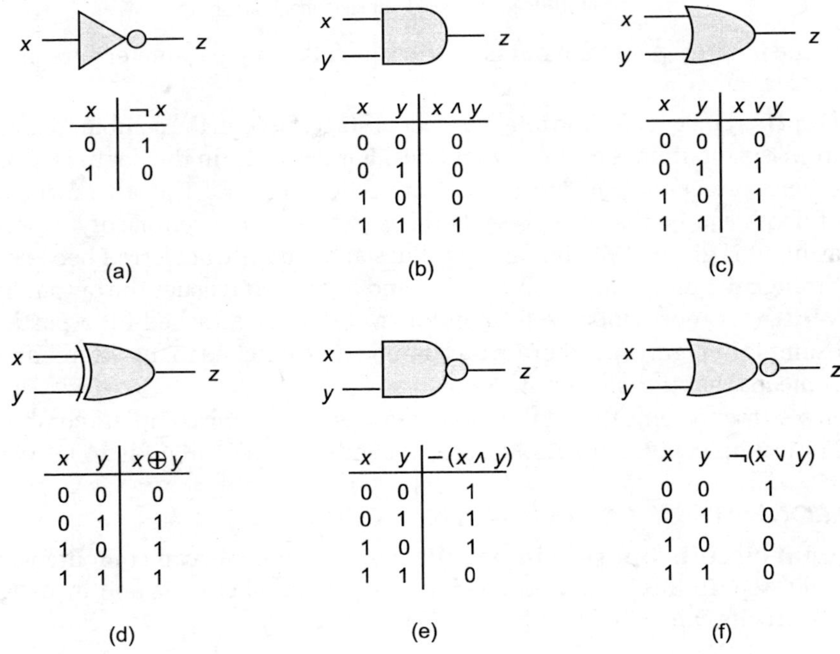

x	¬x
0	1
1	0

x	y	x ∧ y
0	0	0
0	1	0
1	0	0
1	1	1

x	y	x v y
0	0	0
0	1	1
1	0	1
1	1	1

x	y	x⊕y
0	0	0
0	1	1
1	0	1
1	1	1

x	y	−(x ∧ y)
0	0	1
0	1	1
1	0	1
1	1	0

x	y	¬(x ∨ y)
0	0	1
0	1	0
1	0	0
1	1	0

FIGURE 4.3: Six basic logic gates, with binary inputs and outputs. Under each gate is the truth table that describes the gate's operation. (a) The NOT gate (b) The AND gate (c) The OR gate (d) The XOR (exclusive-OR) gate (e) The NAND (NOT-AND) gate (f) The NOR (NOT-OR) gate.

4.2.2.2 COMBINATIONAL CIRCUITS

A **combinational circuit** consists of one or more combinational elements interconnected in an acyclic fashion. The interconnections are called **wires**. A wire can connect the output of one element to the input of another, thereby providing the output value of the first element as an input value of the second. Although a single wire may have no more than one combinational-element output connected to it, it can feed several element inputs. The number of element inputs fed by a wire is called the **fan-out** of the wire. If no element output is connected to a wire, the wire is a **circuit input**, accepting input values from an external source. If no element input is connected to a wire, the wire is a **circuit output**, providing the results of the circuit's computation to the outside world. (An internal wire can also fan out to a circuit output.) Combinational circuits contain no cycles and have no memory elements.

4.2.2.3 FULL ADDERS

As an example, Figure 4.4 shows a combinational circuit, called a **full adder**, that takes as input three bits x, y, and z. It outputs two bits, s and c, according to the following truth table:

x	y	z	c	s
0	0	0	0	0
0	0	1	0	1
0	1	0	0	1
0	1	1	1	0
1	0	0	0	1
1	0	1	1	0
1	1	0	1	0
1	1	1	1	1

Output s is the **parity** of the input bits,

$$s = \text{parity}(x,y,z) = x \oplus y \oplus z,$$

and output c is the **majority** of the input bits,

$$c = \text{majority}(x,y,z) = (x \wedge y) \vee (y \wedge z) \vee (x \wedge z).$$

(In general, the parity and majority functions can take any number of input bits. The parity is 1 if and only if an odd number of the inputs are 1's. The majority is 1 if and only if more than half the inputs are 1's.) Note that the c and s bits, taken together, give the sum of x, y, and z. For example, if x = 1, y = 0, and z = 1, then $\langle c, s \rangle = \langle 10 \rangle$, which is the binary representation of 2, the sum of x, y, and z.

For clarity, we omit the commas between sequence elements when they are bits.

Each of the inputs x, y, and z to the full adder has a fan-out of 3. When the operation performed by a combinational element is commutative and associative with respect to its inputs (such as the functions AND, OR, and XOR), we call the number of inputs the **fan-in** of the element. Although the fan-in of each gate in Figure 4.4 is 2, we could redraw the full adder to replace XOR gates A and E by a single 3-input XOR gate and OR gates F and G by a single 3-input OR gate.

To examine how the full adder operates, assume that each gate operates in unit time. Figure 4.4(a) shows a set of inputs that becomes stable at time 0. Gates A-D, and no other gates, have all their input values stable at that time and therefore produce the values shown in Figure 4.4(b) at time 1. Note that gates A-D operate in parallel. Gates E and F, but not gate G, have stable inputs at time 1 and produce the values shown in Figure 4.4(c) at time 2. The output of gate E is bit s, and so the s output from the full adder is ready at time 2. The c output is not yet ready, however. Gate G finally has stable inputs at time 2, and it produces the c output shown in Figure 4.4(d) at time 3.

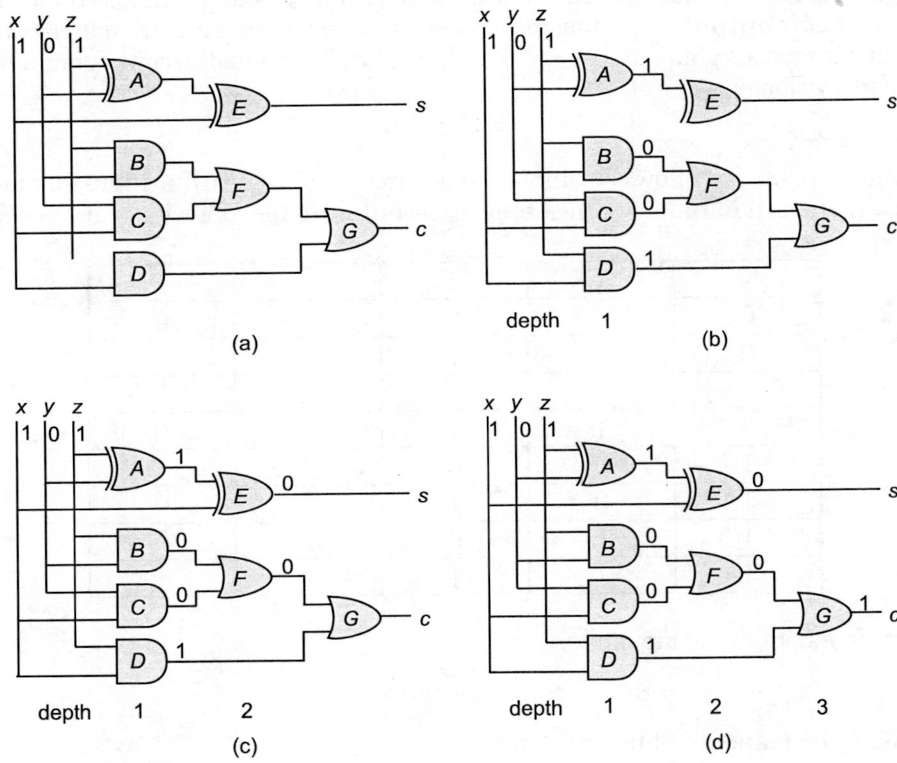

FIGURE 4.4: A full-adder circuit. (a) At time 0, the input bits shown appear on the three input wires. (b) At time 1, the values shown appear on the outputs of gates A-D, which are at depth 1. (c) At time 2, the values shown appear on the outputs of gates E and F, at depth 2. (d) At time 3, gate G produces its output, which is also the circuit output.

4.2.2.4 CIRCUIT DEPTH

We measure the propagation delay of a combinational circuit in terms of the largest number of combinational elements on any path from the inputs to the outputs. Specifically, we define the **depth** of a circuit, which corresponds to its worst-case "running time," inductively in terms of the depths of its constituent wires. The depth of an input wire is 0. If a combinational element has inputs $x_1, x_2, \ldots, x_n$ at depths $d_1, d_2, \ldots, d_n$ respectively, then its outputs have depth $\max\{d_1, d_2, \ldots, d_n\} + 1$. The depth of a combinational element is the depth of its outputs. The depth of a combinational circuit is the maximum depth of any combinational element. Since we prohibit combinational circuits from containing cycles, the various notions of depth are well defined.

If each combinational element takes constant time to compute its output values, then the worst-case propagation delay through a combinational circuit is proportional to its depth. Figure 4.4 shows the depth of each gate in the full adder. Since the gate with the largest depth is gate G, the full adder itself has depth 3, which is proportional to the worst-case time it takes for the circuit to perform its function.

A combinational circuit can sometimes compute faster than its depth. Suppose that a large subcircuit feeds into one input of a 2-input AND gate but that the other input of the AND gate has value 0. The output of the gate will then be 0, independent of the input from the large subcircuit. In general, however, we cannot count on specific inputs being applied to the circuit, and the abstraction of depth as the "running time" of the circuit is therefore quite reasonable.

4.2.2.5 CIRCUIT SIZE

Besides circuit depth, there is another resource that we typically wish to minimize when designing circuits. The **size** of a combinational circuit is the number of combinational elements it contains. Intuitively, circuit size corresponds to the memory space used by an algorithm. The full adder of Figure 4.4 has size 7, for example, since it uses 7 gates.

This definition of circuit size is not particularly useful for small circuits. After all, since a full adder has a constant number of inputs and outputs and computes a well-defined function, it satisfies the definition of a combinational element. A full adder built from a single full-adder combinational element therefore has size 1. In fact, according to this definition, any combinational element has size 1.

The definition of circuit size is intended to apply to families of circuits that compute similar functions. For example, we shall soon see an addition circuit that takes two n-bit inputs. We are really not talking about a single circuit here, but rather a family of circuits--one for each size of input. In this context, the definition of circuit size makes good sense. It allows us to define convenient circuit elements without affecting the size of any implementation of the circuit by more than a constant factor. Of course, in practice, measurements of size are much more complicated, involving not only the choice of combinational elements, but also concerns such as the area the circuit requires when integrated on a silicon chip.

4.2.3 COMMON COMBINATIONAL CIRCUIT

A combinational circuit is one for which the output value is determined solely by the values of the inputs. Such a circuit can be represented by a truth table and computes a Boolean function. The digital devices such as Adders, Subtractions, Multiplexers, Demultiplexers, Encoders and Decoders are all Combinational Circuits.

Unlike Sequential Logic circuits whose outputs are dependant on both the present input and their previous output state giving them some form of Memory, the outputs of Combinational Logic circuits are only determined by their current input state as they have no feedback, and any changes to the signals being applied to their inputs will immediately have an effect at the output. In other words, in a Combination Logic circuit, if the input condition changes state so too does the output as combinational circuits have no memory.

Combination Logic circuits are made up from basic logic AND, OR or NOT gates that are "combined" or connected together to produce more complicated switching circuits. As combination logic circuits are made up from individual logic gates they can also be considered as "decision making circuits" and combinational logic is about combining logic gates together to process two or more signals in order to produce at least one output signal according to the logical function of each logic gate. Common combinational circuits made up from individual logic gates include Multiplexers, Decoders and De-multiplexers, Full and Half Adders etc.

4.2.3.1 HALF ADDER

A **half adder** is a logical circuit that performs an addition operation on two binary digits. The half adder produces a sum and a carry value which are both binary digits. The block diagram and circuit diagram of a Half Adder are shown in figure 4.5 respectively.

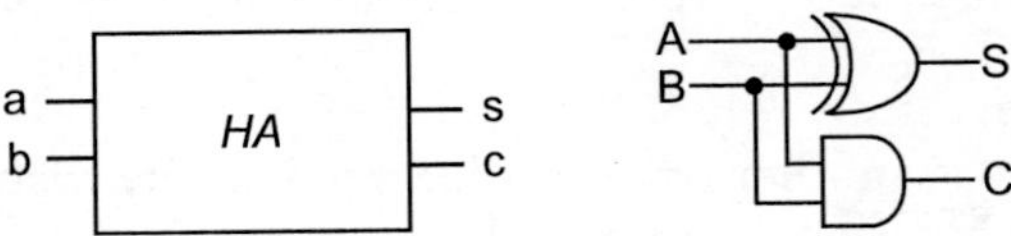

FIGURE 4.5: Half Adder Block Diagram / Circuit Diagram

The drawback of this circuit is that in case of a multi bit addition, it cannot include a carry.

$$S = A \oplus B$$

$$C = A \cdot B$$

The logic table for a half adder is shown in Table 4.1.

A	B	C	S
0	0	0	0
0	1	0	1
1	0	0	1
1	1	1	0

TABLE 4.1: Half Adder Truth Table

4.2.3.2 FULL ADDER

A Full Adder is a combinational circuit which performs the arithmetic addition of three input bits. The noticeable difference between the full- and the half-adder is the ability of the former to handle input carries (C_I). The block diagram for the full adder is shown in Figure 4.6 and the associated truth table in Table 4.2.

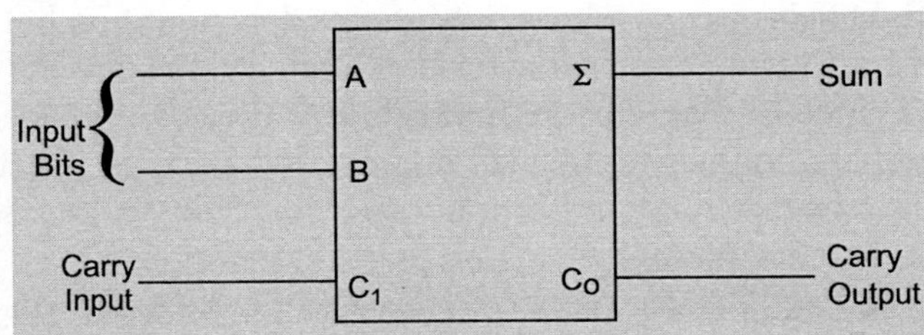

FIGURE 4.6: Block Diagram full-adder

Inputs: {A, B, CarryIn} → Outputs: {Sum, CarryOut}

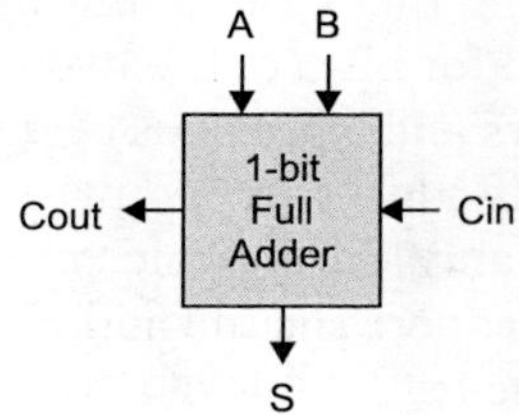

FIGURE 4.7: Schematic symbol for a 1-bit full adder

$$S = (A \oplus B) \oplus C_{in}$$

$$C_{out} = (A \cdot B) + (C_{in} \cdot (A \oplus B)) = (A \cdot B) + (C_{in} \cdot B) + (C_{in} \cdot A)$$

TABLE 4.2: Full-Adder Truth Table

Input			Output	
A	B	C_I	C_O	S
0	0	0	0	0
0	0	1	0	1
0	1	0	0	1
0	1	1	1	0
1	0	0	0	1
1	0	1	1	0
1	1	0	1	0
1	1	1	1	1

By the very nature of the full adder we know that the two input bits must be added to the carry input bit. Recall that for the half-adder the sum of A and B is the XOR of those two variables,

$$\Sigma = A \oplus B$$

Similarly, for the three variables A, B and C_I the sum becomes

$$\Sigma = (A \oplus B) \oplus C_I$$

This is illustrated in Table 4.2. By examining the truth table, observe that the carry output (C_O) is '1' when both the inputs to the first and second XOR gates are '1'. Consequently,

$$C_o = AB + (A \oplus B)\, C_I$$

The complete logic circuit for the full adder is illustrated in Figure 4.8.

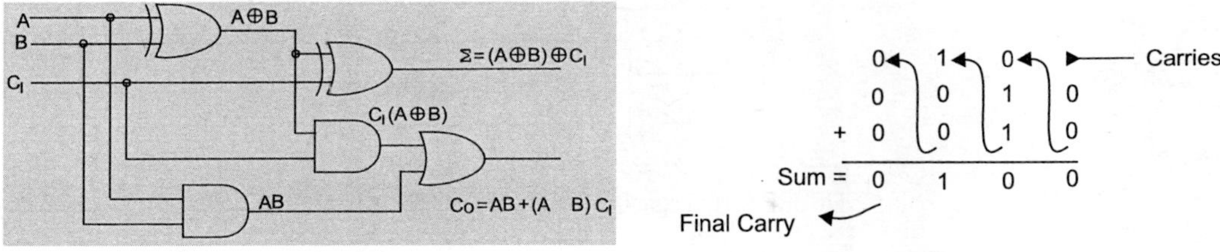

FIGURE 4.8: Logic Circuit for the Full-Adder

This addition of two bits will generate a sum and a carry. The carry may be 0 or 1. Also, there will be no previous carry while adding the least significant bits (bit 0) of the two numbers. This means that two bits need to be added for bit 0 of the two numbers. On the other hand, addition of three bits (two bits of the two numbers and a previous carry, which may be 0 or 1) is required for all the subsequent bits. Note that two half-adders are required to add three bits. A combinational circuit that adds three bits, generating a sum and a carry (which may be 0 or 1), is called a "full adder." Figure 4.6 shows the block diagram of a full adder. The full adder adds three bits, x, y, and z, and generates a sum and a carry. Table 4.2 shows the truth table of a full adder.

4.2.3.3 HALF SUBTRACTOR

A subtractor can be designed using the same approach as that of an adder. As with an adder, three bits are involved in performing the subtraction for each bit: the minuend (X_i), subtrahend (Y_i), and a borrow in from the previous bit order position (B_i). The outputs are the difference bit (D_i) and borrow bit B_{i+1}.

The half-subtractor is a combinational circuit which is used to perform subtraction of two bits. It has two inputs, X (minuend) and Y (subtrahend) and two outputs D (difference) and B (borrow).

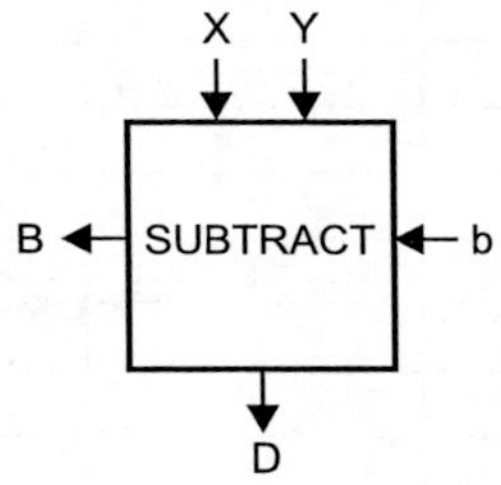

FIGURE 4.9: Half Subtractor

From Figure 4.9, we can see that the subtractor has three inputs and two outputs. This means that one must generate two different K-maps, one for each output. Here are the functions each line performs.

X, Y - The two numbers to be subtracted.
b - Borrow-in.
B - Borrow-out.
D - Difference. This is the result.

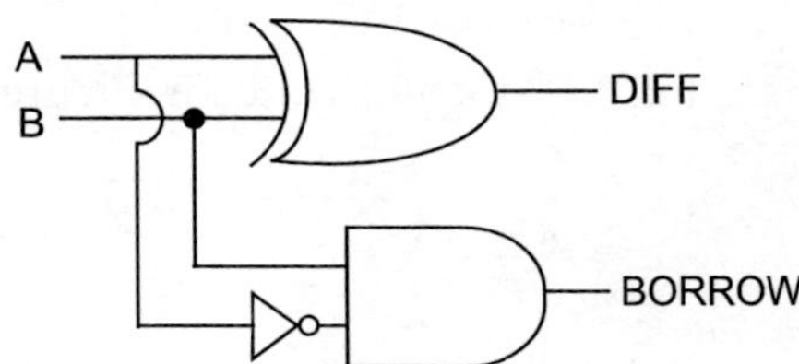

FIGURE 4.10: Logic Diagram for Half Subtractor

The truth table for the half subtractor is given in Table 4.3.

TABLE 4.3: Half Subtractor

X	Y	D	B
0	0	0	0
0	1	1	1
1	0	1	0
1	1	0	0

4.2.3.4 FULL SUBTRACTOR

As in the case of the addition using logic gates, a full subtractor is made by combining two half-subtractors and an additional OR-gate. A full subtractor has the borrow in capability (denoted as $\mathbf{BOR_{IN}}$ in figure 4.11) and so allows cascading which results in the possibility of multi-bit subtraction.

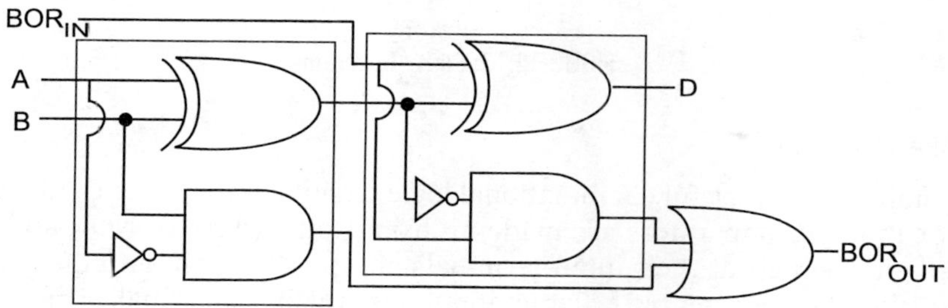

FIGURE 4.11: Full subtractor

The truth table for a full subtractor looks like as shown in table 4.4:

TABLE 4.4

A	B	BOR_{IN}	D	BOR_{OUT}
0	0	0	0	0
0	0	1	1	1
0	1	0	1	0
0	1	1	0	0
1	0	0	1	1
1	0	1	0	1
1	1	0	0	0
1	1	1	1	1

4.2.3.5 PARITY GENERATOR

Parity bits are extra signals which are added to a data word to enable error checking. There are two types of Parity - even and odd. An even parity generator will produce a logic 1 at its output if the data word contains an odd number of ones. If the data word contains an even number of ones then the output of the parity generator will be low. By concatenating the Parity bit to the dataword, a word will be formed which always has an even number of ones i.e. has even parity. Parity is used on communication links (e.g. Modem lines) and is often included in memory systems. If a dataword is sent out with even parity, but has odd parity when it is received then the data has been corrupted and must be resent. As its name implies the operation of an Odd Parity generator, shown in figure 4.12, is similar but it provides odd parity.

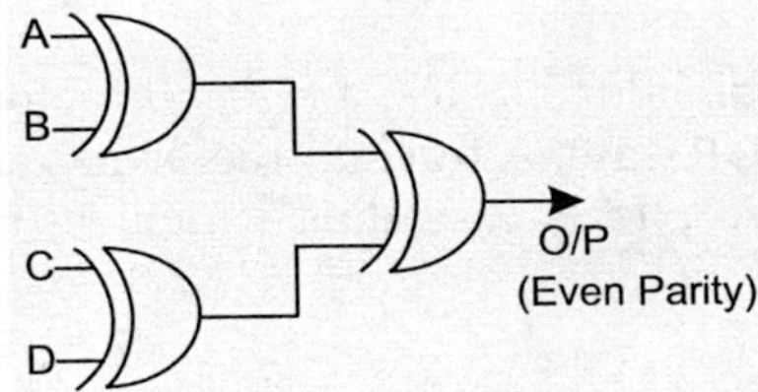

FIGURE 4.12: Parity Generator

4.2.3.6 COMPARATORS

Another common and very useful combinational logic circuit is that of the Digital Comparator circuit. Digital or Binary Comparators are made up from standard AND, NOR and NOT gates that compare the digital signals at their input terminals and produces an output depending upon the condition of the inputs. For example, whether input A is greater than, smaller than or equal to input B etc.

Digital Comparators can compare a variable or unknown number for example A (A1, A2, A3, ... An, etc) against that of a constant or known value such as B (B1, B2, B3,... Bn, etc) and produce an output depending upon the result. For example, a comparator of 1-bit, (A and B) would produce the following three output conditions.

$$A > B, A = B, A < B$$

This is useful if we want to compare two values and produce an output when the condition is achieved. For example, produce an output from a counter when a certain count number is reached. Consider the simple 1-bit comparator below.

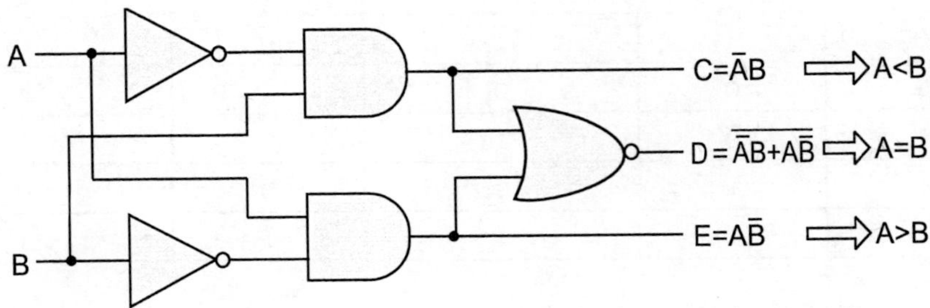

FIGURE 4.13: 1-Bit Comparator

Then the operation of a 1-bit digital comparator is given in the following Truth Table.

TRUTH TABLE 4.5

Inputs	Outputs			
B	A	A > B	A = B	A < B
0	0	0	1	0
0	1	1	0	0
1	0	0	0	1
1	1	0	1	0

You may notice two distinct features about the comparator from the above truth table. Firstly, the circuit does not distinguish between either two “0” or two “1”’s as an output A = B is produced when they are both equal, either A = B = “0” or A = B = “1”. Secondly, the output condition for A = B resembles that of a commonly available logic gate, the Exclusive-NOR or Ex-NOR gate giving Q = AB.

Digital comparators actually use Exclusive-NOR gates within their design for comparing the respective pairs of bits in each of the two words with single bit comparators cascaded together to produce Multi-bit comparators so that larger words can be compared.

4.2.3.7 MULTIPLEXER

Multiplexers which sometimes are simply called “Mux” or “Muxes”, are devices that act like a very fast acting rotary switch. They connect multiple input lines 2, 4, 8, 16 etc one at a time to a common output line and are used as one method of reducing the number of logic gates required in a circuit. Multiplexers are individual Analogue Switches as opposed to the “mechanical” types such as normal conventional switches and relays. They are usually made from MOSFETs devices encased in a single package and are controlled using standard logic gates.

A multiplexer (abbreviated as MUX) is a combinational circuit that selects one of n input lines and provides it on the output. Thus, the multiplexer has several inputs and only one output. The select line identifies or addresses one of several inputs and provides it on the output line. Figure 4.14 shows the block diagram of a 2-to-1 multiplexer. The two inputs can be selected by one select line, S. When S = 0, input line 0 (d_0) will be presented as the output. On the other hand, when S = 1, input line 1 (d_1) will be produced at the output.

Table 4.6 shows the truth table of the 2-to-1 multiplexer. From the truth table, using the K-map of Figure 4.15(a), it can be shown that Z = Sel + Sd_0. Figure 4.15(b) shows the logic diagram. In general, a multiplexer with n select lines can select one of 2” data inputs. Hence, multiplexers are sometimes referred to as “data selectors“. A large multiplexer can be implemented using a small multiplexer as the building block.

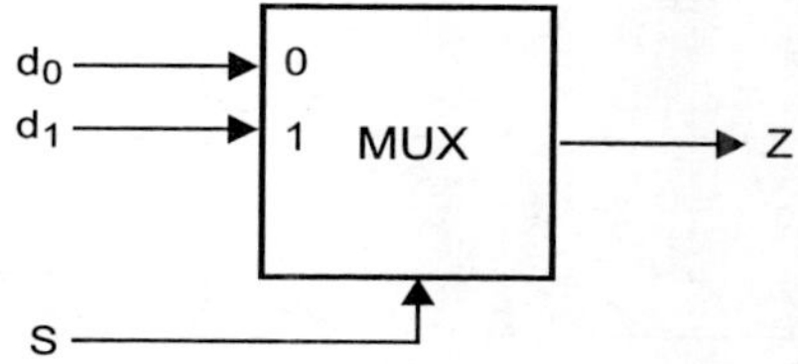

FIGURE 4.14: Block diagram of a 2-to-1 multiplexer

TABLE 4.6: Truth table of the 2-to-1 multiplexer

S	d_0	d_1	Z
0	0	0	0
0	0	1	0
0	1	0	1
0	1	1	1
1	0	0	0
1	0	1	1
1	1	0	0
1	1	1	1

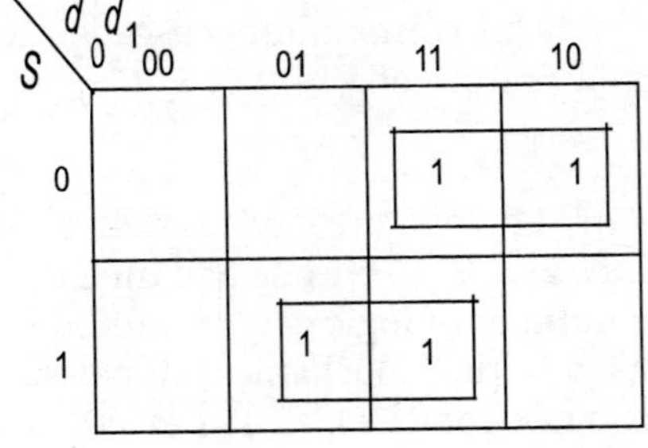

FIGURE 4.15(a): K-Map for the 2-To-1 MUX

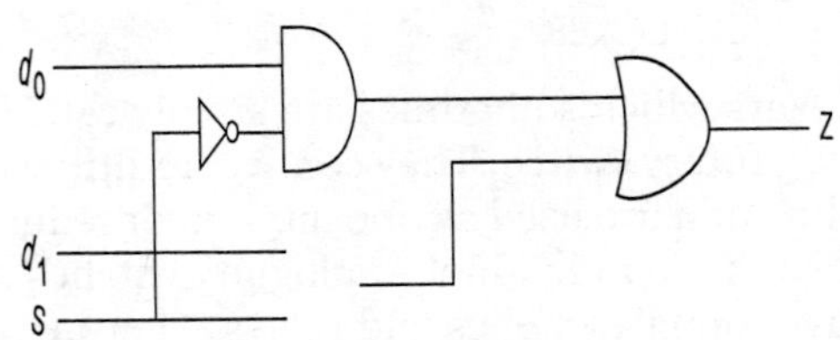

FIGURE 4.15(b): Logic diagram of the 2-to-1 MUX

1. MUX 4:1

A Multiplexer which converts four input signals into a single output signal is a 4:1 MUX. Figure 4.16 show the logic symbol and circuit diagram respectively of 4:1 MUX.

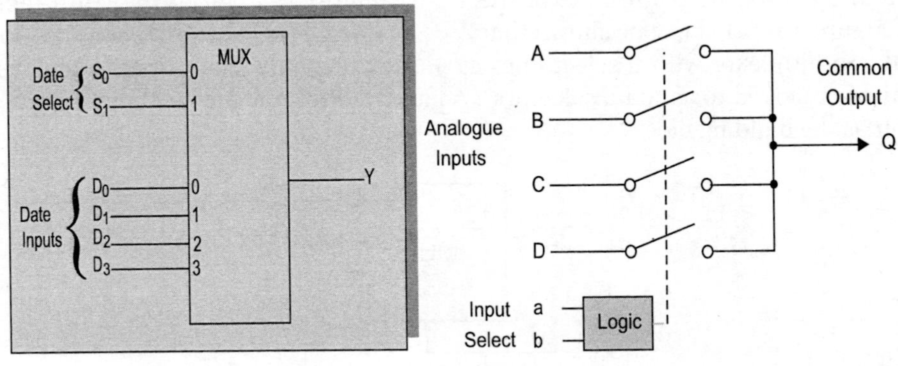

FIGURE 4.16: Logic Symbol for 4:1 MUX

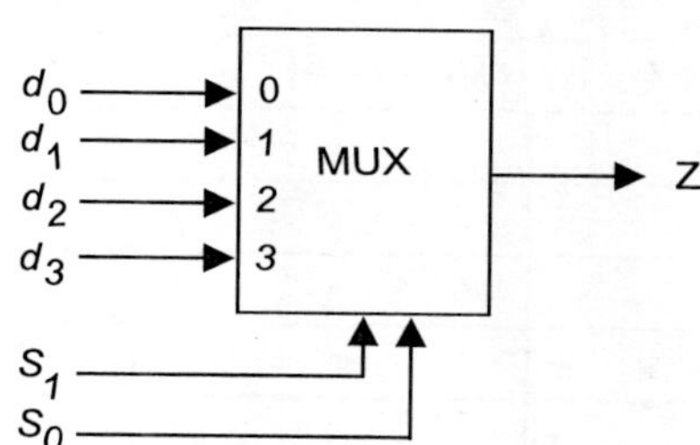

FIGURE 4.17: Block-Diagram of a Four-Input Multiplexer

DATA SELECT INPUTS		INPUT SELECTED
S_1	S_0	
0	0	D_0
0	1	D_1
1	0	D_2
1	1	D_3

TABLE 4.7: Operation of 4:1 MUX

4.2.3.8 DEMULTIPLEXER

De-multiplexers or "De-muxes", are the exact opposite of the Multiplexers we saw in the previous tutorial in that they have one single input data line and then switch it to any one of their individual multiple output lines one at a time. The De-multiplexer converts the serial data signal at the input to a parallel data at its output lines

The demultiplexer is a combinational circuit that performs the reverse operation of a multiplexer. The demultiplexer has only one input and several outputs. One of the outputs is selected by the combination of l's and o's of the select inputs. These inputs determine one of the output lines to be selected; data from the input line is then transferred to the selected output line.

1. DEMULTIPLEXER 1-TO-4 CHANNEL

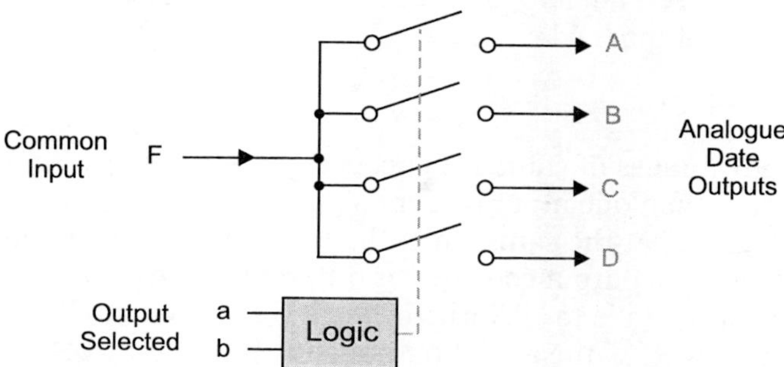

FIGURE 4.18: 1-To-4 Channel De-Multiplexer

Addressing Selected		Output
b	a	
0	0	A
0	1	B
1	0	C
1	1	D

The function of the De-multiplexer is to switch one common data input line to any one of the 4 output data lines A to D in our example above. As with the multiplexer the individual solid state switches are selected by the binary input address code on the output select pins "a" and "b" and by adding more address line inputs it is possible to switch more outputs giving a 1-to-2n data lines output. Some standard De-multiplexer IC´s also have an "enable output" input pin which disables or prevents the input from being passed to the selected output. Also some have latches built into their outputs to maintain the output logic level after the address inputs have been changed. However, in standard decoder type circuits the address input will determine which single data output will have the same value as the data input with all other data outputs having the value of logic "0".

Standard De-multiplexer IC packages available are the TTL 74LS138 1 to 8-output De-multiplexer, the TTL 74LS139 Dual 1 to 4-output De-multiplexer or the CMOS CD4514 1 to 16-output De-multiplexer. Another type of De-multiplexer is the 24-pin, 74LS154 which is a 4-bit to 16-line De-multiplexer/decoder. Here the output positions are selected using the 4-bit binary coded input.

4.2.3.9 ENCODERS

An encoder is a combinational logic circuit that essentially performs the opposite function of the decoder circuit. An encoder accepts an active level (i.e. '1') on one of its inputs representing a digit (e.g. decimal or octal digit) and converts it to a coded output (e.g. binary of BCD). The process of converting from familiar symbols or numbers to a coded format is called encoding.

Unlike a multiplexer that selects one individual data input line and then sends that data to a single output line or switch, an Encoder takes all the data inputs one at a time and converts them to a single encoded output. Then, it is a multi-input data line, combinational logic circuit that converts the logic level "1" data at its inputs to an equivalent binary code at its output. Generally encoders produce outputs of 2-bit, 3-bit or 4-bit codes depending upon the number of data input lines and a "n-bit" encoder has 2n input lines with common types that include 4-to-2, 8-to-3 and 16-to-4 line configurations. Encoders are available to encode either a decimal or hexadecimal input pattern to typically a binary or BCD output code.

I. ENCODER 4-TO-2 BIT

One of the main disadvantages of standard encoders is that they can generate the wrong output code when there is more than one input present at logic level "1". For example, if we make inputs D_1 and D_2 HIGH at logic "1" at the same time, the resulting output is neither at "01" nor at "10" but will be at "11" which is an output code that is different to the actual input present. One simple way to overcome this problem is to "Prioritize" the level of each input pin and if there was more than one input at logic level "1" the actual output code would only correspond to the input with the highest designated priority. Then these types of encoder are known as Priority Encoders or P-encoder.

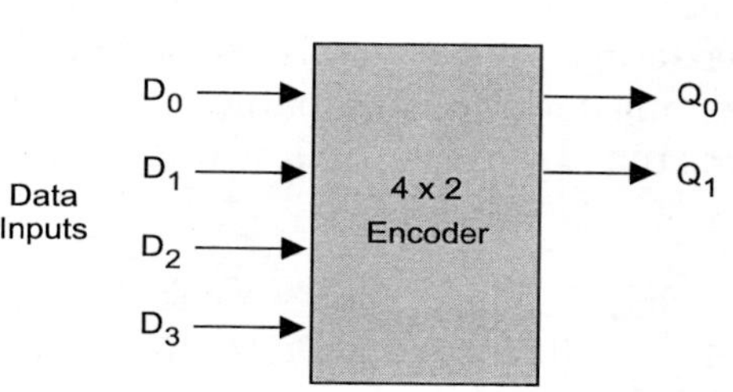

Inputs				Outputs	
D_3	D_2	D_1	D_0	Q_1	Q_0
0	0	0	1	0	0
0	0	1	0	0	1
0	1	0	0	1	0
1		0	0	1	1
0	0	0	0	X	X

FIGURE 4.19: 4-To-2 Bit Encoder

2. PRIORITY ENCODERS

Priority Encoders come in many forma and an example of an 8-input Priority Encoder along with its truth table is as shown below.

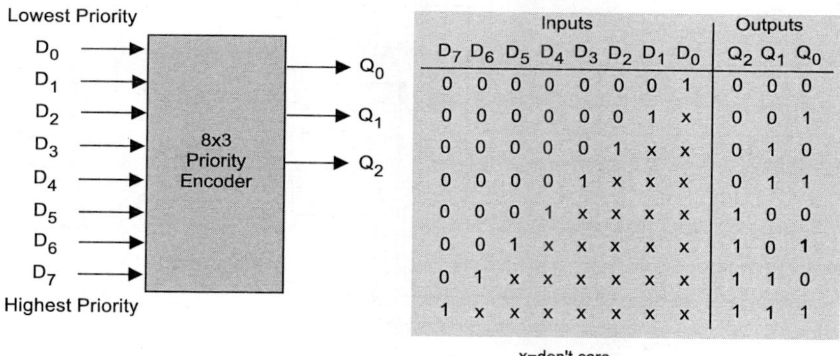

Inputs								Outputs		
D_7	D_6	D_5	D_4	D_3	D_2	D_1	D_0	Q_2	Q_1	Q_0
0	0	0	0	0	0	0	1	0	0	0
0	0	0	0	0	0	1	x	0	0	1
0	0	0	0	0	1	x	x	0	1	0
0	0	0	0	1	x	x	x	0	1	1
0	0	0	1	x	x	x	x	1	0	0
0	0	1	x	x	x	x	x	1	0	1
0	1	x	x	x	x	x	x	1	1	0
1	x	x	x	x	x	x	x	1	1	1

x=don't care

FIGURE 4.20: 8-To-3 Bit Priority Encoder

Priority encoders are available in standard IC form and the TTL 74LS148 is an 8 to 3 bit priority encoder which has eight active LOW (logic "0") inputs and provides a 3-bit code of the highest ranked input at its output. Priority encoders output the highest order input first for example, if input lines "D_2", "D_3" and "D_5" are applied simultaneously the output code would be for input "D_5" ("101") as this has the highest order out of the 3 inputs. Once input "D_5" had been removed the next highest output code would be for input "D_3" ("011"), and so on.

4.2.3.10 DECODERS

A Decoder is the exact opposite to that of an "Encoder" we looked at in the last tutorial. It is basically, a combinational type logic circuit that converts the binary code data at its input into one of a number of different output lines, one at a time producing an equivalent decimal code at its output. Binary Decoders have inputs of 2-bit, 3-bit or 4-bit codes depending upon the number of data input lines, and an "n-bit" decoder has 2n output lines. Typical combinations of decoders include 2-to-4, 3-to-8 and 4-to-16 line configurations. Binary Decoders are available to "decode" either a Binary or BCD input pattern to typically a Decimal output code.

Decoders can detect a code and activate a single output to signal the presence of that code. Decoders have many applications, from producing system alerts in alarm systems to performing the task of driving multiple devices in microprocessor systems e.g. memory. An n-bit binary number provides 2^n minterms or maxterms. For example, a 2-bit binary number will generate 4 (2^2) minterms or maxterms. A decoder is a combinational circuit , when enabled, selects one of 2” minterms or maxterms at the output based on the input combinations. However, a decoder sometimes may have less than 2’ outputs.

I. BINARY DECODERS 2-TO-4

In this simple example of a 2-to-4 line binary decoder, the binary inputs A and B determine which output line from D_0 to D_3 is “HIGH” at logic level “1” while the remaining outputs are held “LOW” at logic “0”. Therefore, whichever output line is “HIGH” identifies the binary code present at the input, in other words it “de-codes” the binary input and these types of binary decoders are commonly used as Address Decoders in microprocessor memory applications.

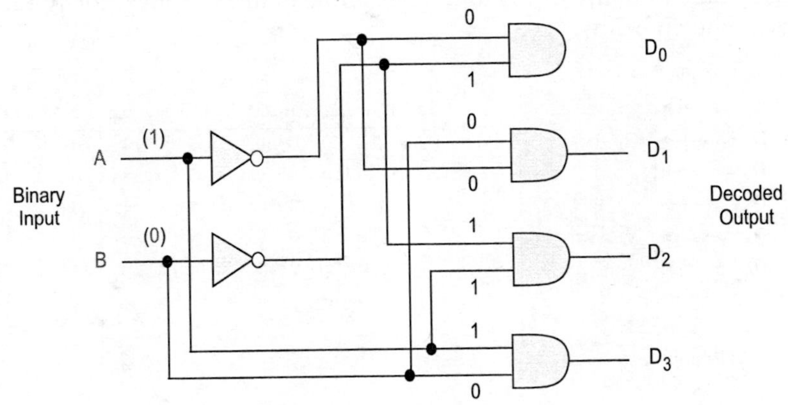

FIGURE 4.21: 2-To-4 Binary Decoders

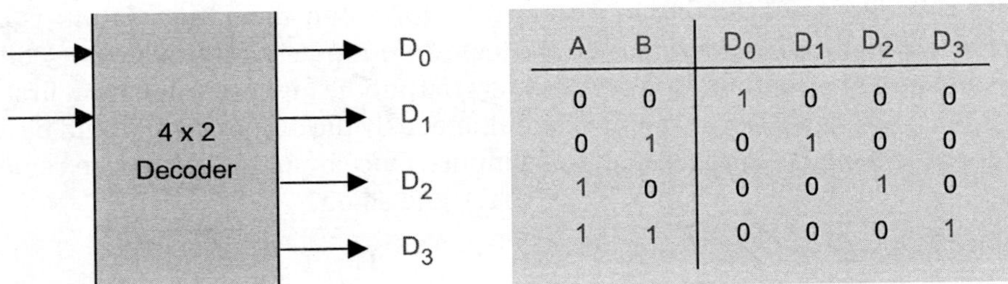

A	B	D_0	D_1	D_2	D_3
0	0	1	0	0	0
0	1	0	1	0	0
1	0	0	0	1	0
1	1	0	0	0	1

TABLE 4.8: 2-To-4 Binary Decoders

4.3 SORTING NETWORK

We examined sorting algorithms for serial computers (random-access machines, or RAM’s) that allow only one operation to be executed at a time. In this section, we investigate sorting algorithms based on a comparison network model of computation in which many comparison operations can be performed simultaneously.

Comparison networks differ from RAM's in two important respects. First, they can only perform comparisons. Thus, an algorithm such as counting sort cannot be implemented on a comparison network. Second, unlike the RAM model, in which operations occur serially--that is, one after another--operations in a comparison network may occur at the same time, or "in parallel." As we shall see, this characteristic allows the construction of comparison networks that sort n values in sublinear time.

A **sorting network** is an abstract mathematical model of a network of wires and comparator modules that is used to sort a sequence of numbers. Each comparator connects two wires and sorts the values by outputting the smaller value to one wire, and the larger to the other. The main difference between sorting networks and comparison sorting algorithms is that the sequence of comparisons is set in advance, regardless of the outcome of previous comparisons. This independence of comparison sequences is useful for parallel execution of the algorithms. Despite the simplicity of the model, sorting network theory is surprisingly deep and complex.

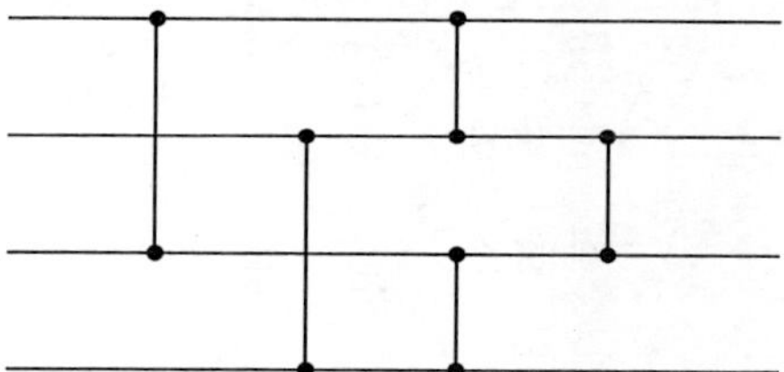

FIGURE 4.22: A simple sorting network consisting of four wires and five connectors

A sorting network consists of two items: comparators and wires. Each wire carries with it a value, and each comparator takes two wires as input and output. When two values enter a comparator, the comparator emits the lower value from the top wire, and the higher value from the bottom wire. A network of wires and comparators that will correctly sort all possible inputs into ascending order is called a sorting network.

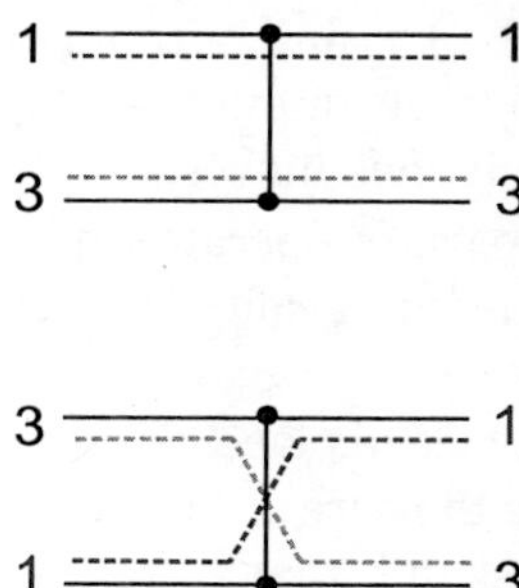

FIGURE 4.23: Demonstration of a comparator in a sorting network.

The full operation of a simple sorting network is shown below. It is easy to see why this sorting network will correctly sort the inputs; note that the first four comparators will "sink" the largest value to the bottom and "float" the smallest value to the top. The final comparator simply sorts out the middle two wires.

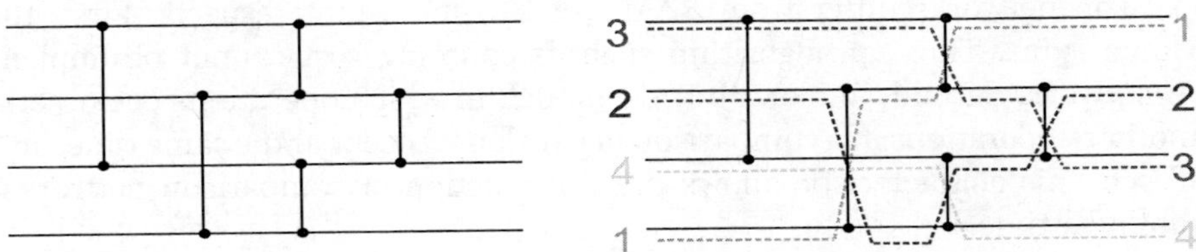

FIGURE 4.24: Sorting network

4.3.1 COMPARISON NETWORKS

Sorting networks are comparison networks that always sort their inputs, so it makes sense to begin our discussion with comparison networks and their characteristics. A comparison network is comprised solely of wires and comparators. A ***comparator***, shown in Figure 4.25 (a), is a device with two inputs, x and y, and two outputs, x' and y', that performs the following function:

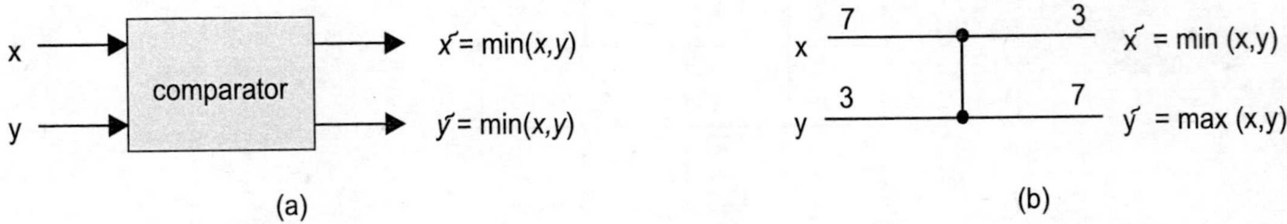

FIGURE 4.25: (a) A comparator with inputs x and y and outputs x′ and y′. (b) The same comparator, drawn as a single vertical line. Inputs x = 7, y = 3 and outputs x′ = 3, y′ = 7 are shown.

$$x' = \min(x, y)$$
$$y' = \max(x, y)$$

Because the pictorial representation of a comparator in Figure 4.25(a) is too bulky for our purposes, we shall adopt the convention of drawing comparators as single vertical lines, as shown in Figure 4.25(b). Inputs appear on the left and outputs on the right, with the smaller input value appearing on the top output and the larger input value appearing on the bottom output. We can thus think of a comparator as sorting its two inputs.

We shall assume that each comparator operates in $O(1)$ time. In other words, we assume that the time between the appearance of the input values x and y and the production of the output values x' and y' is a constant.

A ***wire*** transmits a value from place to place. Wires can connect the output of one comparator to the input of another, but otherwise they are either network input wires or network output wires. Throughout this chapter, we shall assume that a comparison network contains n ***input wires*** $a_1, a_2, \ldots, a_n$, through which the values to be sorted enter the network, and n ***output wires*** $b_1, b_2, \ldots, b_n$, which produce the results computed by the network. Also, we shall speak of the ***input sequence*** $\langle a_1, a_2, \ldots, a_n \rangle$ and the ***output sequence*** $\langle b_1, b_2, \ldots, b_n \rangle$, referring to the values on the input and output wires. That is, we use the same name for both a wire and the value it carries. Our intention will always be clear from the context.

Figure 4.26 shows a ***comparison network***, which is a set of comparators interconnected by wires. We draw a comparison network on n inputs as a collection of n horizontal ***lines*** with comparators stretched vertically. Note that a line does *not* represent a single wire, but rather a sequence of distinct wires connecting various comparators. The top line in Figure 4.26, for example, represents three wires: input wire a_1, which connects to an input of comparator A; a wire connecting the top output of comparator A to an input of comparator C; and output wire b_1, which comes from the top output of comparator C. Each comparator input is connected to a wire that is either one of the network's n input wires $a_1, a_2, \ldots, a_n$ or is connected to the output of another comparator. Similarly, each comparator output is connected to a wire that is either one of the network's n output wires $b_1, b_2, \ldots, b_n$ or is connected to the input of another comparator. The main requirement for interconnecting comparators is that the graph of interconnections must be acyclic: if we trace a path from the output of a given comparator to the input of another to output to input, etc., the path we trace must never cycle back on itself and go through the same comparator twice. Thus, as in Figure 4.26, we can draw a comparison network with network inputs on the left and network outputs on the right; data move through the network from left to right.

Each comparator produces its output values only when both of its input values are available to it. In Figure 4.26 (a), for example, suppose that the sequence ⟨9, 5, 2, 6⟩ appears on the input wires at time 0. At time 0, then, only comparators A and B have all their input values available. Assuming that each comparator requires one time unit to compute its output values, comparators A and B produce their outputs at time 1; the resulting values are shown in Figure 4.26(b). Note that comparators A and B produce their values at the same time, or "in parallel." Now, at time 1, comparators C and D, but not E, have all their input values available. One time unit later, at time 2, they produce their outputs, as shown in Figure 4.26(c). Comparators C and D operate in parallel as well. The top output of comparator C and the bottom output of comparator D connect to output wires b_1 and b_4, respectively, of the comparison network, and these network output wires therefore carry their final values at time 2. Meanwhile, at time 2, comparator E has its inputs available, and Figure 4.26(d) shows that it produces its output values at time 3. These values are carried on network output wires b_2 and b_3, and the output sequence ⟨2, 5, 6, 9⟩ is now complete.

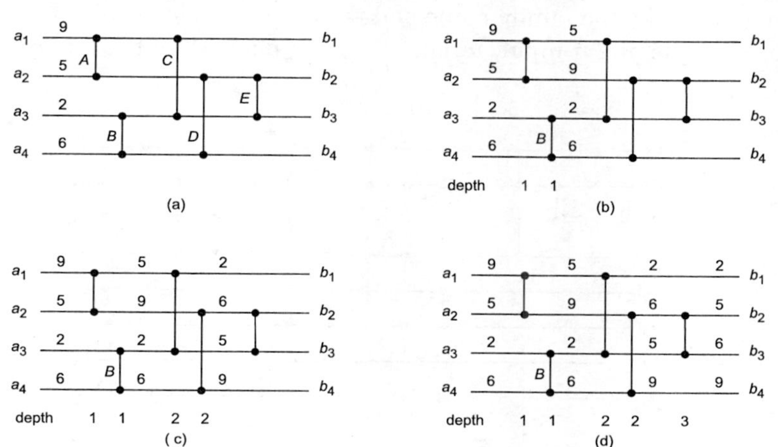

FIGURE 4.26: (a) A 4-input, 4-output comparison network, which is in fact a sorting network. At time 0, the input values shown appear on the four input wires. (b) At time 1, the values shown appear on the outputs of comparators A and B, which are at depth I. (c) At time 2, the values shown appear on the outputs of comparators C and D, at depth 2. Output wires b_1 and b_4 now have their final values, but output wires b_2 and b_3 do not. (d) At time 3, the values shown appear on the outputs of comparator E, at depth 3. Output wires b_2 and b_3 now have their final values.

Under the assumption that each comparator takes unit time, we can define the "running time" of a comparison network, that is, the time it takes for all the output wires to receive their values once the input wires receive theirs. Informally, this time is the largest number of comparators that any input element can pass through as it travels from an input wire to an output wire. More formally, we define the ***depth*** of a wire as follows. An input wire of a comparison network has depth 0. Now, if a comparator has two input wires with depths d_x and d_y, then its output wires have depth max(d_x, d_y) + 1. Because there are no cycles of comparators in a comparison network, the depth of a wire is well defined, and we define the depth of a comparator to be the depth of its output wires. Figure 4.26 shows comparator depths. The depth of a comparison network is the maximum depth of an output wire or, equivalently, the maximum depth of a comparator. The comparison network of Figure 4.26, for example, has depth 3 because comparator *E* has depth 3. If each comparator takes one time unit to produce its output value, and if network inputs appear at time 0, a comparator at depth *d* produces its outputs at time *d*; the depth of the network therefore equals the time for the network to produce values at all of its output wires.

A ***sorting network*** is a comparison network for which the output sequence is monotonically increasing (that is, $b_1 < b_2 < \ldots < b_n$) for *every* input sequence. Of course, not every comparison network is a sorting network, but the network of Figure 4.26 is. To see why, observe that after time 1, the minimum of the four input values has been produced by either the top output of comparator *A* or the top output of comparator *B*. After time 2, therefore, it must be on the top output of comparator *C*. A symmetrical argument shows that after time 2, the maximum of the four input values has been produced by the bottom output of comparator *D*. All that remains is for comparator *E* to ensure that the middle two values occupy their correct output positions, which happens at time 3.

A comparison network is like a procedure in that it specifies how comparisons are to occur, but it is unlike a procedure in that its physical size depends on the number of inputs and outputs. Therefore, we shall actually be describing "families" of comparison networks. For example, the goal of this chapter is to develop a family SORTER of efficient sorting networks. We specify a given network within a family by the family name and the number of inputs (which equals the number of outputs). For example, the *n*-input, *n*-output sorting network in the family SORTER is named SORTER[*n*].

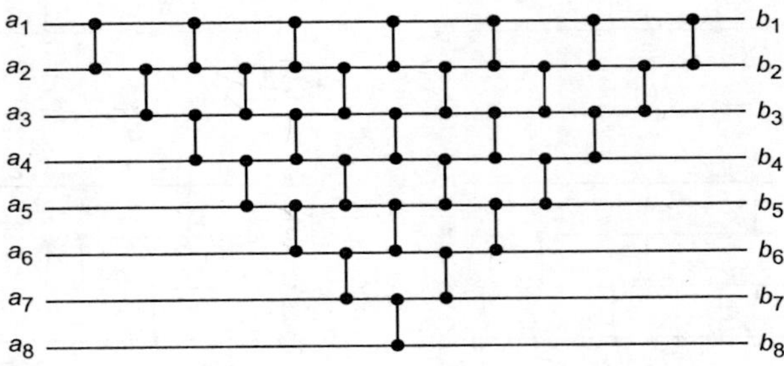

FIGURE 4.27: A sorting network based on insertion sort.

4.3.2 THE ZERO-ONE PRINCIPLE

The ***zero-one principle*** says that if a sorting network works correctly when each input is drawn from the set {0,1}, then it works correctly on arbitrary input numbers. (The numbers can be integers, reals, or, in general, any set of values from any linearly ordered set.) As we construct sorting networks and other comparison networks, the zero-one principle will allow us to focus on their operation for input sequences consisting solely of 0's and 1's. Once we have constructed a sorting network and proved that it can sort all zero-one sequences, we shall appeal to the zero-one principle to show that it properly sorts sequences of arbitrary values.

Lemma 4.1

If a comparison network transforms the input sequence $a = \langle a_1, a_2, \ldots, a_n \rangle$ into the output sequence $b = \langle b_1, b_2, \ldots, b_n \rangle$, then for any monotonically increasing function f, the network transforms the input sequence $f(a) = \langle f(a_1), f(a_2), \ldots, f(a_n) \rangle$ into the output sequence $f(b) = \langle f(b_1), f(b_2), \ldots, f(b_n) \rangle$.

Proof We shall first prove the claim that if f is a monotonically increasing function, then a single comparator with inputs $f(x)$ and $f(y)$ produces outputs $f(\min(x,y))$ and $f(\max(x,y))$. We shall then use induction to prove the lemma.

To prove the claim, consider a comparator whose input values are x and y. The upper output of the comparator is $\min(x,y)$ and the lower output is $\max(x,y)$. Suppose we now apply $f(x)$ and $f(y)$ to the inputs of the comparator, as is shown in Figure 4.28. The operation of the comparator yields the value $\min(f(x), f(y))$ on the upper output and the value $\max(f(x), f(y))$ on the lower output. Since f is monotonically increasing, $x < y$ implies $f(x) f(y)$. Consequently, we have the identities

$$\min(f(x), f(y)) = f(\min(x,y)),$$
$$\max(f(x), f(y)) = f(\max(x,y)).$$

Thus, the comparator produces the values $f(\min(x,y))$ and $f(\max(x,y))$ when $f(x)$ and $f(y)$ are its inputs, which completes the proof of the claim.

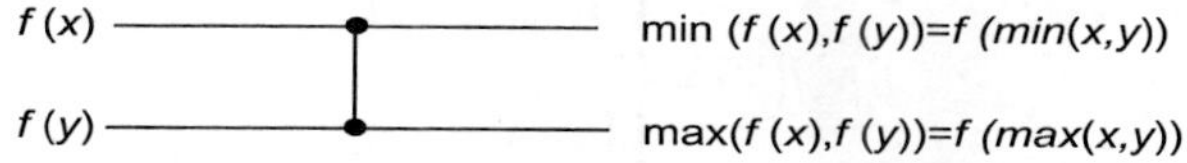

FIGURE 4.28: The operation of the comparator in the proof of Lemma 4.1. The function f is monotonically increasing.

We can use induction on the depth of each wire in a general comparison network to prove a stronger result than the statement of the lemma: if a wire assumes the value a_i when the input sequence a is applied to the network, then it assumes the value $f(a_i)$ when the input sequence $f(a)$ is applied. Because the output wires are included in this statement, proving it will prove the lemma.

For the basis, consider a wire at depth 0, that is, an input wire a_i. The result follows trivially: when $f(a)$ is applied to the network, the input wire carries $f(a_i)$. For the inductive step, consider a wire at depth d, where $d > 1$. The wire is the output of a comparator at depth d, and the input wires to this comparator are at a depth strictly less than d. By the inductive hypothesis, therefore, if the input wires to the comparator carry values a_i and a_j when the input sequence a is applied, then they carry $f(a_i)$ and $f(a_j)$ when the input sequence $f(a)$ is applied. By our earlier claim, the output wires of this comparator then carry $f(\min(a_i, a_j))$ and $f(\max(a_i, a_j))$. Since they carry $\min(a_i, a_j)$ and $\max(a_i, a_j)$ when the input sequence is a, the lemma is proved.

As an example of the application of Lemma 4.1, Figure 4.29 shows the sorting network from Figure 4.26 with the monotonically increasing function $f(x) = (x/2)$ applied to the inputs. The value on every wire is f applied to the value on the same wire in Figure 4.26.

When a comparison network is a sorting network, Lemma 4.1 allows us to prove the following remarkable result.

THEOREM 4.2

If a comparison network with n inputs sorts all 2^n possible sequences of 0's and 1's correctly, then it sorts all sequences of arbitrary numbers correctly.

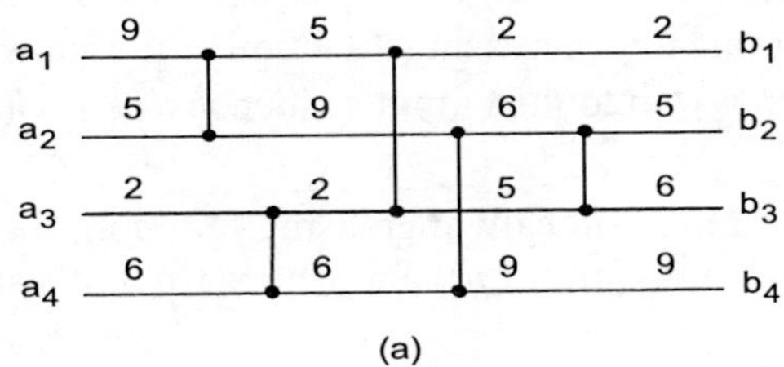

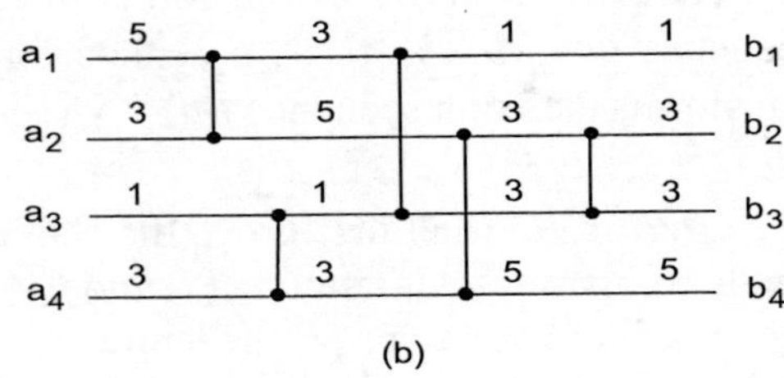

FIGURE 4.29: (a) The sorting network from Figure 28.2 with input sequence ⟨9, 5, 2, 6⟩. (b) The same sorting network with the monotonically increasing function f(x) = f(x/2) applied to the inputs. Each wire in this network has the value of f applied to the value on the corresponding wire in (a).

Proof Suppose for the purpose of contradiction that the network sorts all zero-one sequences, but there exists a sequence of arbitrary numbers that the network does not correctly sort. That is, there exists an input sequence $\langle a_1, a_2, \ldots, a_n \rangle$ containing elements a_i and a_j such that $a_i < a_j$, but the network places a_j before a_i in the output sequence. We define a monotonically increasing function f as

$$f(x) = \begin{cases} 0 & \text{if } x \le a_i \\ 1 & \text{if } x > a_i \end{cases}$$

Since the network places a_j before a_i in the output sequence when $\langle a_1, a_2, \ldots, a_n \rangle$ is input, it follows from Lemma 4.1 that it places $f(a_j)$ before $f(a_i)$ in the output sequence when $\langle f(a_1), f(a_2), \ldots, f(a_n) \rangle$ is input. But since $f(a_j) = 1$ and $f(a_i) = 0$, we obtain the contradiction that the network fails to sort the zero-one sequence $\langle f(a_1), f(a_2), \ldots, f(a_n) \rangle$ correctly.

4.3.3 A BITONIC SORTING NETWORK

The first step in our construction of an efficient sorting network is to construct a comparison network that can sort any ***bitonic sequence:*** a sequence that either monotonically increases and then monotonically decreases, or else monotonically decreases and then monotonically increases. For example, the sequences ⟨1, 4, 6, 8, 3, 2⟩ and ⟨9, 8, 3, 2, 4, 6⟩ are both bitonic. The zero-one sequences that are bitonic have a simple structure. They have the form $0^i 1^j 0^k$ or the form $1^i 0^j 1^k$, for some $i, j, k > 0$. Note that a sequence that is either monotonically increasing or monotonically decreasing is also bitonic. The bitonic sorter that we shall construct is a comparison network that sorts bitonic sequences of 0's and 1's.

THE HALF-CLEANER

A bitonic sorter is comprised of several stages, each of which is called a ***half-cleaner***. Each half-cleaner is a comparison network of depth 1 in which input line i is compared with line $i + n/2$ for $i =$

1, 2, . . . , $n/2$. (We assume that n is even.) Figure 4.30 shows HALF-CLEANER[8], the half-cleaner with 8 inputs and 8 outputs.

When a bitonic sequence of 0's and 1's is applied as input to a half-cleaner, the half-cleaner produces an output sequence in which smaller values are in the top half, larger values are in the bottom half, and both halves are bitonic. In fact, at least one of the halves is ***clean***--consisting of either all 0's or all 1's--and it is from this property that we derive the name "half-cleaner." (Note that all clean sequences are bitonic.) The next lemma proves these properties of half-cleaners.

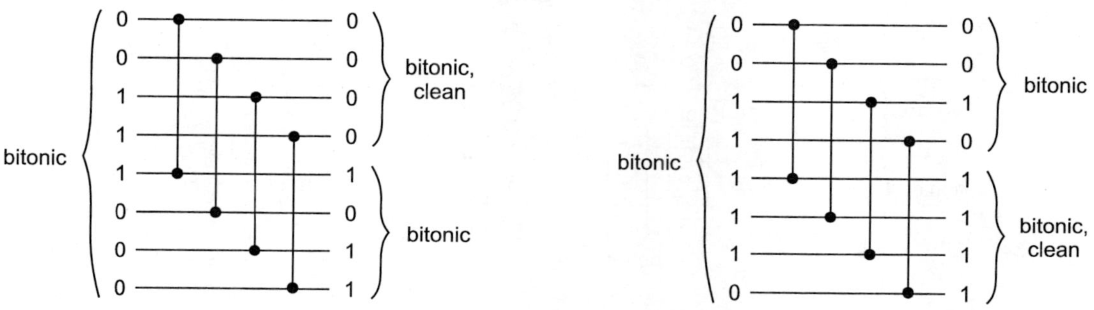

FIGURE 4.30: The comparison network HALF-CLEANER[8]. Two different sample zero-one input and output values are shown. The input is assumed to be bitonic. A half-cleaner ensures that every output element of the top half is at least as small as every output element of the bottom half. Moreover, both halves are bitonic, and at least one half is clean.

LEMMA 4.3

If the input to a half-cleaner is a bitonic sequence of 0's and 1's, then the output satisfies the following properties: both the top half and the bottom half are bitonic, every element in the top half is at least as small as every element of the bottom half, and at least one half is clean.

Proof The comparison network HALF-CLEANER[n] compares inputs i and $i + n/2$ for i = 1, 2, . . . , $n/2$. Without loss of generality, suppose that the input is of the form 00 . . . 011 . . . 100 . . . 0. (The situation in which the input is of the form 11 . . . 100 . . . 011 . . . 1 is symmetric.) There are three possible cases depending upon the block of consecutive 0's or 1s in which the midpoint $n/2$ falls, and one of these cases (the one in which the midpoint occurs in the block of 1's) is further split into two cases. The four cases are shown in Figure 4.31. In each case shown, the lemma holds.

THE BITONIC SORTER

By recursively combining half-cleaners, as shown in Figure 4.32, we can build a ***bitonic sorter***, which is a network that sorts bitonic sequences. The first stage of BITONIC-SORTER[n] consists of HALF-CLEANER[n], which, by Lemma 4.3, produces two bitonic sequences of half the size such that every element in the top half is at least as small as every element in the bottom half. Thus, we can complete the sort by using two copies of BITONIC-SORTER[$n/2$] to sort the two halves recursively. In Figure 4.32(a), the recursion has been shown explicitly, and in Figure 4.32(b), the recursion has been unrolled to show the progressively smaller half-cleaners that make up the remainder of the bitonic sorter. The depth $D(n)$ of BITONIC-SORTER[n] is given by the recurrence whose solution is $D(n) = \lg n$.

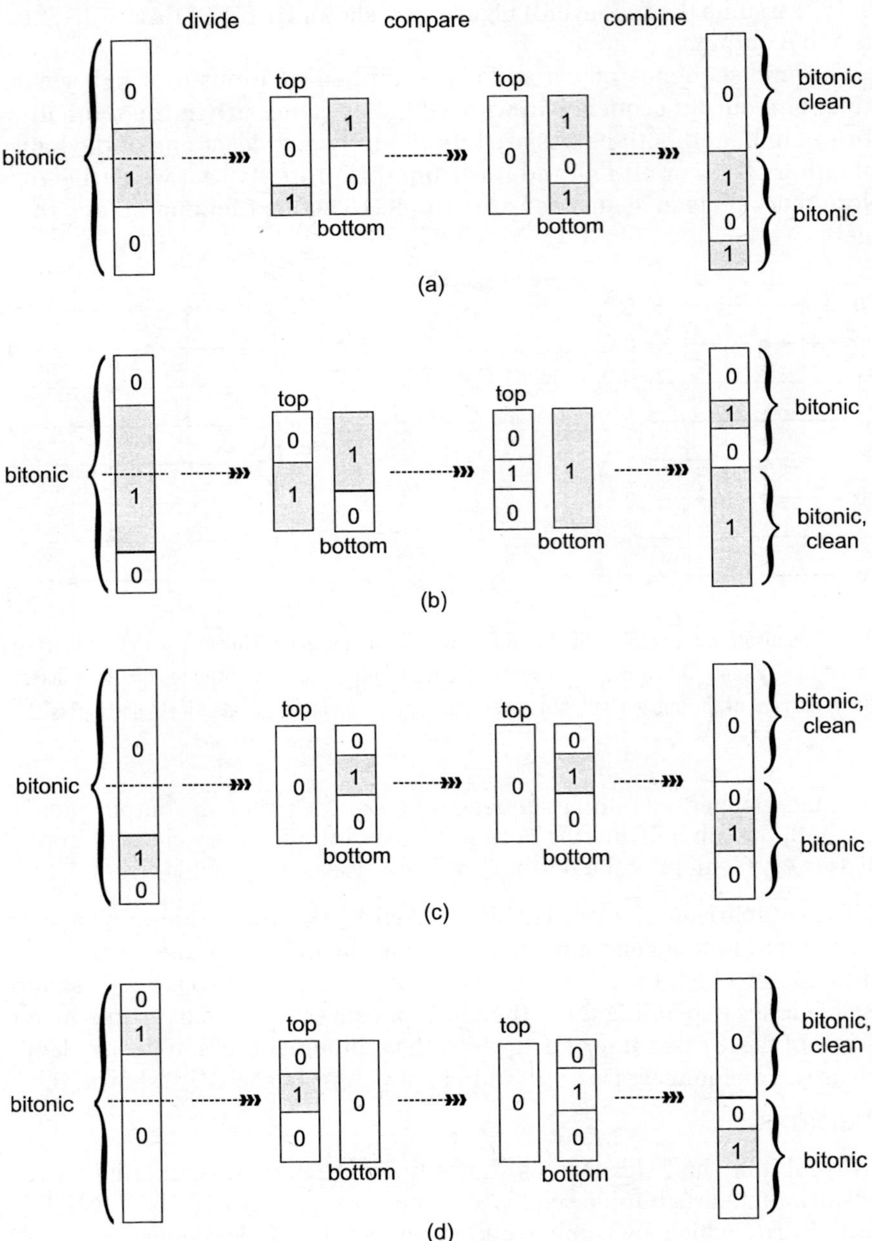

FIGURE 4.31: The possible comparisons in HALF-CLEANER[n]. The input sequence is assumed to be a bitonic sequence of 0's and 1's, and without loss of generality, we assume that it is of the form 00 . . . 011 . . . 100 . . . 0. Subsequences of 0's are white, and subsequences of 1's are gray. We can think of the n inputs as being divided into two halves such that for i = 1, 2, . . . , n/2, inputs i and i + n/2 are compared. (a)-(b) Cases in which the division occurs in the middle subsequence of 1's. (c)-(d) Cases in which the division occurs in a subsequence of 0's. For all cases, every element in the top half is at least as small as every element in the bottom half, both halves are bitonic, and at least one half is clean.

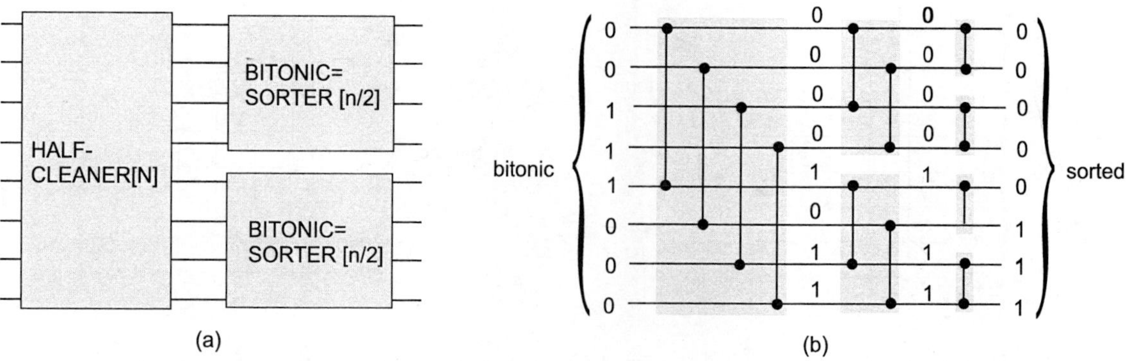

FIGURE 4.32: The comparison network BITONIC-SORTER[n], shown here for n = 8. (a) The recursive construction: HALF-CLEANER[n] followed by two copies of BITONIC-SORTER[n/2] that operate in parallel. (b) The network after unrolling the recursion. Each half-cleaner is shaded. Sample zero-one values are shown on the wires.

$$D(n) = \begin{cases} 0 & \text{if } n = 1 \\ D(n/2) + 1 & \text{if } n = 2^k \text{ and } k \geq 1 \end{cases}$$

Thus, a zero-one bitonic sequence can be sorted by BITONIC-SORTER, which has a depth of lg n. It follows by the analog of the zero-one principle that any bitonic sequence of arbitrary numbers can be sorted by this network.

4.3.4 A MERGING NETWORK

Our sorting network will be constructed from ***merging networks***, which are networks that can merge two sorted input sequences into one sorted output sequence. We modify BITONIC-SORTER[n] to create the merging network MERGER[n]. As with the bitonic sorter, we shall prove the correctness of the merging network only for inputs that are zero-one sequences.

The merging network is based on the following intuition. Given two sorted sequences, if we reverse the order of the second sequence and then concatenate the two sequences, the resulting sequence is bitonic. For example, given the sorted zero-one sequences X = 00000111 and Y = 00001111, we reverse Y to get Y^R = 11110000. Concatenating X and Y^R yields 0000011111110000, which is bitonic. Thus, to merge the two input sequences X and Y, it suffices to perform a bitonic sort on X concatenated with Y^R.

We can construct MERGER[n] by modifying the first half-cleaner of BITONIC-SORTER[n]. The key is to perform the reversal of the the second half of the inputs implicitly. Given two sorted sequences $\langle a_1, a_2, \ldots, a_{n/2} \rangle$ and $\langle a_{n/2+1}, a_{n/2+2}, \ldots, a_n \rangle$ to be merged, we want the effect of bitonically sorting the sequence $\langle a_1, a_2, \ldots, a_{n/2}, a_n, a_{n-1}, \ldots, a_{n/2+1} \rangle$. Since the half-cleaner of BITONIC-SORTER[n] compares inputs i and $n/2 + i$, for $i = 1, 2, \ldots, n/2$, we make the first stage of the merging network compare inputs i and $n - i + 1$. Figure 4.33 shows the correspondence. The only subtlety is that the order of the outputs from the bottom of the first stage of MERGER[n] is reversed compared with the order of outputs from an ordinary half-cleaner. Since the reversal of a bitonic sequence is bitonic, however, the top and bottom outputs of the first stage of the merging network satisfy the properties in Lemma 4.3, and thus the top and bottom can be bitonically sorted in parallel to produce the sorted output of the merging network.

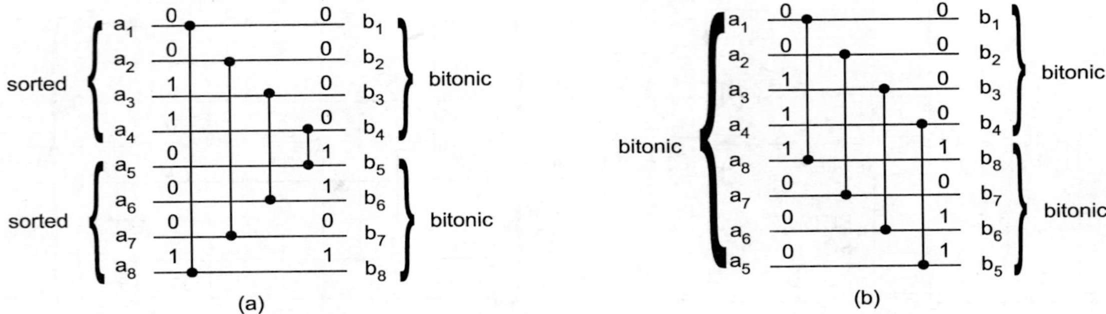

FIGURE 4.33: Comparing the first stage of MERGER[n] with HALF-CLEANER[n], for n = 8. (a) The first stage of MERGER[n] transforms the two monotonic input sequences $\langle a_1, a_2, \ldots, a_{n/2} \rangle$ and $\langle a_{n/2+1}, a_{n/2+2}, \ldots, a_n \rangle$ into two bitonic sequences $\langle b_1, b_2, \ldots, b_{n/2} \rangle$ and $\langle b_{n/2+1}, b_{n/2+2}, \ldots, b_n \rangle$. (b) The equivalent operation for HALF-CLEANER[n]. The bitonic input sequence $\langle a_1, a_2, \ldots, a_{n/2-1}, a_{n/2}, a_n, a_{n-1}, \ldots, a_{n/2+2}, a_{n/2+1} \rangle$ is transformed into the two bitonic sequences $\langle b_1, b_2, \ldots, b_{n/2} \rangle$ and $\langle b_n, b_{n-1}, \ldots, b_{n/2+1} \rangle$.

The resulting merging network is shown in Figure 4.34. Only the first stage of MERGER[n] is different from BITONIC-SORTER[n]. Consequently, the depth of MERGER[n] is lg n, the same as that of BITONIC-SORTER[n].

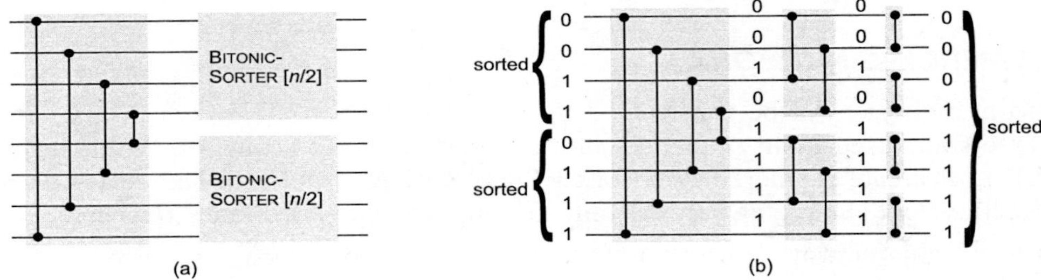

FIGURE 4.34: A network that merges two sorted input sequences into one sorted output sequence. The network MERGER[n] can be viewed as BITONIC-SORTER[n] with the first half-cleaner altered to compare inputs i and n - i + 1 for i = 1, 2, . . . , n/2. Here, n = 8. (a) The network decomposed into the first stage followed by two parallel copies of BITONIC-SORTER[n/2]. (b) The same network with the recursion unrolled. Sample zero-one values are shown on the wires, and the stages are shaded.

4.3.5 A SORTING NETWORK

We now have all the necessary tools to construct a network that can sort any input sequence. The sorting network SORTER[n] uses the merging network to implement a parallel version of merge sort. The construction and operation of the sorting network are iFigure 4.35(a) shows the recursive construction of SORTER[n]. The n input elements are sorted by using two copies of SORTER[$n/2$] recursively to sort (in parallel) two subsequences of length $n/2$ each. The two resulting sequences are then merged by MERGER[n]. The boundary case for the recursion is when $n = 1$, in which case we can use a wire to sort the 1-element sequence, since a 1-element sequence is already sorted. Figure 4.35(b) shows the result of unrolling the recursion, and Figure 4.35(c) shows the actual network obtained by replacing the MERGER boxes in Figure 4.35(b) with the actual merging networks.

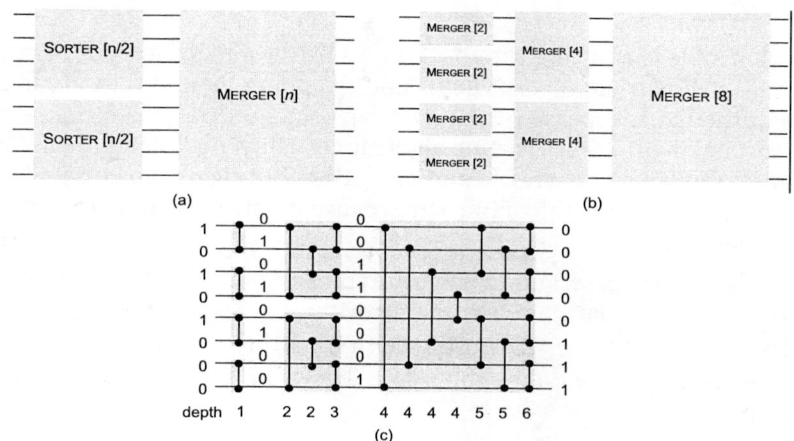

FIGURE 4.35: The sorting network SORTER[n] constructed by recursively combining merging networks. (a) The recursive construction. (b) Unrolling the recursion. (c) Replacing the MERGER boxes with the actual merging networks. The depth of each comparator is indicated, and sample zero-one values are shown on the wires.

Data pass through lg n stages in the network SORTER[n]. Each of the individual inputs to the network is already a sorted 1-element sequence. The first stage of SORTER[n] consists of $n/2$ copies of MERGER[2] that work in parallel to merge pairs of 1-element sequences to produce sorted sequences of length 2. The second stage consists of $n/4$ copies of MERGER[4] that merge pairs of these 2-element sorted sequences to produce sorted sequences of length 4. In general, for $k = 1, 2, \ldots, \lg n$, stage k consists of $n/2^k$ copies of MERGER[2^k] that merge pairs of the 2^{k-1}-element sorted sequences to produce sorted sequences of length 2^k. At the final stage, one sorted sequence consisting of all the input values is produced. This sorting network can be shown by induction to sort zero-one sequences, and consequently, by the zero-one principle (Theorem 4.2), it can sort arbitrary values.

We can analyze the depth of the sorting network recursively. The depth $D(n)$ of SORTER[n] is the depth $D(n/2)$ of SORTER[$n/2$] (there are two copies of SORTER[$n/2$], but they operate in parallel) plus the depth lg n of MERGER[n]. Consequently, the depth of SORTER[n] is given by the recurrence

$$D(n) = \begin{cases} 0 & \text{if } n = 1 \\ D(n/2) + \lg n & \text{if } n = 2^k \text{ and } k \geq 1 \end{cases}$$

whose solution is $D(n) = \Theta(\lg^2 n)$. Thus, we can sort n numbers in parallel in $O(\lg^2 n)$ time.

The following table summarizes the complexities of some sorting networks:

	comparator stages	**comparators**
Odd-even transposition sort	$O(n)$	$O(n^2)$
Bubblesort	$O(n)$	$O(n^2)$
Bitonic sort	$O(\log(n)^2)$	$O(n \cdot \log(n)^2)$
Odd-even mergesort	$O(\log(n)^2)$	$O(n \cdot \log(n)^2)$
Shellsort	$O(\log(n)^2)$	$O(n \cdot \log(n)^2)$

4.3.6 BUBBLE SORT

Bubble sort is a simple sorting algorithm. It works by repeatedly stepping through the list to be sorted, comparing each pair of adjacent items and swapping them if they are in the wrong order. The pass through the list is repeated until no swaps are needed, which indicates that the list is sorted. Bubble sort belongs to $O(n^2)$ sorting algorithms, which makes it quite inefficient for sorting large data volumes. Bubble sort is **stable** and **adaptive**.The algorithm gets its name from the way smaller elements "bubble" to the top of the list. Because it only uses comparisons to operate on elements, it is a comparison sort.

Bubble sort has worst-case and average complexity both $O(n^2)$, where n is the number of items being sorted. There exist many sorting algorithms with substantially better worst-case or average complexity of O(n log n). Even other $O(n^2)$ sorting algorithms, such as Insertion sort, tend to have better performance than bubble sort. Therefore bubble sort is not a practical sorting algorithm when n is large.

However, one significant advantage that bubble sort has over most other implementations, even QuickSort, is that the ability to detect that the list is sorted is efficiently built into the algorithm. Performance of bubble sort over an already-sorted list (best-case) is O(n). By contrast, most other algorithms, even those with better average-case complexity, perform their entire sorting process on the set and thus are more complex. However, Insertion sort also has this mechanism, and also performs better on a list that is substantially sorted (having a small number of inversions).

A bubble sort makes use of an array and some sort of "swapping" mechanism. Most programming languages have a built-in function to swap elements of an array. Even if a swapping function does not exist, only a couple of extra lines of code are required to store one array element in a temporary field in order to swap a second element into its place. Then the first element is moved out of the temporary field and back into the array at the second element's position.

Example 4.1: How a bubble sort works: Suppose you have a row of children's toy blocks with letters on them. They are in random order and you wish to arrange them in alphabetical order from left to right.

Step 1: Begin with the first block. In this case, the letter **G.** (a)

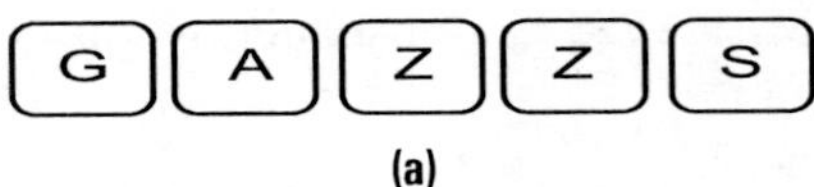

(a)

Step 2: Look at the block just to the right of it.

Step 3: If the block to the right should come before the block on the left, swap them so that they are in order (b)

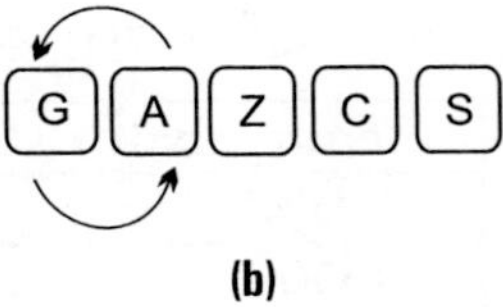

(b)

If you were doing this by hand, you might just pick the blocks to be moved with one in each hand and cross your arms to swap them. Or you might move the first one out of it's position temporarily, move the second one in its place, them move the first one to the now empty position (this is the difference between having a single function to do the swap, or writing some code to do it).

Step 4: Compare the next block in line with the first and repeat step 3. Do this until you run out of blocks. Then begin step one again with the second block. (c,d,e)

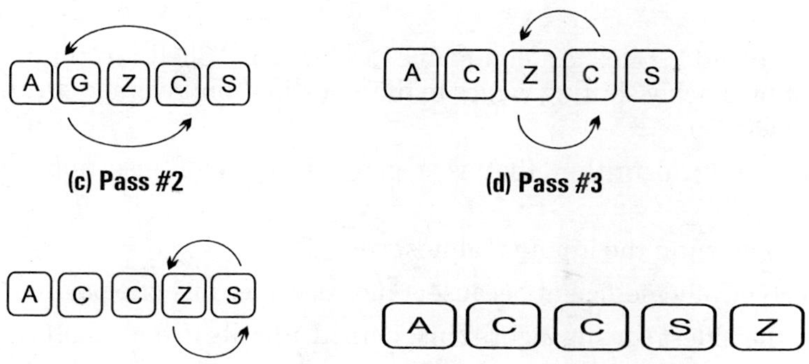

(c) Pass #2 (d) Pass #3

FIGURE 4.36: Bubble Sort.

Example 4.2: Sort {5, 1, 12, -5, 16} using bubble sort.

5	1	12	-5	16	unsorted
5	1	12	-5	16	5 > 1, swap
1	5	12	-5	16	5 < 12, ok
1	5	12	-5	16	12>-5, swap
1	5	-5	12	16	12 > 6, ok
1	5	-5	12	16	1 < 5, ok
1	5	-5	12	16	5 > -5, swap
1	-5	5	12	16	5 < -12, ok
1	-5	5	12	16	1 > -5, swap
-5	1	5	12	16	1 < -5, ok
-5	1	5	12	16	1 < -1, ok
5	1	5	12	16	sorted

FIGURE 4.37: Example of bubble sort.

COMPLEXITY ANALYSIS

Average and worst case complexity of bubble sort is $O(n^2)$. Also, it makes $O(n^2)$ swaps in the worst case. Bubble sort is adaptive. It means that for almost sorted array it gives O(n) estimation. Avoid implementations, which don't check if the array is already sorted on every step (any swaps made). This check is necessary, in order to preserve adaptive property.

4.3.7 SHELL SORT

Shell sort developed by Donald L. Shell is a non-stable in-place sort. Shell sort improves on the efficiency of insertion sort by quickly shifting values to their destination. Average sort time is $\mathbf{O}(n^{7/6})$ while worst-case time is $\mathbf{O}(n^{4/3})$.

Shell sort is a sorting algorithm that is a generalization of insertion sort, with two observations:

- insertion sort is efficient if the input is "almost sorted", and
- insertion sort is typically inefficient because it moves values just one position at a time.

Shellsort is one of the oldest sorting algorithms, named after its inventor D.L. Shell (1959). It is fast, easy to understand and easy to implement. However, its complexity analysis is a little more sophisticated.

The idea of shellsort is the following:

a. arrange the data sequence in a two-dimensional array
b. sort the columns of the array

The effect is that the data sequence is partially sorted. The process above is repeated, but each time with a narrower array, i.e. with a smaller number of columns. In the last step, the array consists of only one column. In each step, the sortedness of the sequence is increased, until in the last step it is completely sorted. However, the number of sorting operations necessary in each step is limited, due to the presortedness of the sequence obtained in the preceding steps.

Example 4.3: Let 3 7 9 0 5 1 6 8 4 2 0 6 1 5 7 3 4 9 8 2 be the data sequence to be sorted. First, it is arranged in an array with 7 columns (left), then the columns are sorted (right):

3	7	9	0	5	1	6
8	4	2	0	6	1	5
7	3	4	9	8	2	

→

3	3	2	0	5	1	5
7	4	4	0	6	1	6
8	7	9	9	8	2	

3	3	2
0	5	1
5	7	4
4	0	6
1	6	8
7	9	9
8	2	

→

0	0	1
1	2	2
3	3	4
4	5	6
5	6	8
7	7	9
8	9	

Data elements 8 and 9 have now already come to the end of the sequence, but a small element (2) is also still there. In the next step, the sequence is arranged in 3 columns, which are again sorted:

Now the sequence is almost completely sorted. When arranging it in one column in the last step, it is only a 6, an 8 and a 9 that have to move a little bit to their correct position.

4.3.8 SELECTION SORT

Selection sort is one of the $O(n^2)$ sorting algorithms, which makes it quite inefficient for sorting large data volumes. Selection sort is notable for its programming simplicity and it can over perform other sorts in certain situations (see complexity analysis for more details).

Selection sort is a sorting algorithm, specifically an in-place comparison sort. It has $O(n^2)$ complexity, making it inefficient on large lists, and generally performs worse than the similar insertion sort. Selection sort is noted for its simplicity, and also has performance advantages over more complicated algorithms in certain situations.

Such algorithms construct the sorted sequence one element at a time by adding elements to the sorted sequence *in order*. At each step, the next element to be added to the sorted sequence is selected from the remaining elements.

Because the elements are added to the sorted sequence in order, they are always added at one end. This is what makes selection sorting different from insertion sorting. In insertion sorting elements are added to the sorted sequence in an arbitrary order. Therefore, the position in the sorted sequence at which each subsequent element is inserted is arbitrary.

Consequently, the sorts are implemented by exchanging array elements. Nevertheless, selection differs from exchange sorting because at each step we *select* the next element of the sorted sequence from the remaining elements and then we move it into its final position in the array by exchanging it with whatever happens to be occupying that position.

The simplest of the selection sorts is called *straight selection* illustrates how straight selection works. In the version shown, the sorted list is constructed from the right (i.e., from the largest to the smallest element values).

At each step of the algorithm, a linear search of the unsorted elements is made in order to determine the position of the largest remaining element. That element is then moved into the correct position of the array by swapping it with the element which currently occupies that position.

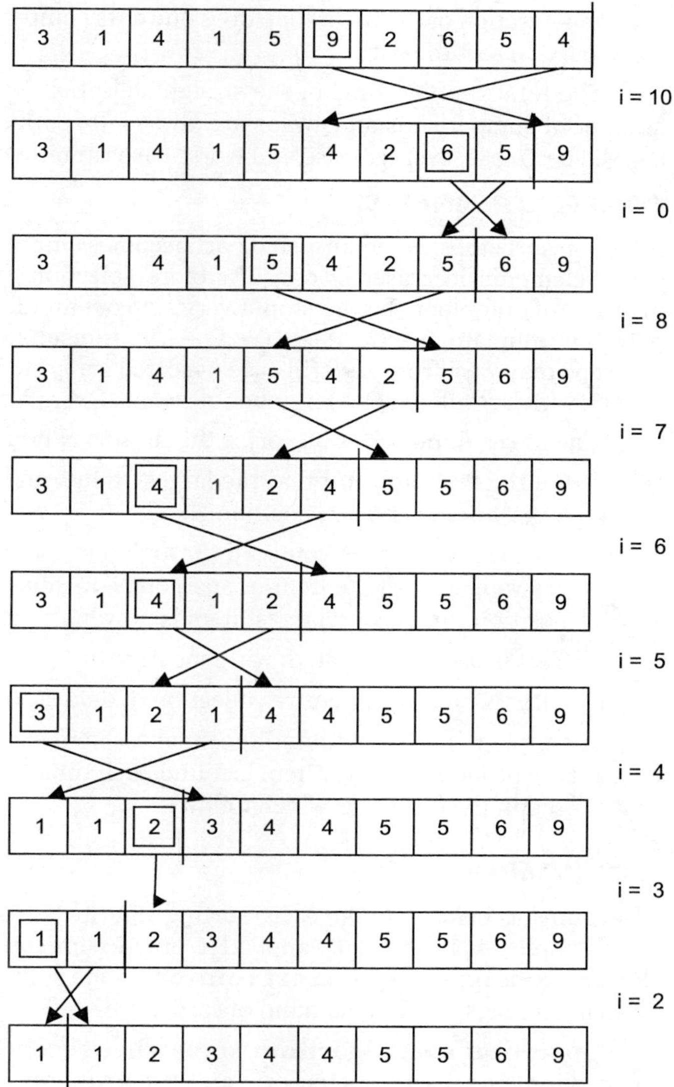

FIGURE 4.38: Straight Selection Sorting.

Example 4.4: In the first step shown in Figure a linear search of the entire array reveals that 9 is the largest element. Since 9 is the largest element, it belongs in the last array position. To move it there, we swap it with the 4 that initially occupies that position. The second step of the algorithm identifies 6 as the largest remaining element an moves it next to the 9. Each subsequent step of the algorithm moves one element into its final position. Therefore, the algorithm is done after n-1 such steps.

In all n-1 iterations of the outer loop are needed to sort the array. Notice that exactly one swap is done in each iteration of the outer loop. Therefore, n-1 data exchanges are needed to sort the list.

Furthermore, in the ith iteration of the outer loop, i-1 iterations of the inner loop are required and each iteration of the inner loop does one data comparison. Therefore, $O(n^2)$ data comparisons are needed to sort the list.

The total running time of the straight selection Do Sort routine is $O(n^2)$. Because the same number of comparisons and swaps are always done, this running time bound applies in all cases. i.e., the best-case, average-case and worst-case running times are all $O(n^2)$.

COMPLEXITY ANALYSIS

Selection sort stops, when unsorted part becomes empty. As we know, on every step number of unsorted elements decreased by one. Therefore, selection sort makes n steps (n is number of elements in array) of outer loop, before stop. Every step of outer loop requires finding minimum in unsorted part. Summing up, n + (n - 1) + (n - 2) + ... + 1, results in $O(n^2)$ number of comparisons. Number of swaps may vary from zero (in case of sorted array) to n - 1 (in case array was sorted in reversed order), which results in O(n) number of swaps. Overall algorithm complexity is $O(n^2)$.

The idea behind selection sort is that to sort N items you make N passes through them.

1. On the first pass you find the largest value, and then swap it with the last item. Thus the largest item is now in position N.
2. On the second pass you scan through just the first N-1 entries. The largest of those items is swapped with the item in position N-1. Hence the largest item overall is now in the last position; the second largest item is now in the second last position.
3. This process is repeated, with one item being placed in its correct location each time.
4. After N passes, the entire collection of data is sorted.

A simple variation is to find the smallest item each time and put it at the front. To sort into descending order, the largest item is found each time and moved to the front (this is the algorithm that is used in the examples which follow).

4.3.9 INSERTION SORT

Insertion sort belongs to the $O(n^2)$ sorting algorithms. Unlike many sorting algorithms with quadratic complexity, it is actually applied in practice for sorting small arrays of data. **For instance, it is used to improve quicksort routine.** Some sources notice, that people use same algorithm ordering items, for example, hand of cards.

Insertion sort algorithm somewhat resembles selection sort. Array is imaginary divided into two parts - sorted one and unsorted one. At the beginning, sorted part contains **first element** of the array and unsorted one contains the rest. At every step, algorithm takes **first element** in the unsorted part and **inserts** it to the right place of the sorted one.

When unsorted part becomes **empty**, algorithm *stops*. Sketchy, insertion sort algorithm step looks like this:

Sorted partitial result		Unsorted dada	
≤ x	> x	x	. . .

becomes

Sorted partitial result			Unsorted Data
≤ x	x	> x	. . .

The idea of the sketch was originally posted here. Let us see an example of insertion sort routine to make the idea of algorithm clearer.

Example 4.5: Sort {7, -5, 2, 16, 4} using insertion sort.

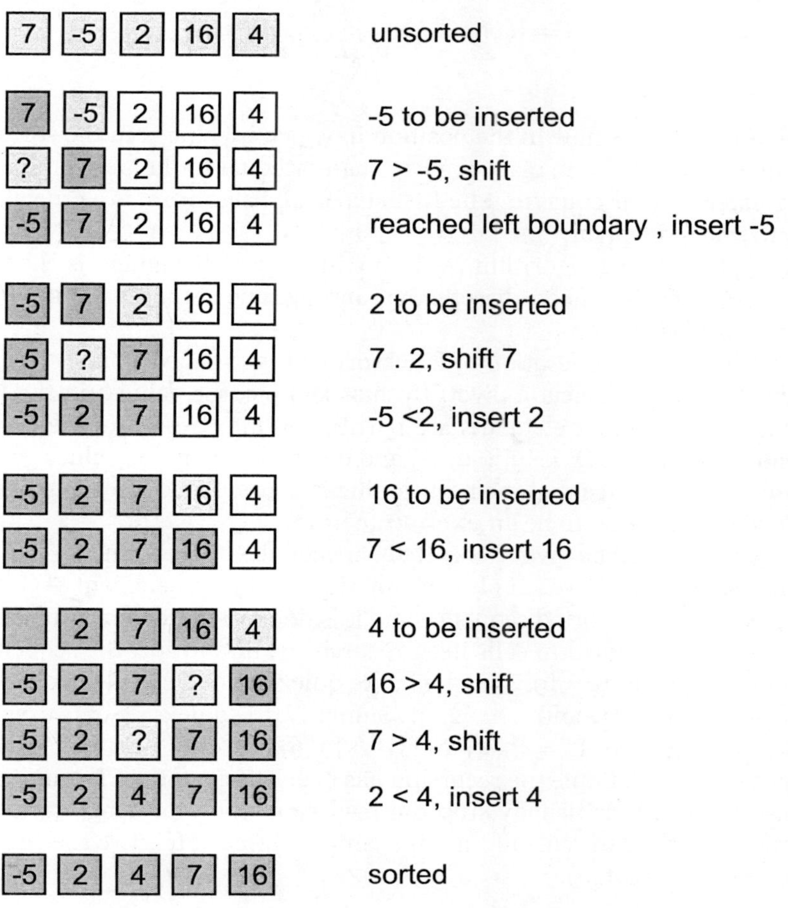

FIGURE 4.39: Example of Insertion Sort.

4.3.10 QUICKSORT

One of the most popular sorting algorithms is Quick Sort. Quick Sort executes in **O**(n lg n) on average, and **O**(n^2) in the worst-case. However, with proper precautions, worst-case behavior is very unlikely. Quick Sort is a non-stable sort. It is not an in-place sort as stack space is required.

Quicksort is a *divide-and-conquer* style algorithm. A divide-and-conquer algorithm solves a given problem by splitting it into two or more smaller subproblems, recursively solving each of the subproblems, and then combining the solutions to the smaller problems to obtain a solution to the original one.

To sort the sequence $S = \{s_0, s_1, s_2, \ldots\ldots, s_n\}$, quicksort performs the following steps:

1. Select one of the elements of S. The selected element, p, is called the *pivot* .
2. Remove p from S and then partition the remaining elements of S into two distinct sequences, L and G, such that every element in L is less than or equal to the pivot and every element in G is greater than or equal to the pivot. In general, both L and G are *unsorted*.
3. Rearrange the elements of the sequence as follows:

$$S' = \{\underbrace{l_1; l_2; \ldots, l_{|L|};}_{L} \underbrace{\; p \;}_{pivot} \underbrace{; g_1; g_2; \ldots; g_{|G|}}_{G}\}$$

Notice that the pivot is now in the position in which it belongs in the sorted sequence, since all the elements to the left of the pivot are less than or equal to the pivot and all the elements to the right are greater than or equal to it.he first step of the algorithm is a crucial one. We have not specified how to select the pivot.

Fortunately, the sorting algorithm works no matter which element is chosen to be the pivot. However, the pivot selection affects directly the running time of the algorithm. If we choose poorly the running time will be poor.

Illustrates the detailed operation of quicksort as it sorts the sequence {3, 1, 4, 1, 5, 9, 2, 6, 5, 4}. To begin the sort, we select a pivot. In this example, the value 4 in the last array position is chosen. Next, the remaining elements are partitioned into two sequences, one which contains values less than or equal to 4 (L = {3, 1, 2, 1}) and one which contains values greater than or equal to 4 (G = {5, 9, 4, 6, 5). Notice that the partitioning is accomplished by exchanging elements. This is why quicksort is considered to be an **exchange sort.**

After the partitioning, the pivot is inserted between the two sequences. This is called *restoring* the pivot. To restore the pivot, we simply exchange it with the first element of G. Notice that the 4 is in its correct position in the sorted sequence and it is not considered any further.

Now the quicksort algorithm calls itself recursively, first to sort the sequence L = {3, 1, 2, 1}; second to sort the sequence G = {9, 4, 6, 5, 5}. The quicksort of L selects 1 as the pivot, and creates the two subsequences L' = {1} and G' = {2, 3}. Similarly, the quicksort of G uses 5 as the pivot and creates the two subsequences L" = {5, 4} and G" = {9, 6}.

At this point in the example the recursion has been stopped. It turns out that to keep the code simple; quicksort algorithms usually stop the recursion when the length of a subsequence falls below a critical value called the cut-off. In this example, the cut-off is two (i.e., a subsequence of two or fewer elements is not sorted).

Example 4.6:

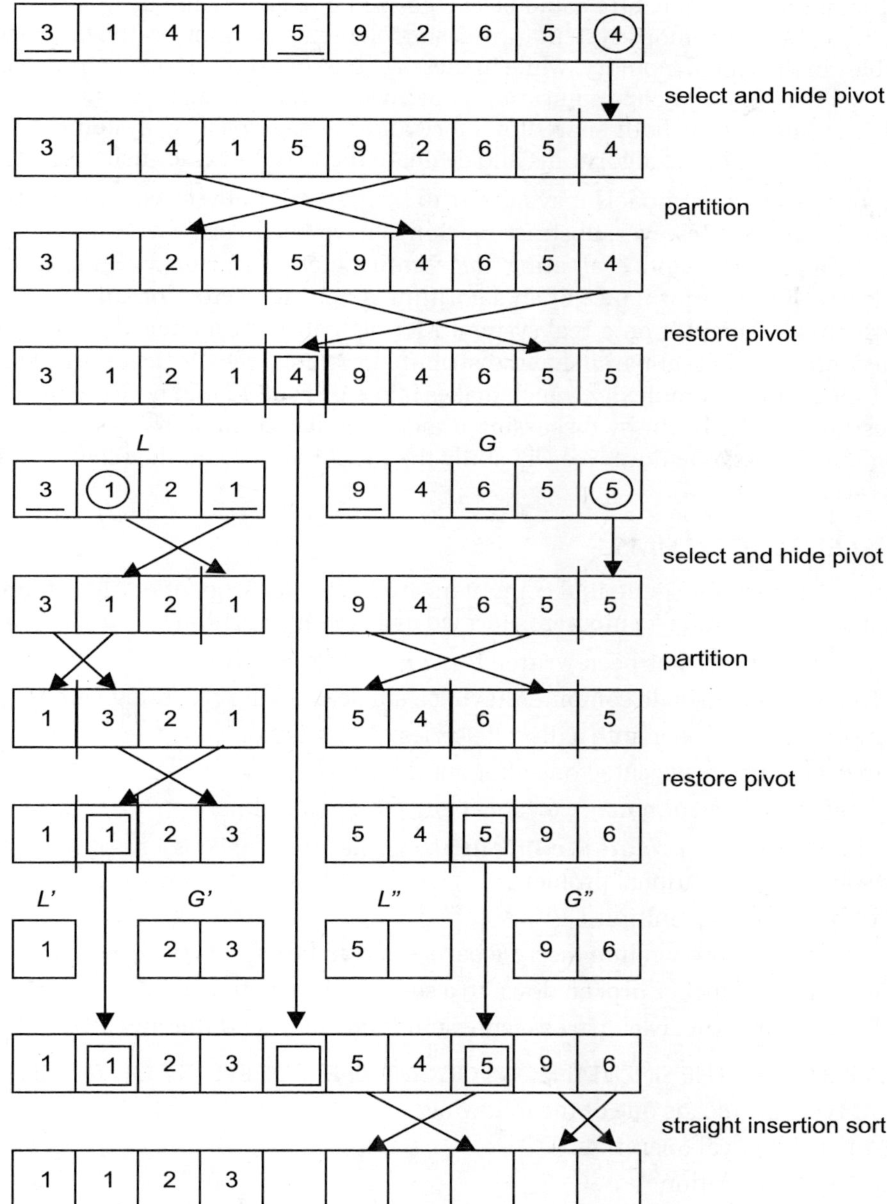

FIGURE 4.40: Quick Sorting

This means that when the algorithm terminates, the sequence is not yet sorted. However as Figure 4.40 shows, the sequence is *almost* sorted. In fact, every element is guaranteed to be less than two positions away from its final resting place. In fact, if we know that every element of the sequence is at most d positions from its final resting place, the running time of straight insertion is O(dn) and since d=2 is a constant, the running time is O(n).

4.4 PRAM MODELS

We learned that parallel architecture could be categorized into shared memory and message passing systems. In a shared memory system, processing elements communicate with each other via shared variables in the global memory, while in message passing systems, each processing element has its own local memory and communication is performed via message passing. In this chapter, we study abstract models for both shared memory and message passing systems. We will study several parallel and distributed algorithms and evaluate their complexities using these models.

At first glance, abstract models may appear to be inappropriate in real-world situations due to their idealistic nature. However, abstract machines have been very useful in studying parallel and distributed algorithms and evaluating their anticipated performance independent of real machines. Clearly, if the performance of an algorithm is not satisfactory on an abstract system, it is meaningless to implement it on a real system. Although abstract models do not consider some practical considerations in real parallel and distributed systems, they focus on the computational aspects of the algorithmic complexity, which makes it less difficult to find performance bounds and complexity estimates. We begin by discussing a model of shared memory systems called PRAM (Parallel Random Access Machine). We will study the PRAM model and the relationships between its different variations.

4.4.1 PARALLEL ALGORITHMS

The Algorithms designed for sequential computers are known as Sequential Algorithms. The algorithm worked out for a parallel computer is termed as Parallel algorithms.

Traditionally, software has been written for ***serial*** computation:

- To be run on a single computer having a single Central Processing Unit (CPU);
- A problem is broken into a discrete series of instructions.
- Instructions are executed one after another.
- Only one instruction may execute at any moment in time.

In the simplest sense, ***parallel computing*** is the simultaneous use of multiple compute resources to solve a computational problem.

- To be run using multiple CPUs.
- A problem is broken into discrete parts that can be solved concurrently.
- Each part is further broken down to a series of instructions.
- Instructions from each part execute simultaneously on different CPUs.

PARALLELISM REFERS TO THE SIMULTANEOUS OCCURRENCE OF EVENTS ON A COMPUTER.

An event typically means one of the following:

- An arithmetical operation
- A logical operation
- Accessing memory
- Performing input or output (I/O)

4.4.2 RANDOM ACCESS MACHINE (RAM)

The basic functional units if the RAM is:

1. A memory unit with M locations. M can be unbounded.

2. A processor that operates under the control of sequential algorithm. The processor can read data from a memory location, write to a memory location, and can perform basic Arithmetic and logical operations.
3. A memory Access unit (MAU) which creates path from the processor to an arbitrary location in the memory.

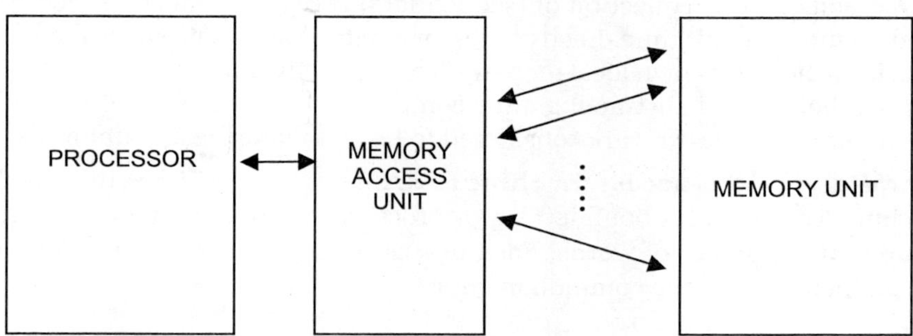

FIGURE 4.41 RAM Model

RAM model consists of three phases namely

- **Read:** The processor reads a datum from the memory. This datum is usually stored in one of its local registers.
- **Write:** The processor writes the content of one register into an arbitrary memory location.
- **Execute:** The processor performs a basic arithmetic and logic operations on the contents of one or two of its registers.

Each PRAM step consists of three phases, executed in the following order:

- A **read phase** in which each processor may read a value from shared memory
- A **compute phase** in which each processor may perform basic arithmetic/logical operations on their local data.
- A **write phase** where each processor may write a value to shared memoNote that this prevents reads and writes from being simultaneous.
- Above requires a PRAM step to be sufficiently long to allow processors to do different arithmetic/logic operations simultaneously.

STRENGTHS OF PRAM MODEL

- PRAM model removes algorithmic details concerning synchronization and communication, allowing designers to focus on problem features
- A PRAM algorithm includes an explicit understanding of the operations to be performed at each time unit and an explicit allocation of processors to jobs at each time unit.
- PRAM design paradigms have turned out to be robust and have been mapped efficiently onto many other parallel models and even network models.

EACH ACTIVE PROCESSOR EXECUTES SAME INSTRUCTION

- Synchronous
- Memory Access

Shared memory computers can be classified as follows depending on whether two or more processors can gain access to the same memory simultaneously.

4.4.3 OVERVIEW OF PRAM

The Parallel Random Access Machine (PRAM) is one of the simplest ways to model a parallel computer. A PRAM consists of a collection of (sequential) processors that can synchronously access a global shared memory in unit time. Each processor can thus access its shared memory as fast (and efficiently) as it can access its own local memory. The main advantages of the PRAM is its simplicity in capturing parallelism and abstracting away communication and synchronization issues related to parallel computing. Processors are considered to be in abundance and unlimited in number.

The **parallel random-access machine (PRAM)** (see Figure 4.42), the canonical structured parallel machine, consists of a bounded set of processors and a common memory containing a potentially unlimited number of words. Each processor is similar to the random-access machine random-access memory and the common memory.

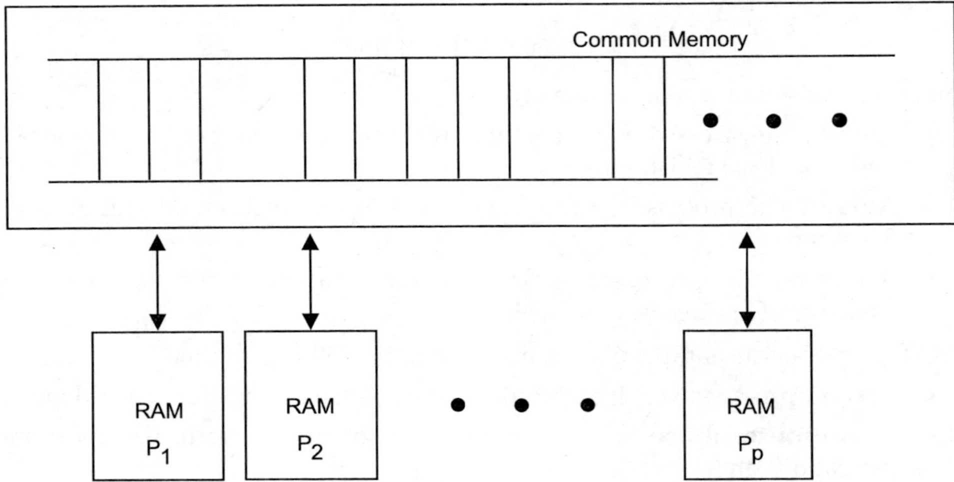

FIGURE 4.42: The PRAM consists of synchronous RAMs accessing a common memory.

The resulting PRAM algorithms thus exhibit unlimited parallelism (number of processors used is a function of problem size). The abstraction thus offered by the PRAM is a fully synchronous collection of processors and a shared memory which makes it popular for parallel algorithm design. It is, however, this abstraction that also makes the PRAM unrealistic from a practical point of view. Full synchronization offered by the PRAM is too expensive and time demanding in parallel machines currently in use. Remote memory (i.e. shared memory) access is considerably more expensive in real machines than local memory access as well. Depending on how concurrent access to a single memory cell (of the shared memory) is resolved, there are various PRAM variants. ER (Exclusive Read) or EW (Exclusive Write) PRAMs do not allow concurrent access of the shared memory. It is allowed, however, for CR (Concurrent Read) or CW (Concurrent Write) PRAMs. Combining the rules for read and writes access there are four PRAM variants: EREW, ERCW, CREW and CRCW PRAMs. Moreover, for CW PRAMs there are various rules that arbitrate how concurrent writes are handled.

(1) In the arbitrary PRAM, if multiple processors write into a single shared memory cell, then an arbitrary processor succeeds in writing into this cell,
(2) In the common PRAM, processors must write the same value into the shared memory cell,
(3) In the priority PRAM the processor with the highest priority (smallest or largest indexed processor) succeeds in writing,
(4) In the combining PRAM if more than one processors write into the same memory cell, the result written into it depends on the combining operator. If it is the sum operator, the sum of the values is written; if it is the maximum operator the maximum is written.

The EREW PRAM is the weakest among the four basic variants. A CREW PRAM can simulate an EREW one. Both can be simulated by the more powerful CRCW PRAM. An algorithm designed for the common PRAM can be executed on a priority or arbitrary PRAM and exhibit similar complexity. The same holds for an arbitrary PRAM algorithm when run on a priority PRAM.

4.4.4 PRAM MODEL OF PARALLEL COMPUTATION

A PRAM consists of a control unit, global memory, and an unbounded set of processors, each with its own private memory. Processors are identified by an index, the value of which can be used to enable or disable the processor or change the memory locations which it can access. Active processors will usually execute identical instructions.

A PRAM computation begins with the input stored in global memory and a single active processing element. In every step of execution, an enabled processor will do either of the following two:

- Activate another processor.
- Read a value from a single private or global memory location, perform a single RAM operation, and write into one local or global memory location.

Every active, enabled processor executes the same instructions (on different memory locations).

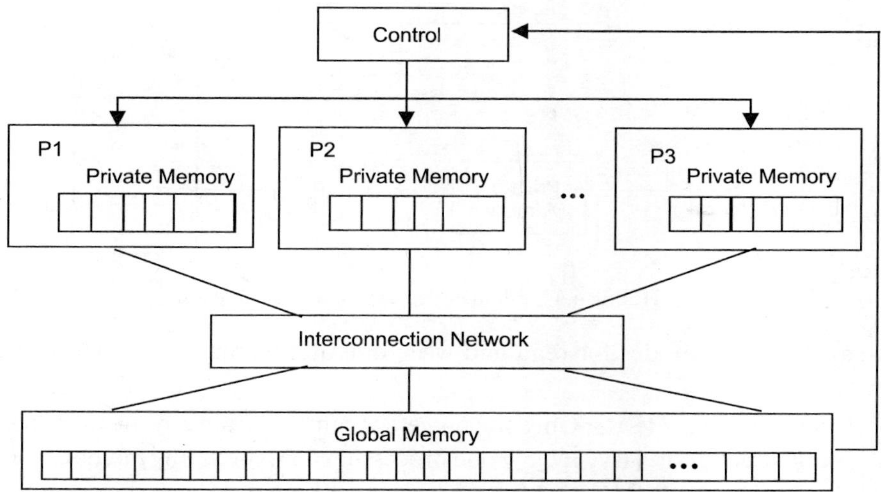

FIGURE 4.43: PRAM model

4.4.5 THE PRAM MODEL AND ITS VARIATIONS

The purpose of the theoretical models for parallel computation is to give frameworks by which we can describe and analyze algorithms. These ideal models are used to obtain performance bounds and complexity estimates. One of the models that have been used extensively is the parallel random access machine (PRAM) model. The PRAM model was introduced by Fortune and Wyllie in 1978 for modeling idealized parallel computers in which communication cost and synchronization overhead are negligible.

A PRAM consists of a control unit, a global memory shared by p processors, each of which has a unique index as follows: P1, P2, . . . , Pp. In addition to the global memory via which the processors can communicate, each processor has its own private memory. Figure 4.44 shows a diagram illustrating the components in the PRAM model.

The p processors operate on a synchronized read, compute, and write cycle. During a computational step, an active processor may read a data value from a memory location, perform a single operation, and finally write back the result into a memory location. Active processors must execute the same instruction, generally, on different data. Hence, this model is sometimes called the shared memory, single instruction, and multiple data (SM SIMD) machine. Algorithms are assumed to run without interference as long as only one memory access is permitted at a time. We say that PRAM guarantees atomic access to data located in shared memory. An operation is considered to be atomic if it is completed in its entirety or it is not performed at all (all or nothing).

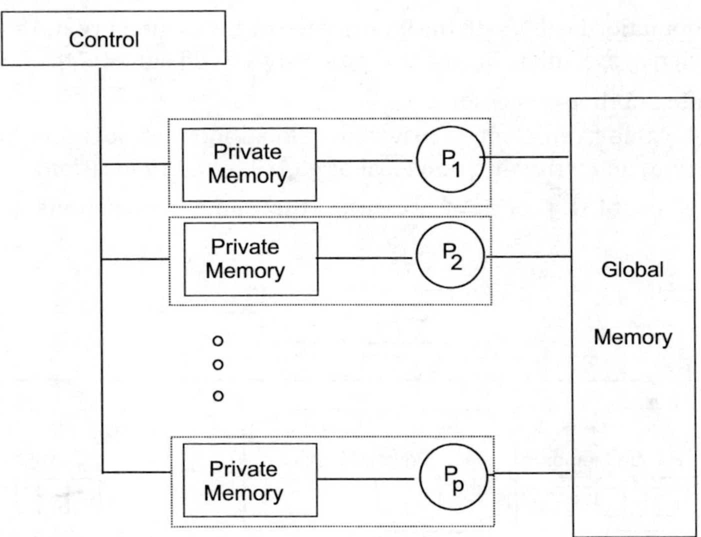

FIGURE 4.44: PRAM model for parallel computations.

There are different modes for read and write operations in a PRAM. These different modes are summarized as follows:

- **Exclusive read (ER):** Only one processor can read from any memory location at a time.
- **Exclusive write (EW):** Only one processor can write to any memory location at a time.
- **Concurrent read (CR):** Multiple processors can read from the same memory location simultaneously.

- **Concurrent write (CW):** Multiple processors can write to the same memory location simultaneously. Write conflicts must be resolved using a well-defined policy such as:

Common: All concurrent writes store the same value.

Arbitrary: Only one value selected arbitrarily is stored. The other values are ignored.

Minimum: The value written by the processor with the smallest index is stored. The other values are ignored.

Reduction: All the values are reduced to only one value using some reduction function such as sum, minimum, maximum, and so on.

Based on the different modes described above, the PRAM can be further divided into the following subclasses:

- **EREW PRAM:** Access to any memory cell is exclusive. This is the most restrictive PRAM model.
- **ERCW PRAM:** This allows concurrent writes to the same memory location by multiple processors, but read accesses remain exclusive.
- **CREW PRAM:** Concurrent read accesses are allowed, but write accesses are exclusive.
- **CRCW PRAM:** Both concurrent read and write accesses are allowed.

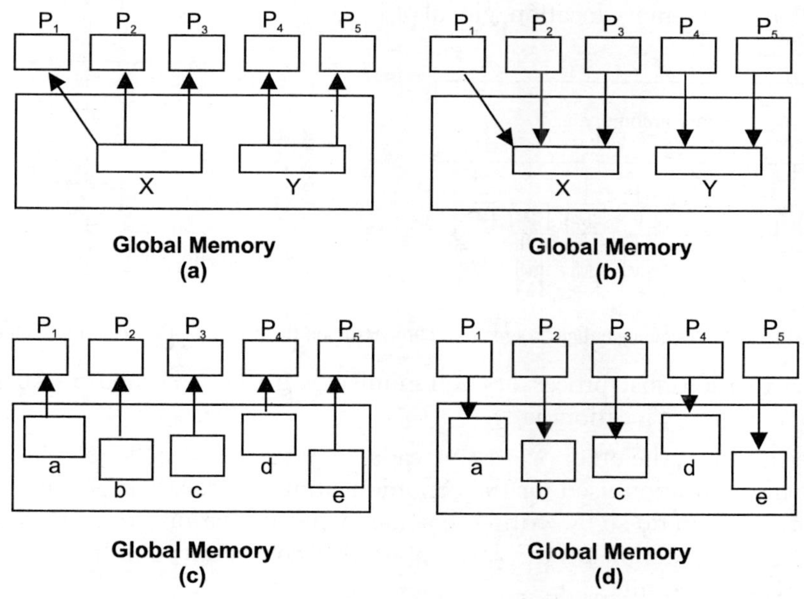

FIGURE 4.45: Computational models for accessing the memory locations regarding read and write operations. (a) Concurrent read. (b) Concurrent write. (c) Exclusive read. (d) Exclusive write.

4.4.6 DESCRIPTION OF THE PRAM MODEL

The PRAM is an idealized parallel machine which was developed as a straightforward generalization of the sequential RAM. Because we will be using it often, we give here a detailed description of it.

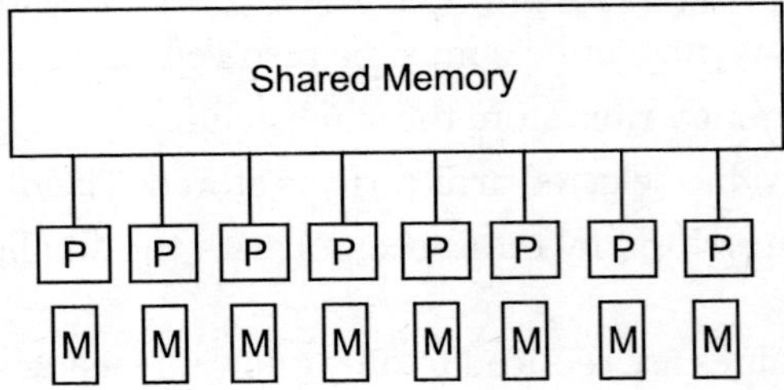

FIGURE 4.46: The PRAM model.

A PRAM uses p identical processors, each one with a distinct id-number, and able to perform the usual computation of a sequential RAM that is equipped with a finite amount of local memory. The processors communicate through some shared global memories (Figure 4.46) to which all are connected. The shared memory contains a finite number of memory cells. There is a global clock that sets the pace of the machine execution. In one *time-unit* period each processor can perform, if so wishes, any or all of the following three steps:

1. **Read** from a memory location, global or local;
2. **Execute** a single RAM operation, and
3. **Write** to a memory location, global or local.

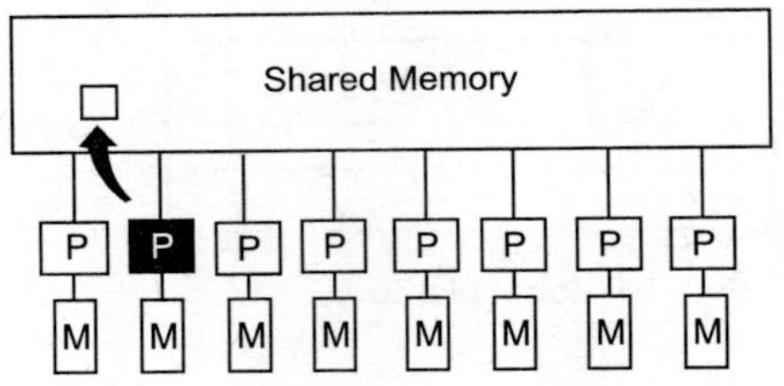

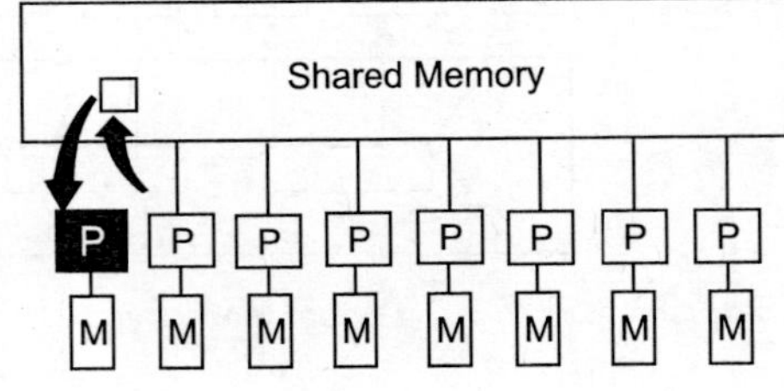

FIGURE 4.47: Communication between two processors in the PRAM model takes two time-units.

Here, the two leftmost processors communicate. In the first step one processor writes a message to some memory location (left).

In the second step, the other processor reads the message. It is the job of the programmer to specify the memory location used for the communication. If processor *pi* wants to communicate with processor *pj*, it can do so by writing to some memory location from which *pj* will read. (See figure 4.47.) So, the model makes the assumption that communication between processors takes constant time (two time-units).

4.4.6.1 AN EXAMPLE: ADDING MATRICES

Let us see how the PRAM works, with a simple example: Adding two matrices *A* and *B* to produce a new matrix *SUM* using a PRAM with p processors. We assume that *A* and *B* have been loaded into the shared memory, and each matrix contains n integers. To make things simple, we also assume that $n \le p$. How the PRAM does perform the addition?

We allocate n consecutive memory locations indexed 1 through n into the shared memory to represent the array *SUM*. We assign one processor per memory location, so that processor with id-number i is assigned to location $SUM[i]$. We can do that since we have enough processors ($p \geq n$). The remaining processors, if any, will remain idle throughout the computation.

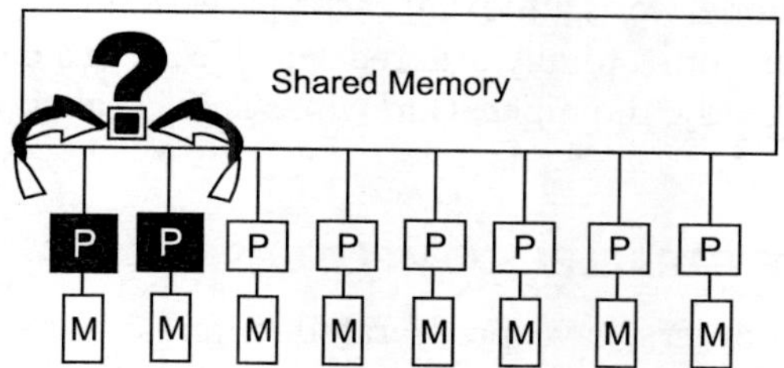

FIGURE 4.48: A conflict occurs when two or more processors try to access the same memory location for reading or writing.

Now, each non-idle processor with id-number i will execute the following three steps:

1. Read $A[i]$ into some register;
2. Read $B[i]$ and add it to the register;
3. Write the contents of the register into $SUM[i]$.

Note that the parallel algorithm we described takes only 3 steps, while a sequential algorithm would take $3n$ steps. Of course, it also uses n processors while the sequential would only use one.

4.4.7 HANDLING CONCURRENT ACCESSES

The fact that the communication between the processors in the PRAM is implemented via accesses to the shared memory makes access conflicts possible. These conflicts may be caused by concurrent accesses to a memory cell by two or more processors for either reading or writing. (See figure 4.48.)

Depending on the way the access of the processors to the global memory is handled, PRAMs are classified as EREW, CREW and CRCW.

EREW: In the exclusive-read-exclusive-write (EREW) PRAM model, no conflicts are permitted for either reading or writing. If, during the execution of a program on this model, some conflict occurs, the program's behavior is undefined.

CREW: In the concurrent-read-exclusive-write (CREW) PRAM model, simultaneous readings by many processors from some memory cell are permitted. However, if a writing conflict occurs, the behavior of the program is undefined. The idea behind this model is that it may be cheap to implement some broadcasting primitive on a real machine, so one needs to examine the usefulness of such a decision.

CRCW: Finally, the concurrent-read-concurrent-write (CRCW) PRAM, the strongest of these models, permits simultaneous accesses for both reading and writing. In the case of multiple processors trying to write to some memory cell, one must define which of the processors eventually does the writing. There are several answers that researchers have given to this question. The most commonly used are:

COMMON: All processors attempting to write to a memory location must write the same value, so the outcome of some writing is the same, no matter which processor wins. This is called the COMMON CRCW PRAM model.

ARBITRARY: Any processor may win. No restriction is placed on the values written. This is called the ARBITRARY CRCW PRAM. Note that, if the program runs a second time, the outcome of a concurrent writing may be different. However, the outcome of the computation in *every* case must be correct.

PRIORITY: In this model we assume that each processor has some unique value *id* associated with it, the *id*'s being drawn from a totally ordered set. In case of a concurrent write, the processor with the lowest (or, equivalently, the highest) *id* wins. This is called the PRIORITY CRCW PRAM model.

4.4.8 ALGORITHMS FOR PARALLEL COMPUTERS

As parallel-processing computers have proliferated, interest has increased in ***parallel algorithms:*** algorithms that perform more than one operation at a time. The study of parallel algorithms has now developed into a research area in its own right. Indeed, parallel algorithms have been developed for many of the problems we have solved in this text using ordinary serial algorithms. In this chapter, we shall describe a few simple parallel algorithms that illustrate fundamental issues and techniques.

In order to study parallel algorithms, we must choose an appropriate model for parallel computing. The random-access machine, or RAM, which we have used throughout most of this book, is, of course, serial rather than parallel. The parallel algorithms in this section are presented in terms of one popular theoretical model: the parallel random-access machine or PRAM (pronounced "PEE-ram"). Many parallel algorithms for arrays, lists, trees, and graphs can be easily described in the PRAM model. Although the PRAM ignores many important aspects of real parallel machines, the essential attributes of parallel algorithms tend to transcend the models for which they are designed. If one PRAM algorithm outperforms another PRAM algorithm, the relative performance is not likely to change substantially when both algorithms are adapted to run on a real parallel computer.

4.4.9 ARCHITECTURE OF THE PRAM MODEL

Figure 4.49 shows the basic architecture of the ***parallel random-access machine (PRAM)***. There are p ordinary (serial) processors $P_0, P_1, \ldots, P_{p-1}$ that have as storage a shared, global memory. All processors can read from or write to the global memory "in parallel" (at the same time). The processors can also perform various arithmetic and logical operations in parallel.

The key assumption regarding algorithmic performance in the PRAM model is that running time can be measured as the number of parallel memory accesses an algorithm performs. This assumption is a straight- forward generalization of the ordinary RAM model, in which the number of memory accesses is asymptotically as good as any other measure of running time. This simple assumption will serve us well in our survey of parallel algorithms, even though real parallel computers cannot perform parallel accesses to global memory in unit time: the time for a memory access grows with the number of processors in the parallel computer.

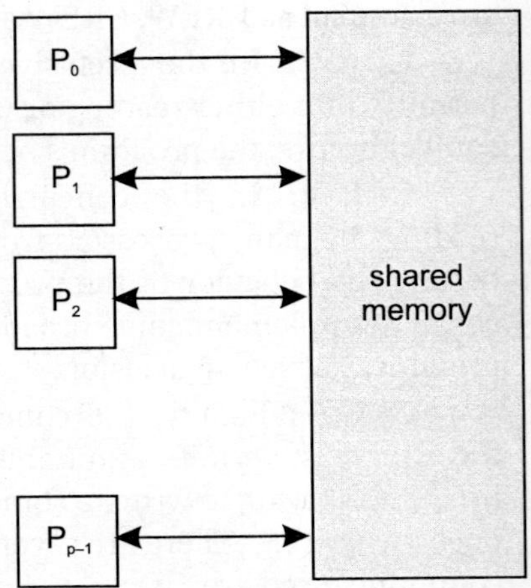

FIGURE 4.49: The basic architecture of the PRAM. There are p processors $P_0, P_1, \ldots, P_{p-1}$ connected to a shared memory. Each processor can access an arbitrary word of shared memory in unit time.

Nevertheless, for parallel algorithms that access data in an arbitrary fashion, the assumption of unit-time memory operations can be justified. Real parallel machines typically have a communication network that can support the abstraction of a global memory. Accessing data through the network is a relatively slow operation in comparison with arithmetic and other operations. Thus, counting the number of parallel memory accesses executed by two parallel algorithms does, in fact, yield a fairly accurate estimate of their relative performances. The principal way in which real machines violate the unit-time abstraction of the PRAM is that some memory-access patterns are faster than others. As a first approximation, however, the unit-time assumption in the PRAM model is quite reasonable.

The running time of a parallel algorithm depends on the number of processors executing the algorithm as well as the size of the problem input. Generally, therefore, we must discuss both time and processor count when analyzing PRAM algorithms; this contrasts with serial algorithms, in whose analysis we have focused mainly on time. Typically, there is a trade-off between the number of processors used by an algorithm and its running time.

4.4.10 CONCURRENT VERSUS EXCLUSIVE MEMORY ACCESSES

A ***concurrent-read*** algorithm is a PRAM algorithm during whose execution multiple processors can read from the same location of shared memory at the same time. An ***exclusive-read*** algorithm is a PRAM algorithm in which no two processors ever read the same memory location at the same time. We make a similar distinction with respect to whether or not multiple processors can write into the same memory location at the same time, dividing PRAM algorithms into ***concurrent-write*** and ***exclusive-write*** algorithms. Commonly used abbreviations for the types of algorithms we encounter are

- **EREW:** exclusive read and exclusive write,
- **CREW:** concurrent read and exclusive write,
- **ERCW:** exclusive read and concurrent write, and
- **CRCW:** concurrent read and concurrent write.

(These abbreviations are usually pronounced not as words but rather as strings of letters.)

Of these types of algorithms, the extremes--EREW and CRCW--are the most popular. A PRAM that supports only EREW algorithms is called an ***EREW PRAM***, and one that supports CRCW algorithms is called a ***CRCW PRAM***. A CRCW PRAM can, of course, execute EREW algorithms, but an EREW PRAM cannot directly support the concurrent memory accesses required in CRCW algorithms. The underlying hardware of an EREW PRAM is relatively simple, and therefore fast, because it needn't handle conflicting memory reads and writes. A CRCW PRAM requires more hardware support if the unit-time assumption is to provide a reasonably accurate measure of algorithmic performance, but it provides a programming model that is arguably more straightforward than that of an EREW PRAM.

Of the remaining two algorithmic types--CREW and ERCW--more attention has been paid in the literature to the CREW. From a practical point of view, however, supporting concurrency for writes is no harder than supporting concurrency for reads. In this chapter, we shall generally treat an algorithm as being CRCW if it contains either concurrent reads or concurrent writes, without making further distinctions.

When multiple processors write to the same location in a CRCW algorithm, the effect of the parallel write is not well defined without additional elaboration. In this chapter, we shall use the

common-CRCW model: when several processors write into the same memory location, they must all write a common (the same) value. There are several alternative types of PRAM's in the literature that handle this problem with a different assumption. Other choices include

- ***arbitrary:*** an arbitrary value from among those written is actually stored,
- ***priority:*** the value written by the lowest-indexed processor is stored, and
- ***combining:*** the value stored is some specified combination of the vaIn the last case, the specified combination is typically some associative and commutative function such as addition (store the sum of all the values written) or maximum (store only the maximum value written).

4.4.11 SYNCHRONIZATION AND CONTROL

PRAM algorithms must be highly synchronized to work correctly. How is this synchronization achieved? Also, the processors in PRAM algorithms must often detect termination of loop conditions that depend on the state of all processors. How is this control function implemented?

We won't discuss these issues extensively. Many real parallel computers employ a control network connecting the processors that helps with synchronization and termination conditions. Typically, the control network can implement these functions as fast as a routing network can implement global memory references.

For our purposes, it suffices to assume that the processors are inherently tightly synchronized. All processors execute the same statements at the same time. No processor races ahead while others are further back in the code. As we go through our first parallel algorithm, we shall point out where we assume that processors are synchronized.

For detecting the termination of a parallel loop that depends on the state of all processors, we shall assume that a parallel termination condition can be tested through the control network in $O(1)$ time. Some EREW PRAM models in the literature do not make this assumption, and the (logarithmic) time for testing the loop condition must be included in the overall running time. CRCW PRAM's do not need a control network to test termination: they can detect termination of a parallel loop in O(1) time through the use of concurrent writes.

4.4.11.1 SIMULATING TREES, ARRAYS, AND HYPERCUBES ON THE PRAM

We have shown that 1D array can be embedded into 2D meshes and that d-dimensional mesh can be embedded into hypercubes while preserving the neighborhood structure of the first graph in the second. Also, we have demonstrated that any balanced tree algorithm can be simulated as a normal algorithm on a hypercube. As a consequence, in each case, an algorithm designed for the first network carries over to the second without any increase in the number of steps executed. We now show that normal hypercube algorithms are efficiently simulated on an EREW PRAM.

With each d-dimensional hypercube processor, associate an EREW PRAM processor and a reserved location in the common memory. In a normal algorithm each hypercube processor communicates with its neighbor along a specified direction. To simulate this communication, each associated PRAM processor writes the data to be communicated into its reserved location.

The processor for which the message is destined knows which hypercube neighbor is providing the data and reads the value stored in its associated memory location. When a hypercube algorithm is not normal, as many as d−1 neighbors can send messages to one processor. Since EREW PRAM processors can access only one cell per unit time, simulation of the hypercube can require a running time that is about d times that of the hypercube.

4.4.11.2 THE POWER OF CONCURRENCY

The CRCW PRAM is a very powerful model. As we show, any Boolean function can be computed with it in a constant number of steps if a sufficient number of processors are available. For this reason, the CRCW PRAM is of limited interest: it represents an extreme that does not reflect reality as we know it. The CREW and EREW PRAMs are more realistic. We first explore the power of the CRCW and then show that an EREW PRAM can simulate a p-processor CRCW PRAM with a slowdown by a factor of O(log2 p).

4.4.11.3 SIMULATING THE PRAM ON A HYPERCUBE NETWORK

As stated above, each PRAM cycle involves reading from the global memory, performing a local computation, and writing to the common memory. Of course, a processor need not access common memory when given the chance. Thus, to simulate a PRAM on a network computer, one has to take into account the fact that not all PRAM processors necessarily read from or write to common memory locations on each cycle. It is important to remember that the latency of network computers can be large. Thus, for the simulation described below to be useful, each PRAM processor must be able to do a lot of work between network accesses.

The EREW PRAM is simulated on a network computer by executing three phases, two of which correspond to reading and writing common memory. (To simulate the CRCWPRAM, we need only add the time given above to simulate a CRCW PRAM by an EREW PRAM.) We simulate an access to common memory by routing a message over the network to the site containing the simulated common memory location. It follows that a message must contain the name of a site as well as the address of a memory location at that site. If the simulated access is a memory read, a return message is generated containing the value of the memory location. If it is a memory write, the transmitted message must also contain the datum to write into the memory location. We assume that the sites are numbered consecutively from 1 to p, the number of processors.

The first problem to be solved is the routing of messages from source to destination processors. The new wrinkle here is that the mapping from source to destination sites defined by a set of messages is not necessarily a permutation. Not all sources may send a message and not all destinations are guaranteed to receive only one message. In fact, some destination may be sent many messages, which can result in their waiting a long time for receipt.

To develop an appreciation for the various approaches to this problem, we describe an algorithm that distributes messages from sources to destinations, though not as efficiently as possible. Each processor prepares a message to be sent to other processors. Processors not accessing the common memory send messages containing dummy site addresses larger than any other address. All messages are sorted by destination address cooperatively by the processors. It can be sorted by a normal algorithm on an p-vertex hypercube, p = 2d, in O(log2 p) steps using Batcher's bitonic sorting network. The k ≤ p non-dummy messages are the first k messages in this sorted list. If the sites at which these messages reside after sorting are the sites for which they were destined, the message routing problem is solved. Unfortunately, this is generally not the case. To route the messages from their positions in the sorted list to their destinations, we first identify duplicates of destination addresses and compute D, the maximum number of duplicates. We then route messages in D stages. In each stage at most one of the D duplicates of each message is routed to its destination. To identify duplicates, we assign a processor to each message in the sorted list that compares its destination site with that of its predecessor, setting a flag bit to 0 if equal and to 1 otherwise. To compare destinations, move messages to adjacent vertices on the hypercube, compare, and then reverse the process. (Move them by sorting by appropriate addresses.) The first processor also sets its flag bit to 1. A segmented integer addition prefix operation that segments its messages with these flag bits assigns to each message an integer (a **priority**) between 1 and D that is q if the site address of this message is the qth such address. (Prefix computations can be done on a p-vertex hypercube in O(log p) steps.) A message with priority q is routed to its destination in the qth stage.

An unsegmented prefix operation with max as the operator is then used to determine D. In the qth stage, $1 \le q \le D$, all non-dummy messages with priority q are routed to their destination site on the hypercube as follows:

a) one processor is assigned to each message;
b) each such processor computes the **gap**, the difference between the destination and current site of its message;
c) each gap g is represented as a binary d-tuple g = (gd−1, . . . , g0);
d) For t = d − 1, d − 2, . . . , 0, those messages whose gap contains 2t are sent to the site reached by crossing the tth dimension of the hypercube.

We show that in at most O(Dlog p) steps all messages are routed to their destinations.

Let the sorted message sites form an ascending sequence. If there are k non-dummy messages, let gapi, $0 \le i \le k - 1$, be the gap of the ith message. Observe that these gaps must also form a nondecreasing sequence. For example, shown below is a sorted set of destinations and a corresponding sequence of gaps:

gap_i	1	1	2	2	3	6	7	8							
$dest_i$	1	2	4	5	7	11	13	15							
i	0	1	2	3	4	5	6	7	8	9	10	11	12	13	15

All the messages whose gaps contain 2d−1 must be the last messages in the sequence because the gaps would otherwise be out of order. Thus, advancing messages with these gaps by 2d−1 positions, which is done by moving them across the largest dimension of the hypercube, advances them to positions in the sequence that cannot be occupied by any other messages, even after these messages have been advanced by their full gaps. For example, shown below are the positions of the messages given above after those whose gaps contain 8 and 4 have been moved by this many positions:

$dest_i$	1	2	4	5	7					11	13				15
i	0	1	2	3	4	5	6	7	8	9	10	11	12	13	15

Repeating this argument on subsequent smaller powers of 2, we find that no two messages that are routed in a given stage occupy the same site. As a consequence, after D stages, each taking d steps, all messages are routed.

4.4.11.4 CIRCUITS AND THE CREW PRAM

Algebraic and logic circuits can also be simulated on PRAMs, in particular the CREWPRAM. For simplicity we assign one processor to each vertex of a circuit (a gate). We also assume that each vertex has bounded fan-in, which for concreteness is assumed to be 2. We also reserve one memory location for each gate and one for each input variable. Each processor now alternates between reading values from its two inputs (concurrently with other processors, if necessary) and exclusively writing values to the location reserved for its value. Two steps are devoted to reading the values of gate inputs. Let D(f) be the depth of the circuit for a function f. After 2D(f) steps the input values have propagated to the output gates, the values computed by them are correct and the computation is complete. We show a stronger result, that CREW PRAMs and circuits are equivalent as language recognizers. We also explore the parallel computation thesis, which states that sequential space and parallel time are polynomially related. It follows that the PRAM and the logic circuit are both excellent models in terms of which to measure the minimal computation time required for a problem on a parallel machine. We exhibit complexity classes, that is, classes of languages defined in terms of the depth of circuits recognizing them.

4.4.12 PROBLEMS OF PRAM IMPLEMENTATION

We have identified two key difficulties in PRAM implementation:

- *Global fine-grained synchronisation*
- *Uniform global concurrent shared-memory access time*

4.4.12.1 SYNCHRONISATION

Realistic parallel architectures involve multiple processors being connecting by fixed-degree networks (or Bounded Degree Networks - BDN).

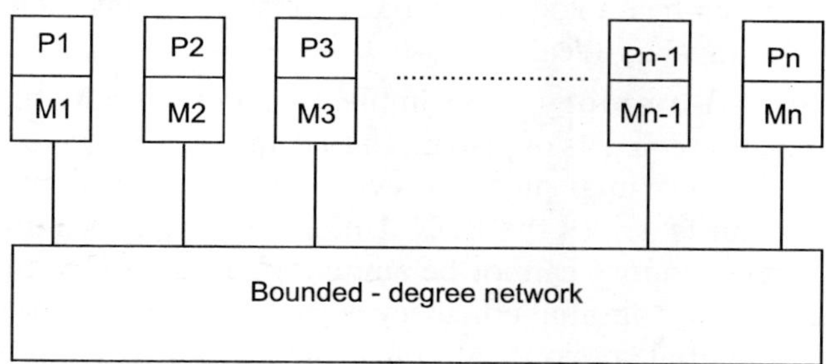

FIGURE 4.50: The Bounded Degree Network.

This means that each node is connected to a finite number of neighbours. At best O(log n) (proportional to the diameter of the network) routing time can be achieved. Global fine-grained synchronisation requires every processor to execute a single-step before stopping to wait for other processors to complete - thus a processor executing step n+1 is guaranteed that all other processors have completed step n. The programmer can thus be assured that data-dependencies between successive instructions on different processors will be maintained. Specifically, a multiprocessor system is said to be sequentially consistent if

"The result of any execution (of the program) is the same as if the operations of all the processors were executed in some sequential order and the operations of each individual processor appear in the sequence in the order specified by its program."[Lamport 1979]

The message to continue will take at least O(log n) time to propagate. Thus as n increases the ratio of arithmetic instruction execution time to synchronisation time decreases. For large n such a machine is inefficient. The programmer will favour a more realistic and efficient model over the PRAM. Consequently, more practical variations on the PRAM model have been developed.

4.4.12.2 GLOBAL CONCURRENT SHARED-MEMORY

Following are the global concurrent shared-memory:

(i) Concurrent Memory Access: Large-scale multi-ported memories are prohibitively expensive at the moment. However an EREW PRAM can simulate a CRCW variant with some slowdown O(log n). Memory requests are sorted by address first followed by processor. Concurrent accesses are eliminated according to access method i.e. ARBITRARY randomly selects a value and eliminates the others; COMMON checks that all values are the same; PRIORITY takes the highest (lowest) processor number; COMBINE merges all values according to the algebraic manipulation into a single written value. This mergesort can be performed in O(log n) using binary trees with log n depth. Reads are performed by reversing the tree into a fan-out structure.

The O(log n) slowdown invalidates the at-first-sight infeasibly fast CRCW results. However optical computing technology might yet yield constant time concurrent access architecture.

(ii) An Optical Solution: [Fietelson 1988] suggests that holograms or lenslet arrays may duplicate data elements while photodetectors can integrate the light falling on them. The former allow *duplicate* writes and concurrent reads while the latter enable summing concurrent writes. However these techniques effectively make it analog computing which can cause inaccuracies, hence limiting the fan-in and the range of values. A digital binary system could be implemented which would ameliorate this but would lead to a multi-step solution. However the number of steps would at least be proportional to the required accuracy rather than the number of inputs being summed. Unfortunately this technology is still at a very early stage and single step concurrent access is yet to be proven on a large scale.

(iii) Virtual shared-memory*:* The implementation of a virtual shared-memory on a distributed memory machine consists of placing shared-memory into memory modules, equipping each processor with an address map such that every global address can be resolved to a module and then routing the requests across the BDN. Unfortunately, by definition, the bandwidth of a BDN is restricted. Shared-memory cannot be simulated on a BDN while still retaining optimal efficiency [Kruskal et al 1990] (optimal efficiency is where the time-processor product is within a constant ratio of the sequential version). Although the latency from the routing delay across the network can be hidden with parallel slackness (multiple PRAM processors are simulated on one physical simulating processor), network congestion delays cannot. If requests are initiated at times 0 and 1 then a network delay of L will lead to replies in L and L+1 but if the delay L is caused by congestion then the replies will come in L and 2L time. However while memory requests are limited in number contention can be restricted using hashing. Universal hashing functions guarantee that the probability of placing two distinct shared-memory addresses onto the same module is proportional to the number of modules squared. This result is further extended for log n-wise independent hashing functions that guarantee the queue size at a given module is no greater than log n. The chosen hash function is used to place the memory locations across memory modules. If the queue size is found to be too large during the simulation then a different hash function is chosen and the memory is rehashed. This can take some time but the probability of rehashing is low and decreases asymptotically as the length of the simulation increases.

(iv) Caches: Alternatively shared-memory machines can be constructed with a shared bus connection to a global memory. Contention on the bus will increase with the number of processors. Caches are placed between the processors and the shared-memory to reduce this contention. Sparse interconnection networks are also proposed to reduce contention. Unfortunately this increases the coherency problem. If multiple copies are distributed amongst the processors a write to the same location has to invalidate them all. Coherency strategies have been evolved to cope with this problem.

Snooping could be used on the bus where each processor invalidated or updated cache entries when a write was seen on the shared bus. In a large multi-processor system the shared bus becomes a bottleneck and so the snooping strategy is not used beyond a few processors. With a sparse network either a *directory* of cached locations is maintained such that writes are propagated to each copy or *compilers* detect data dependencies and automatically invalidate cached copies. With the directory scheme, processors must communicate with a common directory whenever an inconsistency may occur between caches and memory. The processor involved requests mutually exclusive access to the directory writes the new value of the cached item, updates the directory, releases mutual exclusion, and then the new value is passed to all the affected caches. The compiler coherence method inserts instructions into the object code at compile time in portions of the code where the compiler anticipates a value becoming 'stale'. The choice of cache coherence method depends on the task to be executed. The directory method may perform better under certain conditions than the compilers method and *vice-versa*. Large cache block sizes exploit spatial locality, but may further increase contention as a whole since a write to a location in the cache line requires invalidation of the whole line.

Caching and hashing are two different approaches to the same goal of implementing shared-memory. Caching seeks to exploit locality to reduce access time while hashing destroys the locality in an attempt to reduce the worst-case access time. It remains to be seen which is superior or whether a combination is possible.

4.4.13 PRAM HARDWARE IMPLEMENTATION

Although a number of simulations of PRAMs have been undertaken on real distributed machines until recently there was no hardware implementation. The Universistat des Saarlandes at Saarbrucken in Germany is in the process of changing that. They have taken the Fluent Machine architecture of Ranade and streamlined it, improving the slowdown constant by a claimed factor of 5. The Fluent machine implements a butterfly (see diagram (butterfly with n=3) below) routing network with distributed memory and RISC processors at each node. Unfortunately the results are not yet available. The theoretical appraisal actually claims that some applications run faster than a message passing implementation. This is probably due to the hardware support for parallel constructs such as multiprefix and synchronisation. A *Multiprefix* operation is executed by a group of processors on a single memory location. The combined operation result is written into the memory location while each processor is returned the result of the operations performed by processors with a lower index number. For instance, synchronisation is performed with MP A,+,1. If four processors were to synchronise a BSP superstep location A would go from an initialised value of 0 to the number of processors, 4. Processor 1 would be returned 1, number 2 would be given 2, and so on. Once a processor has finished then MP,A,-,1 is performed. In order to ensure that location A is not written and read simultaneously the Saarbrucken prototype restricts reads to even numbered processor instruction cycles and writes to odd cycles. Once A returns to 0 the processors can consider their BSP superstep complete. Most commercially available machines use caches together with a deterministic memory placement. A comparison of the Saarbrucken prototype with such machines will provide vital information on the validity of the hashing approach when applied to real machnes.

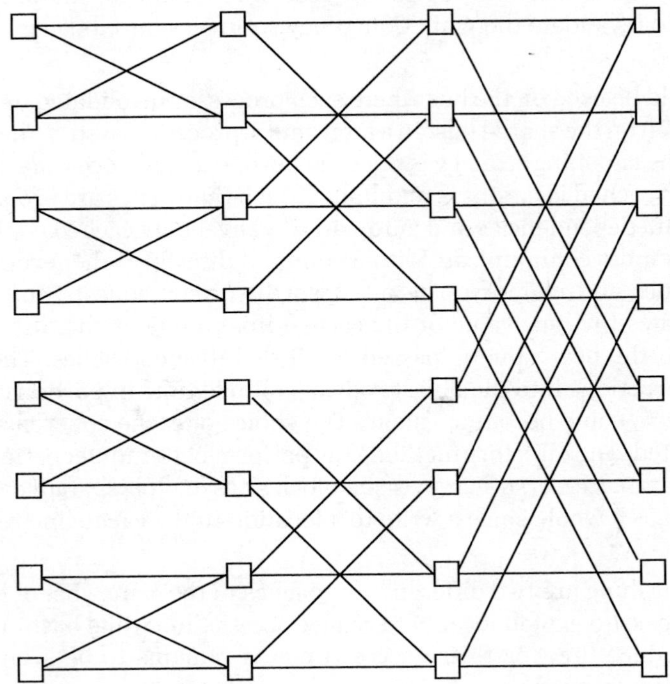

FIGURE 4.51: Butterfly network of degree n=3

4.4.14 MORE REALISTIC PRAMS

In order to make the PRAM more practical, variations on the basic model have been suggested:

4.4.14.1 APRAM

The Asynchronous PRAM aims to overcome the problems introduced by global fine grained synchronisation. Realistic, massively parallel machines must be asynchronous, and so algorithms should be designed for an asynchronous model. Real machines cannot efficiently support the synchrony required by the PRAM because explicit synchronisation induces serious performance penalties. Hence, the more practical asynchronous PRAM (APRAM). The argument for asynchrony is clear: in order to effectively support a large number of processors, multiple users, and multiple instruction streams, the model must permit each processor to execute its instructions independently of the other processors. The pure PRAM model does not allow for this.

The APRAM consists of a collection of processors each with its own local memory and interprocessor communication is through shared global shared memory (as in the PRAM). The individual processors of the APRAM operate asynchronously and no assumption is made by any one of the processors on where another processor is in its program execution. The APRAM can issue one of four instruction types in a time step:

- Global read: read the contents of a shared memory location into local memory;
- Local operation: any RAM operation on local memory only;

- Global writes: writing the contents of a local memory location into a shared memory location;
- Synchronisation: determines a logical point in the computation where each processor waits for all the processors to arrive before continuing the local program.

In addition to being asynchronous, APRAMs differ from PRAMs in that there is an explicit cost for synchronisation. Synchronisation is required to resolve conflicting memory accesses. [Gibbons 90] proposes a novel way to minimise synchronisation costs that uses a 'simple' shared write-through cache policy. The method defines a synchronised read operation which places a value into private memory after a successful read from a shared memory location. The read is supported at the shared cache level in that no access is actually needed to a global shared memory location. The first set of processors places a return address in the cache line, and when the second set of processors arrives a reply is sent to each member of the first set. If a cache collision occurs the first set is dropped from the cache and is told to re-issue the synchronised read instruction. The method ensures that delays are minimised when no collisions occur and unmatched synchronisation accesses do not block the cache line.

4.4.14.2 LPRAM

The LPRAM extends the PRAM by allowing for local memory. This models caching more accurately. The authors in the references do define the PRAM differently. Some allow for local memory as part of the RAM definition of registers and hence local operations on data. Although there is a broad agreement that strictly speaking a PRAM with local memory would then require either some coherency mechanism or care on the part of the programmer not to use stale data which the PRAM model is intended to prevent. Thus the LPRAM explicitly provides for local memory and hence a more realistic approach to locality.

4.4.14.3 BLOCK PRAM

The Block PRAM further extends the LPRAM notion of locality by adding a time penalty l for shared-memory access latency. A block can be read in l + b. There is unbounded shared memory as well as unbounded local memory. The access mechanism is EREW. The Block PRAM takes no account of network topology.

4.4.14.4 BSP

The bulk-synchronous parallel computer (BSPC) is proposed by Valiant as a bridging model between hardware and software for general purpose parallel computing that the von Neumann model provides for sequential processing. In some ways it can be seen as a combination of the Asynchronous PRAM and the Block PRAM. The BSPC is defined as the combination of 3 attributes:

1. A number (p) of components providing memory or processing.
2. A router that delivers messages point-to-point between pairs of components
3. Synchronisation facilities that enable a subset of components to perform super-steps consisting of L (called the periodicity parameter) time units. At the end of each super-step a global check is made to ensure that all components have completed their super-steps consisting of local computations and message deliveries. It can be regarded as a measure of programmability since simultaneous super-steps must not have data dependencies. It relaxes the stringent synchronisation requirement of the PRAM model (equivalent to an L of 1) that we have seen is difficult to achieve in practice.

Another parameter g is introduced that measures the communications granularity. It is defined as the ratio of the total number of computations per second to the total number of words delivered by the router per second. Again g provides an indication of how close a routing system gets to the ideal PRAM model which is equivalent to a g value of 1.

BSP improves upon the PRAM model by providing quantitative measures of the quality of the routing system. As a good bridging model it does not dictate implementation details but shows that optimal efficiency can still be achieved given that the parameters g, L and p are within certain bounds. For instance matrix multiplication needs g=O(n/ p^1/2) and L=O(n^3 /p).

4.5 INTERCONNECTION RAM NETWORKS

Multiprocessors interconnection RAM networks (INs) can be classified based on a number of criteria. Interconnection networks helps in sharing resources, one is between the processor and the memory modules and the other between the processor and the I/O Systems. There are different physical forms available for interconnection networks. These include:

(1) Mode of operation (synchronous versus asynchronous),

(2) Control strategy (centralized versus decentralized),

(3) Switching techniques (circuit versus packet), and

(4) Topology (static versus dynamic).

4.5.1 MODE OF OPERATION

According to the mode of operation, INs are classified as synchronous versus asynchronous. In synchronous mode of operation, a single global clock is used by all components in the system such that the whole system is operating in a lock–step manner. Asynchronous mode of operation, on the other hand, does not require a global clock. Handshaking signals are used instead in order to coordinate the operation of asynchronous systems. While synchronous systems tend to be slower compared to asynchronous systems, they are race and hazard-free.

4.5.2 CONTROL STRATEGY

According to the control strategy, INs can be classified as centralized versus decentralized. In centralized control systems, a single central control unit is used to oversee and control the operation of the components of the system. In decentralized control, the control function is distributed among different components in the system. The function and reliability of the central control unit can become the bottleneck in a centralized control system. While the crossbar is a centralized system, the multistage interconnection networks are decentralized.

4.5.3 SWITCHING TECHNIQUES

Interconnection networks can be classified according to the switching mechanism as circuit versus packet switching networks. In the circuit switching mechanism, a complete path has to be established prior to the start of communication between a source and a destination. The established path will remain in existence during the whole communication period. In a packet switching mechanism, communication between a source and destination takes place via messages that are divided into smaller entities, called packets. On their way to the destination, packets can be sent from a node to another in a store-and-forward manner until they reach their destination. While packet switching tends to use the network resources more efficiently compared to circuit switching, it suffers from variable packet delays.

4.5.4 TOPOLOGY

An interconnection network topology is a mapping function from the set of processors and memories onto the same set of processors and memories. In other words, the topology describes how to connect processors and memories to other processors and memories. A fully connected topology, for example, is a mapping in which each processor is connected to all other processors in the computer. A ring topology is a mapping that connects processor k to its neighbors, processors (k-1) and (k+1). In general, interconnection networks can be classified as static versus dynamic networks. In static networks, direct fixed links are established among nodes to form a fixed network, while in dynamic networks, connections are established as needed. Switching elements are used to establish connections among inputs and outputs. Depending on the switch settings, different interconnections can be established.

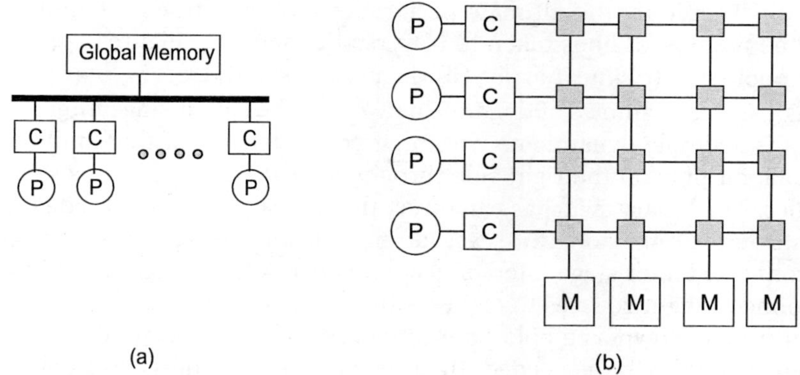

FIGURE 4.52: Shared memory interconnection networks

Nearly all multiprocessor systems can be distinguished by their interconnection network topology. However, in this section, we give a brief introduction to interconnection networks for shared memory and message passing systems. Shared memory systems can be designed using bus-based or switch-based INs. The simplest IN for shared memory systems is the bus. However, the bus may get saturated if multiple processors are trying to access the shared memory (via the bus) simultaneously. A typical bus-based design uses caches to solve the bus contention problem. Other shared memory designs rely on switches for interconnection. For example, a crossbar switch can be used to connect multiple processors to multiple memory modules. A crossbar switch, which can be visualized as a mesh of wires with switches at the points of intersection. Figure 4.52 shows (a) bus-based and (b) switch-based shared memory systems. Figure 4.53 shows bus-based systems when a single bus is used versus the case when multiple buses are used.

Message passing INs can be divided into static and dynamic. Static networks form all connections when the system is designed rather than when the connection is needed. In a static network, messages must be routed along established links.

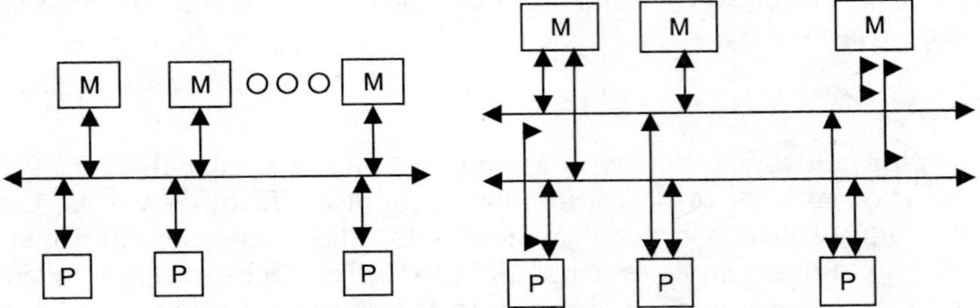

FIGURE 4.53: Single bus and multiple bus systems.

Dynamic INs establishes a connection between two or more nodes on the fly as messages are routed along the links. The number of hops in a path from source to destination node is equal to the number of point-to-point links a message must traverse to reach its destination. In either static or dynamic networks, a single message may have to hop through intermediate processors on its way to its destination. Therefore, the ultimate performance of an interconnection network is greatly influenced by the number of hops taken to traverse the network. Figure 4.54 shows a number of popular static topologies: (a) linear array, (b) ring, (c) mesh, (d) tree, (e) hypercube.

Figure 4.55 shows examples of dynamic networks. The single-stage interconnection network of Figure 4.55a is a simple dynamic network that connects each of the inputs on the left side to some, but not all, outputs on the right side through a single layer of binary switches represented by the rectangles. The binary switches can direct the message on the left-side input to one of two possible outputs on the right side. If we cascade enough single-stage networks together, they form a completely connected multistage interconnection network (MIN), as shown in Figure 4.55b. The omega MIN connects eight sources to eight destinations. The connection from the source 010 to the destination 010 is shown as a bold path in Figure 4.55b. These are dynamic INs because the connection is made on the fly, as needed. In order to connect a source to a destination, we simply use a function of the bits of the source and destination addresses as instructions for dynamically selecting a path through the switches. For example, to connect source 111 to destination 001 in the omega network, the switches in the first and second stage must be set to connect to the upper output port, while the switch at the third stage must be set to connect to the lower output port (001). Similarly, the crossbar switch of Figure 4.55c provides a path from any input or source to any other output or destination by simply selecting a direction on the fly. To connect row 111 to column 001 requires only one binary switch at the intersection of the 111 input line and 011 output line to be set.

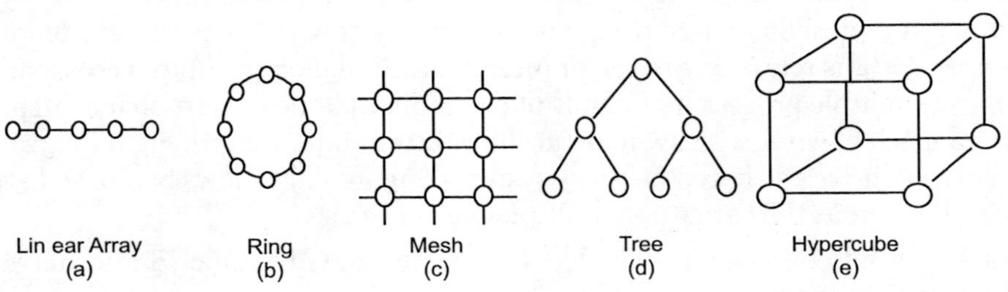

FIGURE 4.54: Examples of static topologies.

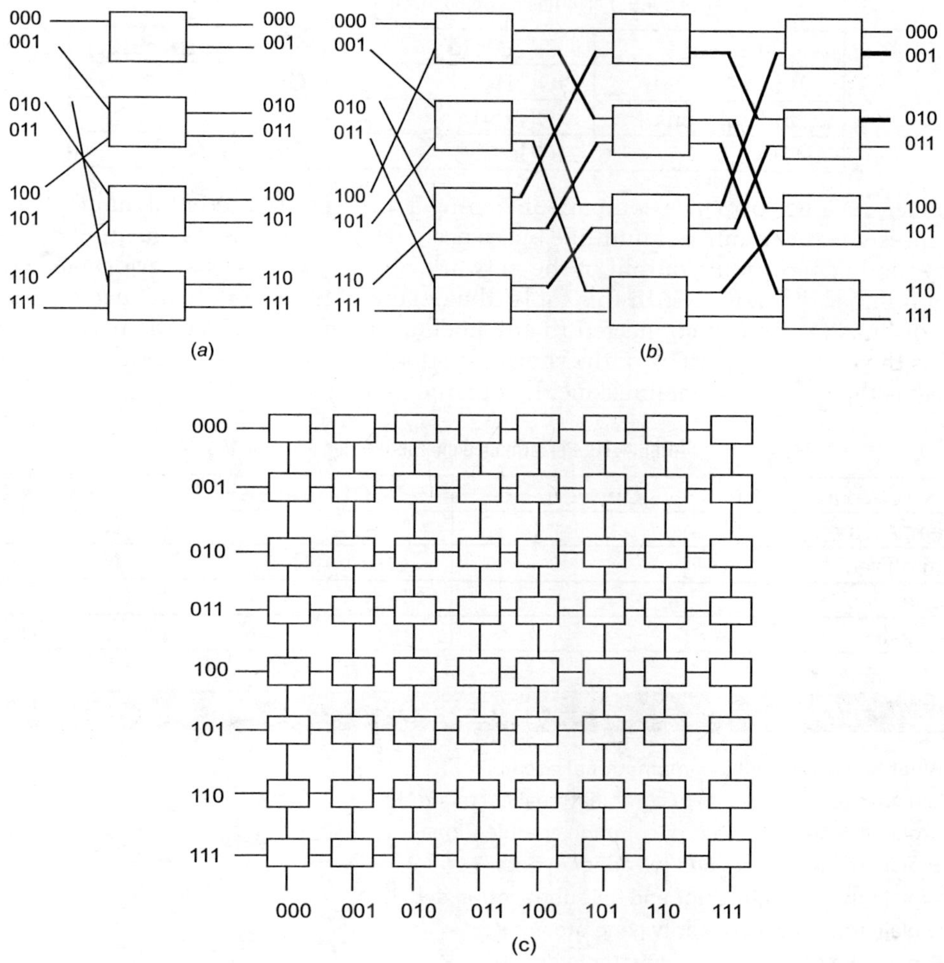

FIGURE 4.55: Example dynamic INs: (a) single-stage, (b) multistage, and (c) crossbar switch.

The crossbar switch clearly uses more binary switching components; for example, N^2 components are needed to connect N X N source/destination pairs. The omega MIN, on the other hand, connects N X N pairs with N/2 (log N) components. The major advantage of the crossbar switch is its potential for speed. In one clock, a connection can be made between source and destination. The diameter of the crossbar is one. (Note: Diameter, D, of a network having N nodes is defined as the maximum shortest paths between any two nodes in the network.) The omega MIN, on the other hand requires log N clocks to make a connection. The diameter of the omega MIN is therefore log N. Both networks limit the number of alternate paths between any source/destination pair. This leads to limited fault tolerance and network traffic congestion. If the single path between pairs becomes faulty, that pair cannot communicate. If two pairs attempt to communicate at the same time along a shared path, one pair must wait for the other. This is called blocking, and such MINs are called blocking networks. A network that can handle all possible connections without blocking is called a nonblocking network.

TABLE 4.9: Performance Comparison of Some Dynamic INs

Network	Delay	Cost (Complexity)
Bus	O(N)	O(1)
Multiple-bus	O(mN)	O(m)
MINs	O(log N)	O(N log N)

Table 4.9 shows a performance comparison among a number of different dynamic INs. In this table, m represents the number of multiple buses used, while N represents the number of processors (memory modules) or input/output of the network. Table 4.10 shows a performance comparison among a number of static INs. In this table, the degree of a network is defined as the maximum number of links (channels) connected to any node in the network. The diameter of a network is defined as the maximum path, p, of the shortest paths between any two nodes. Degree of a node, d, is defined as the number of channels incident on the node.

TABLE 4.10: Performance characteristics of static INs

Network	Degree	Diameter	Cost (# links)
Linear Array	2	N – 1	N – 1
Binary Tree	3	$2([\log_2 N] - 1$	N – 1
n-cube	$\log_2 N$	$\log_2 N$	nN/2
2D-mesh	4	2(n – 1)	2(N – n)

QUESTIONS

1. What do you mean by combinational circuits?
2. Explain the components of combinational circuits?
3. Explain the various types of common combinational circuits?
4. Explain the half adder and full adder in detail?
5. Explain the half subtractor and full subtractor in detail?
6. Explain the concept of parity generator?
7. Explain the concept of comparator in detail?
8. Explain the concept of multiplexer and de-multiplexer in detail?
9. Explain the concept of encoder and decoder in detail?
10. What are sorting networks?
11. Explain the various techniques of sorting networks?
12. Explain the concept of bitonic and merging sorting networks?
13. What do you mean by PRAM models?
14. Explain the PRAM model of parallel computation?
15. Explain the PRAM and its variations in detail?
16. How can you handling concurrent accesses in PRAM?
17. Explain the architecture of PRAM model?
18. Distinguish between concurrent and exclusive memory accesses?
19. Explain the synchronization and control in PRAM?
20. Explain the problems of PRAM implementation?
21. Explain the hardware implementation of PRAM?
22. Explain the various interconnection RAM networks?

CHAPTER 5 PARALLELISM IN UNIPROCESSOR SYSTEMS

5.1 INTRODUCTION

Nowadays, commercial applications are most used on parallel computers. A computer that runs such an application has to be able to process large amount of data in sophisticated ways. We can say with no doubt that commercial applications will define future parallel computers architecture. But scientific applications will still remain important users of parallel computing technology. Trends in commercial and scientific applications are merging as commercial applications perform more sophisticated computations and scientific applications become more data intensive. Today, a lot of parallel programming languages and compilers, based on dependencies detected in source code, are able to automatically split a program into multiple processes and/or threads to be executed concurrently on the available processors from a parallel system.

Parallel computing is an efficient form of information processing which emphasizes the exploitation of concurrent events in the computing process. Concurrency implies parallelism, simultaneity and pipelining. Parallel events may occur in multiple resources during the same time interval; simultaneous events may occur at the same time instant; and pipelined events may occur in overlapped time spans. Parallel processing demands concurrent execution of many programs in the computer. It is a cost effective means to improve system performance through concurrent activities in the computer. The highest level of parallel processing is conducted among multiple jobs or programs through multiprogramming, time-sharing, and multiprocessing. This presentation covers the basics of parallel computing. Beginning with a brief overview and some concepts and terminology associated with parallel computing, the topics of parallel memory architectures, Parallel computer architectures and Parallel programming models are then explored.

5.2 PARALLEL COMPUTING

Traditionally, software has been written for ***serial*** computation. To be executed by a single computer having a single Central Processing Unit (CPU). Problems are solved by a series of instructions, executed one after the other by the CPU. Only one instruction may be executed at any moment in time.

Where as ***parallel computing*** is the simultaneous use of multiple compute resources to solve a computational problem. The compute resources can include a single computer with multiple processors, an arbitrary number of computers connected by a network, a combination of both.

The computational problem usually demonstrates characteristics such as the ability to be:

1) Broken apart into discrete pieces of work that can be solved simultaneously.
2) Execute multiple program instructions at any moment in time.
3) Solved in less time with multiple compute resources than with a single compute resource.

5.3 TRENDS TOWARDS PARALLEL PROCESSING

From an application point of view, the mainstream of usage of computer is experiencing a trend of four ascending levels of sophistication:

1. Data processing
2. Information processing
3. Knowledge processing
4. Intelligence processing

Computer data processing is any process that a computer program does to enter data and summarise, analyse or otherwise convert data into usable information. The process may be automated and run on a computer. It involves recording, analysing, sorting, summarising, calculating, disseminating and storing data. Because data are most useful when well-presented and actually informative, data-processing systems are often referred to as information systems.

The relationships between data, information, knowledge, and intelligence are demonstrated in Figure 5.1. The data space is the largest, including numeric numbers in various formats, character symbols, and multidimensional measures. Data objects are considered mutually unrelated in the space. Huge amounts of data are being generated daily in all walks of life, especially among the scientific, business, and government sectors. An information item is a collection of data objects that are related by some syntactic structure or relation. Therefore, information items form a subspace of the data space. Knowledge consists of information items plus some semantic meanings. Thus knowledge items form a subspace of the information space.

Finally, intelligence is derived from a collection of knowledge items. The intelligence space is represented by the innermost and highest triangle in the Venn diagram.

Computer usage started with data processing, while is still a major task of today's computers. With more and more data structures developed, many users are shifting to computer roles from pure data processing to information processing. A high degree of parallelism has been found at these levels. As the accumulated knowledge bases expanded rapidly in recent years, there grew a strong demand to use computers for knowledge processing. Intelligence is very difficult to create; it's processing even more so. Today's computers are very fast and obedient and have many reliable memory cells to be qualified for data-information-knowledge processing. Computers are far from being satisfactory in performing theorem proving, logical inference and creative thinking.

Many computer scientists feel that the degree of parallelism exploitable at the two highest processing levels should be higher than that at the data-information processing levels.

From an operating point of view, computer systems have improved chronologically in four phases:

1. Batch processing
2. *Multiprogramming*
3. *Time sharing*
4. *Multiprocessing*

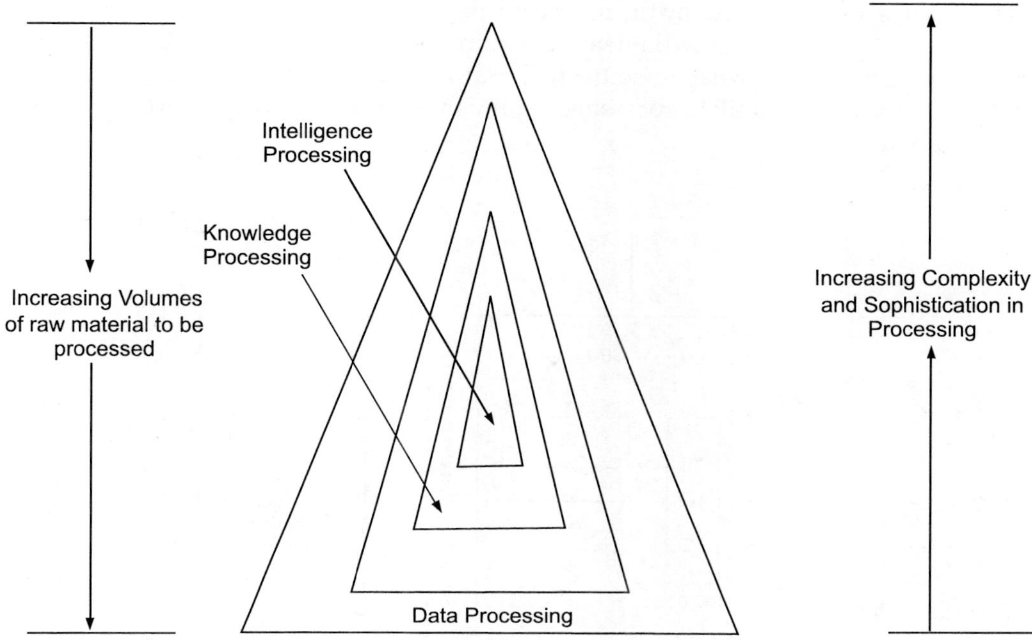

FIGURE 5.1: The spaces of data, information, knowledge and intelligence from the viewpoint of computer processing

In these four operating modes, the degree of parallelism increase sharply from phase to phase. We define parallel processing as parallel processing is an efficient form of information processing which emphasizes the exploitation of concurrent events in the computing process. Concurrency implies parallelism, simultaneity, and pipelining. Parallel processing demands concurrent execution of many programs in the computer. The highest level of parallel processing is conducted among multiple jobs or programs through multiprogramming, time sharing, and multiprocessing. This level requires the development of parallel processable algorithms. The implementation of parallel algorithms depends on the efficient allocation of limited hardware-software resources to multiple programs being used to solve a large computation problem. The next highest level of parallel processing is conducted among procedures or tasks (program segments) within the same program. This involves the decomposition of a program into multiple tasks. The third level is to exploit concurrency among multiple instructions. Data dependency analysis is often performed to reveal parallelism among instructions.

Parallel processing can be challenged in four programmatic levels:

1. Job or program level
2. Task or procedure level
3. Inter-instruction level
4. Intra-instruction level

The highest job level is often conducted algorithmically. The lowest intra-instruction level is often implemented directly by hardware means. Hardware roles increase from high to low levels. On the other hand, software implementations increase from low to high levels.

The trend is also supported by the increasing demand for a faster real-time, resource sharing and fault-tolerant computing environment. It requires a broad knowledge of and experience with all aspects of algorithms, languages, software, hardware, performance evaluation and computing alternatives. To achieve parallel processing requires the development of more capable and cost effective computer system.

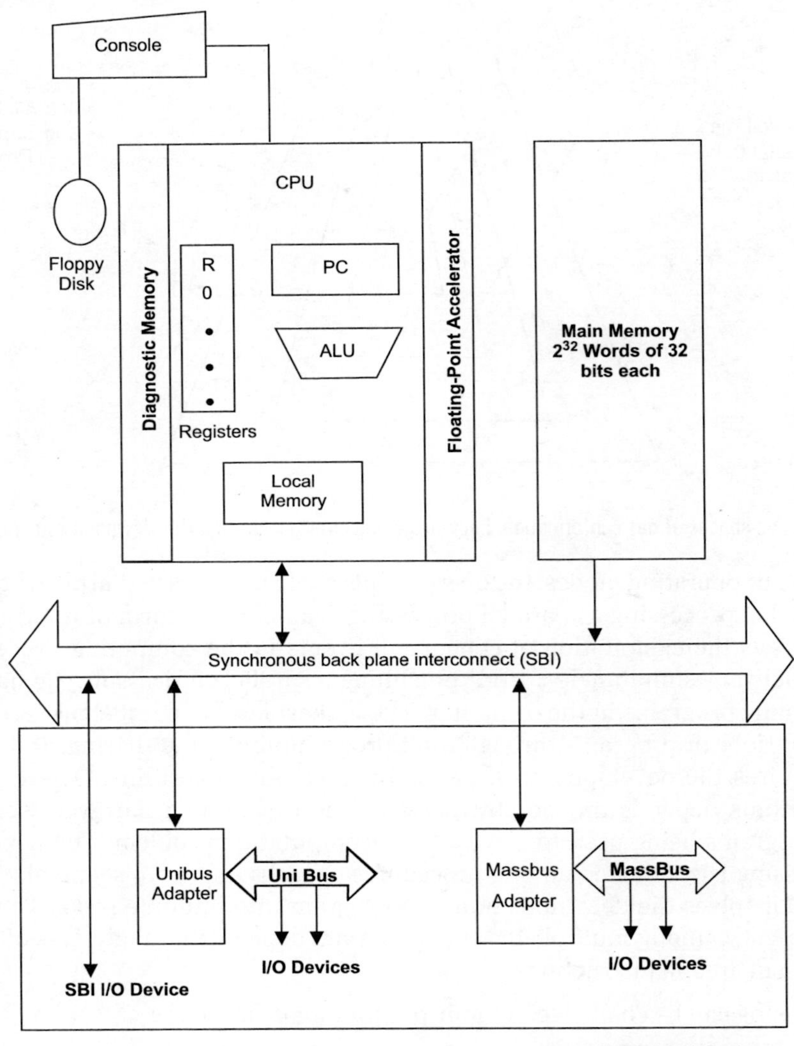

FIGURE 5.2: The system architecture of the super mini VAX – 11/780 microprocessor system

The CPU, the main memory and the I/O subsystems are all connected to a common bus; the synchronous backplane interconnect (SBI) through this bus, all I/O device scan communicate with each other, with the CPU, or with the memory. Peripheral storage or I/O devices can be connected directly to the SBI through the unibus and its controller or through a mass bus and its controller.

5.4 PARALLELISM IN UNIPROCESSOR SYSTEMS

The typical Uniprocessor system consists of three major components: the main memory, the Central processing unit (CPU) and the Input-output (I/O) sub-system. The CPU contains an arithmetic and logic unit (ALU) with an optional floating-point accelerator, and some local cache memory with an optional diagnostic memory. The CPU, the main memory and the I/O subsystems are all connected to a common bus, the synchronous backplane interconnect (SBI) through this bus, all I/O device scan communicate with each other, with the CPU, or with the memory. A number of parallel processing mechanisms have been developed in uniprocessor computers and they are identified as multiplicity of functional units, parallelism and pipelining within the CPU, overlapped CPU and I/O operations, use of a hierarchical memory system, multiprogramming and time sharing, multiplicity of functional units.

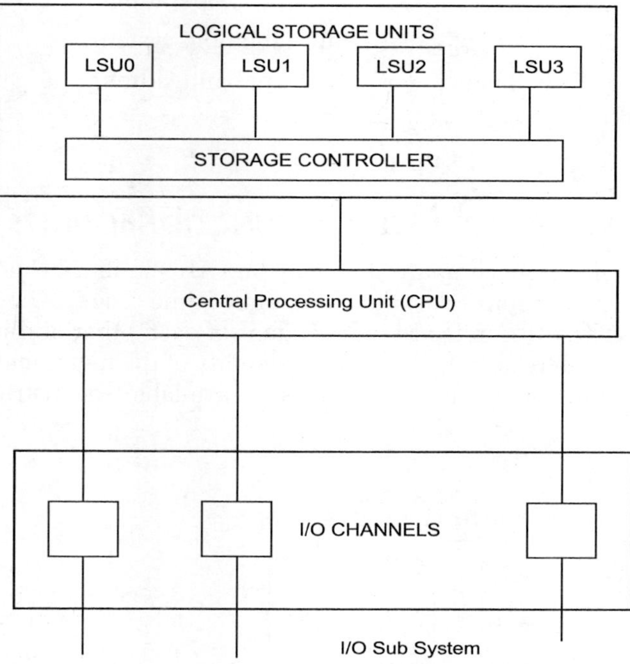

FIGURE 5.3: The System Architecture of the mainframe IBM System

The CPU contains the instruction decoding and execution units as well as a cache. Main memory is divided into four units, referred to as logical storage units that are four-way interleaved. The storage controller provides mutltiport connections between the CPU and the four LSUs. Peripherals are connected to the system via high speed I/O channels which operate asynchronously with the CPU.

5.4.1 BASIC UNIPROCESSOR ARCHITECTURE

A typical uniprocessor computer consists of three major components: the main memory, the central processing unit (CPU), and the input-output (I/O) subsystem. The architectures of two commercially available uniprocessor computers are given below to show the possible interconnection of structures among the three subsystems. There are sixteen 32-bit general purpose registers, one of which serves as the program Counter (pc).there is also a special CPU status register containing information about the current state of the processor and of the program being executed. The CPU contains an arithmetic and logic unit (ALU) with an optional floating-point accelerator, and some local cache memory with an optional diagnostic memory.

5.5 PARALLEL PROCESSING MECHANISMS

A number of parallel processing mechanisms have been developed in uniprocessor computers.

We identify them in the following seven categories:

1. Multiplicity of functional units

2. Parallelism and pipelining within the CPU
3. Overlapped CPU and I/O operations
4. Use of a hierarchical memory system
5. Balancing of subsystem bandwidths
6. Multiprogramming
7. Time sharing

5.5.1 MULTIPLICITY OF FUNCTIONAL UNITS

The early computer has only one ALU in its CPU and hence performing a long sequence of ALU instructions takes more amount of time. The CDC-6600 has 10 functional units built into its CPU. These 10 units are independent of each other and may operate simultaneously. A score board is used to keep track of the availability of the functional units and registers being demanded. With 10 functional units and 24 registers available, the instruction issue rate can be significantly increased.

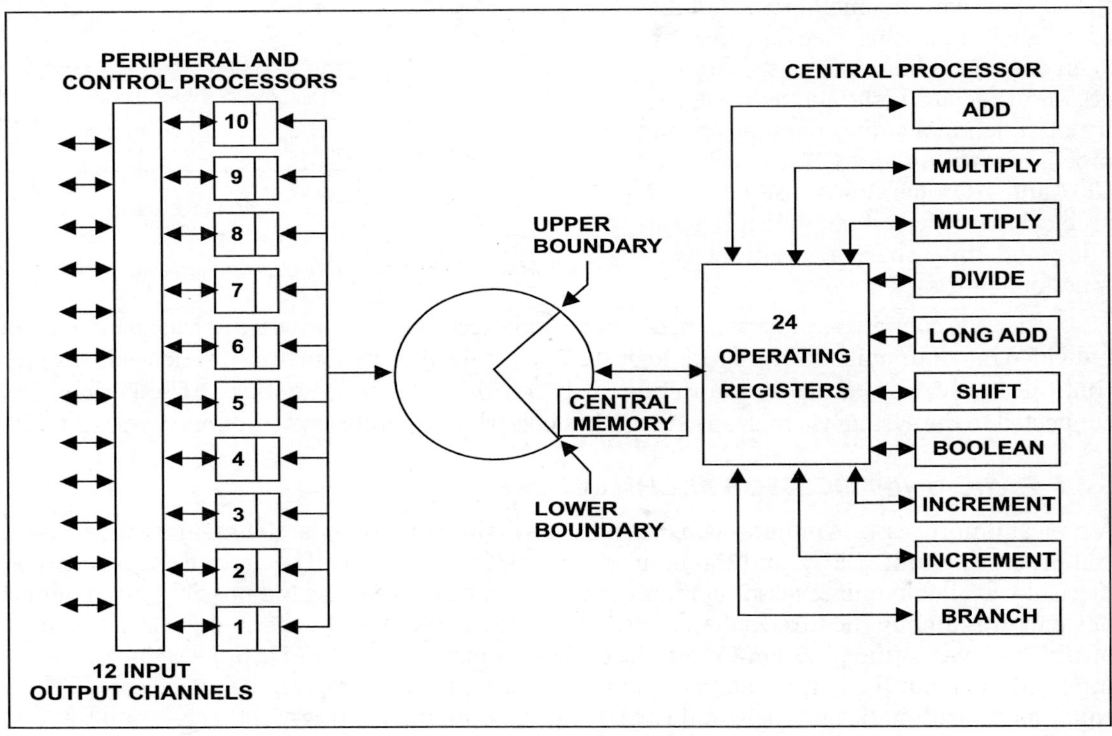

FIGURE 5.4: Block diagram of CDC 6600.

Another good example of a multifunction uniprocessor is the IBM 360/91 which has two parallel execution units. One for fixed point arithmetic and the other for floating point arithmetic. Within the floating point E-unit are two functional units: one for floating point add- subtract and other for floating point multiply – divide. IBM 360/91 is a highly pipelined, multifunction scientific uniprocessor.

5.5.2 PARALLELISM AND PIPELINING WITHIN THE CPU

Parallel adders, using such techniques as carry-look ahead and carry –save, are now built into almost all ALUs. This is in contrast to the bit serial adders used in the first generation machines. High speed multiplier recording and convergence division are techniques for exploring parallelism and the sharing of hardware resources for the functions of multiply and divide. The use of multiple functional units is a form of parallelism with the CPU. Various phases of instructions executions are now pipelined, including instruction fetch, decode, operand fetch, arithmetic logic execution, and store result.

5.5.2.1 INSTRUCTION LEVEL PARALLEL PROCESSING

Following are the various phases of instructions executions:

1. Pipelining of Processing Elements: One of the important methods of increasing the speed of PEs is pipelined execution of instructions. Pipelining is an effective method of increasing the execution speed of processors provided the following "ideal" conditions are satisfied:

1. It is possible to break an instruction into a number of independent parts, each part taking nearly equal time to execute.
2. There is so called locality in instruction execution. If the instructions are not executed in sequence but "jump around" due to many branch instructions, then pipelining is not effective.
3. Successive instruction is such that the work done during the execution of an instruction can be effectively used by the next and successive instruction. Successive instructions are also independent of one another.
4. Sufficient resources are available in a processor so that if a resource is required by successive instructions in the pipeline it is readily available.

In actual practice these "ideal" conditions are not always satisfied. The non-ideal situation arises because of the following reasons:

1. It is not possible to break up an instruction execution into a number of parts each taking exactly the same time. For ex., executing a floating point division will normally take much longer than say, decoding an instruction. It is, however, possible to introduce delays (if needed) so that different parts of an instruction take equal time.
2. All real programs have branch instructions which disturb the sequential execution of instructions. Fortunately statistical studies show that the probability of encountering a branch instruction is low; around 17%. Further it may be possible to predict when branches will be taken a little ahead of time and take some pre-emptive action.
3. Successive instructions are not always independent. The results produced by an instruction may be required by the next instruction and must be made available at the right time.
4. There are always resource constraints in a processor as the chip size is limited. It will not be cost effective to duplicate some resources indiscriminately. For ex., it may not be useful have more than two floating point arithmetic units.

The challenges is thus to make pipelining work under these non-ideal conditions.

The computer is a Reduced Instruction Set Computer (RISC) which is designed to facilitate pipelined instruction execution. The computer is similar to SMAC2. It has the following units.

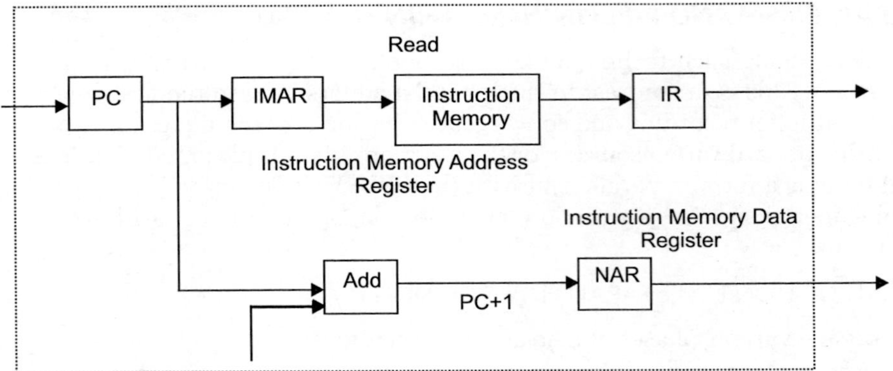

FIGURE 5.5: Block diagram for Fetch Instruction

Step 1: Fetch an instruction from the instruction memory (FI)

- A data cache (or memory) and an instruction cache (or memory). It is assumed that the instructions to be executed are stored in the instruction memory and the data to be read or written are stored in the data memory. These two memories have their own address and data registers. (IMAR- Memory Address Register of instruction memory, DMAR – Memory Address Register of data memory, IR - Data Register of Instruction memory, MDR – Data Register of Data memory)
- A Program Counter (PC) which contains the address of the next instruction to be executed. The machine is word addressable. Each word is 32 bits long.
- A register file with 32 registers. These are general purpose registers used to store operands and index values.
- The instructions are all of equal length and the relative positions of operands are fixed. There are 3 instruction types shown in the figure.
- The only instructions which access memory are load and store instructions. A load instruction reads a word from the data memory and stores it in a specified in the register file and a store instruction stores the contents of a register in the data memory. This is called Load-Store Architecture.
- An ALU which carries out one integer arithmetic or one logic operation in one clock cycle.

Solid lines indicate Data paths and dashed lines indicate control signal.

$$IMAR \leftarrow PC$$

$$IP \leftarrow IMEM[IMAR]$$

$$NAR \leftarrow PC + 1$$

All the above operations are carried out in one cycle.

Step 2: Decode Instructions and Fetch Register (DE)

The instructions are decoded and the operands fields are used to read values of specified registers. The operations carried out during this step are shown below:

B1 ← Reg [IR21...25]
B2 ← Reg [IR16...20]
IMM ← IR0...15 (Mtype instruction)

All these operations are carried out in one clock cycle. Observe that the outputs from the register file are stored in two buffer registers B1 and B2.

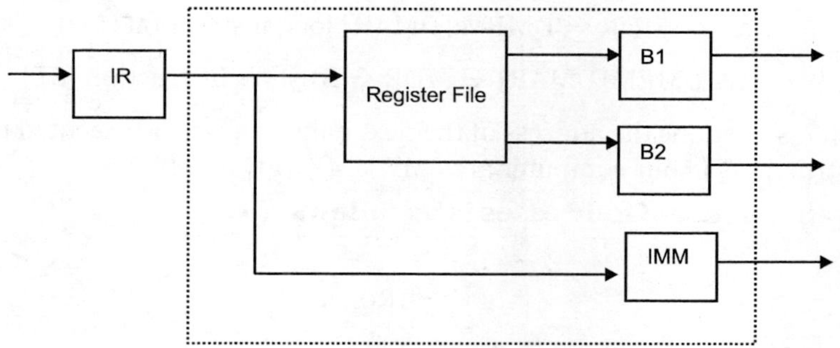

FIGURE 5.6: Data flow in decode and fetch register step

Step 3: Execute instruction and calculate effective address (EX)

The ALU operations are carried out. The instructions where ALU is used may be classified as shown below:

- **Two registers are operands** B3 ← B1 <operation> B2

Where operation is ADD, SUB, MUL or DIV and B3 is the register where ALU output is stored.

- **Increment/Decrement (INC/DEC/BCT)** B3 ← B1 + 1 (Increment)
  B3 ← B1 – 1 (Decrement or BCT)
- **Branch on equal (JEQ)** B3 ← B1 – B2
  If B3 = 0 set zero flag in Status Register = 1
- **Effective address calculation(for LD/ST)**
  For load and store instructions the effective address is stored in B3 B3 ← B2 + IMM

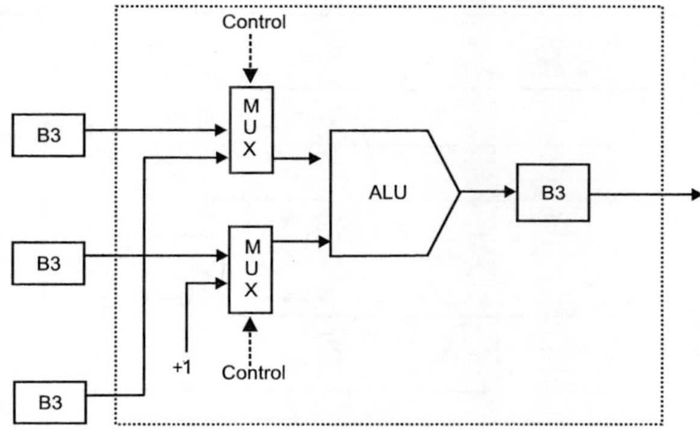

FIGURE 5.7: Data Flow for ALU operation

Step 4: Memory Access (MEM)

Load/Store and address determination are carried out here. The address for load or store operation was computed in the previous step and is in B3. The following operations are carried out for load/store.

DMAR ← B3

Where DMAR is data memory address register

MDR ← DMEM [DMAR] load instruction (LD)

DMEM[DMAR] ← MDR ← B1 store instruction (ST)

For branch instructions the address of the next instruction to be executed must be found. The four branch instructions in our computer are JMP, JMI, JEQ and BCT.

The PC value in these four cases is as follows:

For JMP:

PC ← IR0...25

For JMI:

If (negative flag = 1)PC ← IR0...25
Else PC ← NAR

For JEQ and BCT:

If (zero flag = 1) PC ← IR0...15
Else PC ← NAR

For other instructions:

PC ← NAR

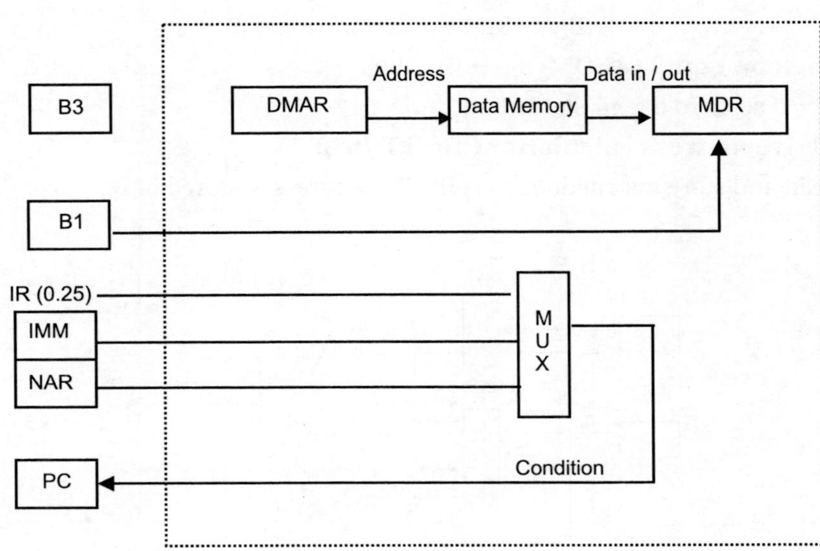

FIGURE 5.8: Data flow for load / store, next address step

Step 5: Store register (SR)

The result of ALU operation or load immediate or load from memory instruction is stored back in the specified register in the register file. The three cases are:

Store ALU output in register file:

$$Reg[IR11...15] \leftarrow B3$$

Load immediate (LDI):

$$Reg[IR21...25] \leftarrow IMM \ (IMM=IR(0...15))$$

Load data retrieved from data memory in register file (LD):

$$Reg[IR21...25] \leftarrow MDR$$

Conditional branch instruction JEQ, JMI and BCT require three cycles. Instructions INC, DEC and LDI do not need a memory access cycle and can complete in three cycles. The proportion of these instructions in actual programs has to be found statistically by executing a large number of programs and counting the number of such instructions.

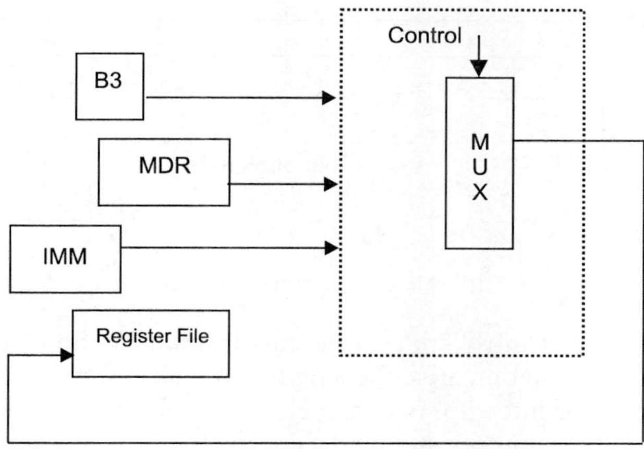

FIGURE 5.9: Data Flow for the store register step

5.5.3 *OVERLAPPED CPU AND I/O OPERATIONS*

I/O operations can be performed simultaneously with the CPU competitions by using separate I/O controllers, channels, or I/O processors. The direct memory access (DMA) channel can be used to provide direct information transfer between the I/O devices and the main memory. The DMA is conducted on a cycle stealing basis, which is apparent to the CPU.

5.5.3.1 DIRECT MEMORY ACCESS (DMA)

The main idea of direct memory access (DMA) is to enable peripheral devices to cut out the "middle man" role of the CPU in data transfer. It allows peripheral devices to transfer data directly from and to memory without the intervention of the CPU. Having peripheral devices access memory directly would allow the CPU to do other work, which would lead to improved performance, especially in the cases of large transfers.

The DMA controller is a piece of hardware that controls one or more peripheral devices. It allows devices to transfer data to or from the system's memory without the help of the processor. In a typical DMA transfer, some event notifies the DMA controller that data needs to be transferred to or from memory. Both the DMA and CPU use memory bus and only one or the other can use the memory at the same time. The DMA controller then sends a request to the CPU asking its permission to use the bus. The CPU returns an acknowledgment to the DMA controller granting it bus access. The DMA can now take control of the bus to independently conduct memory transfer. When the transfer is complete the DMA relinquishes its control of the bus to the CPU. Processors that support DMA provide one or more input signals that the bus requester can assert to gain control of the bus and one or more output signals that the CPU asserts to indicate it has relinquished the bus. Figure 5.10 shows how the DMA controller shares the CPU's memory bus.

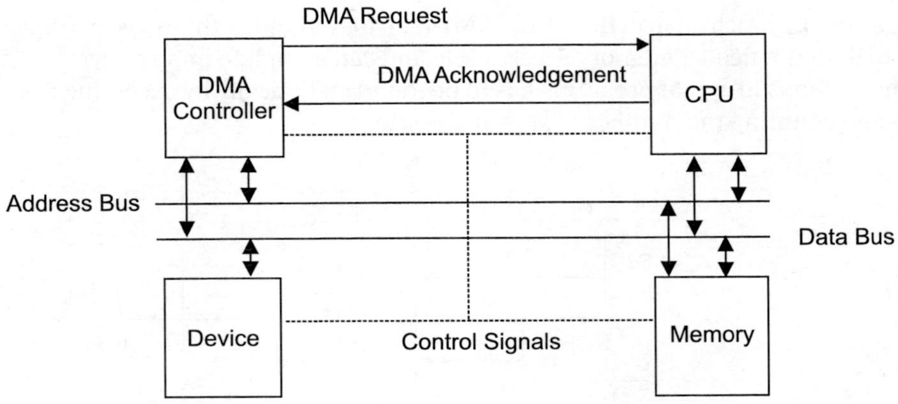

FIGURE 5.10: DMA controller shares the CPU's memory bus

Direct memory access controllers require initialization by the CPU, address of the source area, the address of the destination area, the length of the block, and whether the DMA controller should generate a processor interrupt once the block transfer is complete. A DMA controller has an address register, a word count register, and a control register. The address register contains an address that specifies the memory location of the data to be transferred. It is typically possible to have the DMA controller automatically increment the address register after each word transfer, so that the next transfer will be from the next memory location. The word count register holds the number of words to be transferred. The word count is decremented by one after each word transfer. The control register specifies the transfer mode.

Direct memory access data transfer can be performed in burst mode or single- cycle mode. In burst mode, the DMA controller keeps control of the bus until all the data has been transferred to (from) memory from (to) the peripheral device. This mode of transfer is needed for fast devices where data transfer cannot be stopped until the entire transfer is done. In single-cycle mode (cycle stealing), the DMA controller relinquishes the bus after each transfer of one data word. This minimizes the amount of time that the DMA controller keeps the CPU from controlling the bus, but it requires that the bus request/acknowledge sequence be performed for every single transfer. This overhead can result in a degradation of the performance. The single-cycle mode is preferred if the system cannot tolerate more than a few cycles of added interrupt latency or if the peripheral devices can buffer very large amounts of data, causing the DMA controller to tie up the bus for an excessive amount of time.

The following DMA operations:

1. DMA controller initiates data transfer.
2. Data is moved (increasing the address in memory, and reducing the count of words to be moved).
3. When word count reaches zero, the DMA informs the CPU of the termination by means of an interrupt.
4. The CPU regains access to the memory bus.

A DMA controller may have multiple channels. Each channel has associated with it an address register and a count register. To initiate a data transfer the device driver sets up the DMA channel's address and count registers together with the direction of the data transfer, read or write. While the transfer is taking place, the CPU is free to do other things. When the transfer is complete, the CPU is interrupted. Direct memory access channels cannot be shared between device drivers. A device driver must be able to determine which DMA channel to use. Some devices have a fixed DMA channel, while others are more flexible, where the device driver can simply pick a free DMA channel to use.

1. DMA function: DMA involves an additional module on the system bus. The DMA module (Figure 5.11) is capable of mimicking the processor and, indeed, of taking over control of the system from the processor. It needs to do this to transfer data to and from memory over the system bus. For this purpose, the DMA module must use the bus only when the processor does not need it, or it must force the processor to suspend operation temporarily. The latter technique is more common and is referred to as cycle stealing, because the DMA module in effect steals a bus cycle. When the processor wishes to read or write a block of data, it issues a command to the DMA module, by sending to the DMA module the following information:

1. Whether a read or write is requested, using the read or write control line between the processor and the DMA module.
2. The address of the I/O device involved, communicated on the data lines
3. The starting location in memory to read from or write to, communicated on the data lines and stored by the DMA module in its address register
4. The number of words to be read or written, again communicated via the data lines and stored in the data count register.

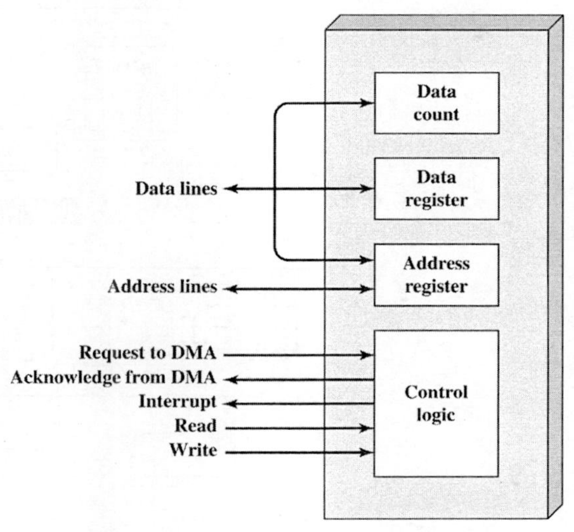

FIGURE 5.11: Typical DMA Block Diagram

The DMA module transfers the entire block of data, one word at a time, directly to or from memory, without going through the processor. When the transfer is complete, the DMA module sends an interrupt signal to the processor. Thus, the processor is involved only at the beginning and end of the transfer. Figure 5.12 shows where in the instruction cycle the processor may be suspended. In each case, the processor is suspended just before it needs to use the bus. The DMA module then transfers one word and returns control to the processor. Note that this is not an interrupt; the processor does not save a context and do something else. Rather, the processor pauses for one bus cycle. The overall effect is to cause the processor to execute more slowly. Nevertheless, for a multiple-word I/O transfer, DMA is far more efficient than interrupt-driven or programmed I/O.

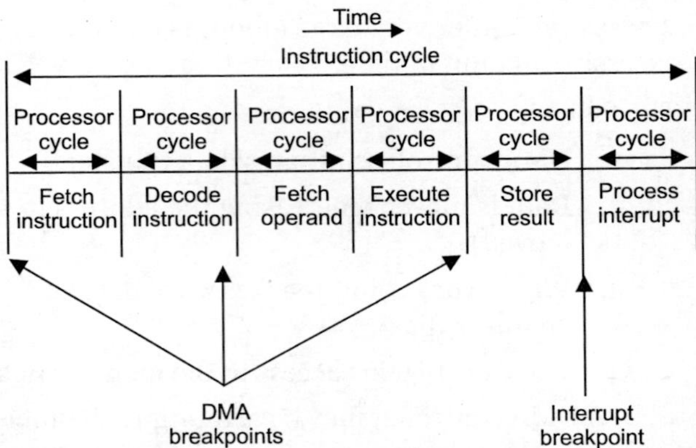

FIGURE 5.12: DMA and Interrupt Breakpoints during an Instruction Cycle

The DMA mechanism can be configured in a variety of ways. Some possibilities are shown in Figure 5.13. In the first example, all modules share the same system bus. The DMA module, acting as a surrogate processor, uses programmed I/O to exchange data between memory and an I/O module through the DMA module. This configuration, while it may be inexpensive, is clearly inefficient. As with processor-controlled programmed I/O, each transfer of a word consumes two bus cycles.

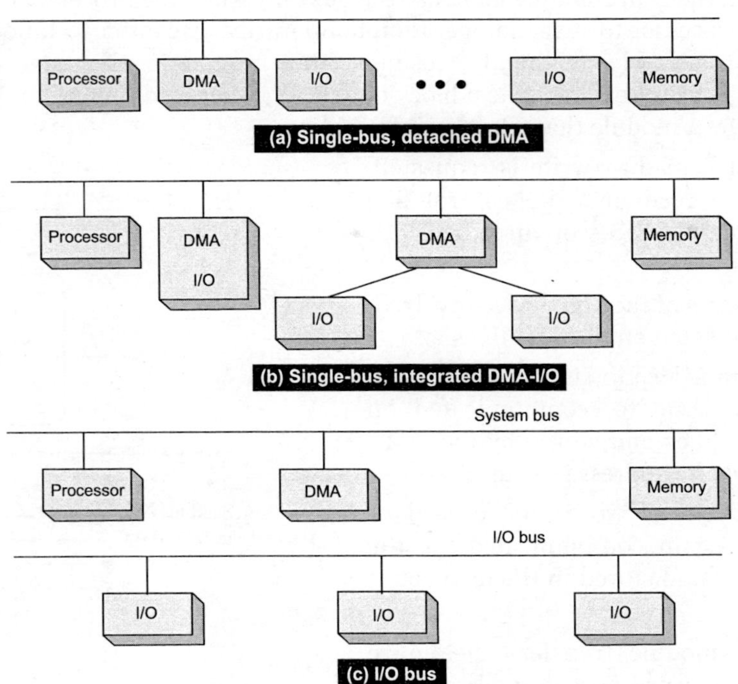

FIGURE 5.13: Alternative DMA Configurations

The number of required bus cycles can be cut substantially by integrating the DMA and I/O functions. As Figure 5.13(b) indicates, this means that there is a path between the DMA module and one or more I/O modules that does not include the system bus. The DMA logic may actually be a part of an I/O module, or it may be a separate module that controls one or more I/O modules. This concept can be taken one step further by connecting I/O modules to the DMA module using an I/O bus (Figure 5.13(c)). This reduces the number of I/O interfaces in the DMA module to one and provides for an easily expandable configuration. In both of these cases (Figures 5.13(b) and 5.13(c)), the system bus that the DMA module shares with the processor and memory is used by the DMA module only to exchange data with memory. The exchange of data between the DMA and I/O modules takes place off the system bus.

2. Example of DMA Transfer: The basic DMA operation interconnection among the four players: the CPU, memory, DMA controller, and the I/O device. In figure 5.14, the address bus is connecting the DMA controller to the memory and the data bus connecting the memory and I/O controller. However, note that these two buses, which are part of the standard system bus, also connect the processor and other components of the system. Each DMA channel is initialized to support a specific I/O device. The processor does this initialization by writing appropriate commands into the DMA controller. After that the I/O channel is dedicated to service that specific I/O device. We illustrate the DMA operation with the aid of the timing diagram given in Figure 5.14. Let us assume that the DMA operation is a read operation (i.e., transferring data from the I/O device to memory) and the channel is initialized to transfer two words of data.

When the I/O device is ready to transfer data, it sends its request through the DMA request (DREQ) line to the DMA controller. On receiving this signal, the DMA controller raises the HOLD signal to indicate that it wants the bus for a DMA transfer. The processor releases the bus after completing its current instruction. The CPU then floats all the control signals it normally generates (such as memory read, memory write, I/O read, I/O write). The granting of the bus to the DMA controller is conveyed by asserting the hold acknowledge (HLDA) signal. This signifies that the DMA controller is in control of the bus. Then the DMA controller notifies the I/O device that the data transfer can begin by sending a DMA acknowledgment (DACK) signal to the I/O controller. For standard transfers, the DMA request can be removed after the DACK signal.

The DMA controller is responsible for generating the control signals I/O read $(\overline{IORD})$ and memory write $(\overline{MEMWR})$. The I/O device responds to the I/O read control signal and places the data on the data bus, which is written directly to the memory using the $(\overline{MEMWR})$ signal. After the data word has been transferred, the word count is decremented. In addition, the memory address is incremented. If

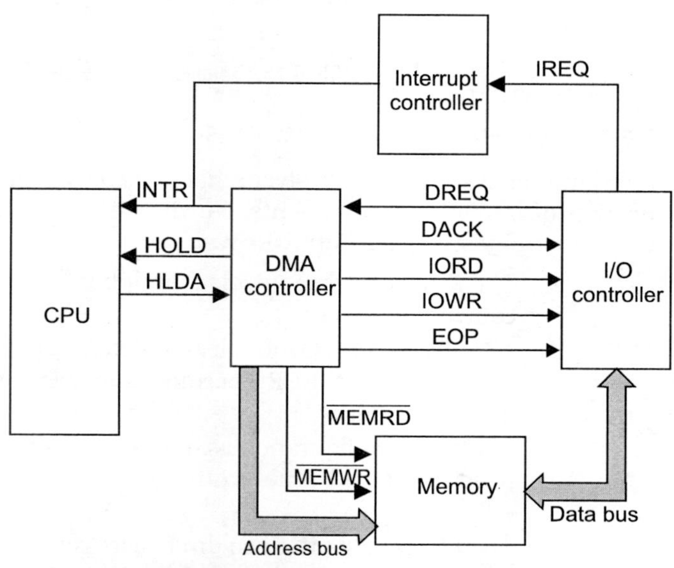

FIGURE 5.14: Simplified diagram giving the DMA controller

the word count is not zero, another data transfer cycle is initiated, as shown in Figure 5.15. Once the two data transfers have been completed, the DMA controller indicates the termination of the operation by sending an "end of process" $(\overline{EOP})$ signal.

It also removes the DACK signal, which in turn removes the HOLD signal, to return the bus to the processor. In this mode, the DMA transfer is done continuously without releasing the bus. For slow devices, this may unnecessarily block the bus from the processor. DMA transfer can also be done on a word-by-word basis. In this mode, the DMA controller requests the bus and releases it after transferring one word. The DMA controller decrements the count value and increments the buffer address, as before. When the device is ready to transfer the next word, it repeats the process by asserting the DREQ signal. This process is repeated until all the words are transferred, at which time the $(\overline{EOP})$ signal is sent to the device to indicate that the data transfer has been completed and it should not send any more data.

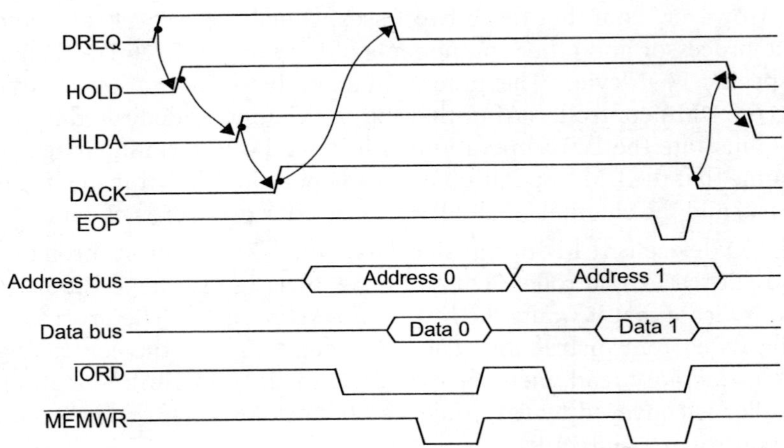

FIGURE 5.15: Example DMA transfer showing two transfer cycles

5.5.3.2 I/O CHANNELS AND PROCESSORS

As computer systems have evolved, there has been a pattern of increasing complexity and sophistication of individual components. Nowhere is this more evident than in the I/O function. **The evolutionary steps can be follows:**

1. The CPU directly controls a peripheral device. This is seen in simple microprocessor-controlled devices.
2. A controller or I/O module is added. The CPU uses programmed I/O without interrupts. With this step, the CPU becomes somewhat divorced from the specific details of external device interfaces.
3. The same configuration as in step 2 is used, but now interrupts are employed. The CPU need not spend time waiting for an I/O operation to be performed, thus increasing efficiency.
4. The I/O module is given direct access to memory via DMA. It can now move a block of data to or from memory without involving the CPU, except at the beginning and end of the transfer.

5. The I/O module is enhanced to become a processor in its own right, with a specialized instruction set tailored for I/O. The CPU directs the I/O processor to execute an I/O program in memory. The I/O processor fetches and executes these instructions without CPU intervention. This allows the CPU to specify a sequence of I/O activities and to be interrupted only when the entire sequence has been performed.
6. The I/O module has a local memory of its own and is, in fact, a computer in its own right. With this architecture, a large set of I/O devices can be controlled, with minimal CPU involvement. A common use for such architecture has been to control communication with interactive terminals. The I/O processor takes care of most of the tasks involved in controlling the terminals.

As one proceeds along this evolutionary path, more and more of the I/O function is performed without CPU involvement. The CPU is increasingly relieved of I/O-related tasks, improving performance. With the last two steps (5–6), a major change occurs with the introduction of the concept of an I/O module capable of executing a program. For step 5, the I/O module is often referred to as an I/O channel. For step 6, the term I/O processor is often used. However, both terms are on occasion applied to both situations. In what follows, we will use the term I/O channel.

1. Input-Output Processor (IOP) An input-output processor (IOP) may be classified as a processor with direct memory access capability that communicates with I/O devices. The computer system can be divided into a memory unit and number of processor comprised of the CPU and one or more IOP's. CPU has following control signals: BR, BG, DB, AB, RD, WR. DMA has following control signals: DS, RS, WR, BR, BG, Interrupt, Address Bus & Data bus and Memory has AD, DB, RD, WR I/O devices has data.

1. I/O device sends DMA request to DMA controller.
2. When DMA controller receive DMA request. DMA enable BR signal which is send to CPU.
3. CPU will then initialize the DMA register giving starting address of memory, block to be accessed. It also supplies the word count.
4. CPU activates the BG to give permission for control of buses to DMA controller.
5. DMA will send the read or write signal to the memory. It also gives address to memory through address bus.
6. DMA controller will send DMA acknowledge to I/O device to inform the device that DMA transfer can take place.
7. Now overall controller is DMA till CPU is idle/disabled. After every word is transference AR is increase and luck is decrease.
8. When WCR reaches zero, DMA will send initial signal to CPU & will disable BR line. CPU will disable the BG lines & control of buses will be returned to CPU.
9. CPU check WCR, if it's zero then it will indicate that transfer is successfully completed.

I/O processor, it's an additional processor available in computer system which handles all the input & output process CPU performs the entire computation or calculation task and it relieved from input/output functions. The work of CPU is divided between the CPU and I/O processor. CPU can continue with its own work and IOP can handle input output processing simultaneously. Thus this will increase the speed of the computer and also the efficiency of the system increases. CPU acts as the master processor and top acts as a slave processor. Thus, CPU initializes the IOP and once the IOP gets the Inst. CPU start I/O, IOP can then after words work independently of the CPU.

Memory occupies the central position b/w the CPU & IOP. CPU and IOP communicate with each other through main memory. IOP communicate with peripheral device through I/O bus.

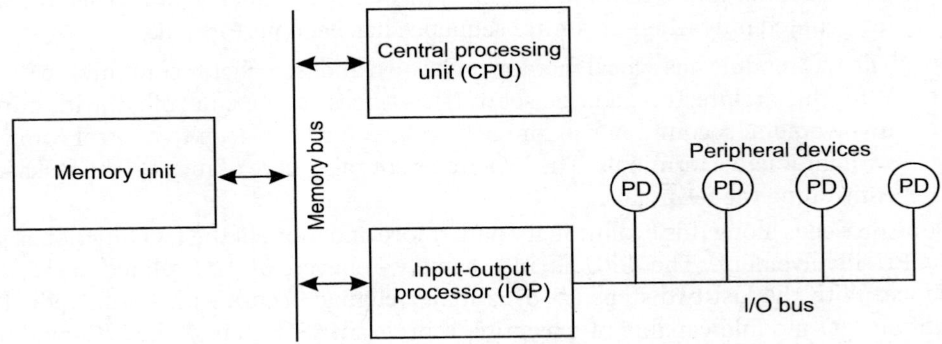

FIGURE 5.16: Block diagram of computer with I/O processor

2. CPU-IOP COMMUNICATION

Following are the steps for CPU-IOP communication:

1. CPU first of all sends an Instruction to IOP to determine whether IOP is free or not or whether IOP is working properly or not.
2. Then the IOP responds back to CPU by giving the status information.
3. CPU checks the status if the status is OK then CPU sends an Instruction to IOP to start I/O transfer.
4. IOP will then conduct the I/O transfers and CPU will continue with another task.
5. When the I/O transfer is completed. Then I/O sends an interrupt to the CPU.
6. CPU then again request for the status of transfer from IOP.
7. IOP responds back by giving the status of transfer.
8. CPU checks the status for correct transfer of data & the whole process is respected again for the next transfer.

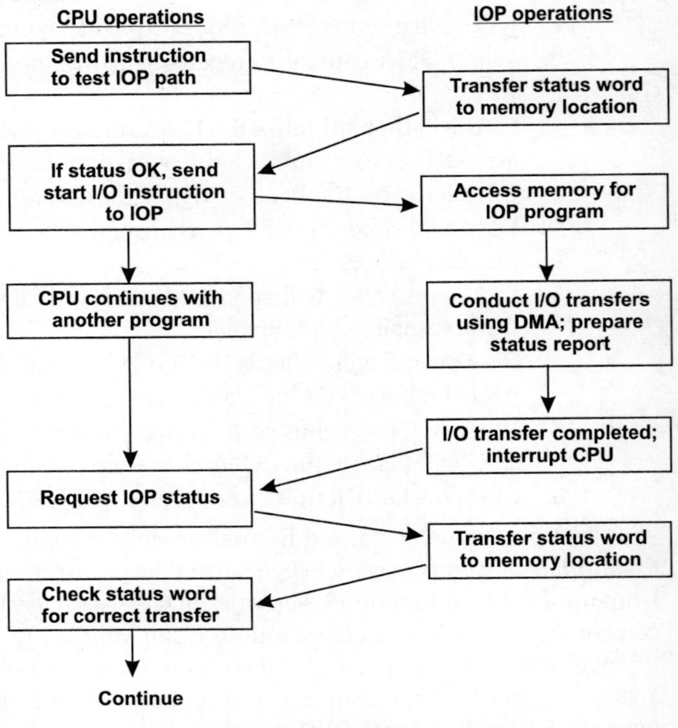

FIGURE 5.17: CPU-IOP Communications

5.5.4 USE OF HIERARCHICAL MEMORY SYSTEM

The CPU is 1000 times faster than memory access. A hierarchical memory system can be used to close up the speed gap. The hierarchical order listed is

- Registers
- Cache
- Main Memory
- Magnetic Disk
- Magnetic Tape

The inner most level is the register files directly addressable by ALU.

Cache memory can be used to serve as a buffer between the CPU and the main memory. Virtual memory space can be established with the use of disks and tapes at the outer levels.

Memory speeds have historically had an inverse nonlinear relationship to cost. Great advances in memory capacity, speed, and cost have been made over the years, and there will be more in the future. However, the shape of the curve and the relative performance of the different technologies have remained essentially unchanged. Memory speeds that were the state of the art a few years ago are considered relatively slow today and today's state of the art will be commonplace in the future. The only certainty is that memory speeds and capacities will continue to increase and relative costs per byte of storage will continue to decrease. The many trade-offs in designing for high performance will include the structure of the memory hierarchy, i.e. the size and technology of each component. So the various components can be viewed as forming a hierarchy of memories ($m_1, m_2, \ldots, m_n$) in which each member m_i is in a sense subordinate to the next highest member m_{i-1} of the hierarchy. To limit waiting by higher levels, a lower level will respond by filling a buffer and then signaling to activate the transfer.

There are four major storage levels:

1. **Internal:** Processor registers and cache.
2. **Main:** the system RAM and controller cards.
3. **On-line mass storage:** Secondary storage.
4. **Off-line bulk storage:** Tertiary and Off-line storage.

This is a most general memory hierarchy structuring. Many other structures are useful. For example, a paging algorithm may be considered as a level for virtual memory when designing computer architecture.

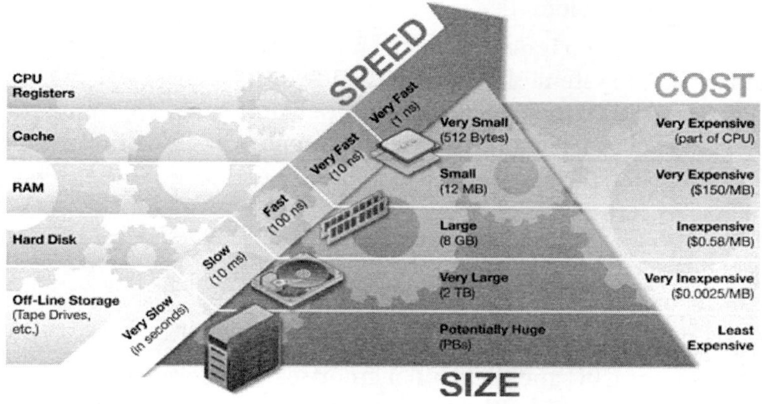

FIGURE 5.18: Memory Hierarchy

Primary Storage is the top level and is made up of CPU registers, CPU cache and memory which are the only components that are directly accessible to the systems CPU. The CPU can continuously read data stored in these areas and execute all instructions as required quickly in a uniform manner. Secondary Storage differs from primary storage in that it is not directly accessible by thy CPU. A system uses input/output (I/O) channels to connect to the secondary storage which control the data flow through a system when required and on request.

Secondary storage is non-volatile so does not lose data when it is powered down so consequently modern computer systems tend to have a more secondary storage than primary storage. All secondary storage today consist of hard disk drives (HDD), usually set up in a RAID configuration, however older installations also included removable media such us magneto optical or MO.

Tertiary Storage is mainly used as backup and archival of data and although based on the slowest devices can be classed as the most important in terms of data protection against a variety of disasters that can affect an IT infrastructure. Most devices in this segment are automated via robotics and software to reduce management costs and risk of human error and consist primarily of disk & tape based back up devices.

Offline Storage is the final category and is where removable types of storage media sit such as tape cartridges and optical disc such as CD and DVD. Offline storage is can be used to transfer data between systems but also allow for data to be secured offsite to ensure companies always have a copy of valuable data in the event of a disaster.

5.5.5 BALANCING OF SUBSYSTEM BANDWIDTH

The CPU is the fastest unit in a computer, with a processor cycle t_p of tens of nanoseconds; the main memory has a cycle time t_m of hundreds of nanoseconds; and the I/O devices are the slowest with an average access time t_d of a few milliseconds. It is thus observed that—

$$t_d > t_m > t_p$$

For example, the IBM 370/168 has t_d = 5 ms (disk), t_m = 320 ns, and t_p = 80 ns. With these speeds gaps between the subsystems, we need to match their processing bandwidths in order to avoid a system bottleneck problem.

The bandwidth of a system is defined as the number of operations performed per unit time. In the case of a main memory system, the memory bandwidth is measured by the number of memory words that can be accessed (either fetch or store) per unit time. Let W be the number of words delivered per memory cycle t_m. Then the maximum memory bandwidth B_m is equal to

$$B_m = \frac{W}{t_m} \text{ (words/s or bytes/s)}$$

5.5.5.1 BANDWIDTH BALANCING BETWEEN CPU AND MEMORY

The speed gap between the CPU and the main memory can be closed up by using fast cache memory between them. The cache should have an access time $t_c = t_p$. A block of memory words is moved from the main memory into the cache so that immediate instructions can be available most of the time from the cache.

5.5.5.2 BANDWIDTH BALANCING BETWEEN MEMORY AND I/O DEVICES

Input-output channels with different speeds can be used between the slow I/O devices and the main memory. The I/O channels perform buffering and multiplexing functions to transfer the data from multiple disks into the main memory by stealing cycles from the CPU.

Furthermore, intelligent disk controllers or database machines can be used to filter out the irrelevant data just off the tracks of the disk. This filtering will alleviate the I/O channel saturation problem. The combined buffering, multiplexing, and filtering operations thus can provide a faster, more effective data transfer rate, matching that of the memory. In the ideal case, we wish to achieve a totally balanced system, in which the entire memory bandwidth matches the bandwidth sum of the processor and I/O devices; that is—

$$B_p^u + B_d = B_m^u$$

where $B_p^u = B_p$ and $B_m^u = B_m$ are both maximized. Achieving this total balance requires tremendous hardware and software supports beyond any of the existing systems.

5.5.6 MULTIPROGRAMMING

Early computer systems were extremely expensive to purchase and to operate. Unfortunately they often sat idle as their human operators tended to their duties at a humans pace. Even a group of highly trained computer operators could not work fast enough to keep even the earliest tape-fed batch systems CPU busy. The advent of multiprogramming broke through the utilization barrier by removing most of the human factor in CPU utilization.

Multiprogramming is the technique of running several programs at a time using timesharing. It allows a computer to do several things at the same time. Multiprogramming creates logical parallelism. The concept of multiprogramming is that the operating system keeps several jobs in memory simultaneously. The operating system selects a job from the job pool and starts executing a job, when that job needs to wait for any I/O operations the CPU are switched to another job. So the main idea here is that the CPU is never idle.

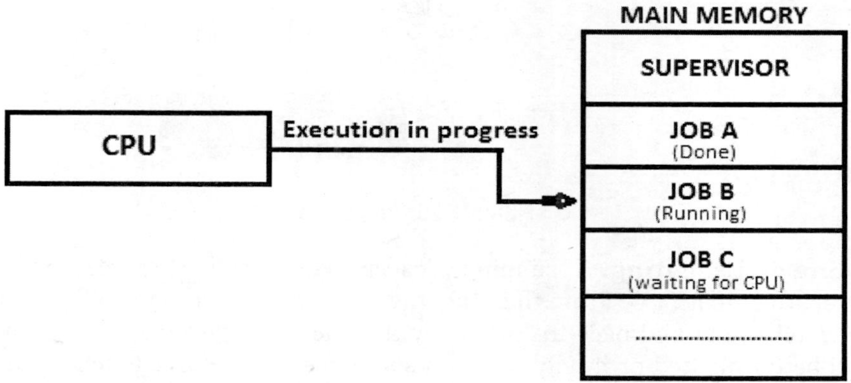

FIGURE 5.19: Execution in progress

5.5.6.1 PROCESS STATES

Following are the various process states:

Created or New: When a process is first created, it occupies the "created" or "new" state. In this state, the process awaits admission to the "ready" state. This admission will be approved or delayed by process scheduler. Typically in most desktop computer systems, this admission will be approved automatically, however for real time operating systems this admission may be delayed.

Ready: A "ready" or "waiting" process has been loaded into main memory and is awaiting execution on a CPU (to be context switched onto the CPU). There may be many "ready" processes at any one point of the systems execution - for example, in a one processor system, only one process can be executing at any one time, and all other "concurrently executing" processes will be waiting for execution.

A ready queue is used in computer scheduling. Modern computers are capable of running many different programs or processes at the same time. However, the CPU is only capable of handling one process at a time. Processes that are ready for the CPU are kept in a queue for "ready" processes. Other processes that are waiting for an event to occur, such as loading information from a hard drive or waiting on an internet connection, are not in the ready queue.

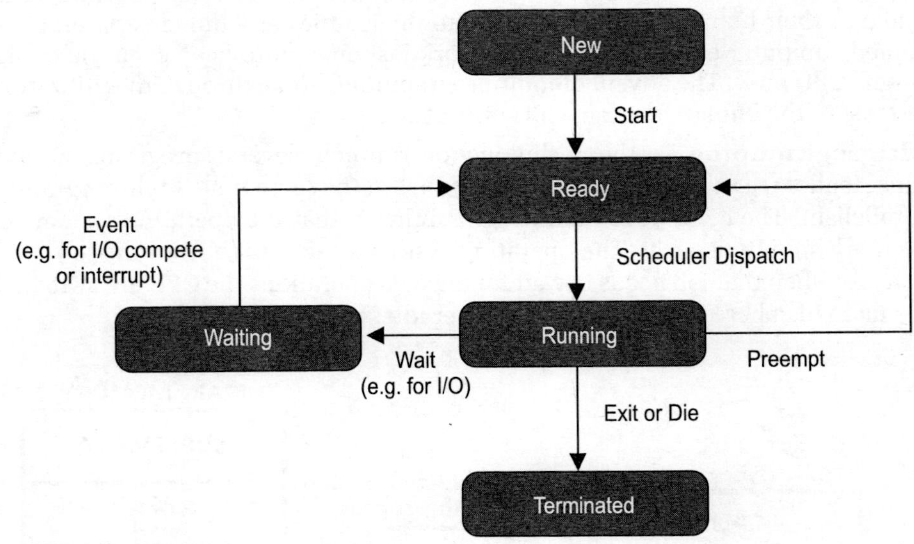

FIGURE 5.20: Process States

Running or Executing: A "running", "executing" or "active" process is a process which is currently executing on a CPU. From this state the process may exceed its allocated time slice and be context switched out and back to "ready" by the operating system, it may indicate that it has finished and be terminated or it may block on some needed resource (such as an input / output resource) and be moved to a "blocked" state.

Blocked or Sleeping: Should a process "block" on a resource (such as a file or a device), it will be removed from the CPU (as a blocked process cannot continue execution) and will be in the blocked state. The process will remain "blocked" until its resource becomes available, which can unfortunately lead to deadlock. From the blocked state, the operating system may notify the process of the availability of the resource it is blocking on (the operating system itself may be alerted to the resource availability by an interrupt). Once the operating system is aware that a process is no longer blocking, the process is again "ready" and can from there be dispatched to its "running" state, and from there the process may make use of its newly available resource.

Terminated: A process may be terminated, either from the "running" state by completing its execution or by explicitly being killed. In either of these cases, the process moves to the "terminated" state.

The prime reason for multiprogramming is to give the CPU something to do while waiting for I/O to complete. If there is no DMA, the CPU is fully occupied doing I/O, so there is nothing to be gained (at least in terms of CPU utilization) by multiprogramming. No matter how much I/O a program does, the CPU will be 100% busy. This of course assumes the major delay is the wait while data is copied. A CPU could do other work if the I/O were slow for other reasons (arriving on a serial line, for instance).

- I/O operations are exceedingly slow (compared to instruction execution)
- A program containing even a very small number of I/O ops, will spend most of its time waiting for them

Hence: poor CPU usage when only single program is present in memory

Single Program

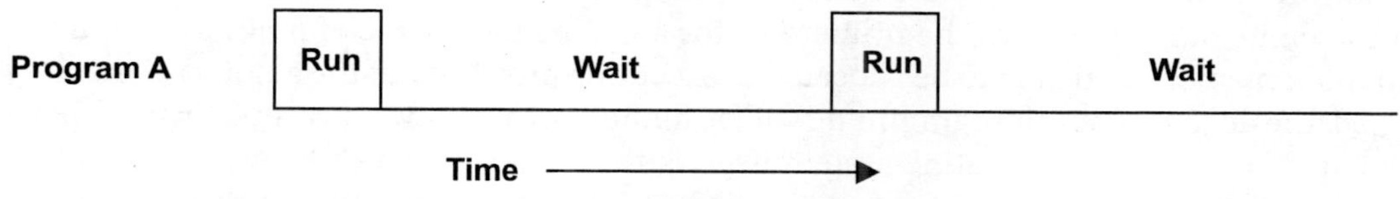

FIGURE 5.21: Uniprogramming

	Uniprogramming	Multiprogramming
Processor use	17%	33%
Memory use	33%	67%
Disk Use	33%	67%
Printer Use	33%	67%
Elapsed time	30 min.	15 min.
Throughput rate	6 jobs/hr.	12 jobs/hr.
Mean response time	18 min.	10 min.

5.5.6.2 MULTIPROGRAMMING-CAPABLE SYSTEM

In a multiprogramming-capable system, jobs to be executed are loaded into a pool. Some number of those jobs is loaded into main memory, and one is selected from the pool for execution by the CPU. If at some point the program in progress terminates or requires the services of a peripheral device, the control of the CPU is given to the next job in the pool. As programs terminate, more jobs are loaded into memory for execution, and CPU control is switched to another job in memory. In this way the CPU is always executing some program or some portion thereof, instead of waiting for a printer, tape drive, or console input.

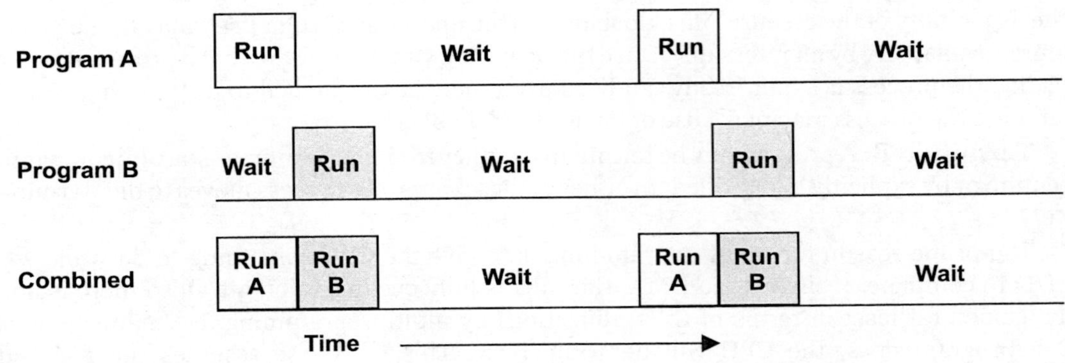

FIGURE 5.22: Multiprogramming using two programs

Memory management- to have several jobs ready to run, they must be kept in main memory.

Job scheduling- the processor must decide which program to run.

An important concept in multiprogramming is the degree of multiprogramming. The degree of multiprogramming describes the maximum number of processes that a single-processor system can accommodate efficiently. The primary factor affecting the degree of multiprogramming is the amount of memory available to be allocated to executing processes. If the amount of memory is too limited, the degree of multiprogramming will be limited because fewer processes will fit in memory. A factor inherent in the operating system itself is the means by which resources are allocated to processes. If the operating system can not allocate resources to executing processes in a fair and orderly fashion, the system will waste time in reallocation, or process execution could enter into a deadlock state as programs wait for allocated resources to be freed by other blocked processes. Other factors affecting the degree of multiprogramming are program I/O needs, program CPU needs, and memory and disk access speed.

Processes maintained in the computers main memory are considered to be executing concurrently even though the CPU is (usually) capable of executing only one instruction at a time. The number of processes that can be held in memory is dependent on the amount of memory available to the system. That amount may be any combination of real or virtual memory, virtual memory being a portion of on-line mass-storage allocated to hold code in the process of being executed which can not fit into available real memory. If a process is too large to fit into the memory allocated to it, portions of its code may be stored temporarily on disk. When this code is required the operating system will load the code into memory and execution will continue. The management process by which this code is swapped into and out of memory is referred to a paging. A similar system can be used to manage data-segment memory.

As the number of processes (degree of multiprogramming) increases in a system that supports paging, the amount of memory available to execute processes in decreases and the number of paging operations required increases. At some point the amount of time the CPU spends paging code and data will drag system performance down. This phenomenon, called "thrashing," is a manifestation of exceeding the degree of multiprogramming for a system.

5.5.6.3 FEATURES AND ADVANTAGES OF MULTIPROGRAMMING

Multiprogramming is the rapid switching of the CPU between multiple processes in memory. It is done only when the currently running process requests I/O, or terminates. It was commonly used to keep the CPU busy while one or more processes are doing I/O. It is now mostly superceded by multitasking, in which processes also lose the CPU when their time quantum expires.

Multiprogramming makes efficient use of the CPU by overlapping the demands for the CPU and its I/O devices from various users. It attempts to increase CPU utilization by always having something for the CPU to execute.

5.5.6.4 REQUIREMENTS OF MULTIPROGRAMMING SYSTEMS

Multiprogramming systems have better throughput than uniprogramming systems because CPU idle time is reduced. They are more sophisticated because they require following additional hardware and software features:

1. **Large memory:** It requires large main memory to hold a good number of user programs along with operating system.
2. **Memory protection:** Multiprogramming requires a memory protection mechanism to prevent a job (in one memory partition) from changing another job's program/data (in another memory partition). A combination of hardware and software protection mechanism is used for this. It prevents one job from addressing beyond the limits of its own allocated memory area.
3. **Job status preservation:** In multiprogramming, when a running job is blocked for I/O processing, CPU is taken away from it and given to another job that is ready for execution. The blocked job resumes its execution sometime later. However, this requires preserving the job's complete status information when CPU is taken away from it and restoring this information back before CPU is given to it again. This can be done by process control block (PCB) for each loaded process.
4. **Proper job mix:** A proper mix of I/O-bound and a CPU-bound job is required to overlap the operations of CPU and I/O devices effectively. If all loaded need I/O at the same time, CPU will again be idle. Hence, jobs resident simultaneously in main memory should contain a good mix of CPU-bound and I/O-bound jobs so that at least one job is always ready to utilize CPU.
5. **CPU scheduling:** In a multiprogramming system, often there are multiple jobs in ready state (waiting for CPU to be allocated). Hence, when CPU becomes free, operating system must decide which of these ready jobs should be allocated to CPU for execution. Part of the operating system that takes this decision is called CPU scheduler, and the algorithm it uses for this is called CPU scheduling algorithm.

5.5.7 BASIC CONCEPT OF TIMESHARING

Timesharing, also called "time slicing" or "time division multiplexing", or even "multitasking", is a system whereby system focus is switched between each of its users. Ideally, users of a timesharing system will not be aware that they are sharing the computer with one or more users.

Timesharing came about as an extension of multiprogramming. Old batch systems, including multiprogramming batch systems, were usually isolated from their end-users. Due to this isolation, programmers were required to plan for every contingency in designing the input for their code. Many times a programmer would receive an output printout or a memory dump of their program. Interaction with the computer system was not possible due to the inefficiency introduced by extensive human interaction.

Timesharing provided a means by which system users could interact with the computer and the computer could direct its idle time toward other users or other processes. Now programmers could write programs that interacted with the user; they even had the opportunity to debug their code in a live environment rather than a stack of paper printout.

To provide service to individual users and maintain their operating environment, timesharing systems employ some means of context switching. In context switching, a users execution environment is loaded into memory, some operation is performed, and then the environment is placed back into temporary storage until the CPU comes back to service the next request.

Timeshare systems allowed multiple users access to the same system, so protection must be provided for each user's environment and for the operating system itself. Also, timeshare systems had to provide the illusion of immediate system interaction in order to be practical and attractive to users demanding real-time interaction.

To achieve effective user interaction, processes were executed in a defined order, and were only given a certain amount of CPU time. This way everyone gets the CPUs attention at some point, and no one can take complete control. Two common schemes are FIFO and round robin. The FIFO scheme processes requests in the order in which they are received. Unfortunately FIFO is not conducive to interactive processing because it permits jobs to run to completion. Thus short jobs wait for long jobs, and job priority can not be defined.

On the other hand, round-robin scheduling is a preemptive method of allocating CPU time. In this scheme, processes gain CPU control in a FIFO method, but after a certain amount of time are stopped, or preempted, and placed back into the queue. It is in this scheme that context switching becomes a central issue. Efficiency in setup and clean up for processes determines the overhead introduced by the system. TSS, the time sharing system for the IBM System 360/67, used a scheduling scheme similar to a combination FIFO/round-robin.

Compared to a timeshare system, the scheduling policy of a batch system is a hybrid of round-robin and FIFO, but with more emphasis on FIFO. Earlier systems relied entirely on a FIFO scheme; one job was loaded into the system and ran to completion before another could start. Later batch systems improved on this theme to provide one job with the CPU for as long as it could execute without requesting an I/O device. Upon such a request, the CPU switched execution to the next job in the queue.

To make them practical, timesharing systems usually supported some sort of on-line central file system and a means of organizing it. MUTLICS, Multiplexed Information and Computing Service, was the first timesharing system to support a centralized file system organized hierarchically.

Timesharing systems, the evolution of multiprogrammed systems, brought the computer to the user. Utilizing process scheduling and queuing schemes; individual users were provided the illusion of being sole user of the system, unlike batch systems where jobs had the opportunity to capture the attention of the CPU from other users. These systems typically incorporated a shared file system where user code and data could be maintained and developed. The timesharing system leveraged the computing investment and at the same time increased the level of service to the end user.

5.5.7.1 TIME-SHARING SYSTEMS

For many jobs, it is desirable to provide a mode in which the user interacts directly with the computer. For jobs like transaction processing, an interactive mode is needed. Multiprogramming can be used to handle multiple interactive jobs and the technique is referred to as **Time-sharing**. In other words the processor's time is shared among multiple users. The basic technique is to have multiple users simultaneously using the system through terminals, with the operating system interleaving the execution of each user program in a short burst, or quantum, of computation.

How It Works: In time-sharing, a number of independent, relatively low-speed stations have access to a CPU and its programs. Multiple users can be accessing the same programs simultaneously. But other users cannot access your data storage. Basically, time-sharing works by dividing up a period of time, such as a second, among many users. Each user gets a fraction of every second devoted to him or her exclusively. Since input/output operations from peripheral devices and terminals are very slow compared to the electronic speed of the computer, the fraction of a second is sufficient to handle the user's primary storage and processing requirements. None of the many users is even aware that other users are getting time. This gives the user the impression that he or she has the entire machine to himself or herself.

Bulletin Board System: A bulletin board system (BBS) is a form of remote time-sharing that links computers though dedicated phone lines. The computer answers the phone, verifies the user's identity, checks what he or she did the last time, keeps track of the length of the interaction, and ensures that the user logged out appropriately. The computer can handle multiple users at the same time that may be playing games, researching term papers, etc.

Remote system: a communication system in which the terminals are widely separated so that telephone lines, microwave stations, or satellites must be used to link up to the central computer.

Example: Assume that there are four interactive users with the following memory requirements:

Job1 – 15K

Job2 – 20K

Job3 – 05K

Job4 – 10K

Initially the monitor loads in Job1 and transfers control to it (Figure 5.23 a). Later, the monitor decides to transfer control to Job2. Because Job2 requires more memory than Job1, Job1 must be written out first, and then Job2 can be loaded (Figure 5.23 b). Next Job 3, is loaded in to be run. However, because Job3 is smaller than Job2, a portion of Job2 can remain in the memory, reducing disk writ time (Figure 5.23 c). Later, the monitor decides to transfer control back to Job 1. An additional portion of Job2 must be written out when Jb1 is loaded back into memory (Figure 5.23 d). When Job4 is loaded, part of Job1 and the portion of Job2 remaining in memory are retained (Figure 5.23 e). At this point, if either Job1 or Job2 is activated, only a partial load will be required. In this example, it is Job2 that runs next. This requires that Job4 and the remaining resident portion of Job1 be written out and that the missing portion of Job2 is read in.

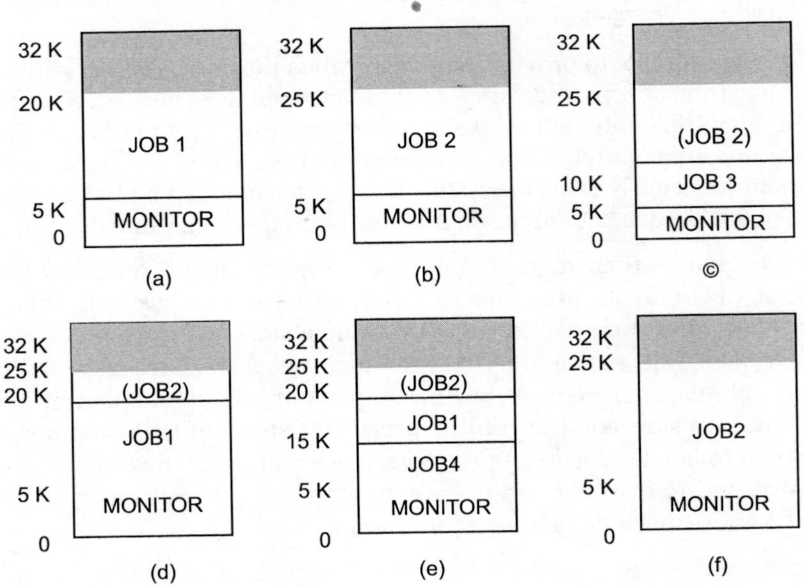

FIGURE 5.23: Compatible Time Sharing System (CTSS) operation

5.5.7.2 REQUIREMENTS OF TIME-SHARING SYSTEMS

Time-sharing systems require following additional hardware and software:

1. A number of terminals connected to a system simultaneously, so that multiple users can use the system simultaneously in interactive mode.
2. Relatively large memory to support multiprogramming.
3. Memory protection mechanism to prevent a job's instructions and data from other jobs in a multiprogramming environment.
4. Job status preservations mechanism to preserve a job's status information when CPU is taken away from it, and restoring this information back, before CPU is given to it again.
5. A special CPU scheduling algorithm that allocates CPU for a short period one-by-one to each user process in a circular fashion.
6. Alarm clock mechanisms to send an interrupt signal to CPU after every time slice.

5.5.7.3 ADVANTAGES OF TIME-SHARING SYSTEMS

Although time-sharing systems are complex to design, they provide the following advantages to their users:

1. **Reduces CPU idle time:** The speed of system is very fast than the user. While a user is busy in thinking or typing, a time sharing system services to many other users. Hence, it gives high utilization of CPU time and reduces CPU idle time. For that reason, the throughput of the system is also increases.
2. **Quick response time:** The special CPU scheduling algorithm used in time-sharing systems to ensures quick response time to all users. It also improve programmers

efficiency by making interactive programming and debugging much simpler and quicker. Multiple programmers can work simultaneously for writing, testing, and debugging their programs, or for trying out various approaches to a problem solving.

3. **Good facility to small users:** Small users can easily and directly access to more sophisticated hardware and software than they could otherwise justify or afford. In time-sharing systems, user have to pay a fee for resources used and are relieved of hardware, software, and personnel problems associated with acquiring and maintaining their own installation.

5.5.7.4 DISADVANTAGES OF TIMESHARING SYSTEMS

1. **Security and protection:** Since thousands of users use a time sharing system simultaneously, so to provide security and protection to user programs and data is difficult.
2. **Problem of reliability:** The time sharing system must be highly reliable because it caters the need of several users.
3. **High overhead involved:** In the timesharing system, programs have to swap for different time slice period according to given time. So the problem of high overhead give rise to high cost.

QUESTIONS

1. What do you mean by parallel computing?
2. Explain the various trends towards parallel processing?
3. Explain the concept of parallelism in uniprocessor systems?
4. Explain the basic architecture of uniprocessor?
5. Explain the various parallel processing mechanisms in detail?
6. Explain the various phases of ILP processing?
7. Explain the concept of DMA in detail?
8. Explain the concept of I/O channels and processors?
9. Explain the concept of memory hierarchy?
10. Explain the concept of multiprogramming and timesharing?

CHAPTER 6 PARALLEL COMPUTER STRUCTURES

6.1 INTRODUCTION

The design and analysis of uniprocessors and pointing out the main limitations of a single-stream machine, we begin in this chapter to pursue the issue of multiple processors. Here a number of processors (two or more) are connected in a manner that allows them to share the simultaneous execution of a single task. The main argument for using multiprocessors is to create powerful computers by simply connecting many existing smaller ones. We then point to the different topologies used for interconnecting multiple processors. Different classification schemes for computer architectures are then introduced and analyzed. We then introduce a topology-based taxonomy for interconnection networks. Two memory-organization schemes for MIMD (multiple instruction multiple data) multiprocessors are also introduced.

Parallel processing has been advocated as a promising approach for building high-performance computer systems. Two basic requirements are inevitable for the efficient use of the employed processors. These requirements are (1) low communication overhead among processors while executing a given task and (2) a degree of inherent parallelism in the task. A number of communication styles exist for multiple processor networks. These can be broadly classified according to (1) the communication model (CM) or (2) the physical connection (PC). According to the CM, networks can be further classified as (1) multiple processors (single address space or shared memory computation) or (2) multiple computers (multiple address space or message passing computation). According to PC, networks can be further classified as (1) bus-based or (2) network based multiple processors. The organization and performance of a multiple processor system are greatly influenced by the interconnection network used to connect them.

On the one hand, a single shared bus can be used as the interconnection network for multiple processors. On the other hand, a crossbar switch can be used as the interconnection network. While the first technique represents a simple easy-to-expand topology, it is, however, limited in performance since it does not allow more than one processor/memory transfer at any given time. The crossbar provides full processor/memory distinct connections but it is expensive. Multistage interconnection networks (MINs) strike a balance between the limitation of the single, shared bus system and the expense of a crossbar-based system. In a MIN more than one processor/memory connection can be established at the same time. The cost of a MIN can be considerably less than that of a crossbar, particularly for a large number of processors and/or memories. The use of multiple buses to connect multiple processors to multiple memory modules has also been suggested as a compromise between the limited single bus and the expensive crossbar.

6.2 PARALLEL ORGANIZATION

Traditionally, the computer has been viewed as a sequential machine. Most computer programming languages require the programmer to specify algorithms as sequences of instructions. Processors execute programs by executing machine instructions in a sequence and one at a time. Each instruction is executed in a sequence of operations (fetch instruction, fetch operands, perform operation, store results).

This view of the computer has never been entirely true. At the micro-operation level, multiple control signals are generated at the same time. Instruction pipelining, at least to the extent of overlapping fetch and execute operations, has been around for a long time. Both of these are examples of performing functions in parallel. This approach is taken further with superscalar organization, which exploits instruction-level parallelism. With a superscalar machine, there are multiple execution units within a single processor, and these may execute multiple instructions from the same program in parallel. As computer technology has evolved, and as the cost of computer hardware has dropped, computer designers have sought more and more opportunities for parallelism, usually to enhance performance and, in some cases, to increase availability. After an overview, this chapter looks at some of the most prominent approaches to parallel organization.

First, we examine symmetric multiprocessors, one of the earliest and still the most common example of parallel organization. In a symmetric multiprocessor organization, multiple processors share a common memory. Another approach to the use of multiple processors that we examine is that of nonuniform memory access machines. The NUMA approach is relatively new and not yet proven in the marketplace, but is often considered as an alternative to the symmetric multiprocessor or cluster approach. Finally, this chapter looks at hardware organizational approaches to vector computation. These approaches optimize the ALU for processing vectors or arrays of floating-point numbers. They are common on the class of systems known as *supercomputers*.

6.3 PARALLEL COMPUTER STRUCTURES

Parallel computers are those systems that emphasize parallel processing. The basic architectural features of parallel computers are introduced below. We divide parallel computers into three architectural configurations:

- Pipeline computers
- Array processors
- Multiprocessor systems

A pipeline computer performs overlapped computations to exploit temporal parallelism. An array processor uses multiple synchronized arithmetic logic units to achieve spatial parallelism. A multiprocessor system achieves asynchronous parallelism through a set of interactive processors with shared resources (memories, database, etc.). These three parallel approaches to computer system design are not mutually exclusive. In fact, most existing computers are now pipelined, and some of them assume also an "array" or a "multiprocessor" structure. The fundamental difference between an array processor and a multiprocessor system is that the processing elements in an array processor operate synchronously but processors in a multiprocessor system may operate asynchronously.

New computing concepts to be introduced in this section include the data flow computers and some VLSI algorithmic processors. All these new approaches demand extensive hardware to achieve parallelism. The rapid progress in the VLSI technology has made these new approaches possible.

6.4 PIPELINE COMPUTERS

In a pipelined computer successive instructions are executed in an overlapped fashion. In a non pipelined computer these four steps must be completed before the next instructions can be issued.

- **Instruction fetch:** Instruction is fetched from the main memory
- **Instruction decoding:** Identifying the operation to be performed.
- **Operand Fetch:** If any operands is needed is fetched.
- **Execution:** Execution of the Arithmetic and logical operation

An instruction cycle consists of multiple pipeline cycles. The flow of data (input operands, intermediate results and output results) from stage to stage is triggered by a common clock of the pipeline. The operations of all stages are triggered by a common clock of the pipeline. For non pipelined computer, it takes four pipeline cycles to complete one instruction. Once a pipe line is filled up, an output result is produced from the pipeline on each cycle. The instruction cycle has been effectively reduced to 1/4th of the original cycle time by such overlapped execution.

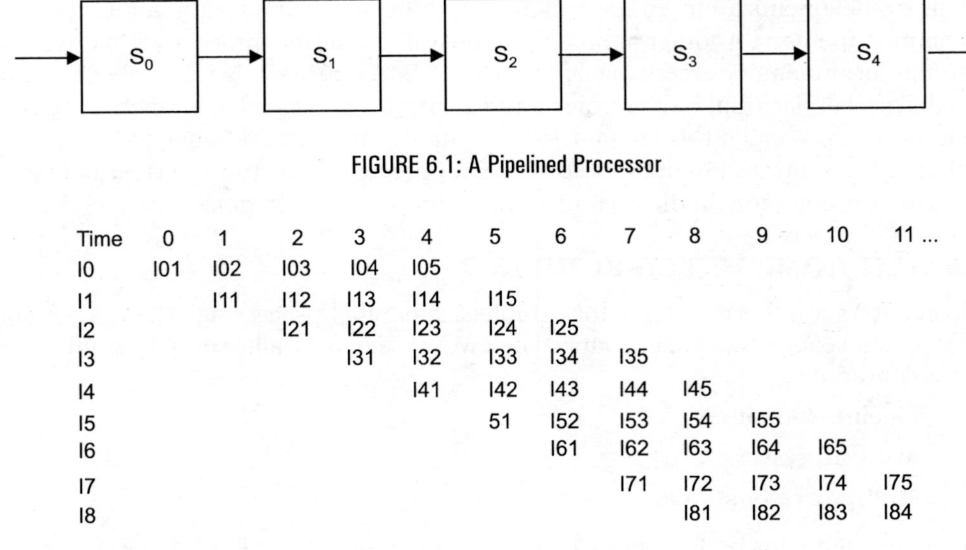

FIGURE 6.1: A Pipelined Processor

Time	0	1	2	3	4	5	6	7	8	9	10	11 ...
I0	I01	I02	I03	I04	I05							
I1		I11	I12	I13	I14	I15						
I2			I21	I22	I23	I24	I25					
I3				I31	I32	I33	I34	I35				
I4					I41	I42	I43	I44	I45			
I5						51	I52	I53	I54	I55		
I6							I61	I62	I63	I64	I65	
I7								I71	I72	I73	I74	I75
I8									I81	I82	I83	I84
...										...		
Completion					I0	I1	I2	I3	I4	I5	16	I7...

FIGURE 6.2: Space Diagram for a Pipelined Processor

6.4.1 PIPELINING

Pipelining refers to the technique in which a given task is divided into a number of subtasks that need to be performed in sequence. Each subtask is performed by a given functional unit. The units are connected in a serial fashion and all of them operate simultaneously. The use of pipelining improves the performance compared to the traditional sequential execution of tasks. Figure 6.3 shows the basic difference between executing four subtasks of a given instruction (in this case fetching F, decoding D, execution E, and writing the results W) using pipelining and sequential processing.

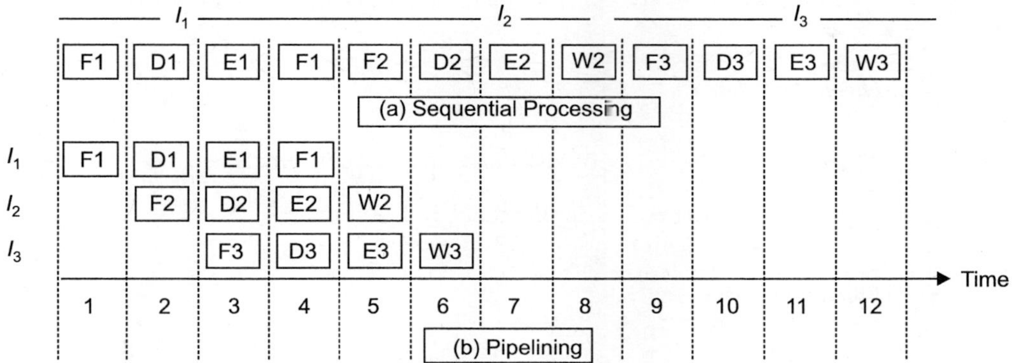

FIGURE 6.3: Pipelining versus sequential processing

It is clear from the figure 6.3 that the total time required to process three instructions (I_1, I_2, I_3) is only six time units if four-stage pipelining is used as compared to 12 time units if sequential processing is used. A possible saving of up to 50% in the execution time of these three instructions is obtained. In order to formulate some performance measures for the goodness of a pipeline in processing a series of tasks, a space time chart (called the Gantt's chart) is used. The chart shows the succession of the subtasks in the pipe with respect to time. Figure 6.4 shows a Gantt's chart. In this chart, the vertical axis represents the subunits (four in this case) and the horizontal axis represents time (measured in terms of the time unit required for each unit to perform its task). In developing the Gantt's chart, we assume that the time (T) taken by each subunit to perform its task is the same; we call this the unit time. The 13 time units are needed to finish executing 10 instructions (I_1 to I_{10}). This is to be compared to 40 time units if sequential processing is used (ten instructions each requiring four time units). In the following analysis, we provide three performance measures for the goodness of a pipeline. These are the Speed-up S(n), Throughput U(n), and Efficiency E(n). It should be noted that in this analysis we assume that the unit time T = t units.

Speed-up S(n): Consider the execution of m tasks (instructions) using n-stages (units) pipeline. As can be seen, n+m-1 time units are required to complete m tasks.

U_4				I_1	I_2	I_3	I_4	I_5	I_6	I_7	I_8	I_9	I_{10}
U_3			I_1	I_2	I_3	I_4	I_5	I_6	I_7	I_8	I_9	I_{10}	
U_2		I_1	I_2	I_3	I_4	I_5	I_6	I_7	I_8	I_9	I_{10}		
U_1	I_1	I_2	I_3	I_4	I_5	I_6	I_7	I_8	I_9	I_{10}			
Time	1	2	3	4	5	6	7	8	9	10	11	12	13

FIGURE 6.4: Space–Time Chart (Gantt chart)

$$\textit{Speed-up } S(n) = \frac{\text{Time using sequential processing}}{\text{Time using pipeline processing}} = \frac{m \times n \times t}{(n+m-1) \times t}$$

$$= \frac{m \times n}{n+m-1}$$

$$\lim_{m\to\infty} S(n) = n \quad \text{(i.e., } n\text{-fold increase in speed is theoretically possible)}$$

2. *Throughput U(n)*

$$\textit{Throughput } U(n) = \text{no. of tasks executed per unit time} = \frac{m}{(n+m-1) \times t}$$

$$\lim_{m\to\infty} U(n) = 1 \text{ assuming that } t = 1 \text{ unit time}$$

3. *Efficiency E(n)*

$$\textit{Efficiency } E(n) = \text{Ratio of the actual speed-up to the maximum speed-up}$$

$$= \frac{\textit{Speed-up}}{n} = \frac{m}{n+m-1}$$

$$\lim_{m\to\infty} E(n) = 1$$

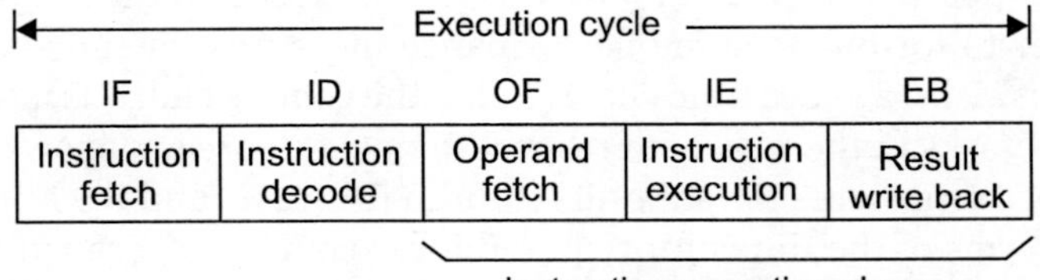

(a) Instruction pipeline stages

Unpack | Align | Add | Normalize

(b) Floating-point add pipeline stages

FIGURE 6.5: Pipelining to divide work into several smaller, preferably equal, parts.

Pipelining allows overlapped execution to improve throughput. The pipeline concept can be applied to various functions of a computer system. The key idea behind pipelining is to divide the work into smaller pieces and use assembly line processing to complete the work. In the instruction execution pipeline, we divided the execution cycle into five steps. For easy reference, we have reproduced these five steps in Figure 6.5(a). In pipeline terminology, each step is called a stage because we will eventually have a dedicated piece of hardware to perform each step. Pipelining can also be applied to arithmetic operations. As an example, we show a floatingpoint add pipeline in Figure 6.5(b).

The floating-point add unit has several stages:

1. **Unpack**: The unpack stage partitions the floating-point numbers into the three fields: the sign field, exponent field, and mantissa field. Any special cases such as not-a-number (NaN), zero, and infinities are detected during this stage.

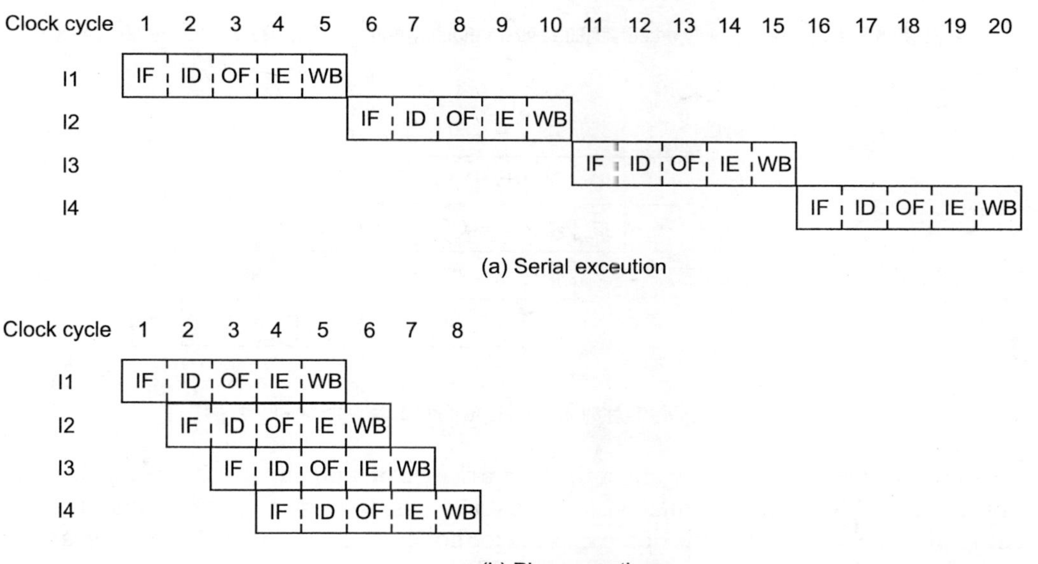

FIGURE 6.6: Pipelining overlaps execution among the stages. This improves instruction execution rate, even though each instruction takes the same amount of time

1. **Align:** This stage aligns the binary points of the two mantissas by right-shifting the mantissa with the smaller exponent.
2. **Add:** This stage adds the two aligned mantissas.
3. **Normalize:** This stage packs the three fields of the result after normalization and rounding into the IEEE-754 floating-point format. Any output exceptions are detected during this stage.

Pipelining works best if we divide the work into equal parts so that each stage takes the same amount of time. Pipelining substantially reduces the execution time by overlapping execution of several instructions. In figure 6.6, serial execution takes 20 clock cycles to execute four instructions I1 through I4. On the other hand, pipelined execution takes only 8 clock cycles. However, pipelining requires hardware support. For the five-stage instruction pipeline, we need four buffers as shown in Figure 6.7. Each of these buffers holds only one value, the output produced by the previous stage. This is possible because the pipeline follows the just-in-time principle. In some processors, the ID stage uses the IF stage buffers by placing the decoded instruction back in the B1 buffer. As we show later, just-in-time arrival of input causes problems because any delay in one stage can seriously affect the entire pipeline flow.

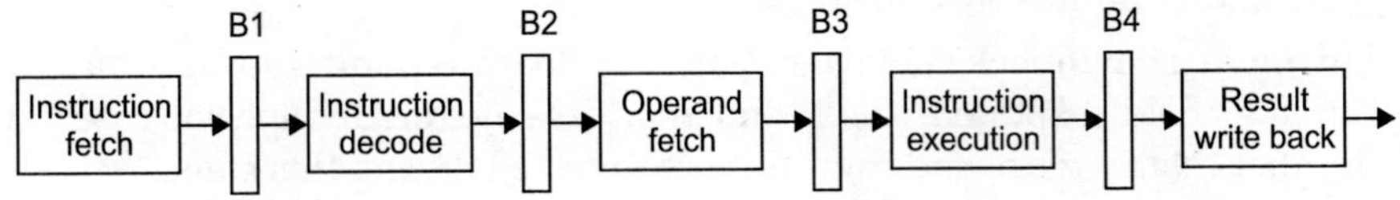

FIGURE 6.7: Pipelines typically do not require substantial buffering as they use the just-in-time concept.

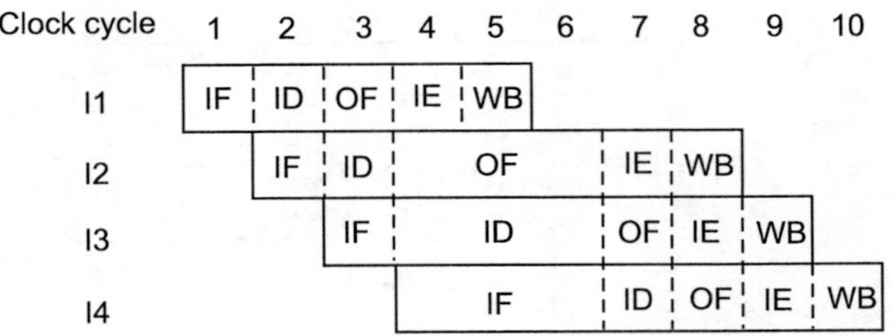

FIGURE 6.8: Delay in any stage can cause pipeline stalls.

Several factors can adversely affect the performance of a pipeline. For starters, it is not always possible to divide the work into equal parts. In that case, the slowest stage determines the flow rate in the entire pipeline. What are some of the reasons for not having equal work for all stages? Sometimes this is due to a complex step that cannot be subdivided conveniently. In some instances, it may be due to the operation that takes a variable amount of time to execute. For example, consider the operand fetch (OF) step in the instruction pipeline. The time required to execute this step depends on where the operands are located: in registers, cache memory, or main memory. If the operands are in registers rather than in memory, it takes less time. In some cases, the complexity of the operation depends on the type of operation performed by the instruction. For example, an integer addition operation may take only one cycle but a multiplication operation may take several cycles.

Let's assume that the operand fetch of the I2 instruction takes more time: three clock cycles rather than one. Figure 6.8 shows how the increased execution time for I2's OF stage causes the pipeline to stall for two clock cycles. As you can see from this figure, the stalled pipeline reduces the overall throughput. One of the goals in designing a pipeline is to minimize pipeline stalls. Pipeline stalls can be caused by several factors. These are called hazards. There are three types of hazards: resource, data, and control hazards. Resource hazards result when two or more instructions in the pipeline want to use the same resource. Such resource conflicts can result in serialized execution, reducing the scope for overlapped execution.

Data hazards are caused by data dependencies among the instructions in the pipeline. As a simple example, suppose that the result produced by instruction I1 is needed as an input to instruction I2. We have to stall the pipeline until I1 has written the result so that I2 reads the correct input. If the pipeline is not designed properly, data hazards can produce wrong results by using incorrect operands. We can use a technique called interlocking to ensure that only correct operands are used. There is another technique called forwarding that actually improves the performance by reducing the amount of time the pipeline is stalled waiting for the result of a previous instruction.

6.4.2 INSTRUCTION PIPELINING

In a pipeline, new inputs are accepted at one end before previously accepted inputs appear as outputs at the other end. Instruction processing subdividing into two stages: fetch instruction and execute instruction. There are times during the execution of an instruction when main memory is not being accessed. This time could be used to fetch the next instruction in parallel with the execution of the current one.

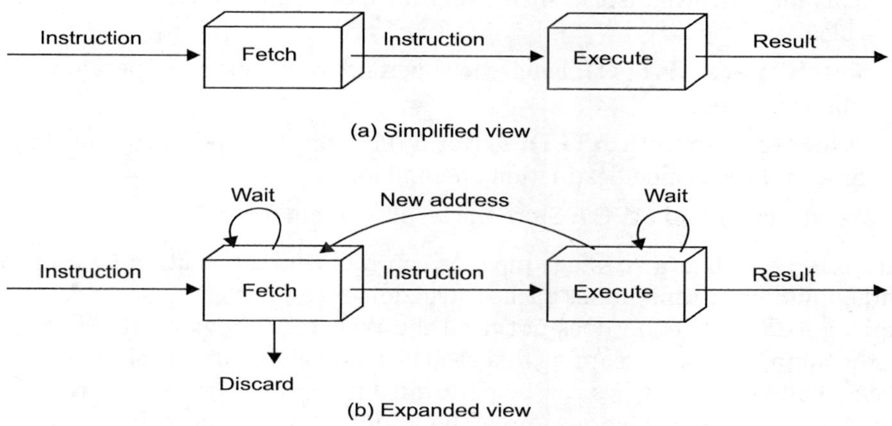

FIGURE 6.9: Two-Stage Instruction Pipeline

Figure 6.9(a) pipeline has two independent stages. The first stage fetches an instruction and buffers it. When the second stage is free, the first stage passes it the buffered instruction. While the second stage is executing the instruction, the first stage takes advantage of any unused memory cycles to fetch and buffer the next instruction. These are called instruction prefetch or fetch overlap. Note that this approach, which involves instruction buffering, requires more registers. In general, pipelining requires registers to store data between stages. It should be clear that this process will speed up instruction execution. If the fetch and execute stages were of equal duration, the instruction cycle time would be halved. However, if we look more closely at this pipeline (Figure 6.9(b)), we will see that this doubling of execution rate is unlikely for two reasons:

1. The execution time will generally be longer than the fetch time. Execution will involve reading and storing operands and the performance of some operation. Thus, the fetch stage may have to wait for some time before it can empty its buffer.
2. A conditional branch instruction makes the address of the next instruction to be fetched unknown. Thus, the fetch stage must wait until it receives the next instruction address from the execute stage. The execute stage may then have to wait while the next instruction is fetched.

When a conditional branch instruction is passed on from the fetch to the execute stage, the fetch stage fetches the next instruction in memory after the branch instruction. Then, if the branch is not taken, no time is lost. If the branch is taken, the fetched instruction must be discarded and a new instruction fetched. While these factors reduce the potential effectiveness of the two-stage pipeline, some speedup occurs. To gain further speedup, the pipeline must have more stages. Let us consider the following decomposition of the instruction processing.

- **Fetch instruction (FI):** Read the next expected instruction into a buffer.
- **Decode instruction (DI):** Determine the opcode and the operand specifiers.
- **Calculate operands (CO):** Calculate the effective address of each source operand. This may involve displacement; register indirect, indirect, or other forms of address calculation.
- **Fetch operands (FO):** Fetch each operand from memory. Operands in registers need not be fetched.
- **Execute instruction (EI):** Perform the indicated operation and store the result, if any, in the specified destination operand location.
- **Write operand (WO):** Store the result in memory.

Figure 6.10 show that a six-stage pipeline can reduce the execution time for 9 instructions from 54 time units to 14 time units. Each instruction goes through all six stages of the pipeline. For example, a load instruction does not need the WO stage. However, to simplify the pipeline hardware, the timing is set up assuming that each instruction requires all six stages. Also, the figure 6.10 assumes that all of the stages can be performed in parallel. In particular, it is assumed that there are no memory conflicts. For example, the FI, FO, and WO stages involve a memory access. Most memory systems will not permit that. However, the desired value may be in cache, or the FO or WO stage may be null. Thus, much of the time, memory conflicts will not slow down the pipeline.

Time →

	1	2	3	4	5	6	7	8	9	10	11	12	13	14
Instruction 1	F1	DI	CO	FO	EI	WO								
Instruction 2		F1	DI	CO	FO	EI	WO							
Instruction 3			F1	DI	CO	FO	EI	WO						
Instruction 4				F1	DI	CO	FO	EI	WO					
Instruction 5					F1	DI	CO	FO	EI	WO				
Instruction 6						F1	DI	CO	FO	EI	WO			
Instruction 7							F1	DI	CO	FO	EI	WO		
Instruction 8								F1	DI	CO	FO	EI	WO	
Instruction 9									F1	DI	CO	F0	EI	WO

FIGURE 6.10: Timing Diagram for Instruction Pipeline Operation

Several other factors serve to limit the performance enhancement. If the six stages are not of equal duration, there will be some waiting involved at various pipeline stages. Another difficulty is the conditional branch instruction, which can invalidate several instruction fetches. A similar unpredictable event is an interrupt. Figure 6.11 the effects of the conditional branch, using the same program as Figure 6.10. Assume that instruction 3 is a conditional branch to instruction 15. Until the instruction is executed, there is no way of knowing which instruction will come next. The pipeline, in this example, simply loads the next instruction in sequence (instruction 4) and proceeds.

In Figure 6.10, the branch is not taken, and we get the full performance benefit of the enhancement. In Figure 6.11, the branch is taken. This is not determined until the end of time unit 7.At this point, the pipeline must be cleared of instructions that are not useful. During time unit 8, instruction 15 enters the pipeline. No instructions complete during time units 9 through 12; this is the performance penalty incurred because we could not anticipate the branch. Figure 6.12 indicates the logic needed for pipelining to account for branches and interrupts.

The CO stage may depend on the contents of a register that could be altered by a previous instruction that is still in the pipeline. Other such register and memory conflicts could occur. The system must contain logic to account for this type of conflict. To clarify pipeline operation, it might be useful to look at an alternative depiction. Figure 6.13 shows same sequence of events, with time progressing vertically down the figure, and each row showing the state of the pipeline at a given point in time. In Figure 6.13(a) the pipeline is full at time 6, with 6 different instructions in various stages of execution, and remains full through time 9; we assume that instruction I9 is the last instruction to be executed. In Figure 6.13(b) the pipeline is full at times 6 and 7. At time 7, instruction 3 is in the execute stage and executes a branch to instruction 15. At this point, instructions I4 through I7 are flushed from the pipeline, so that at time 8, only two instructions are in the pipeline, I3 and I15.

Time → ← Branch penalty →

	1	2	3	4	5	6	7	8	9	10	11	12	13	14
Instruction 1	FI	DI	CO	FO	EI	WO								
Instruction 2		FI	DI	CO	FO	EI	WO							
Instruction 3			FI	DI	CO	FO	EI	WO						
Instruction 4				FI	DI	CO	FO							
Instruction 5					FI	DI	CO							
Instruction 6						FI	DI							
Instruction 7							FI							
Instruction 15								FI	DI	CO	FO	EI	WO	
Instruction 16									FI	DI	CO	FO	EI	WO

FIGURE 6.11: Effect of Conditional Branch on Instruction Pipeline Operation

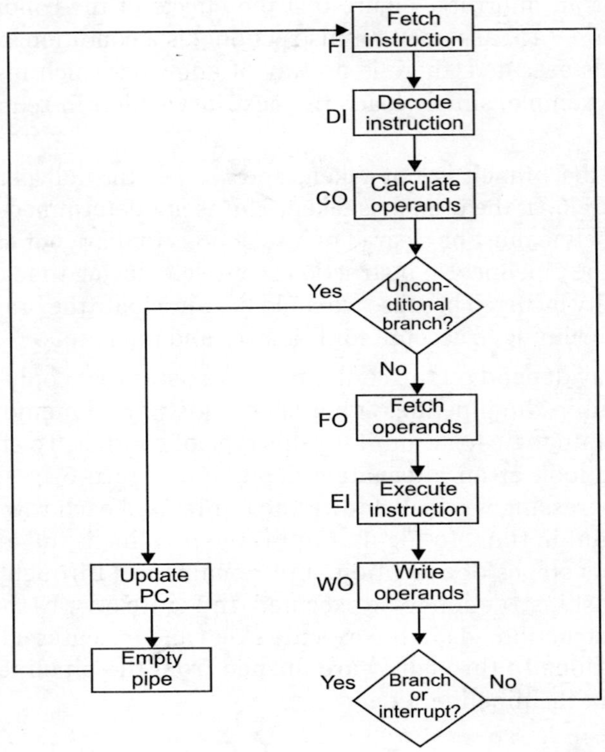

FIGURE 6.12: Six-Stage CPU Instruction Pipeline

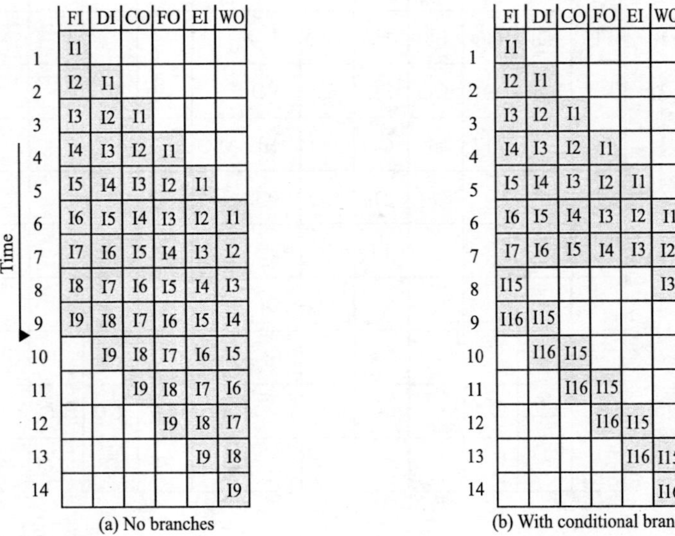

Time	FI	DI	CO	FO	EI	WO
1	I1					
2	I2	I1				
3	I3	I2	I1			
4	I4	I3	I2	I1		
5	I5	I4	I3	I2	I1	
6	I6	I5	I4	I3	I2	I1
7	I7	I6	I5	I4	I3	I2
8	I8	I7	I6	I5	I4	I3
9	I9	I8	I7	I6	I5	I4
10		I9	I8	I7	I6	I5
11			I9	I8	I7	I6
12				I9	I8	I7
13					I9	I8
14						I9

(a) No branches

	FI	DI	CO	FO	EI	WO
1	I1					
2	I2	I1				
3	I3	I2	I1			
4	I4	I3	I2	I1		
5	I5	I4	I3	I2	I1	
6	I6	I5	I4	I3	I2	I1
7	I7	I6	I5	I4	I3	I2
8	I15					I3
9	I16	I15				
10		I16	I15			
11			I16	I15		
12				I16	I15	
13					I16	I15
14						I16

(b) With conditional branch

FIGURE 6.13: Alternative Pipeline Depiction

The number of stages in the pipeline and the faster the execution rate pointed out two factors that pattern for high-performance design must be following:

1. At each stage of the pipeline, there is some overhead involved in moving data from buffer to buffer and in performing various preparation and delivery functions. This overhead can appreciably lengthen the total execution time of a single instruction. This is significant when sequential instructions are logically dependent, either through heavy use of branching or through memory access dependencies.
2. The amount of control logic required to handle memory and register dependencies and to optimize the use of the pipeline increases enormously with the number of stages. This can lead to a situation where the logic controlling the gating between stages is more complex than the stages being controlled.

Another consideration is latching delay: It takes time for pipeline buffers to operate and this adds to instruction cycle time. Instruction pipelining is a powerful technique for enhancing performance but requires careful design to achieve optimum results with reasonable complexity.

6.4.3 PIPELINE PERFORMANCE

In this subsection, we develop some simple measures of pipeline performance and relative speedup. The cycle time of an instruction pipeline is the time needed to advance a set of instructions one stage through the pipeline; each column represents one cycle time. The cycle time can be determined as

$$\tau = \max[\tau_i] + d = \tau_m + d \quad 1 \leq i \leq k$$

where

τ_i= time delay of the circuitry in the ith stage of the pipeline

τ_m= maximum stage delay (delay through stage which experiences the largest delay)

k= number of stages in the instruction pipeline

d= time delay of a latch, needed to advance signals and data from one stage to the next

In general, the time delay d is equivalent to a clock pulse and $\tau_m >> d$ Now suppose that n instructions are processed, with no branches. Let τ_{km} be the total time required for a pipeline with k stages to execute n instructions. Then

$$T_{km} = [k + (n - 1)]\tau$$

A total of k cycles are required to complete the execution of the first instruction, and the remaining n-1 instructions require n-1 cycles. The ninth instruction completes at time cycle 14:

$$14 = [6 + (9 - 1)]$$

Now consider a processor with equivalent functions but no pipeline, and assume that the instruction cycle time is $k\tau$. The speedup factor for the instruction pipeline compared to execution without the pipeline is defined as

$$S_k = \frac{T_{1,n}}{T_{k,n}} = \frac{nk\tau}{[k+(n-1)]\tau} = \frac{nk}{K+(n-1)}$$

Figure 6.14(a) plots the speedup factor as a function of the number of instructions that are executed without a branch. As might be expected, at the limit we have a k-fold speedup. Figure

6.14(b) shows the speedup factor as a function of the number of stages in the instruction pipeline. In this case, the speedup factor approaches the number of instructions that can be fed into the pipeline without branches. Thus, the larger the number of pipeline stages, the greater the potential for speedup. However, as a practical matter, the potential gains of additional pipeline stages are countered by increases in cost, delays between stages, and the fact that branches will be encountered requiring the flushing of the pipeline.

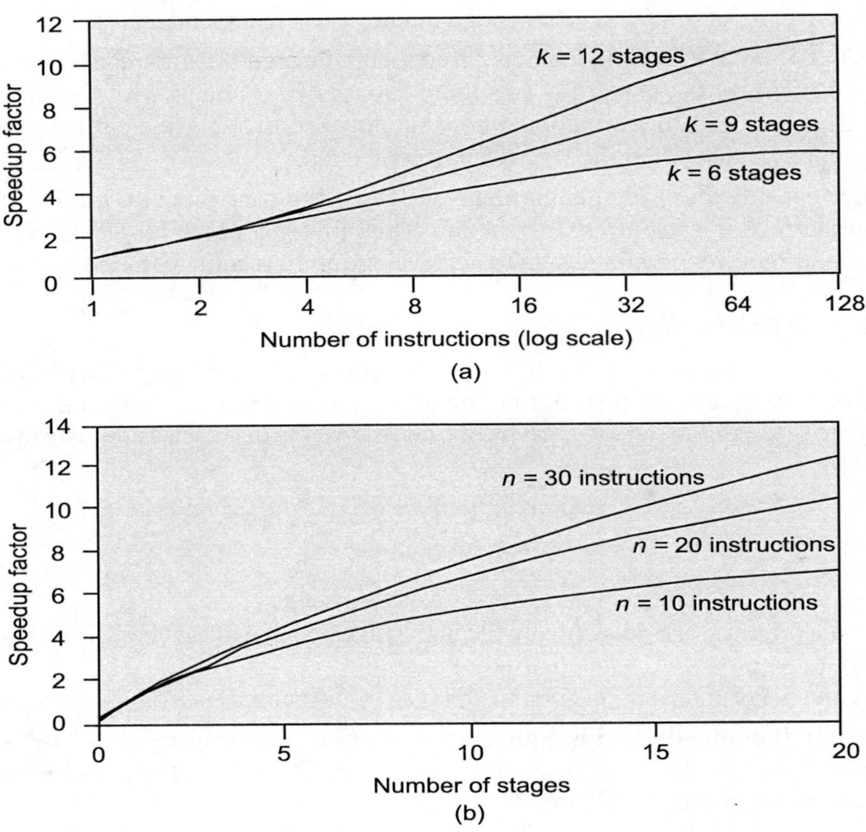

FIGURE 6.14: Speedup Factors with Instruction Pipelining

6.5 ARRAY PROCESSOR

An array processor is a processor that performs computations on large arrays of data. It may be composed of a group of special processors designed to calculate math procedures at very high speeds, often under the control for another central processor. Some computers use array processors to speed up video operations or for fast floating-point math operations. The term is used to refer to two different types of processors, an *attached array processor* and a *SIMD array Processor*. A processor capable of executing instructions in which the operands may be arrays rather than data elements. An array processor is a processor that performs computations on large arrays of data. There are two different types of processors:-

(a) an attached array processor

(b) SIMD array processor.

Array processor, also called a vector processor, is a microprocessor or computer that is capable of performing simultaneous computations on elements of an array of data in some number of dimensions. Common uses of such processor include analysis of fluid dynamics and rotation of 3D objects as well as data retrieval, in which elements in a database are scanned simultaneously that executes one instruction at a time but on an array or table of data at the same time rather than on single data elements.

An array processor is a synchronous parallel computer with multiple arithmetic logic units called processing elements (PE) that can operate in parallel in lock step fashion. By replication one can achieve spatial parallelism. The PEs is synchronized to perform the same function at the same time. Scalar and control type of instructions are directly executed in the control unit (CU). Each PE consists of an ALU registers and a local memory. The PEs is interconnected by a data routing network. Vector instructions are broadcasted to the PEs for distributed execution over different component operands fetched directly from local memories. Array processors designed with associative memories are called as associative processors.

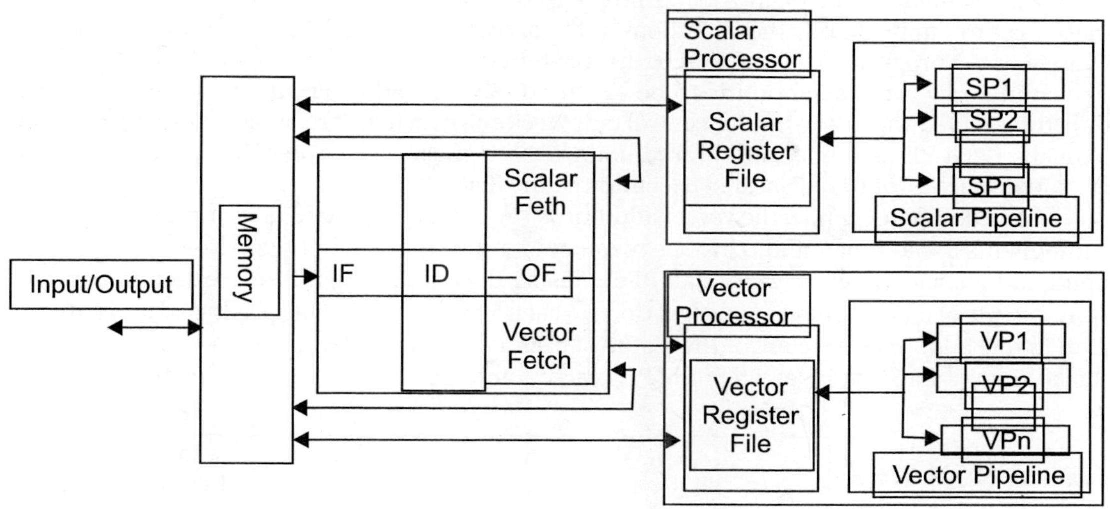

FIGURE 6.15: Functional structure of a modern pipeline computer with scalar and vector Capabilities

6.5.1 ATTACHED ARRAY PROCESSOR

An *attached array processor* is an auxiliary processor attached to a general-purpose computer, designed as a peripheral for a conventional host computer. The array processor can be programmed by the user to accommodate a variety of complex arithmetic problems. The host computer is a general-purpose commercial computer and the attached processor is a back-end machine driven by the host computer. The array processor is connected through an input output controller to the computer and the computer treats it like an external interface. The data for the attached processor are transferred from main memory to a local memory through a high-speed bus. The general-purpose computer without the attached processor serves the users that need conventional data processing.

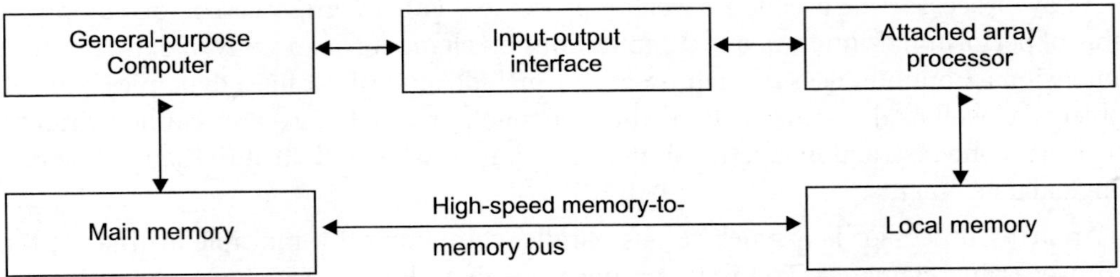

FIGURE 6.16: Attached array processor with host computer

6.5.2 SIMD ARRAY PROCESSOR

An SIMD *array processor* is a processor that has a single-instruction multiple-data organization. It manipulates vector instructions by means of multiple functional units responding to a common instruction. It contains a set of identical processing elements (PEs), each having a local memory M. Each processor element includes an ALU, a floating-point arithmetic unit, and working registers. The master control unit controls the operations in the processor elements. The main memory is used for storage of the program. The function of the master control unit is to decode the instructions and determine how the instruction is to be executed. Scalar and program control instructions are directly executed within the master control unit. Vector instructions are broadcast to all PEs simultaneously. Each PE uses operands stored in its local memory. Vector operands are distributed to the local memories prior to the parallel execution of the instruction.

Consider, for example, the vector addition $C = A + B$. The master control unit first stores the ith components a_i and b_i of A and B in local memory M_i for $i = 1, 2, 3, . n$. It then broadcasts the floating-point add instruction $c_i = a_i + b_i$ to all PEs, causing the addition to take place simultaneously. The components of c_i are stored in fixed locations in each local memory. This produces the desired vector sum in one add cycle. To control the status of each PE during the execution of vector instructions, Each PE has a flag that is set when the PE is active and reset when the PE is inactive.

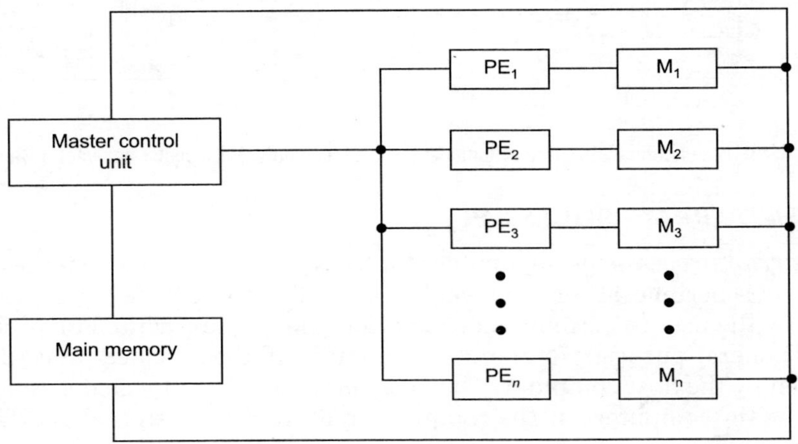

FIGURE 6.17: SIMD array processor organizations

6.6 MULTIPLE PROCESSOR ORGANIZATIONS

A multiprocessor system is an interconnection of two or more CPUs with memory and input—output equipment. The term "processor" in *multiprocessor* can mean either a central processing unit (CPU) or an input—output processor (IOP). However, a system with a single CPU and one or more IOPs is usually not included in the definition of a multiprocessor system unless the IOP has computational facilities comparable to a CPU. As it is most commonly defined, a multiprocessor system implies the existence of multiple CPUs, although usually there will be one or more IOPs as well. Multiprocessors are classified as multiple instruction stream, multiple data stream (MIMD) systems.

There are some similarities between multiprocessor and multicomputer systems since both support concurrent operations. However, there exists an important distinction between a system with multiple computers and a system with multiple processors. Computers are interconnected with each other by means of communication lines to form a *computer network*. The network consists of several autonomous computers that may or may not communicate with each other. A multiprocessor system is controlled by one operating system that provides interaction between processors and all the components of the system cooperate in the solution of a problem.

Although some large-scale computers include two or more CPUs in their overall system, it is the emergence of the microprocessor that has been the major motivation for multiprocessor systems. The fact that microprocessors take very little physical space and are very inexpensive brings about the feasibility of interconnecting a large number of microprocessors into one composite system. Very-large-scale integrated circuit technology has reduced the cost of computer components to such a low level that the concept of applying multiple processors to meet system performance requirements has become an attractive design possibility.

6.6.1 HOW MULTIPROCESSORS CAN IMPROVED PERFORMANCE?

A multiple processor system consists of two or more processors that are connected in a manner that allows them to share the simultaneous (parallel) execution of a given computational task. A multiprocessor is expected to reach a faster speed than the fastest uniprocessor. In addition, a multiprocessor consisting of a number of single uniprocessors is expected to be more cost-effective than building a high-performance single processor. An additional advantage of a multiprocessor consisting of n processors is that if a single processor fails, the remaining fault-free n-1 processors should be able to provide continued service, albeit with degraded performance.

Following are the characteristics of multiprocessors:

1. Multiprocessing improves the reliability of the system so that a failure or error in one part has a limited effect on the rest of the system. If a fault causes one processor to fail, a second processor can be assigned to perform the functions of the disabled processor. The system as a whole can continue to function correctly with perhaps some loss in efficiency.
2. The benefit derived from a multiprocessor organization is an improved system performance. The system derives its high performance from the fact that computations can proceed in parallel in one of two ways.
   - Multiple independent jobs can be made to operate in parallel.
   - A single job can be partitioned into multiple parallel tasks.

An overall function can be partitioned into a number of tasks that each processor can handle individually. System tasks may be allocated to special- purpose processors whose design is optimized to perform certain types of processing efficiently.

For example is a computer system where one processor performs the computations for an industrial process control while others monitor and control the various parameters, such as temperature and flow rate. Another example is a computer where one processor performs high-speed floating-point mathematical computations and another takes care of routine data-processing tasks.

3. Multiprocessing can improve performance by decomposing a program into parallel executable tasks. The user can explicitly declare that certain tasks of the program be executed in parallel. This must be done prior to loading the program by specifying the parallel executable segments.

Most multiprocessor manufacturers provide an operating system with programming language constructs suitable for specifying parallel processing. The other, more efficient way is to provide a compiler with multiprocessor software that can automatically detect parallelism in a user's program. The compiler checks for *data dependency* in the program. If a program depends on data generated in another part, the part yielding the needed data must be executed first. However, two parts of a program that do not use data generated by each can run concurrently. The parallelizing compiler checks the entire program to detect any possible data dependencies. These that have no data dependency are then considered for concurrent scheduling on different processors.

6.6.2 MEMORY ORGANIZATION OF MULTIPROCESSORS

Multiprocessors are classified by the way their memory is organized. A multiprocessor system with common shared memory is classified as a *shared-memory or tightly coupled multiprocessor*. This does not preclude each processor from having its own local memory. In fact, most commercial tightly coupled multiprocessors provide a cache memory with each CPU. In addition, there is a global common memory that all CPUs can access. Information can therefore be shared among the CPUs by placing it in the common global memory. An alternative model of microprocessor is the *distributed-memory or loosely coupled multiprocessor*. Each processor element in a loosely coupled system has its own private local memory. The processors are tied together by a switching scheme designed to route information from one processor to another through a message-passing scheme. The processors relay program and data to other processors in packets. A packet consists of an address, the data content, and some error detection code. The packets are addressed to a specific processor or taken by the first available processor, depending on the communication system used. Loosely coupled systems are most efficient when the interaction between tasks is minimal, whereas tightly coupled systems can tolerate a higher degree of interaction between tasks.

6.6.3 MULTIPROCESSOR SYSTEMS

A basic multiprocessor contains two or more processors of comparable capabilities. All processors share access to common sets of memory modules, I/O channels and peripheral devices. The entire system must be controlled by a single integrated operating system providing interactions between processors and their programs at various levels. Multiprocessor hardware system organization is determined by the interconnection structure to be used between the memories and processors. The interconnection between the components can have different physical configurations, depending on the number of transfer paths that are available between the processors and memory in a shared memory system or among the processing elements in a loosely coupled system. There are several physical forms available for establishing an interconnection network.

Some of these schemes are presented in this section:

1. Time-shared common bus
2. Multiport memory
3. Crossbar switch
4. Multistage switching network
5. Hypercube system

6.6.3.1 TIME-SHARED COMMON BUS

A common-bus multiprocessor system consists of a number of processors connected through a common path to a memory unit. A time-shared common bus for five processors is shown in Figure 6.18. Only one processor can communicate with the memory or another processor at any given time. Transfer operations are conducted by the processor that is in control of the bus at the time. Any other processor wishing to initiate a transfer must first determine the availability status of the bus, and only after the bus becomes available can the processor address the destination unit to initiate the transfer. A command is issued to inform the destination unit what operation is to be performed. The receiving unit recognizes its address in the bus and responds to the control signals from the sender, after which the transfer is initiated. The system may exhibit transfer conflicts since one common bus is shared by all processors. These conflicts must be resolved by incorporating a bus controller that establishes priorities among the requesting units.

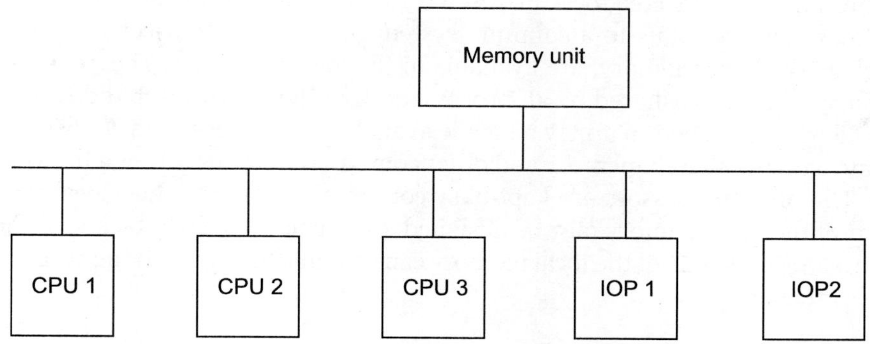

FIGURE 6.18: Time-shared common bus organization.

A single common-bus system is restricted to one transfer at a time. This means that when one processor is communicating with the memory, all other processors are either busy with internal operations or must be idle waiting for the bus. As a consequence, the total overall transfer rate within the system is limited by the speed of the single path. The processors in the system can be kept busy more often through the implementation of two or more independent buses to permit multiple simultaneous bus transfers. However, this increases the system cost and complexity.

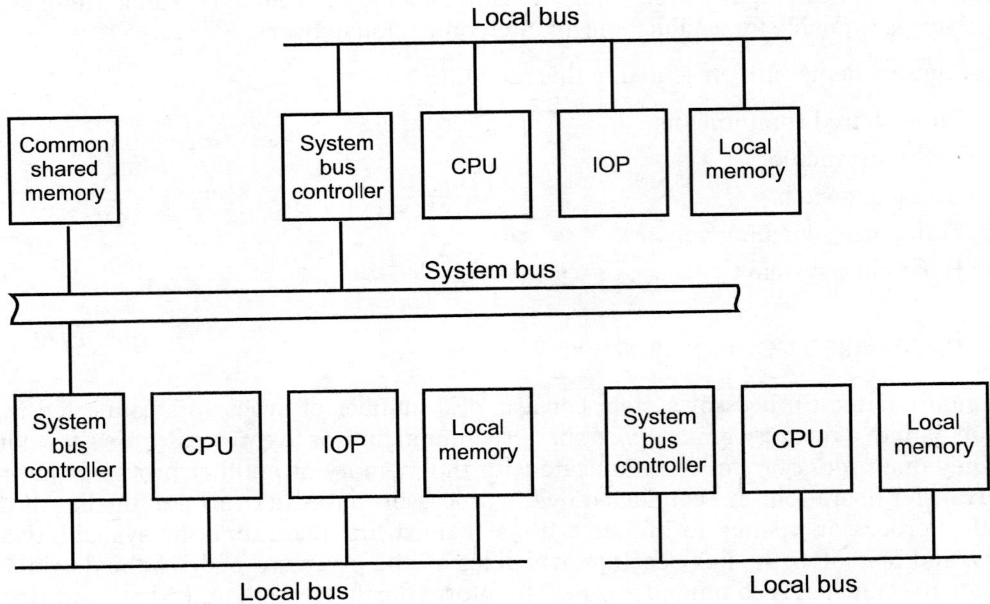

FIGURE 6.19: System bus structure for multiprocessors.

A more economical implementation of a dual bus structure is depicted in Figure 6.19. Here we have a number of local buses each connected to its own local memory and to one or more processors. Each local bus may be connected to a CPU, an IOP, or any combination of processors. A system bus controller links each local bus to a common system bus. The 1/0 devices connected to the local TOP, as well as the local memory, are available to the local processor. The memory connected to the common system bus is shared by all processors. If an IOP is connected directly to the system bus, the I/O devices attached to it may be made available to all processors. Only one processor can communicate with the shared memory and other common resources through the system bus at any given time. The other processors are kept busy communicating with their local memory and I/O devices. Part of the local memory may be designed as a cache memory attached to the CPU. In this way, the average access time of the local memory can be made to approach the cycle time of the CPU to which it is attached.

6.6.3.2 MULTIPORT MEMORY

A multiport memory system employs separate buses between each memory module and each CPU. This is shown in Figure 6.20 for four CPUs and four memory modules (MMs). Each processor bus is connected to each memory module. A processor bus consists of the address, data, and control lines required communicating with memory. The memory module is said to have four ports and each port accommodates one of the buses. The module must have internal control logic to determine which port will have access to memory at any given time. Memory access conflicts are resolved by assigning fixed priorities to each memory port. The priority for memory access associated with each processor may be established by the physical port position that its bus occupies in each module. Thus CPU 1 will have priority over CPU 2, CPU 2 will have priority over CPU 3, and CPU 4 will have the lowest priority.

The advantage of the multiport memory organization is the high transfer rate that can be achieved because of the multiple paths between processors and memory. The disadvantage is that it requires expensive memory control logic and a large number of cables and connectors. As a consequence, this interconnection structure is usually appropriate for systems with a small number of processors.

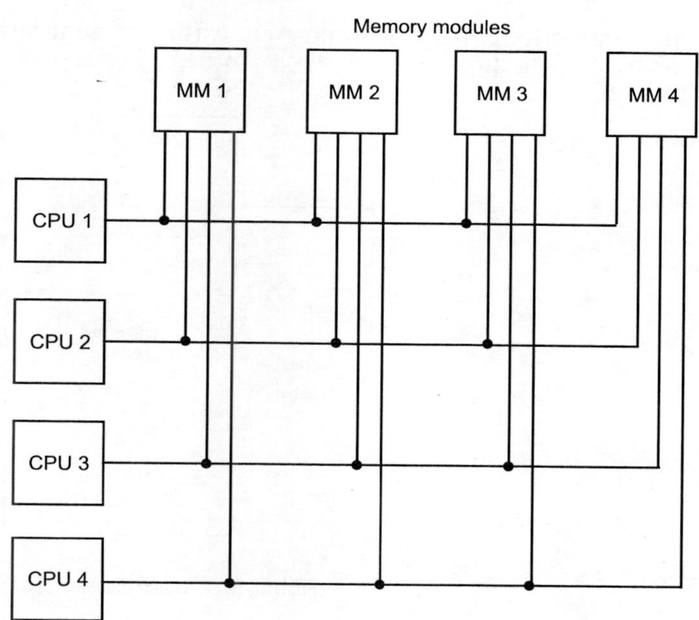

FIGURE 6.20: Multiport memory organization.

6.6.3.3 CROSSBAR SWITCH

The crossbar switch organization consists of a number of crosspoints that are placed at intersections between processor buses and memory module paths. Figure 6.21 shows a crossbar switch interconnection between four CPUs and four memory modules. The small square in each crosspoint is a switch that determines the path from a processor to a memory module. Each switch point has control logic to set up the transfer path between a processor and memory. It examines the address that is placed in the bus to determine whether its particular module is being addressed. It also resolves multiple requests for access to the same memory module on a predetermined priority basis.

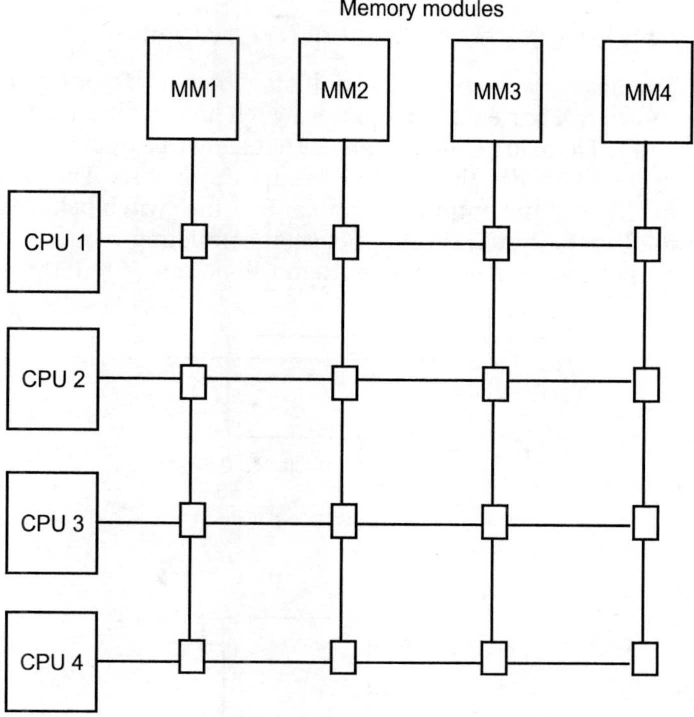

FIGURE 6.21: Crossbar switch

Figure 6.22 shows the functional design of a crossbar switch connected to one memory module. The circuit consists of multiplexers that select the data, address, and control from one CPU for communication with the memory module. Priority levels are established by the arbitration logic to select one CPU when two or more CPUs attempt to access the same memory. The multiplex are controlled with the binary code that is generated by a priority encoded within the arbitration logic.

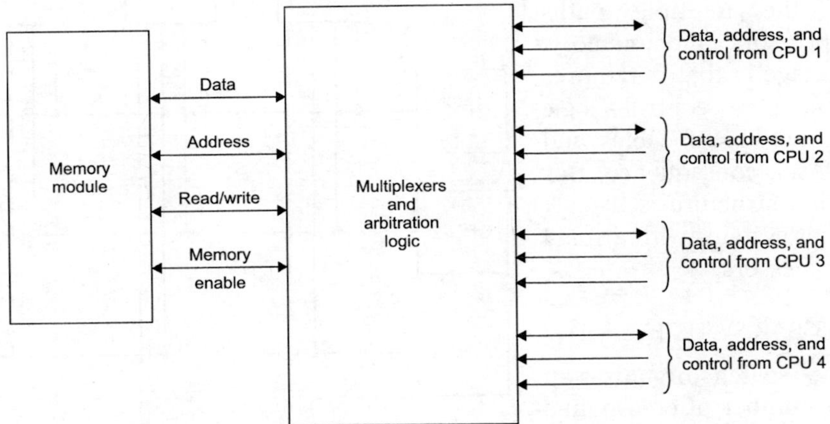

FIGURE 6.22: Block diagram of crossbar switch

A crossbar switch organization supports simultaneous transfers from memory modules because there is a separate path associated with each module. However, the hardware required to implement the switch can become quite large and complex.

6.6.3.4 MULTISTAGE SWITCHING NETWORK

The basic component of a multistage network is a two-input, two-output interchange switch. As shown in Figure 6.23, the 2 × 2 switch has two inputs, labeled A and B, and two outputs, labeled 0 and 1. There are control signals (not shown) associated with the switch that establish the interconnection between the input and output terminals. The switch has the capability connecting input A to either of the outputs. Terminal B of the switch behaves in a similar fashion. The switch also has the capability to arbitrate between conflicting requests. If inputs A and B both request the same output terminal only one of them will be connected; the other will be blocked.

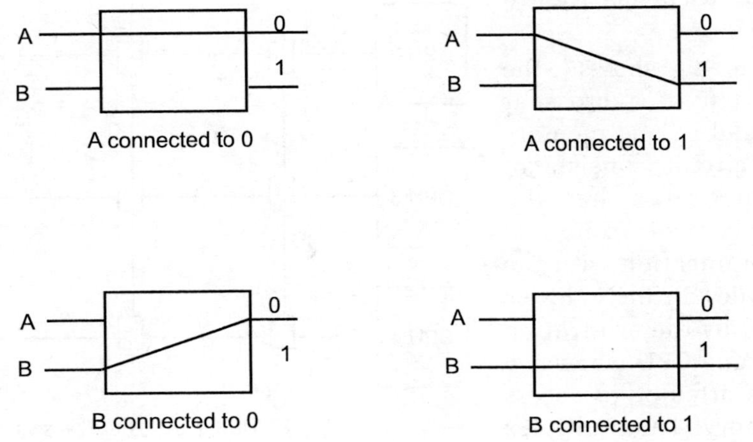

FIGURE 6.23: Operation of a 2×2 interchange switch.

Using the 2×2 switch as a building block, it is possible to build a multistage network to control the communication between a number of sources and destinations. To see how this is done, consider the binary tree shown Figure 6.24. The two processors P_1 and P_2 are connected through switches to eight memory modules marked in binary from 000 through 111. The path from a source to a destination is determined from the binary bits of the destination number. The first bit of the destination number determines the switch output in the first level. The second bit specifies the output of the switch in the second level, and the third bit specifies the output of the switch in the third level. For example, to connect P_1 to memory 101, it is necessary to form a path from P_1 to output 1 in the first-level switch, output 0 in the second-level switch, and output 1 in the third-level switch. It is clear that either P_1 or P_2 can be connected to any one of the eight memories. Certain request patterns, however, cannot be satisfied simultaneously. For example, if P_1 is connected to one of the destinations 000 through 011, P_2 can be connected to only one of the destinations 100 through 111.

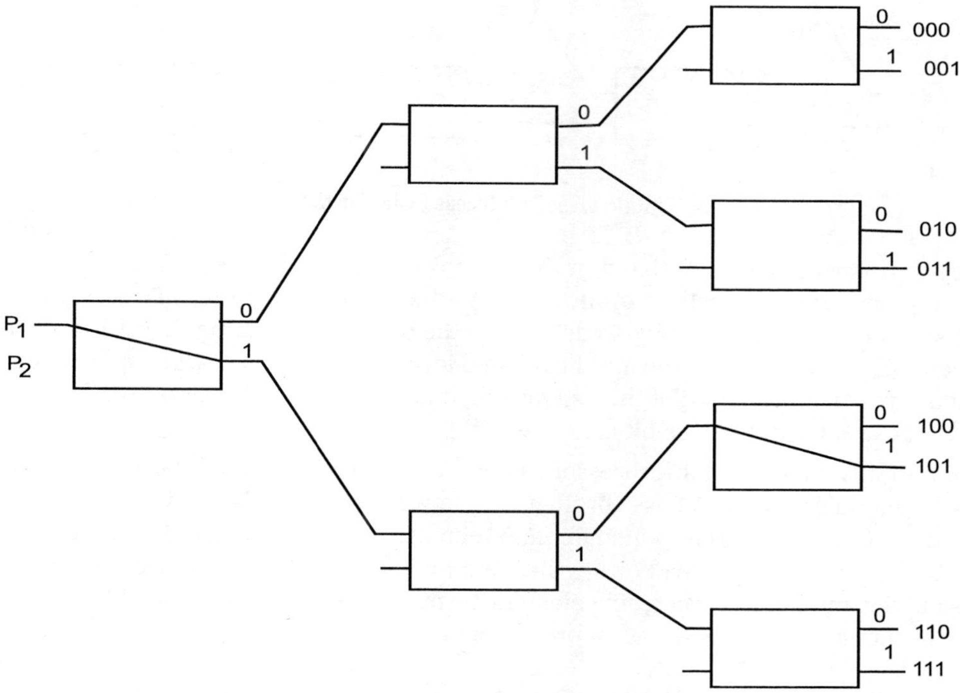

FIGURE 6.24: Binary tree with 2 × 2 switches.

Many different topologies have been proposed for multistage switching networks to control processor—memory communication in a tightly coupled multiprocessor system or to control the communication between the processing elements in a loosely coupled system. One such topology is the omega switching network shown in Figure 6.25. In this configuration, there is exactly one path from each source to any particular destination. Some request patterns, however, cannot be connected simultaneously. For example, any two sources cannot be connected simultaneously to destinations 000 and 001.

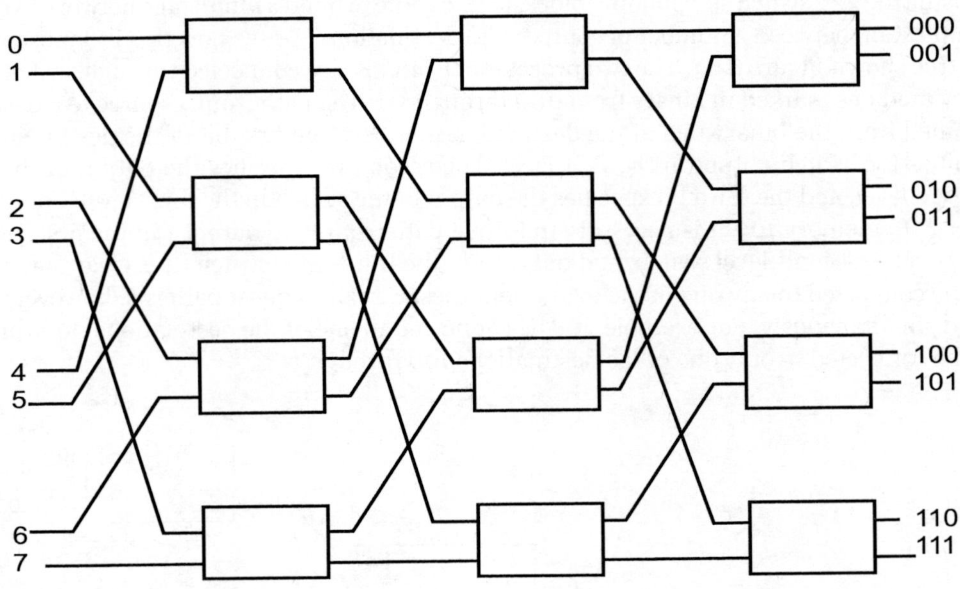

FIGURE 6.25: 8 × 8 Omega Switching Network.

A particular request is initiated in the switching network by the source, which sends a 3-bit pattern representing the destination number. As the binary pattern moves through the network, each level examines a different bit to determine the 2×2 switch setting. Level 1 inspects the most significant bit, level 2 inspects the middle bit, and level 3 inspects the least significant bit. When the request arrives on either input of the 2×2 switch, it is routed to the upper output if the specified bit is 0 or to the lower output if the bit is 1.

In a tightly coupled multiprocessor system, the source is a processor and the destination is a memory module. The first pass through the network sets up the path. Succeeding passes are used to transfer the address into memory and then transfer the data in either direction, depending on whether the request is a read or a write. In a loosely coupled multiprocessor system, both the source and destination are processing elements. After the path is established, the source processor transfers a message to the destination processor.

6.6.3.5 HYPERCUBE INTERCONNECTION

The hypercube or binary n-cube multiprocessor structure is a loosely coupled system composed of $N = 2^n$ processors interconnected in an n-dimensional binary cube. Each processor forms a node of the cube. Although it is customary to refer to each node as having a processor, in effect it contains not only a CPU but also local memory and I/O interface. Each processor has direct communication paths to n other neighbor processors. These paths correspond to the edges of the cube. There are 2" distinct n-bit binary addresses that can be assigned to the processors. Each processor address differs from that of each of its n neighbors by exactly one bit position.

Figure 6.26 shows the hypercube structure for n = 1, 2, and 3. A one-cube structure has n = 1 and $2^n = 2$. It contains two processors interconnected by a single path. A two-cube structure has n = 2 and $2^n = 4$. It contains four nodes interconnected as a square. A three-cube structure has eight nodes interconnected as a cube. An n-cube structure has 2" nodes with a processor residing in each node. Each node is assigned a binary address in such a way that the addresses of two neighbors differ in exactly one bit position. For example, the three neighbors of the node with address 100 in a three-cube structure are 000, 110, and 101. Each of these binary numbers differs from address 100 by one bit value.

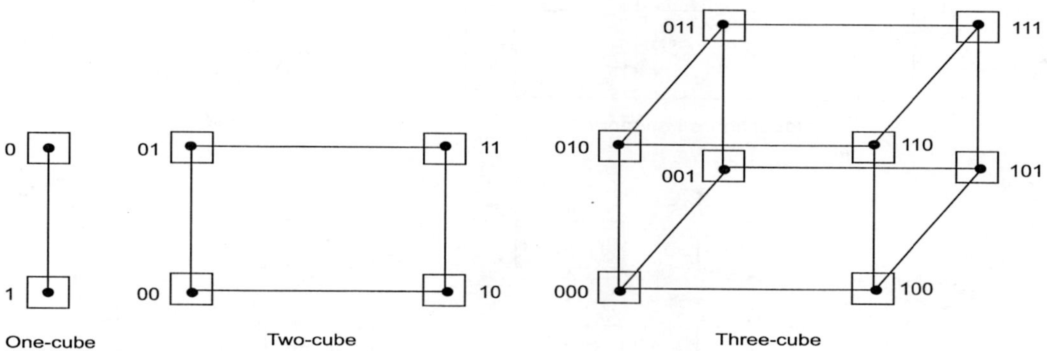

FIGURE 6.26: Hypercube structures for n= 1, 2, 3.

Routing messages through an n -cube structure may take from one to n links from a source node to a destination node. For example, in a three-cube structure, node 000 can communicate directly with node 001. It must cross at least two links to communicate with 011 (from 000 to 001 to 011 or from 000 to 010 to 011). It is necessary to go through at least three links to communicate from node 000 to node 111. A routing procedure can be developed by computing the exclusive-OR of the source node address with the destination node address. The resulting binary value will have 1 bits corresponding to the axes on which the two nodes differ. The message is then sent along any one of the axes. For example, in a three-cube structure, a message at 010 going to 001 produces an exclusive-OR of the two addresses equal to 011. The message can be sent along the second axis to 000 and then through the third axis to 001.

A representative of the hypercube architecture is the Intel iPSC computer complex. It consists of 128 (n = 7) microcomputers connected through communication channels. Each node consists of a CPU, a floating-point processor, local memory, and serial communication interface units. The individual nodes operate independently on data stored in local memory according to resident programs. The data and programs to each node come through a message-passing system from other nodes or from a cube manager. Application programs are developed and compiled on the cube manager and then downloaded to the individual nodes. Computations are distributed through the system and executed concurrently.

6.7 SHARED MEMORY MULTIPROCESSORS

We have mentioned that multiprocessors are classified by how memory is organized. Tightly coupled systems use the same memory and are thus known as *shared memory processors*. This does not mean all processors must share one large memory. Each processor could have a local memory, but it must be shared with other processors. It is also possible that local caches could be used with a single global memory. These three ideas are illustrated in Figure 6.27.

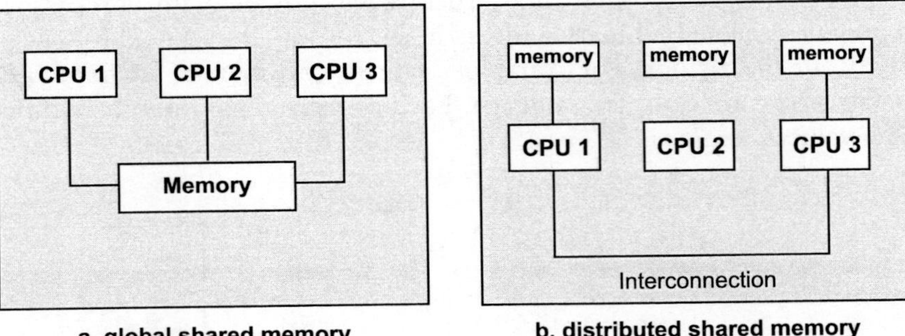

a. global shared memory

b. distributed shared memory

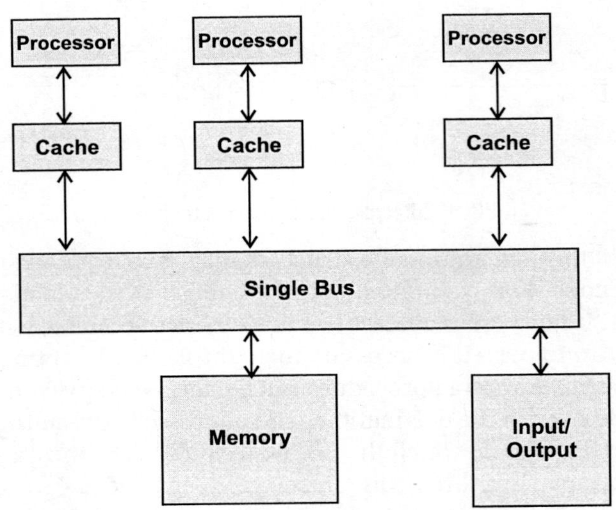

c. global shared memory with separate cache at processors

FIGURE 6.27: Shared Memory

The concept of shared memory multiprocessors (SMM) dates back to the 1970s. The first SMM machine was built at Carnegie-Mellon University using crossbar switches to connect 16 processors to 16 memory modules. The most widely acclaimed of the early SMM machines was the cm* system with its 16 PDP-11 processors and 16 memory banks, all of which were connected using a tree network. The global shared memory was divided equally among the processors. If a processor generated an address, it would first check its local memory. If the address was not found in local memory, it was passed on to a controller. The controller would try to locate the address within the processors that occupied the subtree for which it was the root. If the required address still could not be located, the request was passed up the tree until the data was found or the system ran out of places to look.

There are some commercial SMMs in existence, but they are not extremely popular. One of the first commercial SMM computers was the BBN (Bolt, Beranek, and Newman) Butterfly, which used 256 Motorola 68000 processors. The KSR-1 (from Kendall Square Research) has recently become available, and should prove quite useful for computational science applications. Each KSR-

1 processor contains a cache, but the system has no primary memory. Data is accessed through cache directories maintained in each processor. The KSR-1 processing elements are connected in a unidirectional ring topology, as shown in Figure 6.28. Messages and data travel around the rings in only one direction. Each first-level ring can connect from 8 to 32 processors. A second level ring can connect up to 34 first-level rings, for a maximum of 1088 processors. When a processor references an item in, say, location *x*, the processor cache that contains address *x* places the requested cache slot on the ring. The cache entry (containing the data) migrates through the rings until it reaches the processor that made the request. Distributed shared memory systems of this type are called *shared virtual memory systems*.

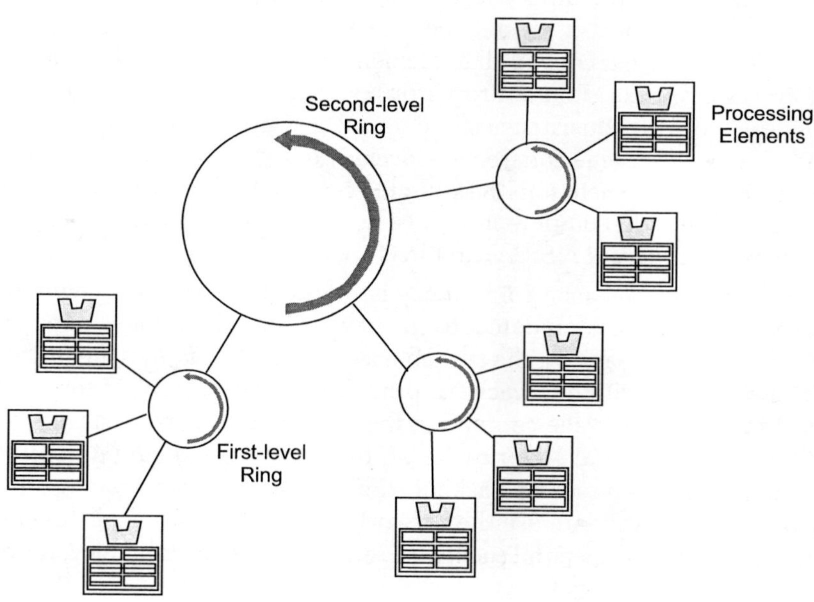

FIGURE 6.28: KSR-1 Hierarchical Ring Topology

Shared memory MIMD machines can be divided into two categories according to how they synchronize their memory operations. In *Uniform Memory Access* (*UMA*) systems, all memory accesses take the same amount of time. A UMA machine has one pool of shared memory that is connected to a group of processors through a bus or switch network. All processors have equal access to memory, according to the established protocol of the interconnection network. As the number of processors increases, a switched interconnection network (requiring 2^n connections) quickly becomes very expensive in a UMA machine. Bus-based UMA systems saturate when the bandwidth of the bus becomes insufficient for the number of processors in the system. Multistage networks run into wiring constraints and significant latency if the number of processors becomes very large. Thus the scalability of UMA machines is limited by the properties of interconnection networks. Symmetric multiprocessors are well-known UMA architectures. Specific examples of UMA machines include Sun's Ultra Enterprise, IBM's iSeries and pSeries servers, the Hewlett-Packard 900, and DEC's AlphaServer.

Nonuniform memory access (*NUMA*) machines get around the problems inherent in UMA architectures by providing each processor with its own piece of memory. The memory space of the machine is distributed across all of the processors, but the processors see this memory as a contiguous addressable entity. Although NUMA memory constitutes a single addressable entity, its distributed nature is not completely transparent. Nearby memory takes less time to read than memory that is further away. Thus, memory access time is inconsistent across the address space of the machine. An example of NUMA architectures includes Sequent's NUMA-Q and the Origin2000 by Silicon Graphics.

NUMA machines are prone to *cache coherence* problems. To reduce memory access time, each NUMA processor maintains a private cache. However, when a processor modifies a data element that is in its local cache, other copies of the data become inconsistent. For example, suppose Processor A and Processor B both have a copy of data element x in their cache memories. Let's say x has a value of 10. If Processor A sets x to 20, Processor B's cache (which still contains a value of 10) has an old, or *stale*, value of x. Inconsistencies in data such as this cannot be allowed, so mechanisms must be provided to ensure cache coherence. Specially designed hardware units known as *snoopy cache controllers* monitor all caches on the system. They implement the system's cache consistency protocol. NUMA machines that employ snoopy caches and maintain cache consistency are referred to as *CC-NUMA* (*cache coherent NUMA*) architectures.

The easiest approach to cache consistency is to ask the processor having the stale value to either void x from its cache or to update x to the new value. When this is done immediately after the value of x is changed, we say that the system uses a *write-through* cache update protocol. With this approach, the data is written to cache and memory concurrently. If the *write-through with update* protocol is used, a message containing the new value of x is broadcast to all other cache controllers so that they can update their caches. If the *write-through with invalidation* protocol is used, the broadcast contains a message asking all cache controllers to remove the stale value of x from their caches. Write-invalidate use the network only the first time x is updated, thus keeping bus traffic light. Write-update keeps all caches current, which reduces latency; however, it increases communications traffic.

A second approach to maintaining cache coherency is the use of a *write-back* protocol that changes only the data in cache at the time of modification. Main memory is not modified until the modified cache block must be replaced and thus written to memory. With this protocol, data values are read in the normal manner, but before data can be written, the processor performing the modification must obtain exclusive rights to the data. It does so by requesting ownership of the data. When ownership is granted, any copies of the data at other processors are invalidated. If other processors wish to read the data, they must request the value from the processor that owns it. The processor with ownership then relinquishes its rights and forwards the current data value to main memory.

6.8 DISTRIBUTED COMPUTING

Distributed computing is another form of multiprocessing. Although it has become an increasingly popular source of computational power, it means different things to different people. In a sense, all multiprocessor systems are also distributed systems because the processing load is divided among a group of processors that work collectively to solve a problem. When most people use the term *distributed system*, they are referring to a very loosely coupled multicomputer system. Recall that multiprocessors can be connected using local buses (as in Figure 6.27c), or they can be connected through a network, as indicated in Figure 6.29. Loosely coupled distributed computers depend on a network for communication among processors.

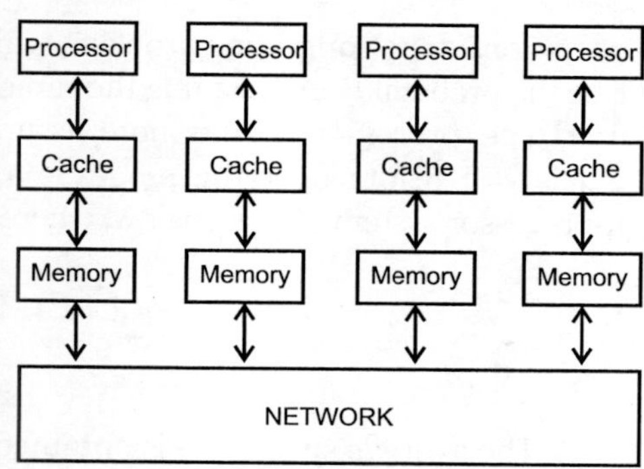

FIGURE 6.29: Multiprocessors Connected by a Network

This idea is exemplified by the recent practice of using individual microcomputers and NOWs for distributed computing systems. These systems allow idle PC processors to work on small pieces of large problems. A recent cryptographic problem was solved through the resources of thousands of personal computers, each performing brute-force cryptanalysis using a small set of possible message keys.

The University of California at Berkeley hosts a radio astronomy group, SETI (Search for Extra Terrestrial Intelligence), that analyzes data from radio telescopes. To help with this project, PC users can install a SETI screen saver on their home computers that will analyze signal data during the processor's normal idle time. SETI is a NOW architecture. The project has been highly successful, with half a million years of CPU time being accumulated in about 18 months.

For general-use computing, the concept of transparency is very important in distributed systems. As many details about the distributed nature of the network should be hidden as possible. Using remote system resources should require no more effort than using the local system.

Remote procedure calls (*RPCs*) extend the concept of distributed computing and help provide the necessary transparency for resource sharing. Using RPCs, a computer can invoke a procedure to use the resources available on another computer. The procedure itself resides on the remote machine, but the invocation is done as if the procedure were local to the calling system. RPCs are used by Microsoft's Distributed Component Object Model (DCOM), the Open Group's Distributed Computing Environment (DCE), the Common Object Request Broker Architecture (CORBA), and Java's Remote Method Invocation (RMI). Today's software designers are leaning toward an object-oriented view of distributed computing, which has fostered the popularity of DCOM, CORBA, and RMI.

6.9 PERFORMANCE OF PARALLEL COMPUTERS

The speedup that can be achieved by a parallel computer with n identical processors working concurrently on a single problem is at most n times faster than a single processor. In practice, the speedup is much less, since some processors are idle at a given time because of conflicts over memory access or communication paths, inefficient algorithms for exploting the natural concurrency in the computing problem or many other reasons to be discussed in subsequent chapters. Figure 6.30 shows the various estimates of the actual speedup, ranging from a lower-bound $\log_2 n$ to an upper-bound n/In n.

The lower-bounding $\log_2$ n is known as the Minsky's conjecture. Most commercial multiprocessor systems have from n = 2 to n = 4 processors. Exploratory research multiprocessors have challenged n = 16 processors in the C.mmp and S-1 systems. Using Minsky's conjecture, only a speedup of 2 to 4 can be expected from existing multiprocessors with 4 to 16 processors. This sounds rather pessimistic. A more optimistic speedup estimate is upper bounded by n/In n as derived below.

Consider a computing problem, which can be executed by a uniprocessor in unit time, $T_1 = 1$. Let f_i be the probability of assigning the same problem to i procesors working equally with an average load $d_i = 1/i$ per processor. Furthermore, assume equal probability of each operating mode using i processor, that is $f_i = 1/n$, for n operating modes:i = 1, 2, ..., n. The average time required to solve the problem on an n-processor system is given below, where the summation represents n operating modes.

$$T_n = \sum_{i=1}^{n} f_i . d_i = \frac{\sum_{i=1}^{n} \frac{1}{i}}{n}$$

The average speedup S is obtained as the ratio of $T_1 = 1$ to T_n; that is,

$$S = \frac{T_1}{T_n} = \frac{n}{\sum_{i=1}^{n}} \leq \frac{n}{\text{In}\, n}$$

For a given multiprocessor system with 2, 4, 8 or 16 processors, the respective average speedups (using Eq. 1) are 1.33, 1.92, 3.08 and 6.93. The speedup obtained in Eq. 1 can be approximated by n/In n for large n. For example, S = 1000/In 1000 = 144.72 for a system with n = 1000 processors. We have plotted the upper bound, the lower bound, and the speedup using Eq. 1 in Figure 6.30.

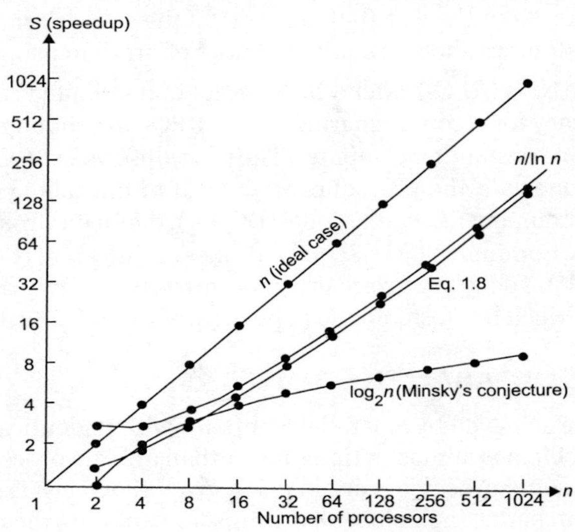

FIGURE 6.30: Various estimates of the speedup of an n-processor system over a single processor

The above analysis explains the reason why a typical commercial multiprocessor system consists of only two to four processors. Dr. John Worlton of the United States Los Alamos Scientific Laboratory said once: "The designers of supercomputers will do better at exploiting concurrency in the computing problems if they use a small number of fast processors instead of a large number of slower processors." This conclusion coincides with the analytical prediction given in Eq. 1.

To measure the real performance of a computer system, one cannot ignore the computation cost and the ease in programming. Comparing multiprocessor systems with other computer structures, we conclude the following: Pipelined uniprocessor systems are still dominating the commercial market in both business and scientific applications. Pipelined computers cost less and their operating systems are well developed to achieve better resource utilization and higher performance. Array processors are mostly custom designed for specific applications, they might be effective. The performance/cost ratio of such special-purpose machines might be low. Programming on an array processor is much more difficult due to the rigid architecture. Multiprocessor systems represent state-of-the-art design in parallel processing computers. Many of the computer manufacturers are taking this route is upgrading their exis

6.10 ARCHITECTURAL CLASSIFICATION SCHEMES

A classification means to order a number of objects into categories, each having common features, among which certain relationship(s) exist(s). In this regard, a classification scheme for computer architectures aims at categorizing them such that those architectures that have common features fall into one category and such that different categories represent distinct groups of architectures. In addition, a classification scheme for computer architecture should provide a basis for information ordering and a basis for predicting the features of a given architecture.

TABLE 6.1: Typical Sizes of Some Multiprocessor Systems

Category	Subcategories	Number of Processors
Communication Model	Multiple processors	2–256
	Multiple computers	8–256
Physical connection	Bus-based	2–32
	Network-based	8–256

Two broad schemes exist for computer architecture classification. The first is based on external (morphological) features of architectures and the second is based on the evolutionary features of architectures. The first scheme emphasizes the finished form of architectures; while the second scheme emphasizes the way architecture has been derived from its predecessor and suggests speculative views on its successor. Morphological classification provides a basis for predictive power, while evolutionary classification provides a basis for better understanding of architectures. Examining the extent to which a classification scheme is satisfying its stated objective(s) could assess the pros and cons of that scheme.

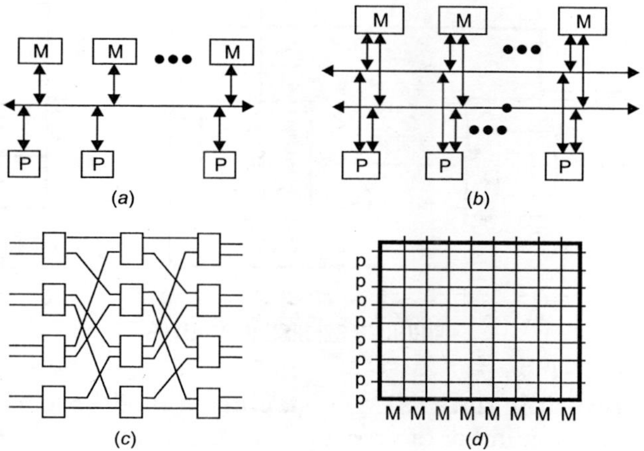

FIGURE 6.31: Four types of multiprocessor interconnection networks. (a) Single-bus system, (b) multi-bus system, (c) multi-stage interconnection network, (d) crossbar system

A number of classification schemes have been proposed over the last three decades. These include the Flynn's classification (1966), the Kuck (1978), the Hwang and Briggs (1984), the Erlangen (1981), the Giloi (1983), the Skillicorn (1988), and the Bell (1992). A number of these are briefly discussed below.

6.10.1 FLYNN'S CLASSIFICATION

The Flynn's classification scheme is based on the multiplicity of instruction streams and data streams in a computer system. Feng's scheme is based on serial versus parallel processing. Handler's classification is determined by the degree of parallelism and pipelining in various subsystem levels.

6.10.1.1 TYPES OF PARALLEL PROCESSOR SYSTEMS

The most popular taxonomy of computer architecture was defined by Flynn in 1966. Flynn's classification scheme is based on the notion of a stream of information. Two types of information flow into a processor: instructions and data. The instruction stream is defined as the sequence of instructions performed by the processing unit. The data stream is defined as the data traffic exchanged between the memory and the processing unit. According to Flynn's classification, either of the instruction or data streams can be single or multiple.

Computer architecture can be classified into the following four distinct categories:

- single-instruction single-data streams (SISD);
- single-instruction multiple-data streams (SIMD);
- multiple-instruction single-data streams (MISD); and
- multiple-instruction multiple-data streams (MIMD).

Single instruction, single data (SISD) stream: A single processor executes a single instruction stream to operate on data stored in a single memory. Uniprocessors fall into this category. **Examples:** most PCs, single CPU workstations and mainframes

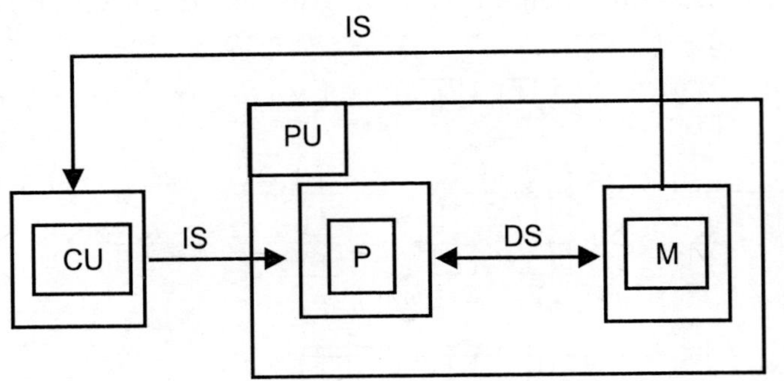

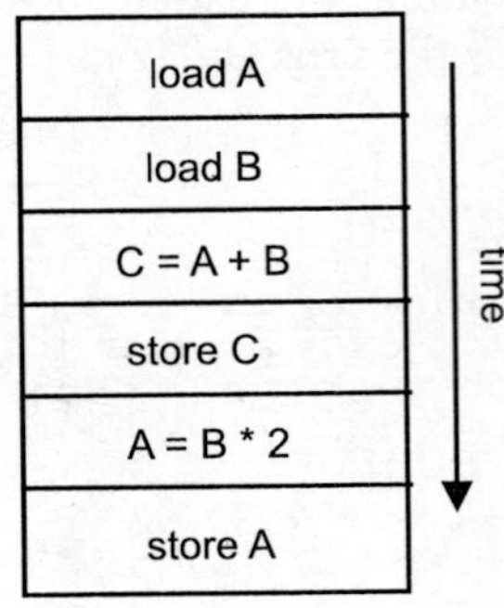

FIGURE 6.32: SISD COMPUTER

Single instruction, multiple data (SIMD) stream: A single machine instruction controls the simultaneous execution of a number of processing elements on a lockstep basis. Each processing element has an associated data memory, so that each instruction is executed on a different set of data by the different processors.

CU-control unit
MM-memory module
IS-instruction stream
PU-processor unit
SM-Shared memory
DS-data stream

EXAMPLES:

- Processor Arrays: Connection Machine CM-2, Maspar MP-1, MP-2
- Vector Pipelines: IBM 9000, Cray C90, Fujitsu VP, NEC SX-2, Hitachi S820

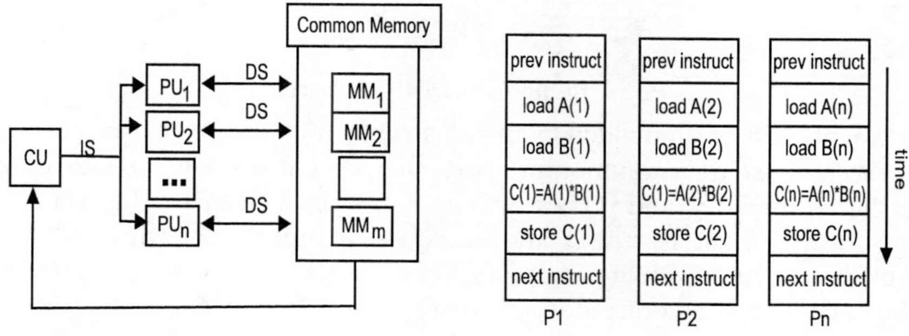

FIGURE 6.33: SIMD Computer

- **Multiple instruction, single data (MISD) stream:** A sequence of data is transmitted to a set of processors, each of which executes a different instruction sequence. This structure is not commercially implemented.

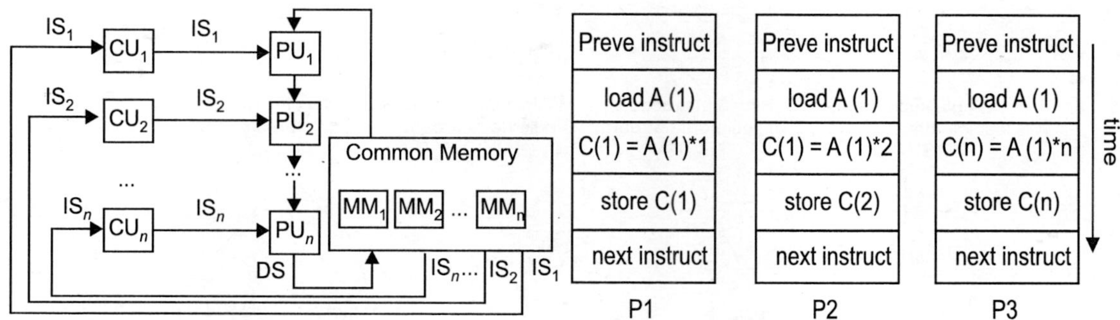

FIGURE 6.34: MISD Computer

- **Multiple instruction, multiple data (MIMD) stream:** A set of processors simultaneously execute different instruction sequences on different data sets. Symmetric multiprocessors, clusters, and NUMA systems fit into this category. With the MIMD organization, the processors are general purpose; each is able to process all of the instructions necessary to perform the appropriate data transformation.

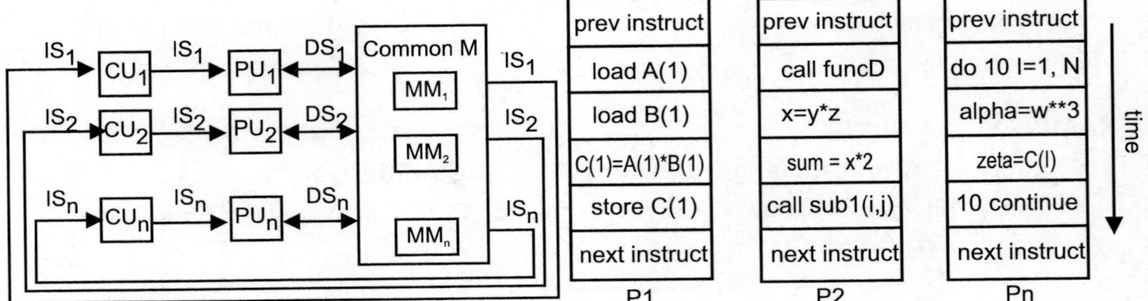

FIGURE 6.35: MIMD Computer

MIMDs can be further subdivided by the means in which the processors communicate (Figure 6.36). If the processors share a common memory, then each processor accesses programs and data stored in the shared memory, and processors communicate with each other via that memory. The most common form of such system is known as a **symmetric multiprocessor (SMP)**. In a symmetric multiprocessor, multiple processors share a single memory or pool of memory by means of a shared bus or other interconnection mechanism; a distinguishing feature is that the memory access time to any region of memory is approximately the same for each processor. A more recent development is the **nonuniform memory access (NUMA)** organization. As the name suggests, the memory access time to different regions of memory may differ for a NUMA processor. A collection of independent uniprocessors or symmetric multiprocessors may be interconnected to form a **cluster**. Communication among the computers is either via fixed paths or via some network facility.

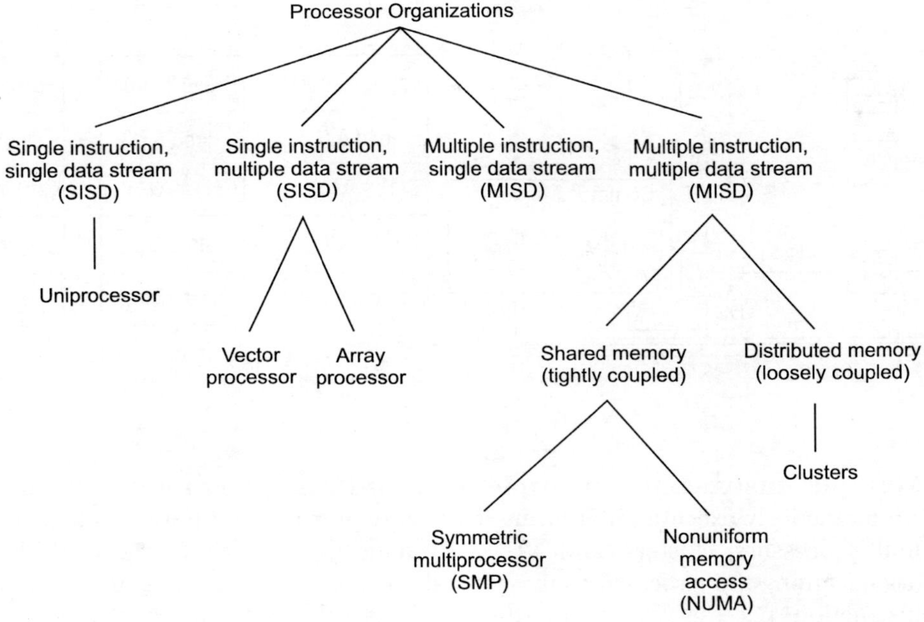

FIGURE 6.36: Taxonomy of Parallel Processor Architectures

6.10.2 PARALLEL ORGANIZATIONS

Figure 6.37 illustrates the general organization of the taxonomy of Figure 6.36. Figure 6.37a shows the structure of an SISD. There is some sort of control unit (CU) that provides an instruction stream (IS) to a processing unit (PU). The processing unit operates on a single data stream (DS) from a memory unit (MU). With an SIMD, there is still a single control unit, now feeding a single instruction stream to multiple PUs. Each PU may have its own dedicated memory (illustrated in Figure 6.37b), or there may be a shared memory. Finally, with the MIMD, there are multiple control units, each feeding a separate instruction stream to its own PU. The MIMD may be a shared-memory multiprocessor (Figure 6.37c) or a distributed-memory multicomputer (Figure 6.37d).

The design issues relating to symmetric multiprocessors, clusters, and NUMAs are complex, involving issues relating to physical organization, interconnection structures, interprocessor communication, operating system design, and application software techniques. Our concern here is primarily with organization, although we touch briefly on operating system design issues.

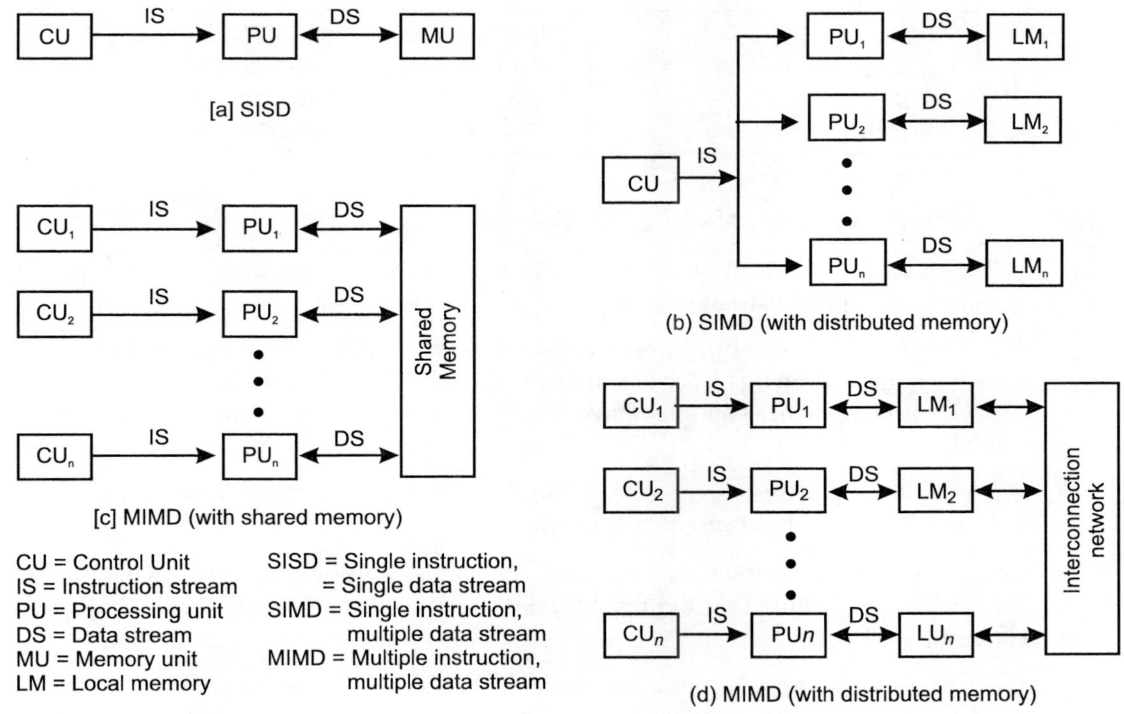

FIGURE 6.37: Alternative Computer Organizations

Figure 6.38 shows the orthogonal organization of the streams according to Flynn's classification.

Schematics for the four categories of architectures resulting from Flynn's classification are shown in Figure 6.39. Table 6.2 lists some of the commercial machines belonging to each of the four categories.

		Data	Stream
		Single	Multiple
Instruction	Single	SISD	SIMD
Stream	Multiple	MISD	MIMD

FIGURE 6.38: Flynn's classification

Table 6.2: Example Machines and Their Flynn's Classification

Classification Category	Example Machines
SISD	IBM 704, VAX 11/780, CRAY-1
SIMD	ILLIAC-IV, MPP, CM-2, STARAN
MISD	See Observation 5 on page 238
MIMD	Cm, CRAY XMP, IBM 370/168M

6.10.2.1 OBSERVATIONS ON FLYNN'S CLASSIFICATION

1. Flynn's classification is among the first of its kind to be introduced and as such it must have inspired subsequent classifications.
2. The classification helped in categorizing architectures that were available and those that have been introduced later. For example, the introduction of the SIMD and MIMD machine models in the classification must have inspired architects to introduce these new machine models.
3. The classification stresses the architectural relationship at the memory processor level. Other architectural levels are totally overlooked.
4. The classification stresses the external (morphological) features of architectures. No information is included on the revolutionary relationship of architectures that belong to the same category.
5. Owing to its pure abstractness, no practically viable machine has exemplified the MISD model introduced by the classification (at least so far). It should, however, be noted that some architects have considered pipelined machines (and perhaps systolic-array computers) as examples for MISD.
6. A very important aspect that is lacking in Flynn's classification is the issue of machine performance. Although the classification gives the impression that machines in the SIMD and the MIMD are superior to their SISD and MISD counterparts, it gives no information on the relative performance of SIMD and MIMD machines.

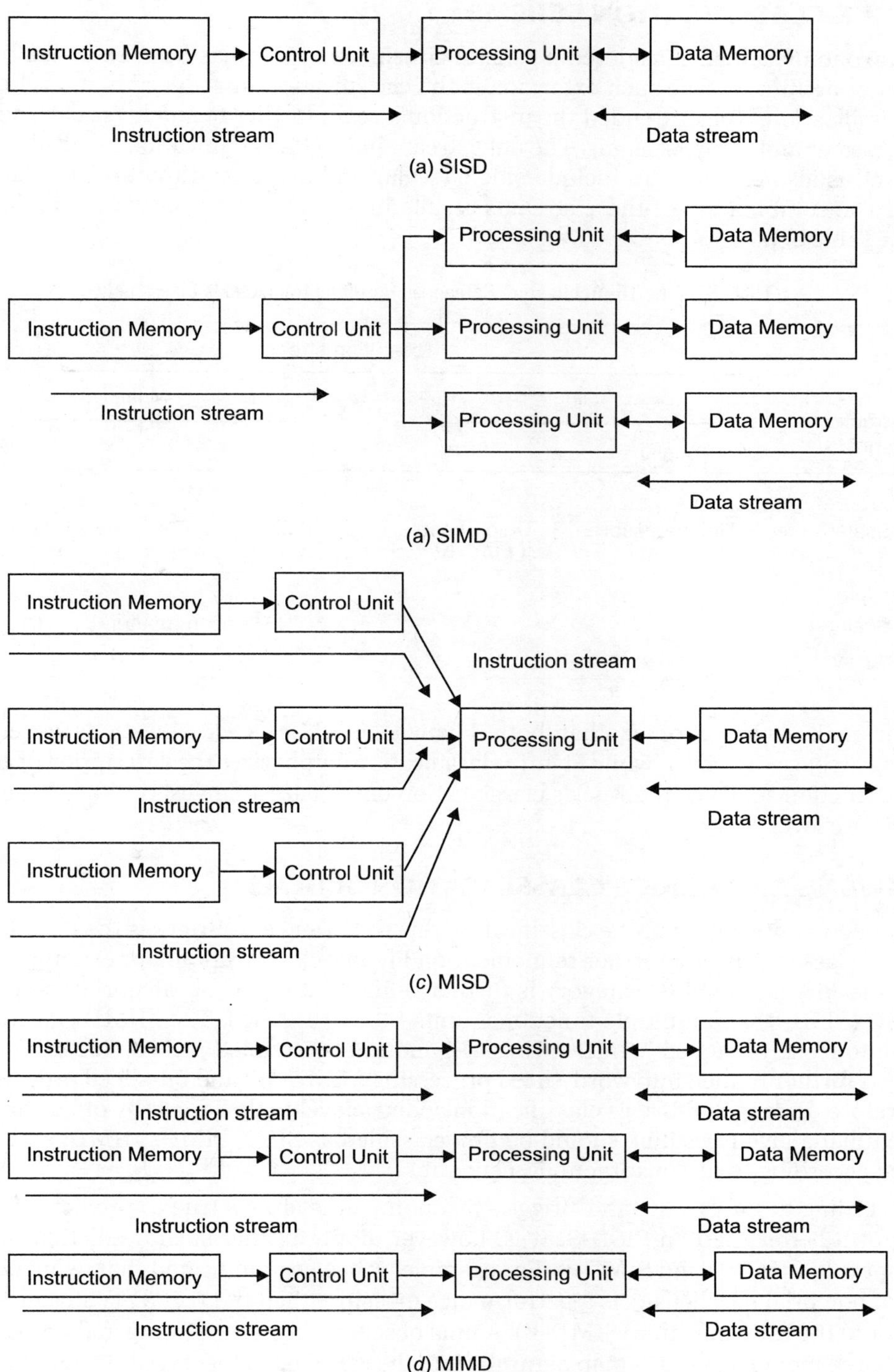

FIGURE 6.39: The four architecture classes resulting from Flynn's taxonomy. (a) SISD,(b) SIMD, (c) MISD, (d) MIMD

6.11 KUCK CLASSIFICATION SCHEME

Flynn's taxonomy can be considered a general classification that has been extended by a number of computer architects. One such extension is the classification introduced by D. J. Kuck in 1978. In his classification, Kuck extended the instruction stream further to single (scalar and array) and multiple (scalar and array) streams. The data stream in Kuck's classification is called the execution stream and is also extended to include single (scalar and array) and multiple (scalar and array) streams. The combination of these streams results in a total of 16 categories of architectures, as shown in Table 6.3.

Table 6.3: The 16-Architecture Categories Resulting from Kuck's Classification

Instruction stream	Execution streams			
	Single		Multiple	
	Scalar	Array	Scalar	Array
Single				
Scalar	Uniprocessor	Uniprocessor ILLIAC-IV	SIMD	
Array				
Multiple				
Scalar			NYU Ultracommputer	Cray X MP
Array				

Our main observation is that both Flynn's and Kuck's classifications cover the entire architecture space. However, while Flynn's classification emphasizes the description of architectures at the instruction set level, the Kuck's classification emphasizes the description of architectures at the hardware level.

6.12 HWANG AND BRIGGS CLASSIFICATION SCHEME

The main new contribution of the classification due to Hwang and Briggs is the introduction of the concept of classes. This is a further refinement on Flynn's classification. For example, according to Hwang and Briggs, the SISD category is further refined into two subcategories: single functional unit SISD (SISD-S) and multiple functional units SISD (SISD-M). The MIMD category is further refined into loosely coupled MIMD (MIMD-L) and tightly coupled MIMD (MIMD-T). The SIMD category is further refined into word-sliced processing (SIMD-W) and bit-sliced processing (SIMD-B). Therefore, Hwang and Briggs classification added a level to the hierarchy of machine classification such that a given machine should be first classified as SISD, SIMD, MIMD, and then further classified according to its constituent descendant.

According to the Hwang and Briggs's taxonomy, it is always true to predict that an SISD-M will perform better than an SISD-S. It is, however, doubtful that such predictions can be made with respect to SIMD-Wand SIMD-B. For example, it has been indicated that using the maximum degree of potential parallelism as a performance measure, then the ILLAC-IV machine (SIMD-W) is inferior to the MPP machine (SIMD-B). A final observation on the Hwang and Briggs's taxonomy is that shared memory systems map naturally into the MIMD-T category, while non shared memory systems map into the MIMD-L category.

6.13 ERLANGEN CLASSIFICATION SCHEME

In its simplest form, this classification scheme adds one more level of details to the internal structure of a computer, compared to Flynn's scheme. In particular, this scheme considers that in addition to the control (CNTL) and processing (ALU) units, a third subunit, called the elementary logic unit (ELU), can be used to characterize a given computer architecture. The ELU represents the circuitry required to perform the bit-level processing within the ALU. An architecture is characterized using a three-tuple system (k, d, w) such that k = number of CNTLs, d = number of ALU units associated with one control unit, and w = number of ELUs per ALU (the width of a single data word). For example, in one of its models, the ILLAC-IV was made up of a mesh connected array of 64 64-bit ALUs controlled by a Burroughs B6700 computer. According to Erlangen, this model of the ILLAC-IV is characterized as (1, 64, 64).

Postulating that pipelining can exist at all three levels of hardware processing, the classification includes three additional parameters. These are w' = the number of pipeline stages per ALU, d' = the number of functional units per ALU, and k' = the number of ELUs forming the control unit. Given the expected multi-unit nature of each of the three hardware processing levels, a more general six-tuple can be used to characterize an architecture as follows: (k×k', d×d', w×w'). Figure 6.40 illustrates the Erlangen classification system. More complex systems can still be characterized using the Erlangen system by using two additional operators, the AND operator, denoted by ×, and the ALTERNATIVE operator, denoted as V. For example, an architecture consisting of two computational subunits each having a six-tuple $(k_0 \times k'_0, d_0 \times d'_0, w_0 \times w'_0)$ and $(k_1 \times k'_1, d_1 \times d'_1, w_1 \times w'_1)$ is characterized using both subunits as $(k_0 \times k'_0, d_0 \times d'_0, w_0 \times w'_0)\ (k_1 \times k'_1, d_1 \times d'_1, w_1 \times w'_1)$, while an architecture that can be expressed using either of the two subunits is characterized as $< k_0 \times k'_0, d_0 \times d'_0, w_0 \times w'_0 > V < k_1 \times k'_0, d_1 \times d'_0, w_1 \times w'_0 >$.

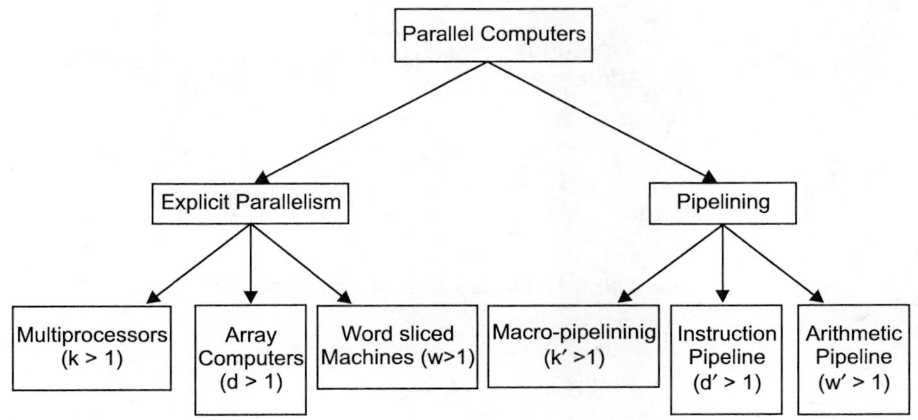

FIGURE 6.40: The Erlangen classification scheme

For example, a later design of the ILLAC-IV consisted of two DEC PDP-10 as the front-end controller where data can only be accepted from one PDP-10 at a time. This version of the ILLAC-IV can be characterized as (2, 1, 36) × (1, 64, 64). Now, since the ILLAC-IV can also work in a half-word mode whereby there are 128 32-bit processors rather than the 64 64-bit processors, then an overall characterization of the ILLAC-IV is given by (2, 1, 36) × [(1, 64, 64) V (1, 128, 32)]. As can be seen, this classification scheme can be regarded as a hierarchical classification that puts more emphasis on the internal structure of the processing hardware. It does not provide any basis for the classification and/or grouping of computer architectures. In particular, the classification overlooks the interconnection among different units.

6.14 SKILLICORN CLASSIFICATION SCHEME

Owing to its inherent nature, Flynn's classification may end up grouping computer systems with similar architectural characteristics but with diverse functionality into one class. This same observation has been the main motive behind the Skillicorn classification introduced in 1988. According to this classification, an abstract von Neumann machine is modeled as shown in Figure 6.41. As can be seen, the abstract model includes two memory subdivisions, instruction memory (IM) and data memory (DM), in addition to the instruction processor (IP) and the data processor (DP). In developing the classification scheme, the following possible interconnection relationships were considered: (IP–DP), (IP–IM), (DP–DM), and (DP–IP).

The interconnection scheme takes into consideration the type and number of connections among the data processors, data memories, instruction processors, and instruction memories. There may exist no, one-to-many, and many-to-many such connections. Table 6.4 illustrates the different connection schemes identified by the classification.

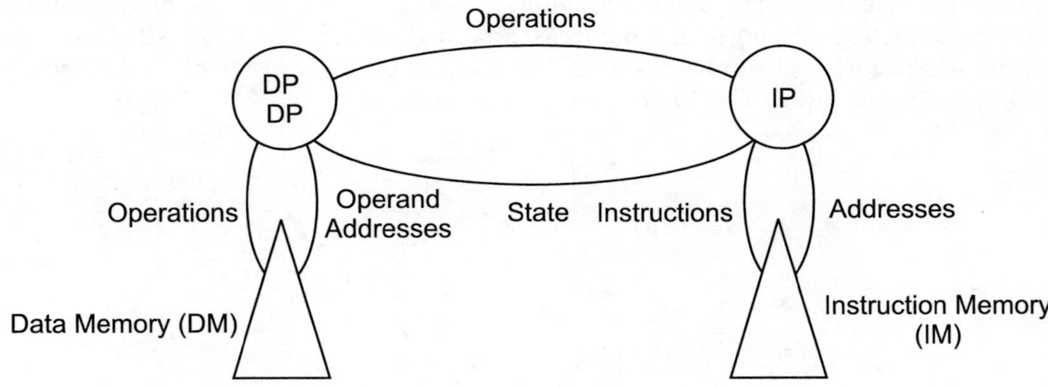

FIGURE 6.41: Abstract model of a simple machine

TABLE 6.4: Possible Connection Schemes

Connection Type	Meaning
1 – 1	A connection between two single units.
1 – n	A connection between a single unit and n other units.
n – n	n (1 – 1) connections.
n × n	n (1 – n) connections.

Using the given connection schemes, Skillicorn arrived at 28 different classes. Sample classes are shown in Table 6.5. The rightmost column of the table indicates the corresponding Flynn's class. Figure 6.42 illustrates four example classes according to the classification.

Major advantages of the Skillicorn classification include:

(1) Simplicity

(2) The proper consideration of the interconnectivity among units

(3) Flexibility

(4) The ability to represent most current computer systems.

However, the classification

(1) Lacks the inclusion of operational aspects such as pipelining

(2) Has difficulty in predicting the relative power of machines belonging to the same class without explicit knowledge of the interconnection scheme used in that class.

Multiple processor systems can be further classified as tightly coupled versus loosely coupled. In a tightly coupled system, all processors can equally access a global memory. In addition, each processor may also have its own local or cache memory. In a loosely coupled system, the memory is divided among processors such that each processor will have its own memory attached to it. However, processors still share the same memory address space. Any processor can directly access any remote memory. Examples of tightly coupled multiple processors include the CMU C.mmp, Encore Computer Multimax, and the Sequent Corp. Balance series. Examples of loosely coupled multiple processors include CMU Cm, the BBN Butterfly, and the IBM RP3.

TABLE 6.5: Sample Connection Classes

Class	IP	DP	IP–DP	IP–IM	DP–DM	DP–DP	Description	Flynn
1	1	1	1 – 1	1 – 1	1 – 1	None	Von Neumann	SISD
2	1	N	1 – n	1 – 1	n – n	n × n	Type 1 array processors	SIMD
3	1	N	1 – n	1 – 1	n × n	None	Type 2 array processors	SIMD
4	N	N	n – n	n – n	n – n	n × n	Loosely coupled Von Neumann	MIMD
5	N	N	n – n	n – n	n × n	None	Tightly coupled Von Neumann	MIMD

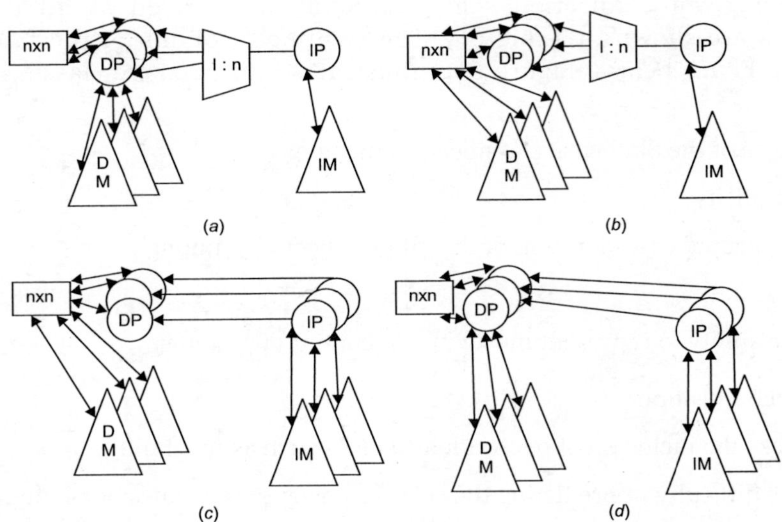

FIGURE 6.42: Example connection classes. (a) Array 1 class, (b) array 2 class, (c) tightly coupled multiprocessor, (d) loosely coupled multiprocessor

6.15 SYMMETRIC MULTIPROCESSORS

Until fairly recently, virtually all single-user personal computers and most workstations contained a single general-purpose microprocessor. As demands for performance increase and as the cost of microprocessors continues to drop, vendors have introduced systems with a symmetric multiprocessor organization. The term symmetric multiprocessor refers to computer hardware architecture and also to the operating system behavior that reflects that architecture.

A symmetric multiprocessor can be defined as a standalone computer system with the following characteristics:

1. There are two or more similar processors of comparable capability.
2. These processors share the same main memory and I/O facilities and are interconnected by a bus or other internal connection scheme, such that memory access time is approximately the same for each processor.
3. All processors share access to I/O devices, either through the same channels or through different channels that provide paths to the same device.
4. All processors can perform the same functions (hence the term *symmetric*).
5. The system is controlled by an integrated operating system that provides interaction between processors and their programs at the job, task, file, and data element levels.

Points 1 to 4 should be self-explanatory. Point 5 illustrates one of the contrasts with a loosely coupled multiprocessing system, such as a cluster. In the latter, the physical unit of interaction is usually a message or complete file. In a symmetric multiprocessor, individual data elements can constitute the level of interaction, and there can be a high degree of cooperation between processes. The operating system of a symmetric multiprocessor schedules processes or threads across all of the processors.

6.15.1 ADVANTAGES OF SYMMETRIC MULTIPROCESSORS

A symmetric multiprocessor organization has a number of potential advantages over a uniprocessor organization, including the following:

- **Performance:** If the work to be done by a computer can be organized so that some portions of the work can be done in parallel, then a system with multiple processors will yield greater performance than one with a single processor of the same type (Figure 6.43).

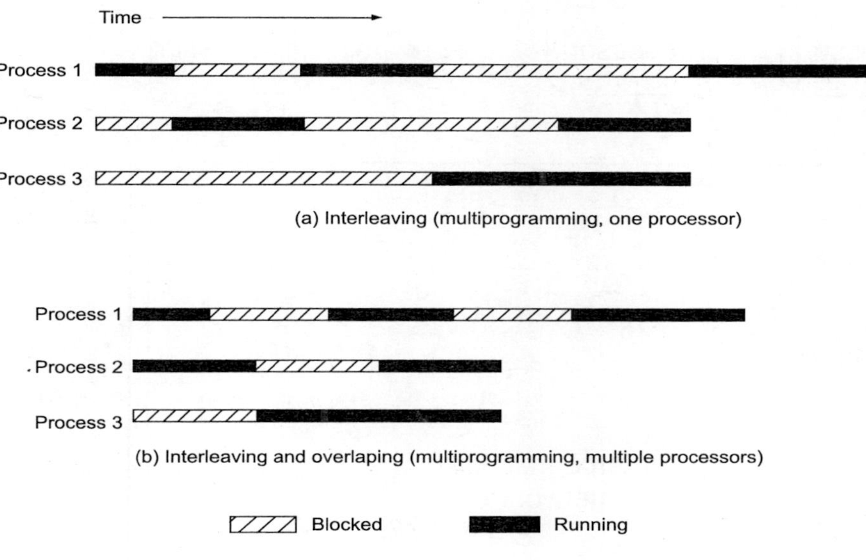

FIGURE 6.43: Multiprogramming and Multiprocessing

- **Availability:** In a symmetric multiprocessor, because all processors can perform the same functions, the failure of a single processor does not halt the machine. Instead, the system can continue to function at reduced performance.
- **Incremental growth:** A user can enhance the performance of a system by adding an additional processor.
- **Scaling:** Vendors can offer a range of products with different price and performance characteristics based on the number of processors configured in the system.

It is important to note that these are potential, rather than guaranteed; benefits. The operating system must provide tools and functions to exploit the parallelism in an symmetric multiprocessor system.

An attractive feature of a symmetric multiprocessor is that the existence of multiple processors is transparent to the user. The operating system takes care of scheduling of threads or processes on individual processors and of synchronization among processors.

6.16 ORGANIZATION OF A MULTIPROCESSOR SYSTEM

Figure 6.44 depicts in general terms the organization of a multiprocessor system. There are two or more processors. Each processor is self-contained, including a control unit, ALU, registers, and, typically, one or more levels of cache. Each processor has access to a shared main memory and the

I/O devices through some form of interconnection mechanism. The processors can communicate with each other through memory (messages and status information left in common data areas). It may also be possible for processors to exchange signals directly. The memory is often organized so that multiple simultaneous accesses to separate blocks of memory are possible. In some configurations, each processor may also have its own private main memory and I/O channels in addition to the shared resources.

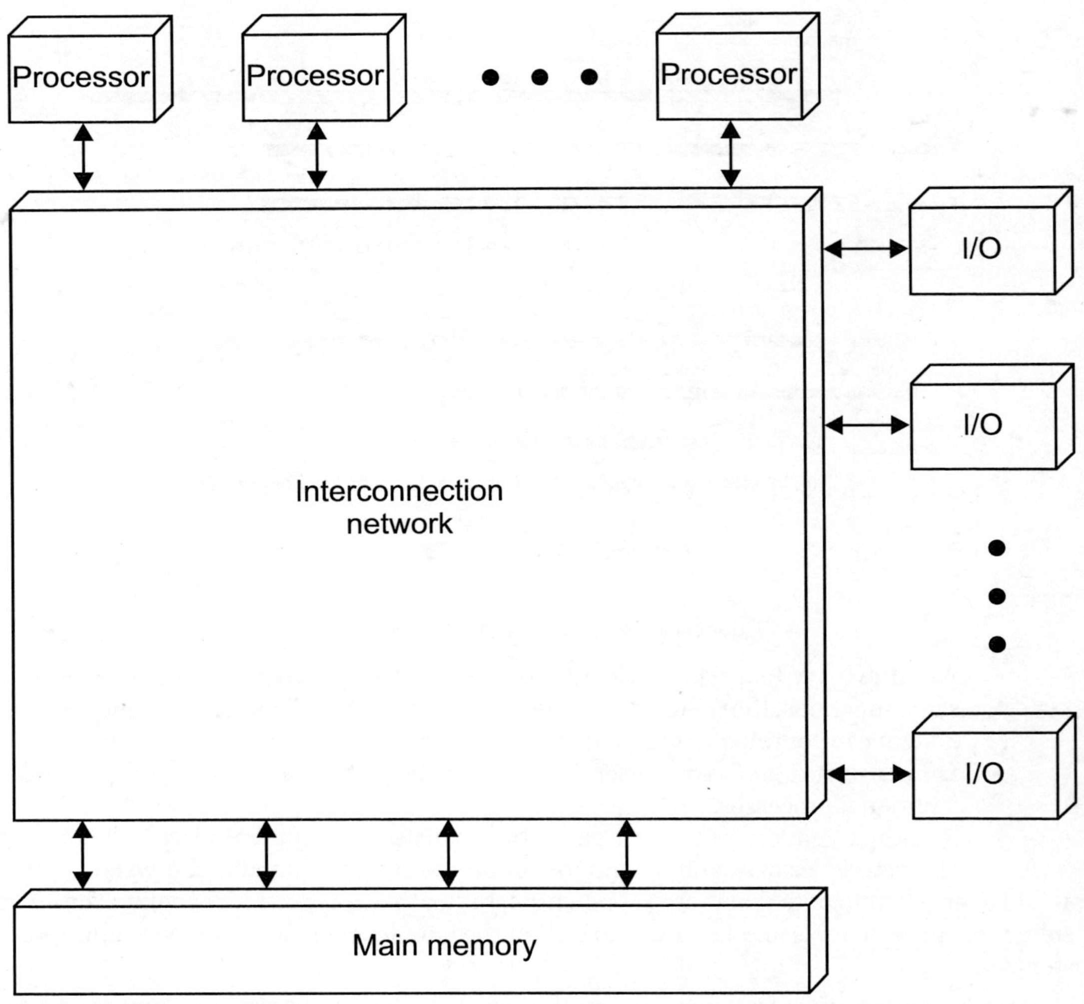

FIGURE 6.44: Generic Block Diagram of a Tightly Coupled Multiprocessor

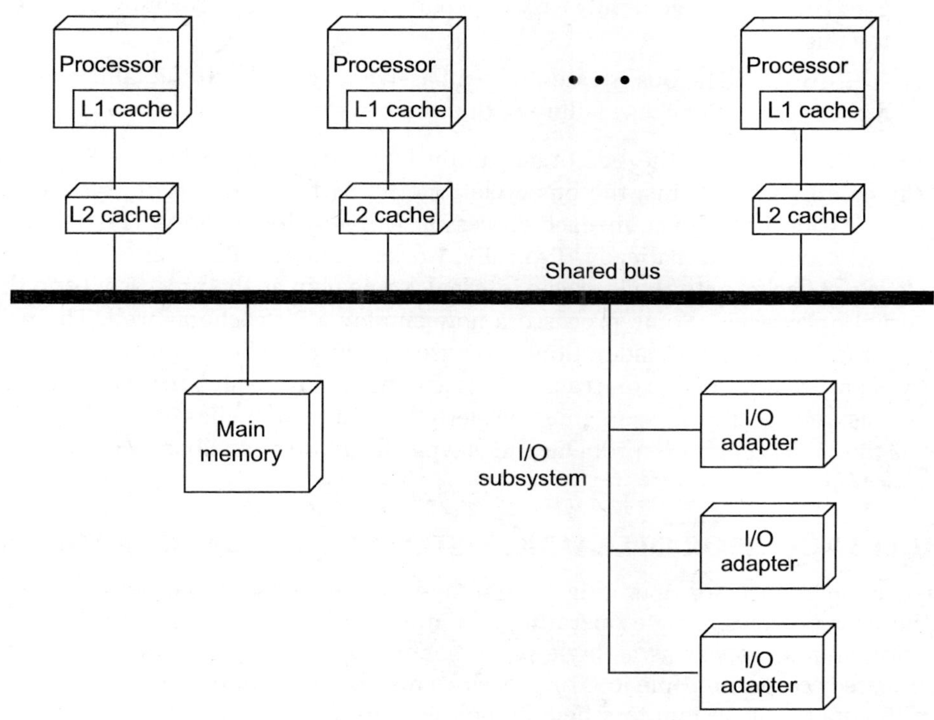

FIGURE 6.45: Symmetric Multiprocessor Organization

The most common organization for personal computers, workstations, and servers is the time-shared bus. The time-shared bus is the simplest mechanism for constructing a multiprocessor system (Figure 6.45).The structure and interfaces are basically the same as for a single-processor system that uses a bus interconnection. The bus consists of control, address, and data lines.

To facilitate DMA transfers from I/O processors, the following features are provided:

- **Addressing:** It must be possible to distinguish modules on the bus to determine the source and destination of data.
- **Arbitration:** Any I/O module can temporarily function as "master." A mechanism is provided to arbitrate competing requests for bus control, using some sort of priority scheme.
- **Time-sharing:** When one module is controlling the bus, other modules are locked out and must, if necessary, suspend operation until bus access is achieved. These uniprocessor features are directly usable in a symmetric multiprocessor organization. In this latter case, there are now multiple processors as well as multiple I/O processors all attempting to gain access to one or more memory modules via the bus.

The bus organization has several attractive features:

- **Simplicity:** This is the simplest approach to multiprocessor organization. The physical interface and the addressing, arbitration, and time-sharing logic of each processor remain the same as in a single-processor system.

- **Flexibility:** It is generally easy to expand the system by attaching more processors to the bus.
- **Reliability:** The bus is essentially a passive medium, and the failure of any attached device should not cause failure of the whole system.

The main drawback to the bus organization is performance. All memory references pass through the common bus. Thus, the bus cycle time limits the speed of the system. To improve performance, it is desirable to equip each processor with a cache memory. This should reduce the number of bus accesses dramatically. Typically, workstation and PC symmetric multiprocessors have two levels of cache, with the L1 cache internal (same chip as the processor) and the L2 cache either internal or external. Some processors now employ a L3 cache as well. The use of caches introduces some new design considerations. Because each local cache contains an image of a portion of memory, if a word is altered in one cache, it could conceivably invalidate a word in another cache. To prevent this, the other processors must be alerted that an update has taken place. This problem is known as the *cache coherence* problem and is typically addressed in hardware rather than by the operating system.

6.17 MULTIPROCESSOR OPERATING SYSTEM DESIGN CONSIDERATIONS

A symmetric multiprocessor operating system manages processor and other computer resources so that the user perceives single operating system controlling system resources. In fact, such a configuration should appear as a single-processor multiprogramming system. In both the SMP and uniprocessor cases, multiple jobs or processes may be active at one time, and it is the responsibility of the operating system to schedule their execution and to allocate resources. A user may construct applications that use multiple processes or multiple threads within processes without regard to whether a single processor or multiple processors will be available. Thus a multiprocessor operating system must provide all the functionality of a multiprogramming system plus additional features to accommodate multiple processors.

Various key design issues:

- **Simultaneous concurrent processes:** OS routines need to be reentrant to allow several processors to execute the same IS code simultaneously. With multiple processors executing the same or different parts of the OS, OS tables and management structures must be managed properly to avoid deadlock or invalid operations.
- **Scheduling:** Any processor may perform scheduling, so conflicts must be avoided. The scheduler must assign ready processes to available processors.
- **Synchronization:** With multiple active processes having potential access to shared address spaces or shared I/O resources, care must be taken to provide effective synchronization. Synchronization is a facility that enforces mutual exclusion and event ordering.
- **Memory management:** Memory management on a multiprocessor must deal with all of the issues found on uniprocessor machines. In addition, the operating system needs to exploit the available hardware parallelism, such as multiported memories, to achieve the best performance. The paging mechanisms on different processors must be coordinated to enforce consistency when several processors share a page or segment and to decide on page replacement.

- **Reliability and fault tolerance:** The operating system should provide graceful degradation in the face of processor failure. The scheduler and other portions of the operating system must recognize the loss of a processor and restructure management tables accordingly.

6.18 PARALLEL AND MULTIPROCESSOR ARCHITECTURES

Since the beginning of computing, scientists have endeavoured to make machines solve problems better and faster. Miniaturization technology has resulted in improved circuitry, and more of it on a chip. Clocks have become faster, leading to CPUs in the gigahertz range. However, we know that there are physical barriers that control the extent to which single-processor performance can be improved. Heat and electromagnetic interference limit chip transistor density. Even if (when?) these problems are solved, processor speeds will always be constrained by the speed of light. On top of these physical limitations, there are also economic limitations. At some point, the cost of making a processor incrementally faster will exceed the price that anyone is willing to pay. Ultimately, we will be left with no feasible way of improving processor performance except to distribute the computational load among several processors. For these reasons, parallelism is becoming increasingly popular.

It is important to note, however, that not all applications can benefit from parallelism. For example, multiprocessing parallelism adds cost (such as process synchronization and other aspects of process administration). If an application isn't amenable to a parallel solution, generally it is not cost effective to port it to a multiprocessing parallel architecture.

Implemented correctly, parallelism results in higher throughput, better fault tolerance, and a more attractive price/performance ratio. Although parallelism can result in significant speedup, this speedup can never be perfect. Given n processors running in parallel, perfect speedup would imply that a computational job could complete in time, leading to an n-fold increase in power (or a runtime decrease by a factor of n).

We need only recall Amdahl's Law to realize why perfect speedup is not possible. If two processing components run at two different speeds, the slower speed will dominate. This law also governs the speedup attainable using parallel processors on a problem. No matter how well you parallelize an application; there will always be a small portion of work done by one processor that must be done serially. Additional processors can do nothing but wait until the serial processing is complete. The underlying premise is that every algorithm has a sequential part that ultimately limits the speedup achievable through a multiprocessor implementation. The greater the sequential processing, the less cost effective it is to employ a multiprocessing parallel architecture.

Using multiple processors on a single task is only one of many different types of parallelism. In earlier sections, we introduced a few of these including pipelining, VLIW, and ILP, giving motivations for each particular type. Other parallel architectures deal with multiple (or parallel) data. Examples include SIMD machines such as vector, neural, and systolic processors. There are many architectures that allow for multiple or parallel processes, characteristic of all MIMD machines. It is important to note that "parallel" can have many different meanings, and it is equally important to be able to differentiate among them.

We begin this section with a discussion of examples of ILP architectures, and then move on to SIMD and MIMD architectures. The last section introduces alternative (fewer mainstreams) parallel processing approaches, including systolic arrays, neural networks, and dataflow computing.

6.18.1 SUPERSCALAR AND VLIW

In this section we revisit the concept of superscalar architectures and compare them to VLIW architectures. Superscalar and VLIW architectures both exhibit instruction-level parallelism, but differ in their approach. To set the stage for our discussion, we start with a definition of superpipelining. Recall that pipelining divides the fetch-decode-execute cycle into stages, in which a set of instructions is in different stages at the same time. In a perfect world, one instruction would exit the pipe every clock cycle. However, because of branching instructions and data dependencies in the code, the goal of one instruction per cycle is never quite achieved.

Superpipelining occurs when a pipeline has stages that require less than half a clock cycle to execute. An internal clock can be added which, when running at double the speed of the external clock, can complete two tasks per external clock cycle. Although superpipelining is equally applicable to both RISC and CISC architectures, it is most often incorporated in RISC processors. Superpipelining is one aspect of superscalar design, and for this reason, there is often confusion regarding which is which.

So, what exactly is a superscalar processor? We know that the Pentium processor is superscalar, but have yet to discuss what this really means. *Superscalar* is a design methodology that allows multiple instructions to be executed simultaneously in each cycle. Although superscalar differs from pipelining in several ways that will be discussed shortly, the net effect is the same. The way in which superscalar designs achieve speedup is similar to the idea of adding another lane to a busy single lane highway. Additional "hardware" is required, but in the end, more cars (instructions) can get from point A to point B in the same amount of time.

The superscalar components analogous to our additional highway lanes are called *execution units*. Execution units consist of floating-point adders and multipliers, integer adders and multipliers, and other specialized components. Although the units may also work independently, it is important that the architecture have a sufficient number of these specialized units to process several instructions in parallel. It is not uncommon for execution units to be duplicated; for example, a system could have a pair of identical floating-point units. Often, the execution units are pipelined, providing even better performance.

A critical component of this architecture is a specialized *instruction fetch unit*, which can retrieve multiple instructions simultaneously from memory. This unit, in turn, passes the instructions to a complex *decoding unit* that determines whether the instructions are independent (and can thus be executed simultaneously) or whether a dependency of some sort exists (in which case not all instructions can be executed at the same time).

As an example, consider the IBM RS/6000. This processor had an instruction fetch unit and two processors, each containing a 6-stage floating-point unit and a 4-stage integer unit. The instruction fetch unit was set up with a 2-stage pipeline, where the first stage fetched packets of four instructions each, and the second stage delivered the instructions to the appropriate processing unit.

Superscalar computers are architectures that exhibit parallelism through pipelining and replication. Superscalar design includes superpipelining, simultaneous fetching of multiple instructions, a complex decoding unit capable of determining instruction dependencies and dynamically combining instructions to ensure no dependencies are violated, and sufficient quantities of resources for parallel execution of multiple instructions. We note that although this type of parallelism requires very specific hardware, a superscalar architecture also requires a sophisticated compiler to schedule operations that make the best use of machine resources.

Whereas superscalar processors rely on the hardware (to arbitrate dependencies) and the compiler (to generate approximate schedules), VLIW processors rely *entirely* on the compiler. VLIW processors pack independent instructions into one long instruction, which, in turn, tells the execution units what to do. Many argue that because the compiler has a better overall picture of dependencies in the code, this approach results in better performance. However, the compiler cannot have an overall picture of the run-time code so it is compelled to be conservative in its scheduling.

As a VLIW compiler creates very long instructions, it also arbitrates all dependencies. The instructions, which are fixed at compile time, typically contain four to eight instructions. Because the instructions are fixed, any modification that could affect scheduling of instructions (such as changing memory latency) requires a recompilation of the code, potentially causing a multitude of problems for software vendors. VLIW supporters point out that this technology simplifies the hardware by moving complexity to the compiler. Superscalar supporters counter with the argument that VLIW can, in turn, lead to significant increases in the amount of code generated. For example, when program control fields are not used, memory space and bandwidth are wasted. In fact, a typical FORTRAN program explodes to double and sometimes triple its normal size when compiled on a VLIW machine.

Intel's Itanium, IA-64, is one example of a VLIW processor. Recall that the IA-64 uses an EPIC style of VLIW processor. An EPIC architecture holds some advantages over an ordinary VLIW processor. Like VLIW, EPIC bundles its instructions for delivery to various execution units. However, unlike VLIW, these bundles need not be the same length. A special delimiter indicates where one bundle ends and another begins. Instruction words are prefetched by hardware, which identifies and then schedules the bundles in independent groups for parallel execution. This is an attempt to overcome the limitations introduced by the compiler's lack of total knowledge of the run-time code. Instructions within bundles may be executed in parallel with no concern for dependencies, and thus no concern for ordering. By most people's definition, EPIC is really VLIW. Although Intel might argue the point, and die-hard architects would cite the minor differences mentioned above (as well as a few others), EPIC is in reality an enhanced version of VLIW.

6.18.2 VECTOR PROCESSORS

Often referred to as supercomputers, *vector processors* are specialized, heavily pipelined processors that perform efficient operations on entire vectors and matrices at once. This class of processor is suited for applications that can benefit from a high degree of parallelism, such as weather forecasting, medical diagnoses, and image processing.

To understand vector processing, one must first understand vector arithmetic. A vector is a fixed-length, one-dimensional array of values, or an ordered series of scalar quantities. Various arithmetic operations are defined over vectors, including addition, subtraction, and multiplication.

Vector computers are highly pipelined so that arithmetic operations can be overlapped. Each instruction specifies a set of operations to be carried over an entire vector. For example, let's say we want to add vectors V1 and V2 and place the results in V3. On a traditional processor our code would include the following loop:

```
for i = 0 to Vector Length
V3[i] = V1[i] + V2[i];
```

However, on a vector processor, this code becomes—

```
LDV   V1, R1;  load vector1 into vector register R1
LDV   V2, R2
ADDV  R3, R1, R2
STV   R3, V3;  store vector register R3 in vector V3
```

Vector registers are specialized registers that can hold several vector elements at one time. The register contents are sent one element at a time to a vector pipeline, and the output from the pipeline is sent back to the vector registers one element at a time. These registers are, therefore, FIFO queues capable of holding many values. Vector processors generally have several of these registers. The instruction set for a vector processor contains instructions for loading these registers, performing operations on the elements within the registers, and storing the vector data back to memory.

Vector processors are often divided into two categories according to how the instructions access their operands. *Register-register vector processors* require that all operations use registers as source and destination operands. *Memory-memory vector processors* allow operands from memory to be routed directly to the arithmetic unit. The results of the operation are then streamed back to memory. Register-to-register processors are at a disadvantage in that long vectors must be broken into fixed length segments that are small enough to fit into the registers. However, memory-to-memory machines have a large startup time due to memory latency. (Startup time is the time between initializing the instruction and the first result emerging from the pipeline.) After the pipeline is full, however, this disadvantage disappears.

Vector instructions are efficient for two reasons. First, the machine fetches significantly fewer instructions, which means there is less decoding, control unit overhead, and memory bandwidth usage. Second, the processor knows it will have a continuous source of data and can begin prefetching corresponding pairs of values. If interleaved memory is used, one pair can arrive per clock cycle. The most famous vector processors are the Cray series of supercomputers. Their basic architecture has changed little over the past 25 years.

6.19 ALTERNATIVE PARALLEL PROCESSING APPROACHES

Entire books have been devoted to particular alternative and advanced architectures. Although we cannot discuss all of them in this brief section, we can introduce you to a few of the more notable systems that diverge from the traditional von Neumann architecture. These systems implement new ways of thinking about computers and computation. They include dataflow computing, neural networks, and systolic processing.

6.19.1 DATAFLOW COMPUTING

Von Neumann machines exhibit sequential control flow. A program counter determines the next instruction to execute. Data and instructions are segregated. The only way in which data may alter the execution sequence is if the value in the program counter is changed according to the outcome of a statement that references a data value.

In *dataflow* computing, the control of the program is directly tied to the data itself. It is a simple approach: An instruction is executed when the data necessary for execution become available. Therefore, the actual order of instructions has no bearing on the order in which they are eventually executed. Execution flow is completely determined by data dependencies. There is no concept of shared data storage in these systems, and there are no program counters to control execution. Data flows continuously and is available to multiple instructions at the same time. Each instruction is considered to be a separate process. Instructions do not reference memory; instead, they reference other instructions. Data is passed from one instruction to the next.

We can understand the computation sequence of a dataflow computer by examining its *data flow graph*. In a data flow graph, nodes represent instructions, and arcs indicate data dependencies between instructions. Data flows through this graph in the form of *data tokens*. When an instruction has all of the data tokens it needs, the node *fires*. When a node fires, it consumes the data tokens, performs the required operation, and places the resulting data token on an output arc. This idea is illustrated in Figure 6.46.

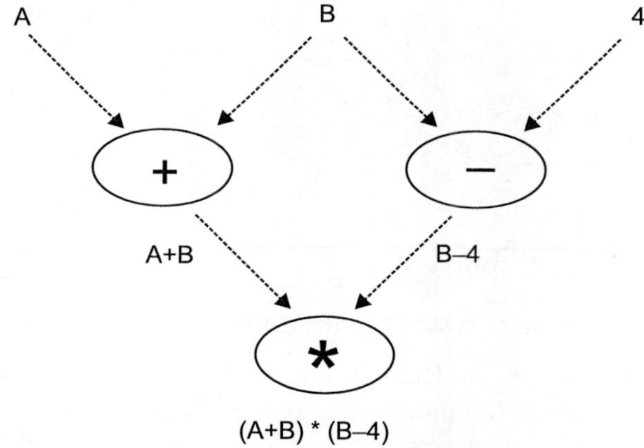

FIGURE 6.46: Data Flow Graph Computing N = (A + B) * (B - 4)

The data flow graph shown in Figure 6.46 is an example of a *static* dataflow architecture in which the tokens flow through the graph in a staged pipelined fashion. In *dynamic* dataflow architectures, tokens are tagged with context information and are stored in a memory. During every clock cycle, memory is searched for the set of tokens necessary for a node to fire. Nodes fire only when they find a complete set of input tokens within the same context.

Programs for dataflow machines must be written in languages that are specifically designed for this type of architecture; these include VAL, Id, SISAL, and LUCID. Compilation of a dataflow program results in a data flow graph much like the one illustrated in Figure 6.46. The tokens propagate along the arcs as the program executes.

Consider the sample code that calculates *N*!:

```
(initial j <- n; k <- 1
while j > 1 do
new k <- k * j;
new j <- j - 1; return k)
```

The corresponding data flow graph is shown in Figure 6.47. The two values, *N* and 1, are fed into the graph. *N* becomes token *j*. When *j* is compared to 1, if it is greater than 1, the *j* token is passed through and doubled, with one copy of the token passed to the "-1 node" and one copy passed to the multiply node. If *j* is not greater than 1, the value of *k* is passed through as the output of the program. The multiply node can only fire when both a new *j* token and a new *k* token are available. The "right facing" triangles that *N* and 1 feed into are "merge" nodes and fire whenever either input is available. Once *N* and 1 are fed into the graph, they are "used up" and the new *j* and new *k* values cause the merge nodes to fire.

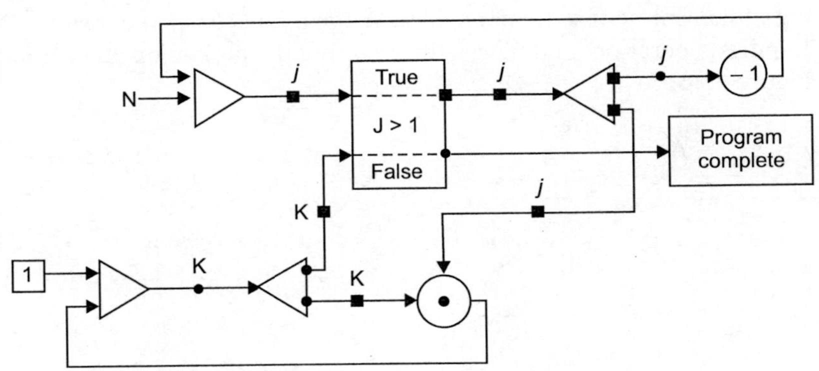

FIGURE 6.47: Data Flow Graph Corresponding to the Program to Calculate N!

Al Davis, of the University of Utah, built the first dataflow machine in 1977. The first multiprocessor dataflow system (containing 32 processors) was developed at CERT-ONERA in France in 1979. The University of Manchester created the first tagged-token dataflow computer in 1981. The commercially available *Manchester tagged dataflow model* is a powerful dataflow paradigm based on dynamic tagging. This particular architecture is described as tagged because data values (tokens) are tagged with unique identifiers to specify the current iteration level. The tags are required because programs can be *re-entrant*, meaning the same code can be used with different data. By comparing the tags, the system determines which data to use during each iteration. Tokens that have matching tags for the same instruction cause the node to fire.

A loop serves as a good example to explain the concept of tagging. A higher level of concurrency can be achieved if each iteration of the loop is executed in a separate instance of a subgraph. This subgraph is simply a copy of the graph. However, if there are many iterations of the loop, there will be many copies of the graph. Rather than copying the graph, it would be more efficient to share the nodes among different instances of a graph. The tokens for each instance must be identifiable, and this is done by giving each of them a tag. The tag for each token identifies the instance to which it belongs. That way, tokens intended for, say, the third iteration cannot cause nodes for the fourth iteration to fire.

The architecture of a dataflow machine consists of a number of processing elements that must communicate with each other. Each processing element has an *enabling unit* that sequentially accepts tokens and stores them in memory. If the node to which this token is addressed fires, the input tokens are extracted from memory and are combined with the node itself to form an executable packet. The processing element's *functional unit* computes any necessary output values and combines them with destination addresses to form more tokens. These tokens are then sent back to the enabling unit, at which time they may enable other nodes. In a tagged-token machine, the enabling unit is split into two separate stages: the *matching unit* and the *fetching unit*. The matching unit stores tokens in its memory and determines whether an instance of a given destination node has been enabled. In tagged architectures, there must be a match of both the destination node address and the tag. When all matching tokens for a node are available, they are sent to the fetching unit, which combines these tokens with a copy of the node into an executable packet, which is then passed on to the functional unit.

Because data drives processing on dataflow systems, dataflow multiprocessors do not suffer from the contention and cache coherency problems that are so vexing to designers of control driven multiprocessors. It is interesting to note that von Neumann, whose name is given to the von Neumann bottleneck in traditional computer architectures, studied the possibility of data-driven architectures similar in nature to dataflow machines. In particular, he studied the feasibility of neural networks, which are data-driven by nature and discussed in the next section.

6.19.2 NEURAL NETWORKS

Traditional architectures are quite good at fast arithmetic and executing deterministic programs. However, they are not so good at massively parallel applications, fault tolerance, or adapting to changing circumstances. Neural networks, on the other hand, are useful in dynamic situations where we can't formulate an exact algorithmic solution, and where processing is based on an accumulation of previous behavior.

Whereas von Neumann computers are based on the processor/memory structure, neural networks are based on the parallel architecture of human brains. They attempt to implement simplified versions of biological neural networks. Neural networks represent an alternative form of multiprocessor computing with a high degree of connectivity and simple processing elements. They can deal with imprecise and probabilistic information and have mechanisms that allow for adaptive interaction between the processing elements. Neural networks (or neural nets), like biological networks, can learn from experience.

Neural network computers are composed of a large number of simple processing elements that individually handle one piece of a much larger problem. Simply stated, a neural net consists of processing elements (PEs), which multiply inputs by various sets of weights, yielding a single output value. The actual computation involved is deceptively easy; the true power of a neural network comes from the parallel processing of the interconnected PEs and the adaptive nature of the sets of weights. The difficulties in creating neural networks lie in determining which neurons (PEs) should be connected to which, what weights should be placed on the edges, and the various thresholds that should be applied to these weights. Furthermore, as a neural network is learning, it can make a mistake. When it does, weights and thresholds must be changed to compensate for the error. The network's *learning algorithm* is the set of rules that governs how these changes are to be made.

Neural networks are known by many different names, including *connectionist systems*, *adaptive systems*, and *parallel distributed processing systems*. These systems are particularly powerful when a large database of previous examples can be used by the neural net to learn from prior experiences. They have been used successfully in a multitude of real world applications including quality control, weather forecasting, financial and economic forecasting, speech and pattern recognition, oil and gas exploration, health care cost reduction, bankruptcy prediction, machine diagnostics, securities trading, and targeted marketing. It is important to note that each of these neural nets has been specifically designed for a certain task, so we cannot take a neural network designed for weather forecasting and expect it to do a good job for economic forecasting.

The simplest example of a neural net is the *perceptron*, a single trainable neuron. A perceptron produces a Boolean output based on the values that it receives from several inputs. A perceptron is trainable because its threshold and input weights are modifiable. Figure 6.48 shows a perceptron with inputs $x_1, x_2, \ldots, x_n$, which can be Boolean or real values. Z is the Boolean output. The w_i's represent the weights of the edges and are real values. T is the real-valued threshold. In this example, the output Z is true (1) if the net input $w_1x_1 + w_2x_2 + \ldots + w_nx_n$, is greater than the threshold T. Otherwise, Z is zero.

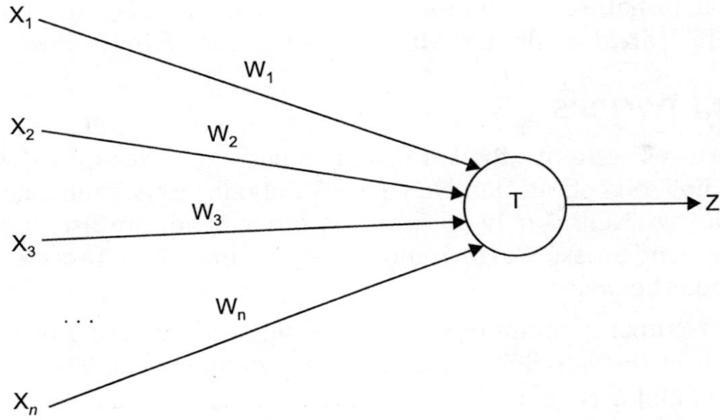

FIGURE 6.48: A Perceptron

A perceptron produces outputs for specific inputs according to how it is trained. If the training is done correctly, we should be able to give it any input and get reasonably correct output. The perceptron should be able to determine a reasonable output even if it has never before seen a particular set of inputs. The "reasonableness" of the output depends on how well the perceptron is trained.

Perceptrons are trained by use of either supervised or unsupervised learning algorithms. *Supervised* learning assumes prior knowledge of correct results, which are fed to the neural net during the training phase. While it is learning, the neural net is told whether its final state is correct. If the output is incorrect, the network modifies input weights to produce the desired results. *Unsupervised* learning does not provide the correct output to the network during training. The network adapts solely in response to its inputs, learning to recognize patterns and structure in the input sets. We assume supervised learning in our examples.

The best way to train a neural net is to compile a wide range of examples that exhibit the very characteristics in which you are interested. A neural network is only as good as the training data, so great care must be taken to select a sufficient number of correct examples. For example, you would not expect a small child to be able to identify all birds if the only bird he had ever seen was a chicken. Training takes place by giving the perceptron inputs and then checking the output. If the output is incorrect, the perceptron is notified to change its weights and possibly the threshold value to avoid the same mistake in the future. Moreover, if we show a child a chicken, a sparrow, a duck, a hawk, a pelican, and a crow, we cannot expect the child to remember the similarities and differences after seeing them only once. Similarly, the neural net must see the same examples many times in order to infer the characteristics of the input data that you seek.

A perceptron can be trained to recognize the logical AND operator quite easily. Assuming there are n inputs, the output should be 1 only if all inputs are equal to 1. If the threshold of the perceptron is set to n, and the weights of all edges are set to 1, the correct output is given. On the other hand, to compute the logical OR of a set of inputs, the threshold simply needs to be set to 1. In this way, if at least one of the inputs is 1, the output will be 1.

For both the AND and OR operators, we know what the values for the threshold and weights should be. For complex problems, these values are not known. If we had not known the weights for AND, for example, we could start the weights at 0.5 and give various inputs to the perceptron, modifying the weights as incorrect outputs was generated. This is how neural net training is done. Typically, the network is initialized with random weights between -1 and 1. Correct training requires thousands of steps. The training time it depends on the size of the network. As the number of perceptrons increases, the number of possible "states" also increases.

Let's consider a more sophisticated example, that of determining whether a tank is hiding in a photograph. A neural net can be configured so that each output value correlates to exactly one pixel. If the pixel is part of the image of a tank, the net should output a one; otherwise, the net should output a zero. The input information would most likely consist of the color of the pixel. The network would be trained by feeding it many pictures with and without tanks. The training would continue until the network correctly identified whether the photos included tanks.

The U.S. military conducted a research project exactly like the one we just described. One hundred photographs were taken of tanks hiding behind trees and in bushes, and another 100 photographs were taken of ordinary landscape with no tanks. Fifty photos from each group were kept "secret," and the rest were used to train the neural network. The network was initialized with random weights before being fed one picture at a time. When the network was incorrect, it adjusted its input weights until the correct output was reached. Following the training period, the 50 "secret" pictures from each group of photos were fed into the network. The neural network correctly identified the presence or absence of a tank in each photo.

The real question at this point has to do with the training-had the neural net actually learned to recognize tanks? The Pentagon's natural suspicion led to more testing. Additional photos were taken and fed into the network, and to the researchers' dismay, the results were quite random. The neural net could not correctly identify tanks within photos. After some investigation, the researchers determined that in the original set of 200 photos, all photos with tanks had been taken on a cloudy day, whereas the photos with no tanks had been taken on a sunny day. The neural net had properly separated the two groups of pictures, but had done so using the color of the sky to do this rather than the existence of a hidden tank. The government was now the proud owner of a very expensive neural net that could accurately distinguish between sunny and cloudy days!

This is a great example of what many consider the biggest issue with neural networks. If there are more than 10 to 20 neurons, it is impossible to understand how the network is arriving at its results. One cannot tell if the net is making decisions based on correct information, or, as in the above example, something totally irrelevant. Neural networks have a remarkable ability to derive meaning and extract patterns from data that are too complex to be analyzed by human beings. However, some people trust neural networks to be experts in their area of training. Neural nets are used in such areas as sales forecasting, risk management, customer research, undersea mine detection, facial recognition, and data validation. Although neural networks are promising, and the progress made in the past several years has led to significant funding for neural net research, many people are hesitant to put confidence in something that no human being can completely understand.

6.19.3 SYSTOLIC ARRAYS

Systolic array computers derive their name from drawing an analogy to how blood rhythmically flows through a biological heart. They are a network of processing elements that rhythmically compute data by circulating it through the system. Systolic arrays are a variation of SIMD computers that incorporates large arrays of simple processors that use vector pipelines for data flow, as shown in Figure 6.49b. Since their introduction in the 1970s, they have had a significant impact on special-purpose computing. One well-known systolic array is CMU's iWarp processor, which was manufactured by Intel in 1990. This system consists of a linear array of processors connected by a bidirectional data bus.

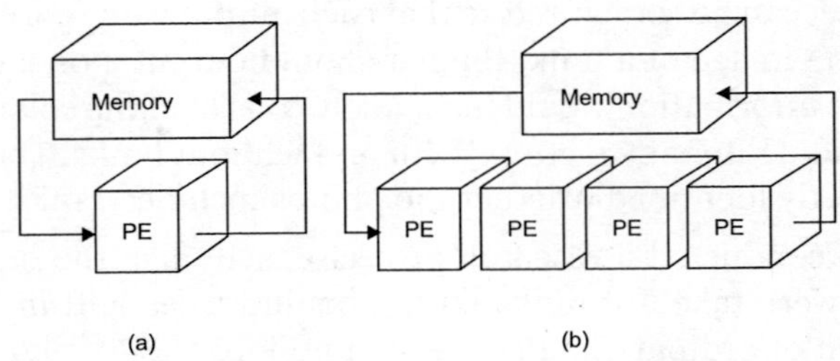

FIGURE 6.49: a. A Simple Processing Element (PE) b. A Systolic Array Processor

Although Figure 6.49b illustrates a one-dimensional systolic array, two-dimensional arrays are not uncommon. Three-dimensional arrays are becoming more prevalent with the advances in VLSI technology.

Systolic arrays employ a high degree of parallelism (through pipelining) and can sustain a very high throughput. Connections are typically short, and the design is simple and thus highly scalable. They tend to be robust, highly compact, efficient, and cheap to produce. On the down side, they are highly specialized and thus inflexible as to the types and sizes of problems they can solve.

A good example of using systolic arrays can be found in polynomial evaluation. To evaluate the polynomial $y = a_0 + a_1x + a_2x^2 + \ldots + a_kx^k$, we can use Horner's Rule:

$$y = ((((a_n x + a_{n-1}) \times x + a_{n-2}) \times x + a_{n-3}) \times x \ldots a_1) \times x + a_0$$

A linear systolic array, in which the processors are arranged in pairs, can be used to evaluate a polynomial using Horner's Rule, as shown in Figure 6.50. One processor multiplies its input by x and passes the result to the right. The next processor adds a_j and passes the result to the right. After an initial latency of $2n$ cycles to get started, a polynomial is computed in every cycle.

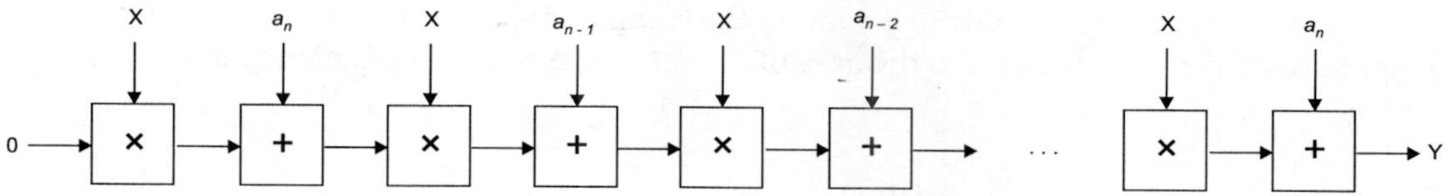

FIGURE 6.50: Using a Systolic Array to Evaluate a Polynomial

Systolic arrays are typically used for repetitive tasks, including Fourier transformations, image processing, data compression, shortest path problems, sorting, signal processing, and various matrix computations (such as inversion and multiplication). In short, systolic array computers are suitable for computational problems that lend themselves to a parallel solution using a large number of simple processing elements.

6.20 FENG'S CLASSIFICATION

Tse-yun Feng suggested the use of degree of parallelism to classify various computer architectures.

6.20.1 SERIAL VERSUS PARALLEL PROCESSING

The maximum number of binary digits (bits) that can be processed within a unit time by a computer system is called the maximum parallelism degree P. Let Pi be the number of bits that can be processed within the ith processor cycle (or the ith clock period). Consider T processor cycles indexed by i = 1, 2,..., T. The average parallelism degree, P_a is defined by

$$P_a = \frac{\sum_{i=1}^{T} P_i}{T}$$

In general, $P_i < P$. Thus, we define the utilization rate m of a computer system within T cycles by

$$\mu = \frac{P_a}{P} = \frac{\sum_{i=1}^{T} P_i}{T \cdot P}$$

If the computing power of the processor is fully utilized (or the parallelism is fully exploited), then we have Pi = P for all i and $\mu = 1$ for 100 percent utilization. The utilization rate depends on the application program being executed.

Figure 6.51 demonstrates the classification of computers by their maximum parallelism degrees. The horizontal axis shows the word length n. The vertical axis corresponds to the bit-slice length m. Both length measures are in terms of the number of bits contained in a word or in a bit slice. A bit slice is a string of bits, one from each of the words at the same vertical bit position. For example, the TI-ASC has a word length of 64 and four arithmetic pipelines. Each pipe has eight pipeline stages. Thus there are 8×4 = 32 bits per each bit slice in the four pipes. TI-ASC is represented as (64, 32). The maximum parallelism degree P(C) of a given computer system C is represented by the product of the word length w and the bit-slice length m; that is, $P(C) = n \cdot m$.

The pair (n, m) corresponds to a point in the computer space shown by the coordinate system in Figure 6.51. The P(C) is equal to the area of the rectangle defined by the integer's n and m.

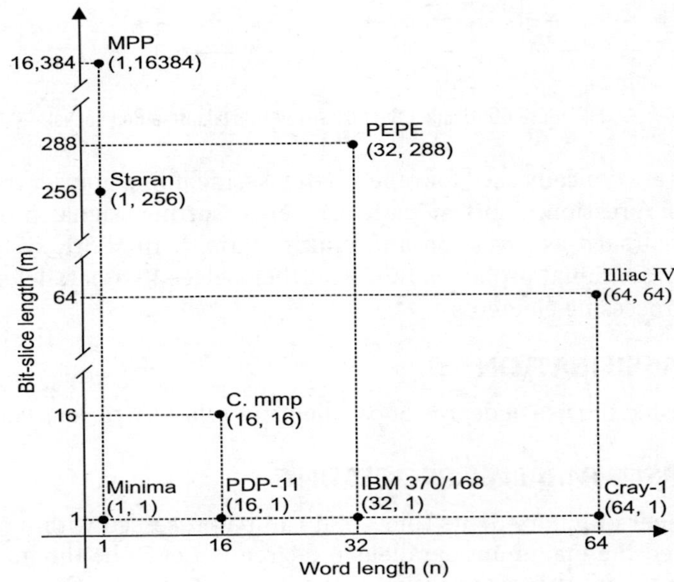

FIGURE 6.51: Feng's classification of computer systems in terms of parallelism exhibited by word length and bit-slice length

There are four types of processing methods that can be seen from this diagram:

- Word-serial and bit-serial (WSBS)
- Word-serial and bit-parallel (WSBP)
- Word-parallel and bit-serial (WPBS)
- Word-parallel and bit-parallel (WPBP)

WSBS has been called bit-serial processing because one bit (n = m = 1) is processed at a time, a rather slow process. This was done only in the first-generation computers.

TABLE 6.6: Feng's Computer Classification

Mode	Computer Model	Degree of Parallelism
WSPS N = 1; M = 1	The 'MINIMA'	(1,1)
WPBS N=1; M>1	STARAN MPP DAP	(1,256) (1,16384) (1,4096)
WSBP n>1; m=1 (Word Slice Processing)	IBM 370/168 UP CDC 6600 Burrough 7700 VAX 11/780	(64,1) (60,1) (48,1) (16/32,1)
WPBP n>1; m>1 (fully parallel processing)	Illiav IV	(64, 64)

WPBS (n = 1, m > 1) has been called bis (bit-slice) processing because an m-bit slice is processed at a time. WSBP (n > 1, m = 1), as found in most existing computers, has been called word-slice processing because one word of n bits is processed at a time. Finally, WPBP (n > 1, m > 1) is known as fully parallel processing (or simply parallel processing, if no confusion exists), in which an array of n.m bits is processed at one time, the fastest processing mode of the four. In Table 6.6, we have listed a number of computer systems under each processing mode. The system parameters n, m are also shown for each system. The bit-slice processors, like STARAN, MPP and DAP, all have long bit slices. Illiac-IV and PEPE are two word-slice array processors.

6.21 HANDLER'S CLASSIFICATION (PARALLELISM VERSUS PIPELINING)

Wolfgang Handler has proposed a classification scheme for identifying the parallelism degree and pipelining degree built into the hardware structures of a computer system. He considers parallel-pipeline processing at three subsystem levels:

- Processor control unit (PCU)
- Arithmetic logic unit (ALU)
- Bit-level circuit (BLC)

The functions of PCU and ALU should be clear to us.

- Each PCU corresponds to one processor or one CPU.
- The ALU is equivalent to the processing element (PE) we specified for SIMD array processors.
- The BLC corresponds to the combinational logic circuitry needed to perform 1-bit operations in the ALU.

A computer system C can be characterized by a triple containing six independent entities, as defined below:

$$T(C) = (K \times K', D \times D', W \times W')$$

where K = the number of processors (PCUs) within the computer

D = the number of ALUs (or PEs) under the control of one PCU

W = the word length of an ALU or of a PE

W' = the number of pipeline stages in all ALUs or in a PE

D' = the number of ALUs that can be pipelined

K' = the number of PCUs that can be pipelined

Several real computer examples are used to clarify the above parametric descriptions. The Texas Instrument's Advanced Scientific Computer (TI – ASC) has one controller controlling four arithmetic pipelines; each has 64-bit word lengths and eight stages. Thus, we have

$$T(ASC) = (1 \times 1, 4 \times 1, 64 \times 8) = (1, 4, 64 \times 8)$$

Whenever the second entity, K', D', or W', equals 1, we drop it, since pipelining of one stage or of one unit is meaningless.

Another example is the Control Data 6600, which has a CPU with an ALU that has 10 specialized hardware functions, each of a word length of 60 bits. Up to 10 of these functions can be linked into a longer pipeline. Furthermore, the CDC-6600 has 10 peripheral I/O processors which can operate in parallel. Each I/O processor has one ALU with a word length of 12 bits. Thus, we specify 6600 in two parts, using the operator x to link them:

$$T\,(\text{CDC 6600}) = T\,(\text{central processor}) \times T\,(\text{I/O processors})$$
$$= (1, 2 \times 10, 60) \times (10, 1, 12)$$

Another sample system is the C.mmp multiprocessor system developed at Carnegie-Mellon University. This system can be used in a number of ways, as illustrated in Figure 6.52. The system consists of 16 PDP-11 minicomputers of a word length of 16 bits. Normally, it will operate in MIMD mode, as shown in Figure 6.52a. Theoretically, it can also operate in SIMD mode, provided all the minicomputers are synchronized by one master controller, as illustrated in Figure 6.52b. Finally, the system can be rearranged to operate in MISD mode, as shown in Figure 6.52c. Based on these three operating modes, we specify C.mmp in three parts, using the operator + to separate them.

$$T\,(\text{C.mmp}) = (16, 1, 16) + (1 \times 16, 1, 16) + (1, 16, 16)$$

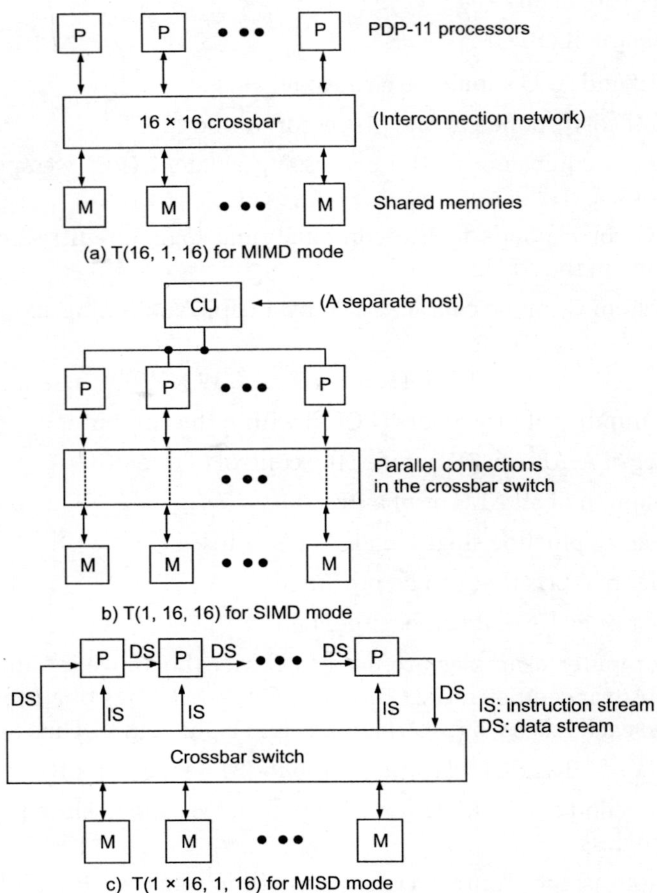

FIGURE 6.52: Operation modes in C.mmp system (al double-arrowed paths are for both IS and DS)

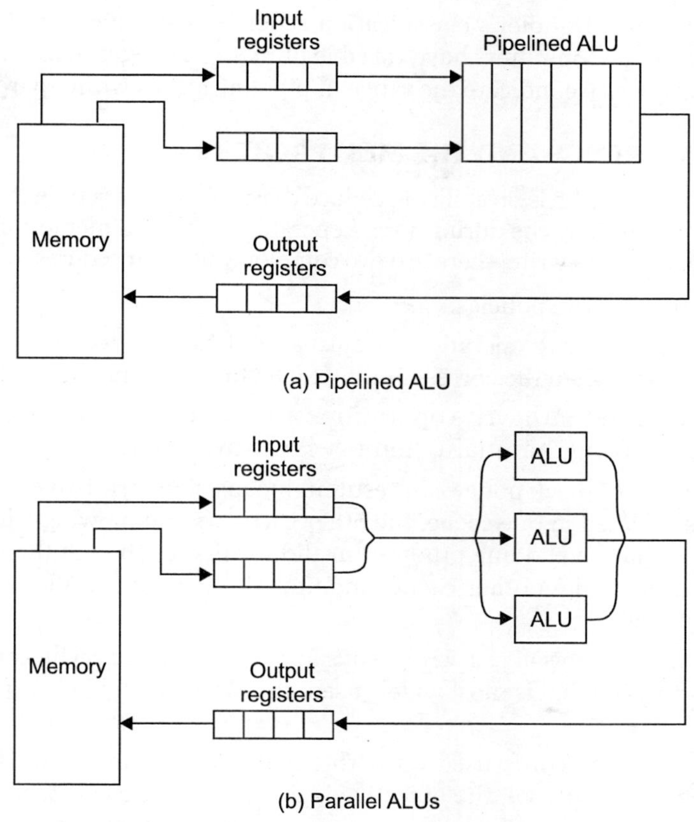

FIGURE 6.53: Pipelined and Parallel ALU

TABLE 6.8: Handler's computer system classification

Computer model T(C)	**System Signification†** **$\langle K\times K', D\times D', W\times W'\rangle$**
T (TI–ASC)	$\langle 1, 4, 64 \times 8\rangle$
T(CDC–6600)	$\langle 1, 1 \times 10, 60\rangle \times \langle 10, 1, 12\rangle$ central processor I/O processor
T(Illiac IV)	$\langle 1, 64, 64\rangle$
T(MPP)	$\langle 1, 16384, 1\rangle$
T(C.mmp)	$\langle 16, 1, 16\rangle + \langle 1 \times 16, 1, 16\rangle + \langle 1, 16, 16\rangle$
T(PEPC)	$\langle 1 \times 3, 288, 32\rangle$
T(IBM 360/91)	$\langle 1, 3, 64 \times (3 \sim 5)\rangle$
T(Prime)	$\langle 5, 1, 16\rangle$
T(Cray-1)	$\langle 1, 12 \times 8‡, 64 \times (1 \sim 14)\rangle$
T(AP-120B)	$\langle 1, 2, 38 \times (2 \sim 3)\rangle$

† K, D', and W' are omitted when equal to 1.

‡ For Cray-I, the pipeline chaining degree is a variable with a maximum value equal to 8.

In Table 6.8, we use Handler's classification scheme to specify some computer systems. It should be noted that many computers have variable numbers of stages in different functional units. Under such circumstances we indicate the range of pipeline stages within parentheses.

6.22 CACHE COHERENCE AND THE MESI PROTOCOL

The primary advantage of cache is its ability to reduce the average access time in uniprocessors. When the processor finds a word in cache during a read operation, the main memory is not involved in the transfer. If the operation is to write, there are two commonly used procedures to update memory.

We defined two common write policies:

- **Write back:** Write operations are usually made only to the cache. Main memory is only updated when the corresponding cache line is flushed from the cache.
- **Write through:** All write operations are made to main memory as well as to the cache, ensuring that main memory is always valid.

It is clear that a write-back policy can result in inconsistency. If two caches contain the same line, and the line is updated in one cache, the other cache will unknowingly have an invalid value. Subsequent reads to that invalid line produce invalid results. Even with the write-through policy, inconsistency can occur unless other caches monitor the memory traffic or receive some direct notification of the update.

In this section, we will briefly survey various approaches to the cache coherence problem and then focus on the approach that is most widely used: the MESI modified/exclusive/shared/invalid) protocol.

A version of this protocol is used on both the Pentium 4 and PowerPC implementations. For any cache coherence protocol, the objective is to let recently used local variables get into the appropriate cache and stay there through numerous reads and write, while using the protocol to maintain consistency of shared variables that might be in multiple caches at the same time. Cache coherence approaches have generally been divided into software and hardware approaches. Some implementations adopt a strategy that involves both software and hardware elements. Nevertheless, the classification into software and hardware approaches is still instructive and is commonly used in surveying cache coherence strategies. In a shared memory multiprocessor system, all the processors share a common memory. In addition, each processor may have a local memory, part or all of which may be a cache. The compelling reason for having separate caches for each processor is to reduce the average access time in each processor. The same information may reside in a number of copies in some caches and main memory. To ensure the ability of the system to execute memory operations correctly, the multiple copies must be kept identical. This requirement imposes a *cache coherence* problem. A memory scheme is *coherent* if the value returned on a load instruction is always the value given by the latest store instruction with the same address. Without a proper solution to the cache coherence problem, caching cannot be used in bus-oriented multiprocessors with two or more processors.

6.22.1 SOFTWARE SOLUTIONS

Software cache coherence schemes attempt to avoid the need for additional hardware circuitry and logic by relying on the compiler and operating system to deal with the problem. Software approaches are attractive because the overhead of detecting potential problems is transferred from run time to compile time, and the design complexity is transferred from hardware to software. On the other hand, compile-time software approaches generally must make conservative decisions, leading to inefficient cache utilization.

Compiler-based coherence mechanisms perform an analysis on the code to determine which data items may become unsafe for caching, and they mark those items accordingly. The operating system or hardware then prevents noncacheable items from being cached.

The simplest approach is to prevent any shared data variables from being cached. This is too conservative, because a shared data structure may be exclusively used during some periods and may be effectively read-only during other periods. It is only during periods when at least one process may update the variable and at least one other process may access the variable that cache coherence is an issue. More efficient approaches analyze the code to determine safe periods for shared variables. The compiler then inserts instructions into the generated code to enforce cache coherence during the critical periods. A number of techniques have been developed for performing the analysis and for enforcing the results; see [LILJ93] and [STEN90] for surveys.

6.22.2 HARDWARE SOLUTIONS

Hardware-based solutions are generally referred to as cache coherence protocols. These solutions provide dynamic recognition at run time of potential inconsistency conditions. Because the problem is only dealt with when it actually arises, there is more effective use of caches, leading to improved performance over a software approach. In addition, these approaches are transparent to the programmer and the compiler, reducing the software development burden. Hardware schemes differ in a number of particulars, including where the state information about data lines is held, how that information is organized, where coherence is enforced, and the enforcement mechanisms. In general, hardware schemes can be divided into two categories: directory protocols and snoopy protocols.

Directory Protocols Directory protocols collect and maintain information about where copies of lines reside. Typically, there is a centralized controller that is part of the main memory controller, and a directory that is stored in main memory. The directory contains global state information about the contents of the various local caches. When an individual cache controller makes a request, the centralized controller checks and issues necessary commands for data transfer between memory and caches or between caches. It is also responsible for keeping the state information up to date; therefore, every local action that can affect the global state of a line must be reported to the central controller. Typically, the controller maintains information about which processors have a copy of which lines. Before a processor can write to a local copy of a line, it must request exclusive access to the line from the controller. Before granting this exclusive access, the controller sends a message to all processors with a cached copy of this line, forcing each processor to invalidate its copy. After receiving acknowledgments back from each such processor, the controller grants exclusive access to the requesting processor. When another processor tries to read a line that is exclusively granted to another processor, it will send a miss notification to the controller. The controller then issues a command to the processor holding that line that requires the processor to do a write back to main memory. The line may now be shared for reading by the original processor and the requesting processor.

Directory schemes suffer from the drawbacks of a central bottleneck and the overhead of communication between the various cache controllers and the central controller. However, they are effective in large-scale systems that involve multiple buses or some other complex interconnection scheme.

Snoopy Protocols Snoopy protocols distribute the responsibility for maintaining cache coherence among all of the cache controllers in a multiprocessor. A cache must recognize when a line that it holds is shared with other caches. When an update action is performed on a shared cache line, it must be announced to all other caches by a broadcast mechanism. Each cache controller is able to "snoop" on the network to observe these broadcasted notifications, and react accordingly. Snoopy protocols are ideally suited to a bus-based multiprocessor, because the shared bus provides a simple means for broadcasting and snooping. However, because one of the objectives of the use of local caches is to avoid bus accesses, care must be taken that the increased bus traffic required for broadcasting and snooping does not cancel out the gains from the use of local caches. Two basic approaches to the snoopy protocol have been explored: write invalidate and write update (or write broadcast).With a write-invalidate protocol, there can be multiple readers but only one writer at a time. Initially, a line may be shared among several caches for reading purposes. When one of the caches wants to perform a write to the line, it first issues a notice that invalidates that line in the other caches, making the line exclusive to the writing cache. Once the line is exclusive, the owning processor can make cheap local writes until some other processor requires the same line.

With a write-update protocol, there can be multiple writers as well as multiple readers. When a processor wishes to update a shared line, the word to be updated is distributed to all others, and caches containing that line can update it. Neither of these two approaches is superior to the other under all circumstances. Performance depends on the number of local caches and the pattern of memory reads and writes. Some systems implement adaptive protocols that employ both write-invalidate and write-update mechanisms. The write-invalidate approach is the most widely used in commercial multiprocessor systems, such as the Pentium 4 and PowerPC. It marks the state of every cache line (using two extra bits in the cache tag) as modified, exclusive, shared, or invalid.

For this reason, the write-invalidate protocol is called MESI. In the remainder of this section, we will look at its use among local caches across a multiprocessor. For simplicity in the presentation, we do not examine the mechanisms involved in coordinating among both level 1 and level 2 locally as well as at the same time coordinating across the distributed multiprocessor. This would not add any new principles but would greatly complicate the discussion.

6.22.3 THE MESI PROTOCOL

To provide cache consistency on an SMP, the data cache often supports a protocol known as MESI. For MESI, the data cache includes two status bits per tag, so that each line can be in one of four states:

- **Modified:** The line in the cache has been modified (different from main memory) and is available only in this cache.

TABLE 6.9: MESI Cache Line States

	(M) Modified	(E) Exclusive	(S) Shared	(I) Invalid
This cache line valid?	Yes	Yes	Yes	No
The memory copy is....	out of date	valid	valid	—
Copies exist in other caches?	No	No	may be	may be
A write to this line	does not go to bus	does not go to bus	goes to bus and update cache	goes directly to bus

- **Exclusive:** The line in the cache is the same as that in main memory and is not present in any other cache.
- **Shared:** The line in the cache is the same as that in main memory and may be present in another cache.
- **Invalid:** The line in the cache does not contain valid data.

Table 6.9 summarizes the meaning of the four states. Figure 6.54 displays a state diagram for the MESI protocol. Keep in mind that each line of the cache has its own state bits and therefore its own realization of the state diagram. Figure 6.54a shows the transitions that occur due to actions initiated by the processor attached to this cache. Figure 6.54b shows the transitions that occur due to events that are snooped on the common bus. This presentation of separate state diagrams for processor-initiated and bus-initiated actions helps to clarify the logic of the MESI protocol. At any time a cache line is in a single state. If the next event is from the attached processor, then the transition is dictated by Figure 6.54a and if the next event is from the bus, the transition is dictated by Figure 6.54b. Let us look at these transitions in more detail.

Read Miss When a read miss occurs in the local cache, the processor initiates a memory read to read the line of main memory containing the missing address. The processor inserts a signal on the bus that alerts all other processor/cache units to snoop the transaction. There are a number of possible outcomes:

- If one other cache has a clean (unmodified since read from memory) copy of the line in the exclusive state, it returns a signal indicating that it shares this line. The responding processor then transitions the state of its copy from exclusive to shared, and the initiating processor reads the line from main memory and transitions the line in its cache from invalid to share.
- If one or more caches have a clean copy of the line in the shared state, each of them signals that it shares the line. The initiating processor reads the line and transitions the line in its cache from invalid to share.
- If one other cache has a modified copy of the line, then that cache blocks the memory read and provides the line to the requesting cache over the shared bus. The responding cache then changes its line from modified to shared.1 The line sent to the requesting cache is also received and processed by the memory controller, which stores the block in memory.
- If no other cache has a copy of the line (clean or modified), then no signals are returned. The initiating processor reads the line and transitions the line in its cache from invalid to exclusive.

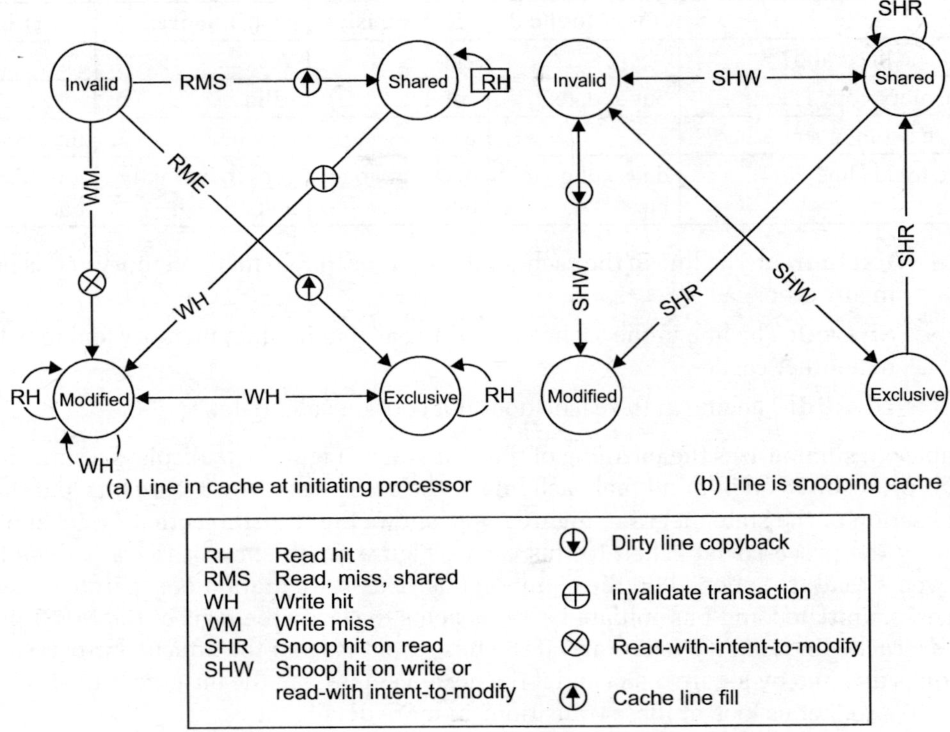

FIGURE 6.54: MESI State Transition Diagram

Read Hit When a read hit occurs on a line currently in the local cache, the processor simply reads the required item. There is no state change: The state remains modified, shared, or exclusive.

Write Miss When a write miss occurs in the local cache, the processor initiates a memory read to read the line of main memory containing the missing address. For this purpose, the processor issues a signal on the bus that means *read-with-intent-to modify* (RWITM).When the line is loaded, it is immediately marked modified. With respect to other caches, two possible scenarios precede the loading of the line of data. First, some other cache may have a modified copy of this line (state = modify).

In this case, the alerted processor signals the initiating processor that another processor has a modified copy of the line. The initiating processor surrenders the bus and waits. The other processor gains access to the bus, writes the modified cache line back to main memory, and transitions the state of the cache line to invalid (because the initiating processor is going to modify this line). Subsequently, the initiating processor will again issue a signal to the bus of RWITM and then read the line from main memory, modify the line in the cache, and mark the line in the modified state.

The second scenario is that no other cache has a modified copy of the requested line. In this case, no signal is returned, and the initiating processor proceeds to read in the line and modify it. Meanwhile, if one or more caches have a clean copy of the line in the shared state, each cache invalidates its copy of the line, and if one cache has a clean copy of the line in the exclusive state, it invalidates its copy of the line.

Write Hit When a write hit occurs on a line currently in the local cache, the effect depends on the current state of that line in the local cache:

- **Shared:** Before performing the update, the processor must gain exclusive ownership of the line. The processor signals its intent on the bus. Each processor that has a shared copy of the line in its cache transitions the sector from shared to invalid. The initiating processor then performs the update and transitions its copy of the line from shared to modify.
- **Exclusive:** The processor already has exclusive control of this line, and so it simply performs the update and transitions its copy of the line from exclusive to modify.
- **Modified:** The processor already has exclusive control of this line and has the line marked as modified, and so it simply performs the update.

L1-L2 Cache Consistency We have so far described cache coherency protocols in terms of the cooperate activity among caches connected to the same bus or other SMP interconnection facility. Typically, these caches are L2 caches, and each processor also has an L1 cache that does not connect directly to the bus and that therefore cannot engage in a snoopy protocol. Thus, some scheme is needed to maintain data integrity across both levels of cache and across all caches in the SMP configuration. The strategy is to extend the MESI protocol (or any cache coherence protocol) to the L1 caches. Thus, each line in the L1 cache includes bits to indicate the state. In essence, the objective is the following: for any line that is present in both an L2 cache and its corresponding L1 cache, the L1 line state should track the state of the L2 line.

A simple means of doing this is to adopt the write-through policy in the L1 cache; in this case the write through is to the L2 cache and not to the memory. The L1 write-through policy forces any modification to an L1 line out to the L2 cache and therefore makes it visible to other L2 caches. The use of the L1 write through policy requires that the L1 content must be a subset of the L2 content. This in turn suggests that the associativity of the L2 cache should be equal to or greater than that of the L1 associativity. The L1 write-through policy is used in the IBM S/390 SMP. If the L1 cache has a write-back policy, the relationship between the two caches is more complex. There are several approaches to maintaining coherence for example, the approach used on the Pentium II.

6.23 PARALLEL PROCESSING APPLICATIONS

Fast and efficient computers are in high demand in many scientific, engineering and energy resource, medical, military, artificial intelligence and the basic research areas. Large scale computations are performed in these application areas. Parallel processing computers are needed to meet these demands. Large scale scientific problem solving involves three interactive disciplines;

- Theories
- Experiments
- Computations

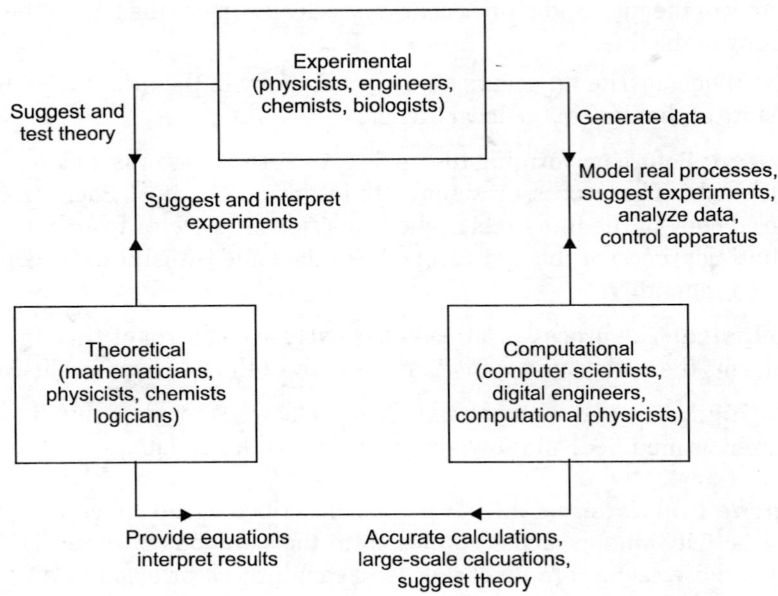

FIGURE 6.55: Interaction among experiments, theories, and computations to solve large-scale scientific problems.

Theoretical scientists develop mathematical models that computer engineers solve numerically, the numerical results then suggest new theories. Experimental science provides data for computational science and the latter can model processes that are hard to approach in the laboratory.

Computer Simulation has several advantages:

1. It is far cheaper than physical experiments.
2. It can solve much wider range of problems that specific laboratory equipments can.
3. Computational approaches are only limited by computer speed and memory capacity, while physical experiments have many special practical constraints.

6.23.1 PREDICTIVE MODELING AND SIMULATIONS

Predictive modeling is done through extensive computer simulation experiments, which often involve large-scale computations to achieve the desired accuracy and turnaround time. Such numerical modeling requires state-of-the-art computing at speeds approaching 1000 million megaflops or beyond.

(A) Numerical Weather Forecasting: Weather modeling is necessary for short range forecasts and do long range hazard predictions such as flood, drought and environment pollutions. The weather analyst needs to solve general circulation model equations with the computer. The atmospheric state is represented by the surface pressure, the wind field, temperature, and the water vapor mixing ratio. These state variables are governed by the Navier-Stokes fluid dynamics equations in a spherical coordinate system.

(B) Oceanography and Astrophysics: Since ocean can store and transfer heat and exchange it with the atmosphere. Understanding of oceans helps us in

- Climate Predictive Analysis
- Fishery Management
- Ocean Resource Exploration
- Costal Dynamics and Tides

(C) Socioeconomics and Government Use: Large computers are in great demand in the areas of econometrics, social engineering, government census, crime control, and the modeling of the world's economy for the year 2000. Nobel laureate W. W. Leontief (1980) has proposed an input-output model of the world economy which performs large-scale matrix operations on a CDC scientific computer. This United Nations – supported world economic simulation suggests how a system of international economic relations that features a partial disarmament could narrow the gap between the rich and the poor.

6.23.2 ENGINEERING DESIGN AND AUTOMATION

Fast computers have been in high demand for solving many engineering design problems, such as the finite element analysis needed for structural designs and wind tunnel experiments for aero dynamics studies.

(A) Finite Element Analysis: The design of dams, bridges, ships, supersonic jets, high buildings, and space vehicles requires the resolution of a large system of algebraic equations. Conventional approaches using predeveloped software packages (written in sequential codes) require intolerable turnaround times. Many researchers and engineers have attempted to build more efficient computers to perform finite-element analysis or to seek finite difference solutions. This would imply a fundamental change of engineering design tools and higher productivity in the future.

(B) Computational Aerodynamics: Large scale computers have made significant contributions in providing new technological capabilities and economies in pressing ahead with aircraft and spacecraft lift and turbulence studies.

(C) Artificial Intelligence and Automation: Intelligent I/O interfaces are being demanded for future supercomputers that must directly communicate with human beings in images, speech, and natural languages. The various intelligent functions that demand parallel processing are:

- Image Processing
- Pattern Recognition
- Computer Vision
- Speech Understanding
- Machien Interface
- CAD/CAM/CAI/OA
- Intelligent Robotics
- Expert Computer Systems
- Knowledge Engineering

(D) Remote Sensing Applications: Computer analysis of remotely sensed earth resource data has many potential applications in agriculture, forestry, geology, and water resource. Explosive amounts of pictorial information need to be processed in this area.

6.23.3 ENERGY RESOURCES EXPLORATION

Energy affects the progress of the entire economy on a global basis. Computer can play the important role in the discovery of oil and gas and the management of their recovery, in the development of workable plasma fusion energy and in ensuring nuclear reactor safety.

(A) Seismic Exploration: Many oil companies are investing in the use of attached array processors or vector supercomputer for seismic data processing, which accounts for about 10 percent of the oil finding costs. Seismic explorations sets off a sonic wave by explosive or by jamming a heavy hydraulic ram into the ground about the spot are used to pick up the echoes.

(B) Reservoir Modeling: Super computers are used to perform three dimensional modeling of oil fields. The reservoir problem is solved by using the finite difference method on the three-dimensional representation of the field. Geologic core samples are examined to project forward into time the field's expected performance. Presently at least 1000 flops needs to be processed per data point tin the three-dimensional model of an oil field. This means a superpower computer must be employed to achieve an accurate performance evaluation in a reasonable time period for a large field.

(C) Plasma Fusion Power: Nuclear fusion researchers to use a computer 100 times more powerful than any existing one to model the plasma dynamics in the proposed Tokamak fusion power generator.

(D) Nuclear Reactor Safety: Nuclear reactor designs and safety control can both be aided by computer simulation studies. These studies attempt to provide for:

- On-Line analysis of reactor conditions
- Automatic control for normal and abnormal operations
- Quick assessment of potential mitigation accidents

6.23.4 MEDICAL, MILITARY AND BASIC RESEARCH

Fast computers are needed in the computer assisted tomography, artificial heart design, liver diagnosis, brain damage estimation, and genetic engineering studies. Military defence needs to use supercomputers for weapon design, effects, simulation and other electronic warfare.

(A) Computer Assisted Tomography: The human body can be modeled by computer assisted tomography (CAT) scanning. The Mayo Clinic in Rochester, Minnesota, is developing a research CAT scanner for three-dimensional, stop-action, cross-action viewing of the human heart. At the Courant Institute of Mathematical Sciences, research scientists are seeking an array processor for time-sequence, three-dimensional modeling of blood flow in the heart, with the goal of pursuing the artificial heart. Similar approaches can be applied to reveal the secrets of other human organs in real time.

(B) Genetic Engineering: Biological system can be simulated on super computers. Genetic engineering is advancing rapidly in recent years. There is a growing need for large-scale computations to study molecular biology for the synthesis of complex organic molecules, such as proteins. Crystallography also can be aided by computer processing.

(C) Weapon Research and Defence: Military Research agencies have used the majority of existing supercomputers. Listed below are several defense-related military applications of supercomputers.

- Multiwarhead nuclear weapon design (Cray-1)
- Simulation of atomic weapon effects by solving hydrodynamics and radiation problems (Cyber-205)
- Intelligence gathering, such as radar signal processing on the associative processor for the antiballistic missile (ABM) program (PEPE)
- Cartographic data processing for automatic map generation (Staran)
- Sea surveillance for antisubmarine warfare (the S-1 multiprocessor)

(D) Basic Research Problem: Many of the aforementioned application areas are related to basic scientific research. Below are several additional areas that demand the use of supercomputers:

1. **Computational chemists** solve problems on quantum mechanics, statistical mechanics, polymer chemistry, and crystal growth.
2. **Computational physicists** analyze particle tracks generated in spark chambers, study fluid dynamics, examine quantum field theory, and investigate molecular dynamics.
3. **Electronic engineers** solve large-scale circuit equations using the multilevel Newton algorithm, and lay out VLSI connections on semiconductor chips.

QUESTIONS

1. Explain the concept of parallel organization in detail?
2. Explain the architectural structures of parallel computers?
3. Explain the concept of pipeline computers in detail?
4. What do you mean by pipelining?
5. Explain the concept of instruction pipeline?
6. How can you calculate the performance of pipelining?
7. Explain the concept of array processor in detail?
8. Explain the various multiple processor organizations in detail?
9. What are the characteristics of multiprocessors?
10. Explain the various types of multiprocessor systems?
11. Explain the memory organization of multiprocessors?
12. Explain the concept of shared memory multiprocessors?
13. What do you mean by distributed computing?
14. How can you calculate the performance of parallel computers?
15. Explain the various architectural classification schemes?
16. Explain the types of parallel organizations?
17. Explain the Kuck classification scheme?

18. Explain the Hwang and Briggs classification scheme?
19. Explain the Erlangen classification scheme?
20. Explain the Skillicorn classification scheme?
21. What are symmetric multiprocessors?
22. Explain the advantages of symmetric multiprocessors?
23. Explain the Organization of multiprocessors?
24. What are the key issues of multiprocessors?
25. Explain the various parallel and multiprocessor architectures?
26. Explain the concept of superscalar and VLIW?
27. What are the vector processors?
28. Explain the concept of dataflow computing?
29. Explain the architecture of neural networks?
30. Explain the concept of systolic processing?
31. Distinguish between serial and parallel processing?
32. Distinguish between parallelism and pipelining?
33. Explain the concept of cache coherence
34. Explain the concept of MESI protocol?
35. Explain the various applications of parallel processing?

CHAPTER 7 PIPELINING

7.1 INTRODUCTION

Pipelining offers an economical way to realize temporal parallelism in digital computers. The concept of pipeline processing in a computer is similar to assembly lines in an industrial plant. To achieve pipelining, one must subdivide the input task (process) into a sequence of subtasks, each of which can be executed by a specialized hardware stage that operates concurrently with other stages in the pipeline. Successive tasks are streamed into the pipe and get executed in an overlapped fashion at the subtask level. The subdivision of labor in assembly lines has contributed to the success of mass production in modern industry; By the same token pipeline processing has led to the tremendous improvement of system throughput in the modern digital computer. In this section, a sample design of a floating point adder is used to illustrate the concept of linear pipelining. Basis prosperities and speedup of a linear-pipeline processor are characterized. Various types of pipeline processors are than classified according to pipelining levels and functional configurations. Finally, we introduce the reservation table as a design tool of general pipelines with either linear or nonlinear data-flow patterns.

7.2 PIPELINING: AN OVERLAPPED PARALLELISM

Pipelining is a technique of decomposing a sequential process into sub-processes, with each sub-process being executed in a special dedicated segment that operates concurrently with all other segments. Any operation that can be decomposed into a sequence of sub-operations of about the same complexity can be implemented by a pipeline processor. Pipeline is similar to the assembly line in industrial plant. To achieve pipelining one must divide the input process into a sequence of sub tasks and each of which can be executed concurrently with other stages. Pipelining offers an economical way to realize temporal parallelism in digital computers. To achieve pipelining, one must subdivide the input task into a sequence of subtasks, each of which can be executed by a specialized hardware stage.

- Pipelining is the backbone of vector supercomputers.
- Widely used in application-specific machine where high throughput is needed.
- Can be incorporated in various machine architectures (SISD, SIMD, MIMD, ...).

Easy to build a powerful pipeline and waste its power because:

- Data can not be fed fast enough

- The algorithm does not have inherent concurrency.
- Programmers do not know how to program it efficiently.

7.2.1 ADVANTAGES AND DISADVANTAGES

Pipelining does not help in all cases. There are several possible disadvantages. An instruction pipeline is said to be fully pipelined if it can accept a new instruction every clock cycle. A pipeline that is not fully pipelined has wait cycles that delay the progress of the pipeline.

Advantages of Pipelining

1. The cycle time of the processor is reduced, thus increasing instruction issue-rate in most cases.
2. Some combinational circuits such as adders or multipliers can be made faster by adding more circuitry. If pipelining is used instead, it can save circuitry vs. a more complex combinational circuit.

Disadvantages of Pipelining

1. A non-pipelined processor executes only a single instruction at a time. This prevents branch delays (in effect, every branch is delayed) and problems with serial instructions being executed concurrently. Consequently the design is simpler and cheaper to manufacture.
2. The instruction latency in a non-pipelined processor is slightly lower than in a pipelined equivalent. This is because extra flip flops must be added to the data path of a pipelined processor.

A non-pipelined processor will have a stable instruction bandwidth. The performance of a pipelined processor is much harder to predict and may vary more widely between different programs.

7.3 PRINCIPLES OF LINEAR PIPELINING

The precedence relation of a set of subtasks $\{T_{1,} T_{2,} ..., T_k\}$ for a given task T implies that some task T_j cannot start until some earlier task T_i ($i < j$) finishes. The interdependencies of all subtasks form the precedence graph. With a linear precedence relation, task T_j cannot start until all earlier subtasks $\{T_i$ for all $i < j\}$ finish. A linear pipeline can process a succession of subtasks with a linear precedence graph.

A basic linear-pipeline processor is depicted in Figure 7.1a. The pipeline consists of a cascade of processing stages. The stages are pure combinational circuit performing arithmetic or logic operations over the data stream flowing through the pipe. The stages are separated by high-speed interface latches. The latches are fast registers for holding the intermediate results between the stages. Information flows between adjacent stages are under the control of a common clock applied to all the latches simultaneously.

7.3.1 CLOCK PERIOD

The logic circuitry in each stage S_i has a time delay denoted by τ_I. Let τ_I be the time delay of each interface latch. The clock period of a linear pipeline is defined by

$$\tau = \max + \tau_{I\,=}\,\tau_m + \tau_I$$

The reciprocal of the clock period is called the frequency $f = 1/\tau$ of a pipeline processor.

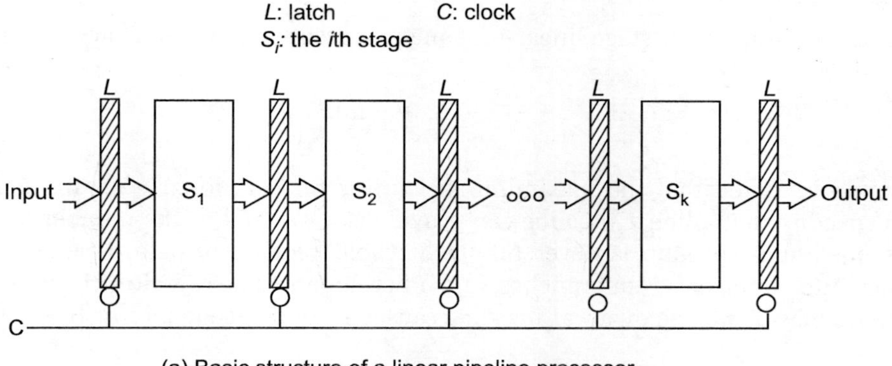

(a) Basic structure of a linear pipeline processor

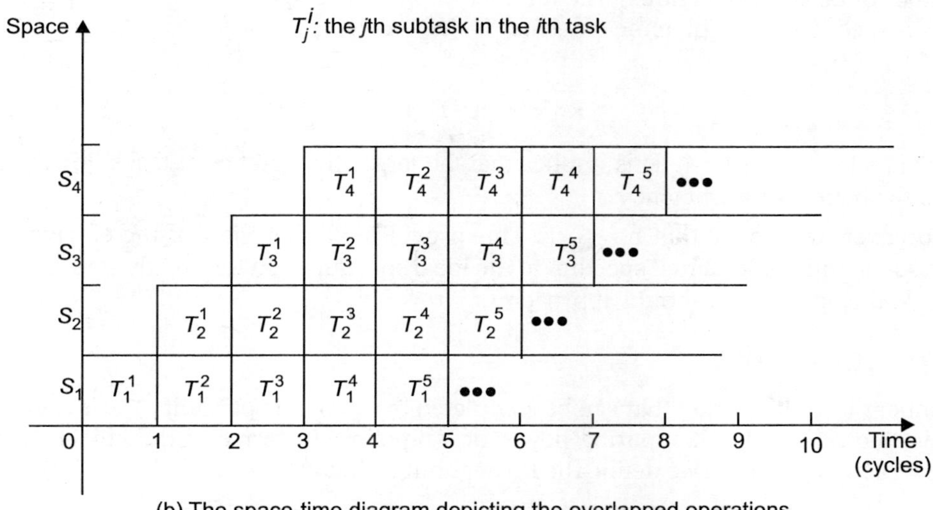

(b) The space-time diagram depicting the overlapped operations

FIGURE 7.1: Linear pipeline processor for overlapped processing of multiple tasks.

SPACE-TIME DIAGRAM

One can draw a space-time diagram to illustrate the overlapped operations in a linear pipeline processor. The space-time diagram of a four-stage pipeline processor is demonstrated in Figure 7.1b. Once the pipe is filled up, it will output one result per clock period independent of the number of stages in the pipe. Ideally, a linear pipeline with k stages can process n tasks in $T_k = k + (n - 1)$ clock periods where k cycle are used to fill up the pipeline or to complete execution of the first task and n – 1cycles are needed to complete the remaining n -1 tasks. The same number of tasks (operand pairs) can be executed in a nonpipeline processor with an equivalent function in $T_i = n.\ k$ time delay.

7.3.2 SPEEDUP

We define the speedup of a k-stage linear-pipeline processor over an equivalent nonpipeline processor as

$$S_k = \frac{T_1}{T_k} = \frac{n \cdot k}{k + (n - 1)}$$

It should be noted that the maximum speedup is $S_k \rightarrow k$, for $n > k$. In other words, the maximum speedup that a linear pipeline can provide is k, where k is the number of stages in the pipe. This maximum speedup is never fully achievable because of data dependencies between instructions. Interrupts, program branches, and other factors to be revealed in later section. Many pipeline cycles may be wasted on a waiting state caused by out-of-sequence instruction executions.

7.3.3 EFFICIENCY

The efficiency of a linear pipeline is measured by the percentage of busy time-space spans over the total time-space span, which equals the sum of all busy and idle time-space spans. Let n, k, τ be the number of tasks (instructions), the number of pipeline stages, and the clock period of a linear pipeline, respectively. The pipeline efficiency is defined by

$$n = \frac{n.k.\tau}{k.[k\tau + (n-1)\tau]} = \frac{n}{k + (n-1)}$$

Note that $n \rightarrow 1$ as $n \rightarrow$. This implies that the larger the number of tasks flowing through the pipeline, the better is its efficiency.

Moreover, we realize that $n = S_k/k$. This provides another view of the efficiency of a linear pipeline as the ratio of its actual speedup to the ideal speedup k. In the steady state of a pipeline, we have $n > k$, the efficiency n should approach 1.

7.3.4 THROUGHPUT

The number of results (tasks) that can be completed by a pipeline per unit time is called is throughput. This rate reflects the computing power of a pipeline. In terms of the efficiency η and clock period τ of a liner pipeline, we define the throughput as follows:

$$w = \frac{\eta}{k\tau + (n+1)\tau} = \frac{\eta}{\tau}$$

where n equals the total number of tasks being processed during an observation period $k\tau + (n - 1)\tau$. In the ideal case, $w = 1/\tau = f$ when $\eta \rightarrow 1$. This means that the maximum throughput of a linear pipeline is equal to its frequency, which corresponds to one output result per clock period.

EXAMPLE

To illustrate the operation principles of a pipeline computation, the design of a pipeline floating point adder is given. It is constructed in four stages. The inputs are

$$A = a \times 2^p$$

$$B = b \times 2^q$$

where **a** and **b** are 2 fractions and p and q are their exponents and here base 2 is assumed.

To compute the sum

$$C = A + B = c \times 2^r = d \times 2^s$$

Operations performed in the four pipeline stages are specified.

1. Compare the two exponents p and q to reveal the larger exponent r = max (p, q) and to determine their difference t = p – q
2. Shift right the fraction associated with the smaller exponent by t bits to equalize the two components before fraction addition.
3. Add the pre-shifted fraction with the other fraction to produce the intermediate sum fraction c where 0 <= c <1.
4. Count the number of leading zeroes, say u, in fraction c and shift left c by u bits to produce the normalized fraction sum $d = c \times 2^u$, with a leading bit 1. Update the large exponent s by subtracting s= r – u to produce the output exponent.

7.4 LINEAR PIPELINE PROCESSORS

A linear pipeline processor is a cascade of processing stages which are linearly connected to perform a fixed function over a stream of data flowing from one end to the other. In modern computers, linear pipelines are applied for instruction execution, arithmetic computation and memory access operations.

7.4.1 ASYNCHRONOUS AND SYNCHRONOUS MODELS

A linear pipeline is constructed with k processing stages (segments). External inputs (operands) are fed into the pipeline at the first stage S1. The processed results are passed from stage Si to stage Si+1 for all i = 1, 2, …., k-1. The final result emerges from the pipeline at the last stage. Depending on the control of data flow along the pipeline, linear pipeline is modeled into two categories: asynchronous and synchronous.

7.4.1.1 ASYNCHRONOUS MODEL

As shown in Figure 7.3a, data flow between adjacent stages in asynchronous pipeline is controlled by a handshaking protocol. When stage Si is ready to transmit, it sends a ready signal to stage Si+1. After stage Si+1 receives the incoming data, it returns an acknowledge signal to Si.

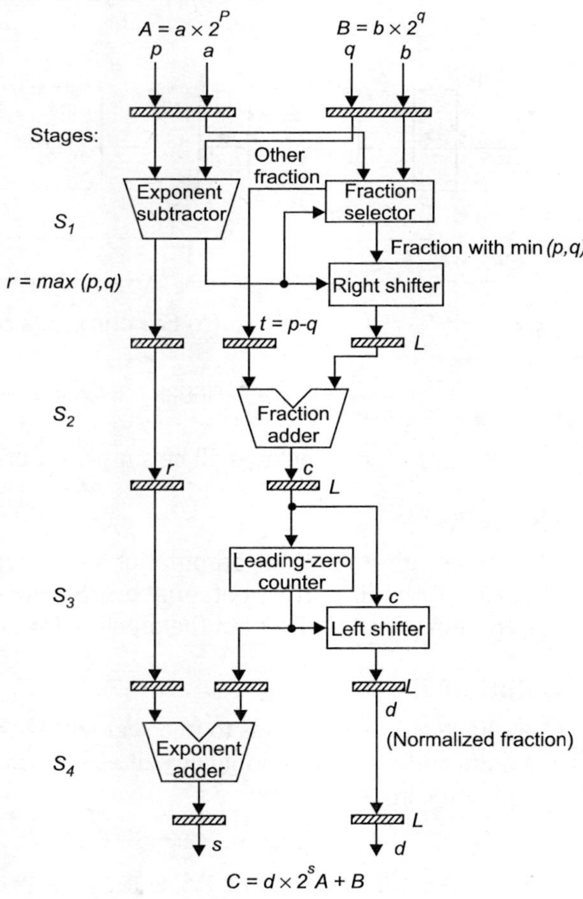

FIGURE 7.2: A pipelined floating-point adder with four processing stages

7.4.1.2 SYNCHRONOUS MODEL

Synchronous pipelines are illustrated in Figure 7.3b. The operands pass through all segments in a fixed sequence. Each segment consists of a combinational circuit Si that performs a suboperation over the data stream flowing through the pipe Isolating registers R (latches) are used to interface between stages and hold the intermediate results between the stages. Upon the arrival of a clock pulse, all registers transfer data to the next stage simultaneously.

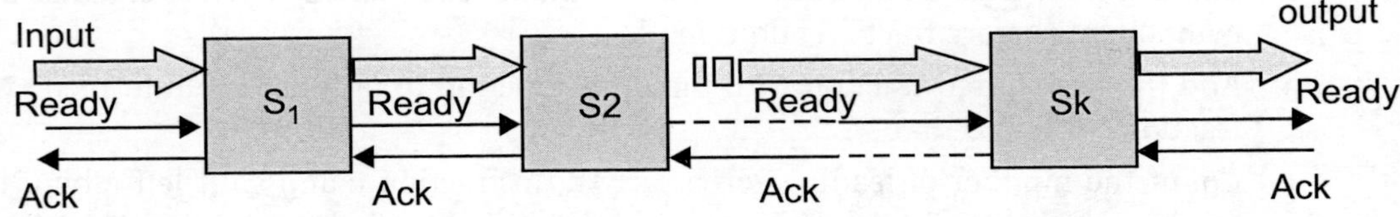

(a) An asynchronous pipeline model

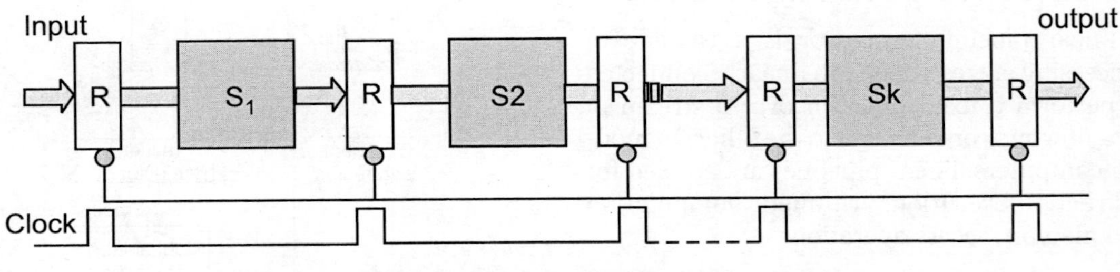

(b) Synchronous pipeline model

FIGURE 7.3: Asynchronous and Synchronous models

Synchronous pipeline will be simply described by the following example.

Example

In certain scientific computations it is necessary to perform the arithmetic operation (Ai + Bi)*(Ci + Di) with a stream of numbers. Specify a pipeline configuration to carry out this task. List the contents of all registers in the pipeline for i = 1 through 6.

Solution

Each sub-operation is to in a segment within a pipeline. Each segment will have one or more registers and a combinational circuit as shown. The sub-operations performed in each segment of the pipeline are as follows:

R1← Ai, R2← Bi, R3← Ci, R4← Di input Ai, Bi, Ci and Di

R5 ← R1 + R2, R6 ← R3 + R4 Perform Addition of Ai + Bi and Ci + Di

R7 ← R5 * R6 Multiply (Ai + Bi)*(Ci + Di)

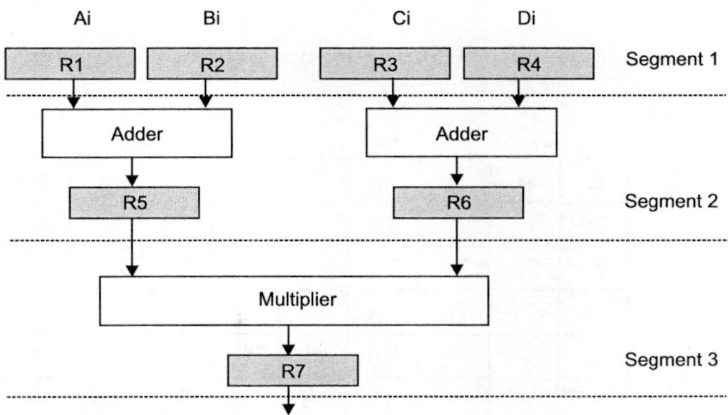

The seven registers are loaded with new data every clock pulse.

The effect of each clock will be as shown:

Clock Pulse	Segment 1				Segment 2		Segment 3
	R1	R2	R3	R4	R5	R6	R7
1	A1	B1	C1	D1	–	–	–
2	A2	B2	C2	D2	A1+B1	C1+D1	–
3	A3	B3	C3	D3	A2+B2	C2+D2	A1+B1 * C1+D1
4	A4	B4	C4	D4	A3+B3	C3+D3	A2+B2 * C2+D2
5	A5	B5	C5	D5	A4+B4	C4+D4	A3+B3 * C3+D3
6	A6	B6	C6	D6	A5+B5	C5+D5	A4+B4 * C4+D4
7	–	–	–	–	A6+B6	C6+D6	A5+B5 * C5+D5
8	–	–	–	–	–	–	A6+B6 * C6+D6

7.4.2 SPACE-TIME DIAGRAM

This is a diagram that shows segment utilization as a function of time. The space-time diagram of a four segment pipeline is shown above. The horizontal axis displays the time in clock cycles and the vertical axis gives the segment number. This diagram shows six tasks T1 through T6 executed in four segments. The first task T1 is completed after the fourth (k) clock cycle. No matter how many segments are there in the system, once the pipeline is full, it takes only one clock period to obtain the output.

Task: A task is defined as the total operation performed going through all the segments in the pipe.

Clock Cycles		**1**	**2**	**3**	**4**	**5**	**6**	**7**	**8**	**9**
Segment	1	T1	T2	T3	T4	T5	T6	–	–	–
	2	–	T1	T2	T3	T4	T5	T6	–	–
	3	–	–	T1	T2	T3	T4	T5	T6	–
	4	–	–	–	T1	T2	T3	T4	T5	T6

Example

Draw the space-time diagram for a six-segment pipeline showing the time it takes to process eight tasks.

Solution

Clock Cycles		**1**	**2**	**3**	**4**	**5**	**6**	**7**	**8**	**9**	**10**	**11**	**12**	**13**
Segment:	1	T1	T2	T3	T4	T5	T6	T7	T8	–	–	–	–	–
	2	–	T1	T2	T3	T4	T5	T6	T7	T8	–	–	–	–
	3	–	–	T1	T2	T3	T4	T5	T6	T7	T8	–	–	–
	4	–	–	–	T1	T2	T3	T4	T5	T6	T7	T8	–	–
	5	–	–	–	–	T1	T2	T3	T4	T5	T6	T7	T8	–
	6	–	–	–	–	–	T1	T2	T3	T4	T5	T6	T7	T8

It takes 13 clock cycles to process 8 tasks.

7.4.3 PIPELINE SPEEDUP

Consider the case where a k-segment pipeline with a clock cycle time tp is used to execute n tasks. The first task T1 will take a time equal to ktp. All remaining n-1 tasks will take a time equal to (n-1) tp. Therefore, to complete n tasks through a k-segment pipeline requires k + (n - 1) clock cycles. Next, consider a non-pipeline that performs the same operation and takes a time equal to tn to complete each task. The total time required for n tasks is ntn. The speedup of a pipeline processing over an equivalent non-pipeline processing is defined by the ratio:

$$S = \frac{Non\text{ - }pipeline\,time}{pipeline\,time} = \frac{nt_n}{(k+n\text{ - }1)t_p}$$

As the number of tasks increases, n becomes much larger than k – 1, and (k + 1 – n) approaches the value of n, under this condition, the speedup becomes

$$S = \frac{t_n}{t_p}$$

If we assume that the time it takes to process a task is the same in the pipeline and non-pipeline circuits, we will have tn = ktp. Including this assumption, the speedup will be reduced to

$$S = \frac{t_n}{t_p} = k$$

This shows that the theoretical maximum speedup that a pipeline can provide is k, where k is the number of segments in the pipeline. In the below graph, plots the speedup as a function of n, the number of tasks performed by the pipeline.

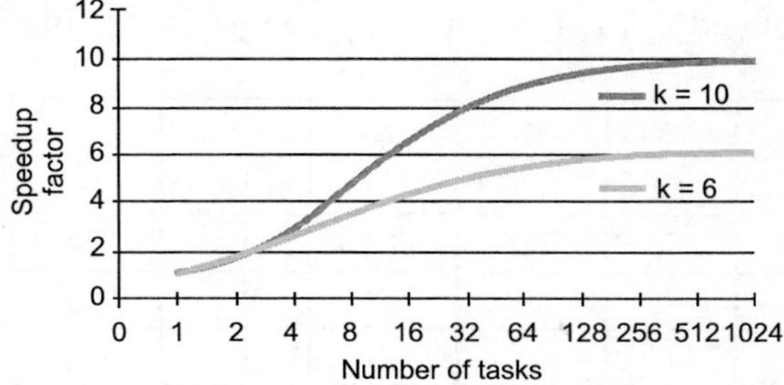

7.4.4 PIPELINE EFFICIENCY

The efficiency Ek of a linear k-segment pipeline is defined as

$$E_k = \frac{Speedup}{Number\ of\ segments} = \frac{S_k}{k}$$

If we assume that the time it takes to process a task is the same in the pipeline and non-pipeline circuits, the speed up will be

$$S_k = \frac{knt_p}{(k+n-1)t_p}$$

Then the efficiency will be defined as

$$E_k = \frac{S_k}{k} = \frac{n}{k+(n-1)}$$

Example

A non-pipeline system takes 50 ns to process a task. The same task can be processed in a six-segment pipeline with a clock cycle of 10 ns. Determine the speedup and the efficiency of the pipeline for 100 tasks. What is the maximum speedup and efficiency that can be achieved?

Solution

Given

- For the non-pipeline system: tn = 50 ns
- For the pipeline system: k = 6, tp = 10 ns
- Number of tasks n = 100

Required

$$\text{Speedup} \Rightarrow S = \frac{nt_n}{(k+n+1)t_p} = \frac{100\times 50}{(6+100+1)\times 10} = 4.76$$

The maximum speedup can be achieved when the number of tasks increases up to a value much larger than k – 1, So we can neglect k–1.

⇒ The ratio will be reduced to

$$S_{max} = \frac{nt_n}{nt_p} = \frac{t_n}{t_p} = \frac{50}{10} = 5$$

$$\text{Efficiency} \Rightarrow E = \frac{\text{Speedup}}{\text{No.of segments}} = \frac{S}{k} = \frac{4.76}{6} = 79.33\%$$

$$\text{Maximum Efficiency} = E_{max} = \frac{\text{Maximum Speedup}}{\text{No.of Segments}}$$

$$\frac{S_{max}}{k} = \frac{5}{6} = 83.33\%$$

7.4.5 PIPELINE THROUGHPUT

The pipeline throughput H_K is defined as the number of tasks (operations) performed per unit time: The maximum throughput f occurs when $E_K \rightarrow 1$ as $n \rightarrow \infty$.

$$H_k = \frac{n}{[k+(n-1)]\tau} = \frac{nf}{k+(n-1)}$$

7.5 CLASSIFICATION OF PIPELINE PROCESSORS

According to the levels of processing, Handler (1977) has proposed the following classification scheme for pipeline processors:

1. **Arithmetic Pipeline:** The arithmetic logic units of a computer can be segmentized for pipeline operations in various data formats. Well-known arithmetic pipeline examples are the four-stage pipes used in Star-100, the eight-stage pipes used in the TI-ASC, the up to 14 pipelines stages used in the Cray-1, and up to 26 stages per pipe in the Cyber-205.
2. **Instruction Pipelining:** The execution of a stream of instruction can be pipelined by overlapping the execution of the current instruction with the fetch, decode, and operand fetch of subsequent instruction. This technique is also known as instruction look ahead. Almost all high-performance computers are now equipped with instruction-execution pipelines.
3. **Processor Pipelining:** This refers to the pipeline processing of the same data stream by a cascade of processors, each of which processes a specific task. The data stream passes the first processor with results stored in a memory block which is also accessible by the second processor. The second processor then passes the refined results to the third, and so on. The pipelining of multiple processors is not yet well accepted as a common practice.

According to pipeline configurations and control strategies, Ramamooorthy and Li (1977) have proposed the following three pipeline classification schemes:

(i) **Unifunction vs. Multifunction Pipelines:** A pipeline unit with a fixed and dedicated function, such as the floating-point adder is called unifunctional. The Cray-1 has 12 unifunctional pipeline units for various scalar, vector, fixed-point, and floating-point operations. A multifunction pipe may perform different subsets of stages in the pipeline. The TI-ASC has four multifunction pipeline processors, each of which is reconfigurable for a variety of arithmetic logic operations at different times.

(ii) **Static vs. Dynamic Pipelines:** A static pipeline may assume only one functional configuration at a time. Static pipelines can be either unifunctional or multi-functional. Pipelining is made possible in static pipes only if instructions of the same type are to be executed continuously. The function performed by a static pipeline should not change frequently. Otherwise, its performance may be very low. A dynamic pipeline processor permits several functional configurations to exist simultaneously. In this sense, a dynamic pipeline must be multifunctional. On the other hand, a unifunctional pipe must be static. The dynamic configuration needs much more elaborate control and sequencing mechanisms than those for static pipelines. Most existing computers are equipped with static pipes, either unifunctional or multifunctional.

(iii) Scalar vs. Vector Pipelines: Depending on the instruction or data types, pipeline processors can be also classified as scalar pipelines and vector pipelines. A scalar pipeline processes a sequence of scalar operands under the control of DO loop. Instructions in a small DO loop are often prefetched into the instruction buffer. The required scalar operands for repeated scalar instructions are moved into a data cache in order to continuously supply the pipeline with operands. The IBM System/360 Model 91 is typical example of a machine equipped with scalar pipelines. However, the Model 91 does not have a cache. Vector pipelines are specially designed to handle vector instructions over vector operands. Computers having vector instructions are often called vector processors. The design of a vector pipeline is expended from that of a scalar pipeline. The handling of vector operands in vector pipelines is under firmware and hardware controls (rather than under software controls as in scalar pipelines).

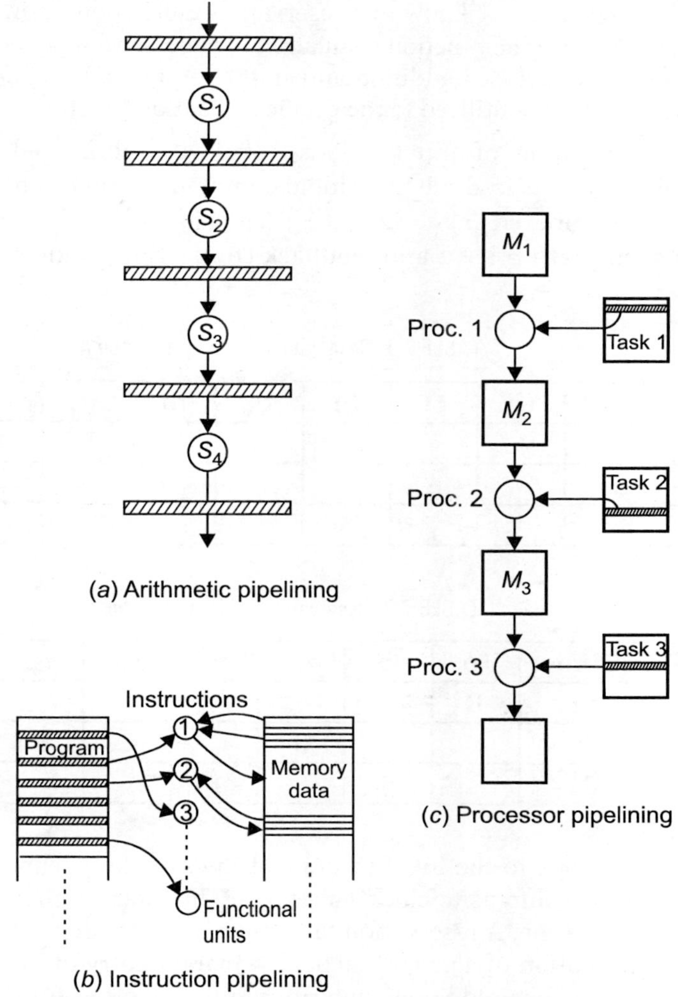

FIGURE 7.4: Classification of pipelined processors.

7.6 GENERAL PIPELINES AND RESERVATION TABLES

What we have studied so far are linear pipelines without feedback connections. The inputs and outputs of such pipelines are totally independent. In some computations, like linear recurrence, the outputs of the pipeline are fed back as future inputs. In other words, the inputs may depend on previous outputs. Pipelines with feedback may have a nonlinear flow of data. The utilization history of pipeline determines the present state of the pipeline. The timing of the feedback inputs becomes crucial to the nonlinear data flow. Improper use of feed-forward or feedback inputs may destroy the inherent advantages of pipelining. On the other hand, proper sequencing with non-linear data flow may enhance the pipeline efficiency. In practice, many of the arithmetic pipeline processors allow nonlinear connection as a mechanism to implement recursion and multiple functions.

The interconnection structures and data flow patterns in general pipelines are characterized either feed-forward or feed-backward connections, in addition to the cascaded connections in a linear pipeline. A TwoD chart known as reservation table shows how the successive pipelines stages are utilized for a specific function evaluation in successive pipeline cycles. Multiplication of two numbers is done by repeated addition and shift operations. Reservation tables are used how successive pipeline stages are utilized for a specific evaluation function.

Consider an example of pipeline structure with both feed forward and feedback connections. The pipeline is dual functional denoted as function A and function B. The pipeline stages are numbered as S1, S2 and S3. The feed forward connection connects a stage Si to a stage Sj such that j ≥ i + 2 and feedback connection connects to Si to a stage Sj such that j <= i.

TABLE 7.1: Reservation Table for function A

Time	t0	t1	t2	t3	t4	t5	t6	t7
S1	A			A			A	
S2		A						A
S3			A		A	A		

TABLE 7.2: Reservation Table for function B

Time	t0	t1	t2	t3	t4	t5	t6
S1	B				B		
S2			B			B	
S3		B		B			B

The row corresponds to the two functions of the sample pipeline. The rows correspond to pipeline stages and the columns to clock time units. The total number of clock units in the table is called the evaluation time. A reservation table represents the flow of data through the pipeline for one complete evaluation of a given function. A market entry in the (i, j)th square of the table indicates the stage Si will be used j time units after initiation of the function evaluation.

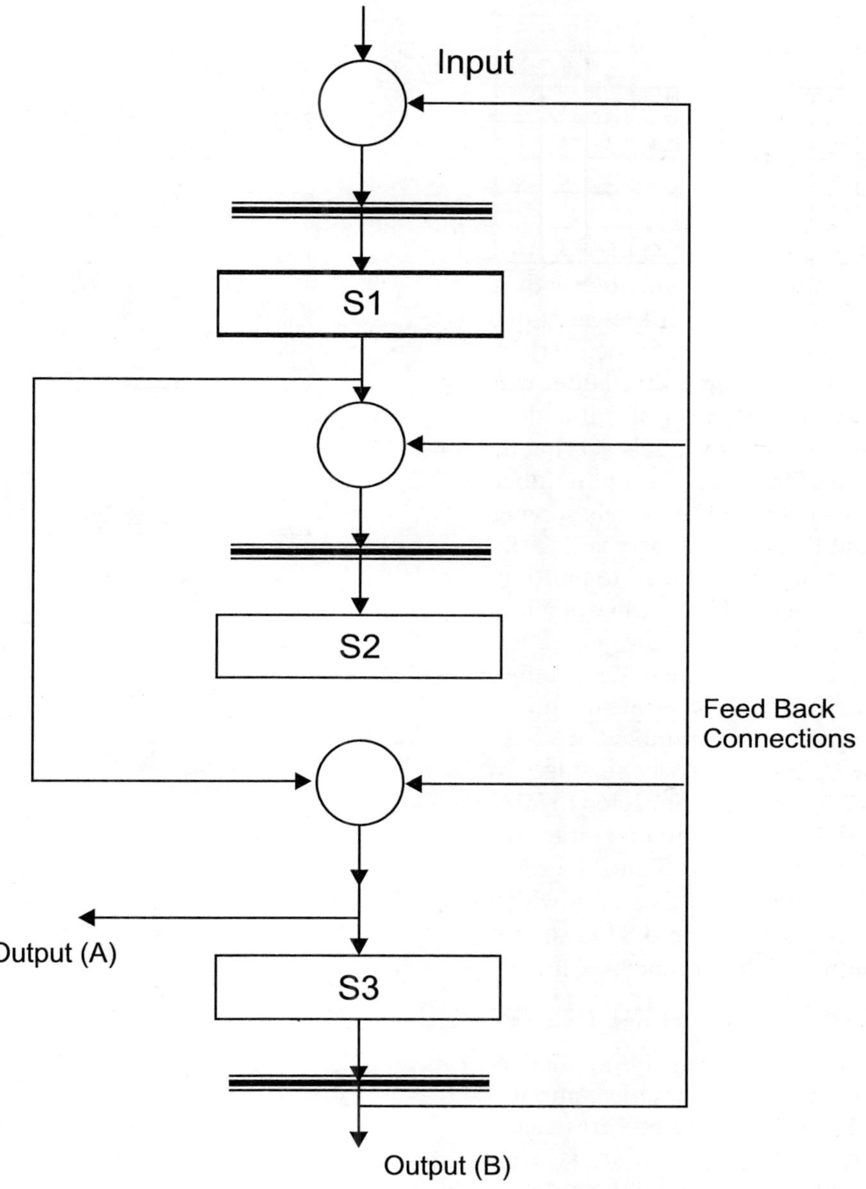

FIGURE 7.5: A sample Pipeline

7.6.1 ARITHMETIC PIPELINE DESIGN EXAMPLES

The multiplication of two fixed point numbers is done by repeated add-shift operations, using ALU which has built in add and shift functions. Multiple number additions can be realized with a multilevel tree adder. The conventional carry propagation adder (CPA) adds two input numbers say A and B, to produce one output number called the sum A+B carry save adder (CSA) receives three input numbers, say A,B and D and two output numbers, the sum S and the Carry vector C.

A	=		1	1	1	1	0	1
B	=		0	1	0	1	1	0
D	=		1	1	0	1	1	1
C	=	1	1	0	1	1	1	
S	=		0	1	1	1	0	0
A+B+D	=	1	1	1	0	0	1	0

A CSA can be implemented with a cascade of full adders with the carry-out of a lower stage connected to the carry-in of a higher stage. A carry-save adder can be implemented with a set of full adders with all the carry-in terminals serving as the input lines for the third input number D, and all the carry-out terminals serving as the output lines for the carry vector C.

This pipeline is designed to multiply two six bit numbers. There are five pipeline stages. The first stage is for the generation of all $6 \times 6 = 36$ immediate product terms, which forms the six rows of shifted multiplicands. The six numbers are then fed into two CSAs in the second stage. In total four CSAs are interconnected to form a three level merges six numbers into two numbers: the sum vector S and the carry vector C. The final stage us a CPA which adds the two numbers C and S to produce the final output of the product A × B.

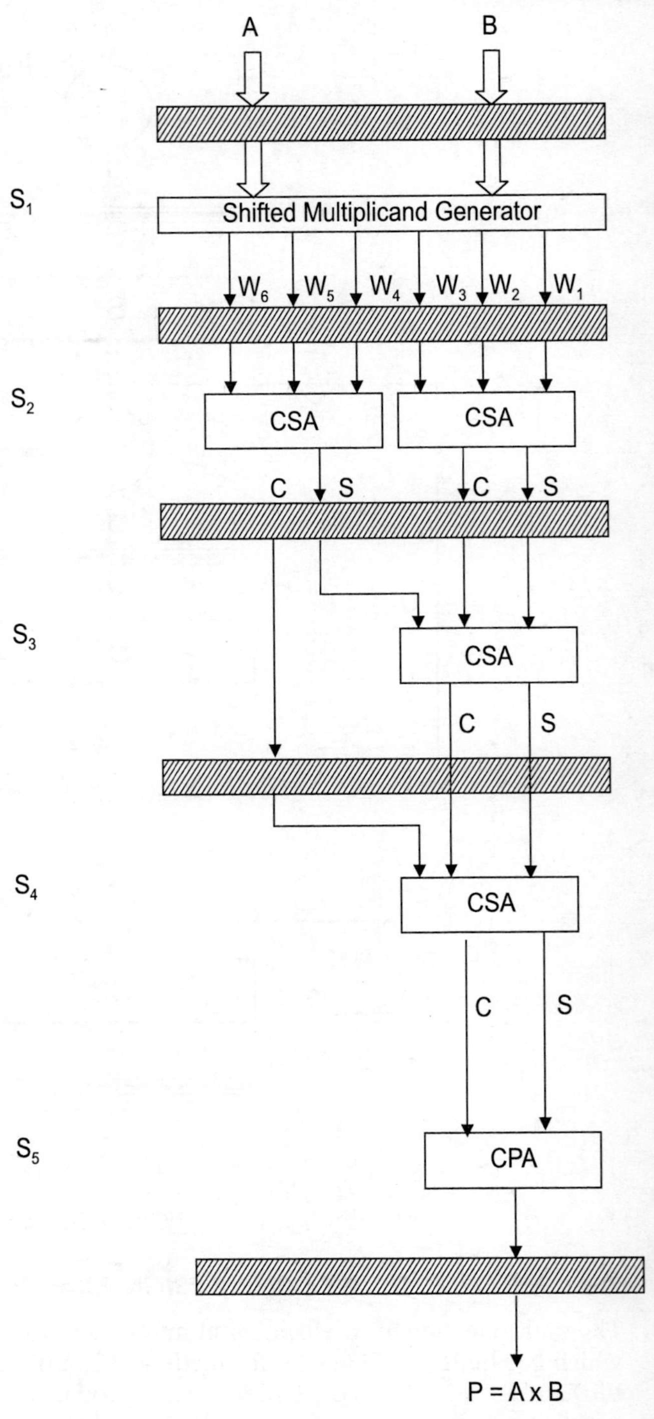

FIGURE 7.6: A Pipelined Multiplier built with a CSA tree

7.7 ARITHMETIC PIPELINE DESIGN

Pipelining techniques can be applied to speed up numerical arithmetic computations. Pipeline arithmetic units are usually found in very high speed computers. They to implement floating point operations, multiplication of fixed point numbers, and similar computations encountered in scientific problems.

7.7.1 FIXED-POINT OPERATIONS

Fixed-point numbers are represented internally in machines in sign-magnitude, one's complement, or two's complement notation. Add, subtract, multiply, and divide are the four primitive arithmetic operations.

7.7.2 FLOATING-POINT NUMBERS

A floating-point number X is represented by a pair (m, e), where m is the mantissa (or fraction) and e is the exponent with an implied base (or radix). The algebraic value is represented as

$$X = m \times r^e$$

The sign of X can be embedded in the mantissa.

7.7.2.1 FLOATING-POINT OPERATIONS

The four primitive arithmetic operations are defined below for a pair of floating-point numbers represented by $X = (m_x, e_x)$ and $Y = (m_y, e_y)$, Assuming $e_x <= e_y$ and base r = 2.

$$X + Y = (m_x \times 2^{e_x - e_y} + m_y) \times 2^{e_y}$$

$$X - Y = (m_x \times 2^{e_x - e_y} - m_y) \times 2^{e_y}$$

$$X \times Y = (m_x \times m_y) \times 2^{e_x + e_y}$$

$$X \div Y = (m_x \div m_y) \times 2^{e_x - e_y}$$

These operations can be divided into two halves:

One half is for exponent operations such as comparing their relative magnitudes or adding/subtracting them; the other half is for mantissa operations including four types of fixed-point operations.

The floating-point addition and subtraction can be performed in four segments as shown in Figure 7.7. The registers labeled R are latches used to interface between segments and to store intermediate results. The sub-operations that are performed in the four segments are:

1. Compare the exponents: The exponents are compared by subtracting them to determine their difference. The larger exponent is chosen as the exponent of the result.

2. Align the mantissa: The mantissa associated with the smaller exponent is shifted to the right a number of times equal to the exponent difference.

3. Add or subtract the mantissa: The two mantissas are added or subtracted.

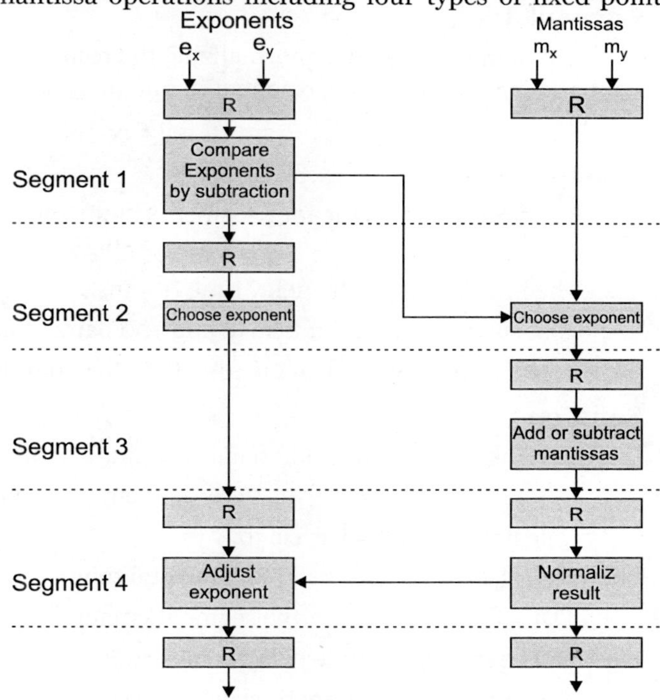

FIGURE 7.7: Arithmetic pipeline operation

4. **Normalize the result:** Normalizing the result so that it has a fraction (mantissa) with nonzero first digit.

Pipeline in Figure 7.7 refers to binary numbers, but in the following numerical example we use decimal numbers for simplicity (r = 10). Consider the two normalized floating-point numbers:

$$X = 0.99 \times 10^5$$
$$Y = 0.5 \times 10^3$$

Sub-operations will be carried out through the four segments as follows:

Segment 1:

The two exponents are subtracted to obtain 4 – 3 = 1. The larger exponent 4 is chosen to be the exponent of the result.

Segment 2:

The mantissa of Y is shifted to the right once to obtain

$$X = 0.99 \times 10^4$$
$$Y = 0.05 \times 10^4$$

This aligns the two mantissas under the same exponent.

Segment 3:

The two mantissas are added to produce the sum

$$Z = 1.04 \times 10^4$$

Segment 4:

The sum is adjusted by normalizing the result. This done by shifting the mantissa once to the right and incrementing the exponent to obtain

$$Z = 1.04 \times 10^5$$

Example

The time delays in the four segments in the pipeline of Fig.2-6 are as follows:

$$t_1 = 50\text{ns},\ t_2 = 30\text{ns},\ t_3 = 95\text{ns},\ t_4 = 45\text{ns}.$$

The interface registers delay time tr =5ns.

a. How long would it take to add 100 pairs of numbers in the pipeline?

b. How can we reduce the total time to about one-half of the time calculated in part (a)?

Solution

(a) The time taken to add n pairs of numbers in an k-segment pipeline = (k + n - 1) tp

Given: k = 4 and n = 100

Calculating the clock cycle tp:

The total time delay in a segment i

TDi = the time delay in the segment circuit + the time delay of the interface register

→ The maximum time delay of all segments

TDmax = the maximum time delay in segment circuits + the time delay of the interface register

= 95ns + 5ns = 100ns

As we have a different time delay in each segment, the clock cycle must be larger than or equal to the maximum delay

→The clock cycle tp = 100ns

→The time taken to add 100 pairs of numbers in the 4-segment pipeline = (k + n - 1) tp

= (4 + 100 - 1) 100 ns

= 10.3ns

(b) To reduce the time calculated in part (a) to one-half, we have to reduce the clock cycle tp. We can achieve this if we could reduce the maximum time delay TDmax to 50ns. This can be reached by reducing 1 t from 50ns to 45ns and 3 t from 95ns to 45ns.

7.8 INSTRUCTION PIPELINE DESIGN

An instruction pipeline reads consecutive instruction from memory while previous instructions are being executed in other segments. This causes the instruction fetch and executes phases to overlap and perform simultaneous operations.

7.8.1 INSTRUCTION CYCLE

Computers with complex instructions (CISC) require other phases in addition to the fetch and execute to process an instruction completely. In the most general case, the computer needs to process each instruction with the following sequence of steps:

1. Fetch the instruction from memory.
2. Decode instruction.
3. Calculate the effective address.
4. Fetch operands from memory.
5. Execute the instruction.
6. Store the result.

There are certain difficulties that will prevent the instruction pipeline from operating at its maximum rate. Different segments may take different times to operate on the incoming information. Therefore, the design the design of an instruction pipeline will be most efficient if the instruction cycle is divided into segments of equal duration.

7.8.1.1 FOUR SEGMENT INSTRUCTION PIPELINE

A pipelined processor may process each instruction in four steps, as follows:

F Fetch: read the instruction from the memory.

D Decode: decode the instruction and fetch the source operand(s).

E Execute: Perform the operation specified by the instruction.

W Write: Store the result in the destination location.

Figure 7.8 shows how the instruction cycle in the CPU can be processed with a four-segment pipeline.

An instruction in the sequence may be a program control type that causes a branch out of normal sequence. In that case, the pending operations in the last two segments are completed and the instruction buffer is emptied. The pipeline then restarts from the new address stored in the program counter. Similarly, an interrupt request, when acknowledged, will cause the pipeline to empty and restart from a new address value, which is the beginning of an interrupt service routine.

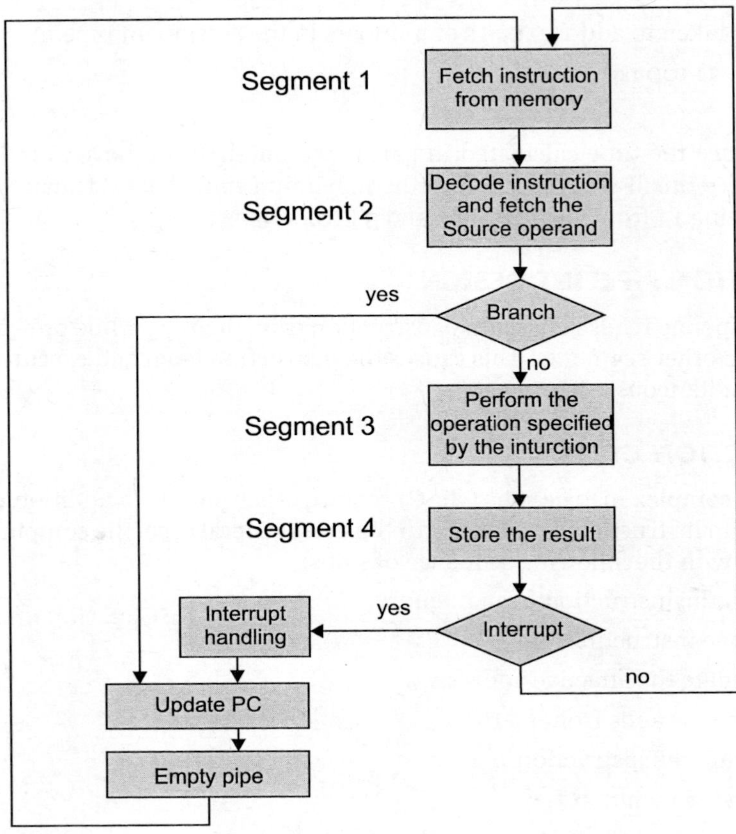

FIGURE 7.8: instruction pipeline

Figure 7.9 shows the operation of the four-segment pipeline. For a variety of reasons, one of the pipeline stages may not be able to complete its processing task for a given instruction in the time allotted. Any condition that causes the pipeline to deviate form its normal operation (to stall) is called a hazard. In general there are three major hazards:

Time →

Clock cycles	1	2	3	4	5	6	7
Instructions							
11	F1	D1	E1	W1			
12		F2	D2	E2	W2		
13			F3	D3	E3	W3	
14				F4	D4	E4	W4

FIGURE 7.9: Four segment pipeline

1. Data hazard
2. Instruction hazard
3. Structural hazard

7.8.1.2 DATA HAZARDS

A data hazard is any condition in which either the source or the destination operands of an instruction are not available at the time expected in the pipeline. As a result some operation has to be delayed, and the pipeline stalls. An example of that situation, when the source operand(s) of an instruction is the result of the previous instruction. The former may be in the D segment while the later is in the E segment, which means that the result of the later instruction is not yet stored in the destination while the former instruction requesting it, which will cause a conflict. Pipelined computers deal with such conflicts in a variety of ways.

Hardware Interlock

The most straight forward method is to insert hardware interlock. An interlock is a circuit that detects instructions whose source operands are destinations of instructions farther up in the pipeline. Detection of this situation causes the instruction whose source is no available to be delayed by enough clock cycles to resolve the conflict. Hardware is used to insert the required delays.

Operand forwarding

Instead of transferring an ALU result into a destination register, hardware checks the destination operand, and if it is needed as a source in the next instruction, it passes the result directly into the ALU input. Figure 7.10 shows a part of a pipeline processor which caries out this task.

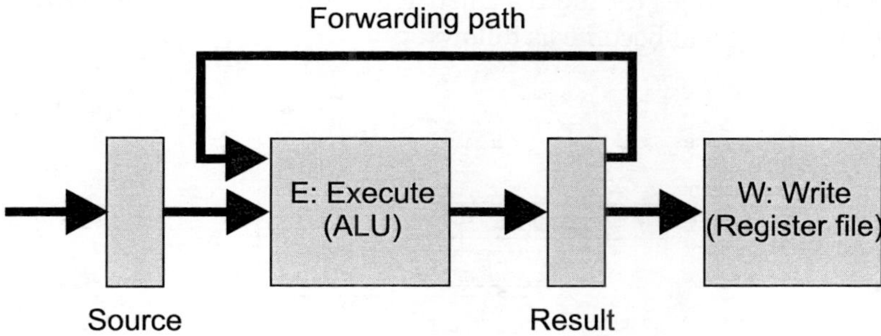

FIGURE 7.10: Pipeline Processor

Example

Consider the four instructions in the following program. Suppose that the first instruction starts from step 1 in the pipeline used in Figure 7.9. Specify what operations are performed in the four segments during step 5 and step 6, assuming:

(a) The pipeline system uses hardware interlock technique to handle data hazards.

(b) The pipeline system uses the operand forwarding technique in Figure 7.10 to handle data hazards.

LOAD R1 ← M[312]

ADD R2 ← R2 + M[313]

INC R3 ← R4 + 1

STORE M[314] ← R3

Solution

The STORE instruction will cause a data conflict as its source operand (R3) is the result of the previous instruction (INC), this will result in a data hazard. The timing for the pipeline of the above program will be as follows:

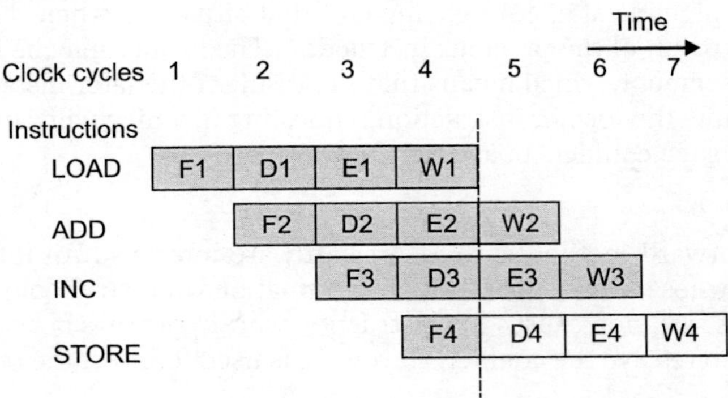

(a) In a pipeline system using hardware interlock, the interlock circuit will detect that the STORE instruction's source operand is the destination of the INC instruction. We assume that the interlock circuit detects such instruction after it passes the F segment. After detecting this situation, the interlock will cause the STORE instruction to be delayed for 2 clock cycles which is the minimum number of cycles for the INC instruction to write the result to the destination (R3). The timing of the pipeline will become as follows:

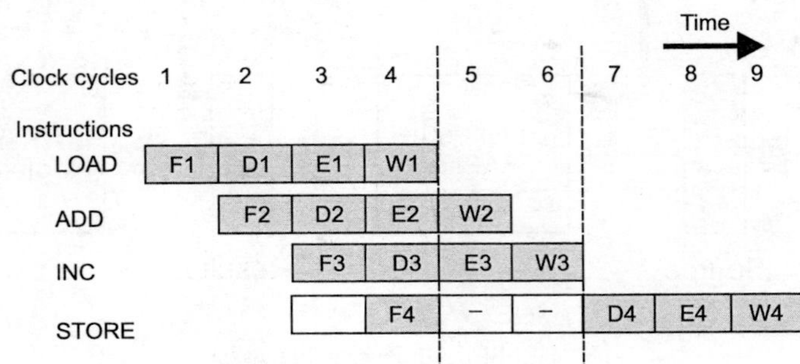

As shown above, at step 5 and 6, the situation will be as follows:

Instructions	Step 5	Step 6
LOAD	Completed	Completed
ADD	Writing the Result to destination (R2)	Completed
INC	Performing the operation (R4+1)	Writing the Result to destination (R3)
STORE	Delayed	Delayed

(b) In a pipeline system using operand forwarding, as sown in Figure 7.10, the result of an instruction can be fed back directly into the E segment in the case of data dependency. In the above program, hardware will detect data dependency between the INC and the STORE instructions. This will cause the result of the INC instruction to be passed directly into the input of the E segment. The timing of the pipeline will become as follows:

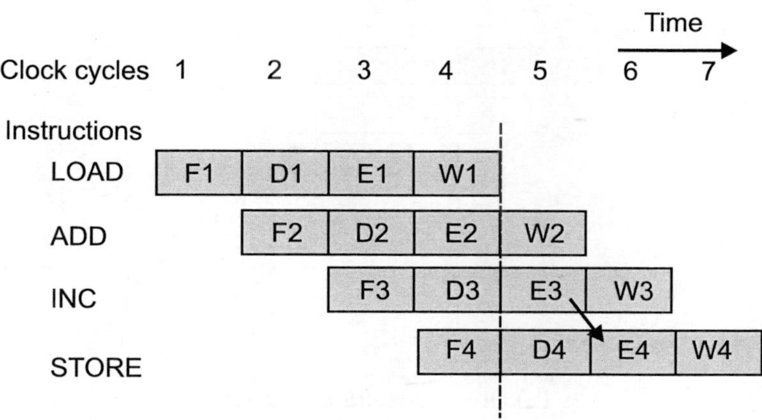

In the above figure, it can be seen that, no delays are needed as the operand will be forwarded directly from the output of the E segment to its input. In this situation in the D segment of the STORE instruction, fetching the source operand will be skipped. At step 5 and 6, the situation will be as follows:

Instructions	Step 5	Step 6
LOAD	Completed	Completed
ADD	Writing the Result to destination (R2)	Completed
INC	Performing the operation (R4+1)	Writing the Result to destination (R3)
STORE	Decode the instruction	Performing the operation (no operation to be performed)

7.8.1.3 INSTRUCTION HAZARDS

The purpose of the instruction fetch unit is to supply the execution units with a steady stream of instructions. Whenever this stream is interrupted, the pipeline stalls, as in the case of a cache miss. A branch instruction may also cause the pipeline to stall. Figure 7.11 illustrates the effect of branching on the instruction stream.

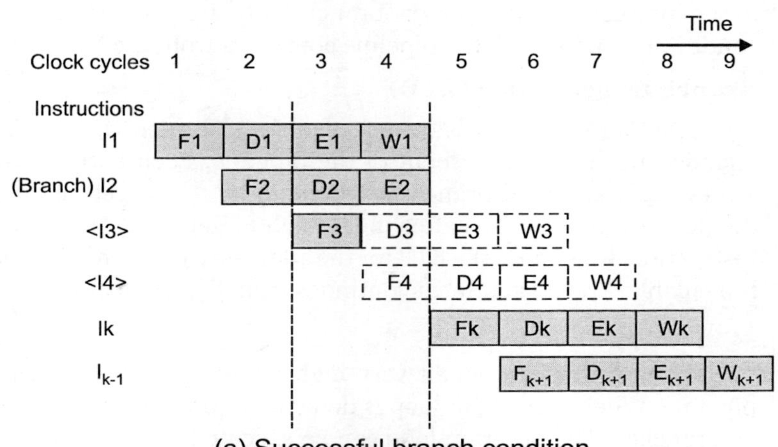

(a) Successful branch condition

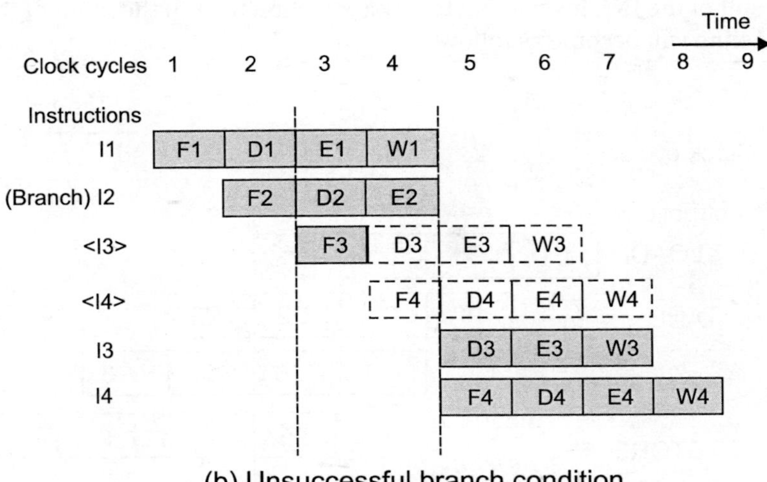

(b) Unsuccessful branch condition

Figure 7.11: Instruction hazards

The above figure shows a sequence of instructions being executed in a four-stage pipeline. Instructions I1 to I4 are stored at successive memory addresses, and I2 is a branch instruction. Let the branch target be instruction Ik. In clock cycle 3, the fetch operation for instruction I3 is in progress at the same time the branch instruction is being decoded and the target address computed. In clock cycle 4, if the branch is taken (Fig.2-10a), the processor must discard I3 and fetch instruction Ik. If the branch is not taken (Fig.2-10b), I3 can be used. In the meantime, the hardware unit responsible for the Execute (E) step must be tolled to do nothing during that clock period. Thus, the pipeline is stalled for two clock cycles. The time lost as a result of a branch instruction is often referred to as branch penalty. Pipelined computers employ various hardware techniques to minimize the performance degradation caused by instruction branching.

Pre-fetch target instruction

One way of handling a conditional branch is to pre-fetch the target instruction in addition to the instruction following the branch. Both are saved until the branch is executed. If the branch condition is successful, the pipeline continues from the branch target instruction.

Branch target buffer (BTB)

Another possibility is the use of a branch target buffer or BTB. BTB is an associative memory included in the fetch segment of the pipeline. Each entry of the BTB consists of the address of a previously executed branch instruction and the target instruction of that branch. It also stores the next few instructions after the branch target instruction. When the pipeline decodes a branch instruction, it searches the BTB for the address of the in instruction. If it is in the BTB, the instruction is available directly and fetch continues from the new path.

Loop buffer

Loop buffer is a small very high speed register file included in the fetch segment of the pipeline. When a program loop is detected in the program, it is stored in the loop buffer including all branches. The program loop can be executed directly without accessing memory until the loop mode is removed by the final branch.

Branch prediction

A pipeline with branch prediction uses some additional logic to guess the outcome of a conditional branch instruction before it is executed. A correct prediction eliminates the wasted time caused by the branch penalties.

7.8.1.4 STRUCTURAL HAZARDS

This is the situation when two instructions require the use of a given hardware resource at the same time. The most common case is in access to memory. One instruction may need to access memory as part as part of Execute(E) or Write(W) stage, while another instruction is being fetched. Many processors use separate instruction and data memories to avoid this conflict.

7.8.2 RISC INSTRUCTION PIPELINE

Reduced Instruction Set Computers (RISC) is able to use an efficient instruction pipeline, taking in advance the following notations over the RISC characteristics:

- Because of the fixed-length instruction format, the decoding of the operation can occur at the same time as the register selection.
- All data manipulated instructions have register-to-register operations. Since all operands are in registers, there is no need for calculating the effective address or fetching of operands from memory.

Single cycle instruction execution

One of the major advantages of RISC over CISC is that RISC can achieve pipeline segments, requiring just one clock cycle, while CISC uses many segments in its pipeline, with the longest segment requiring two or more clock cycles.

Compiler support

Instead of designing hardware to handle difficulties (hazards) associated with data conflicts and branch penalties, RISC processors relay on the efficiency of the compiler to detect and minimize the delays.

7.8.2.1 THREE-SEGMENT INSTRUCTION PIPELINE

The instruction cycle for a RISC computer can be divided into three sub-operations and implemented in three segments:

I Instruction fetch: fetches the instruction from the program memory.

A ALU operation: decodes the instruction and performs an ALU operation. An ALU operation may be one of three types, data manipulation, data transfer, or program control.

E Execute instruction: directs the output of the ALU to the destination.

Figure 7.12 shows the operation of the four-segment pipeline.

The following sections illustrate how RISC computers use the compiler to handle data, instruction hazards.

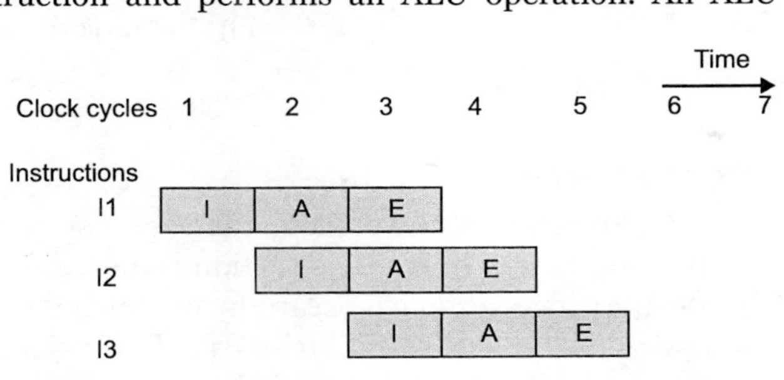

FIGURE 7.12: Three Segment Instruction Pipeline

Delayed load

The compiler of RISC computers is designed to detect the data conflicts (data hazards) and reorder the instructions as necessary to delay the loading of the conflicting data by inserting no operation instructions. For example, the two instructions (written in Berkeley RISC I format).

ADD R1, R2, R3 R3 ← R1 + R2

SUB R3, R4, R5 R5 ← R3 - R4

Give rise to data dependency (data hazard). The result of the Add instruction is placed into register R3, which in tern is one of the two source operands of the Subtract instruction. There will be a conflict in the Subtract instruction. This can be seen from the pipeline timing shown in Figure 7.13a. The A segment in clock cycle 3 is using data from R3 which will not be the correct value since the Addition operation is not yet completed. The compiler when detects such situation, it searches for a useful to put after the Add, if it cannot find such an instruction, it inserts no operation instruction, illustrated in Figure 7.13b. This is the type of instruction that fetched from memory but has no operation, thus wasting a clock cycle.

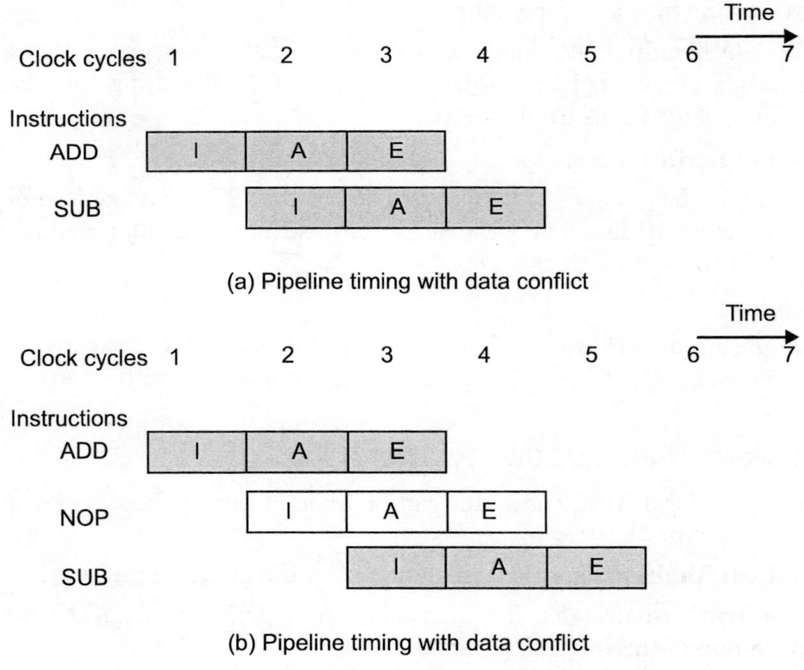

FIGURE 7.13: Pipeline timing diagram

Delayed Branch

In Figure 7.11a, the processor fetches instruction I3 before it determines whether the current instruction I2 is a branch instruction. When execution of I2 is completed and a branch is to be made, the processor must discard I3 and fetch the instruction at the branch target Ik. The location following the branch instruction is called a branch delay slot. The instructions in the delay slots are always fetched and at least partially executed before the branch decision is made and the branch target address is computed. The compiler for a processor that uses delayed branches is designed

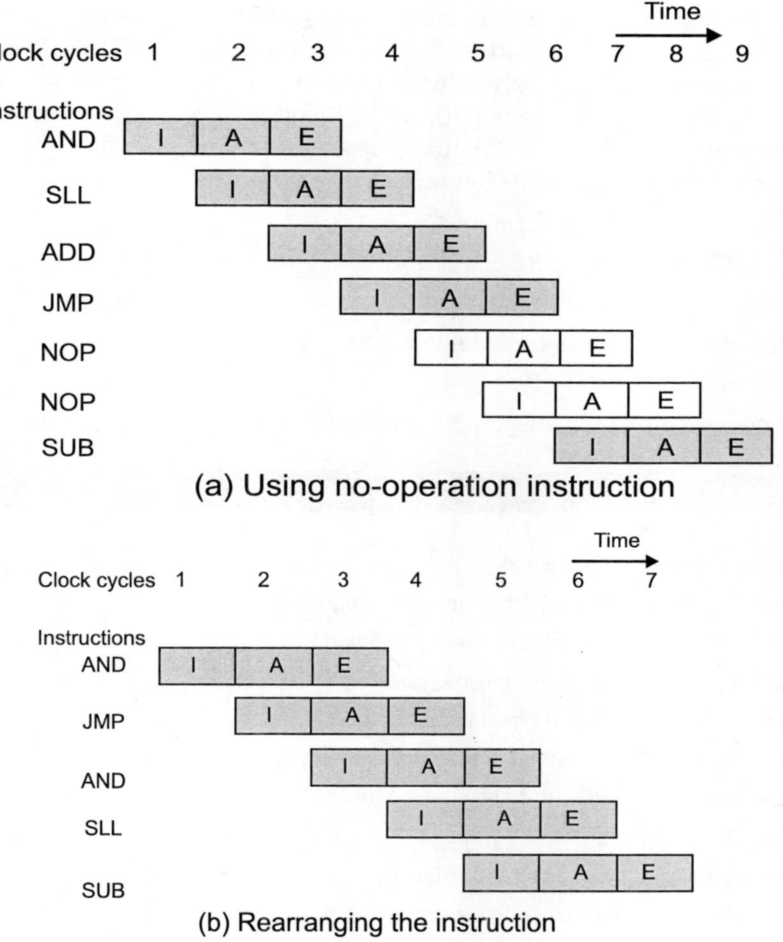

FIGURE 7.14: Rearrange pipeline timing diagram

to analyze the instructions before and after the branch and rearrange the program sequence by inserting useful (or no-operation) instructions in the delay slots.

RISC computers use delayed branch to handle branch related instruction hazards. An example of delayed branch is shown in Figure 7.14. The program sequence for this example consists of the following instructions (written in Berkeley RISC I format).

AND R0, #10, R0	R0 ← R0 #10
SLL R2, #1, R1	R1 ← Shift-left R2 once
ADD R3, R4, R5	R5 ← R3 + R4
JMP Z, #2(R6)	PC ← R6 + 2 (Conditional jump, result = 0)
SUB R7, #3, R6	R6 ← R7 − 3

In the above program sequence, the branch (JMP) instruction must be followed by two delay slots to avoid incorrect fetching for the SUB instruction (in the case of successful branch condition). When the compiler searches for two useful instructions to insert in the delay slots instead of inserting no operation (as in Fig.2-13a), the AND instruction and the shift left (SLL) instruction will be a good choice as there source operands and result are not related to any other instruction. The program will be rearranged as follows.

ADD R3, R4, R5 R5 ←R3 + R4

JMP Z, #2(R6) PC ← R6 + 2 (Conditional jump, result = 0)

AND R0, #10, R0 R0 ← R0 - #10

SLL R2, #1, R1 R1 ← Shift-left R2 once

SUB R7, #3, R6 R6 ← R7 – 3

The pipeline timing for this new arrangement is shown in Figure 7.14b

QUESTIONS

1. What do you mean by pipelining?
2. Explain the advantages and disadvantages of pipelining?
3. Explain the various principles of linear pipelining?
4. What do you mean by linear pipeline processors?
5. Explain the classification of pipeline processors?
6. Explain the concept of general pipelines and reservation tables?
7. Explain the example of arithmetic pipeline design?
8. Explain the design of arithmetic pipeline?
9. Explain the operation of arithmetic pipeline?
10. Explain the design of instruction pipeline?
11. Explain the types of hazards in instruction pipeline?
12. Explain the design of three instruction RISC pipeline?

CHAPTER 8

PRINCIPLES OF DESIGNING PIPELINED PROCESSORS

8.1 INTRODUCTION

We begin with a review of several of various instruction-prefetch and branch-control strategies for designing pipelined instruction units. Data-buffering and busing structures are presented for smoothing pipelined operations to avoid congestion. We will also study internal data-forwarding and register-tagging techniques by examining instruction-dependence relations. The detection and resolution of logic hazards in pipelines will be described. Principles of job sequencing in a pipeline will be studied with reservation tables to avoid collisions in utilizing pipeline resources.

8.2 INSTRUCTION PREFETCH AND BRANCH HANDLING

Instruction prefetch: Formally, a prefetching strategy can be stated as follows: Instruction words ahead of the once currently being decoded are fetched from the memory before the instruction-decoding unit requests them. The prefetch of instructions is modeled in Figure 8.1. The memory is assumed to be interleaved and can accept request at one per cycle. All requests require T cycles to return from memory. There are two prefetch buffers of sizes s and t instruction words. The s-size buffer holds instructions fetched during the sequential part of a run. When a branch is successful, the entire buffer is invalidated. The other buffer holds instructions fetched from the target of a conditional branch. When a conditional branch is resolved and determined to be unsuccessful, the contents of this buffer are invalidated. The decoded requests instruction words at a maximum rate of one per r cycles. If the instruction requested by the decoded is available in the sequential buffer for sequential instructions, or is in the target buffer if a conditional branch has just been resolved and is successful, it enters the decoder with zero delay. Otherwise, the decoder is idle until the instruction returns from memory.

Except for jump instructions, all decoded instructions enter the execution pipeline, where E units are required to complete execution. If the decoded instruction is an unconditional branch, the instruction word at the target of the jump is requested immediately by the decoder and decoding ceases until the target instruction returns from the memory. The pipeline will see the full memory latency time T, since there was no opportunity for target prefetching.

If the decoded instruction is a conditional branch, sequential prefetching is suspended during the E cycles it is being executed. The instruction simultaneously enters the execution pipeline, but no more instructions are decoded until the branch is resolved at the end of E units. Instructions are prefetched from the target memory address of the conditional branch instruction. Requests for t target instructions are issued at the rate of one per cycle. Once the branch is resolved, target prefetching becomes unnecessary.

If the branch is successful, the target instruction stream becomes the sequential stream, and instructions are requested every r time units from this stream. Execution of this new stream begins when the target of the branch returns from memory, or whenever E units have elapsed, whichever is later. If the branch is unsuccessful, instruction requests are initiated every r units of time following the branch resolution and continue until the next branch or jump is decoded.

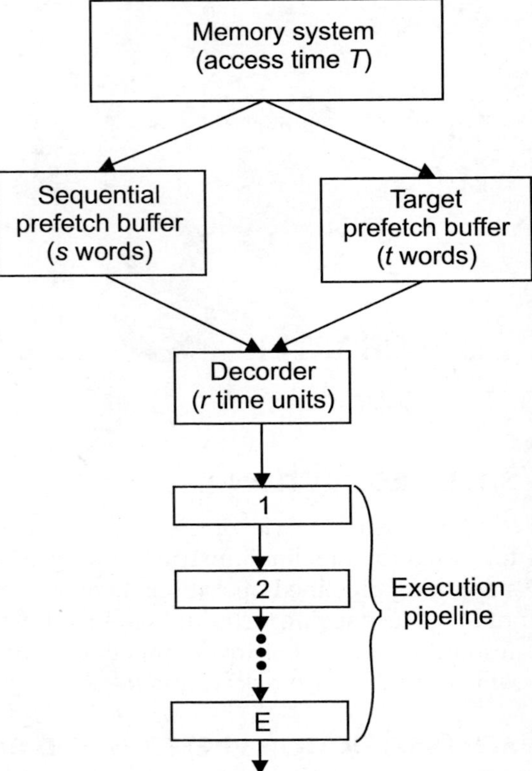

FIGURE 8.1: An instruction pipeline with both sequential and target prefetch buffers.

Instruction prefetching reduces the damaging effects of branching. The idea is to keep a short loop of eight instruction double words or less completely in the branch-target buffer so that no additional memory accesses are needed until the loop mode is removed by the final branching out. This replacement of the condition mode by the local loop mode is established once a successful branch results and the back-eight test is satisfied. The load lookahead mechanism in the ASC system follows a similar approach. Another approach is to prefetch into the instruction buffer one (by guess) or even both instruction sequences forked at a conditional branch instruction. After the test result becomes available, one of the two prefetched instruction sequences will be executed and the other discarded. This branch-target prefetch approach may increase the utilization of the pipeline CPU and thus increase the total system throughput.

Branch handling: From the viewpoint of overlapped execution sequencing for pipelined processing, the instruction mixes in typical computer programs can be classified into four types, as shown in Table 8.1. The arithmetic load operations constitute 60 percent of a typical computer program. These are mainly data manipulation operations which require one or two operand fetches. The execution of different arithmetic operations requires a different number of pipeline cycles. The store-type operation does not require a fetch operand, but memory access is needed to store the data. The branch-type operation corresponds to an unconditional jump. There are two possible paths for a conditional branch operation. The yes path requires the calculation of the new address being branched to, whereas the no path proceeds to the next sequential instruction in the program. The arithmetic-load and store instructions do not alter the sequential execution order of the program. The branch instructions (25 percent in typical programs) may alter the program counter (PC) in order to jump to a program location other than the next instruction. Different types of instructions require different cycle allocations. The branch types of instructions will cause some damaging effects on the pipeline performance.

TABLE 8.1: Typical instruction mix and pipeline cycle allocation

Instruction type and mix rate	**Arithmetic/ load type 60%**	**Store Type 15%**	**Branch Type 5%**	**Conditional branch type**	
Segment function				**Yes 12%**	**No 8%**
Instruction fetch	6	6	6	6	6
Decode	2	2	2	2	2
Condition test				1	1
Operand address calculation	2	2	2	2	2
Operand fetch(es)	6-12				
Arithmetic logic execution	4-8	6			
Store result		1			
Update PC and flags	1	17	1	1	1
Total pipeline cycles	21-31		11	12	12

Some functions, like interrupt and branch, produce damaging effects on the performance of pipeline computers. When instruction I is being executed, the occurrence of an interrupt postpones the execution of instruction I+1 until the interrupting request has been serviced. Generally, there are two types of interrupts. Precise interrupts are caused by illegal operation codes found in instructions, which can be detected during the decoding stage. The other type, imprecise interrupts, is caused by defaults from storage, address, and execution functions.

Since decoding is usually the first stage of an instruction pipeline, and interrupt on instruction I prohibits instruction I+1 from entering the pipeline. However, those instructions preceding instruction I that have not yet emerged from the pipeline continue to run until the pipeline is drained. Then the interrupt routine is serviced. An imprecise interrupt occurs usually when the instruction is halfway through the pipeline and subsequent instructions are already admitted into the pipeline. when an interrupt of this kind occurs, no new instructions are allowed to enter the pipeline, but all the incomplete instructions inside the pipeline, whether they precede or follow the interrupted instruction, will be completed before the processing unit is switched to service the interrupt.

The effect of branching on pipeline performance is described below by a linear instruction pipeline consisting of five segments: instruction fetch, decode, operand fetch, execute, and store results. Possible memory conflicts between overlapped fetches are ignored and a sufficiently large cache memory (instruction-data buffers) is used in the following analysis.

As illustrated in Figure 8.2, the instruction pipeline executes a stream of instructions continuously in an overlapped fashion if branch-type instructions do not appear. Under such circumstances, once the pipeline is filled up with sequential instructions (non-branch type), the pipeline completes the execution of one instruction per a fixed latency (usually one or two clock periods).

On the other hand, a branch instruction entering the pipeline may halfway down the pipe (such as a "successful" conditional branch instruction) before a branch decision is made. This will cause the program counter to be loaded with the new address to which the program should be directed, making all prefetched instructions (either in the cache memory or already in the pipeline) useless. The next instruction cannot be initiated until the completion of the current branch-instruction cyclė. This causes extra time delays in order to drain the pipeline, as depicted in Figure 8.2c. The overlapped action is suspended and the pipeline must be drained at the end of the branch cycle. The continuous flow of instructions into the pipeline is thus temporarily interrupted because of the presence of a branch instruction.

In general, the higher the percentage of branch-type instructions in a program, the slower a program will run on a pipeline processor. This certainly does not merit the concept of pipelining. An analytical estimation of the effect of branching on an n-segment instruction pipeline is given below. The instruction cycle is assumed to include n pipeline cycles.

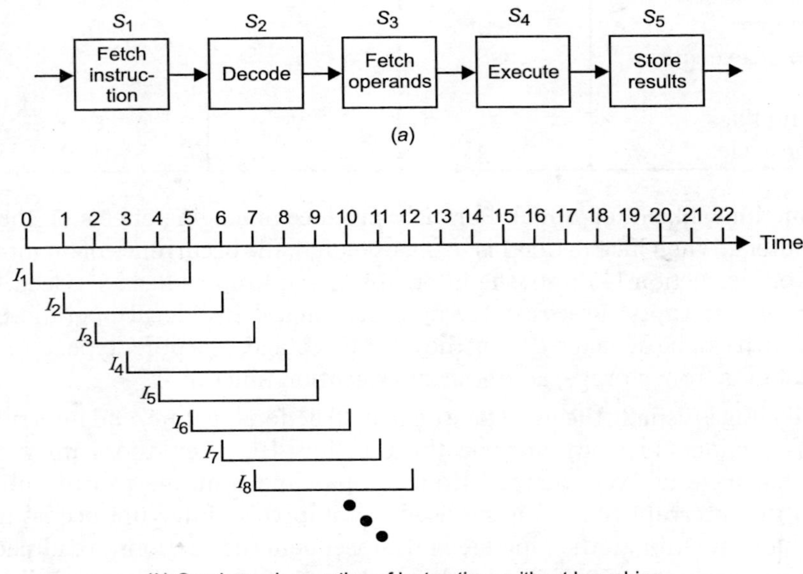

(b) Overlapped execution of instructions without branching

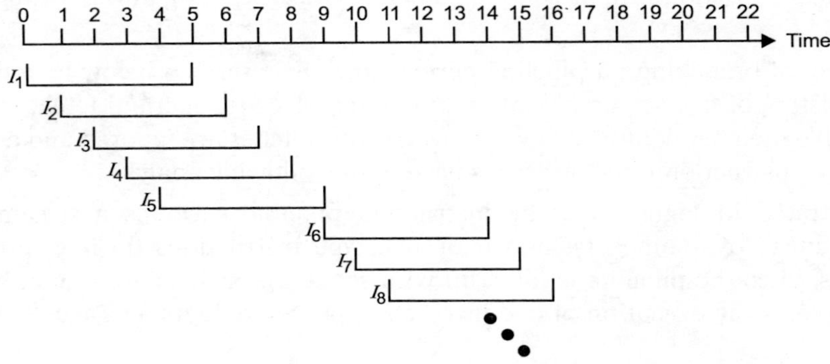

( ) Instruction I_5 is a branch instruction

FIGURE 8.2: The effect of branching on the performance of an instruction pipeline.

For example, one instruction cycle is equal to five pipeline clock periods in Figure 8.2. Clearly, if a branch instruction does not occur, the performance would be one instruction per each pipeline cycle. Let p be the probability of a conditional branch instruction in a typical program (20 percent by table 8.1) and q be the probability that a branch is successful (12/20= 60 percent by Table 8.1). Suppose that there are m instructions waiting to be executed through the pipeline. The number of instructions that cause successful branches equals m. p. q. Since (n – 1)/n extra time delay is needed for each successful branch instruction, the total instruction cycles required to process these m instructions equal (1/n)(n + m – 1) + (m . p . q)(n – 1)/n. As m becomes very large, the performance of the instruction pipeline is measured by the average number of instructions executed per instruction cycle:

$$\lim_{m\to\infty} \frac{m}{(n+m-1)/n+m.p.q.(n-1)/n} = 1\frac{n}{1+pq(n-1)}$$

When p = 0 (no branch instructions encountered), the above measure reduces to n instructions per n pipeline clocks, which is ideal. In reality, the above ratio is always less than n. For example, with n = 5, p = 20 percent, and q = 60 percent, we have the performance of 3.24 instructions per instruction cycle (or 5 pipeline cycles), which is less than the ideal execution rate of 5 instructions per 5 pipeline cycles. In other words, an average of 35.2 percent cycles may be wasted because of branching. In order to cope with the damaging effects of branch instructions, various mechanisms have been developed in pipeline computers.

8.3 BUFFERING

Buffers are used to speed close up the speed gap between memory accesses for either instructions or operands. Buffering can avoid unnecessary idling of the processing stages caused by memory access conflicts or by unexpected branching or interrupts. The concepts of busing is discussed which eliminates the time delay to store and to retrieve intermediate results or to from the registers.

The computer performance can be greatly enhanced if one can eliminate unnecessary memory accesses and combine transitive or multiple fetch-store operations with faster register operations. This is carried by register tagging and forwarding. A pipeline hazard refers to a situation in which a correct program ceases to work correctly due to implementing the processor with a pipeline.

There are three fundamental types of hazard:

- Data hazards,
- Branch hazards, and
- Structural hazards.

8.3.1 DATA BUFFERING

Another method to smooth the traffic flow in a pipeline is to use buffers to close up the speed gap between the memory accesses for either instructions or operands and arithmetic and logic executions in the functional pipes. The instruction or operand buffers provide a continuous supply of instructions or operands to the appropriate pipeline units. Buffering can avoid unnecessary idling of the processing stages caused by memory access conflicts or by unexpected branching or interrupts. Sometimes the entire loop instructions can be stored in the buffer to avoid repeated fetch of the same instructions loop, if the buffer size is sufficiently large. It is very large in the usage of pipeline computers.

Three buffer types are used in various instructions and data types. Instructions are fetched to the instruction fetch buffer before sending them to the instruction unit. After decoding, fixed point and floating point instructions and data are sent to their dedicated buffers. The store address and data buffers are used for continuously storing results back to memory. The storage conflict buffer is used only used when memory.

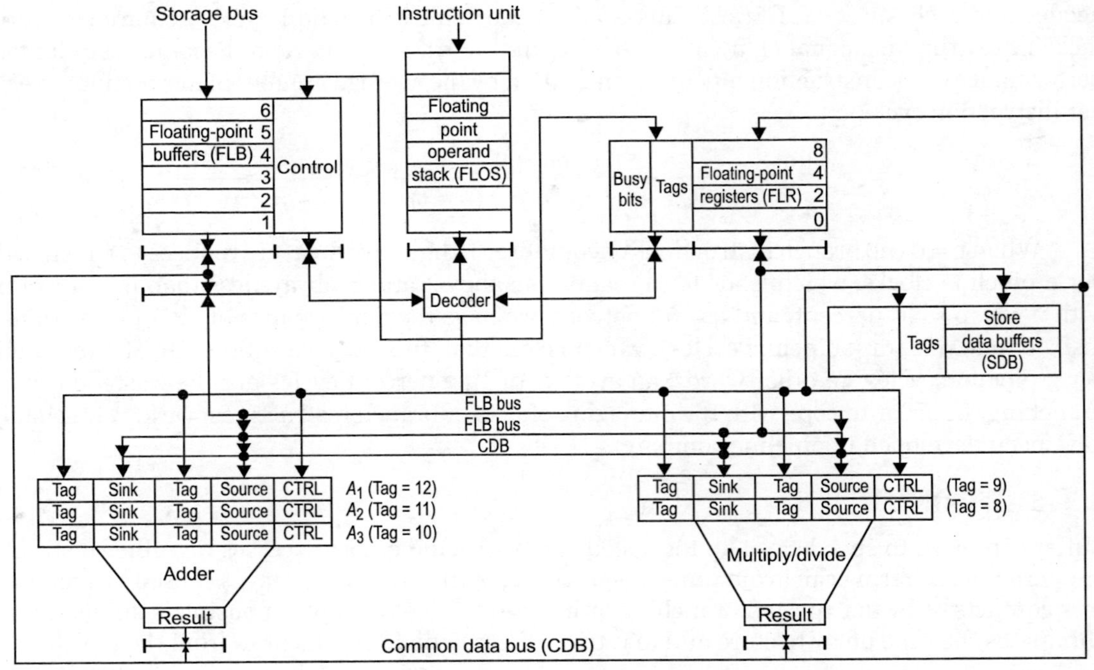

FIGURE 8.3: Data Buffers, transfer paths, reservation stations and common data bus

8.3.2 BUSING STRUCTURES

The sub function being executed by one stage should be independent of the other sub functions being executed by the remaining stages; otherwise some process in the pipeline must be halted until the dependency is removed. When one instruction waiting to be executed is first to be modified by a future instruction, the execution of this instruction must be suspended until the dependency is released.

Another example is the conflicting use of some registers or memory locations by different segments of a pipeline. These problems cause additional time delays. An efficient internal busing structure is desired to route the resulting stations with minimum time delays. In the AP 120B or FPS 164 attached processor the busing structure are even more sophisticated. Seven data buses provide multiple data paths. The output of the floating point adder in the AP 120B can be directly routed back to the input of the floating point adder, to the input of the floating point multiplier, to the data pad, or to the data memory. Similar busing is provided for the output of the floating point multiplier. This eliminates the time delay to store and to retrieve intermediate results or to from the registers.

8.4 INTERNAL FORWARDING AND REGISTER TAGGING

To enhance the performance of computers with multiple execution pipelines

1. **Internal Forwarding** refers to a short circuit technique for replacing unnecessary memory accesses by register -to-register transfers in a sequence of fetch-arithmetic-store operations.
2. **Register Tagging** refers to the use of tagged registers, buffers and reservations stations for exploiting concurrent activities among multiple arithmetic units. The computer performance can be greatly enhanced if one can eliminate unnecessary memory accesses and combine transitive or multiple fetch-store operations with faster register operations. This concept of internal data forwarding can be explored in three directions. The symbols Mi and Rj to represent the ith word in the memory and jth fetch, store and register-to-register transfer. The contents of Mi and Rj are represented by (Mi) and Rj.

Store-Fetch Forwarding

The store the n fetch can be replaced by two parallel operations, one store and one register transfer.

Two memory accesses

Mi ← (R1) (store)

R2 ← (Mi) (Fetch)

Is being replaced by

Only one memory access

Mi ← (R1) (store)

R2 ← (R1) (register Transfer)

Fetch-Fetch Forwarding

The following fetch operations can be replaced by one fetch and one register transfer. One memory access has been eliminated.

Two memory accesses

R1 ← (Mi) (fetch)

R2 ← (Mi) (Fetch)

Is being replaced by

Only one memory access

R1 ← (Mi) (Fetch)

R2 ← (R1) (register Transfer)

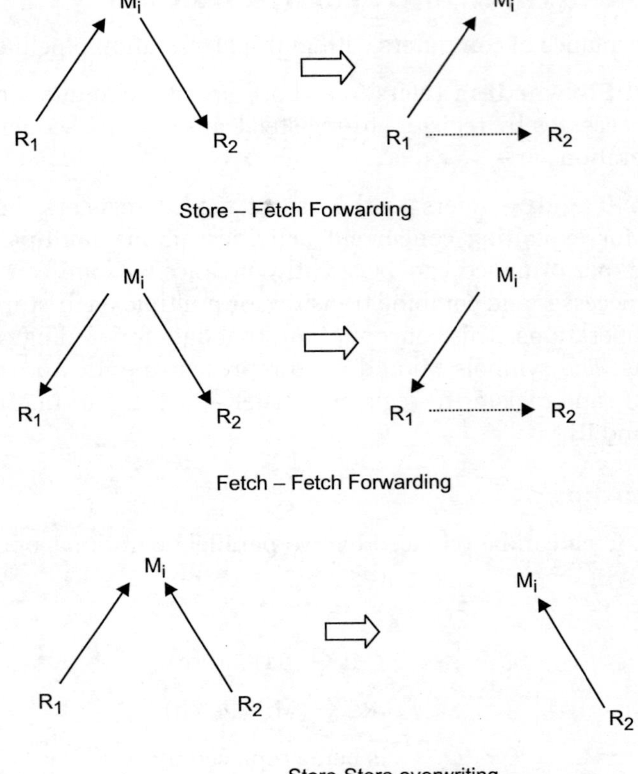

FIGURE 8.4: Internal Forwarding Examples thick arrows for memory accesses and dotted arrows for register transfers

Store-Store Overwriting

The following two memory updates of the same word can be combined into one; since the second store overwrites the first.

Two memory accesses

Mi ← (R1) (store)

Mi ← (R2) (store)

Is being replaced by

Only one memory access

Mi ← (R2) (store)

The above step shows how to apply internal forwarding to simplify a sequence of arithmetic and memory access operations.

8.5 HAZARD DETECTION AND RESOLUTION

The next issue in pipelining is **hazards**. A pipeline hazard refers to a situation in which a correct program ceases to work correctly due to implementing the processor with a pipeline.

There are three fundamental types of hazard:

- Data hazards,
- Branch hazards, and
- Structural hazards.

Data hazards can be further divided into

- Write After Read(WAR)
- Write After Write(WAW)
- Read After Write(RAW)

8.5.1 DATA HAZARDS

This is when reads and writes of data occur in a different order in the pipeline than in the program code. There are three different types of data hazard (named according to the order of operations that must be maintained):

RAW

A Read After Write hazard occurs when, in the code as written, one instruction reads a location after an earlier instruction writes new data to it, but in the pipeline the write occurs after the read (so the instruction doing the read gets stale data).

WAR

A Write After Read hazard is the reverse of a RAW: in the code a write occurs after a read, but the pipeline causes write to happen first.

WAW

A Write After Write hazard is a situation in which two writes occur out of order. We normally only consider it a WAW hazard when there is no read in between; if there is, then we have a RAW and/or WAR hazard to resolve, and by the time we've gotten that straightened out the WAW has likely taken care of itself.

(The text defines data hazards, but doesn't mention the further subdivision into RAW, WAR, and WAW. Their graduate level text mentions those)

We use resource objects to refer to working registers, memory locations, and special flags. The contents of these resource objects are called data objects. Each instruction can be considered a mapping form a set of data objects to a set of data objects. The domain D(I) of an instruction I is the set of resource objects whose data objects may affect the execution of instruction I. The range R(I) of an instruction I is the set of resource objects whose data objects may be modified by the execution of instruction I. Obviously, the operands to be used in an instruction execution are retrieved (read) form its domain, and the result will be stored (written) in its range. In what follows, we considered the execution of the two instructions I and j in a program. Instruction j appears after instruction I in the program. There may be done or other instruction between instructions I and j. The latency between the two instructions is a very subtle matter. Instruction j may enter the execution pipe before or after the completion of the execution of instruction I. The improper timing and data dependencies may create some hazardous situations, as shown in Figure 8.5.

A RAW hazard between the two instructions I and j may occur when j attempts to read some data object that has been modified by I. A WAR hazard may occur when j attempts to modify some data object that is read by I. A WAW hazards may occur if both I and j attempt to modify the same data object. Formally, the necessary conditions for these hazards are stated as follows:

$$R(I) \cap D(J) \neq \varnothing \text{ for RAW}$$

$$R(I) \cap R(J) \neq \varnothing \text{ for WAW}$$

$$D(I) \cap R(J) \neq \varnothing \text{ for WAR}$$

Possible hazards for the four types of instructions (Table 8.1) are listed in Table 8.2 Recognizing the existence of possible hazards, computer designers wish to detect the hazard and then to resolve it effectively. Hazard detection can be done in the instruction-fetch stage of a pipeline processor by comparing domain and range of the incoming of the instruction with those of the instructions being processed in the pipe. Should any of the conditions be detected, a writing signal can be generated to prevent the hazard from taking place.

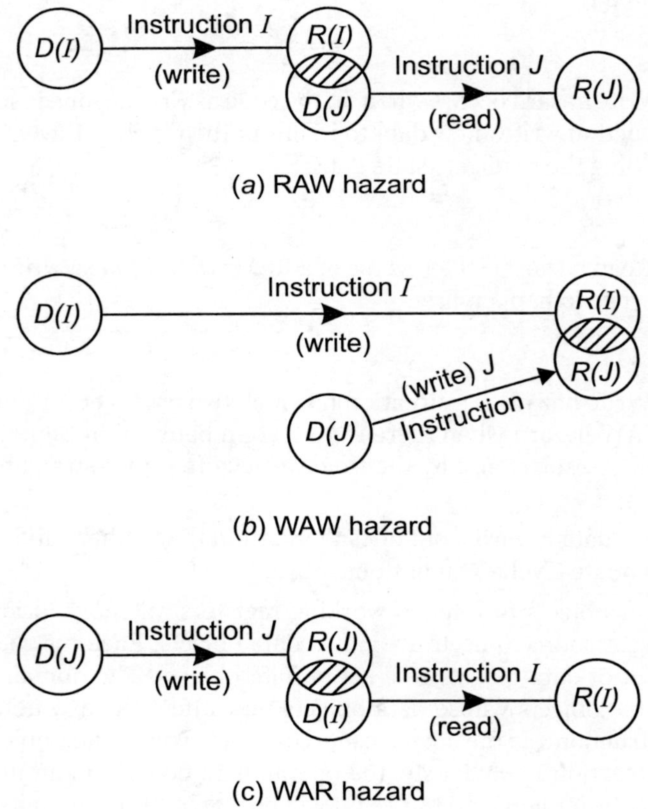

FIGURE 8.5: Illustration of RAW, WAW, and WAR hazard conditions.

Another approach is to allow the incoming instruction through the pipe and distribute the detection to all the potential pipeline stages. This distributed approach offers better flexibility at the expense of increased hardware control.

TABLE 8.2: Possible hazards for various instruction types

Instruction *J* Second	Instruction *I* (first)			
	Arithmetic and load type	**Store Type**	**Branch Type**	**Conditional Branch Type**
Arithmetic and Load Type	RAW WAW WAR	RAW WAR	WAR	WAR
Store Type	RAW WAR	WAW		
Branch Type	RAW		WAW	WAW
Conditional Branch Type	RAW		WAW	WAW

8.5.2 CONTROL HAZARDS

This is when a decision needs to be made, but the information needed to make the decision is not available yet. A Control Hazard is actually the same thing as a RAW data hazard (see above), but is considered separately because different techniques can be employed to resolve it - in effect, we'll make it less important by trying to make good guesses as to what the decision is going to be.

Two notes: First, there is no such thing as a RAR hazard, since it doesn't matter if reads occur out of order. Second, in the MIPS pipeline, the only hazards possible are branch hazards and RAW data hazards.

8.5.3 STRUCTURAL HAZARDS

These occur when a single piece of hardware is used in more than one stage of the pipeline, so it's possible for two instructions to need it at the same time.

So, for instance, suppose we'd only used a single memory unit instead of separate instruction memory and data memories. A simple (non-pipelined) implementation would work equally well with either approach, but in a pipelined implementation we'd run into trouble any time we wanted to fetch an instruction at the same time a lw or sw was reading or writing its data. In effect, the pipeline design we're starting from has anticipated and resolved this hazard by adding extra hardware. Interestingly, the earlier editions of our text used a simple implementation with only a single memory, and separated it into an instruction memory and a data memory when they introduced pipelining. This edition starts right off with the two memories.

Also, the first Sparc implementations (remember, Sparc is almost exactly the RISC machine defined by one of the authors) did have exactly this hazard, with the result that load instructions took an extra cycle and store instructions took two extra cycles.

8.5.4 RESOLVING HAZARDS

There are four possible techniques for resolving a hazard. In order of preference, they are:

Forward: If the data is available somewhere, but is just not where we want it, we can create extra data paths to "forward" the data to where it is needed. This is the best solution, since it doesn't slow the machine down and doesn't change the semantics of the instruction set. All of the hazards in the example above can be handled by forwarding.

Add hardware: This is most appropriate to structural hazards; if a piece of hardware has to be used twice in an instruction, see if there is a way to duplicate the hardware. This is exactly what the example MIPS pipeline does with the two memory units (if there were only one, as was the case with RISC and early SPARC, instruction fetches would have to stall waiting for memory reads and writes), and the use of an ALU and two dedicated adders.

Stall: We can simply make the later instruction wait until the hazard resolves itself. This is undesirable because it slows down the machine, but may be necessary. Handling a hazard on waiting for data from memory by stalling would be an example here. Notice that the hazard is guaranteed to resolve itself eventually, since it wouldn't have existed if the machine hadn't been pipelined. By the time the entire downstream pipe is empty the effect is the same as if the machine hadn't been pipelined, so the hazard has to be gone by then.

Document (AKA punt): Define instruction sequences that are forbidden, or change the semantics of instructions, to account for the hazard. Examples are delayed loads and delayed branches. This is the worst solution, both because it results in obscure conditions on permissible instruction sequences, and (more importantly) because it ties the instruction set to a particular pipeline implementation. A later implementation is likely to have to use forwarding or stalls anyway, while emulating the hazards that existed in the earlier implementation. Both Sparc and MIPS have been bitten by this; one of the nice things about the late, lamented Alpha was the effort they put into creating an exceptionally "clean" sequential semantics for the instruction set, to avoid backward compatibility issues tying them to old implementations.

8.6 JOB SEQUENCING AND COLLISION PREVENTION

When a task is initiated in a static pipeline, its flow pattern is fixed. An initiation refers to the start of a single function evaluation.

Collision: When two or more initiations attempt to use the same stage at the same time.

Problem:

To properly schedule queued tasks awaiting initiation in order to avoid collisions and to achieve high throughput.

Reservation Table + Modified State Diagram + MAL

Fundamental Concepts:

Latency - number of time units between two initiations (any positive integer 1, 2,...)

Latency sequence – sequence of latencies between successive initiations

Latency cycle – a latency sequence that repeats itself

Control strategy – the procedure to choose a latency sequence

Greedy strategy – a control strategy that always minimizes the latency between the current initiation and the very last initiation

Definitions:

1. A collision occurs when two tasks are initiated with latency (initiation interval) equal to the column distance between two "X" on some row of the reservation table.
2. The set of column distances F ={l1,l2,...,lr} between all possible pairs of "X" on each row of the reservation table is called the forbidden set of latencies.
3. The collision vector is a binary vector C = (Cn...C2 C1), Where Ci=1 if i belongs to F (set of forbidden latencies) and Ci=0 otherwise.

Example: Let us consider a Reservation Table with the following set of forbidden latencies F and permitted latencies P (complementation of F).

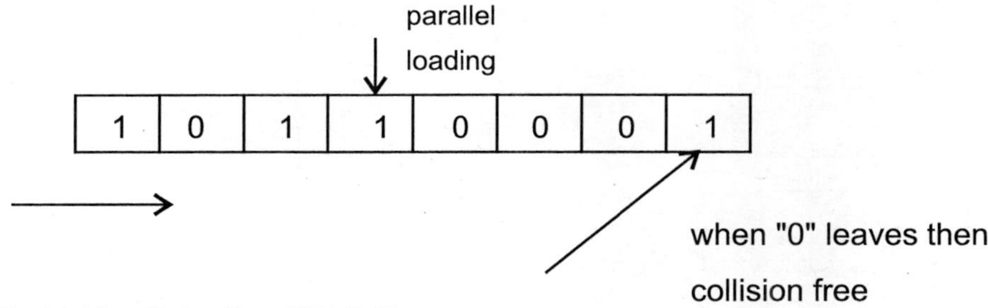

Forbidden list = F = {1,5,6,8}

Collision vector: C={1 0 1 1 0 0 0 1}

8 7 6 5 4 3 2 1

	0	1	2	3	4	5	6	7	8
1	X								X
2		X	X					X	
3				X					
4					X	X			
5							X	X	

```
   1 0 1 1 0 0 0 1
   ---------------
   1 0 1 1 0 1 1 1
OR         1 0 1 1
   ---------------
   1 0 1 1 1 0 1 1
```

FIGURE 8.6: Reservation table

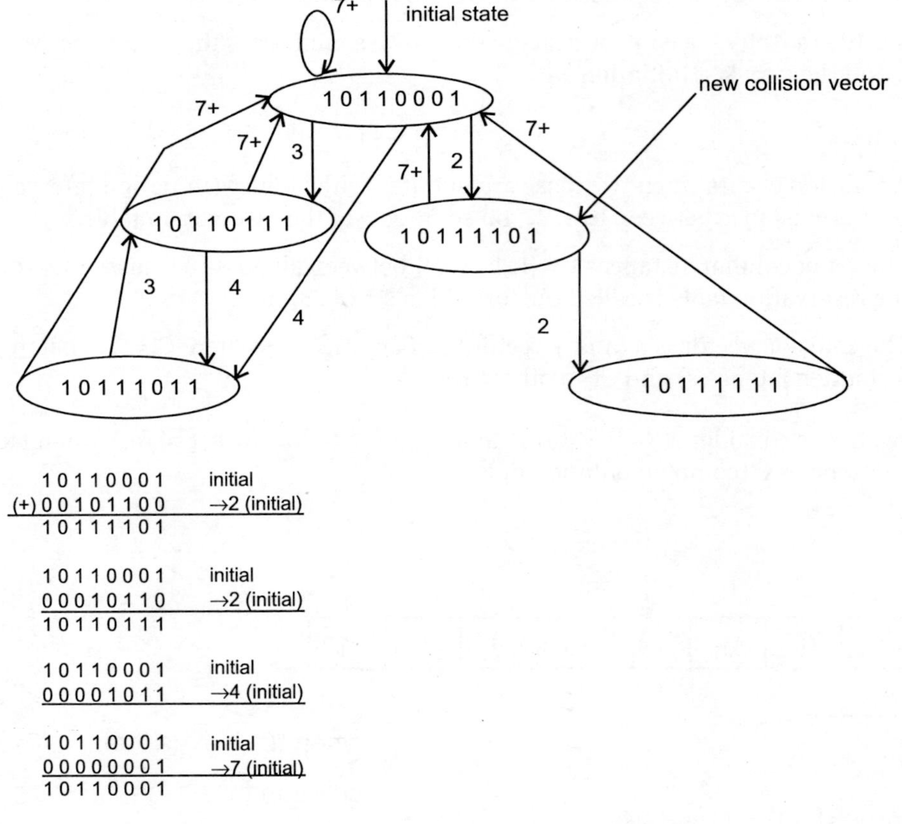

FIGURE 8.7: State diagram

Facts:

1. The collision vector shows both permitted and forbidden latencies from the same reservation table.
2. One can use n-bit shift register to hold the collision vector for implementing a control strategy for successive task initiations in the pipeline. Upon initiation of the first task, the collision vector is parallel-loaded into the shift register as the initial state. The shift register is then shifted right one bit at a time, entering 0's from the left end. A collision free initiation is allowed at time instant t+k a bit 0 is being shifted at of the register after k shifts from time t.

   A **state diagram** is used to characterize the successive initiations of tasks in the pipeline in order to find the shortest latency sequence to optimize the control strategy. A **state** on the diagram is represented by the contents of the shift register after the proper number of shifts is made, which is equal to the latency between the current and next task initiations.
3. The successive collision vectors are used to prevent future task collisions with previously initiated tasks, while the collision vector C is used to prevent possible collisions with the

current task. If a collision vector has a "1" in the ith bit (from the right), at time t, then the task sequence should avoid the initiation of a task at time t+i.

4. Closed logs or cycles in the state diagram indicate the steady – state sustainable latency sequence of task initiations without collisions. The **average latency** of a cycle is the sum of its latencies (period) divided by the number of states in the cycle.
5. The throughput of a pipeline is inversely proportional to the reciprocal of the average latency. A latency sequence is called **permissible** if no collisions exist in the successive initiations governed by the given latency sequence.
6. The maximum throughput is achieved by an optimal scheduling strategy that achieves the (MAL) minimum average latency without collisions.

Corollaries:

1. The job-sequencing problem is equivalent to finding a permissible latency cycle with the MAL in the state diagram.
2. The minimum number of X's in array single row of the reservation table is a lower bound of the MAL.

Simple cycles are those latency cycles in which each state appears only once per each iteration of the cycle. A single cycle is a **greedy cycle** if each latency contained in the cycle is the minimal latency (outgoing arc) from a state in the cycle.

A good task-initiation sequence should include the greedy cycle.

Procedure to determine the greedy cycles

1. From each of the state diagram, one chooses the arc with the smallest latency label unit; a closed simple cycle can formed.
2. The average latency of any greedy cycle is no greater than the number of latencies in the forbidden set, which equals the number of 1's in the initial collision vector.
3. The average latency of any greedy cycle is always lower-bounded by the

   MAL <= ALgreedy <=# of 1' sin the collision vector.

QUESTIONS

1. Explain the concept of instruction prefetch?
2. Explain the technique of branch handling in pipelined processors?
3. Explain the effect of branching on the performance of an instruction pipeline?
4. What do you mean by buffering?
5. Explain the concept of busing structures?
6. Explain the concept of internal forwarding and register tagging?
7. What are hazards? How can you detect hazards?
8. Explain the various types of hazards in detail?
9. How can you resolve hazards in an instruction pipeline?
10. Explain the concept of job sequencing and collision prevention in detail?

CHAPTER 9 SUPERSCALAR AND SUPERPIPELINE DESIGN

9.1 INTRODUCTION

Computer designers and computer architects have been striving to improve uniprocessor computer performance since the first computer was designed. The most significant advances in uniprocessor performance have come from exploiting advances in implementation technology. Architectural innovations have also played a part, and one of the most significant of these over the last decade has been the rediscovery of RISC architectures. Now that RISC architectures have gained acceptance both in scientific and marketing circles, computer architects have been thinking of new ways to improve uniprocessor performance. Many of these proposals such as VLIW, superscalar, and even relatively old ideas such as vector processing try to improve computer performance by exploiting instruction-level parallelism. They take advantage of this parallelism by issuing more than one instruction per cycle explicitly (as in VLIW or superscalar machines) or implicitly (as in vector machines). In this chapter we will limit ourselves to improving uniprocessor performance, and will not discuss methods of improving application performance by using multiple processors in parallel.

As an example of instruction-level parallelism, consider the two code fragments in Figure 9.1. The three instructions in (a) are independent; there are no data dependencies between them, and in theory they could all be executed in parallel. In contrast, the three instructions in (b) cannot be executed in parallel, because the second instruction uses the result of the first, and the third instruction uses the result of the second.

```
Load  C1<-23(R2)        Add   R3<-R3+1
Add   R3<-R3+1          Add   R4<-R3+R2
FPAdd C4<-C4+C3         Store 0[R4]<-R0

(a) parallelism=3       (b) parallelism=1
```

FIGURE 9.1: Instruction-Level Parallelism

The amount of instruction-level parallelism varies widely depending on the type of code being executed. When we consider uniprocessor performance improvements due to exploitation of instruction-level parallelism, it is important to keep in mind the type of application environment. If the applications are dominated by highly parallel code (e.g., weather forecasting), any of a number of different parallel computers (e.g., vector, MIMD) would improve application performance. However, if the dominant applications have little instruction-level parallelism (e.g., compilers, editors, event-driven simulators, lisp interpreters), the performance improvements will be much smaller.

9.2 MACHINE TAXONOMY

There are several different ways to execute instructions in parallel. Before we examine these methods in detail, we need to start with some definitions:

Operation latency: The time (in cycles) until the result of an instruction is available for use as an operand in a subsequent instruction. For example, if the result of an Add instruction can be used as an operand of an instruction that is issued in the cycle after the Add is issued, we say that the Add has an operation latency of one.

Simple operations: The vast majority of operations executed by the machine. Operations such as integer add, logical ops, loads, stores, branches, and even floating-point addition and multiplication are simple operations. Not included as simple operations are instructions which take an order of magnitude more time and occur less frequently, such as divide and cache misses.

Instruction class: A group of instructions all issued to the same type of functional unit.

Issue latency: The time (in cycles) required between issuing two instructions. This can vary depending on the instruction classes of the two instructions.

9.2.1 THE BASE MACHINE

In order to properly compare increases in performance due to exploitation of instruction-level parallelism, we define a base machine that has an execution pipestage parallelism of exactly one.

This base machine is defined as follows:

- Instructions issued per cycle = 1
- Simple operation latency measured in cycles = 1
- Instruction-level parallelism required to fully utilize = 1

The one-cycle latency specifies that if one instruction follows another, the result of the first is always available for the use of the second without delay. Thus, there are never any operation latency interlocks, stalls, or NOP's in a base machine. A pipeline diagram for a machine satisfying the requirements of a base machine is shown in Figure 9.2. The execution pipestage is crosshatched while the others are unfilled. Note that although several instructions are executing concurrently, only one instruction is in its execution stage at any one time. Other pipestages, such as instruction fetch, decode, or write back, do not contribute to operation latency if they are bypassed, and do not contribute to control latency assuming perfect branch slot filling and/or branch prediction.

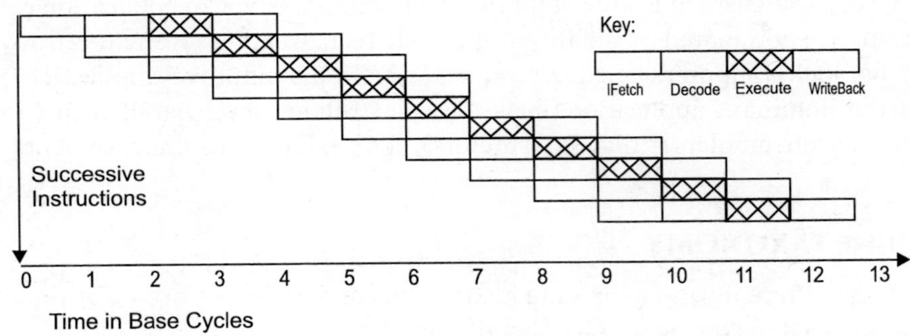

FIGURE 9.2: Execution in a base machine

9.2.2 UNDERPIPELINED MACHINES

The single-cycle latency of simple operations also sets the base machine cycle time. Although one could build a base machine where the cycle time was much larger than the time required for each simple operation, it would be a waste of execution time and resources. This would be an underpipelined machine. An underpipelined machine that executes an operation and writes back the result in the same pipestage is shown in Figure 9.3.

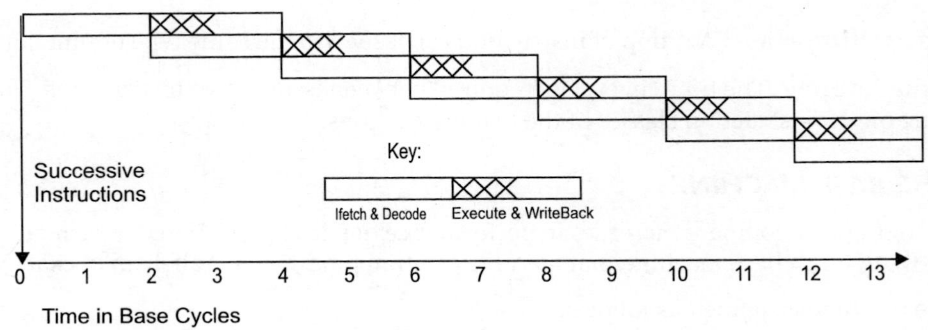

FIGURE 9.3: Underpipelined: cycle > operation latency

The assumption made in many other architecture proposals is that the cycle time of a machine is many times larger than add or load latency, and hence several adders can be stacked in series without affecting the cycle time. If this were really the case, then something would be wrong with the machine cycle time. When the add latency is given as one, for example, we assume that the time to read the operands has been piped into an earlier pipestage, and the time to write back the result has been pipelined into the next pipestage. Then the base cycle time is simply the minimum time required to do a fixed-point add and bypass the result to the next instruction. In this sense machines like the Stanford MIPS chip are underpipelined, because they read operands out of the register file, do an ALU operation, and write back the result all in one cycle.

Another example of underpipelining would be a machine like the Berkeley RISC II chip, where loads can only be issued every other cycle. Obviously this reduces the instruction-level parallelism below one instruction per cycle. An underpipelined machine that can only issue an instruction every other cycle is illustrated in Figure 9.4. Note that this machine's performance is the same as the machine in Figure 9.3, which is half of the performance attainable by the base machine.

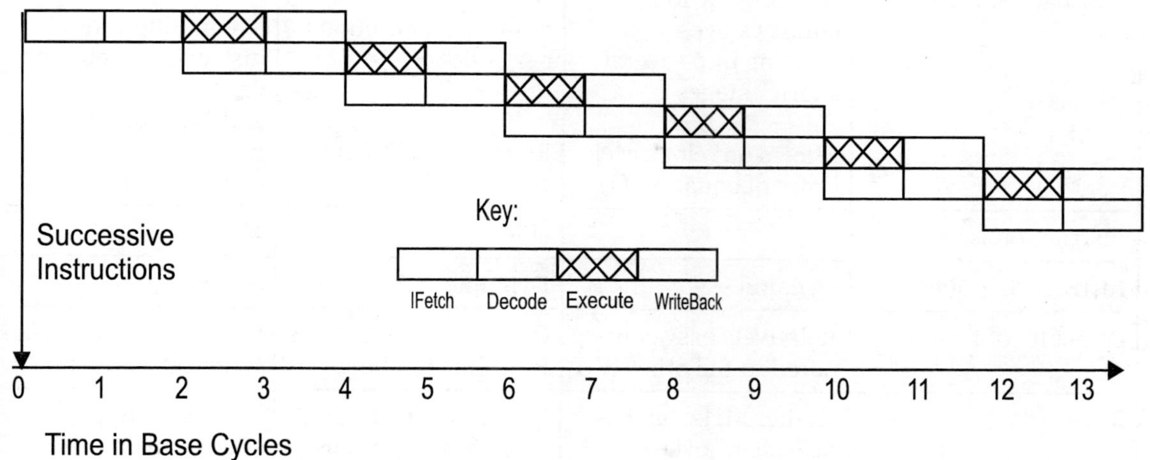

FIGURE 9.4: Underpipelined: issues < 1 instruction per cycle

In summary, an underpipelined machine has worse performance than the base machine because it either has:

- a cycle time greater than the latency of a simple operation, or
- it issues less than one instruction per cycle.

9.3 PERFORMANCE ENHANCEMENTS

In general, the performance of a microprocessor is expressed by equation (1):

$$\text{Execution Time} = \text{IC} \times \text{CPI} \times \text{clock cycle time} \qquad (1)$$

In this equation, IC corresponds to the number of instructions in the program at hand, while CPI represents the average number of clock cycles per instruction. Clock cycle time represents the duration of a clock cycles.

In basic pipeline architecture, only one instruction can be issued at each cycle. Overcoming this limitation has been the subject of much work in the past: more specifically, it has been the goal of computer architects to reduce each variable of equation (1). For one thing, CPI can be improved by designing more advanced organizations and architectures and also by modifying the instruction set architecture (such as providing instructions which may require fewer cycles). Clock cycle time can be improved by better process technology, advanced hardware implementation techniques, and also by more sophisticated architectural organizations. Finally, IC can be improved by implementing advanced compiler and instruction set architectures.

TABLE 9.1: Comparison of Superpipelining, Superscalar, and VLIW

	Superpipelining	Superscalar	VLIW
Approach & Effects	Dividing the long latency stages of a pipeline into several shorter stages Effects on (clock cycle time) of equation (1)	Dynamically issuing multiple instructions per cycle Effects on (CPI) of equation (1)	Utilizing the compiler to combine several instructions into one very long instruction and executing it Effects on (IC) of equation (1)
Instruction issue rate	1	N	M
Instruction issue style	Dynamic	Dynamic	Static
Difficulty of Design	Relatively easy compared to the other two	Complex design issues Run time tracking	Complex design issues Compiler support
Keywords	Higher MHz, latch delay, clock skew	Dynamic scheduling, Out-of-order execution, Register renaming, Score boarding	Compiler support, static scheduling, loop unrolling, trace scheduling

The three main techniques mentioned earlier (superpipelining, superscalar, and VLIW) are such improvements to the architecture. Indeed, superpipelining improves the performance by dividing the long latency stages (such as the memory access stages) of a pipeline into several shorter stages, thereby reducing the clock rate of the pipeline. (In other words, superpipelining has the effect of reducing Clock_cycle_time in equation (1)). Superscalar, on the other hand, improves the performance by dynamically issuing multiple instructions per cycle (this means that superscalar reduces CPI). VLIW (Very Long Instruction Word) improves the performance by utilizing the compiler to combine several instructions into one very long instruction and executing it. (VLIW reduces IC). Table 9.1 highlights the differences among the three techniques.

For the last two decades, each of these techniques and a variety of combinations has had a significant effect on the performance of modern processors. Therefore, in this chapter, we first introduce the concepts and benefits of each technique and then examine examples of each kind.

9.4 SUPERSCALAR

A **superscalar** CPU architecture implements a form of parallelism called instruction level parallelism within a single processor. It therefore allows faster CPU throughput than would otherwise be possible at a given clock rate. A superscalar processor executes more than one instruction during a clock cycle by simultaneously dispatching multiple instructions to redundant functional units on the processor. Each functional unit is not a separate CPU core but an execution resource within a single CPU such as an arithmetic logic unit, a bit shifter, or a multiplier.

In the Flynn taxonomy, a single-core superscalar processor is classified as an SISD processor (Single Instructions, Single Data), while a multi-core superscalar processor is classified as an MIMD processor (Multiple Instructions, Multiple Data).

While a superscalar CPU is typically also pipelined, pipelining and superscalar architecture are considered different performance enhancement techniques.

The superscalar technique is traditionally associated with several identifying characteristics (within a given CPU core):

- Instructions are issued from a sequential instruction stream.
- CPU hardware dynamically checks for data dependencies between instructions at run time (versus software checking at compile time).
- The CPU accepts multiple instructions per clock cycle.

9.4.1 FROM SCALAR TO SUPERSCALAR

The simplest processors are scalar processors. Each instruction executed by a scalar processor typically manipulates one or two data items at a time. By contrast, each instruction executed by a vector processor operates simultaneously on many data items. An analogy is the difference between scalar and vector arithmetic. A superscalar processor is sort of a mixture of the two. Each instruction processes one data item, but there are multiple redundant functional units within each CPU thus multiple instructions can be processing separate data items concurrently.

Superscalar CPU design emphasizes improving the instruction dispatcher accuracy, and allowing it to keep the multiple functional units in use at all times. This has become increasingly important when the number of units increased. While early superscalar CPUs would have two ALUs and a single FPU, a modern design such as the PowerPC 970 includes four ALUs, two FPUs, and two SIMD units. If the dispatcher is ineffective at keeping all of these units fed with instructions, the performance of the system will suffer.

A superscalar processor usually sustains an execution rate in excess of one instruction per machine cycle. But merely processing multiple instructions concurrently does not make an architecture superscalar, since pipelined, multiprocessor or multi-core architectures also achieve that, but with different methods.

In a superscalar CPU the dispatcher reads instructions from memory and decides which ones can be run in parallel, dispatching them to redundant functional units contained inside a single CPU. Therefore a superscalar processor can be envisioned having multiple parallel pipelines, each of which is processing instructions simultaneously from a single instruction thread.

9.4.2 LIMITATIONS ON PARALLEL EXECUTION

Following are the limitations of parallel execution:

1. The situations which prevent instructions to be executed in parallel by a superscalar architecture are very similar to those which prevent an efficient execution on any pipelined architecture.
2. The consequences of these situations on superscalar architectures are more severe than those on simple pipelines, because the potential of parallelism in superscalars is greater and, thus, a greater opportunity is lost.
3. Three categories of limitations have to be considered:

Resource conflicts: They occur if two or more instructions compete for the same resource (register, memory, functional unit) at the same time; they are similar to structural hazards discussed with pipelines. Introducing several parallel pipelined units, superscalar architectures try to reduce a part of possible resource conflicts.

- **Control (procedural) dependency:**
  - The presence of branches creates major problems in assuring an optimal parallelism. How to reduce branch penalties has been discussed in lectures 7&8.
  - If instructions are of variable length, they cannot be fetched and issued in parallel; an instruction has to be decoded in order to identify the following one and to fetch it →superscalar techniques are efficiently applicable to RISCs, with fixed instruction length and format.
- **Data conflicts:**
  - Data conflicts are produced by data dependencies between instructions in the program. Because superscalar architectures provide a great liberty in the order in which instructions can be issued and completed, data dependencies have to be considered with much attention.

9.5 SUPERSCALAR PROCESSORS

Superscalar processors improve performance by replicating the pipeline hardware. One simple technique is to have multiple pipelines. Figure 9.5 shows a dual pipeline design, somewhat similar to that present in the Pentium. The instruction fetch unit fetches two instructions each cycle and loads the two pipelines with one instruction each. Since these two pipelines are independent, instruction execution can proceed in parallel.

In our pipeline example, we assumed that all stages take the same amount of time. Although simple integer instructions can be executed in one cycle, complex instructions such as integer division and floating-point operations can take longer (often by several cycles). If we have only one execution unit at stage 4, execution of these complex instructions can bring the pipeline to a crawl! We can improve the situation by providing multiple execution units, linked to a single pipeline, as shown in Figure 9.6. In this figure, we are using four execution units: two integer units and two floating-point units. Such designs are referred to as superscalar processors.

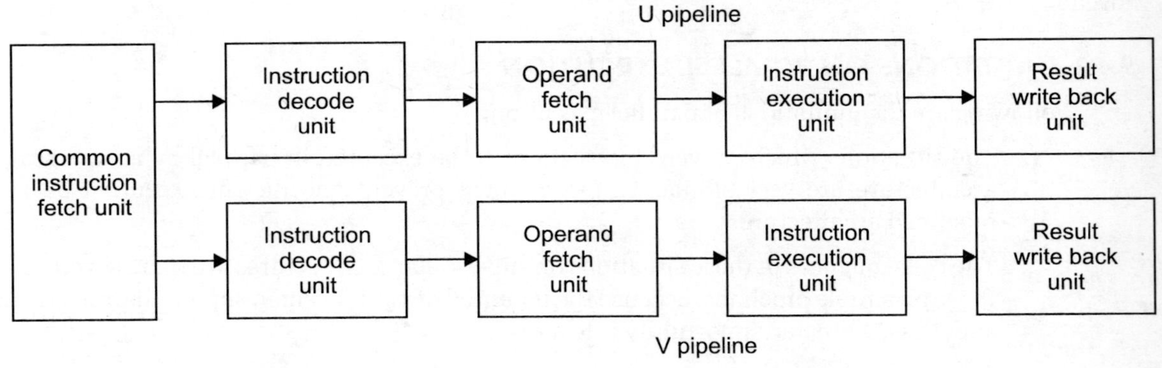

FIGURE 9.5: dual pipeline based on the five stages used

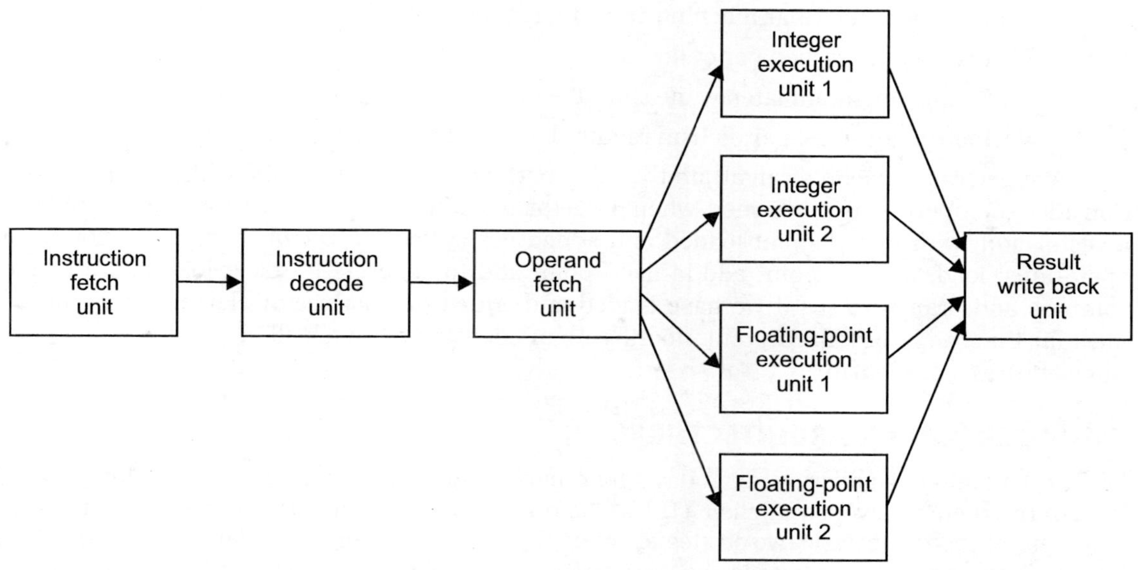

FIGURE 9.6: Superscalar Pipeline with four functional units

9.5.1 SUPERSCALAR MACHINES

As their name suggests, superscalar machines were originally developed as an alternative to vector machines. A superscalar machine of degree n can issue n instructions per cycle. A superscalar machine could issue all three parallel instructions in Figure 9.1(a) in the same cycle. Superscalar execution of instructions is illustrated in Figure 9.7.

In order to fully utilize a superscalar machine of degree n, there must be n instructions executable in parallel at all times. If an instruction-level parallelism of n is not available, stalls and dead time will result where instructions are forced to wait for the results of prior instructions.

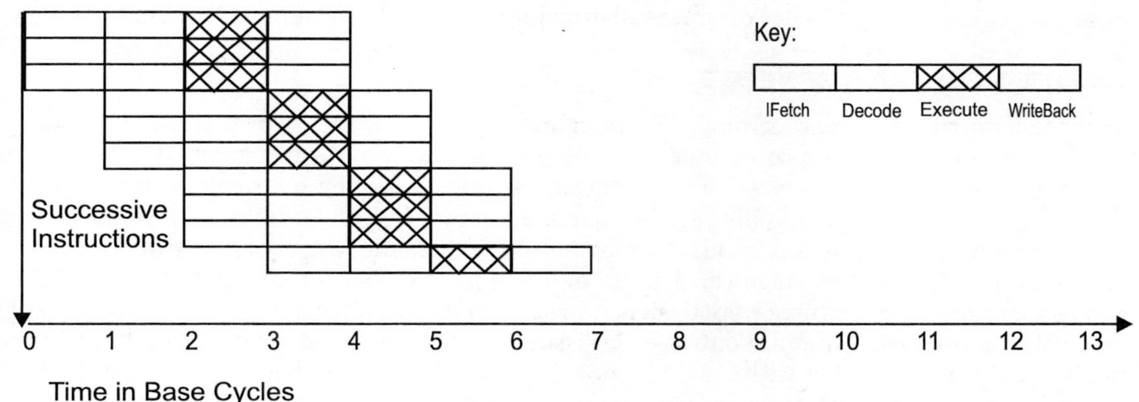

FIGURE 9.7: Execution in a superscalar machine (n = 3)

Formalizing a superscalar machine according to our definitions:

- Instructions issued per cycle = n
- Simple operation latency measured in cycles = 1
- Instruction-level parallelism required to fully utilize = n

A superscalar machine can attain the same performance as a machine with vector hardware. Consider the operations performed when a vector machine executes a vector load chained into a vector add, with one element loaded and added per cycle. The vector machine performs four operations: load, floating-point add, a fixed-point add to generate the next load address, and a compare and branch to see if we have loaded and added the last vector element. A superscalar machine that can issue a fixed-point, floating-point, load and a branch all in one cycle achieves the same effective parallelism.

9.6 SUPERSCALAR ARCHITECTURES

One of the main design issues for today's high-performance microprocessors is exploiting a high level of Instruction Level Parallelism (ILP). The ILP is a primary way to improve the parallelism of a sequential code. The basic two strategies for exploiting Instruction Level Parallelism are multiple instruction issue and out-of-order execution. Those two techniques were invented to execute as many instructions as possible in a given clock cycle. In addition, sophisticated branch prediction schemes and speculative execution techniques were proposed to overcome the limited amount of parallelism available within a basic block. Both techniques have successfully provided many opportunities to discover more parallelism across the control flow limit.

Traditionally, superscalar and Very Long Instruction Word (VLIW) architectures were developed as the main microprocessor models for exploiting ILP. Although both architectures target multiple instruction issue and out-of-order execution, they have adopted fundamentally different approaches. The significant differences lie in the way to schedule the instructions. Superscalar processors are mainly characterized with dynamic scheduling which uses hardware to schedule the instructions at run-time. On the contrary, VLIW architectures depend on static scheduling which schedules the instructions at compile time in a static way. We will discuss the design features and some example architectures of superscalar and VLIW in this and the following section. First, the basic concept and design issues of superscalar architectures will be presented in detail.

9.6.1 CONCEPT AND BENEFITS

Superscalar architectures are strongly based on previous pipelined RISC processors. The most significant advantage of RISC processors is the inherent simplicity of the instruction set architecture. The early pipelined RISC processors were designed to execute one instruction for one pipeline stage. The major innovation of the super-scalar architecture over the traditional pipelined processor is the multiple instruction issue advantage through dynamic instruction scheduling. In those approaches, each pipeline stage can handle multiple instructions simultaneously. Although the early superscalar architectures were designed to issue multiple instructions in an in-order fashion, this would consequently require out-of-order issue to maximize the effect of the multiple instruction issue feature. Together with the dynamic scheduling and enough backward compatibility, the multiple issue characteristic becomes the main advantage of the current superscalar processors.

The basic working mechanism of dynamic scheduling is quite simple. The instructions are simply fetched in the instruction sequence. They are then stored in a pool of instructions (also referred to as the scheduling window, instruction window or instruction buffer). Just as in the basic RISC architecture, the instructions are fetched sequentially following the program counter (PC). However, once the instructions are decoded, the dependencies among the instructions are analyzed. Then, the processor can deduce which instructions inside the pool can be executed without causing data hazards. Concurrent execution or out-of-order execution is made possible by hardware-based run-time dependency checking.

1. A Basic Model of Superscalar Pipeline: Figure 9.8 shows a typical model of a basic five-stage pipelined processor. In the single instruction issue RISC processor model, each stage handles only one instruction per cycle. In addition, the execution of the instructions should be made in-order, following the fetching sequence of the original binary code. On the contrary, each of the processing stage is able to handle a number of instructions in the superscalar pipeline model. For example, the IF (Instruction Fetch) stage can fetch multiple instructions from the instruction cache and the EX (Execution) stage can execute multiple instructions simultaneously. This multiple instruction issue characteristic inherently means out-of-order execution of the instruction sequence. It has been developed to reduce the execution time of a fixed size of code by exploiting fine-grain parallelism as low as at the instruction level.

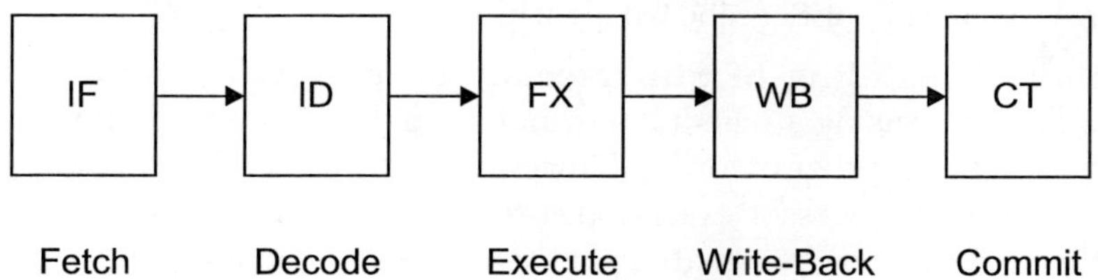

FIGURE 9.8: Five-stage pipelined processor

However, executing multiple instructions simultaneously means the sequential characteristic of the original code cannot be guaranteed. This brings out highly critical problems since the current programming languages are strongly based on a sequential programming model, and the binary code is correctly executed only if its sequential characteristic is respected. An inappropriate execution order between instructions could cause data hazards due to the register naming dependencies. Figure 9.9 depicts possible data hazards due to an out-of-order execution.

```
ld  r2, 0(r7)     -- (a)
add r4, r2, r7    -- (b)
add r3, r4, r5    -- (c)
sub r9, r4, r4    -- (d)
sub r9, r2, r7    -- (e)
```

Data dependencies

RAW : Read After Write

WAR : Write After Read

WAW : Write After Write

FIGURE 9.9: Data dependencies in a sequential code

The instruction stream on the left side of Figure 9.9 shows an example of a sequential instruction stream. In the previous pipelined RISC processor model, those instructions are fetched, executed, and committed in program order. This means that none of the instructions can be executed before any instruction ahead of it is committed. However, in the superscalar model, the processor aims at executing in a cycle as many instructions as possible through multiple instruction issue and out-of-order execution (within the allowed bandwidth).

Now, can the five instructions in Figure 9.9 be executed simultaneously? Obviously, executing those five instructions in parallel without considering the program order does not produce correct results. Indeed, there are some data dependencies. For example, instructions (b) and (e) cannot be executed until instruction (a) completes, since both (b) and (e) need to read r2; there exists a RAW (Read After Write) data dependency. On the other hand, a WAR (Write After Read) dependency exists between the instruction (b) and (c) due to r3. Also, a WAW (Write After Write) dependency can be found between instructions (d) and (e). In the superscalar architecture model, the data dependencies which can cause data hazards are detected during the instruction decode stage. Based on those data dependencies, the instruction execution order is decided dynamically. It will be explained shortly in the next part. The dynamic scheduling of the Superscalar model is strongly based on the early Tomasulo or Scoreboard algorithms.

2. Dynamic Scheduling of Superscalar: Superscalar architectures achieve dynamic instruction scheduling by using a scheduling window. In dynamic scheduling, the instructions are still fetched sequentially in program order. However, those instructions are decoded and stored in a scheduling window of a processor execution core. After decoding the instructions, the processor core obtains the dependency information between the instructions and can also identify the instructions which are ready for execution (ready instructions mean the instructions of which the source registers have been calculated). Indeed, there must be no data hazard in issuing the ready instructions.

In essence, the execution of an instruction i is decided by the previous instruction k which produces the value for the source registers of the instruction i. This means that the superscalar processors can execute the instructions as soon as the input values are available (also, the corresponding functional units should be available). The processor dynamically achieves parallel execution of the instructions by performing a run-time dependency check and waking up the following instructions. However, at the same time, it also implies that every instruction should broad-cast the register name and value across the issue window to wake up and select any ready instruction. This means that a superscalar architecture needs a complex wake-up and selection logic inside of the scheduling window. It should be also noted that a superscalar architecture is expected to deliver high degrees of Instruction-Level Parallelism, together with a large issue width which consequently requires more complex hardwired instruction scheduling logic. This will cause a significant overhead for future superscalar processors.

Although superscalar architectures require complex issue logic and scheduling mechanisms, they have been the standard general-purpose processor during the last decade. This is mostly due to the fact that this model possesses an inherent backward compatibility. This adaptability to legacy code and the ability to continue using conventional compilers make superscalar architectures quite attractive. That is the main reason why all major processor venders have focused on developing superscalar-styled ILP processors since the 1990s.

3. Register Renaming: Register renaming is a technique which increases the chance to uncover independent instructions by removing the false dependencies. Those false dependencies are caused by using the same register name. More specifically, the register renaming can eliminate the WAW (write after write) and WAR (write after read) dependencies among the instructions. Figure 9.10 shows one such example. The four instructions on the right side of Figure 9.10 show the original instruction stream produced by the compiler. Through register r2, there exists a WAW dependency between instructions (a) and (c) and a WAR dependency between instructions (b) and (c). Those dependencies limit the parallel execution (or out-of-order execution) of the instructions. Clearly, the instruction (c) cannot be executed before instruction (b) reads r2. However, this data dependency can be removed when the register r2 in instruction (c) and (d) is given another register name. The four instructions on the right side show the instruction stream with register renaming.

		< after renaming>	
add r2, r3, r4	-- (a)	add r2, r3, r4	-- (a)
add r4, r2, r3	-- (b)	add r4, r2, r3	-- (b)
sub r2, r6, r7	-- (c)	sub r2, r6, r7	-- (c)
mul r9, r2, r8	-- (d)	mul r9, r2, r8	-- (d)

FIGURE 9.10: Register renaming example

Now, instruction (c) can be issued and executed, regardless of the execution of instruction (a), since it writes into register r2'. The register renaming scheme was originally developed as an compiling technique for an ILP processor such as VLIW. However, the superscalar architecture also uses a register renaming scheme for the same purpose. Its implementation is a purely hardware-based dynamic method. There are two ways we can implement the register renaming scheme in the superscalar model. The first method explicitly provides a larger number of physical registers than the logical registers. Then, at run-time, the processor can map any available physical register to the logical register. This technique requires a register mapping table. The second method uses a reorder buffer (ROB). In this approach, each entry of reorder buffer works as a physical register.

4. Reorder Buffer: A Reorder buffer (ROB) provides two main functions in modern superscalar processor. The first task is to guarantee the in-order completion of a sequential instruction stream. Especially, the in-order completion is crucial for correct speculative execution and the implementation of precise interrupts. As seen in Figure 9.8, a basic superscalar processor has two stages for instruction completion: the Write Back (WB) stage and the Commit (CT) stage. The WB stage allows the later instructions to use the result of the instruction. However, it does not allow the instruction to write the value into the register file or memory. The instruction still has to wait inside the ROB until it retires from the CT stage. The retire process in the CT stage strictly follows the program order (in-order completion). This in-order completion guarantees that the program can return to the precise state in any point of the program execution. The precise state means the sequentially of the program execution is guaranteed. This is extremely important for interrupt or miss-speculation cases. The ROB is implemented as a circular FIFO and retires the instructions following the program order; each entry of the ROB is assigned at the decoding stage and must hold the original program order. During the commit stage, the instructions at the head of the ROB are scanned and an instruction is committed if all the previous instructions are committed (multiple instructions within the commit-width can also be committed during the same cycle).

The second function of the ROB is to achieve register renaming through the slots of the ROB. When the processor uses an ROB, an available entry in the ROB is assigned to an instruction at the decoding stage. Each entry of the ROB contains three fields which indicate the instruction type, the destination register, and the result. The destination register field indicates the logical name of the register and the result field holds the value for the register. It also has a single bit ready indicator. When the ready bit indicates the value is ready, the later instructions which need the values can simply read the value; otherwise the later instruction should be left to wait inside a scheduling window until the value is ready.

5. Branch Prediction: A superscalar architecture is capable of delivering instructions beyond the current basic block by predicting the future control path. Therefore, excellent branch prediction is essential if we are to have a large pool of instructions to choose from. More particularly, the current trend in superscalar design is to achieve large issue-width with a large scheduling window. To satisfy those demands, the number of in-flight instructions (in other words, the instruction inside the processor in a clock cycle) should be large enough to find the ready instructions to issue or execute. By using efficient branch prediction and speculation techniques, fetching many instructions from the correct control path is possible.

The simplest way to predict branch is static branch prediction; it means the branch instructions are either always taken or always not-taken. However, this static method does not accurately predict the branch outcome. Therefore, current superscalar processors mainly depend on dynamic branch prediction which utilizes the previous history to decide the behavior of future branches. In current super-scalar designs, many dynamic branch prediction techniques have been proposed and developed. A basic form of branch prediction consists in using the local history of a branch instruction. The Branch History Table (BHT) is accessed by indexing a certain number of lower bits of the PC of the branch instruction, where the table provides the history of the branch behavior. In addition, other prediction schemes also consider the global branch history together with the local history. Those combined schemes significantly enhance the branch prediction success rate. Such schemes include two-level adaptive branch predictions and branch correlation. The interested reader is referred to these publications for details on the working mechanism and design features of those branch schemes. Besides predicting the branch direction (either taken or not-taken), there had been one more prediction on the target address. It is possibly achieved by using a Branch Target Buffer to provide the target address prediction. This operation can determine the expected target address at the instruction fetch stage; therefore, the BTB is accessed during the IF stage and the next PC can be obtained for the very next cycle.

9.6.2 DESIGN CHALLENGES

In a conventional superscalar design, wake up and select operation cannot be pipelined nor be implemented as a one-cycle operation. Therefore, as far as the size of an issue window is concerned, more instructions within an issue window mean more communication overhead (wire delay) for the wake up and select operations in a clock cycle time. In fact, wires tend to scale poorly compared to semiconductor devices, and the amount of state that can be reached in a single clock period eventually ceases to grow. Consequently, there is a scaling problem with regard to the issue window size of the superscalar design. The goals of a larger instruction window and of a faster clock become directly antagonistic in the issue window design of future superscalar processors. This phenomenon will be even more noticeable as higher degrees of parallelism are needed. It is well recognized that the centralized scheduling logic would be the most critical part of a processor and would limit the ultimate clock rate.

Another important issue in processor design is how to solve the problem caused by the dramatically growing speed-gap between the processor and main memory. An obvious solution would be the use of a large scheduling window: searching across a wider range of instructions can offer more opportunities to uncover independent instructions which can hide long access latencies. However, since a large instruction window will cause a lower clock rate, other approaches for processor design must be investigated. As an example, the partitioning of a single scheduling window can reduce the complexity of the centralized design as well as the size of each component. Indeed, a higher clock rate can be achieved since the decentralized model reduces the length of the wire for communication. This microarchitecture technique is called clustering.

The last design challenge of the dynamic scheduling is the considerable amount of power consumption. According to Gowan et al., 18% of total power consumption of the Alpha 21264 processor is used by the instruction issue unit. A large amount of power is dissipated by the wake up and the selection logic. This is mainly due to the global communication of the centralized scheduling unit. As an alternative design, the clustered architectures can reduce the power consumption of the centralized instruction issue unit. Separating a single scheduling window into multiple structures can reduce the power consumption of the aggressive scheduling unit of a superscalar architecture.

9.6.3 EXAMPLE ARCHITECTURES

We consider two microprocessor models as being good representatives of superscalar architectures: the Alpha 21264 and the MIPS R10000.

1. Alpha 21264 : The Alpha 21264 (EV6) processor (Figure 9.11) was introduced in 1998 with a 0.35μm CMOS process technology operating at 600MHz frequency. It is the first Alpha processor designed with an out-of-order issue strategy. The Alpha 21264 has a 4 way issue bandwidth. However, the execution stage supports 6-way issue in a cycle with four integer functional units and two floating-point functional units. It is also designed to support 80 in-flight instructions in a processor. Alpha 21264 has only two floating-point units and a single physical register file. Both floating-point units are fully pipelined.

The Alpha 21264 processor is implemented with a 64-KB, two-way set-associative L1 data cache. The earlier model of the processor (Alpha 21164) had only a 8-KB data cache which resulted in many more cache misses than the more modern 21264 processor. It now has a huge L1 data cache. As a result, the access latency to the data cache requires two clock cycles. However, two concurrent accesses to the level 1 data cache are supported.

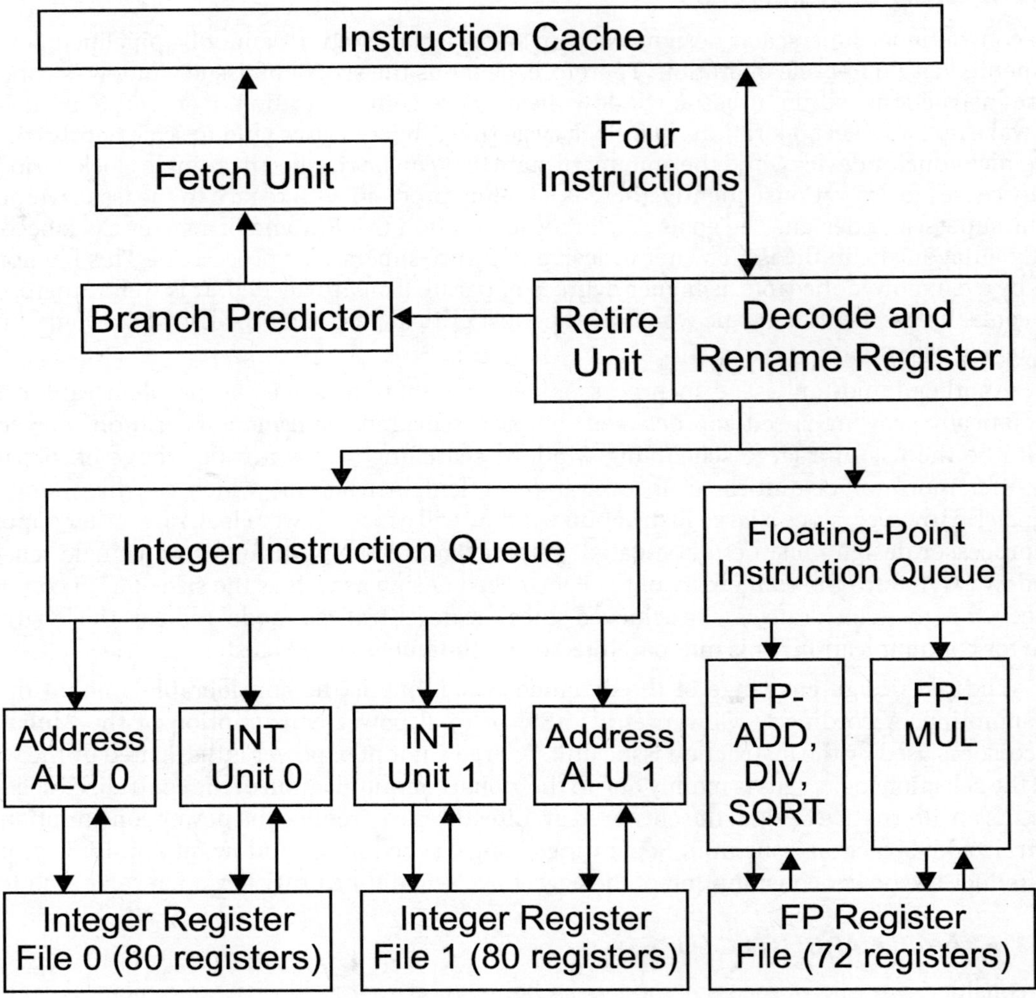

FIGURE 9.11: Alpha 21264 Block Diagram

Figure 9.12 shows a detailed description of the Alpha 21264 pipeline. In its basic inception, an instruction is required to go through all seven stages until it can write back the results. Since the 64KB data cache needs two clock cycles to deliver the data, load/store pipeline operations require two more clock cycles than normal operations.

One distinct feature of the Alpha 21264 is in that the fetch stage uses line and way prediction for the next instruction to fetch. It is possibly achieved by using the next line predictor and set predictor. The purpose of those predictors is similar to that of the Branch Target Buffer: it provides the address for the next instruction to fetch. As for the control flow prediction, the processor still has a branch prediction mechanism: a hybrid branch predictor is implemented. One more interesting feature of the processor is the load hit/miss prediction which helps to schedule load instructions.

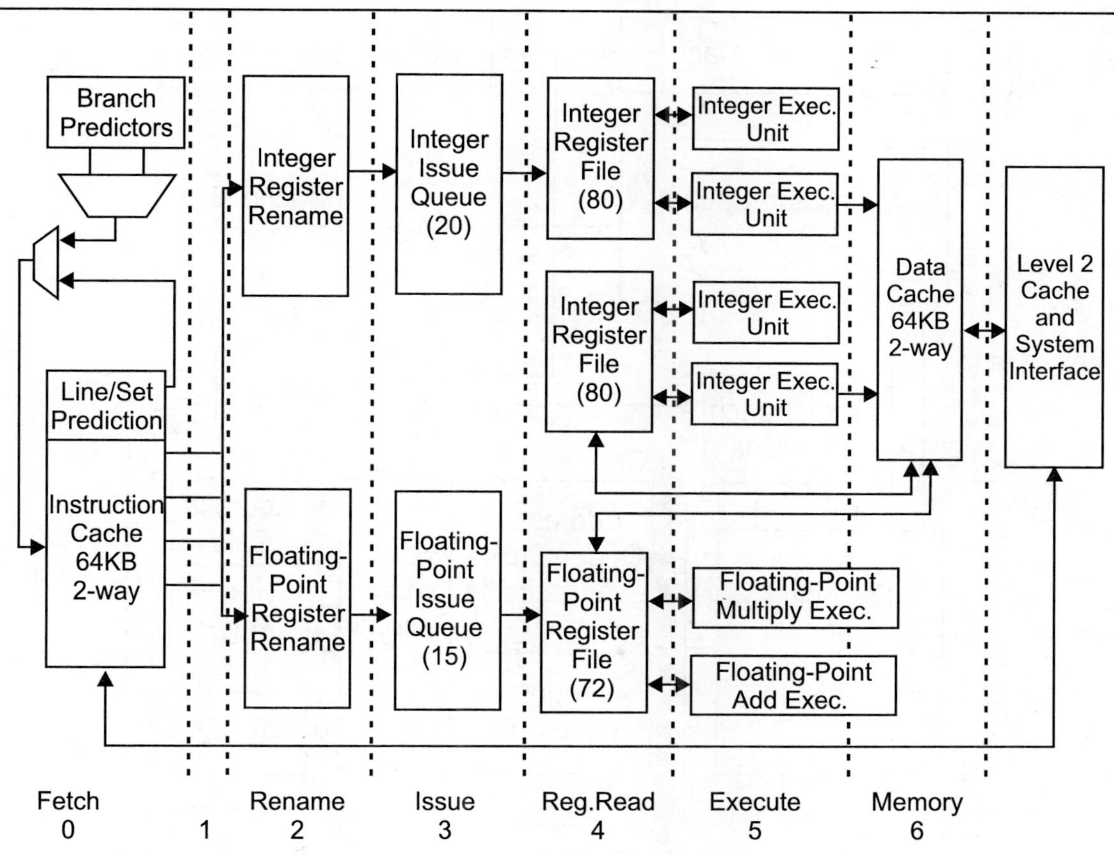

FIGURE 9.12: Alpha 21264 Pipeline

The EV7 architecture (Alpha 21364), the fourth generation of the Alpha processor, inherited many characteristics from the Alpha 21264 processor. Indeed, the Alpha 21364 is designed to be the System-On-Chip version of the Alpha 21264. It uses the EV6 as the core processing element and adds peripheral features such as integrated second level cache, memory controller, and network interface.

2. MIPS R10000: The MIPS R10000 is based on the previous MIPS processors. The previous MIPS processors were mainly single issue pipelined RISC processors. The MIPS R10000 is the first out-of-order issue superscalar processor which is implemented for the MIPS IV ISA. The MIPS R1000 processor fetches four instructions from the instruction cache in every cycle and decodes those instructions. Any branch is immediately predicted upon detection.

The first implementation of the MIPS IV ISA architecture is the 4-issue superscalar processor (R8000). The R8000 is able to execute two ALU and two memory operations per cycle. However, the R8000 processor does not have a dynamic scheduling capability. The most distinguishable advantage of the R10000 (Figure 9.13) is the out-of-order execution feature which is enabled by the dynamic scheduling.

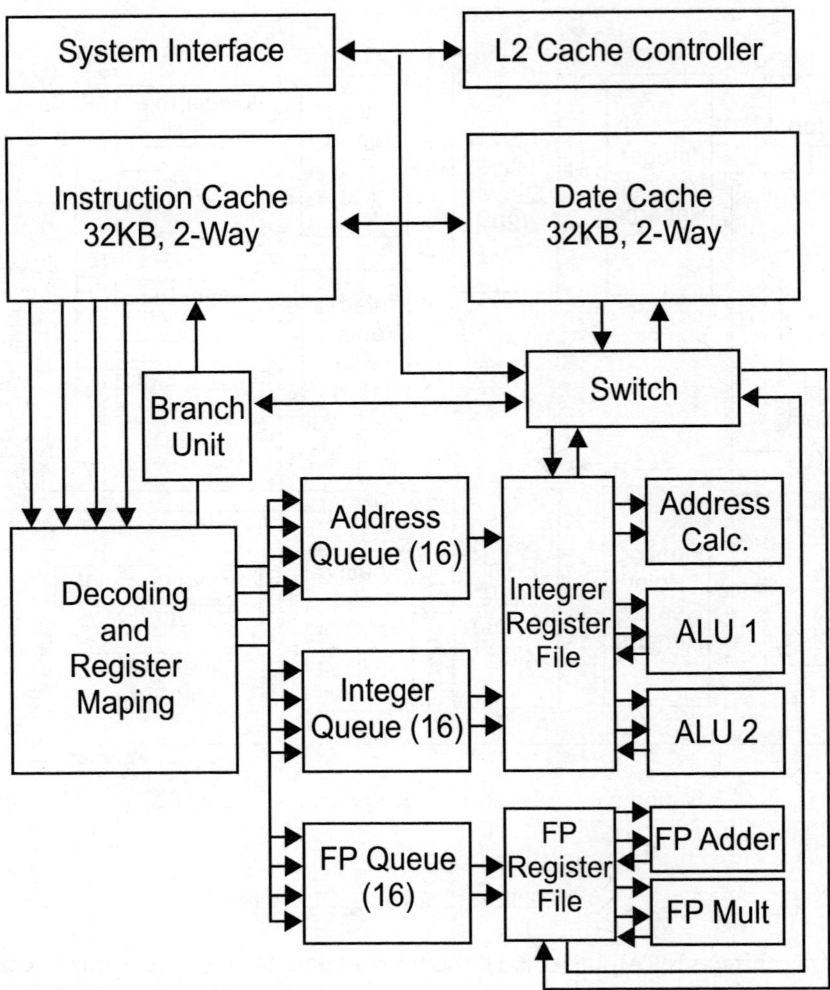

FIGURE 9.13: MIPS R10000 Block Diagram

Four instructions can be fetched and decoded at each clock cycle. Those instructions are stored in one of the three instruction queues after the decoding stage. Each queue has 16 entries for instructions. Those issue queues can also read operands from the register file. Once the register dependencies are resolved and functional units are available, the instructions can be executed in one of the five functional units. Normal integer operations take one clock cycle while load store instructions requires two clock cycles in the execution stage. The floating-point operations need three clock cycles for their execution.

Both level 1 caches are 32KB in size and two-way interleaved. The core processor chip also controls a large external level 2 cache. The R10000 is implemented with a 64-bit split-transaction system bus used to communicate with the outside of the chip. Up to four R10000 chips can be integrated using this bus architecture. As a summary of the two example architectures, Table 9.2 shows a comparison between the Alpha 21264 processor and the MIPS R10000 processor.

TABLE 9.2: Comparison of the two Commercial Superscalar Processors

Processor	Alpha 21264	MIPS R1000
Issue Width	4 way	4 way
Integer Unit	4	2
Address Unit	0	1
Floating Point Units	2	2
L1 I-Cache	64 KB	32 KB
L1 D-Cache	64 KB	32 KB
Integer instruction Queue	20 entries	16 entries
Floating Point Instruction Queue	15 entries	16 entries
Integer Register	80	64
Floating Point Register	72	64
System Bus Width	64 bits	64 bits
Technology	0.35 μm	0.35 μm

9.7 SUPER-PIPELINED PROCESSORS

Super-pipelined processors divide each processor cycle into two or more sub-cycles. A new instruction is fetched in each sub-cycle. As you can see from Figure 9.14(b), the five instructions complete two cycles earlier than in the pipelined version. After the pipeline is full, the super-pipeline version executes two instructions per cycle (i.e., one instruction per sub-cycle).

Clock cycle	1	2	3	4	5	6	7	8	9
I1	IF	ID	OF	IE	WB				
I2		IF	ID	OF	IE	WB			
I3			IF	ID	OF	IE	WB		
I4				IF	ID	OF	IE	WB	
I5					IF	ID	OF	IE	WB

(a) Pipelined execution

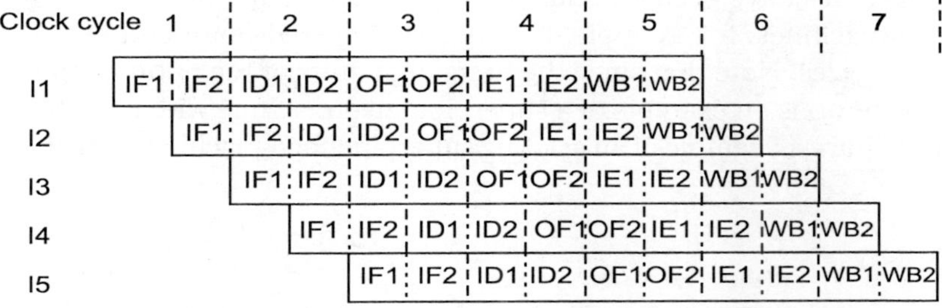

(b) Superpipelined execution

FIGURE 9.14: Super-pipelined execution tends to achieve better performance by dividing each step into sub-steps

It uses an eight-stage instruction pipeline; each stage takes half of the master clock cycle. Thus, execution of each instruction takes four master clock cycles. The instruction fetch and memory access stages are split into two sub-operations. The EX stage computes the operations. In load and store operations, the ALU computes the address during this stage. For the branch instructions, the ALU determines whether the branch is taken (and computes the target address) during the EX stage. The TC stage is used to check the tag field of the cache.

9.7.1 SUPERPIPELINED MACHINES

Superpipelined machines exploit instruction-level parallelism in another way. In a superpipelined machine of degree m, the cycle time is 1/m the cycle time of the base machine. Since a fixed-point add took a whole cycle in the base machine, given the same implementation technology it must take m cycles in the superpipelined machine. The three parallel instructions in Figure 9.1(a) would be issued in three successive cycles, and by the time the third has been issued, there are three operations in progress at the same time. Figure 9.15 shows the execution of instructions by a superpipelined machine.

Formalizing a superpipelined machine according to our definitions:

- Instructions issued per cycle = 1, but the cycle time is 1/m of the base machine
- Simple operation latency measured in cycles = m
- Instruction-level parallelism required to fully utilize = m

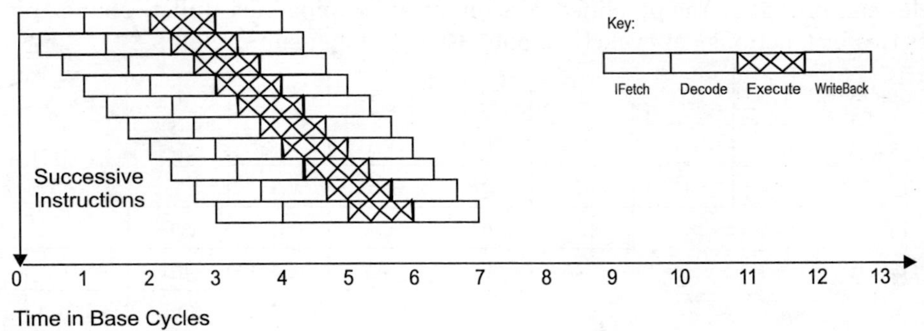

FIGURE 9.15: Superpipelined execution (m = 3)

Superpipelined machines have been around a long time. Seymour Cray has a long history of building superpipelined machines: for example, the latency of a fixed-point add in both the CDC 6600 and the Cray-1 is 3 cycles. Note that since the functional units of the 6600 are not pipelined (two are duplicated), the 6600 is an example of a superpipelined machine with class conflicts. The CDC 7600 is probably the purest example of an existing superpipelined machine since its functional units are pipelined.

9.8 SUPERPIPELINING

Superpipelining simply allows a processor to improve its performance by running the pipeline at a higher clock rate. The higher clock rate is achieved by identifying the pipeline stages that determine the clock cycle (in other words, the most time consuming stages) and decomposing them into smaller stages. Superpipelining is the simplest technique of the three. It does not require additional hardware (such as functional units and fetch units) that a superscalar architecture does. It also does not require the complex controls (no multiple issue control or need to keep track of the instructions issued). Finally, it should be noted that superpipelining does not need the advanced compiler technologies required by the VLIW model.

9.8.1 CONCEPTS AND BENEFITS

The concept of superpipelining is best explained by an illustration. Imagine the pipeline shown in Figure 9.16 (the simple pipeline of the DLX Architecture). In this figure, each stage is drawn with a white box (with the corresponding name inside) while the gray skinny sticks represent the latches between the stages. The length of the double arrows represents the length of time required by each stage for completion of its task. From the Figure 9.16, either the IF (Instruction Fetch) stage or the MEM (Data memory access) stage determine the clock rate because they are the longest time consuming stages of the pipeline (assume for the moment that the IF and MEM stages are nearly twice as long as the other stages).

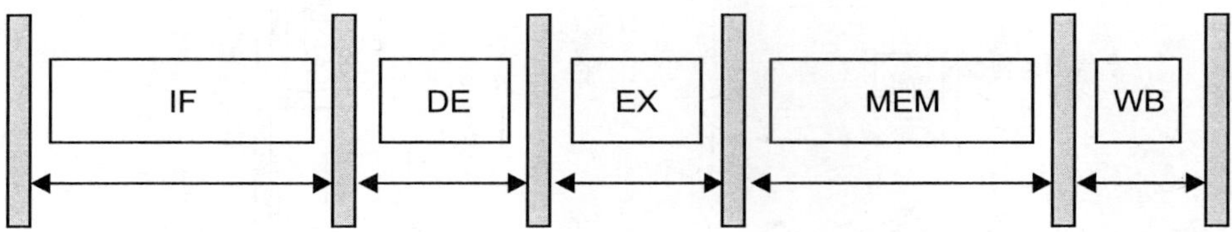

FIGURE 9.16: Pipe Latency Dominated by Memory Accesses

We can increase the performance of the pipeline in Figure 9.15 by dividing the IF and the MEM (Data memory access) stages into two halves (and placing latches in between the new stages as in Figure 9.17). This allows the clock_cycle_time of equation (1) to be reduced (by half). This is the key point about superpipelining. (Organizing a pipeline with stages that have approximately the equal amount of execution time.) This reduced clock rate improves the performance. This is because the clock cycle for the pipeline is determined by the longest stage and as in Figure 9.18, if the pipeline has few long stages and the rest are nominal compared to the longer ones; there are wasted time when executing the shorter stages. Thus, if there are hundreds and thousands of instructions in a program, the aggregated wasted time will be significant (this wasted time is denoted with dotted lines in Figure 9.18-(a)). On the other hand, if the pipeline was superpipelined with discrete design principles as it was in Figure 9.17, most of the stages will be balanced and the wasted time will be minimal as in Figure 9.18-(b).

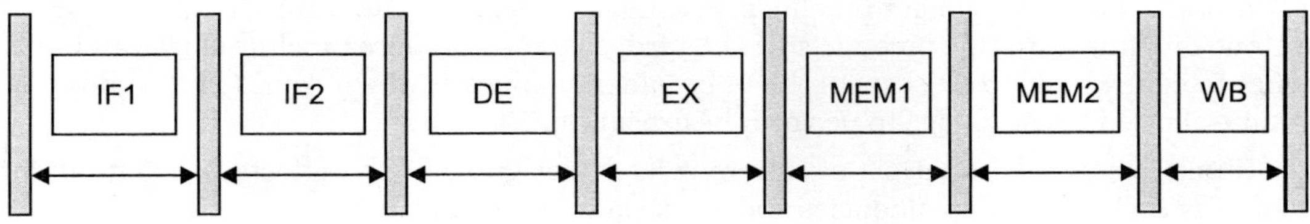

FIGURE 9.17: Pipe Latency Not Dominated by Memory Accesses

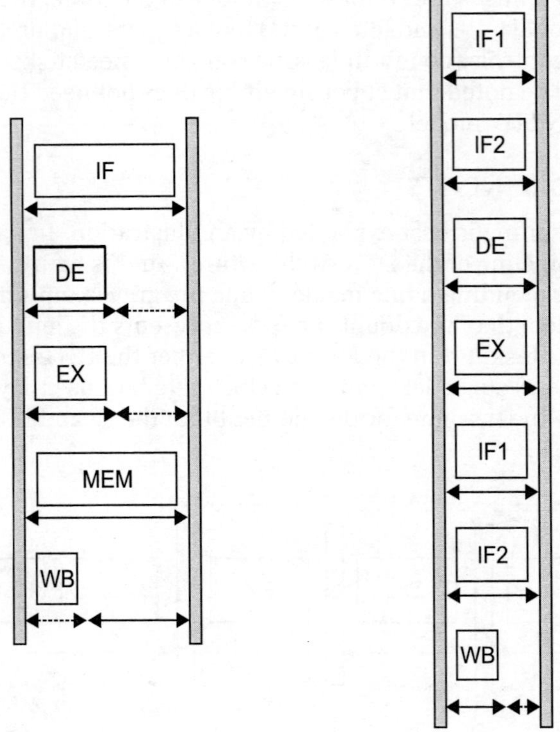

(a) Pipeline with imbalanced stages (b) Pipeline with balanced stages

FIGURE 9.18: Determination of Pipeline Clock Cycle

9.8.2 DESIGN CHALLENGES

At least superficially, superpipelining could appear easy to attain: simply divide the most time consuming stages into small units (and continue this process until all the stages are infinitely small). However, as we know, there is a limit to the efficiency (and potential of such a subdivision). Indeed, it can be observed from Figure 9.19 that a pipeline stage can be meaningfully pipelined only if the stage between two latches executes in more time (A in Figure 9.19) than one latch (B in Figure 9.19). Hwang reports that in general, the time delay of a latch is about one or two order of magnitude shorter compared to the delay of the longest pipeline stage. Otherwise, we just spend more time on additional latches for longer pipelines. Second, after some point, it may simply be infeasible to continue dividing a specific pipeline stage). Third, as there are more pipeline stages and thus more latches to control, the clock skew problem becomes significant which would in turn directly affect the time allotted to each stage to perform its execution.

Kunkel shows the analysis of different latch designs and the effects of latch overhead in pipeline as well as data dependencies and clock skew overhead.

He reports that if pipeline stages get extremely short, it becomes necessary to pad some delay to obtain performance improvement. He also says that eight to ten gate levels per pipeline stage lead to optimal overall performance.

Superpipelining also brings a number of major side effects. As the number of stages is increased, so is the number of forwarding paths (stages) and the delay (stall cycles) caused by branches and loads. The combination of the above two factors has strong adverse affects on the performance of the processor since it increases the CPI (therefore, techniques to improve CPI, such as hardware-based pipeline scheduling, branch prediction, multiple issue, and compiler-assisted parallelism exploiting techniques have been developed). These topics will be discussed in the context of superscalar and VLIW. However, it should be noted that when the above techniques are considered, superpipelining can improve CPI as well.)

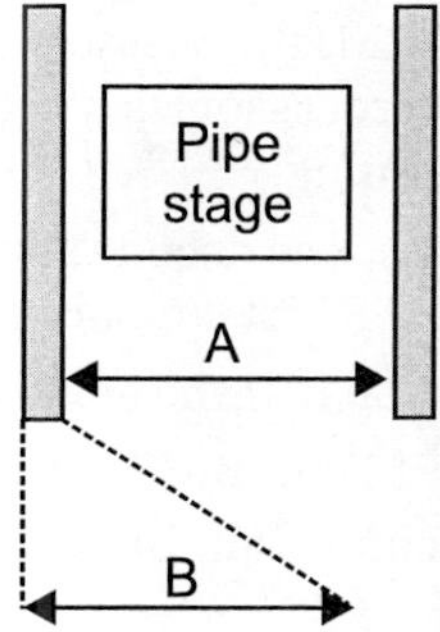

FIGURE 9.19: Pipe Latency Restriction by the Latency of a Latch

9.8.3 EXAMPLE ARCHITECTURES

Three processor architectures can show possible implementations of superpipelining. In those examples, we focus on how superpipelining has helped improve the performance of each architecture and show the design techniques to exploit the benefits of using superpipelining.

We first show an early version of a superpipelined architecture (MIPS R4000) and then move on to more modern and advanced models. The modern processors are not only superpipelined but also based on a combination of superpipelining and superscalar architecture.

1. MIPS R4000: The MIPS R4000 is a superpipelined version of the MIPS R3000 which implemented only a 5-stage pipeline whereas the MIPS R4000 had 8 stages. The MIPS R4000 operates at double the speed (100 MHz) of the MIPS R3000. This was achieved by advances in the process technology and improved circuit design techniques.

One of the main goals of the architects of the MIPS R4000 was to improve the performance over that of MIPS R3000. The choice was between superpipelining and superscalar (and actually VLIW as well). Superpipelining was ultimately selected because:

(1) Less logic is required compared to superscalar,
(2) The control logic is much simpler (no multiple issues and no need to keep track of the instructions issued and of the flow),
(3) (1) and (2) result in a faster cycle time, short design and test time, and
(4) No need for new compiler development.

The MIPS R4000 has a branch delay of three cycles and a load delay of two cycles. The MIPS R3000 had IF (Instruction Fetch), RF (Register Read), ALU (Add, logical, shift computation), DC (Data cache Access and tag check), and WB (Register File write) stages. The eight stages of R4000 are listed below:

- IF - Instruction Fetch, First Half
- IS - Instruction Fetch, Second Half
- RF - Register Fetch
- EX - Execution Instruction Fetch
- DF - Data Fetch, First Half
- DS - Data Fetch, Second Half
- TC - Tag Check
- WB - Write Back

2. The ARM11 Processor: ARM cores are famous for their simple and cost-effective design. However, ARM cores have also evolved and show superpipelining characteristics in their architectures and have architectural features to hide the possible long pipeline stalls.

Amongst of the ARM cores, the ARM11 processor is based on the ARM architecture v6. The ARM11 (specifically, the ARM1136JF-S processor) is a high-performance and low-power processor which is equipped with eight stage pipelining.

The core consists of two fetch stages, one decode stage, one issue stage, and four stages for the integer pipeline. The eight stages of the ARM11 core are depicted in Figure 9.20.

Below is described the function of each of the eight stages:

- Fe1 - Instruction Fetch, First Half, Branch Prediction
- Fe2 - Instruction Fetch, Second Half, Branch Prediction
- De - Instruction Decode
- Iss - Register read and instruction issue
- Sh - Shifter stage
- ALU - Main integer operation calculation
- Sat - Pipeline stage to enable saturation of integer results

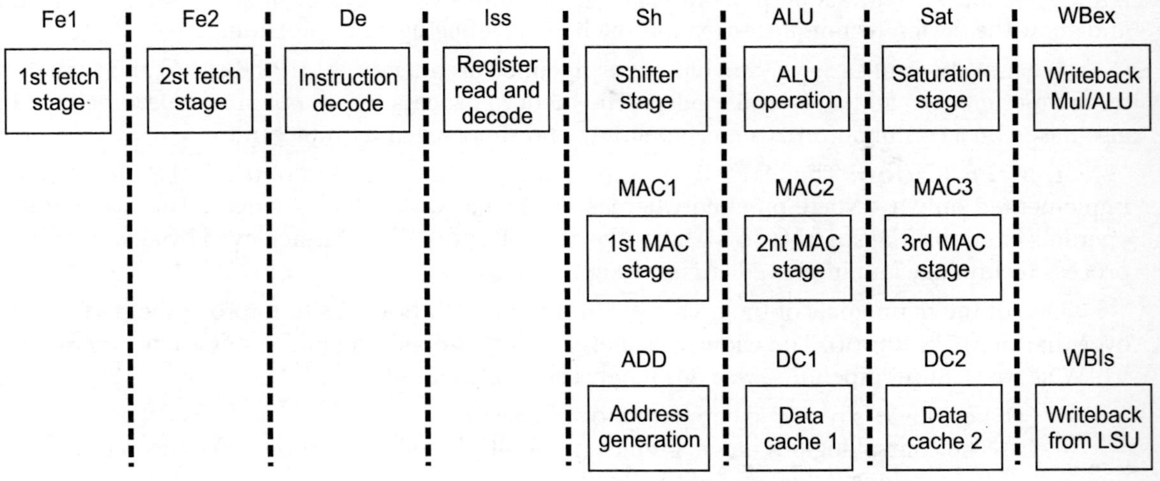

FIGURE 9.20: Eight Pipe Stages of ARM11 Core

- WBex - Write Back of data from the multiply or main execution pipelines
- MAC1 - First stage of the multiply-accumulate pipeline
- MAC2 - Second stage of the multiply-accumulate pipeline
- MAC3 - Third stage of the multiply-accumulate pipeline
- ADD - Address generation stage
- DC1 - First stage of Data Cache access
- DC2 - Second stage of Data Cache access
- WBls - Write back of data from the Load Store Unit

The ARM11 core uses both dynamic (using branch target address cache and branch history) and static (using the direction of the branches) predictions to hide the deep penalty caused by having increased the length of the pipeline. The instruction prefetch unit of the ARM11 core buffers up to three instructions in its FIFO in order:

1) Detect branch instructions before they enter the integer units,
2) Dynamically predict those branches (to be taken), and
3) Provide branch folding of the predicted branches if possible.

By using this prefetch unit, the ARM11 core reduces the cycle time of the branch instructions and improves the performance. Previous ARM processors without the prefetch unit suffered from a one cycle delay when a branch was not taken and three or more cycles for the taken branches (since the target address was known only at the end of the execute stage).

3. The Intel Netburst Microarchitecture: In this section, we discuss the Intel NetBurst micro-architecture (again, we focus on the superpipelining feature of the design). It is a deeply pipelined design (called hyper-pipelined technology) and it can, not only run at high clock rates (up to 10 GHz), but it also allows different part of the processor run at different clock rates. For instance, the most frequently-executed instruction in common cases (such as cache hit) are decoded efficiently and executed with short latencies therefore, improving the overall performance. The pipeline is also equipped with branch penalty hiding techniques such as speculation, buffering,

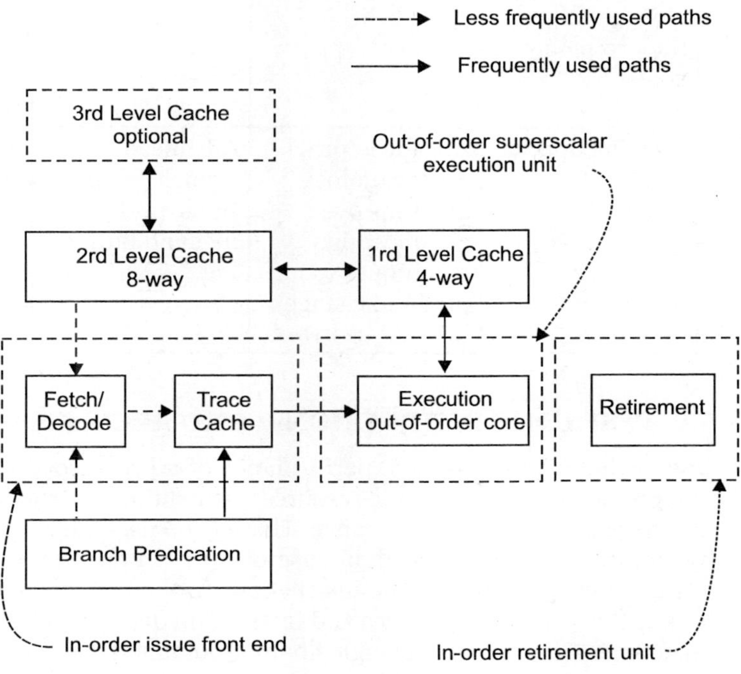

FIGURE 9.21: Intel NetBurst Pipeline Architecture

superscalar, and out-of-order execution. The Pentium 4 processor and the Xeon processor are based on the Intel NetBurst micro-architecture. However, in some modern complex processor designs (such as the NetBurst architecture), the number of cycles through which an instruction must go cannot be specifically determined because of the concept of "out-of-order execution." However, we can categorize the different parts of the pipeline through which an instruction must go. Thus, let us examine how these different parts of the NetBurst pipeline are correlated.

The NetBurst pipeline consists of three main parts and the pipeline architecture of Netburst is depicted in Figure 9.21. Those three main parts are:

- the in-order issue front end
- the out-of-order superscalar execution core
- the in-order retirement unit

In the NetBurst pipeline, the in-order issue front end feeds instructions to the out-or-order execution core. It fetches and decodes instructions. Instructions are decoded and translated into micro-ops (μops). The main responsibility of the front-end is to feed these micro-ops to the execution core in program order. It also utilizes the trace cache to store the program execution flow and it possesses a branch prediction unit. The execution core executes the micro-ops in an out-of-order fashion. The retirement unit retires the micro-ops in program order. The comparison of the features of the pipeline of the example superpipelining architectures are shown in Table 9.3.

TABLE 9.3: Comparison of MIPS R4000, ARM11 Core, and Intel NetBurst

	MIPS R4000	**ARM 11 Core**	**Intel Net Burst**
Number of Superpipeline stages	8	8	3 distinguished groups of pipe stages (Front end, Execution unit and Retirement Unit. Each with different number of pipestages)
Pipeline Special Features	Advanced process technology and improved circuit design techniques (compared to 5 stage MIPS R3000)	Advanced branch predictions, prefetching, and buffering	Hyper-pipelined technology (Pipe stages have different clock frequencies) speculation, buffering, superscalar and out of order execution

9.9 VERY LONG INSTRUCTION WORD ARCHITECTURES

One of the ways to improve performance of a processor is to increase the number of functional units. When we have multiple resources, scheduling instructions to keep these units busy is important to realize higher performance. There is no use in having a large number of functional units if we cannot keep them busy doing useful work. In most processors, instruction scheduling is done at run-time by looking at the instructions in the instruction queue. Instruction scheduling needs to take the available resources and instruction dependencies into account. For example, if we have one integer add unit and a single floating-point add unit, we can schedule one integer add instruction and another floating-point add instruction. Obviously, we cannot schedule two integer add instructions or two floating-point add instructions.

In the code sequence:—

```
add     R1,R2,R3 ;    R1 = R2+R3
sub     R5,R6,R7 ;    R5 = R6-R7
and     R4,R1,R5 ;    R4 = R1 AND R5
```

We cannot schedule these three instructions even if we have add, subtract, and logical AND functional units due to the dependency between them AND and add/sub instructions. We can schedule add and sub in one instruction cycle and the AND instruction can be scheduled in the next cycle. Instruction scheduling is more complex than this case might suggest. For example, we can use out-of-order scheduling as in the following:

```
add     R1,R2,R3 ;    R1 = R2+R3
sub     R5,R6,R7 ;    R5 = R6-R7
and     R4,R1,R5 ;    R4 = R1 AND R5
xor     R9,R9,R9 ;    R9 = R9 XOR R9
```

We can schedule these four instructions in two cycles:

Cycle 1: add, sub, xor

Cycle 2: and

Even though we schedule the xor instruction ahead and, this out-of-order execution does not cause any semantic problems. Such out-of-order execution allows us to exploit instruction level parallelism (ILP) to improve performance. Very long instruction word (VLIW) architectures move the job of instruction scheduling from run-time to compile-time. An advantage of such a scheme is that we can do more comprehensive offline analysis to determine the best scheduling, as we have complete knowledge of the program. This transfer of complexity from hardware to software leads to simpler, more efficient, and easier-to-design processors. At the same time, we get all the flexibility that we normally associate with a software-based approach to handle difficult tasks.

Each VLIW instruction consists of several primitive operations that can be executed in parallel. Each word in a VLIW processor may be tens of bytes wide. For example, the Multi-flow TRACE system uses a 256-bit instruction word. It packs 7 different operations into each word. A more powerful model of the TRACE system uses 1024-bit instructions and packs as many as 28 operations. Branches and memory access (load and store operations) invariably cause performance problems. These processors can minimize the branch prediction errors by executing all branch results and then selecting the result that corresponds to the taken branch.

9.9.1 VLIW MACHINES

VLIW, or very long instruction word, machines typically have instructions hundreds of bits long. Each instruction can specify many operations, so each instruction exploits instruction-level parallelism. Many performance studies have been performed on VLIW machines. The execution of instructions by an ideal VLIW machine is shown in Figure 9.22. Each instruction specifies multiple operations, and this is denoted in the Figure by having multiple crosshatched execution stages in parallel for each instruction.

VLIW machines are much like superscalar machines, with three differences. First, the decoding of VLIW instructions is easier than superscalar instructions. Since the VLIW instructions have a fixed format, the operations specifiable in one instruction do not exceed the resources of the machine. However in the superscalar case, the instruction decode unit must look at a sequence of instructions and base the issue of each instruction on the number of instructions already issued of each instruction class, as well as checking for data dependencies between results and operands of instructions. In effect, the selection of which operations to issue in a given cycle is performed at compile time in a VLIW machine, and at run time in a superscalar machine. Thus the instruction decode logic for the VLIW machine should be much simpler than the superscalar.

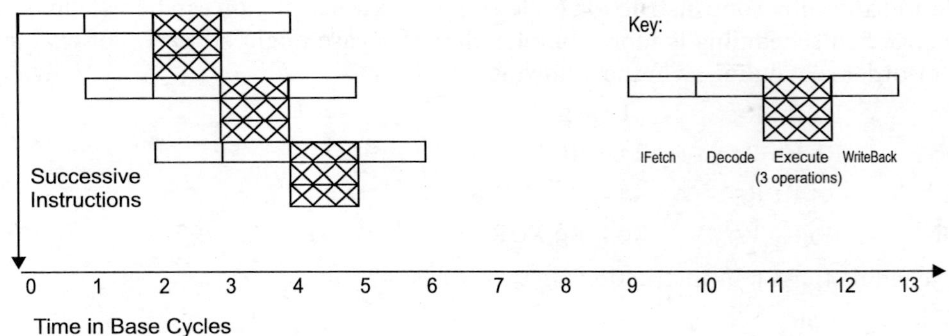

FIGURE 9.22: Execution in a VLIW machine

A second difference is that when the available instruction-level parallelism is less than that exploitable by the VLIW machine, the code density of the superscalar machine will be better. This is because the fixed VLIW format includes bits for unused operations while the superscalar machine only has instruction bits for useful operations.

A third difference is that a superscalar machine could be object-code compatible with a large family of non-parallel machines, but VLIW machines exploiting different amounts of parallelism would require different instruction sets. This is because the VLIW's that are able to exploit more parallelism would require larger instructions.

In spite of these differences, in terms of run time exploitation of instruction-level parallelism, the superscalar and VLIW will have similar characteristics. Because of the close relationship between these two machines, we will only discuss superscalar machines in general and not dwell further on distinctions between VLIW and superscalar machines.

9.9.2 CLASS CONFLICTS

There are two ways to develop a superscalar machine of degree n from a base machine.

1. Duplicate all functional units' n times; including register ports, bypasses, busses, and instruction decode logic.
2. Duplicate only the register ports, bypasses, busses, and instruction decode logic.

Of course these two methods are extreme cases, and one could duplicate some units and not others. But if all the functional units are not duplicated, then potential class conflicts will be created. A class conflict occurs when some instruction is followed by another instruction for the same functional unit. If the busy functional unit has not been duplicated, the superscalar machine must stop issuing instructions and wait until the next cycle to issue the second instruction.

Thus class conflicts can substantially reduce the parallelism exploitable by a superscalar machine. (We will not consider superscalar machines or any other machines that issue instructions out of order. Techniques to reorder instructions at compile time instead of at run time are almost as good, and are dramatically simpler than doing it in hardware.)

9.10 VLIW (VERY LONG INSTRUCTION WORD)

VLIW has been developed to exploit Instruction-Level Parallelism by using a long instruction word which contains multiple fixed numbers of operations. Those operations can be fetched, decoded, issued, and executed at the same time without causing any data or control hazards. Therefore, all operations within a single VLIW instruction must be absolutely independent.

Superscalar architecture was designed to improve the speed of the scalar processor. But it has been realized that it is not easy to implement as we discussed earlier.

Following are some problems faced in the superscalar architecture:

- It is required that extra hardware must be provided for hardware parallelism such as instruction registers, decoder and arithmetic units, etc.
- Scheduling of instructions dynamically to reduce the pipeline delays and to keep all processing units busy is very difficult.

Another alternative to improve the speed of the processor is to exploit a sequence of instructions having no dependency and may require different resources, thus avoiding resource conflicts. The idea is to combine these independent instructions in a compact long word incorporating many operations to be executed simultaneously. That is why; this architecture is called **very long instruction word (VLIW) architecture**. In fact, long instruction words carry the opcodes of different instructions, which are dispatched to different functional units of the processor. In this way, all the operations to be executed simultaneously by the functional units are synchronized in a VLIW instruction. The size of the VLIW instruction word can be in hundreds of bits. VLIW instructions must be formed by compacting small instruction words of conventional program. The job of compaction in VLIW is done by a compiler.

The processor must have the sufficient resources to execute all the operations in VLIW word simultaneously.

For example, one VLIW instruction word is compacted to have load/store operation, floating point addition, floating point multiply, one branch, and one integer arithmetic as shown in Figure 9.23.

Load/Store	FP Add	FP Multiply	Branch	Integer arithmetic

FIGURE 9.23: VLIW instruction word

A VLIW processor to support the above instruction word must have the functional components as shown in Figure 9.24. All the functions units have been incorporated according to the VLIW instruction word. All the units in the processor share one common large register file.

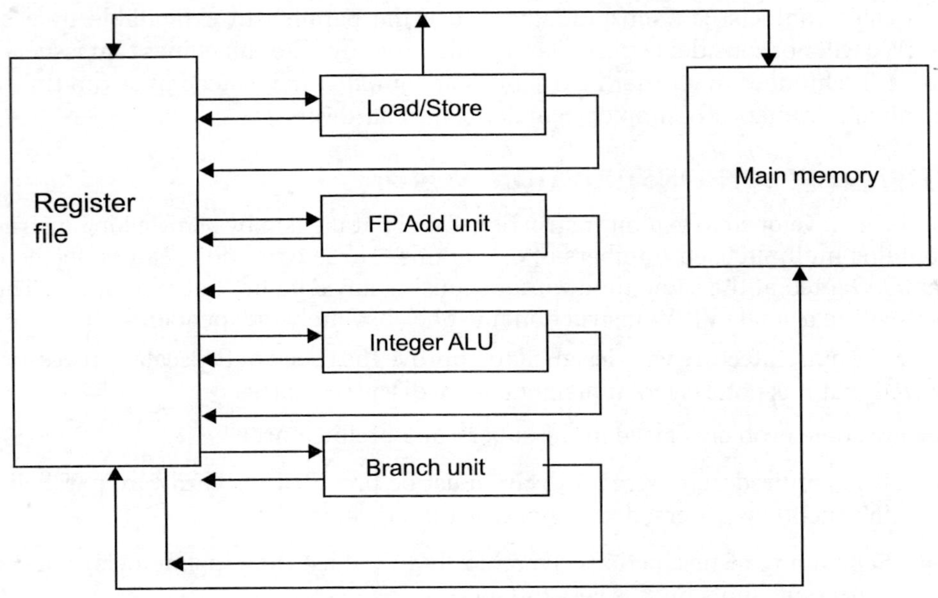

FIGURE 9.24: VLIW Processor

Parallelism in instructions and data movement should be completely specified at compile time. But scheduling of branch instructions at compile time is very difficult. To handle branch instructions, trace scheduling is adopted. Trace scheduling is based on the prediction of branch decisions with some reliability at compile time. The prediction is based on some heuristics, hints given by the programmer or using profiles of some previous program executions.

9.10.1 CONCEPT AND BENEFITS

In VLIW architecture, parallel execution of multiple instructions is made possible by issuing a long instruction word. A single long instruction word is designed to achieve simultaneous execution of a fixed number of multiple operations. Those operations must be independent of each other to avoid possible data hazards. Indeed, several independent instructions are integrated inside a very long instruction word.

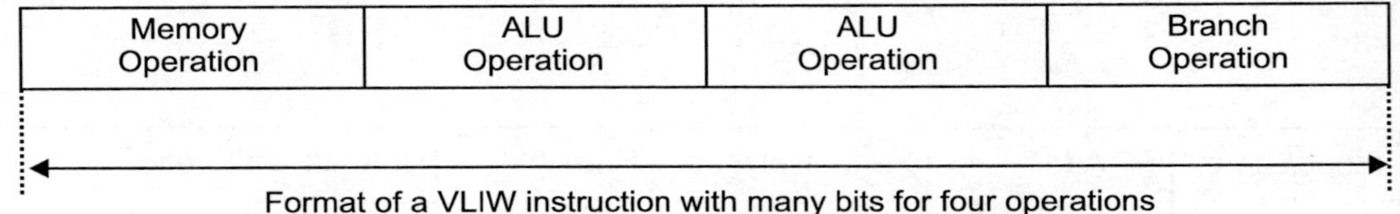

FIGURE 9.25: An example of VLIW instructions

The VLIW instruction is wide enough to allow the concurrent operation of multiple functional units. Its size normally ranges from 64 to 128 bits, and even up to 1024 bits. Figure 9.25 shows a typical format of VLIW instructions. Many bits on the long instruction enable a single instruction word to sufficiently control the several functional units directly and independently in every cycle.

Since it is the long instruction word which delivers the potential ILP to the hardware, a VLIW processor can be designed with a simpler hardware compared to an equivalent superscalar processor: it need not include the special units the run-time dependency check and instruction scheduling. The block diagram of a simple VLIW processor is shown in Figure 9.26.

VLIW architecture is, by essence, meant to activate multiple functional units at the same time. Therefore, the VLIW compiler should uncover independent operations to be executed in parallel. This means that the compiler must perform a detailed analysis on the data-flow and control-flow at compile time (which is when the potential ILP is fixed). When the compiler cannot find enough instructions to fill in the width of the long instruction, it simply inserts a NOP.

When the interaction between the compiler and the hardware for instruction scheduling is considered, the fundamental differences between the VLIW and the superscalar design approaches can be explained as shown in Figure 9.27: in superscalar architectures, most of the scheduling is handled by hardware at run-time. However, in VLIW architecture, the scheduling is decided by the compiler in a static way. Indeed, an intelligent compiler is the key component which ultimately decides the performance of VLIW architecture. Since the ILP within a basic block is quite limited, the VLIW architecture needs to examine more instructions to find more ILP. It is possibly achieved by looking at the instruction stream beyond the control-flow limits. For that purpose, several techniques such as loop unrolling and trace scheduling have been introduced in the VLIW design techniques. Those techniques will be explained shortly.

Compared to the dynamic scheduling of superscalar architectures, static scheduling does not require a complex scheduling logic. In addition, VLIW can uncover more parallelism by searching over a wider range of static code. Also, it is quite beneficial to know the source code structure to find parallelism in the VLIW architecture. However, several limitations such as long compilation time, not enough compatibility, and code explosion make VLIW architectures difficult to use in practice. In conclusion, we can say that VLIW architectures do not have the hardware complexity of current superscalar architectures. However, they impose a much heavier burden on the compiler than superscalar architectures. This means that there exists a clear trade-off between the two approaches in the current high-performance microprocessor design. In the following part, more detailed techniques for the VLIW architecture are explained.

1. Loop Unrolling: Loop Unrolling is one basic technique to find more Instruction Level Parallelism out of the sequential instruction stream. It is based on the idea of expanding the multiple instances of a simple loop-body. Then, a wider range of instructions is at our disposal since we can have more instructions from the multiple iterations. It is most beneficial to unroll loops when the loop body does not include any complex control flow.

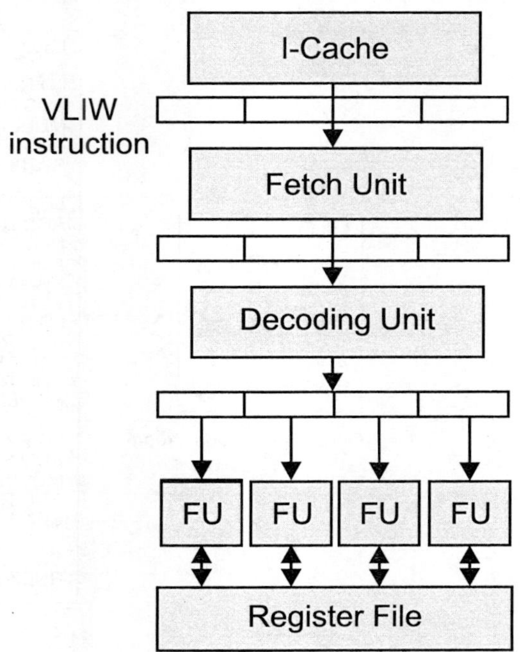

FIGURE 9.26: VLIW hardware

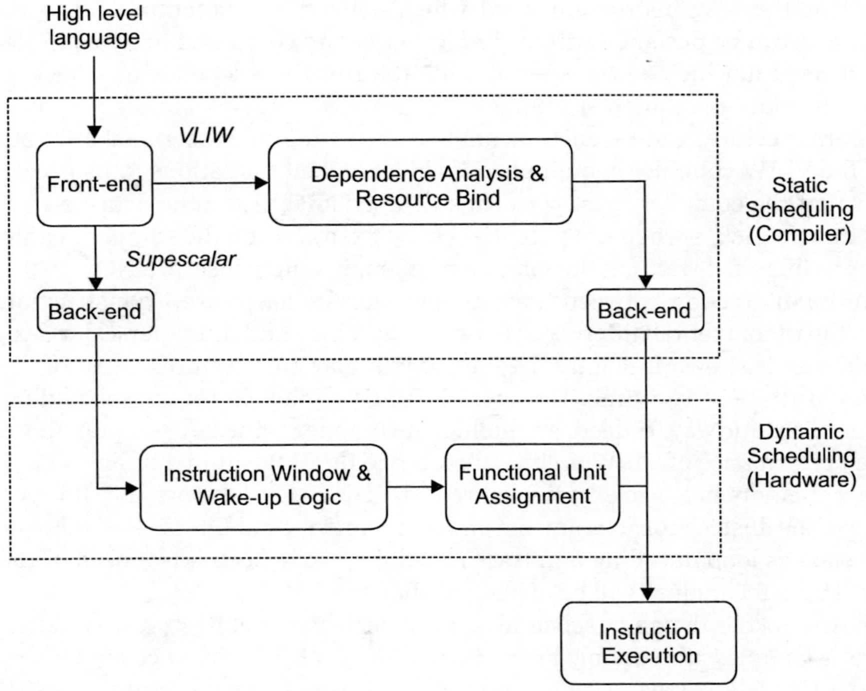

FIGURE 9.27: Instruction Scheduling in the Superscalar and VLIW architectures

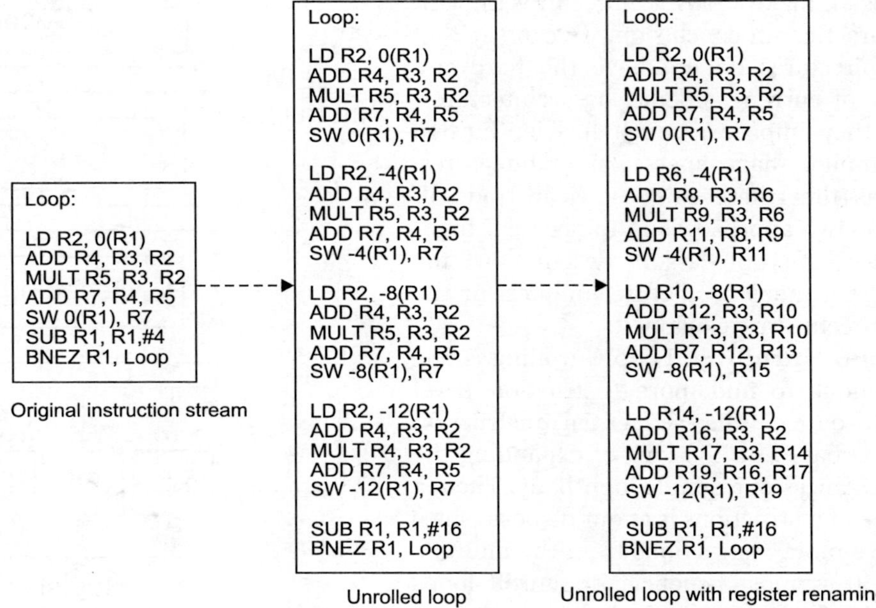

FIGURE 9.28: An example of loop unrolling

As seen in Figure 9.28, the original loop body has a sequence of seven instructions. Therefore, without loop unrolling, the compiler can only pick from a pool of seven instructions to uncover parallelism (assuming there is no branch prediction). Loop unrolling will maximize the size of instruction window across the control flow limits by expanding the loop body. The loop body can be expanded by unrolling the several loop iterations. For example, in Figure 9.28, the next four iterations of the loop can be integrated as the single loop of the second diagram. Now, the basic block has four times many instructions than before. Therefore, more instructions can be examined for possible parallel execution.

Although we can have more instructions after loop unrolling, there are name dependencies between iterations. To reduce the false dependencies between instructions (since they may use the same register names), register renaming is imperatively before the final instruction stream can be obtained. However, some instructions might have loop-carried dependencies, which occur that later iterations of the loop body depend on the computation results of the previous iteration. Therefore, those dependencies must be carefully respected during register renaming.

2. Software Pipelining: Software pipelining is a technique which enables the later iterations of a loop to start before the previous iterations have finished the loop. Therefore, the later iterations of a loop can be executed, pipelined with the previous iterations. Of course, the loop unrolling technique also achieves the same scheduling as software pipelining, which is merely a subset of loop unrolling. However, in loop unrolling, a simple form of instruction pool is obtained from the multiple instances of the same loop body. The compiler can then schedule each of the instructions in turn. On the contrary, in software pipelining, the parallelism is obtained between the different parts of the same loop body by executing later iterations a couple of clock cycles later.

The main advantage of software pipelining over a simple loop unrolling technique is the following; loop unrolling requires overhead for each instance of an unrolled loop, whereas software pipelining only imposes start-up and wind-down overhead. For example, assume in a simple example that there are 100 iterations and that the loop body contains 4 instructions for the normal computation and 2 instructions for its control flow. If we unroll the loop over 4 iterations, those results in 16+2 instructions for an extended loop (the loop which includes 4 iterations in this example). Just assume that four iterations of an instruction can be executed in parallel, and the parallel execution of four instructions takes one clock cycle. Therefore, in the loop unrolling case, one unrolled loop execution requires 4 cycles for the computation and 2 cycles for the control instructions. Since the unrolled loop needs to be iterated 25 times, the total required cycle time is 150 cycles. However, we first can eliminate the control flow instructions in the software pipelining. Then, the first iteration starts alone and the second iteration starts when the second instruction of the first iteration starts. Both operations can be executed in parallel. Since execution can support up to four instructions in parallel, the fifth iteration can start just after the first iteration finishes (recall that one loop execution includes the execution of four instructions). In this particular case, the 100th iteration starts at 100 cycles and it requires 4 more clock cycles to finish. Therefore, 104 cycles are required for the overall execution.

Software pipelining sometimes provides an easier approach to parallelize a loop with loop-carried dependencies. In the previous example, there are no loop-carried dependencies. Therefore, each iteration of the original loop can be executed in parallel. However, if there existed loop-carried dependencies, those would have to be carefully taken into account. Figure 9.29 shows one example of software pipelining which includes a loop carried dependency; the second instruction

Add R4, R5, R2 requires the updated value of R5 in the previous loop iteration. Therefore, simple loop unrolling should consider this dependency to schedule the instruction. As seen in the Figure 9.29, the software pipelined code can yield some added ILP. As seen in the example, software pipelining can be an easier approach to schedule parallel execution of a loop body with loop-carried dependencies; however, if the distance between the instructions for loop-carried dependencies is too high, software pipelining does not provide much of a benefit: the later iteration cannot be executed until the previous iteration finishes and provides the results.

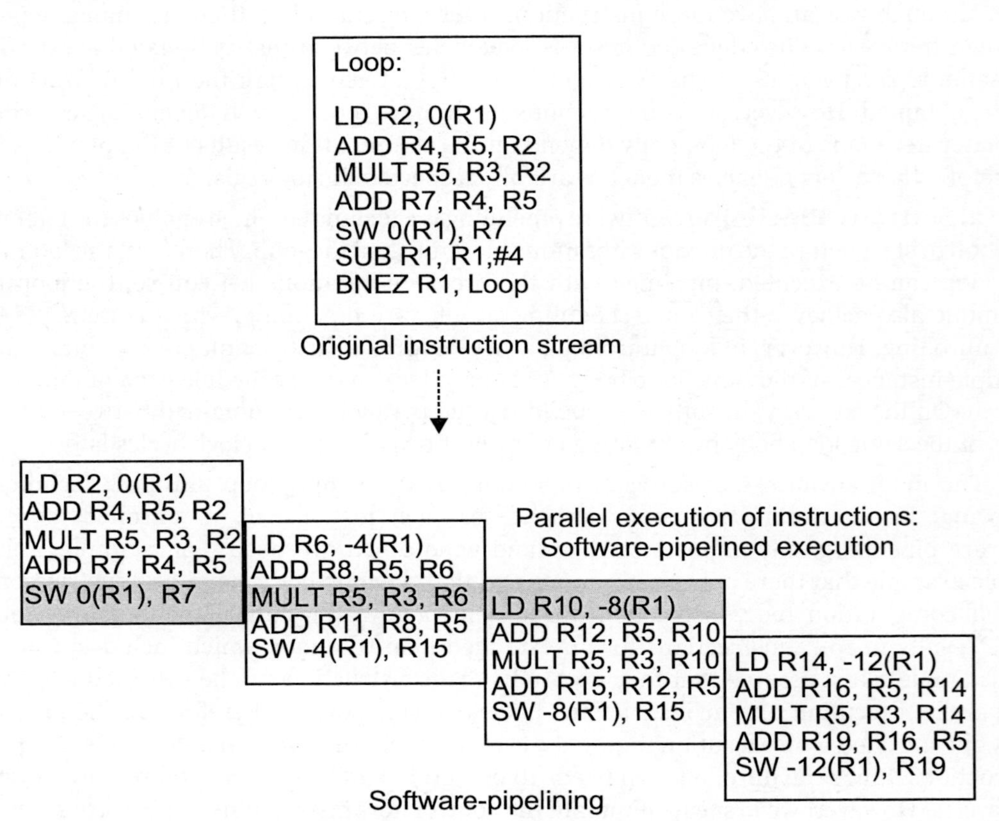

FIGURE 9.29: An example of software pipelining

3. Trace Scheduling: Loop unrolling and software pipelining is quite beneficial to extend the range of the instruction window for a simple loop body. However, when the loop contains very complex control flow, it cannot be easily unrolled. The Trace Scheduling technique has been developed to find more ILP across the basic block boundary even with a complex control flow. Trace is considered a large extended basic block considering the control path which is frequently taken. This technique considers the branch instructions as jump instructions inside a trace, and it schedules the instructions inside the trace as a large basic block.

However, to guarantee the correct computation of the other path execution, Trace Scheduling requires some compensating code to be inserted for the case when the program flows out of the trace. Trace scheduling depends on the frequent occurrence of the Trace path. Since the VLIW compiler decides traces in a static way, the traces may not be sufficiently well predicted. Therefore, if the predicted path execution does not happen frequently, the compensation code overhead can be higher than the advantage given by trace scheduling.

The above three techniques can be used to increase the amount of parallelism by extending the instruction pool. All three approaches strongly depend on an appropriate and accurate control flow prediction; using them is beneficial only when the behavior of branches is predictable by the compiler. To cope more aggressively with dynamic events inside the control flow, ISA supported techniques such as conditional instructions and predication have been introduced in addition to the traditional VLIW concept.

9.10.2 DESIGN CHALLENGES

The largest challenge for VLIW architecture is the code explosion problem. Code explosion is caused by the need for the compiler to insert NOPs in the object code when the available parallelism of the code is not sufficient to fill each VLIW instruction. These NOPs may waste considerable amount of bits in the VLIW code.

Also, a large number of registers are required in the VLIW architecture due to transformations such as loop unrolling, register renaming, and trace scheduling. In addition, a large data transport capability between functional units and register file is required. Since the VLIW instructions are, by definition, very long, they will require a high bandwidth between the instruction cache and the fetch unit. Although static scheduling has several advantages over dynamic scheduling, pure VLIW has not enjoyed a successful commercial implementation. The main weakness of the architectures has to do with backward compatibility; conventional compiler or binary must be considerably modified in the VLIW architectures. In fact, superscalar architectures have a huge advantage due to the compatibility which is one reason why they have been chosen by almost all processor vendors.

Indeed, the VLIW instruction should be adjusted to the hardware configuration. Therefore, the compiler should be notified the hardware characteristic in advance. It consequently means that there is not even compatibility between different VLIW processors.

9.10.3 EXAMPLE ARCHITECTURES

Following are the examples of VLIW architectures:

1. The IA-64 ISA and Itanium Processor: The Intel Itanium is the first commercial processor which implements the IA-64 ISA. The IA-64 ISA is a 64-bit instruction set architecture implementing EPIC (Explicitly Parallel Instruction Computing), a design which is a joint project of Intel and HP. Although the Itanium processor is not a pure VLIW processor, many features of Itanium resemble that of VLIW architecture. First of all, a 128-bit wide instruction bundle is used for the long instruction word. Indeed, a single bundle holds three instructions. Each base instruction requires 41-bit wide, and 123 bits on a bundle are used for those three instruction. The remaining 5 bits can be used as the template. Those template bits are used to deliver the execution information of the bundle. The template bits are very useful to avoid empty operations (NOPs), and allow higher flexibility in the exploitation of parallelism. Figure 9.30 shows the format of a three-instruction bundle.

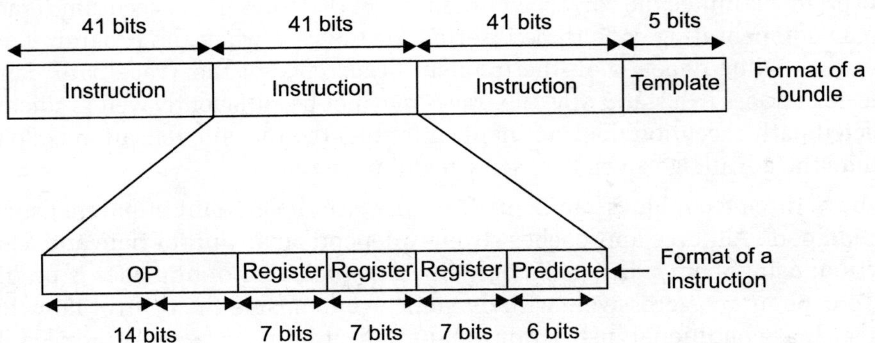

FIGURE 9.30: Format of an instruction bundle

The IA-64 provides 128 65-bit general registers with 65 bits for each register and 128 82-bit floating-point registers. It also has 64 1-bit registers designed to indicate the result of conditional expression instructions. In addition, eight 64-bit branch registers are implemented for function call linkage and return. This ISA also provides space for up to 128 64-bit special-purpose application registers. Two distinct features of the IA-64 are predication and load speculation. Originally, the predication requires the instructions for predicated execution. For example, the instruction itself detects a conditional variable to decide whether the instruction can be executed or not. In other words, the instruction is executed only when its predication is true. However, in the IA-64 architecture, all the branch paths are eagerly executed and the instructions inside those paths are committed only when the predication is true. Under the predication, the execution of each instruction needs to be accompanied by a dedicated predicate register among 64 predicated registers. Then, the instructions can only be committed when the specified predicate register is confirmed as true.

Figure 9.31 shows a simple example of the predicated execution. The CMPEQ instruction sets the value of the predication registers based on the comparing operation. Then, the later predicated instructions are committed according to the contents of the dedicated predication registers. The predication in IA-64 means both paths of a branch instruction must execute in parallel. After finding the branch result, only the

Source Code

```
if (a = b)
a = 0;
else
b = 0;
```

Normal Code without Predication

```
beq r1, r2, L1
J   L2
L1:
move r1, 0
J   L3
L2:
move r2, 0
L3:
```

Predicated Code

```
CMPEQ r1, r2, p1/p2    // check (a == b) sets p1, p2
[p1] MOV r1, 0         // if (p1 == true) r1 = 0
[p2] MOV r2, 0         // if (p2 == true) r2 = 0
```

FIGURE 9.31: Predication Example

correct path execution is committed and can affect the program execution. Indeed, it is very similar to the multi-path execution or eager execution.

The other technique called speculative load execution of the IA-64 enables to move load instructions across the control flow boundary. Speculative loading, indeed, has been proposed to reduce the access latencies of load instructions. For speculative loading, a load instruction is converted into two other instructions: the speculative load instruction which is moved before a branch instruction and the checking instruction which stays in the original location to check the proper execution of the program flow. An example of the speculative load execution is shown in Figure 9.32. The lw.s instruction is a speculative load instruction which is moved across a control flow boundary, and the chk.s instruction is the checking instruction in the original location. The checking instruction confirms the validity of the speculative execution.

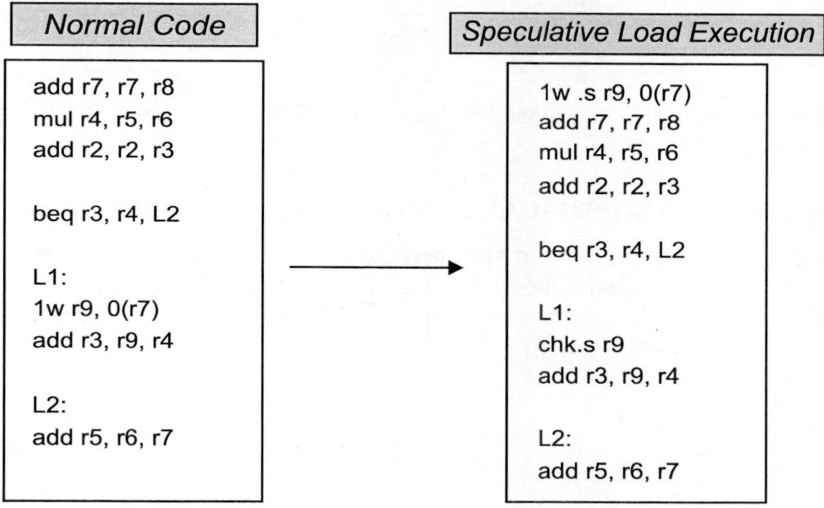

FIGURE 9.32: Speculative Load Execution

The first IA-64 processor, Itanium, is implemented with a six-wide and 10-stage pipeline. It is designed to operate at a frequency of 800 MHz. It has four integer units, four multimedia units, two load/store units, three branch units, two extended-precision floating-point units, and two additional single-precision floating-point units. Two bundles are fetched in every clock cycle. Therefore, the machine can fetch six instructions at each clock cycle.

9.10.4 ADVANTAGES AND PROBLEMS WITH VLIW PROCESSORS

Following are the Advantages with VLIW processors:

- Simpler hardware:
  - the number of FUs can be increased without needing additional sophisticated hardware to detect parallelism, like in superscalars.
  - Power consumption can be reduced.

- Good compilers can detect parallelism based on global analysis of the whole program (no window of execution problem).

Following are the Problems with VLIW processors:

- Large number of registers needed in order to keep all FUs active (to store operands and results).
- Large data transport capacity is needed between FUs and the register file and between register files and memory.
- High bandwidth between instruction cache and fetch unit.

Example: one instruction with 7 operations, each 24 bits →168 bits/instruction.

- Large code size, partially because unused operations →wasted bits in instruction word.
- Incomputability of binary code

For example:

If for a new version of the processor additional FUs are introduced →the number of operations possible to execute in parallel is increased →the instruction word changes →old binary code cannot be run on this processor.

9.11 SUPERPIPELINED SUPERSCALAR MACHINES

Since the number of instructions issued per cycle and the cycle time are theoretically orthogonal, we could have a superpipelined superscalar machine. A superpipelined superscalar machine of degree (m, n) has a cycle time 1/m that of the base machine, and it can execute n instructions every cycle. This is illustrated in Figure 9.33.

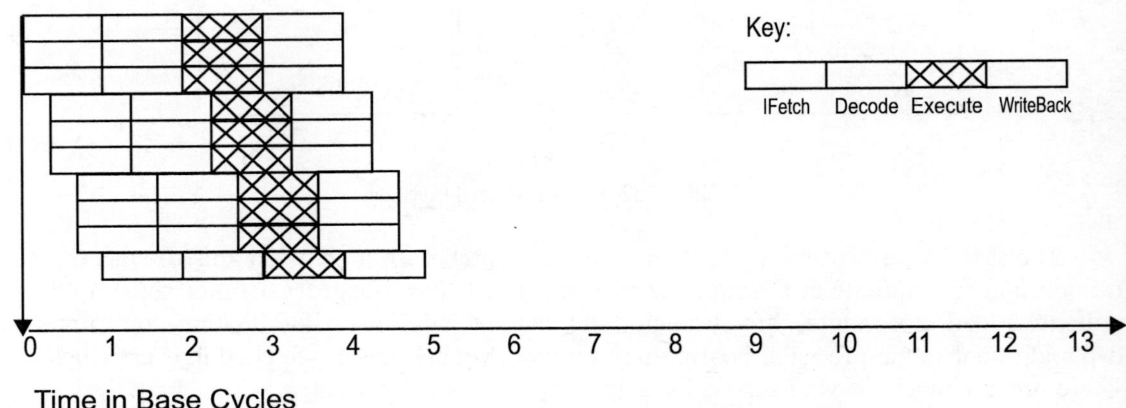

FIGURE 9.33: A Superpipelined Superscalar (n = 3, m = 3)

Formalizing a superpipelined superscalar machine according to our definitions:

- Instructions issued per cycle = n, and the cycle time is 1/m that of the base machine
- Simple operation latency measured in cycles = m

Instruction-level parallelism required to fully utilize = n*m.

QUESTIONS

1. Explain the concept of machine taxonomy?
2. Explain the execution of base machine?
3. What do you mean by underpipelined machine?
4. Explain the comparison between Superpipelining, Superscalar, and VLIW?
5. What do you mean by superscalar?
6. What are the limitations of parallel execution?
7. Explain the concept of superscalar processors?
8. What are superscalar machines?
9. Explain the architecture of superscalar processor?
10. Explain the basic model of superscalar pipeline?
11. What are the design challenges of superscalar machines?
12. Explain the examples of superscalar machines?
13. What are super-pipelined processors?
14. Explain the concept of superpipelined machines?
15. Explain the concept of superpipelining in detail?
16. Explain the design challenges of superpipelined machines?
17. Explain the examples of superpipelined machines?
18. Explain the architecture of VLIW machine?
19. Explain the concept of VLIW machines?
20. Explain the design challenges of VLIW machines?
21. Explain the examples of VLIW machines?
22. Explain the advantages and problems with VLIW processors?
23. Explain the concept of superpipelined superscalar machines?

CHAPTER 10

DESIGN STRUCTURES AND ALGORITHMS FOR ARRAY PROCESSORS

10.1 INTRODUCTION

A synchronous array of parallel processors is called an array processor which consists of multiple processing elements (PE) under supervision of one control unit (CU). Some array processor may use 2 routing register, one for input and the other for output. Each PE_i is either active or in the inactive mode during each instruction cycle. If a PE_i is active, it executes the instruction broadcast to it by the CU. If a PE_i is inactive, it will not execute the broadcast instruction. The masking schemes are used to specify the status flag of PE_i. There are fundamental decisions in determining the appropriate structure of an interconnection network for an SIMD machine. They are made between Operation Modes, Control Strategies, Switching methodologies, Network Topologies.

10.2 ARRAY PROCESSOR

An array processor is a processor that performs computations on large arrays of data. It may be composed of a group of special processors designed to calculate math procedures at very high speeds, often under the control for another central processor. Some computers use array processors to speed up video operations or for fast floating-point math operations. The term is used to refer to two different types of processors, an *attached array processor* and a *SIMD array Processor*. A processor capable of executing instructions in which the operands may be arrays rather than data elements. An array processor is a processor that performs computations on large arrays of data. There are two different types of processors; a) an attached array processor b) SIMD array processor.

Array processor, also called a vector processor, is a microprocessor or computer that is capable of performing simultaneous computations on elements of an array of data in some number of dimensions. Common uses of such processor include analysis of fluid dynamics and rotation of 3D objects as well as data retrieval, in which elements in a database are scanned simultaneously that executes one instruction at a time but on an array or table of data at the same time rather than on single data elements.

10.2.1 ATTACHED ARRAY PROCESSOR

An *attached array processor* is an auxiliary processor attached to a general-purpose computer, designed as a peripheral for a conventional host computer. The array processor can be programmed by the user to accommodate a variety of complex arithmetic problems. The host computer is a general-purpose commercial computer and the attached processor is a back-end machine driven by the host computer. The array processor is connected through an input output controller to the computer and the computer treats it like an external interface. The data for the attached processor are transferred from main memory to a local memory through a high-speed bus. The general-purpose computer without the attached processor serves the users that need conventional data processing.

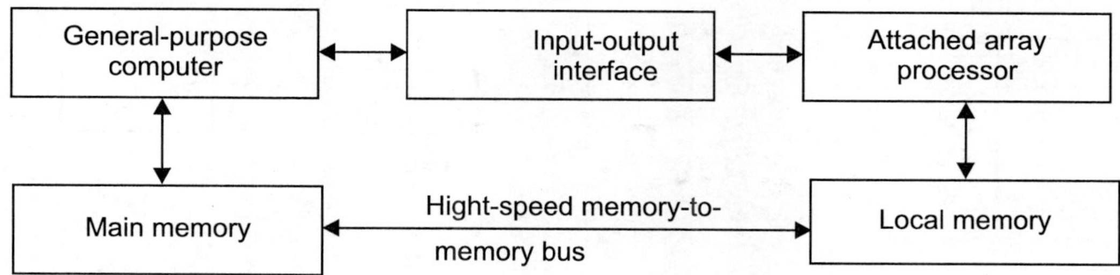

FIGURE 10.1: Attached Array Processor with Host Computer

10.2.2 SIMD ARRAY PROCESSOR

A synchronous array of parallel processors is called an array processor which consists of multiple processing elements (PE) under supervision of one control unit (CU). An array processor can handle single instruction multiple data streams (SIMD). It is also known as SIMD computers.

SIMD appears in two basic architectural organizations:

- Array Processors using random access memory
- Associative Processors

Depending on whether there is one or several of these streams we have four classes of computers.

- Single Instruction Stream, Single Data Stream: SISD
- Multiple Instruction Stream, Single Data Stream: MISD
- Single Instruction Stream, Multiple Data Stream: SIMD
- Multiple Instruction Stream, Multiple Data Stream: MIMD

An SIMD *array processor* is a processor that has a single-instruction multiple-data organization. It manipulates vector instructions by means of multiple functional units responding to a common instruction. It contains a set of identical processing elements (PEs), each having a local memory M. Each processor element includes an ALU, a floating-point arithmetic unit, and working registers. The master control unit controls the operations in the processor elements. The main memory is used for storage of the program. The function of the master control unit is to decode the instructions and determine how the instruction is to be executed. Scalar and program control instructions are directly executed within the master control unit. Vector instructions are broadcast to all PEs simultaneously. Each PE uses operands stored in its local memory. Vector operands are distributed to the local memories prior to the parallel execution of the instruction.

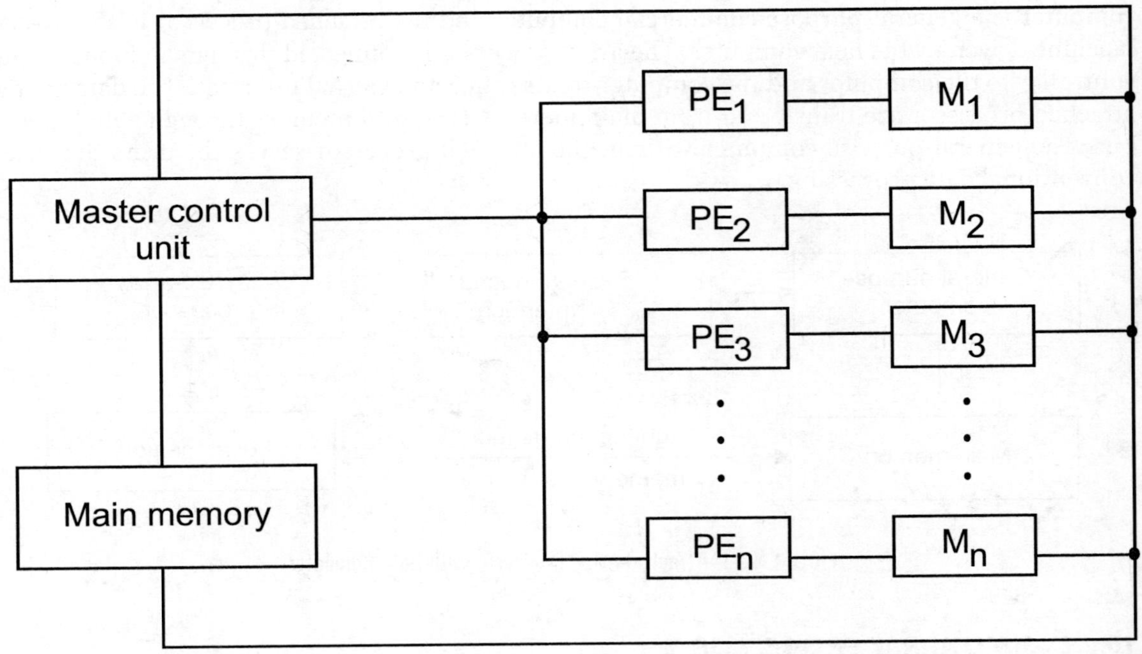

FIGURE 10.2: SIMD array processor organizations

Consider, for example, the vector addition $C = A + B$. The master control unit first stores the ith components a_i and b_i of A and B in local memory M_i for $i = 1, 2, 3, \ldots, n$. It then broadcasts the floating-point add instruction $c_i = a_i + b_i$ to all PEs, causing the addition to take place simultaneously. The components of c_i are stored in fixed locations in each local memory. This produces the desired vector sum in one add cycle. To control the status of each PE during the execution of vector instructions, Each PE has a flag that is set when the PE is active and reset when the PE is inactive.

10.3 SIMD ARCHITECTURE

The SIMD model of parallel computing consists of two parts: a front-end computer of the usual von Neumann style, and a processor array as shown in Figure 10.3. The processor array is a set of identical synchronized processing elements capable of simultaneously performing the same operation on different data. Each processor in the array has a small amount of local memory where the distributed data resides while it is being processed in parallel. The processor array is connected to the memory bus of the front end so that the front end can randomly access the local processor memories as if it were another memory. Thus, the front end can issue special commands that cause parts of the memory to be operated on simultaneously or cause data to move around in the memory. A program can be developed and executed on the front end using a traditional serial programming language. The application program is executed by the front end in the usual serial way, but issues commands to the processor array to carry out SIMD operations in parallel.

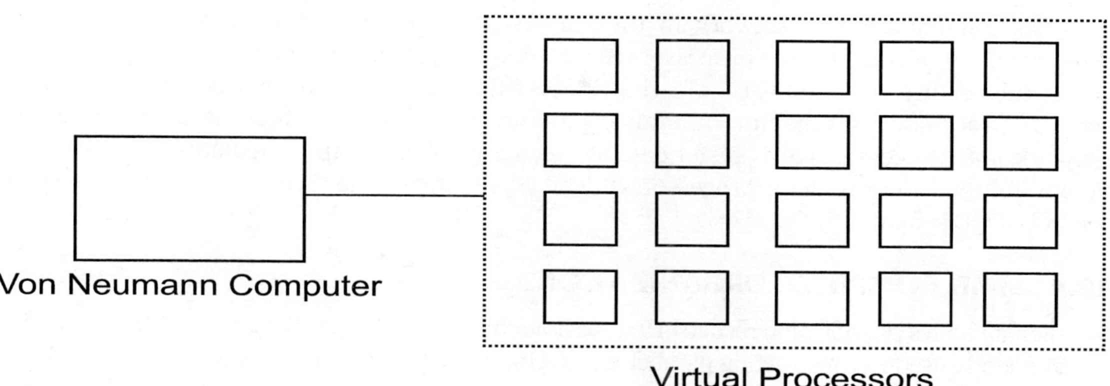

FIGURE 10.3: SIMD architecture model

The similarity between serial and data parallel programming is one of the strong points of data parallelism. Synchronization is made irrelevant by the lock–step synchronization of the processors. Processors either do nothing or exactly the same operations at the same time. In SIMD architecture, parallelism is exploited by applying simultaneous operations across large sets of data. This paradigm is most useful for solving problems that have lots of data that need to be updated on a wholesale basis. It is especially powerful in many regular numerical calculations.

There are two main configurations that have been used in SIMD machines (see Figure 10.4). In the first scheme, each processor has its own local memory. Processors can communicate with each other through the interconnection network. If the interconnection network does not provide direct connection between a given pair of processors, then this pair can exchange data via an intermediate processor. The ILLIAC IV used such an interconnection scheme.

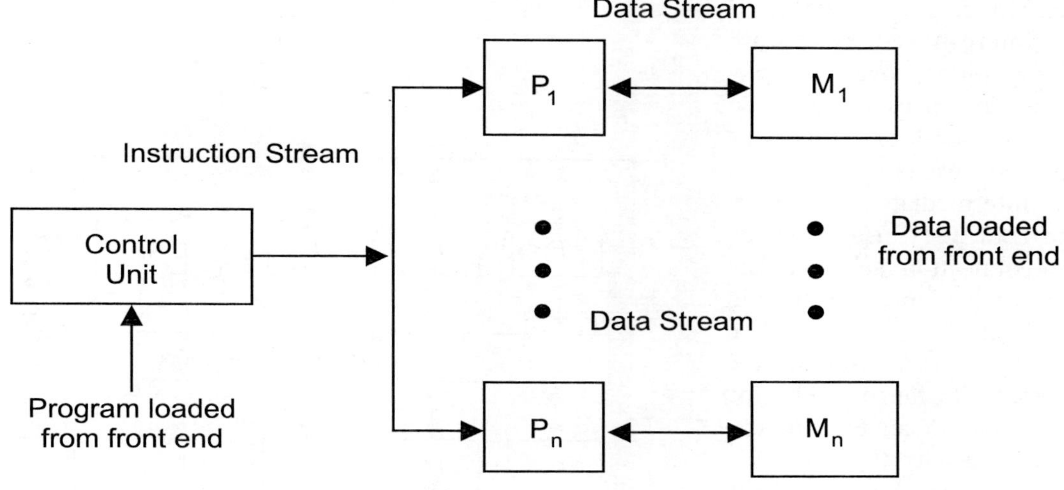

FIGURE 10.4: SIMD architecture

The interconnection network in the ILLIAC IV allowed each processor to communicate directly with four neighboring processors in an 8 X 8 matrix pattern such that the ith processor can communicate directly with the $(i - 1)^{th}$, $(i + 1)^{th}$, $(i - 8)^{th}$, and $(i + 8)^{th}$ processors. In the second SIMD scheme, processors and memory modules communicate with each other via the interconnection network. Two processors can transfer data between each other via intermediate memory module(s) or possibly via intermediate processor(s). The BSP (Burroughs' Scientific Processor) used the second SIMD scheme.

10.4 SIMD COMPUTER ORGANIZATIONS

Recall that Flynn's classification results in four basic architectures. Among those, the SIMD and the MIMD are frequently used in constructing parallel architectures. In this section, we will provide basic information on the SIMD paradigm. It is important at the outset to indicate that SIMD are mostly designed to exploit the inherent parallelism encountered in matrix (array) operations, which are required in applications such as image processing. Famous real-life machines that have been commercially constructed include the ILLIAC-IV (1972), the STARAN (1974), and the MPP (1982).

Two main SIMD configurations have been used in real-life machines. These are shown in Figure 10.5. In the first scheme, each processor has its own local memory. Processors can communicate with each other through the interconnection network. If the interconnection network does not provide direct connection between a given pair of processors, then this pair can exchange data via an intermediate processor. The ILLIAC-IV used such an interconnection scheme. The interconnection network in the ILLIAC-IV allowed each processor to communicate directly with four neighboring processors in an 8X8 matrix pattern such that the ith processor can communicate directly with the $(i-1)^{th}$, $(i+1)^{th}$, $(i-8)^{th}$, and $(i+8)^{th}$ processors.

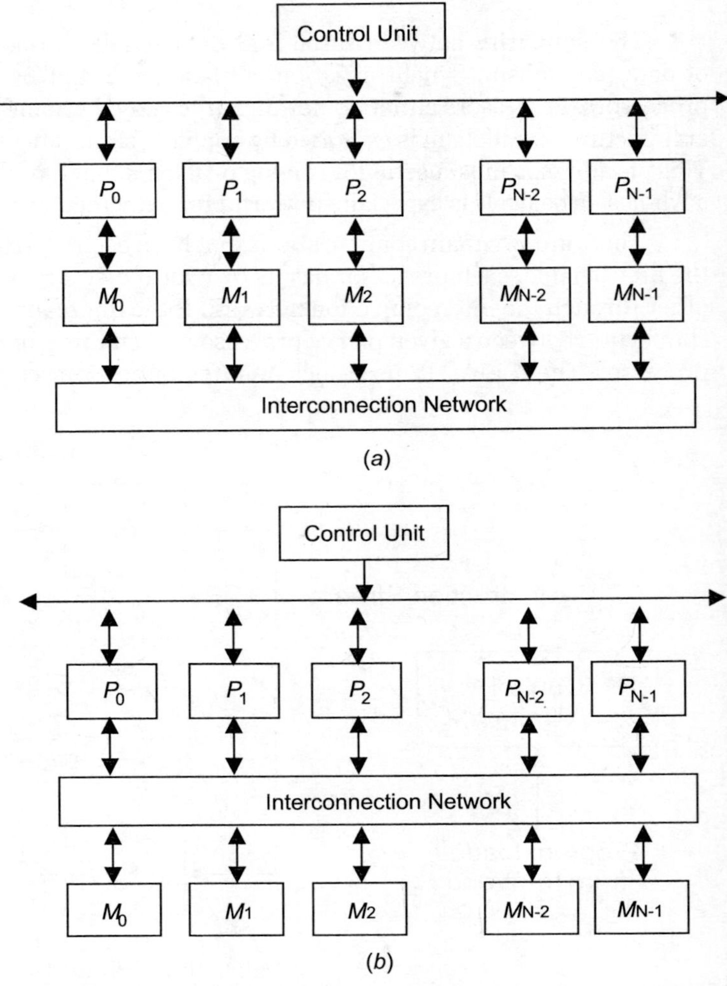

FIGURE 10.5: Two SIMD schemes. (a) SIMD scheme 1, (b) SIMD scheme 2

In the second SIMD scheme, processors and memory modules communicate with each other via the interconnection network. Two processors can transfer data between each other via intermediate memory module(s) or possibly via intermediate processor(s). Assume, for example, that processor i is connected to memory modules (i - 1), i, and (i + 1). In this case, processor 1 can communicate with processor 5 via memory modules 2, 3, and 4 as intermediaries. The BSP (Burroughs' Scientific Processor) used the second SIMD scheme.

In order to illustrate the effectiveness of SIMD in handling array operations, consider, for example, the operations of adding the corresponding elements of two one dimensional arrays A and B and storing the results in a third one-dimensional array C. Assume also that each of the three arrays has N elements. Assume also that SIMD scheme 1 is used. The N additions required can be done in one step if the elements of the three arrays are distributed such that M0 contains the elements A(0), B(0), and C(0), M1 contains the elements A(1), B(1), and C(1), . . . , and MN-1 contains the elements A(N - 1), B(N - 1), and C(N - 1). In this case, all processors will execute simultaneously an add instruction of the form C ← A + B. After executing this single step by all processors, the elements of the resultant array C will be stored across the memory modules such that M0 will store C(0), M1 will store C(1), . . . , and MN-1 will store C(N - 1). It is customary to formally represent an SIMD machine in terms of five-tuples (N, C, I, M, F). The meaning of each argument is given below.

1. N is the number of processing elements ($N = 2^k, k \geq 1$).
2. C is the set of control instructions used by the control unit, for example, do, for, step.
3. I is the set of instructions executed by active processing units.
4. M is the subset of processing elements that are enabled.
5. F is the set of interconnection functions that determine the communication links among processing elements.

10.4.1 CONFIGURATION OF SIMD ARRAY PROCESSOR

All N identical processors operate under the control of a single instruction stream issued by a central control unit. There are N data streams; one per processor, so different data can be used in each processor.

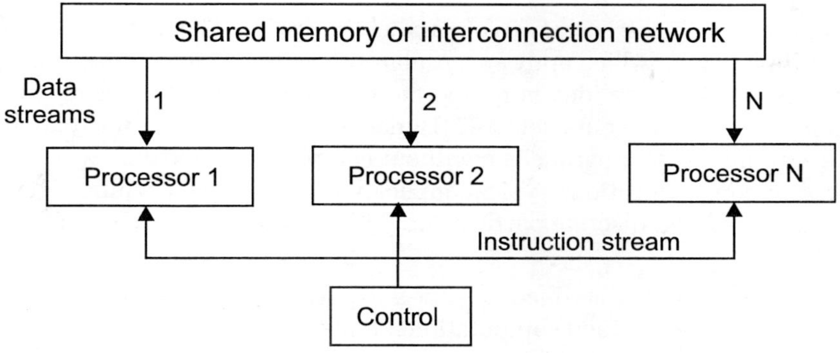

FIGURE 10.6: Configuration of SIMD Array Processor

- The processors operate *synchronously* and a global clock is used to ensure lockstep operation, i.e., at each step (global clock tick) all processors execute the same instruction, each on a different datum.
- Array processors such as the ICL DAP, Connection Machine CM-200, and MasPar are SIMD computers.
- SIMD machines are particularly useful at exploiting data parallelism to solve problems having a regular structure in which the same instructions are applied to subsets of data.

$$\begin{matrix} a_{11} & a_{12} \\ a_{21} & b_{22} \end{matrix} + \begin{matrix} b_{11} & b_{12} \\ b_{21} & b_{22} \end{matrix} = \begin{matrix} c_{11} & c_{12} \\ c_{21} & c_{22} \end{matrix}$$

The same instruction is issued to all 4 processors (add two numbers), and all processors execute the instructions simultaneously. It takes one step to add the matrices, compared with four steps on a SISD machine.

- In this example the instruction is simple, but in general it could be more complex such as merging two lists of numbers.
- The data may be simple (one number) or complex (several numbers).
- Sometimes it may be necessary to have only a subset of the processors executes an instruction, i.e., only some data needs to be operated on for that instruction. This information can be encoded in the instruction itself indicating whether
  - the processor is active (execute the instruction)
  - the processor is inactive (wait for the next instruction)
- SIMD machines usually have 1000's of very simple processors. Shared memory SIMD machines are unrealistic because of the cost and difficulty in arranging for efficient access to shared memory for so many processors. There are no commercial shared memory SIMD machines.
- MIMD machines use more powerful processors and shared memory machines exist for small numbers of processors (up to about 100).

10.5 SIMD MACHINES

SIMD represents one of the earliest styles of parallel processing. The term SIMD stands for "Single-Instruction Multiple-Data," which aptly encapsulates the parallel processing model. Closely related to vector processing, the basic idea is to operate the same instruction sequence simultaneously on a large number of discrete data sets. SIMD machines are geared toward applications that exhibit massive amounts of data parallelism without complicated control flow or excessive amounts of inter-processor communication. Typical applications for SIMD machines include low-level vision and image processing, discrete particle simulation, database searches, and genetic sequence matching.

SIMD machines can be classified as processor-array machines; a SIMD machine basically consists of an array of fine-grained computational units connected together in some sort of simple network topology. This processor array is connected to a control processor, which is responsible for fetching and interpreting instructions. The control processor issues arithmetic and data processing instructions to the processor array, and handles any control flow or serial computation that cannot be parallelized. For flexibility in implementing algorithms, processing elements can usually be individually disabled for conditional execution. The instructions issued by the control processor are executed by the processor array in lockstep operation. Thus, control for a SIMD machine is vastly simplified, and synchronization issues can be avoided. Since the individual processing elements are usually very simple in nature, SIMD machines can typically run at very high clock rates and process data very quickly.

When designing a SIMD machine, the primary factors to consider are:

- Processing element selection
- Communications/network topology
- Instruction issue

The primary trade-off for SIMD machines is between processor simplicity and cost. Traditionally, SIMD processor elements are very rudimentary, shunning complex control and generalized function in favor of simple interfaces and implementation. Oftentimes, SIMD machines employ bit processors which operate on only one bit at a time (bit serial); thus a 32-bit operation would require 32 cycles for a bit processor to work through. One of the chief benefits of using very simple processors is that they are readily optimized and uncomplicated to control. An added benefit is the fact that bit processors can work on arbitrary length data. In addition, since SIMD machines are targeted at specific applications, no silicon is wasted in implementing functionality that is not used. SIMD processing elements are usually connected to their nearest neighbors, forming 2D or 3D meshes. The benefit here is the physical connections often mimic the physical phenomena the program is trying to simulate (e.g., cellular automata for microphysical simluations). SIMD-style processing works best when there is little data exchange between processors, since communication is costly. The ideal case has each processing element munging on data stored locally on each processing node without any data dependencies.

The methods by which instructions are issued to the processor array are of primary concern. The control processor may broadcast instructions to the processor arrays, or each processing node can hold a local cache of instructions to operate. Distribution of instructions to the processing nodes is a serious issue when designing SIMD machines.

10.5.1 SIMD CM-1 MACHINE

Several commercial SIMD machines were introduced in the 1970s, but they were not very widely used. Interest in this class of machines was renewed in the late 1980s with the introduction of the Connection Machine (CM-1) from Thinking Machines, Inc., and the MasPar MP-1. Part of the renewed interest is certainly the result of VLSI technology, which had advanced by that time to the point where several small processors could be put on a single chip. By themselves these processors were too simple to compete with general purpose single-chip processors such as the Motorola 68020 or Intel 80386, but literally thousands of them could be packaged in a small space and built into a cost-effective system. For example, 32 MP-1 processors fit on a single chip, and 32 chips were placed on a single board, for a total of 1024 processors (and their associated memory) in approximately 4 square feet.

The CM-1 was based on 1-bit processors. Every operation in the machine processed 1-bit operands and produced 1-bit results. Operations on larger data elements, for example 32-bit integers, required one cycle per bit. Attached to each processor was a local memory with a capacity of 4K bits. Memory references, like processor operations, were 1-bit operations, i.e. a fetch copied 1 bit from memory into a 1-bit processor register. 16 processors were implemented on a single chip. Within a chip, processors were connected with a grid, and up to 4096 chips were connected via a 12-dimensional hypercube. All processors obeyed instructions issued by a central control processor, which in turn was connected to a front-end workstation.

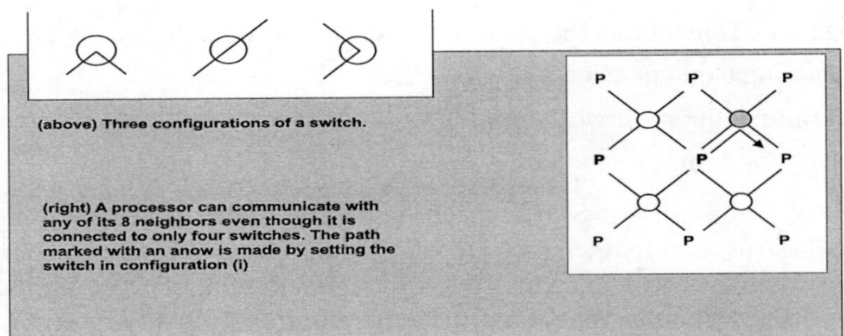

FIGURE 10.7: Switching in an X-net

The MasPar MP-1 was introduced a few years after the CM-1. It also has a very narrow datapath, but it processes data 4 bits at a time instead of 1 bit at a time. Each processor can have up to 64KB of local memory. One of the interesting aspects of the MP-1 is that there are two separate communication systems, and programmers can alternate between them to choose the best performance for different parts of their algorithms. One interconnection network is known as the X-net (Figure 10.7). It connects each processor to its 8 nearest neighbors in a 2D mesh with wraparound connections. The other connection is a global router, which provides point-to-point communication between any two PEs. The router is implemented by a 3-stage switching network, where each stage in a 1024-processor machine contains a 16 × 16 crossbar; together the three stages comprise a 1024 × 1024 crossbar. The processors are controlled by a proprietary RISC processor known as the array control unit, or ACU. The ACU has its own local memory and is used for scalar operations, while the processor array is intended for vector and array operations. An MP-1 can be configured as an n x n square mesh or an n × 2n rectangular mesh. The smallest configuration has 1,024 processors and the largest has 16,384 processors in a 128 × 128 grid.The newest machines from Thinking Machines and MasPar are the CM-5 and MP-2, respectively. The MP-2 has a wider internal data path than the MP-1 - 32 bits vs. 4 bits - but is otherwise very similar to the MP-1 in that it uses both the X-net and global router to connect PEs in a 2D mesh. The largest MP-2, which has 16,384 (2^{14}) processors, has a theoretical peak performance of 550 MFLOPS and reaches 473 MFLOPS on the LINPACK benchmark for parallel machines.

10.6 MASKING AND DATA ROUTING

Each processor PE has its own memory PEM_i (figure 10.8). It has a set of working registers and flags names A_i, B_i, C_i. It contains Arithmetic and Logic unit S_i and a local index register I_i, an address registers D_i and a data routing register R_i. The R_i of each PE_i is connected to the R_j of other PEs via the interconnection network. When data transfer among PEs occurs, it is the content of R_i registers that are being transferred.

Some array processor may use two routing register, one for input and the other for output. Each PE_i is either active or in the inactive mode during each instruction cycle. If a PE_i is active, it executes the instruction broadcast to it by the CU. If a PE_i is inactive, it will not execute the broadcast instruction. The masking schemes are used to specify the status flag S_i of PE_i. The conventions S_i = 1 is chosen for an active PE_i and S_i = 0 for an inactive PE_i. In the CU, there is a global index register I and a Masking register M. The M register has N bits.

The physical length of a vector is determined by the number of PEs. The CU performs the segmentation of a long vector into vector loops, the setting of a global address, and the offset increment.

Two processes are employed:

Master Process

- Holds pool of tasks for worker processes to do
- Sends worker a task when requested
- Collects results from workers

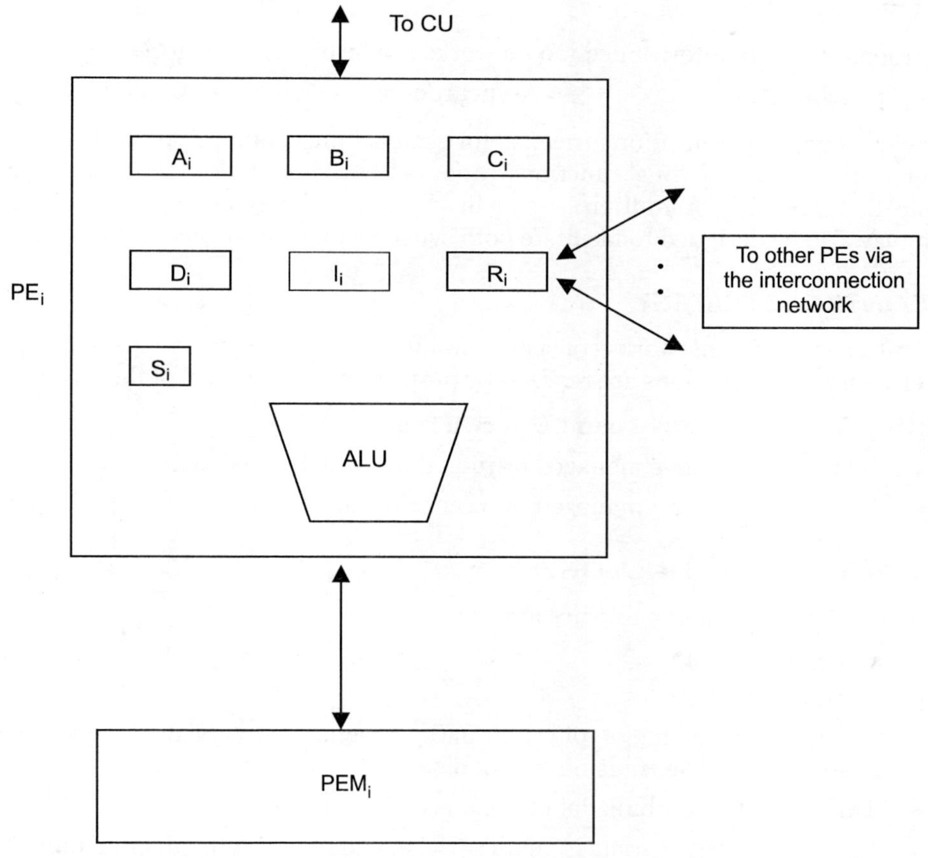

FIGURE 10.8: Components in a Processing element (PE_i)

Worker Process: repeatedly does the following

- Gets task from master process
- Performs computation
- Sends results to master
- Worker processes do not know before runtime which portion of array they will handle or how many tasks they will perform.
- Dynamic load balancing occurs at run time: the faster tasks will get more work to do.

10.7 INTER PE COMMUNICATIONS

These are fundamental decisions in determining the appropriate structure of an interconnection network for an SIMD machine. The decisions are made between

1. Operation Modes
2. Control Strategies
3. Switching methodologies
4. Network Topologies

10.7.1 OPERATION MODE

The operations modes of interconnection networks can be of three categories:

- Synchronous
- Asynchronous
- Combined.

Synchronous communication is needed for establishing communication paths synchronously for either a data manipulating function or for a data instruction broadcast. Asynchronous communication is needed for multiprocessing in which connection requests are issued dynamically. A system may also be designed to facilitate both synchronous and asynchronous operations.

10.7.2 CONTROL STRATEGY

A typical interconnection networks consists of number of switching elements and interconnecting links. Interconnection functions are realized by properly setting control of the switching elements.

The setting function control can be of two types:

- Distributed Control managed by individual switching element.
- Centralized Control managed by a centralized

10.7.3 SWITCHING TECHNOLOGY

The two major switching methodologies are

- Circuit switching
- Packet switching
- In circuit switching a physical path is actually established between source and destination before transmission of data.
- This is suitable for bulk data transmission.
- In packet switching, data is put in a packet and routed through interconnection network without establishing a physical connection path.
- This is suitable for short messages.

10.7.4 NETWORK TOPOLOGY

A network can be depicted by a graph which nodes represent switching points and edges represent communication links. The topologies can be of two types:

- Static
- Dynamic

In static link between two processors are passive and dedicated buses cannot be reconfigured for direct connection to other processors. In dynamic link, configuration can be made by setting the network's active switching elements.

10.8 SIMD INTERCONNECTION NETWORKS

Various interconnection networks have been suggested for SIMD computers. The SIMD networks classified into two categories based on topologies called as Static Networks and Dynamic Networks. The diagrammatical representation of static interconnection networks is shown. Dynamic networks have been further classified as Single stage versus Multistage. Examples of Single stage network are implemented in ILLIAC and an example of multistage network is Omega network.

10.8.1 STATIC VERSUS DYNAMIC NETWORKS

The topological structure of an SIMD array processor is mainly characterized by the data routing network used in interconnecting the processing elements.

Interconnection Networks

- Parallel computers with many processors do not use shared memory hardware.
- Instead each processor has its own local memory and data communication takes place via message passing over an *interconnection network*.
- The characteristics of the interconnection network are important in determining the performance of a multicomputer.
- If network is too slow for an application, processors may have to wait for data to arrive.

Interconnection Networks and Message Passing

In this case each processor has its own private (local) memory and there is no global, shared memory. The processors need to be connected in some way to allow them to communicate data.

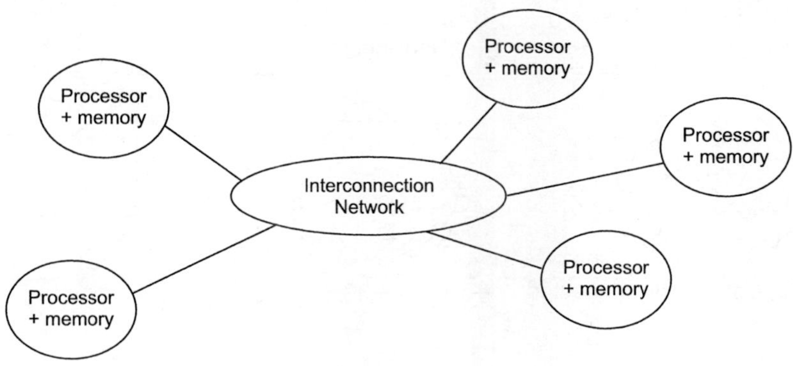

FIGURE 10.9: Interconnection Networks and Message Passing

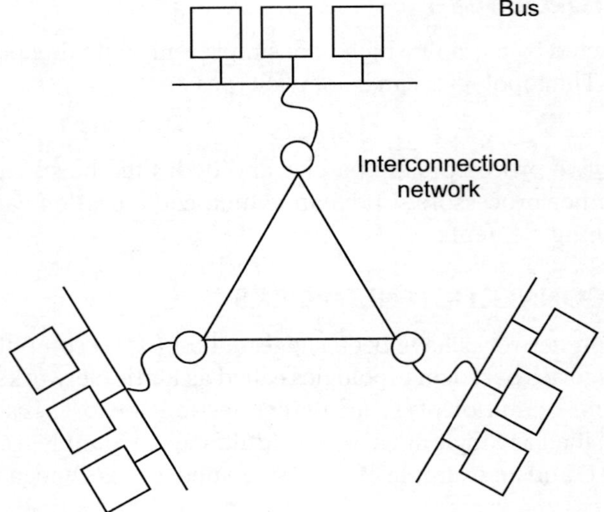

FIGURE 10.10: Interconnection Networks

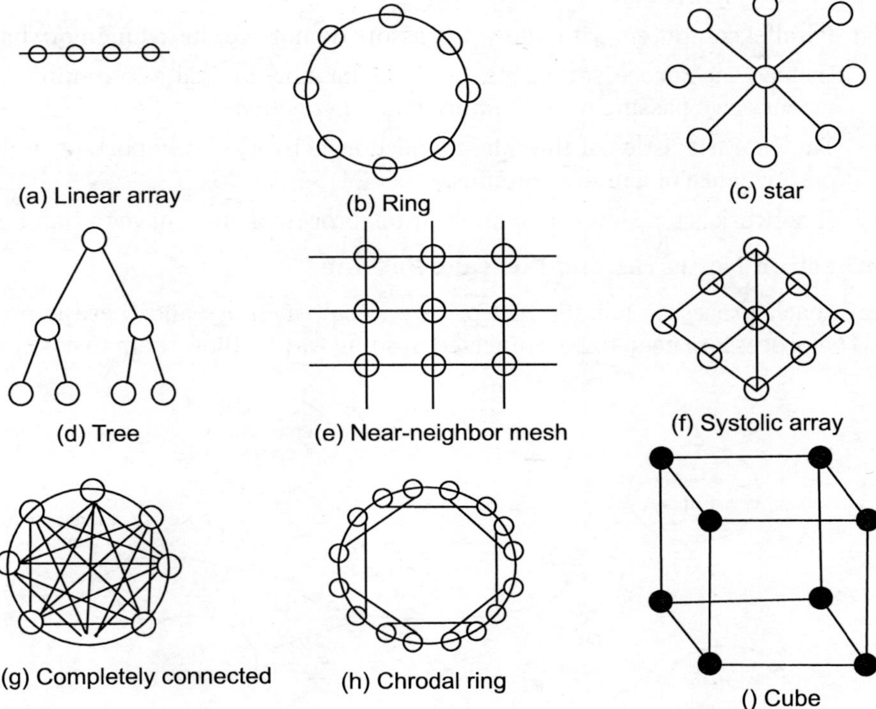

FIGURE 10.11: Static Interconnection Network Topologies

The SIMD interconnection networks are classified into the following two categories based on network topologies:

- Static Networks
- Dynamic Networks

Static Networks

Topologies in the static networks can be classified according to the dimension required for layout. One dimensional topologies include—

- Linear array

Two dimensional topologies include—

- Ring
- Star
- Tree
- Mesh
- Systolic Array

Thee dimensional topologies include

- Completely connected chordal ring
- Three cube
- Three cube connected cycle

Dynamic Networks

Two classes of dynamic networks are

- Single stage
- Multi stage

Single Stage Networks

A single stage switching network with N input selectors (IS) and N output selectors (OS). Each is essentially a 1- to-D demultiplexer and each OS is an M-to-1 multiplexer. Cross bar network is a single stage network. The single stage network is also called as recirculating network. Data items may have to recirculation through the single stage several times before reaching their final destinations. The number of recirculation depends on the connectivity in the single stage network.

Multistage Networks

Multi-stage networks are based on the so called shuffle-exchange switching element, which is basically a 2×2 crossbar. Multiple layers of these elements are connected and form the network.

Many stages of interconnected switches form a multistage SIMD networks.

Three characterizing feature describe multistage networks—

- The Switch Box
- Network Topology
- Control Structure

Each box is essentially an interchange device with two inputs and two outputs. There are four states in a switch box. They are

- Straight
- Exchange
- Upper Broadcast
- Lower broadcast

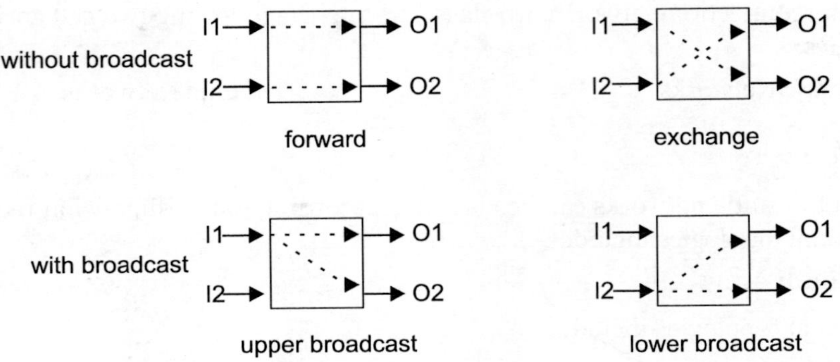

FIGURE 10.12: A two-by-two switching box and its four interconnection states

Examples of Multistage Networks

- Banyan
- Cube
- Flip
- Omega
- Baseline
- Delta
- Indirect cube

All multistage networks that are based on shuffle-exchange elements, is a blocking network because not all possible input-output connections can be made at the same time, since one path might block another (in contrast to a crossbar, which is non-blocking). Using crossbars instead of the shuffle-exchange elements, it is possible, to build non-blocking networks. Such networks are called CLOS-networks. A multistage network is capable of connecting an arbitrary input terminal to an arbitrary output terminal.

Multistage networks can be

- One sided
- Two Sided

The one sided network called as full switches, have input-output ports on the same side. The two sided network have an input side and output side and can be divided into three classes:

- Blocking
- Arrangeable
- Non- Blocking

In blocking networks, simultaneous connections of more than one terminal pair may result conflicts in the use of network communication links.

Examples: Data Manipulator, Flip, N cube, omega

In rearrangeable network, a network can perform all possible connections between inputs and outputs by rearranging its existing connections so that a connection path for a new input-output pair can always be established.

Example: Benes Network

A non-blocking can handle all possible connections without blocking.

Example: Clos Network

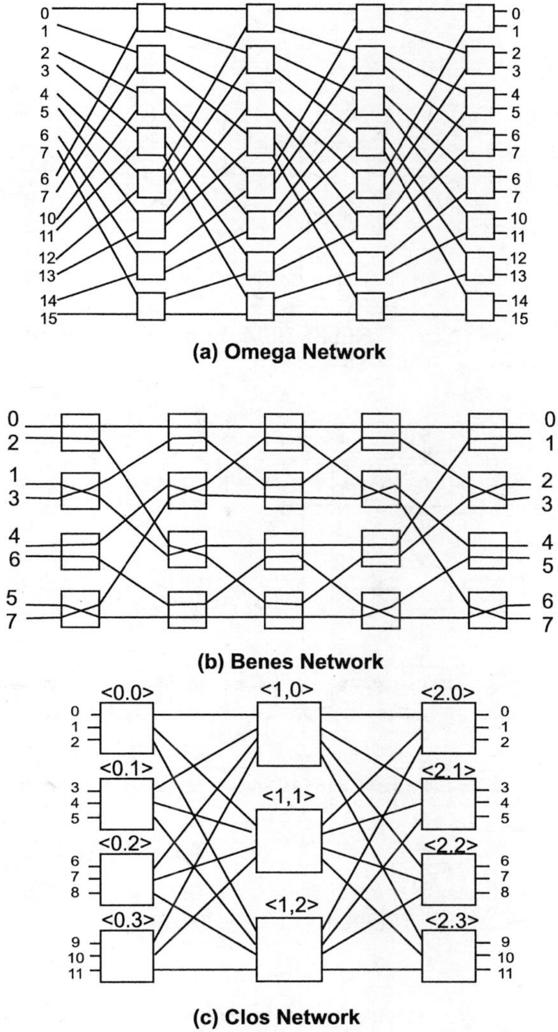

FIGURE 10.13 Several Multistage Interconnection Networks

10.8.2 MESH-CONNECTED ILLIAC NETWORKS

In a mesh network nodes are arranged as a q-dimensional lattice, and communication is allowed only between neighboring nodes. In a *periodic mesh*, nodes on the edge of the mesh have wrap-around connections to nodes on the other side. This is sometimes called a *toroidal mesh.*

Mesh Metrics

For a q-dimensional non-periodic lattice with kq nodes:

- Network connectivity = q
- Network diameter = q(k-1)

- Network narrowness = k/2
- Expansion Increment = kq-1
- Bisection width = kq-1
- Edges per node = 2q

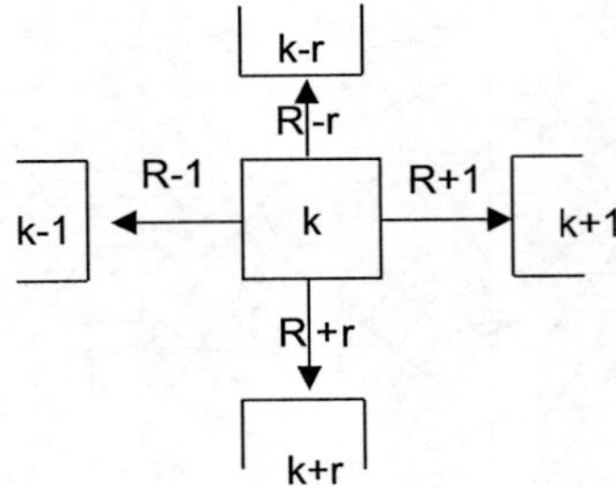

FIGURE 10.14: Topology

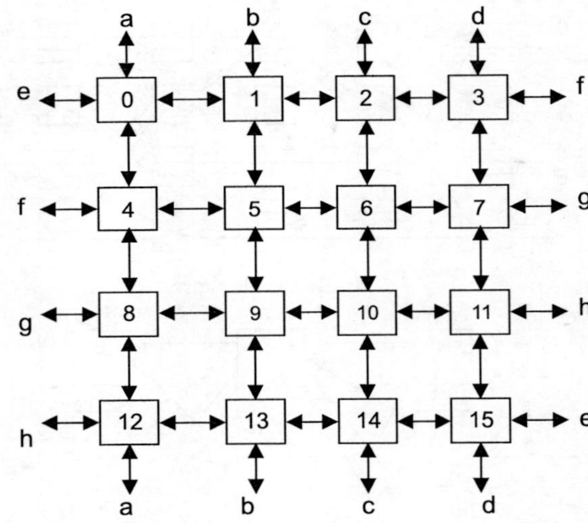

FIGURE 10.15: Mesh Connections

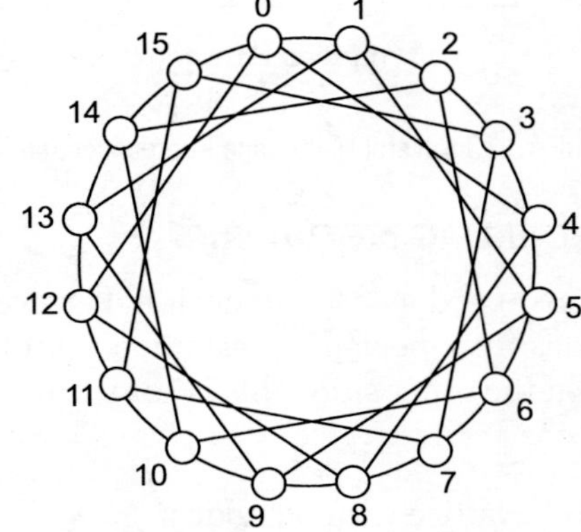

FIGURE 10.16: Mesh Redrawn

The topology is formerly described by the four routing functions:

- R+: I→ i+1 mod N=> (0, 1, 2..., 14, 15)
- R- : I→i-1 mod N=> (15, 14,...,2, 1, 0)
- R+r: I→i+r mod N=> (0,4,8,12)(1,5,9,13)(2,6,10,14)(3,7,11,15)
- R-r: I→i-r mod N=> (15,11,7,3)(14,10,6,2)(13,9,5,1)(12,8,4,0)

where (i j k)(l m n)=> i-->j, j-->k, k-->i ; l-->m, m-->n, n-->l and r = N

Each PEi is directly connected to its four neighbors in the mesh network. Horizontally, all PEs of all rows form a linear circular list as governed by the following two permutations, each with a single cycle of order N. The permutation cycles (a b c) (d e) stands for permutation a→b, b→c, c→a and d→e, e→d in a circular fashion with each pair of parentheses.

R+1 = (0 1 2....N−1)

R−1 = (N−1 ..... 2 1 0)

For the example network of N = 16 and r = √16 = 4, the shift by a distance of four is specifies by the following permutations, each with four cycles of order four each:

R+4 = (0 4 8 12) (1 5 9 13) (2 6 10 14) (3 7 11 15)

R −4 = (12 8 4 0) (13 9 5 1) (14 10 6 2) (15 11 7 3)

10.8.3 CUBE INTERCONNECTION NETWORKS

The cube network consists of m functions defined by $cube_i$

(Pm-i ..Pi+1 PiPi-1 ... Po) = Pm-i ....Pi+1P'iPi-1 .....Po

for 0 <= i < m. When the PE addresses are considered as the corners of an m-dimensional cube this network connects each PE to its m neighbors.

Dimensionality of a cube "n" = log2N

Communication links connect each pair of PEs with addresses that differ in 1 bit only (distance of 1). Examples

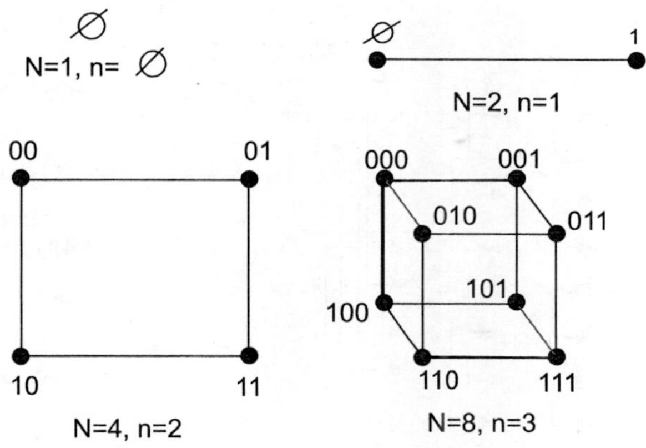

FIGURE 10.17: A 3 Cube of 8 nodes

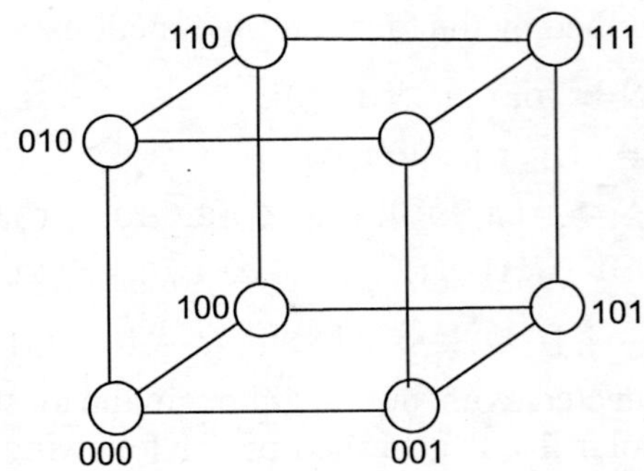

FIGURE 10.18: A 3-cube with nodes denoted as C2 C1 C0 in binary

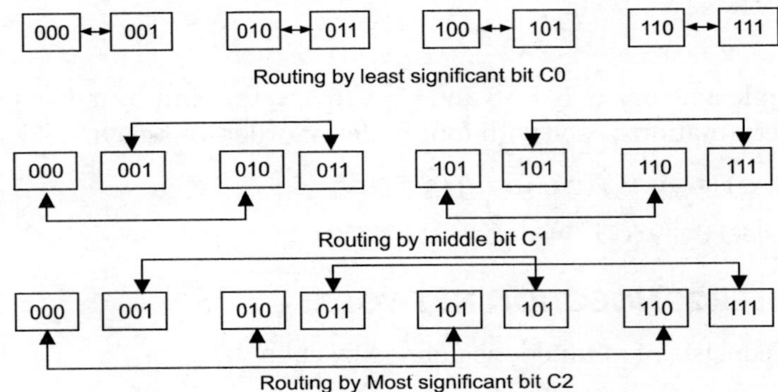

FIGURE 10.19: The recirculating Network

It takes <= log N steps to rotate data from any PE to another.

Routing functions are formerly described as:

Ci (An-1 .... A1 AO) = An-1...Ai+1 A'i Ai-1......AO

Vi = 0, 1, 2,..., n-1

Example: N=8 ⇒ n=3

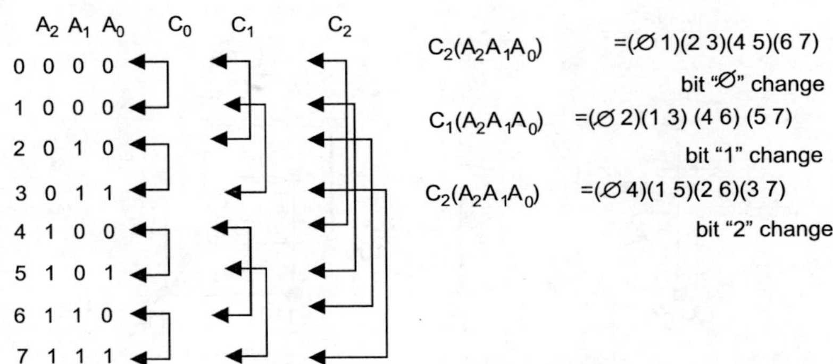

FIGURE 10.20: A multistage Cube network for N = 8

Two functions straight and exchange switch boxes are used in constructing multistage cube networks. The stages are numbered as 0 at input end and increased to n-1 at the output stage.

10.8.4 SHUFFLE-EXCHANGE OMEGA NETWORKS

A shuffle-exchange network consists of n=2k nodes, and two kinds of connections.

Routing:

- Have wide applications in implementing parallel algorithms such as FFT, sorting, AT, and polynomial evaluations.
- Two routing functions: shuffle "S" and Exchange "E".

Shuffle:

$$S(A)=S(An-1...A1A0)=A.n-2...A1A0An-1,\ 0<A<1$$

Which is effectively like shuffling the bottom half of a card deck into the top half?

Exchange:

E(An-1...A1A0)= (An-1...A1A0')=C0 . The complement of LSM means data exchange between two PEs with adjacent addresses.

- *Exchange* connections links nodes whose numbers differ in their lowest bit.
- *Perfect shuffle* connections link node i with node 2i mod(n-1), except for node n-1 which is connected to itself.
- *Example of n = 8*

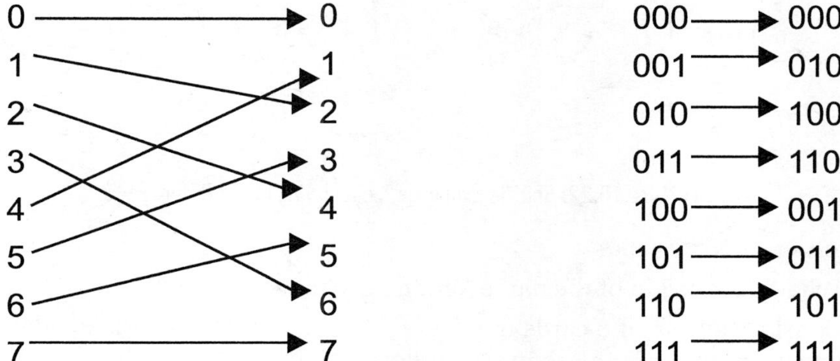

An N by N omega network consists of n identical stages, where each stage is a perfect shuffle interconnection followed by a column of N/2 four-function interchange boxes under individual box control. The shuffle connects output P n-l...Pl P0 of stage i to input P n-2...PlP0Pn-l of stage i-1. Each interchange box in an omega network is controlled by the n-bit destination tags associated with the data on its input lines.

The perfect shuffle cuts the deck into 2 halves from the center and remixes them evenly. The inverse perfect shuffle does the opposite to restore the original ordering.

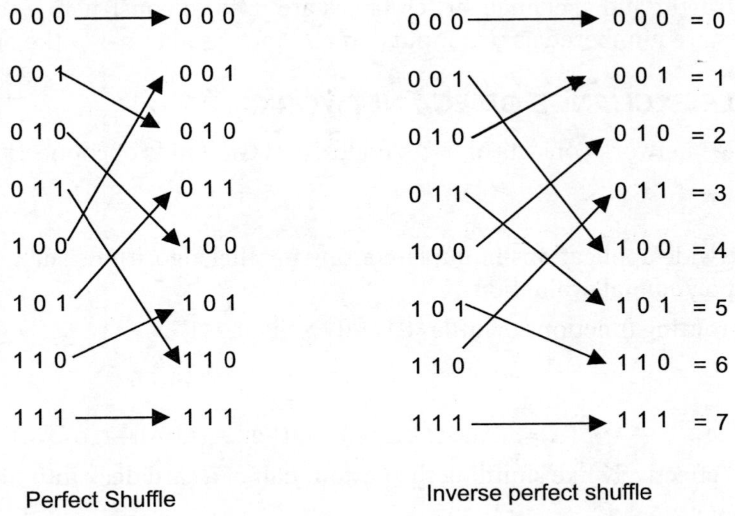

FIGURE 10.21: Perfect Shuffle and Inverse Perfect Shuffle for n = 8

8-Node Shuffle-Exchange Network

Below is an 8-node shuffle-exchange network, in which shuffle links are shown with solid lines, and exchange links with dashed lines.

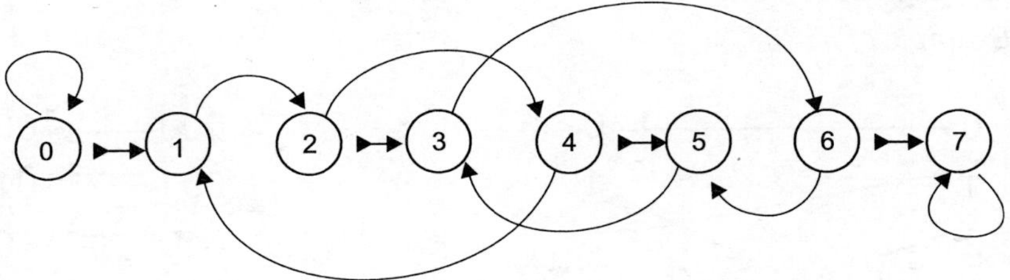

FIGURE 10.22: Shuffle Exchange recirculating network for N = 8

Shuffle-Exchange Networks

- What is the origin of the name "shuffle-exchange"?
- Consider a deck of 8 cards numbered 0, 1, 2,..., 7. The deck is divided into two halves and shuffled perfectly, giving the order: 0, 4, 1, 5, 2, 6, 3, 7
- The final position of a card i can be found by following the shuffle link of node i in a shuffle exchange network.
- Let ak-1, ak-2,..., a1, a0 be the address of a node in a shuffle-exchange network in binary.
- A datum at this node will be at node number ak-2,..., a1, a0, ak-1 after a shuffle operation.
- This corresponds to a cyclic leftward shift in the binary address.
- After k shuffle operations we get back to the node we started with, and nodes through which we pass are called a *necklace*.

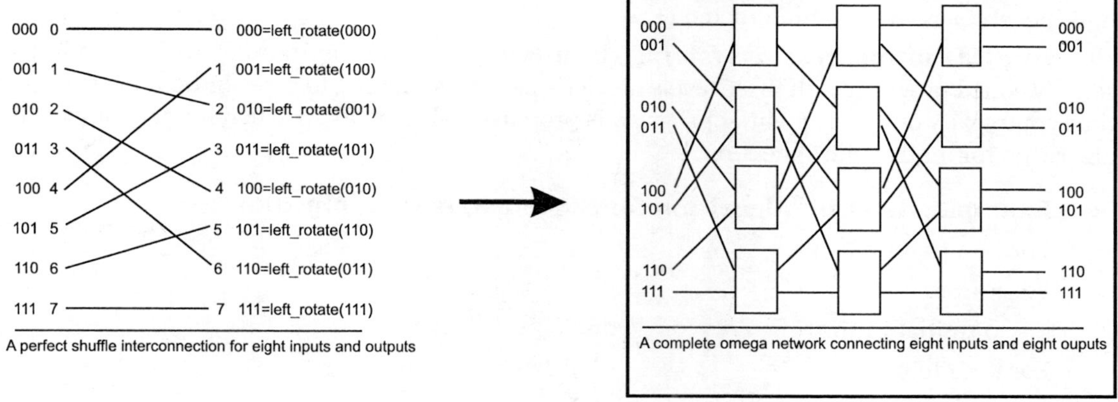

A perfect shuffle interconnection for eight inputs and outputs

A complete omega network connecting eight inputs and eight ouputs

FIGURE 10.23: The Multi stage Omega Network

10.9 PARALLEL ALGORITHMS FOR ARRAY PROCESSORS

The main motivation for developing SIMD array processors was to perform parallel computations on vector or matrix types of data. Parallel processing algorithms have been developed by many computer scientists for SIMD computer. Important SIMD algorithms can be used to perform matrix multiplication, fast Fourier transform (FFT), matrix transposition, summation of vector elements, matrix inversion, parallel sorting, linear recurrence, Boolean matrix operations, and to solve partial differential equations. Here is the representation of SIMD algorithms for matrix multiplication, parallel sorting, and parallel FFT. The physical memory allocations and program implementation depend on the specific architecture of a given SIMD machine.

10.9.1 SIMD MATRIX MULTIPLICATION

Matrix manipulation is needed in solving linear systems of equations. Matrix operations include matrix multiplication, L-U decomposition, and matrix inversion.

Here we present two parallel algorithms for matrix multiplication. The differences between SISD and SIMD matrix algorithms are pointed out in their program structures and speed performance. In general, the inner loop of a multilevel SISD program can be replaced by one or more SIMD vector instructions.

Let $A = [a_{ik}]$ and $B = [b_{kj}]$ be n × n matrices. The multiplication of A and B generates a product matrix $C = A \times B = [c_{ij}]$ of dimension n × n. The elements of the product matrix C is related to the elements of A and B by:

$$c_{ij} = \sum_{k=1}^{n} a_{ik} \times b_{kj} \quad \text{for } 1 \leq i \leq n \text{ and } 1 \leq j \leq n$$

There are n3 cumulative multiplications to be performed in Equation. A cumulative multiplication refers to the linked multiply-add operation $c \neg c + a \times b$. The addition is merged into the multiplication because the multiply is equivalent to multioperand addition. Therefore, we can consider the unit time as the time required to perform one cumulative multiplication, since add and multiply are performed simultaneously.

In SISD uniprocessor system: The n^3 cumulative multiplications are carried out by a serially coded program with three levels of Do loops corresponding to three indices to be used. The time complexity of this sequential program is proportional to n^3, as specified in the following SISD algorithm for matrix multiplication.

Example: An $O(n^3)$ algorithm for SISD matrix multiplication

For i = 1 to n Do

For j = 1 to n Do

$c_{ij} = 0$ (initialization)

For k = 1 to n Do

$c_{ij} = c_{ij} + a_{ik} . b_{kj}$ (scalar additive multiply)

End of k loop

End of j loop

End of i loop

Now we want to implement the matrix multiplication on an SIMD computer with n PEs. The algorithm construct depends on heavily on the memory allocations of the A, B, and C matrices in the PEMs. Suppose we store each row vector of the matrix across the PEMs, as illustrated in Figure 10.24. Column vectors are then stored within the same PEM. This memory allocation scheme allows parallel access of all the elements in each row vector of the matrices. Based in this data distribution, we obtain the following parallel algorithm. The two parallel do operations correspond to vector load for initialization and vector multiply for the inner loop of additive multiplications. The time complexity has been reduced to $O(n^2)$.

Therefore, the SIMD algorithm is n times faster than the SISD algorithm for matrix multiplication.

Example: An $O(n^2)$ algorithm for SIMD matrix multiplication

For j = 1 to n Do

Par for k = 1 to n Do

$c_{jk} = 0$ (vector load)

For j = 1 to n Do

Par for k = 1 to n Do

$c_{ik} = c_{ik} + a_{ij} . b_{jk}$ (vector multiply)

End of j loop

End of i loop

It should be noted that the vector load operation is performed to initialize the row vectors of matrix C one row at a time. In the vector multiply operation, the same multiplier a_{ij} is broadcast from the CU to all PEs to multiply all n elements $\{b_{ik}$ for k = 1, 2, ..., n$\}$ of the ith row vector of B. In total, n^2 vector multiply operations are needed in the double loops.

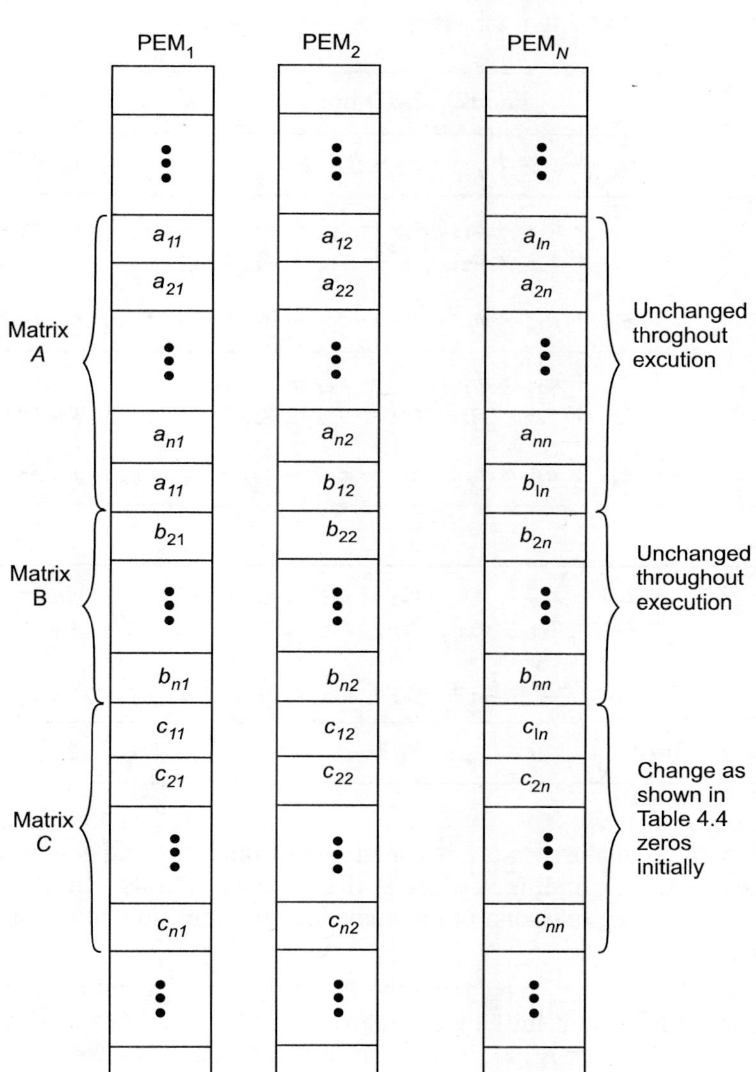

FIGURE 10.24: Memory allocation for SIMD matrix multiplication

The successive memory contents in the execution of the above SIMD matrix multiplication program are illustrated in table 10.1. Each vector multiply instruction implies n parallel scalar multiplications in each of the n2 iterations. This algorithm in Example is implementable on an array of n PEs.

If we increase the number of PEs used in an array processor to n2, an O(n log2 n) algorithm can be devised to multiply the two n × n matrices A and B. Let n = 2m and recall the binary cube network. Consider an array processor whose n2 = 22m PEs are located at the 22m vertices of a 2m-cube network. A 2m-cube network can be considered as two (2m – 1)-cube networks linked together by 2m extra edges.

TABLE 10.1: Successive contents of the C array in memory

Outer loop i	Inner loop j	Parallel SIMD operations on $k = 1, 2, \ldots, n$			
		$c_{i1} \leftarrow c_{i1} + a_{ij} \times b_{j1}$	$c_{i2} \leftarrow c_{i2} + a_{ij} \times b_{j2}$	$\cdots$	$c_{in} \leftarrow c_{in} + a_{ij} \times b_{jn}$
1	1	$c_{11} \leftarrow c_{11} + a_{11} \times b_{11}$	$c_{12} \leftarrow c_{12} + a_{11} \times b_{12}$		$c_{1n} \leftarrow c_{1n} + a_{11} \times b_{1n}$
	2	$c_{11} \leftarrow c_{11} + a_{12} \times b_{21}$	$c_{12} \leftarrow c_{12} + a_{12} \times b_{22}$		$c_{1n} \leftarrow c_{2n} + a_{12} \times b_{2n}$
	$\vdots$	$\vdots$	$\vdots$	$\cdots$	$\vdots$
	n	$c_{11} \leftarrow c_{11} + a_{1n} \times b_{n1}$	$c_{12} \leftarrow c_{12} + a_{1n} \times b_{n2}$		$c_{1n} \leftarrow c_{1n} + a_{1n} \times b_{nn}$
2	1	$c_{21} \leftarrow c_{21} + a_{21} \times b_{11}$	$c_{22} \leftarrow c_{22} + a_{21} \times b_{12}$		$c_{2n} \leftarrow c_{2n} + a_{21} \times b_{1n}$
	2	$c_{21} \leftarrow c_{21} + a_{22} \times b_{21}$	$c_{22} \leftarrow c_{22} + a_{22} \times b_{22}$		$c_{2n} \leftarrow c_{2n} + a_{22} \times b_{2n}$
	$\vdots$	$\vdots$	$\vdots$	$\cdots$	$\vdots$
	n	$c_{21} \leftarrow c_{21} + a_{2n} \times b_{n1}$	$c_{22} \leftarrow c_{22} + a_{2n} \times b_{n2}$		$c_{2n} \leftarrow c_{2n} + a_{2n} \times b_{2n}$
$\vdots$	$\vdots$	$\vdots$	$\vdots$	$\vdots$	$\vdots$
n	1	$c_{n1} \leftarrow c_{n1} + a_{n1} \times b_{11}$	$c_{n2} \leftarrow c_{n2} + a_{n1} \times b_{12}$		$c_{nn} \leftarrow c_{nn} + a_{n1} \times b_{1n}$
	2	$c_{n1} \leftarrow c_{n1} + a_{n2} \times b_{21}$	$c_{n2} \leftarrow c_{n2} + a_{n2} \times b_{22}$		$c_{nn} \leftarrow c_{nn} + a_{n2} \times b_{2n}$
	$\vdots$	$\vdots$	$\vdots$	$\cdots$	$\vdots$
	n	$c_{nn} \leftarrow c_{nn} + a_{nn} \times b_{n1}$	$c_{n2} \leftarrow c_{n2} + a_{nn} \times b_{n2}$		$c_{nn} \leftarrow c_{nn} + a_{nn} \times b_{nn}$
Local memory		PEM_1	PEM_2	$\cdots$	PEM_n

In Figure 10.25, a 4-cube network is constructed from two 3-cube networks by using $8 = 2^3$ extra edges between corresponding vertices at the corner positions. For clarity, we simplify the 4-cube drawing by showing only one of the eight fourth dimension connections. The remaining connections are implied.

Let $(p_{2m-1}\ p_{2m-2} \ldots p_m\ p_m - 1 \ldots p_1 p_0)2)$ be the PE address in the 2m cube. We can achieve the $O(n\log_2 n)$ compute time only if initially the matrix elements are favorably distributed in the PE vertices. The n rows of matrix A are distributed over n distinct PEs whose addresses satisfy the condition

$$p_{2m-1}\ p_{2m-1} \cdots p_m = p_{m-1}\ p_{m-2} \cdots p_o$$

as demonstrated in Figure 10.26a for the initial distribution of four rows of the matrix A in a 4×4 matrix multiplication ($n = 4$, $m = 2$). The four rows of A are then broadcast over the fourth dimension and front to back edges, as marked by row numbers in Figure 10.25b.

The n columns of matrix B (or the n rows of matrix Bt) are evenly distributed over the PEs of the 2m cubes, as illustrated in Figure 10.26c. The four rows of Bt are then broadcast over the front and back faces, as shown in Figure 10.26d. Figure 10.27 shows the combined results of A and Bt broadcasts with the inner product ready to be computed. The n-way broadcast depicted in Figure 10.26b and 10.26d takes log n steps, as illustrated in Figure 10.27 in m = log2n = log24 = 2 steps. The matrix multiplication on a 2m-cube network is formally specified below.

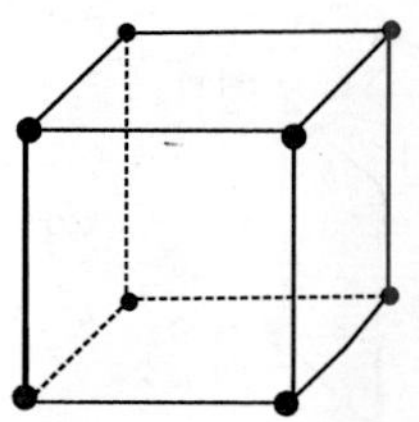

(a) A 3 cube

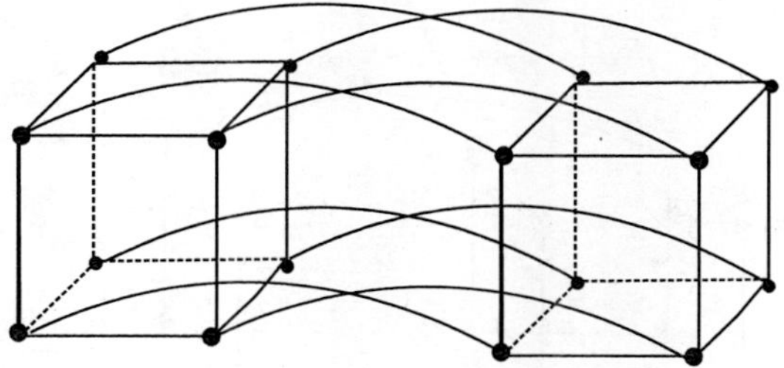

(b) A 4 cube formed from two 3 cubes

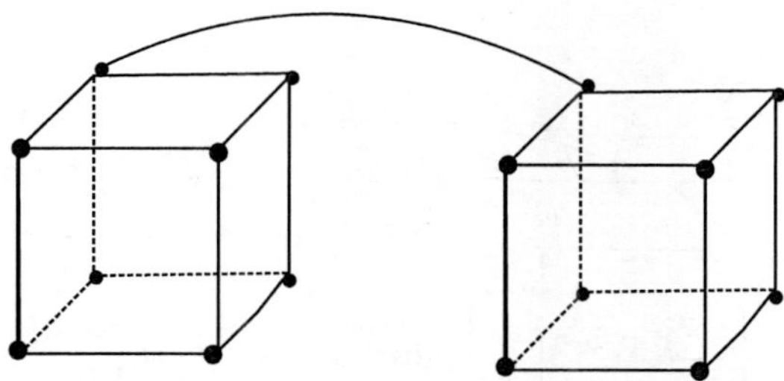

(c) The 4 cube showing only one of eight fourth-dimension connections

FIGURE 10.25: The construction of (m + 1) – cube from two m-cubes.

Example: An O(n $\log_2$ n) algorithm for matrix multiplication

1. Transpose B to form B^t over the m cubes $x_{2m-1} \ldots x_m 0 \ldots 0$ in n $\log_2$ n steps (Figure 10.26c).
2. N-way broadcast each row of B^t to all PEs in the m cube

$$p_{2m-1} \ldots p_m x_{m-1} \ldots x_0$$

   in n $\log_2$ n steps (Figure 10.26d).
3. N-way broadcast each row of A residing in PE $p_{2m-1} \ldots p_m p_{m-1} \ldots p_0$ to all PEs in the m cube $x_{2m-1} \ldots x_m p_{n-1} \ldots p_0$ in n $\log_2$ n steps (Figure 10.26b). All the n rows can be broadcast in parallel.
4. Each PE now contains a row of A and a column of B and can form the inner product in O(n) steps (Figure 10.27). The elements of each result row can be brought together within the same PEs which initially held a row of A in O(n) steps.

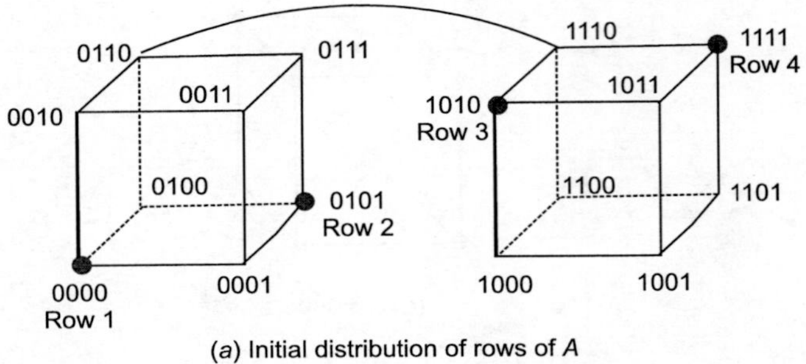

(a) Initial distribution of rows of A

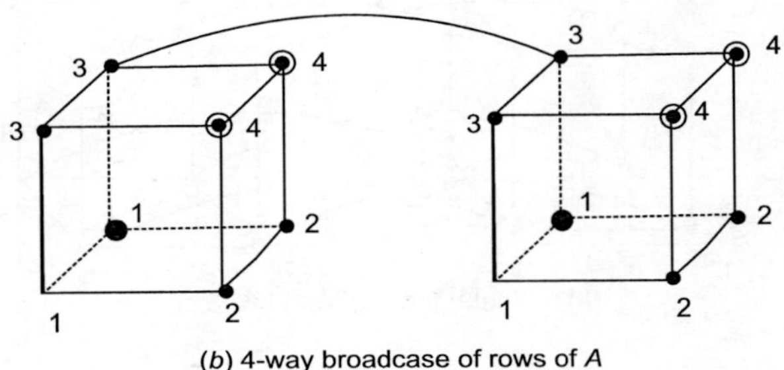
(b) 4-way broadcase of rows of A

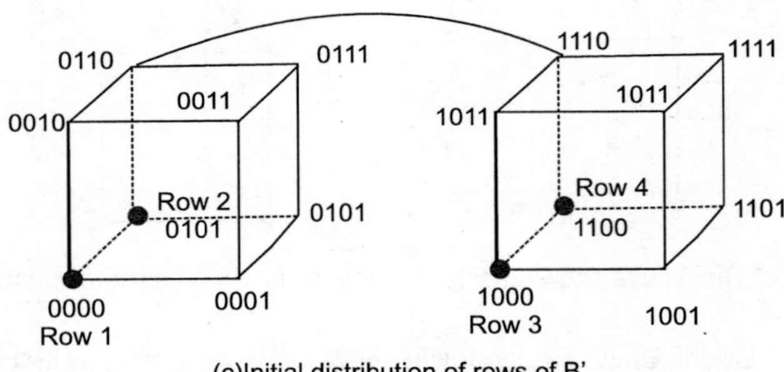

(c)Initial distribution of rows of B'

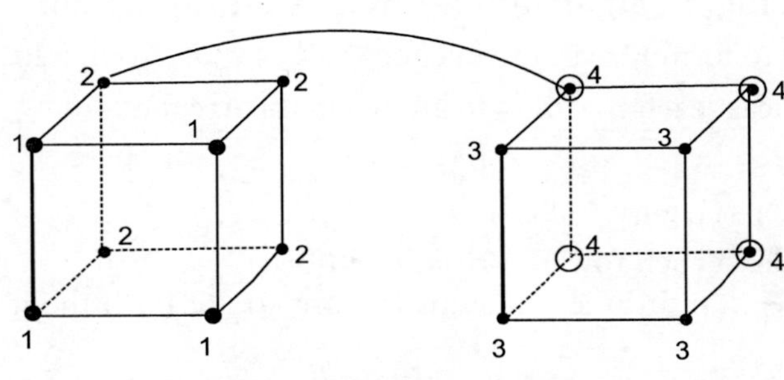
(d)4 way broadcase of rows of B'

FIGURE 10.26: Allocation of the elements of two 4 x 4 matrices in a 4-cube of 16 PEs.

The above algorithm takes a total of $3n \log_2 n + O(n)$ time steps to complete, which equals $O(n \log_2 n)$. This demonstrates a gain in speed over the $O(n^2)$ algorithm in previous Example at the expense of using n^2 PEs over the use of only n PEs in the slow algorithm. A hardware approach VLSI to complete the n-by-n matrix multiplication in O(n) time using $O(n^2/m^2)$ VLSI processor arrays, each consisting of an array of $O(m^2)$ PEs for pipelined inner-product computations.

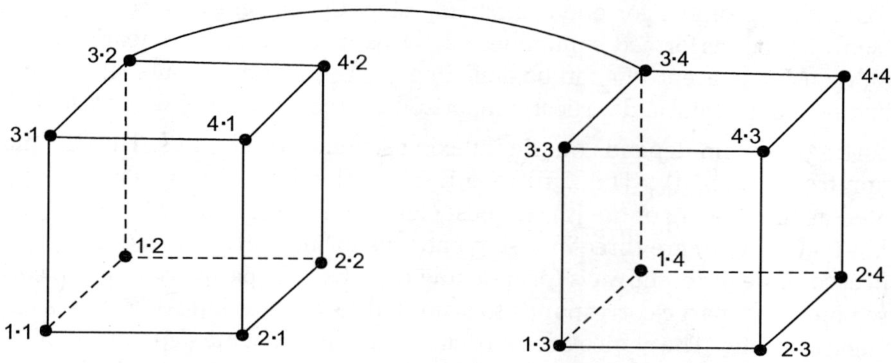

FIGURE 10.27: The final distributions of the rows of matrix A and the columns of matrix B ready for inner product in the 16 PEs of a 4-cube array processor.

10.9.2 PARALLEL SORTING ON ARRAY PROCESSORS

An SIMD algorithm is to be presented for sorting n^2 elements on a mesh-connected (Illiac-IV-like) processor array in O(n) routing and comparison. This shows a speedup of $O(\log_2 n)$ over the best sorting algorithm, which takes $O(n \log_2 n)$ steps on a uniprocessor system. We assume an array processor with $N = n^2$ identical PEs interconnected by a mesh network (Figure 10.28) similar to Illiac-IV except that the PEs at the perimeter have two or three rather than four neighbors. In other words, there are no wraparound connections in simplified mesh network.

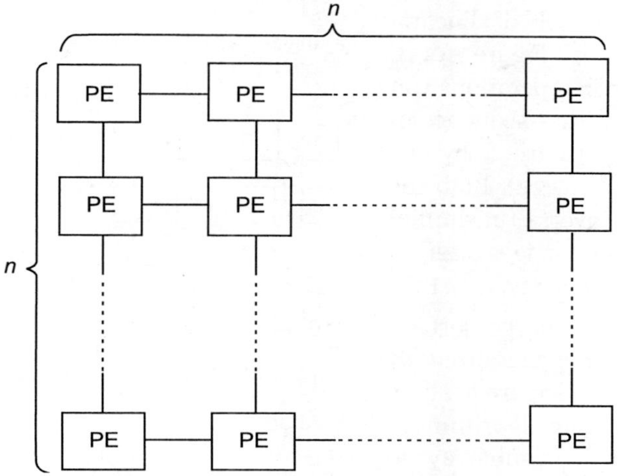

FIGURE 10.28: A mesh connection of PEs without boundary wraparound connections for SIMD sorting.

Eliminating the wraparound connections simplifies the array-sorting algorithm. The time complexity of the array-sorting algorithm would be affected by, at most, a factor of two if the wraparound connections were included.

Two time measures are needed to estimate the time complexity of the parallel sorting algorithm. Let t_R be the routing time required to move one items from a PE to one of its neighbors, and t_C be the comparison time required for one comparison step. Concurrent data routing is allowed. Up to N comparison may be performed simultaneously. This means that a comparison-interchange step between two items in adjacent PEs can be done in $2t_R + t_C$ time units (route left, compare, and route right). A mixture of horizontal and vertical comparison interchanges requires at least $4t_R + t_C$ time units.

The sorting problem depends on the indexing schemes on the PEs. The PEs may be indexed by a bijection from {1,2,...,n} x {1,2,...,n} to{0,1,...,N – 1}, where $N = n^2$. The sorting problem can be formulated as the moving of the jth smallest element in the PE array for all j = 0, 1, 2,..., N – 1. Illustrated in Figure 10.29 are three indexing patterns formed after sorting the given array in part a with respect to three different ways for indexing the PEs. The patterns in part b corresponds to a row-majored indexing, part c corresponds to a snuffed row-major indexing, and is based on snake-like row-major indexing. The choice of a particular indexing scheme depends upon how the sorted elements will be used. We are interested in designing sorting algorithms which minimize the total routing and comparison steps.

The longest routing path on the mesh in a sorting process is the transposition of two elements initially loaded at possible corner PEs, as illustrated in Figure 10.30. This transposition needs at least 4(n – 1) routing steps. This means that no

Algorithm can sort n^2 elements in a time of less than O(n). In other words, an O(n) sorting algorithm is considered optimal on a mesh of n^2 PEs. Before we show one such optimal sorting algorithm on the mesh-connected PEs, let us review Batcher's odd-even merge sort of two sorted sequences on a set of linearly connected PEs shown in Figure 10.31. The shuffle and unshuffle operations can each be implemented with a sequence of interchange operations (marked by the double-arrows in Figure 10.32). Both the perfect shuffle and its inverse (unshuffle) can be done in k – 1 interchanges or 2(k – 1) routing steps on a linear array of 2k PEs.

Batcher,s odd-even merge sort on a linear array has been generalized by Thompson and Kung to a square array of PEs. Let M(j, k) be a sorting algorithm for merging two sorted j-by-k/2 subarrays to form a sorted j-by-k array, where j and k are powers of 2 and k > 1. The snakelike

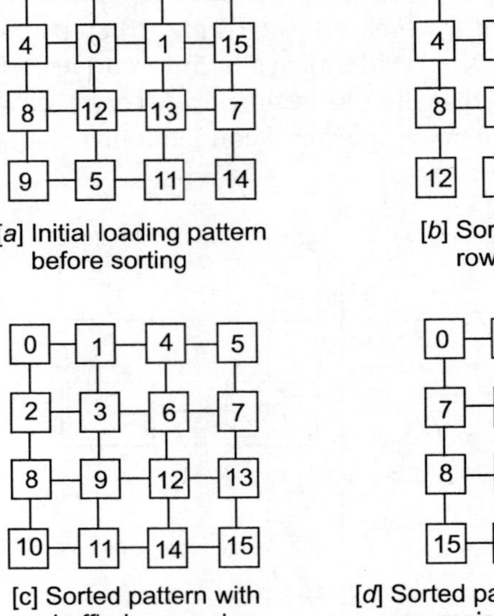

FIGURE 10.29: Sorting patterns with respect to three ways of indexing the PEs.

row-major ordering is assumed in all the arrays. In the degenerate case of M(1, 2)a single comparison-interchange step is sufficient to sort two unit subarrays. Given two sorted columns of length $j \geq 2$, the M(j, 2) algorithm consists of the following steps:

Example: The M(j, 2) sorting algorithm

J1: Move all odds to the left column and all events to the right in $2t_k$ time.

J2: Use the odd-even transposition sort to sort each column in $2jt_k + jt_c$ time.

J3: Interchange on each row in $2t_k$ time.

J4: Perform one comparison-interchange in $2t_k + t_c$ time.

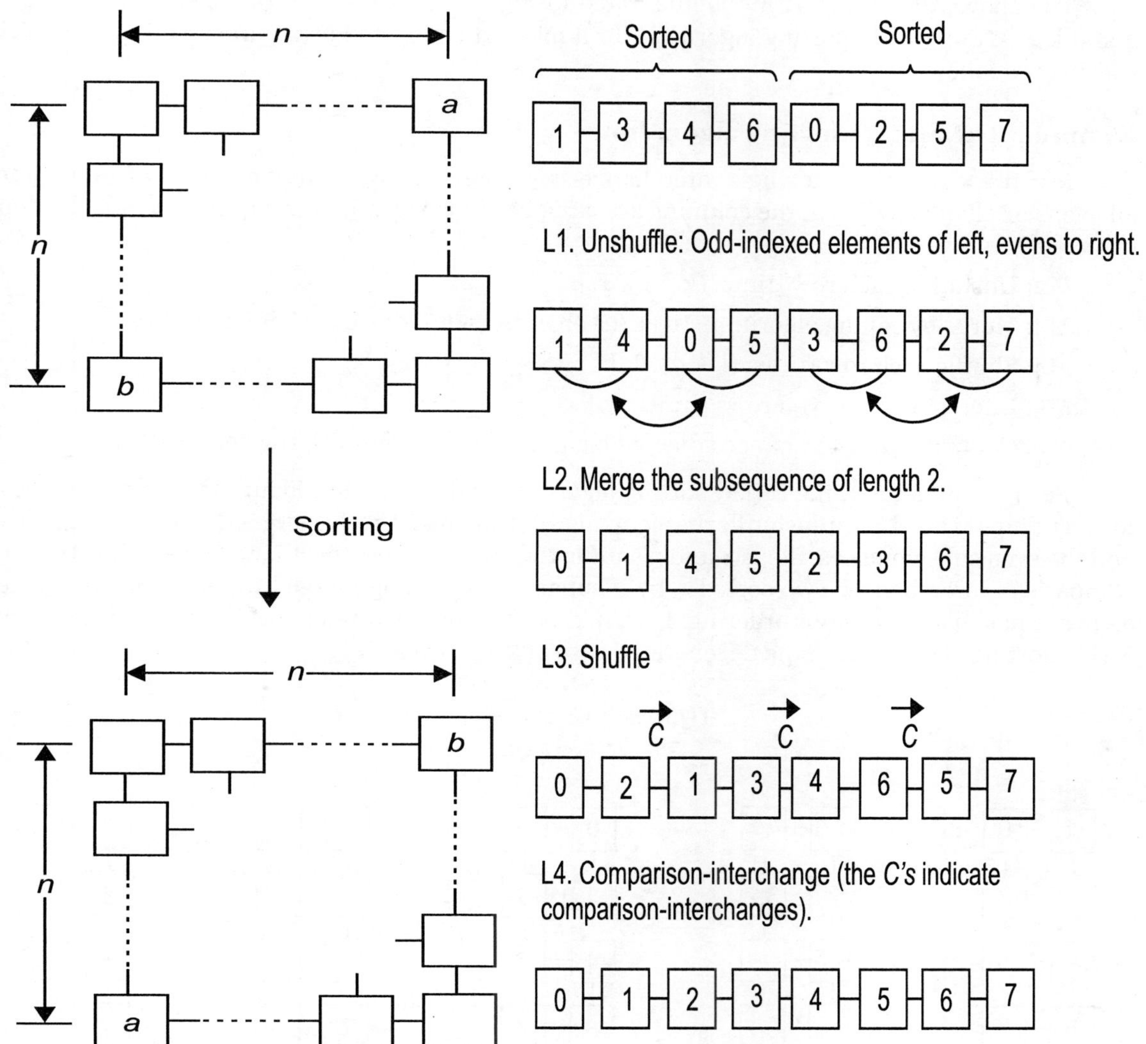

FIGURE 10.30: The transposition of two elements at opposite corner PEs.

FIGURE 10.31: Batcher's odd-even merge of two sorted sequences on a linear array of PEs.

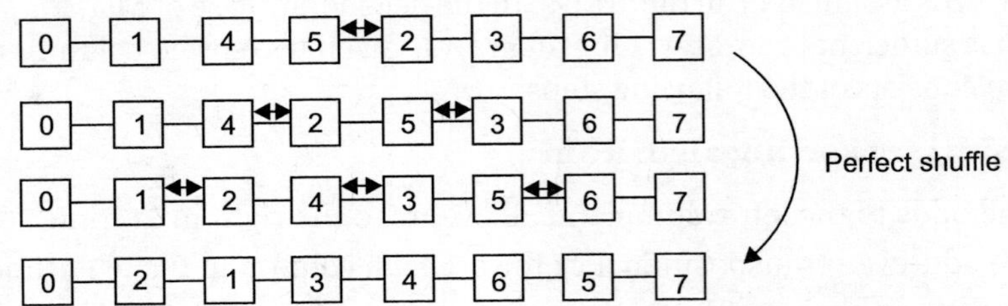

FIGURE 10.32: The implementation of a perfect shuffle by a sequence of interchange operations.

The above M(j, 2) algorithm is illustrated in Figure 10.33 for an M(4, 2) sorting. When $j > 2$ and $k > 2$, the M(j, k) sorting algorithm for a meshed-connected array processor is recursively specified as follows:

Example: The M(j, k) sorting algorithm

M1: If $j > 2$, perform a single interchange step on even rows so that columns contain either all evens or all odds. If $j = 2$, the columns are already segregates, so nothing else needs to be done (time: $2t_k$).

M2: Unshuffle each row [time: $(k - 2). T_k$].

M3: Merge by calling algorithm M(j,k/2) on each half of the array [time: T(j, k/2].

M4: Shuffle each row [time: $(k - 2). T_k$].

M5: Interchange on even rows [time: $2t_k$].

M6: Comparison-interchange adjacent elements (every even with the next odd) [time:– $4t_k$].

For $j > 2$ and $k > 2$, the M(j,k) sorting algorithm is illustrated in Figure 10.34 for the case of M(4,4). Steps M1 and M2 unushuffle the elements. Step M3 recursively merges the odd subsequences and the even subsequences. Steps 4 and 5 shuffle the odd and even together. M6 performs the final comparison interchange. Two sorted 4-by-2 subarrays are being merged to form a 4-by-4 sorted array in snakelike row-major ordering. Let T(j,k) be the time required to perform all the step in the M(j,k) sorting algorithm. In the degenerated case of $k = 2$, we have

$$T(j,k) = (2j + 6)t_R + (j + 1)t$$

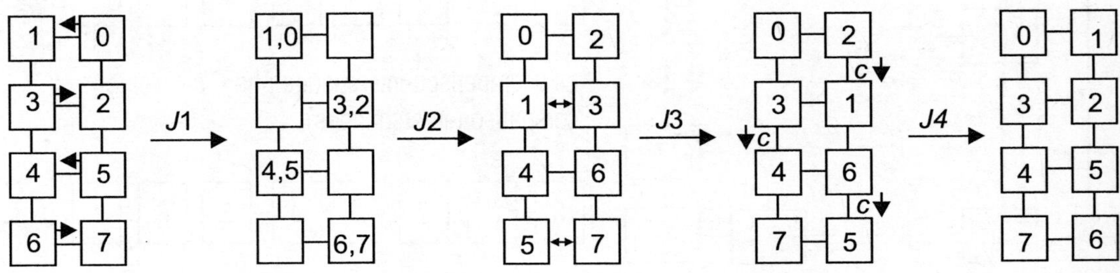

FIGURE 10.33: Data routing, comparison, and interchange operations performed in the M(4,2) sorting algorithm.

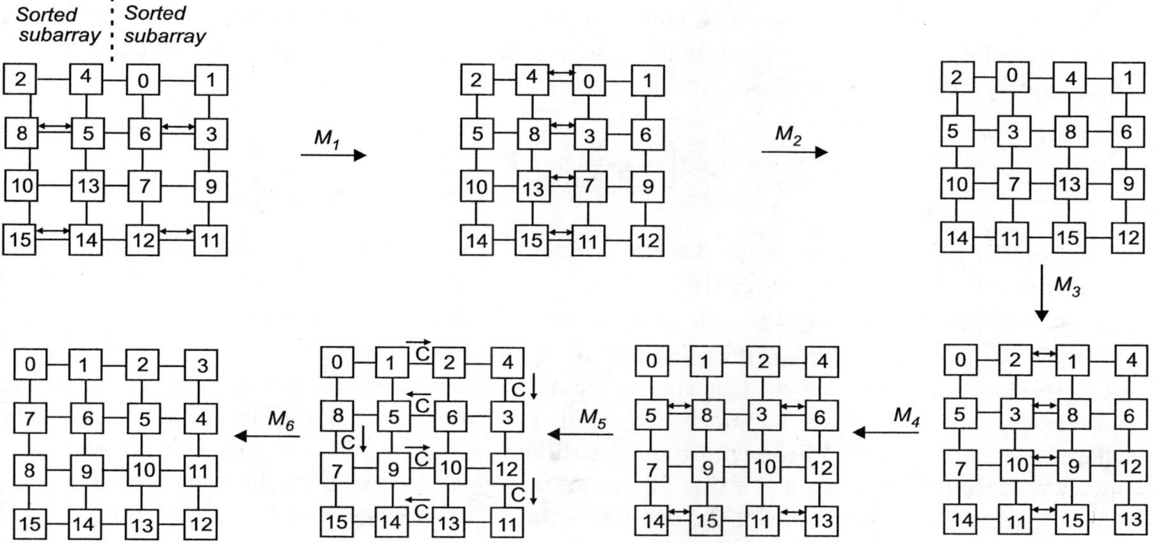

FIGURE 10.34: Merge step sorting in the M(4,4) sorting algorithm (the final sorted 4 × 4 array has snake-like row major ordering).

For k > 2, the time function is recursively computed by:

$$T(j,k) = (2k + 4)t_R + t_C + T(j,k/2)$$

By repeated substitution, we have the following time bound:

$$T(j, k) \leq (2j + 4k + 4\log_2 k)t_k + (j + \log_2 k)t_c$$

For an n x n array of PEs, the M(n, n) sort algorithm can be done in T(n, n) time, which is proportional to O(n).

$$T(n, n) = (6n + 4\log_2 n)t_R + (n + \log_2 n)t_c = O(n)$$

Combining an upwards merge with the sideways merge (just described), one can further tighten the above bound to within a factor of 6n under the assumption that $t_C \leq t_R$. This parallel sorting algorithm has a speedup of $\log_2 n$ over the best $o(n \log_2 n)$ algorithm for serial sorting.

10.9.3 SIMD FAST FOURIER TRANSFORM

SIMD algorithms for performing one-dimensional and two-dimensional fast Fourier transform (FFT) are presented in this section. Let s(k), k = 0, 1, ..., M – 1 be M samples of a time function. The discrete Fourier transform of s(k) is defined to be the discrete function x(j), j = 0, 1, ..., M – 1 where

$$x(j) = \sum_{k=0}^{M-1} s(k).W^{jk} \quad j = 0, 1, ..., M-1$$

$$\text{and } W = e^{2\pi i/M} \text{ and } I = \sqrt{-1}$$

Considered the use of an SIMD machine with N = M/2 PEs to perform an M-point FFT of the discrete signal sequence $\{s(m), 0 \leq m \leq M - 1\}$. The algorithm is a parallel implementation of the decimation-in-frequency (DIF) technique illustrated in Figure 10.35 for the case of M = 16 sampling points. the DIF algorithm divides the input sequence {s(m)} into two half subsequences {f(m)} and {g(m)} such that f(m) = s(m) and

$$G(m)=s\left(m+\frac{M}{2}\right)\text{for}\, m=0,1,\ldots\frac{M}{2}-1$$

The FFT for the M-point sequence can be computers in terms of the two M/2-point FFt of the two sequences {f(m) + g(m)} and {[f(m) – g(m)]. W^m}, where $n \le m < M/2$. For m being a power of 2, repeated applications of this dividing process require O(M $\log_2$ M) array operations.

For the parallel FFT algorithm, PE_i initially contains s(k) and s(k + m/2), where $0 \le k < N$. As in the serial method, $\log_2$ M stages of computations are needed. At each stage, M/2 butterfly operations, shown in Figure 10.36, are executed. The items being paired in a butterfly at stage k where $0 \le k < \log_2 M$ are those whose insides differe in the ($\log_2$ M – k – 1)th bit position of the binary representation. Because of this difference in a given bit position, the cube interconnection network provides a natural means for specifying the interprocessor data transfers required for the FFT algorithm. This network consists of n routing functions C_i for $0 \le I < \log_2 N$ as in Equation above. Figure 10.36 illustrates data transfers and computations performed in the one-dimensional FFT algorithm for an SIMD machine with N = M/2 PEs.

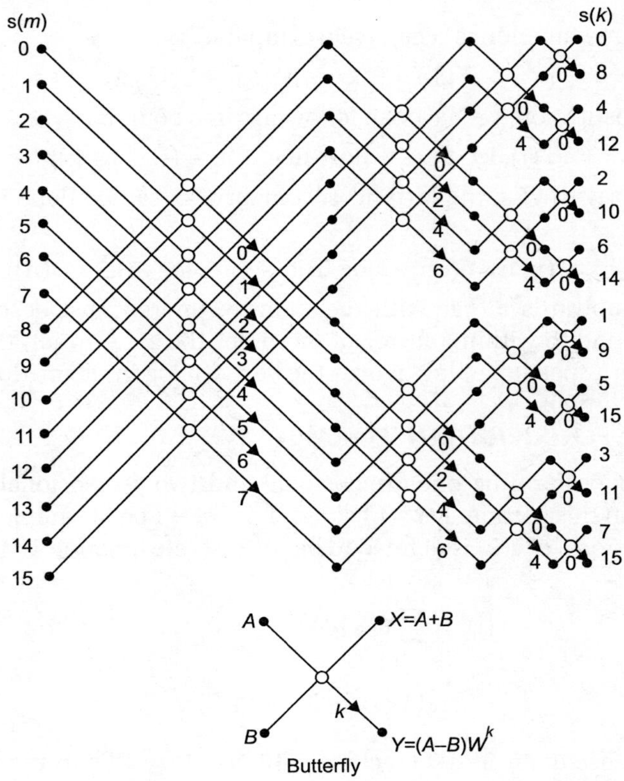

FIGURE 10.35: Operations in a 16-point FFT based on the decimation-in-frequency algorithm.

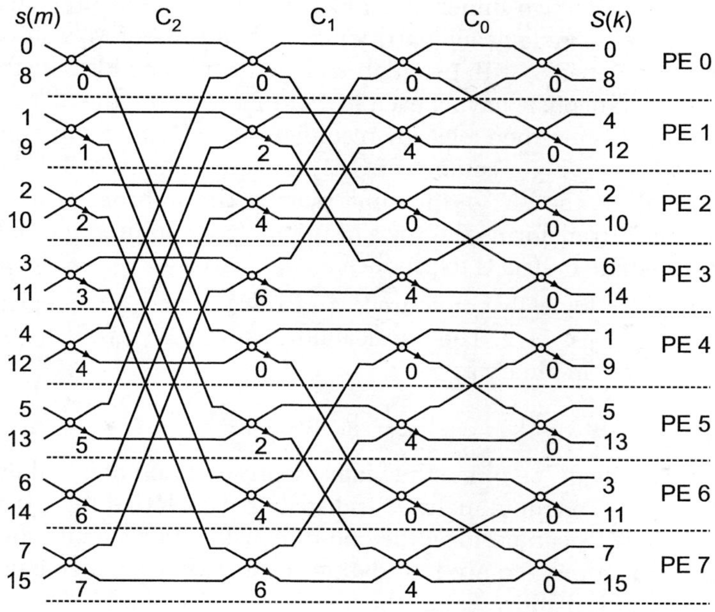

FIGURE 10.36: Computation of a 16-point FFT in an SIMD machine with 8 PEs.

The above algorithm performs the M-point FFT calculations using $\log_2 (M/2)$ parallel data transfers. This is a lower bound of the number of data transfers required to perform an M-point FFT when the M points are initially distributed over M/2 PEs. The number of parallel butterfly operations performed is $\log_2 M$, where butterfly involves two complex additions and one complex multiplication in each PE. The number of butterfly steps is reduced from $(M/2) \log_2 M$ in a serial FFT algorithm to $\log_2 m$ for a parallel FFT algorithm, using M/2 PEs.

Because M/2 PEs may not be available for the computation of an M-point FFT, it is of interest to considered FFT algorithms which use fewer PEs. A simple solution for using fewer PEs is to replicate the steps in the M/2 PE algorithm. For example, if $N = M/4$, two computations that were performed in parallel in different PEs in the M/2 PE algorithm are now performed sequentially in the same PE, as shown for N = 16 in Figure 10.37. The number of butterfly steps performed is $2\log_2 M$. $2(\log_2 M - 2) = 2 [\log_2(M/4)]$ parallel data transfers are required. This approach can be generalized to perform an M-point FFT in $M/2^k$ PEs for $2 \leq k \leq \log_2 M$. For $N = M/2^k$ PEs, each PE will initially contain 2^k elements. The number of parallel butterfly steps performed will be $2^{k-1} \log_2 M$. The data transfer will be performed the C_i functions for $\log_2 M - k - 1 \geq i \geq 0$; each C_i function will be replicated 2^{k-1} times. The total number of parallel data transfers will therefore be $2^{k-1} (\log_2 M - k)$.

We consider next the two-dimensional FFT algorithm for processing an M-by-M signal array. A standard approach to computing the two-dimensional FFT of a signal array S is to perform the one-dimensional FFT on the rows of S, giving an intermediate matrix G, then performing the one-dimensional FFT on the columns of G. The resulting matrix F is the two-dimensional FFT of S. An SIMD algorithm which uses $N = M^2/2$ PEs is presented below.

The implementation of a two-dimensional FFT makes use of the previous work done for one-dimensional FFTs. The PEs are logically partitioned into M rows of M/2 PEs. Each row of PEs is given a row of the input matrix S, with two matrix elements in each PE. The two-dimensional FFT is implemented by simultaneously having each row of PEs compute the FFT of its row of the input matrix to obtain G. The PEs are then logically reconfigured to form M columns of M/2 processors, with each column of PEs having a column of G. Then each column of PEs computes the FFT of its column of G to obtain F, the FFT of the input matrix. This approach can be considered a row-column method in that it transforms the rows of the matrix S to produce G, then transforms the columns of the intermediate matrix G to produce F.

Initially, the PEs are logically configured as M rows of M/2 PEs, logically numbered (i, j), where $0 \leq i < M$ and $0 \leq j < M/2$. The physical address of PE (i, j), is $i(M/2) + j$. The physical address can be represented in binary as

$$p_{2\mu-2}\, p_{2\mu-3} \cdots p_{\mu-1}\, p_{\mu-2} \cdots p_1 p_0$$

where $\mu = \log_2 M$. Bits $p_{\mu-2} \cdots p_0$ are the binary representation of j, and bits $p_{2\mu-2} \cdots p_{\mu-1}$ are the binary representation of i. The input matrix S is distributed such that PE(i, j) has S(i, j) and S(i, j + M/2). Thus, each row of PEs can perform the one-dimensional FFT on its row of S with N = M/2. In this case, the cube functions required for data transfers will exchange data based on the lower order μ - 1 bits of the physical address; i.e., the functions will act on j independently of i. Thus, the one-dimensional FFT can be performed on each row independently and simultaneously. The result G is distributed to each column of PEs which holds two columns of G, with each PE holding one element from each of the two columns of G.

The PEs are now logically reconfigured to form M columns of M/2 PEs, with each column of PEs having one column of G. Two matrix elements are in each PE.

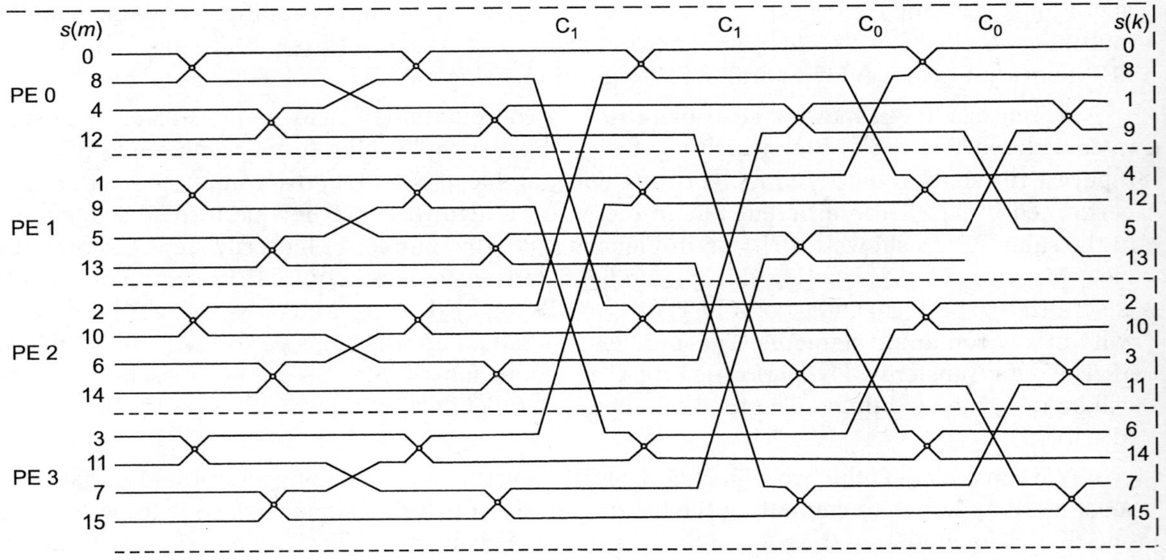

FIGURE 10.37 Computation of a 16-point FFt in an SIMD machine with 4 PEs.

TABLE 10.2: SIMD machine reconfiguration for two-dimensional FFT computations [notation (i, j) denotes the PE_{ij}]

Configuration: *M*-by-*M*/2 array

(0, 0)	(0, 1)	···	(0, M/2 − 1)
(1, 0)	(1, 1)	···	(1, M/2 − 1)
⋮			⋮
(M − 1, 0)	(M − 1, 1)	···	(M − 1, M/2 − 1)

Configuration: *M*/2-by-*M* array

(0, 0)	(M/2, 0)	(0, 1)	(M/2, 1)	···	(0, M/2 − 1)	(M/2, M/2 − 1)
(1, 0)	(M/2 + 1, 0)	(1, 1)	(M/2 + 1, 1)	···		
⋮						⋮
(M/2 − 2, 0)	(M − 1, 0)	(M/2 − 1, 1)	(M − 1, 1)	···	(M/2 − 1, M/2 − 1)	(M − 1, M/2 − 1)

To do this, PE (i, j) renumbered (k, l) where k = i mod (M/2) and l = 2j + [i/(M/2)]. Effectively, this renumbering takes each column of the original configuration, divides it in half, and aligns the halves to form two columns, as shown in Table 10.2. In terms of the binary representation of the physical address, the binary representation of k is $p_{2\mu-3} \cdots p_{\mu-1}$, and the binary representation of l is $p_{\mu-2} \cdots p_0 p_{2\mu-2}$.

After the renumbering, G is distributed to each pair of PE columns PE(k, 2λ) and PE(k, 2λ + 1), where $0 \leq k, \lambda < M/2$. Within such a pair of PE columns, PE(k, 2λ) has two points from the kth row of G, and PE(k, 2λ +1) has two corresponding points from the (k + M/2)th row of G, for $0 \leq k < M/2$. Within each of the two columns of G, these are precisely the points which must be paired at the start of the one-dimensional M-point, M/2 PE algorithm. Using the $C_{2\mu-2}$ function, PE (k, 2λ) and PE(k, 2λ +1), where $0 \leq k, \lambda < M/2$. Within each of the two columns of G, these are precisely the points which must be paired at the start of the one-dimensional M-point, M/2 PE algorithm. Using the $C_{2\mu-2}$ function, PE(k, 2λ) and PE(k, 2λ) + 1), where $0 \leq k, \lambda < M/2$, can exchange data so that each column of PEs gets a different column of G with each PE holding the two elements of G needed to start the one-dimensional FFT. In terms of physical PE addresses, $p_{2\mu-2}$ is the low order bit in the binary representation of the logical column index, so the $C_{2\mu-2}$ routing function effects the exchange of elements between the corresponding rows in columns 2λ and 2λ + 1, for $0 \leq \lambda < M/2$.

Each column of PEs now performs the one-dimensional FFT on its column of G. However, to perform the FFT on a column, it is necessary to perform data transfers based on the row index, which is given by k and represented by $p_{2\mu-3} \cdots p_{\mu-1}$ of the physical PE address. Therefore, whenever C_i is executed in the original algorithm, $C_{i\mu-1}$ is executed in this algorithm. In this way, the cube routing functions allow communication within a column instead of within a row.

The complexity of this SIMD algorithm has been derived from the one-dimensional FFT case. The number of multiplication steps required is $2\log_2 M$; the number of addition steps required is $2(2\log_2 M)$; and the number of data transfer steps required is $2\log_2(M/2) + 1 = 2\log_2 M - 1$. The complexity of a serial FFT algorithm is $M^2 \log_2 M$ multiplications and $2M^2 \log_2 M$ additions. To sum up, the speedup of a parallel two-dimensional FFT algorithm is $M^2/2$ over a serial FFT algorithm. Without surprise, this speedup equals the number of PEs in the SIMD array processor.

10.9.4 CONNECTION ISSUES FOR SIMD PROCESSING

SIMD array processors allow explicit expression of parallelism in user programs. The compiler detects the parallelism and generates object code suitable for execution in the multiple processing elements and the control unit. Program segments which cannot be converted into parallel executable forms are executed in the control unit; program segments which can be converted into parallel executable forms are sent to the PEs and executed synchronously on data fetched from parallel memory modules under the control of the control unit. To enable synchronous manipulation in the PEs, the data is permuted and arranged in vector form. Thus, to run a program more efficiently on an array processor, one must develop a technique for vectorization.

Following are the various connection issues for SIMD processing:

1. Connectivity: In array processing, data is often stored in parallel memory modules in skewed forms that allow a vector of data to be fetched without conflict. However, the fetched data must be realigned in a prescribed order before it can be sent to individual PEs for processing. This alignment is implemented by the routing functions of the interconnection network, which also realigns the data generated by individual PEs into skewed form for storage in the memory modules.

2. Permutation: A rearrangeable network and the nonblocking network can realize every permutation function, but using these networks for alignment requires considerable effort to calculate control settings. A recursive routing mechanism has been suggested for a few families of permutations needed for parallel processing; however, the problem remains for the realization of general permutations. Many attempts have been made on the permutation capabilities of single-stage networks and blocking multistage networks. These networks cannot realize arbitrary permutations in a single pass. Recent results show that the baseline network can realize arbitrary permutations in just two passes while other blocking multistage networks, such as the Omega network, need at least three passes. Wu and Feng (1981) have proved that the shuffle-exchange network can realize arbitrary permutations in $3(\log_2 N) - 1$ passes where N is the network size.

3. Reconfigurability: A configuration concept has been proposed to better use the interconnection network. Under this concept, a network is just a configuration in the same topologically equivalent class. To configure a permutation function as an interconnection network, we can assign input-output link names in a way that realizes the permutation function in one conflict-free pass. Assigning logical names that realize various permutation functions without conflicts is called a reconfiguration problem. Through the reconfiguration process, the baseline network can realize every permutation in one pass without conflicts. This means that concurrent processing throughput could be enhanced by the proper assignment of tasks to processing elements and data to memory modules.

4. Partitioning: When dividing an SIMD interconnection network into independent subnetworks of different sizes, each subnetwork must have all the interconnection capabilities of a complete network of the same type and size. Hence, with a partitionable network, a system can support multiple SIMD machines. By dynamically reconfiguring the system into independent SIMD machines and properly assigning tasks to each partition, we can use resources more efficiently. Siegel (1980) has proved that single-stage networks such as the shuffle-exchange and Illiac networks cannot be partitioned into independent subnetworks, but blocking multistage networks such as a data manipulator can be partitioned.

5. Reliability: The reliable operation of interconnection networks is important to overall system performance.

The reliability issue can be thought of as two problems:

(i) Fault diagnosis: The fault-diagnosis problem has been studied for a class of multistage interconnection networks constructed of switching elements with two valid stages. The problem is approached by generating suitable fault-detection and fault-location test sets for every fault in the assumed fault model. The test sets are then trimmed to a minimal or nearly minimal set.

(ii) Fault tolerance: The second reliability problem concerns mainly the degree of fault tolerance. It is important to design a network that combines full connection capability with graceful degradation in spite of the existence of faults.

6. Bandwidth: A high network bandwidth is often desired at reasonably low network cost. The network bandwidth is defined as the number of PE requests honored per unit of time. Several analytical methods have been used to estimate network bandwidth. Most analytical models suggested by researchers are too simplified and closed-form solutions are not attainable. Numerical experiments can simulate actual PE-connection requests by tracing the program to be executed. Continued research efforts are needed in this area to accurately estimate the bandwidth of various interconnection networks. The cost of a network is primarily determined by the switching complexity. To achieve a cost-effective network design, one must find the optimal trade-off between performance (bandwidth) and cost (complexity). The main difficulty lies in the fact that bandwidth analysis depends on unpredictable program behavior and cost varies rapidly with progress in technology. Cost effectiveness must also insure flexibility in application programming and reliability in achieving fault tolerance. These are wide open areas of further research on interconnection networks for both SIMD and MIMD computers.

QUESTIONS

1. What do you mean by array processor?
2. Explain the attached array processor with the help of diagram?
3. Explain the SIMD array processor in detail?
4. Explain the architecture of SIMD processor?
5. Explain are the various organizations of SIMD computers?
6. Explain the configuration of SIMD array processor?
7. What are SIMD machines?
8. Explain the masking and data routing in detail?
9. Explain the concept of inter PE communications in detail?
10. Explain the various SIMD interconnection networks in detail?
11. Explain the matrix multiplication in SIMD processor?
12. Explain the concept of parallel sorting on array processor?
13. Explain the Fast Fourier Transform in SIMD array processor?
14. Explain the various connection issues for SIMD processing?

Objective Type Questions

1. **What is the primary function of a CPU?**

   a. Memory storage
   b. Data processing
   c. Input/output operations
   d. Network communication

2. **Which of the following architectures is based on the principle of storing instructions and data in the same memory?**

   a. Harvard architecture
   b. Von Neumann architecture
   c. RISC architecture
   d. CISC architecture

3. **What does RISC stand for?**

   a. Reduced Instruction Set Computer
   b. Random Instruction Set Computer
   c. Real-time Instruction Set Computer
   d. Readable Instruction Set Computer

4. **In pipelining, what is a "hazard"?**

   a. A delay in processing
   b. An error in instruction execution
   c. A type of memory fault
   d. A potential conflict in instruction execution

5. **What is the purpose of cache memory?**

   a. To increase the data storage capacity
   b. To speed up data access for frequently used data
   c. To store backup data
   d. To process data

6. **Which of the following is an advantage of pipelining?**

   a. Increased hardware complexity
   b. Reduced clock speed
   c. Increased instruction throughput
   d. Simplified control logic

7. **In which type of memory does data lose its contents when power is turned off?**

   a. ROM
   b. SRAM
   c. DRAM
   d. Flash memory

8. **What is the main difference between CISC and RISC architectures?**
   a. CISC has fewer instructions than RISC
   b. RISC uses complex instructions
   c. CISC has more addressing modes than RISC
   d. RISC supports multitasking while CISC does not

9. **What is the purpose of a Memory Management Unit (MMU)?**
   a. To manage input/output operations
   b. To control memory access and virtual memory management
   c. To process data
   d. To increase CPU clock speed

10. **Which of the following is NOT a type of cache mapping?**
    a. Direct mapping
    b. Associative mapping
    c. Set-associative mapping
    d. Random mapping

11. **What does the term "multithreading" refer to?**
    a. Executing multiple processes simultaneously
    b. Executing multiple threads within a single process
    c. Using multiple processors for a single task
    d. Running multiple operating systems

12. **What is the role of the instruction decoder in a CPU?**
    a. To fetch instructions from memory
    b. To execute instructions
    c. To convert instructions into control signals
    d. To store instructions

13. **Which of the following is a characteristic of SIMD (Single Instruction, Multiple Data)?**
    a. One instruction operates on multiple data points simultaneously
    b. Multiple instructions operate on a single data point
    c. Multiple processors execute different instructions
    d. It does not require a control unit

14. **In computer architecture, what is "latency"?**
    a. The speed of data transfer
    b. The time delay in data access
    c. The capacity of memory
    d. The rate of instruction execution

15. **What is the purpose of virtual memory?**
    a. To increase physical memory
    b. To provide an abstraction of larger memory than physically available

c. To improve cache performance

d. To manage data redundancy

16. Which of the following is an example of an I/O device?

a. CPU

b. RAM

c. Hard drive

d. Cache

17. In computer architecture, what does the acronym ALU stand for?

a. Arithmetic Logic Unit

b. Automatic Logic Unit

c. Advanced Logic Unit

d. Analog Logic Unit

18. What type of instruction allows the CPU to perform arithmetic and logic operations?

a. Control instructions

b. Data transfer instructions

c. Arithmetic and logic instructions

d. Jump instructions

19. What is a "bus" in computer architecture?

a. A type of memory

b. A set of physical connections for data transfer

c. A processor component

d. A software interface

20. Which of the following types of hazards occurs due to data dependencies between instructions?

a. Structural hazard

b. Control hazard

c. Data hazard

d. Timing hazard

21. In pipelining, what is the "fetch" stage responsible for?

a. Retrieving the next instruction from memory

b. Decoding the instruction

c. Executing the instruction

d. Writing back the result

22. What is a "branch prediction" in modern CPUs?

a. A method to execute instructions out of order

b. A technique to predict the outcome of a conditional branch instruction

c. A method to manage cache memory

d. A technique to compress data

23. Which of the following is NOT a type of data hazard?

a. Read after write

b. Write after read

c. Write after write

d. Execute after fetch

24. What does DMA stand for in computer architecture?

a. Direct Memory Access

b. Dynamic Memory Allocation

c. Data Management Access

d. Direct Memory Allocation

25. What is "out-of-order execution" in CPUs?

a. Executing instructions in the order they are received

b. Executing instructions as resources become available, regardless of their order

c. Ignoring some instructions to save time

d. Executing only high-priority instructions

26. Which of the following best describes "symmetric multiprocessing"?

a. Multiple CPUs with shared memory
b. Multiple CPUs with dedicated memory

c. A single CPU with multiple cores
d. A CPU managing multiple I/O devices

27. What is the main advantage of a multi-core processor?

a. Increased clock speed

b. Reduced power consumption

c. Ability to perform multiple tasks simultaneously

d. Simplicity in design

28. What is the purpose of the instruction cache?

a. To store data for quick access

b. To store frequently executed instructions for faster access

c. To manage I/O operations

d. To back up data

29. Which of the following is a characteristic of a supercomputer?

a. High energy consumption
b. High processing speed

c. Low cost
d. Small size

30. What does "bus contention" refer to?

a. Multiple devices trying to use the bus simultaneously

b. A failure in bus transmission

c. An error in data transfer

d. A type of data corruption

31. Which of the following is an example of a sequential access storage device?

a. Hard disk drive
b. Solid-state drive

c. Tape drive
d. RAM

32. What does "instruction set architecture" (ISA. define?

a. The physical layout of the CPU

b. The way data is stored in memory

c. The set of instructions a processor can execute

d. The connection between hardware and software

33. Which of the following technologies allows for the simultaneous execution of multiple threads?

a. Single-core processors

b. Multicore processors

c. Sequential processing

d. Pipeline processing

34. In the context of computer architecture, what is "concurrency"?

a. Executing multiple processes at the same time

b. Executing multiple threads simultaneously within the same process

c. Executing processes in a predefined order

d. Only executing one process at a time

35. What is the role of the control unit in a CPU?

a. To perform arithmetic operations

b. To manage the execution of instructions and direct the flow of data

c. To store data

d. To manage cache memory

36. What does "paging" refer to in memory management?

a. The process of storing data on the hard disk

b. Dividing memory into fixed-size blocks for efficient allocation

c. The transfer of data between CPU and memory

d. The method of organizing data in a database

37. In a multiprocessor system, what does the term "cache coherence" refer to?

a. Ensuring all caches are empty

b. Keeping multiple caches in sync with each other

c. Reducing the number of cache misses

d. Increasing cache size

38. Which of the following is a function of an operating system?

a. Managing hardware resources

b. Providing a user interface

c. Executing programs

d. All of the above

39. What is a "vector processor"?

a. A processor designed for arithmetic operations on vectors

b. A processor that only performs scalar operations

c. A processor designed for graphics rendering

d. A multi-core processor

40. What does "spooling" stand for?

a. Simultaneous Peripheral Operations On-Line

b. Simultaneous Processing Of Large Output

c. Sequential Processing Of Large Output

d. Simple Peripheral Operations On-Line

41. In the context of cache memory, what is a "cache miss"?

a. The required data is found in the cache

b. The required data is not found in the cache, requiring a fetch from main memory

c. The cache is full

d. The cache is invalid

42. Which of the following techniques improves CPU performance by allowing multiple instructions to be executed at the same time?

a. Superscalar architecture

b. Sequential processing

c. Simple pipelining

d. None of the above

43. In a distributed system, what is "data replication"?

a. Storing the same data in multiple locations for redundancy and availability

b. Storing different data at each location

c. A method for data compression

d. A technique for data visualization

44. What is the purpose of a "bus arbiter"?

a. To manage data transfer rates

b. To control which device can use the bus at any given time

c. To store data temporarily

d. To execute instructions

45. What is a "dual-core processor"?

a. A processor with two independent cores for processing

b. A processor that can handle two threads at a time

c. A processor designed for parallel processing

d. All of the above

46. In a pipelined processor, which stage is responsible for executing arithmetic and logic operations?

a. Fetch stage

b. Decode stage

c. Execute stage

d. Write-back stage

47. What does "load balancing" refer to in computer architecture?

a. Distributing workloads across multiple resources

b. Balancing data storage across drives

c. Allocating memory evenly

d. Synchronizing clock speeds

48. What is a "system bus"?

a. A pathway that connects different components of a computer

b. A type of cache memory

c. A component of the CPU

d. A storage device

49. Which of the following is a benefit of using a virtual machine?

a. Increased hardware costs
b. Isolation and security for applications
c. Reduced processing speed
d. Limited resource utilization

50. What does "NUMA" stand for in computer architecture?

a. Non-Uniform Memory Access
b. Non-Universal Memory Architecture
c. Network Unified Memory Access
d. None of the above

51. In a pipelined architecture, what does "stalling" mean?

a. Pausing execution of an instruction to resolve hazards

b. Completing all instructions without delay

c. Increasing the clock speed

d. Fetching data from the cache

52. Which of the following refers to a collection of interconnected computers that work together to provide a unified service?

a. Workstation
b. Server farm
c. Cluster computing
d. Grid computing

53. What is the primary function of a "dispatcher" in a CPU?

a. To allocate CPU time to processes
b. To manage memory allocation
c. To execute instructions
d. To fetch data from storage

54. Which of the following is a common method for increasing memory access speed?

a. Increasing memory size
b. Using cache memory
c. Utilizing slower storage devices
d. Using traditional hard drives

55. In the context of computer organization, what is a "flip-flop"?

a. A type of memory

b. A basic memory element capable of storing one bit of information

c. A data transfer mechanism

d. A CPU instruction

56. What is "task parallelism"?

a. Executing different tasks simultaneously
b. Executing the same task multiple times
c. Performing tasks in a predefined order
d. Running tasks sequentially

57. In computer architecture, what does "addressing mode" refer to?

a. The method of accessing memory locations

b. The type of CPU instruction

c. The speed of data transfer

d. The number of cores in a CPU

58. Which of the following is an example of a "hard real-time" system?

a. Video streaming application
b. Online gaming

c. Airbag deployment system
d. Word processing

59. What is the purpose of the "write-back" stage in a pipelined processor?

a. To fetch the next instruction

b. To write the results of an operation back to memory

c. To decode the instruction
d. To execute the instruction

60. What does "bandwidth" refer to in the context of computer systems?

a. The number of devices connected to a network

b. The amount of data that can be transferred in a given time

c. The speed of a CPU
d. The size of memory

61. In computer architecture, what is a "memory leak"?

a. A failure to release memory that is no longer needed

b. A type of cache miss

c. The loss of data during transmission
d. A failure in memory access

62. Which of the following is a type of parallel processing?

a. Time-sharing
b. Batch processing

c. Data parallelism
d. Sequential processing

63. What is the purpose of an "interrupt" in a CPU?

a. To speed up instruction execution

b. To handle events that require immediate attention

c. To manage memory allocation
d. To transfer data between devices

64. In computer architecture, what is "thermal throttling"?

a. Reducing CPU speed to prevent overheating

b. Increasing clock speed for performance

c. Cooling down the CPU
d. Powering off the system

65. What is a "data bus"?

a. A pathway for control signals

b. A pathway for transferring data between components

c. A storage area for data
d. A type of cache

66. What is the main role of the arithmetic logic unit (ALU)?

a. To store data
b. To perform arithmetic and logical operations
c. To fetch instructions from memory
d. To manage I/O operations

67. In terms of memory hierarchy, which type of memory is the fastest?

a. Cache memory
b. RAM
c. Hard disk
d. Flash memory

68. What does "load-store architecture" refer to?

a. A type of CPU design where all operations are performed on registers
b. A method of storing data in memory
c. A technique for data compression
d. A type of data transfer method

69. What is the role of a "front-side bus" (FSB. in a computer?

a. To connect the CPU to the main memory
b. To connect I/O devices
c. To transfer data between cache and main memory
d. To connect the hard drive

70. What is "speculative execution"?

a. Executing instructions based on predictions before the outcome is known
b. Executing only the highest-priority instructions
c. Ignoring certain instructions to save time
d. Executing instructions in order

71. In computer architecture, what does "non-volatile memory" refer to?

a. Memory that loses its contents when powered off
b. Memory that retains data even when the power is off
c. Memory that can be accessed quickly
d. Temporary memory storage

72. What is "context switching"?

a. Switching between different operating systems
b. The process of storing the state of a process so that it can be resumed later
c. Changing the context of user applications
d. Switching from one CPU to another

73. What does "serial communication" refer to?

a. Sending data one bit at a time over a single channel
b. Sending data in parallel
c. Sending data to multiple devices simultaneously
d. A type of memory access

74. What is a "microcontroller"?

a. A simple CPU with built-in memory and I/O ports

b. A large-scale CPU used in servers

c. A type of RAM

d. A device for managing input/output operations

75. In computer architecture, what does "fault tolerance" mean?

a. The ability to recover from failures without data loss

b. The ability to increase processing speed

c. The ability to manage memory effectively

d. The ability to handle multiple tasks

76. What does "interleaving" refer to in memory organization?

a. Distributing memory accesses across multiple banks to improve performance

b. Combining multiple data streams

c. Merging different memory types

d. A method of data compression

77. Which of the following is a component of a GPU (Graphics Processing Unit)?

a. Control unit

b. ALU

c. Texture mapping unit

d. Cache

78. What is the function of an "operating system kernel"?

a. To manage hardware and software resources

b. To provide a user interface

c. To execute applications

d. To store data

79. In a CPU, what does "pipelining" allow?

a. Parallel execution of multiple processes

b. Overlapping instruction execution to improve performance

c. Simultaneous access to multiple memory locations

d. Increased clock speed

80. Which of the following is a characteristic of a "bus topology" in computer networks?

a. All devices are connected to a central hub

b. Devices are connected in a linear sequence

c. Devices communicate directly with each other

d. It requires a large number of cables

81. In computer architecture, what does "virtualization" refer to?

a. Creating a simulated version of hardware or software

b. The process of optimizing memory usage

c. The ability to run multiple operating systems on a single machine

d. All of the above

82. Which of the following best describes "data mining"?

a. Collecting data for storage

b. Analyzing large datasets to discover patterns and trends

c. Transferring data between devices

d. Encrypting sensitive information

83. What is the main purpose of a "floating-point unit" (FPU)?

a. To perform basic arithmetic operations
b. To handle floating-point calculations

c. To manage memory allocation
d. To execute logical operations

84. What is "instruction-level parallelism"?

a. Executing multiple instructions in parallel

b. Executing multiple processes simultaneously

c. Executing the same instruction multiple times

d. None of the above

85. Which of the following is a disadvantage of using a virtual machine?

a. Increased flexibility
b. Higher overhead and resource usage

c. Improved security
d. Better isolation

86. In the context of CPU design, what does "frequency" refer to?

a. The number of cores in a CPU

b. The number of instructions executed per second

c. The number of cycles per second (measured in Hz)

d. The size of the cache memory

87. What is "data consistency" in databases?

a. Ensuring data is stored efficiently

b. Maintaining accurate and reliable data over time

c. Storing duplicate data
d. Encrypting data

88. In a data warehouse, what is "ETL"?

a. Extract, Transform, Load
b. Evaluate, Transfer, Link

c. Execute, Test, Load
d. Extract, Transfer, Load

89. What is the main function of an "interrupt controller"?

a. To handle memory allocation

b. To manage interrupt requests from various devices

c. To execute instructions

d. To perform arithmetic operations

90. Which of the following is NOT a characteristic of a cloud computing environment?

a. On-demand self-service
b. Resource pooling
c. Limited access to resources
d. Broad network access

91. In terms of memory organization, what is a "cache line"?

a. The smallest unit of data that can be stored in the cache
b. The maximum size of a cache
c. A method of organizing cache memory
d. The speed of cache memory

92. What is the main purpose of a "system call" in an operating system?

a. To execute applications
b. To provide a mechanism for applications to request services from the kernel
c. To manage memory allocation
d. To allocate CPU time to processes

93. In the context of computer networks, what is a "gateway"?

a. A device that connects two different networks
b. A device that provides security
c. A device that increases bandwidth
d. A type of router

94. What is the purpose of a "buffer" in data transfer?

a. To store data temporarily during transfer
b. To increase bandwidth
c. To manage memory allocation
d. To execute instructions

95. Which of the following is a characteristic of "peer-to-peer" networks?

a. Centralized control
b. Direct sharing of resources between devices
c. Only one device can serve as a host
d. Requires a server

96. In computer architecture, what is a "thread pool"?

a. A set of pre-initialized threads that can be reused for executing tasks
b. A collection of data structures
c. A type of cache memory
d. A memory management technique

97. What is the main function of a "memory manager" in an operating system?

a. To allocate and deallocate memory to processes
b. To execute instructions
c. To manage I/O operations
d. To provide a user interface

98. In the context of CPU architecture, what does "out-of-order execution" refer to?

a. Executing instructions in a predetermined order
b. Executing instructions as resources become available, regardless of their original order

c. Ignoring certain instructions to improve performance

d. Executing only the highest-priority instructions

99. Which of the following is a type of non-volatile memory?

a. RAM b. Cache memory

c. Flash memory d. Registers

100. What does "compression" refer to in data storage?

a. Increasing data size for storage

b. Reducing data size for efficient storage and transfer

c. Encrypting data for security

d. None of the above

SOLUTION:

1. b	2. b	3. a	4. d	5. b	6. c	7. c	8. c
9. b	10. d	11. b	12. c	13. a	14. b	15. b	16. c
17. a	18. c	19. b	20. c	21. a	22. d	23. b	24. a
25. b	26. a	27. c	28. b	29. b	30. a	31. c	32. c
33. b	34. b	35. b	36. b	37. b	38. d	39. a	40. a
41. b	42. a	43. a	44. b	45. d	46. c	47. a	48. a
49. b	50. a	51. a	52. c	53. a	54. b	55. b	56. a
57. a	58. c	59. b	60. b	61. a	62. c	63. b	64. a
65. b	66. b	67. a	68. a	69. a	70. a	71. b	72. b
73. a	74. a	75. a	76. a	77. c	78. a	79. b	80. b
81. d	82. b	83. b	84. a	85. b	86. c	87. b	88. a
89. b	90. c	91. a	92. b	93. a	94. a	95. b	96. a
97. a	98. b	99. c	100. b				